Free Money and Help for Women Entrepreneurs

by

Matthew Lesko

and

Mary Ann Martello

Researchers
Zsuzsa Beres; Giovina Taraschi
Melanie Coltan; Nancy Gibson
Mary Courtney Ore; Amy Hollingsworth
Allison Mays; Caroline Pharmer
Cindy Owens; Marcelle McCarthy
Bradley Sowash; Emily Subler; Marty Brinkman

Production
Beth Meserve

Marketing
Kim McCoy

Support
Mercedes Sundeen

Cover
Steve Bonham

Clip art used in this publication © Dynamic Graphics, Inc.; Totem
Graphics; One Mile Up; Tech Pool; Image Club Graphics, Inc.; and
Corel Corp.

FIRST EDITION

Library of Congress Cataloging-in-Publication date
    Lesko, Matthew
    Martello, Mary Ann

Free Money and Help for Women Entrepreneurs

ISBN # 1-878346-51-2

Most books by Matthew Lesko are available at special quantity
discounts for bulk purchases for sales promotions, premiums, fund-
raising or educational use. Special books or book excerpts also can be
created to fit specific needs.

For details, write Information USA, Special Markets, Attention: Kim
McCoy, P.O. Box E, Kensington, MD 20895; or 1-800-797-7811,
Marketing; {www.lesko.com}.

Table of Contents

Over 100 Government Grants For Your Business.. 127

Women Entrepreneurs Rule

Unless you have been living in a cave for the last 15 years,
you can't help but notice that women are taking over the
world of entrepreneurs. Women are responsible for starting
two out of every three new businesses in the United States

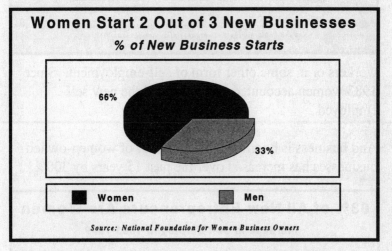

Women Start 2 Out of 3 New Businesses
% of New Business Starts

66%

33%

■ Women   ■ Men

Source: National Foundation for Women Business Owners

and at that rate soon we'll all be working for women.
But more importantly than the number of new startups is
the fact that women are also more successful than men at
starting businesses. If you are a woman, you have a 75%
chance of succeeding, whereas men only have a 67%
chance of success.

Many women who aren't starting their own businesses are
still working for themselves as freelancers, contract

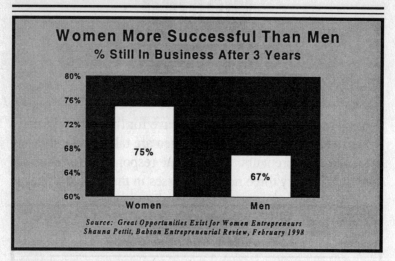

Women More Successful Than Men
% Still In Business After 3 Years

75% Women
67% Men

*Source: Great Opportunities Exist for Women Entrepreneurs
Shauna Pettit, Babson Entrepreneurial Review, February 1998*

workers or in some other form of self-employment. Since 1983 women accounted for 83% of all the new self-employed.

And business is booming! The number of women-owned businesses has increased over the past 15 years by 300%

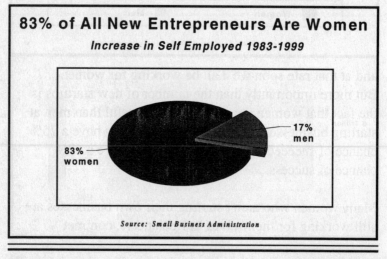

83% of All New Entrepreneurs Are Women
Increase in Self Employed 1983-1999

17% men
83% women

Source: Small Business Administration

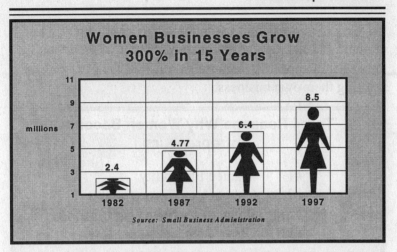

Women Businesses Grow 300% in 15 Years

millions

Source: Small Business Administration

from 2.4 million in 1992 to over 8.5 million in 1997. Sales from women-owned businesses have increased over 1,000% during the same time period and that's after adjusting for inflation. Now that's an impressive number. Increased sales means increased employment. Women-owned businesses are now responsible for employing over 25% of the U.S. workforce.

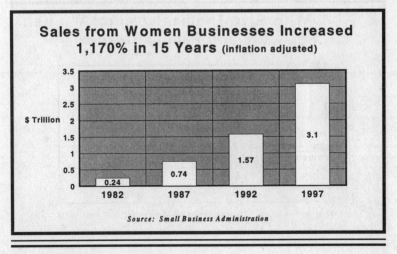

Sales from Women Businesses Increased 1,170% in 15 Years (inflation adjusted)

$ Trillion

Source: Small Business Administration

It's easy to understand that men may be largely ego driven in their reasons for starting businesses, but women, on the other hand, appear to be more practical in their reasons for starting their own business.

Top 4 Reasons Why Women Become Entrepreneurs

#1	Wanted Flexibility
#2	Unhappy or Uncomfortable
#3	Bored or Unchallenged
#4	Glass Ceiling

Source: National Foundation of Women Business Owners

And here's the best part. Women are better at integrating their business into their family life than men are. Over twice as many women as men give themselves an "A" grade in their efforts to balance their work and family life.

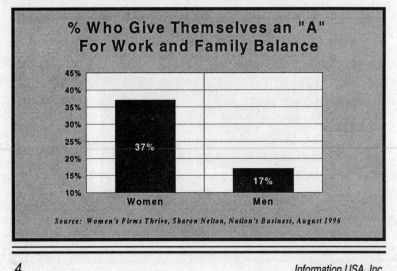

% Who Give Themselves an "A" For Work and Family Balance

Women: 37%
Men: 17%

Source: Women's Firms Thrive, Sharon Nelton, Nation's Business, August 1996

One Million Entrepreneurs A Year Get Government Money

Each year millions of Americans play state government lottery hoping to win enough money so that they might quit their boring jobs and do something they've always dreamed of. Most of these lottery players know that their odds of winning are one in a million. But what they don't realize, is that there are hundreds of other government programs that give out money to people who dream of starting or expanding a business and the odds are terrific!

Each year the government gives out over $300 billion to entrepreneurs who want to start or expand their business. And the important thing is that they give it out to over 1 million entrepreneurs each and every year. The best part is that in some of the major programs over 67% of the people who apply for the money get it. It's not one in one million like in the lottery. In these programs 2 out of every 3 people who apply for money get help!

We all know about the lottery because that's the one government agency that has a lot of money to advertise. But other offices don't spend a nickel advertising that they are giving away billions of dollars each and every year.

Who Gets the Money?

Remember over 1 million businesses a year get money from the government so it goes to all kinds of people. H. Ross Perot, Donald Trump, Lee Iacocca, Paul Newman, and Nike Shoes have been recipients of government money. Other recipients include:

Suzanne Schwartz:
 $12,000 to start a craft business in her home, and
Debra Jefferies:
 $30,000 to start a video production company as well as $30,000 worth of government contracts, and
Diane Gann:
 $25,000 to start a paralegal service, and
Blanca Basson:
 $30,000 to start a jingles business out of her home.

And there is no special kind of business that the government favors.

★ *Irene's Cleaners and Alterations* in Mesa, Arizona got $67,000
★ *Happy Time Day Care Center* in Mt. Vernon, Illinois received $235,000
★ *Beaver Creek Resort* in Monticello, Kentucky got $1,700,000
★ *Han's Hair Design* in Champaign, Illinois received $12,000; and
★ *Sug's Home Care* in Corbib, Kansas got $6,000.

WHY NOW IS THE BEST TIME TO START A BUSINESS

I believe that the current conditions in our society make it an excellent environment for entrepreneurship. Here's why.

1. It Takes Very Little Money

In this country's youth, all you needed was some land to be in your own business, and the government was giving it out to homesteaders who would take it to grow crops and start a business. Then in the last century, the industrial age began and it took more to start a business. In addition to real estate, factories and stores required buildings, employees, and equipment to get them started and this required money, and lots of it.

Now in the information age, entrepreneurialism again requires very little money. There are many businesses today, particularly service-based businesses, that can be started with nothing more than a phone, a desk, and business cards. And if you throw in a computer, the world really opens up for you.

Here's an interesting fact. For the cost of buying one share of Amazon.com you might become an Amazon.com. It costs next to nothing to begin selling things on the Internet. Find a product on consignment! Learn how to design a web page! And then start figuring out how to market the heck out of it!

2. No Job Is Safe Anymore

One reason people didn't start their own businesses in the past was fear. People felt they needed the security of a steady job and a retirement plan. Well the New World order has changed all that. You can't even work for IBM anymore and retire in 30 years with a good pension. They as well as dozens of other big companies including Citicorp

Bank, Kodak, Levis, have laid off thousands of workers, even when they were making good profits. Even the government has been laying off people. No job is safe anymore, no matter how good an employee you are. A new boss, a merger, or a new strategic plan can change your life

overnight. The world has flipped upside down. Now it's actually more secure to work for yourself instead of some big company. Companies are no longer loyal to employees. But if you have your own company, you'll never fire yourself.

3. Jobs Are Boring

Most creative people who work in large companies feel frustrated and believe their real talents go unused. They see that the company they work for is not much different from a government agency. They see that 20% of the people are doing 80% of the work. They also are fed up with having to have 10 months of meetings before any little decision is made.

Few people working in big businesses feel that their efforts go towards making a difference. Office politics seem to be just as important as actual work. People feel unfulfilled and search for ways to feel needed.

As an entrepreneur you know you are needed from the first day you open up for business. You immediately see the direct correlation between your efforts and the success of your business. It's not office politics or 10 months of meetings that will determine your success; it's going to be hard work, fast decision making, mixed with a dose of good luck.

As big business makes employees feel unimportant more entrepreneurs will go out and do things for themselves.

4. *The Best Tax Shelter*
As long as our economy is based on capitalism, having your own business offers the best of all tax advantages, no matter how Congress tinkers with the tax code because under the tax laws, any money spent in an attempt to generate a sale for your business is tax deductible. This is how people who own their own businesses write off their houses, their cars, their country clubs, their travel, their entertainment, and even their boats. When I was a young single entrepreneur, I paid almost no taxes. Almost everything I did was a business expense. But now that I am married with two children, things are a little different. I haven't yet figured a way to deduct such expenses as children's clothes and toys.

5. *Any Economy Is Good*

A healthy economy is obviously good for most businesses. When times are good, people spend more money and that raises the tide for all businesses. But I also believe that a bad economy may be even a better time to start a business.

If you start your business during a boom, customers can come easily, and you can get fat and happy. Then, when the first economic downturn hits, you may not be able to handle it. You won't know how to operate in a mean and lean mode. That is why a lot of  businesses go belly up in bad economic times. However, if you start your business when times are tough, it will make your business stronger. You will figure out ways to make it work when times are bad, and you'll make a bundle when the economy makes a comeback and business gets easier. You will also learn how to handle things when the economy turns sour again. You'll be ready to operate a lean and mean company, and you won't become a business failure statistic.

6. *Big Business Is Creating More Opportunities*

As big business gets bigger and bigger, it creates more and more opportunities for the small entrepreneur. When my Fortune 500 clients look for new business opportunities, the first thing they ask is: "How big will this business be?" And if the answer isn't at least $100 million, they are not interested. It takes them just as much effort to get into a

$100 million business as it does for them to get into a $1 million business. SO they concentrate only on the big ones, and leave the $1 million crumbs for the small entrepreneurs. Well, I don't know about you, but a $1 million business is not a bad living. I see myself as an entrepreneur cockroach, living off $1 million crumbs that fall through the cracks from the big guys. And if my history serves me well, the cockroach outlived the dinosaur by a long shot.

7. *The Information Explosion Has Opened Up Our Society*

The information explosion had greatly expanded what once was just a little club of entrepreneurs. Before the information explosion you had to know someone to get the legal, marketing, technical or competitive information needed to launch a venture. Now you don't have to know someone to get this kind of help, you just have to understand the process of accessing information. Why can anyone tap into this information gold mine? Because this information can be found within our government and by living in an open democracy we all have the same right and access to this information whether you're Donald Trump or a street cleaner.

6 THINGS ENTREPRENEURS DON'T NEED

Everybody is always telling entrepreneurs about all the essentials they need. I think it's just as important to tell entrepreneurs what they don't need. After starting four businesses of my own and even after having two failures, here is what I believe you should be extra careful to avoid.

1. Too Much Professional Advice

If you're starting a business with a limited supply of capital, too much professional advice is going to kill you. If you try to surround yourself with all the trappings of business success, you're soon going to go out of business.

 Remember you and your time are the most important resources in your business. Succeeding in business is a "beat the clock" game. If you're spending a lot of your time meeting with lawyers and accountants or choosing fancy "power" furniture, you'll have little time to concentrate on the ONE thing that is important to your success... getting a client. This is the most critical success factor of any new business. Without a client, everything else is meaningless.

When I started my first business, I got the high priced accountants, the high priced lawyers, the power business cards and power furniture, but I went out of business. And who won? It was the accountants, lawyers, and furniture salesmen! They were all smart enough to get paid up front and I was out on the street.

Your clients don't care what kind of accounting system you use or what legal structure you have formed. And having the right look, whether it is impressive business cards or furniture may only affect your business 5% to 10%. This is a very insignificant percentage if you have no business. Furthermore, it's a waste of time if you're spending a half a day choosing furniture when you could be spending a half a day getting a client. And 99% of the clients don't care what kind of furniture you have. The only person who really cares about what kind of furniture you have is the furniture salesman.

2. Too Much Money

Anyone can start a business if given a million dollars. It doesn't take a lot of creativity to spend money to buy advertising in your local newspaper. But what are you going to do next year when your business doesn't have an extra $1 million lying around? Instead of learning how to buy advertising space, you should first learn how to get your local newspaper to write a FREE story about your business. The price is right and it's more effective than advertising because you're also getting a big, respected institution, the newspaper, to endorse you (or so it seems to most readers).

Too much money for a novice entrepreneur makes you fat, lazy, and uncreative. The key to developing a strong business is learning how to get sales using the least amount of money, not the most amount of money.

3. Too Perfect A Product

A beginning entrepreneur can easily get hung up trying to develop the prefect product. Most of us can never be perfect, but we can still be successful. Entrepreneurs can

easily get trapped into believing that their product or service has to be perfect before they offer it to the public.

Trying to be flawless can lead to failure. Being a perfectionist can cause you to go broke before you get to market. Be careful that your perfectionist attitude isn't really a mask for your own insecurities. What your family and friends will think about your product doesn't matter. The object of a product is to sell it to a customer. Your relatives and friends will probably never be your customers. Customers come with all different kinds of needs, and very few are willing to pay for perfection. Go open up your own closets and look at all the mediocre stuff you have purchased!

Until you start asking people for money, you really don't know what they will buy. Your product is probably going to change dozens of times before it reaches its final form. And this metamorphosis is due to customer feedback, your

most important information source. The most important
thing is to introduce your product as soon as possible, so
that you can stay in business long enough to find out how to
improve it.

Few of us are smart enough to read minds, but we're all
smart enough to listen. If you offer a product to ten people
and five of them say they would buy it if it were green, go
right out and paint the damn thing green, so you can make a
few sales!

4. A Board of Directors

Anytime you get three people in a room and talk about an
idea, there will always be one naysayer. Finding potential
problems is always easy. If an
idea were perfect, it wouldn't
be an idea anymore; it would
already be a product or service.

For ideas to work it usually
takes the passion and
commitment of one person.
This kind of spirit doesn't come
from a board of directors that engages in group decision
making. Although democratic, this process usually results
in ideas where everyone owns a small piece of the end
product and no one person is committed to the complete
picture.

Board meetings can be a waste of time for struggling
entrepreneurs. Entrepreneurs have to live from moment to

moment, often making quick reflexive decisions, so they can immediately move to the next decision. The temperament required for entrepreneurialism is different than the temperament needed to placate a diverse group, such as a board of directors.

5. An MBA

I have a BS in Business and an MBA. I believe it took me

 two failing businesses to unlearn all that I was taught in my six years of business school. I was brainwashed into believing such things as: "if you need money, you go to the bank." When I was starting my businesses

I quickly learned that a bank is the last place an entrepreneur with no money should go. Business schools spend a lion's share of the time teaching you how to run a big business like General Motors. And from what happened to General Motors in the last 20 years, you can see that they didn't do such a good job at that!

The jargon you learn in business school certainly is helpful if you want to get a job in big business. But if you are a small entrepreneur, much of what they teach you will just interfere with your instincts. There is no magic to most operations of running a business. Accounting is keeping a checkbook. Production is making sure that your product costs less than you sell it for. In the beginning, marketing can seem magical. Finding a customer is what any new business is all about, and it doesn't take an MBA to figure out how to do it. It takes a lot of door pounding.

6. *Government Forms*

Don't tell the government what I'm about to say, because I may get into trouble. I believe that entrepreneurs should even forget about government licenses and forms for starting a business.

After I had two businesses that failed, I got rid of the accountants, the lawyers, the power furniture and power business cards, and I also didn't file any local, county, state or federal forms. Don't get me wrong; I did file my tax return. NEVER MESS AROUND WITH THE IRS! The government forms I'm talking about are the permits, licenses and applications to do business. My theory is that filing all these forms takes time and energy. Your time is very important. You'd be better off concentrating on what is the critical success factor to your business, getting customers.

If you don't file the necessary forms, there isn't much that can happen to you. The way the government works, it will take them three years to find you. And by then, you'll either be out of business, or you'll be successful enough to pay the $50 late filing fee or whatever is necessary.

HOW TO CHOOSE THE RIGHT BUSINESS FOR YOU

Trust Your Heart As Well as Your Head

Choosing the business that is right for you can be a daunting prospect. Take heart, however, there are many different businesses as there are ideas. One of them is right for you.

To begin with, choose an area that excites you. To succeed, you must love what you do. I know that this sounds deceptively simple, but everything else depends upon this one principle.

Find out if there's a market for your products or services. Study your competition, suppliers, and new customers. Once this is done, trust your instincts. Choosing a business is a very personal decision. After all, you may end up spending the rest of your life with this business.

Following your heart, as well as your head, will greatly increase your chances of financial and personal success. I'm not advocating that you rely upon your instinct alone, but the elements that lead to success often have little to do with advanced business degrees or perfectly balanced ledgers.

When you love what you do — magic happens. Your business is no longer work. You may find yourself thinking about your business all the time, not because you have to, but because it is fun, fulfilling and exciting.

Your chances of success increase tremendously because you won't be easily discouraged. If you look around at the people who run businesses, you'll see that it doesn't take a rocket scientist to run a successful company. Most of us are bright enough to run a business if we decide to try.

Perseverance, not intelligence, is the key. If you love what you're doing, you won't give up at the first economic downturn and try to find something more profitable. You'll stay and learn to make money even when the economy sours. Eventually, you'll become better at what you do than anyone else.

We pride ourselves at making all our decisions "by the numbers." Numbers are safe. Yet, those who meet the needs of our fast changing society look past the numbers. They see beyond the present and anticipate the future.

Steps In Choosing A Business

1: Use Your Imagination: Clear your mind and let your imagination go. Explore new ideas and opportunities. Ask yourself questions such as:
   a) What is my fantasy business?
   b) What would I do even if I didn't get paid for doing it?

c) What do people I really admire in the world do and
why do I admire them?

2: *Research Your Idea Now*: Reach for the calculator and
explore as many ideas as you can. Your job
is to take the best ideas that you have at the
moment and see how they grow. You can
expect a lot of duds. Don't worry if all of
your ideas aren't winners. With work
and the help of a calculator, your ideas
will lead you to other interesting
opportunities you've never even
considered. Do the research. Study
the options. Remember all the
information you need to find out
about any business is out there. Start by
looking through this book. It will give you plenty of ideas
of where to begin your search.

3: *Trust Your Instincts*: The final decision can be difficult.
If you did enough research, you probably came up with
more than one potentially good idea. But, be sure to make
the final decision with your heart, as well as your head.
You are the one who has to be happy. And when you are,
you will work like heck to make that business a success.

DON'T BELIEVE IN INSTANT SUCCESS

Everybody fails, but no one ever tells you about it. I had two failing business before I got lucky with what I am doing now. In 1975 I even had a computer software company that failed. Looking back at the growth of the computer business since then, I feel that I must have been the only person in the country with a computer company that didn't make it.

It's not only me. Everybody who does anything in the world has to experience failure. We all know that Henry Ford was responsible for manufacturing the first mass-produced automobile called the Model T. But very few people are **Model T** aware that the Model T was not the first automobile. He went through models A to S that were all failures before he got it right. Coca-Cola was only selling a dozen cases a week for a long time while they got it right. Even Thomas Edison failed over 1,000 different times while working on the filament for the light bulb before he was successful.

Our society should glorify failure the same way it glorifies success. The stories we read about in the general press and in special interest magazines like Success, all make success sound easy. They tell you stories of some housewife who was selling her "Can't Beat Em" cookies at school bake sales when her son's teacher suggested she should sell them in stores. In no time at all she's a millionaire. Face it: that's probably not going to happen to you.

A millionaire friend of mine, Dr. Fad, didn't make money instantly either. Maybe you've heard of him. He's **WACKY** responsible for the Wacky Wall Walker fad a number of year ago and he made a **WALL** bundle from it. He was successful with the Wall Walker only after dozens of other **WALKER** products failed. His business sounds glamorous now. He got his own television show and 60 Minutes did a story on him. But when he started, his little import/export business struggled for years, as he lived in an efficiency apartment with his wife and his business shared a one-room office. Some of his early failures included importing Japanese fish parts and facemasks for industrial use. He struggled with his unglamorous business for years before he hit the jackpot.

SUCCESS MERCHANTS LIE TO YOU

Go out and fail.... This is the only way you are going to get anywhere. The odds of being an instant success are about the same as you being hit by lightning. If you live in Florida, where lightning has a habit of striking often, your odds may not be that bad. If you're waiting for the right idea that is sure to be an instant success like you see in the magazines, you'll never do anything. Magazines lie by making you believe that you too can be an instant success, just like the people they profile. This is how they sell magazines.

Success Stories Can Stop YOUR Success

The problem with these instant success stories is instead of encouraging you they are more likely to stop you from fulfilling your dream. When the announcer introduces one of the panel members, it's usually, something like this ... "Do you see Joe and his wife here? Yesterday Joe was a garbage collector in Chattanooga, Tennessee. Last night he listened to my 15-hour 'How to Make a Million' success tapes and today Joe owns 15 beautiful properties in Southern California."

Any rational person knows that kind of instant success probably won't happen to him. But now you feel jealous. You are thinking... "If that garbage collector can do it, why can't I?" And then you think about **Instant Success** buying the 15-hour cassette program, but you don't because **Stories** your rational side knows that you can't listen to hours of tapes at night and own 15 properties by the next morning. If that garbage collector really did it and you can't, you're going to feel dumb. How can a garbage collector be smarter than you are? No one wants to know that a garbage collector is smarter, even if he may be, so you don't do anything about it.

Or, if you buy the tapes and listen to them, you get angry because your life didn't change overnight. You get discouraged, throw the tapes in the closet and hang up your success dreams, leaving it for the folks on TV.

Failure Is the Only Way to Unlearn What You Learned in School

It took me two failing businesses to unlearn all I was taught in my six years of business school. I marched out into the world with an MBA in Computer Science and that was why my first two businesses failed. I was trying to put into practice what I learned in school. They were telling me things like..."If you need money go to the bank." No matter how good the economy is, a bank is the last place an entrepreneur with no assets is likely to find money for his or her business.

In my consulting business, I was trying to do things just like the big consultants, such as preparing mahogany-bound reports and renting fancy offices. I couldn't perform the services of a big consulting firm as well as a big consulting firm could. The clients who expected that from me were not satisfied in the end. What I learned was that I was a small consulting firm, but there were a lot of companies who didn't want a big consulting firm. They wanted someone who was operating out of their bedroom. I discovered my niche and that uniqueness gave me a real edge.

Friends, Loved Ones, and Teachers Are Bad for Entrepreneurs

We all have misconceptions about the way things work and what will be successful. We are inundated from all sides with opinions. Our associates, friends, families, and teachers all continually tell us why they believe someone is a success. They don't really know. If they did, they would be doing it too. The truth is what makes one person a success is not likely to make you a success. The reason for your success will be because you are different than anyone else and your product will be different than anyone else's.

Another way all sorts of well-meaning folks hinder your success is by protecting you. All these people who care for you will not want to see you hurt. They will show you 15 ways your idea is likely to fail. Teachers are the worst. It seems that the more schooling you receive in this country, the more reasons you can think of as to why the idea won't work. Remember, the founder of Federal Express first presented his idea as a paper in business school, and the professor barely gave him a passing grade because he thought the idea wouldn't work. And that was at Harvard! So trust your instincts and set your idea in motion, regardless of what some people might say.

If you want to succeed, most likely you are going to experience failure. And you shouldn't let anyone protect you from it. It's the best springboard to your future success.

KEY POINTERS WHEN APPLYING FOR MONEY

The following are tips meant to offer advice and encouragement to both the novice and the "old pro" government money seeker.

1) Don't Always Believe A "NO" Answer

If you call a government office and ask about a particular money program and they tell you that no such program exists, don't believe them. No one person in the government can know everything.

Senator Kerry of Massachusetts recently surveyed all the local Small Business Administration offices to see how they were administering a program that provides money to Vietnam era veterans starting their own businesses. Only half the offices knew that such a program existed. These are the same offices that are in charge of giving out the money.

Other times, programs are consolidated under new names. For example, there used to be a program at the U.S. Department of Agriculture which gave money to farmers to build golf courses and tennis courts in their fields so that they could get into the resort business. The program was called the Recreation Facility Loan Program. I think the name made politicians uneasy, so they folded the money into the Farm Operating Loan Program.

The lesson here is not to throw up your hands when told that a program does not exist. Keep asking questions like:

- ➡ "Did such a program ever exist?"
- ➡ "What happened to the program?"
- ➡ "Are there any similar programs?"
- ➡ "Can I get a descriptive listing of all your current programs?"
- ➡ "What other programs or agencies might offer money in similar areas?"
- ➡ "Is there anyone who may know more about this program?"

2) Apply To More Than One Program

There is no rule that says that you can apply only to one program for your business. For example, if you want to build condominiums in a town of less than 50,000, investigate programs at the Small Business Administration, the Department of Housing and Urban Development, the Department of Agriculture, as well as programs at the state and city level. The worst that can happen to you is that all of your applications are approved. This is a nice predicament to be in. You may not be able to accept the money from everyone. Many of the applications do not even ask if you are applying for money elsewhere.

3) Don't Be Discouraged If You Think You Are Not Eligible

If you happen to contact a program office and they tell you that the program was changed so that only non-profit organizations can now receive the money, don't let this discourage you. What you can do is find a non-profit or existing organization to work with you. This is done every day in Washington, DC. Entrepreneurs locate federal money programs and find passive partners who will get a percentage of the money.

4) Talk To Those Who Give the Money

Before you actually fill out any application, it is well worth your time to review the forms with the program officials, either in person if at all possible, or over the telephone. Many of the funding agencies have offices throughout the country to assist you. Such contact should help you tailor your answers to meet the government's expectations. It will give them what they want to see.

5) Give Them What They Want

When you prepare your application, give the government exactly what it asks for, even though it may not make much sense to you. Don't fight it. You will need all your energy to get your money. It is unlikely that you will have any chance in changing the government's ways even if you are right.

6) Starting Small or Big?

You have to be careful about when to ask for a lot of money and when to ask for just a little. This depends upon the program. So before you say how much money you need, be sure you have some understanding of the maximum amount as well as the average amount of monies given to applicants. Each program office listed can give you this information.

7) *Try Again*
If your proposal is rejected, learn what you did wrong and try again next year, or try with a different program. Many proposals are rejected because of bad timing or a relatively minor hitch. Don't worry. Being turned down will not be held against you. Some programs deny first time applications just for drill. They want to make sure that you are serious about your project.

8) *When the Bureaucracy Is Stuck, Use Your Representative*
Contact the office of your U.S. Senator or Congressperson only when the bureaucracy comes to a halt on your paperwork. Sometimes this is the only way to get action. Playing constituent is a very effective resource but should be used only when all else fails.

9) *Don't Overlook State Programs*
Investigate opportunities from the state agencies at the same time you are exploring federal financial assistance. State business money programs are listed under "State Money and Help for Your Business."

JUMPING OVER
BUREAUCRATIC HURDLES

Remember you are not going to make one telephone call
and as a result, some bureaucrat will send you a check. If it
were that easy, our mammoth deficit would be 10 times as
big as it is now. What normally happens is
that bureaucratic hurdles will be put in your
way, and how you handle them will
determine the success or failure of your
getting the money. A Boston
entrepreneur named Steven Stern
depicts an example of the ultimate
success in overcoming such
bureaucratic roadblocks. His story
follows:

A few years ago, Steven Stern saw
me on the David Letterman Show one night when I talked
about a government program which gave money to teenage
entrepreneurs. The next day Steven called my office and
asked for more details about the program. He explained that
he was 16 years old and wanted to start a lawn mowing
business in Boston. I told him that I really didn't know
much about the details of the program, but I did give him
the name and address of the office that runs the program.

Steven called me back about two days later and said that
the Washington DC office told him to contact the regional
office located in Boston. When he called the regional

office, he was told that he could not apply for that program because the money was set aside for teenagers in rural areas. He asked me what he could do now, and I suggested he call Washington back and get a copy of the law authorizing the program. I told him that the law would give him all the facts.

When Steven got a copy of the law, he was surprised to find that it stated that the money was indeed intended for teenagers in rural areas, but it also said that it could be used to start lawn mowing businesses anywhere. What a match! So he took a copy of the law to the government office in Boston and rubbed their noses in the facts. The local office then conceded that he should apply for the money, and gave him an application.

But, at this point Steven was stopped again. Just as they handed him an application, they asked if he belonged to a 4-H club. This was another eligibility requirement for the financial assistance. Well, Steven attended a city high school where students didn't know one end of a cow from another, let alone belong to a 4-H club. But this did not stop Steven. He went to school the next day and rounded up four of his buddies and started what may have been one of the first and only inner city 4-H clubs.

Now completely eligible to apply for the money, Steven sent in his application and three months later received $3,000 to start his business. Within two years, Steven was

making $10,000 a year and able to support himself through
Babson College.

Not all cases are going to be as difficult as Steven's, but
they can be. You have to have the stamina to overcome any
hurdle the government puts in your path. Remember that
someone is going to get the money every year, and it might
as well be you.

TIPS ON FINDING INFORMATION

The Art of Getting A Bureaucrat to Help You

Our greatest asset as information seekers is that we live in a society inhabited by people who are dying to talk about what they do for a living. However, in this world of big bureaucracies and impersonal organizations, it is rare that any of us get a chance to share what we know with someone who is truly interested. Perhaps this is why psychiatrists are in such great demand.

This phenomenon can work to your advantage; almost anyone can find an expert on any topic providing you expect that the search will take an average of seven telephone calls.

The Value of Experts in Today's Information Age

Using experts can be your answer to coping with the information explosion. Computers handle some problems of the information explosion because they are able to categorize and index vast amounts of data. However, many computerized databases fail to contain information that is generated by non-traditional sources, for example, documents that are buried in state and federal agencies.

Another problem is that many databases suffer from lack of timeliness because they offer indexes to articles and most publishers have long lead times for getting the material into print. And in our fast changing society, having the most current information is crucial.

Computers also contribute to a more serious problem. Because of their ability to store such large quantities of data, computers aggravate the information explosion by fueling the information overload. If you access one of the major databases on a subject such as Maine potatoes, most likely you will be confronted with a printout of 500 or more citations. Do you have the time to find and read all of them? How can you tell a good article from a bad one?

The first step to cut through this volume of information is to find an expert specializing in Maine potatoes. Yes, such an individual exists. This person already will have read those 500 articles and will be able to identify the relevant ones that meet your information needs. This expert will also be able to tell you what will be in the literature next year, because probably he is in the midst of writing or reviewing forthcoming articles. And if you are in search of a fact or figure, this government bureaucrat might know the answer right off the top of his head. And the best part of this research strategy is that all the information can be accumulated for just the price of a telephone call.

CASE STUDY: HOW TO FIND MR. POTATO

The techniques for locating an expert can best be illustrated by a classic story from the days when I was struggling to start my first information brokerage company in 1975.

At the time the business amounted only to a desk and telephone crowded into the bedroom of my apartment. As so often happens in a fledgling enterprise, my first client was a friend. His problem was this: "I must have the latest information on the basic supply and demand of Maine potatoes within 24 hours."

My client represented a syndicate of commodity investors, which invests millions of dollars in Maine potatoes. When he called, these potatoes were selling at double their normal price and he wanted to know why. I knew absolutely nothing about potatoes, but thought I knew where to find out. The agreement with my client was that I would be paid only if I succeeded in getting the information (no doubt you've guessed I no longer work that way).

Luck With the First Telephone Call

The first call I made was to the general information office of the U.S. Department of Agriculture. I asked to speak to an expert on potatoes. The operator referred me to Mr. Charlie Porter. At that point I wondered if this Mr. Porter was a department functionary with responsibility for handling crank calls, but the operator assured me that he was an agriculture economist specializing in potatoes. I called Mr. Porter and explained how I was a struggling entrepreneur who knew nothing about potatoes and needed his help to answer a client's request. Charlie graciously gave me much of the information I needed, adding that he would be happy to talk at greater length either over the phone or in person at his office. I decided to go see him.

Only Problem Was Getting Out Of Charlie Porter's Office

For two and a half hours the next morning, the federal government's potato expert explained in intimate detail the supply and demand of Maine potatoes. Charlie Porter showed me computer printouts that reflected how the price had doubled in recent weeks. For any subject that arose during our conversation, Charlie had immediate access to a reference source. Rows of books in his office 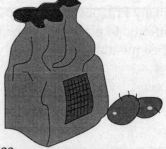 covered every conceivable aspect of the potato market. A strip of ticker tape that tracked the daily price of potatoes from all over the country lay across his desk.

Here in Charlie's office was everything anyone might ever want to know about potatoes. The problem, it turned out, was not in getting enough information, but how to gracefully leave his office. Once Charlie started talking, it was hard to stop him. It seemed that Charlie Porter had spent his lifetime studying the supply and demand of potatoes and finally someone with a genuine need sought his expertise.

One Potato...Two Potato...

When I was finally able to let Charlie know I had to leave, he pointed across the hall in the direction of a potato statistician whose primary responsibility was to produce a monthly report showing potato production and consumption in the United States. From the statistician I was to learn about all the categories of potatoes that are tallied. It turns out the U.S. Department of Agriculture counts all the potato chips sold every month, even how many Pringles potato chips are consumed. The statistician offered to place me on the mailing list to receive all this free monthly data.

THE ART OF GETTING AN EXPERT TO TALK

The information explosion requires greater reliance on experts in order to sift through the proliferation of data. Cultivating an expert, however, demands an entirely different set of skills from using a library or a publication. You must know how to treat people so that they are ready, willing, and able to give the information you need. It is human nature for almost anyone to want to share his or her knowledge, but your approach will determine whether you ultimately get the expert to open up. So it is your job to create an environment that  makes an individual want to share his expertise. Remember when dealing with both public and private sector experts, they will all get the same paycheck whether they give you two weeks worth of free help or if they cut the conversation short.

Expectations: The 7-Phone Call Rule

There is no magic to finding an expert. It is simply a numbers game, which takes an average of seven telephone calls. Telephone enough people and keep asking each for a lead. The magic lies in how much information the expert will share once you find that individual. This is why it is essential to remember "the 7-phone call rule."

If you make several calls and begin to get upset because you are being transferred from one person to another, you will be setting yourself up to fail once you locate the right expert. What is likely to happen is that when your "Charlie Porter" picks up his telephone he is going to hear you complaining about how sick and tired you are of getting the runaround from his organization. Well, to Charlie, you don't sound like you are going to be the highlight of his day. He will instantly figure out how to get rid of you.

This explains why some people are able to get information and others fail. Seasoned researchers know it is going to take a number of telephone calls and they will not allow themselves to get impatient. After all, the runaround is an unavoidable part of the information gathering process. Consequently, the first words that come out of your mouth are extremely important because they set the stage for letting the expert want to help you.

Ten Basic Telephone Tips

Here are a few pointers to keep in mind when you are casting about for an expert. These guidelines amount to basic common sense but are very easy to forget by the time you get to that sixth or seventh phone call.

1) Introduce Yourself Cheerfully

The way you open the conversation will set the tone for the entire interview. Your greeting and initial comment should be cordial and cheerful. They should give the feeling that this is not going to be just another telephone call, but a pleasant interlude in his or her day.

2) Be Open and Candid

You should be as candid as is possible with your source since you are asking the same of him. If you are evasive or deceitful in explaining your needs or motives, your source will be reluctant to provide you with information. If there are certain facts you cannot reveal such as client confidentiality, explain just that. Most people will understand and admire your honesty.

3) Be Optimistic

Throughout the entire conversation you should exude a sense of confidence. If you call and say "You probably aren't the right person" or "You don't have any information, do you?" it makes it easy for the person to say, "You're right, I cannot help you." A positive attitude will encourage your source to stretch his mind to see how he might be able to help you and give you what you need.

4) Be Humble and Courteous

You can be optimistic and still be humble. Remember the old adage that you can catch more flies with honey than you can with vinegar. People in general, and experts in particular, love to tell others what they know, as long as their position of authority is not questioned or threatened.

5) Be Concise

State your problem simply. A long-winded explanation may bore your contact and reduce your chances for getting a thorough response. No one, not even a government bureaucrat, enjoys speaking to a bore.

6) Don't be A "Gimme"

A "gimme" is someone who says "give me this" or "give me that", and has little consideration for the other person's time or feelings.

7) *Be Complimentary*

This goes hand in hand with being humble. A well-placed compliment about your source's expertise or insight about a particular topic will serve you well. In searching for information in large organizations, you are apt to talk to many colleagues of your source, so it wouldn't hurt to convey the respect that your "Charlie Porter" commands, for example, "Everyone I spoke to said you are the person I must talk with." It is reassuring to anyone to know that they have the respect of their peers.

8) *Be Conversational*

Avoid spending the entire time talking about the information you need. Briefly mention a few irrelevant topics such as the weather, the Washington Redskins, or the latest political campaign. The more social you are without being too chatty, the more likely that your source will open up and really give you the information that you're looking for.

9) *Return the Favor*

You might share with your source information or even gossip you have picked up elsewhere. However, be certain not to betray the trust of either your client or another source. If you do not have any relevant information to share at the moment, it would still be a good idea to call back when you are further along in your research.

10) *Send Thank You Notes*

A short note, typed or handwritten, will help ensure that your source will be just as cooperative in the future.

Women Business Programs

Uncle Sam Is Getting A Sex Change

It wasn't very long ago that most small businesses in this country were headed by men. Now, women head 2 out of every 3 new businesses that start. The government's lead office for supporting small business, The *Small Business Administration*, has wised up and now has special staff in almost every area of the country that cater strictly to the specific needs of women entrepreneurs. They can help you network with other women business owners, tell you where to find financial assistance, or tell you how to obtain government procurement contracts.

To locate the nearest Women's Business Ownership Representative, contact your local Small Business Administration Office, or Office of Women's Business Ownership, U.S. Small Business Administration, 409 3rd St., SW, Washington, DC 20416; 202-205-6673; 800-8-ASK-SBA; {www.sba.gov}.

Women's Business Ownership Representatives

Alabama
Susan Dunham
U.S. Small Business Administration
2121 8th Ave., North, Suite 200
Birmingham, AL 35203-2398
205-731-1334
Fax: 205-731-1404

Alaska
Joyce Courtney
U.S. Small Business Administration
222 West 8th Ave., Room 67
Anchorage, AK 99513-7559
907-271-4022
Fax: 907-271-4545

Arizona
Gail Gesell
U.S. Small Business Administration
2828 North Central, Suite 800
Phoenix, AZ 85004-1025
602-640-2316
602-640-2325
Fax: 602-640-2360

Arkansas
Valerie Coleman
U.S. Small Business Administration

2120 Riverfront, Suite 100
Little Rock, AR 72202
501-324-5871, ext. 236
Fax: 501-324-5199/5149

California
Gloria Minarik
U.S. Small Business Administration
455 Market St., 6th Floor
San Francisco, CA 94105
415-744-8491
Fax: 415-744-6812

Gilda Perez
U.S. Small Business Administration
660 J St., Suite 215
Sacramento, CA 95814-2413
916-498-6430
Fax: 916-498-6422

Delores Braswell
U.S. Small Business Administration
550 W. C St., Suite 550
San Diego, CA 92188
619-557-7250, ext. 1147
Fax: 619-557-5894

Rose Kim
U.S. Small Business Administration
200 W. Santa Ana Blvd., Suite 700
Santa Ana, CA 92703-2352
714-950-7420
Fax: 714-836-2528

Theresa Leets
U.S. Small Business Administration
330 N. Brand Blvd., Suite 1200
Glendale, CA 91203-2304
818-552-3215
Fax: 818-552-3260

Leslie Lang Lopez
U.S. Small Business Administration
2719 N. Air Fresno Dr.
Suite 107
Fresno, CA 93727-1547
209-487-5791, ext. 526
Fax: 209-487-5803

Colorado
Marsha Summerlin
Cindy Cronin
U.S. Small Business Administration
721 19th St., Suite 426
Denver, CO 80202-2599
303-844-3461
Fax: 303-844-6539

Connecticut
Kathleen Duncan
U.S. Small Business Administration
330 Main St., 2nd Floor
Hartford, CT 06106
860-240-4842
Fax: 860-240-4659

Delaware
Carlotta Catullo
U.S. Small Business Administration
824 Market St., Suite 610
Wilmington, DE 19801
302-573-6380
Fax: 302-573-6060

District of Columbia
Ms. Cynthia Pope
U.S. Small Business Administration
1110 Vermont Ave. NW, 9th Floor
Washington, DC 20005
(P.O. Box 34500
Washington, DC 20043-4500)
202-606-4000, ext. 345
Fax: 202-606-4225

Florida
Judy Dunn
U.S. Small Business Administration
7825 Bay Meadows Way
Suite 100B
Jacksonville, FL 32256-7504
904-443-1900/1933
Fax: 904-443-1980

Patricia McCartney
U.S. Small Business Administration
1320 S. Dixie Hwy.
Suite 501, 3rd Floor
Coral Gables, FL 33146-2911
305-536-5833
Fax: 305-536-5058

Georgia
Dorothy Fletcher
U.S. Small Business Administration
1720 Peachtree St., NW, 6th Floor
Atlanta, GA 30309
404-853-7674
Fax: 404-853-7677

Hawaii
Doreen Ezuka
U.S. Small Business Administration
300 Ala Moana
Room 2314
Honolulu, HI 96850-4981
808-541-2971
808-541-3024
Fax: 808-541-2976

Idaho
Pat Hunt
U.S. Small Business Administration
1020 Main St., Suite 290
Boise, ID 83702-5745
208-334-9079
Fax: 208-334-9353

Illinois

Sam McGrier
U.S. Small Business Administration
500 W. Madison St., Suite 1250
Chicago, IL 60661-2511
312-353-4528/5429
Fax: 312-886-5108

Indiana

Ms. Betty McDonald
U.S. Small Business Administration
429 N. Pennsylvania Ave.
Suite 100
Indianapolis, IN 46204
317-226-7272
Fax: 317-226-7259

Valerie Ross
U.S. Small Business Administration
511 W. Capitol St., Suite 302
Springfield, IL 62704
217-492-4416
Fax: 217-492-4867

Iowa

Carolyn Tonn
U.S. Small Business Administration
215 4th Ave. SE, Suite 200
Cedar Rapids, IA 52401
319-362-6405
Fax: 319-362-7861

Deb Anderson
U.S. Small Business Administration
210 Walnut St., Room 749
Des Moines, IA 50309
515-284-4761
Fax: 515-284-4572

Kansas

Iris Newton
U.S. Small Business Administration
100 E. English, Suite 510

Wichita, KS 67202
316-269-6631
Fax: 316-269-6499

Kentucky

Carol Halfield
U.S. Small Business Administration
600 Dr. Martin Luther King, Jr. Pl.
Room 188
Louisville, KY 40202
502-582-5971
Fax: 502-582-5009

Louisiana

Loretta Puree
U.S. Small Business Administration
365 Canal St., Suite 2250
New Orleans, LA 70130
504-589-6685, ext. 231
Fax: 504-589-2339

Maine

Patricia Knowles
U.S. Small Business Administration
40 Western Ave., Room 512
Augusta, ME 04330
207-622-8242
Fax: 207-622-8277

Maryland

Martha Brown
U.S. Small Business Administration
10 S. Howard St., Suite 6220
Baltimore, MD 21201
410-962-6195
Fax: 410-962-1805

Beatrice Checket
SCORE
907 Sextant Way
Annapolis, MD 21401
410-366-8746
Fax: 410-266-8754

Massachusetts
Lisa Gonzalez
U.S. Small Business Administration
10 Causeway St., Room 265
Boston, MA 02222-1093
617-565-5588
Fax: 617-565-5598

Harry Webb
U.S. Small Business Administration
1441 Main St., Room 410
Springfield, MA 01103
413-785-0268
Fax: 413-785-0267

Michigan
Catherine Gase
U.S. Small Business Administration
477 Michigan Ave.
Room 515
Detroit, MI 48226
313-226-6075, ext. 404
Fax: 313-226-4769

Minnesota
Cynthia Collett
U.S. Small Business Administration
100 N. 6th St., Suite 610C
Minneapolis, MN 55403-1563
612-370-2324
612-370-2312
Fax: 612-370-2303

Missouri
U.S. Small Business Administration
911 Walnut St.
Kansas City, MO 64106
816-426-3608
Fax: 816-426-5559

Patty Ingram
U.S. Small Business Administration
323 W 8th, 5th Floor
Kansas City, MO 64105

816-374-6762
Fax: 816-374-6759

Laverne Johnson
U.S. Small Business Administration
815 Olive St., Suite 242
St. Louis, MO 63101
314-539-6600
Fax: 314-539-3785

LuAnn Hancock
U.S. Small Business Administration
620 S. Glenstone, Suite 110
Springfield, MO 65802-3200
417-864-7670
Fax: 417-864-4108

Mississippi
Charles Gillis
U.S. Small Business Administration
One Government Plaza
2909 13th St., Suite 203
Gulfport, MS 39501-7758
228-863-4449
Fax: 228-864-0179

Valencia Jamila
U.S. Small Business Administration
101 W. Capitol St., Suite 400
Jackson, MS 39201
601-965-5342
Fax: 601-965-5629

Montana
U.S. Small Business Administration
301 South Park Ave.

Room 334
Helena, MT 59626
406-441-1081
Fax: 406-441-1090

Nebraska
Barbara Foster
U.S. Small Business Administration
11145 Mill Valley Rd.
Omaha, NE 68154
402-221-3604
Fax: 402-221-3680

Nevada
Donna Hopkins
U.S. Small Business Administration
301 E. Stewart Ave.
P.O. Box 7527
Las Vegas, NV 89125-2527
702-388-6611
Fax: 702-388-6469

New Hampshire
Sandra Sullivan
U.S. Small Business Administration
143 N. Main St.
Concord, NH 03301
603-225-1400
Fax: 603-225-1409

New Jersey
Frank Burke
U.S. Small Business Administration
Two Gateway Center, 4th Floor
Newark, NJ 07102
201-645-2434
Fax: 201-645-6265

New Mexico
Susan Chavez
U.S. Small Business Administration
625 Silver SW, Room 320
Albuquerque, NM 87102

505-766-1879
Fax: 505-766-1057

New York
Carol White
U.S. Small Business Administration
26 Federal Plaza
Room 3100
New York, NY 10278
212-264-1482
Fax: 212-264-4963

U.S. Small Business Administration
100 S. Clinton St.
Room 1073
P.O. Box 7317
Syracuse, NY 13261
315-448-0428
Fax: 315-448-0410

James Cristofaro
U.S. Small Business Administration
333 E. Water St., 4th Floor
Elmira, NY 14901
607-734-8142
Fax: 607-733-4656

Donald Butzek
U.S. Small Business Administration
111 W. Huron St., Room 1311
Buffalo, NY 14202
716-551-5670
Fax: 716-551-4418

U.S. Small Business Administration
35 Pinelawn Rd., Room 207W
Melville, NY 11747
516-454-0763
Fax: 516-454-0769

Howard Daly
SCORE
431 Woodland Lane

Webster, NY 14580
716-671-4550

Marcia Ketchum
U.S. Small Business Administration
100 State St., Room 410
Rochester, NY 14614
716-263-6700
Fax: 716-263-3146

North Carolina
Cassandra Smith
U.S. Small Business Administration
200 N. College St., Suite A2015
Charlotte, NC 28202-2173
704-344-6587
Fax: 704-344-6769

North Dakota
Marlene Koenig
U.S. Small Business Administration
657 2nd Ave. North, Room 219
Fargo, ND 58102
701-239-5131
Fax: 701-239-5645

Ohio
Rosemary Darling
U.S. Small Business Administration
1111 Superior Ave., Suite 630
Cleveland, OH 44144
216-522-4180 ext. 128
Fax: 216-522-2038

Janice Sonnenberg
U.S. Small Business Administration
2 Nationwide Plaza, Suite 1400
Columbus, OH 43215-2542
614-469-6860
Fax: 614-469-2391

Bonnie Schenck
U.S. Small Business Administration

525 Vine St., Suite 870
Cincinnati, OH 45202
513-684-6907
Fax: 513-684-3251

Oklahoma
Joyce Jones
U.S. Small Business Administration
210 Park Ave.
Oklahoma City, OK 73102
405-231-4301
Fax: 405-231-4876

Oregon
Leann Earley
U.S. Small Business Administration
1515 SW 5th Ave.
Suite 1050
Portland, OR 97207
503-326-5101
Fax: 503-326-2808

Pennsylvania
Ana Gallardo
U.S. Small Business Administration
900 Market St.
Philadelphia, PA 19107
215-580-2707
Fax: 215-580-2800

Linda Carey
U.S. Small Business Administration
1000 Liberty Ave.
Federal Bldg. #1128
Pittsburgh, PA 15222
412-644-2780
Fax: 416-644-5446

Rhode Island
Patricia O'Rourke
U.S. Small Business Administration
380 Westminister St., 5th Floor
Providence, RI 02903

401-528-4688
Fax: 401-528-4539

South Carolina
Teresa Singleton
U.S. Small Business Administration
1835 Assembly St., Room 358
Columbia, SC 29201
803-765-5298
Fax: 803-765-5962

South Dakota
Darlene Michael
U.S. Small Business Administration
101 S. Phillips Ave.
Suite 200
Sioux Falls, SD 57104-6727
605-330-4231
Fax: 605-330-4215

Tennessee
Saundra Jackson
U.S. Small Business Administration
50 Vantage Way, Suite 201
Nashville, TN 37228-1550
615-736-5881
615-736-7935
Fax: 615-736-7232

Texas
Terry Ruiz
U.S. Small Business Administration
10737 Gateway West, Suite 320
El Paso, TX 79925

915-540-5154
Fax: 915-540-5636

Wila Lewis
U.S. Small Business Administration
9301 SW Freeway, Suite 550
Houston, TX 77074
713-773-6519
Fax: 713-773-6550

Thelma Ruelas
U.S. Small Business Administration
222 E. Van Buren St., Suite 500
Harlingen, TX 78550
210-427-8533
Fax: 210-427-8537

Vicky Norton
U.S. Small Business Administration
1611 10th St., Suite 200
Lubbock, TX 79401
806-472-7462
Fax: 806-472-7487

U.S. Small Business Administration
727 E. Durango, Room A527
San Antonio, TX 78206
210-472-5900
Fax: 210-472-5935

Diane Cheshier
U.S. Small Business Administration
4300 Amon Carter Blvd., Suite 114
Ft. Worth, TX 76155
817-885-6504
Fax: 817-885-6543

Mr. Jesus Sendejo
U.S. Small Business Administration
606 N. Caranchua
Corpus Christi, TX 78476
512-888-3331
Fax: 512-888-3481

Utah
Jean Fox
U.S. Small Business Administration
125 S. State St., Room 2229
Salt Lake City, UT 84138-1195
801-524-6831
Fax: 801-524-4160

Vermont
Brenda Fortier
U.S. Small Business Administration
87 State St., Room 205
Montpelier, VT 05601-0605
802-828-4422
Fax: 802-828-4485

Virginia
Fannie Gergoudis
U.S. Small Business Administration
1504 Santa Rosa Rd., Suite 200
Richmond, VA 23229
804-771-2765, ext. 112
Fax: 804-771-8018

Washington
Carol McIntosh
U.S. Small Business Administration
1200 Sixth Ave., Suite 1700
Seattle, WA 98101
206-553-7310
206-553-7315
Fax: 206-553-7044

U.S. Small Business Administration
Seattle, WA 98174-1088
206-220-6520
Fax: 206-220-6570

Coralie Myers
U.S. Small Business Administration
1020 W. Riverside Ave.

Spokane, WA 99201
509-353-2800
509-353-2630
Fax: 509-353-2600

Diana Wilhite
617 N. Helena
Spokane, WA 99202
509-534-9001
Fax: 509-534-3003

West Virginia
Sharon Weaver
U.S. Small Business Administration
168 W. Main St., 6th Floor
Clarksburg, WV 26301
304-623-5631
Fax: 304-623-0023

Wisconsin
U.S. Small Business Administration
212 E. Washington Ave.
Room 213
Madison, WI 53703
608-264-5516
Fax: 608-264-5541

Jerry Polk
U.S. Small Business Administration
310 W. Wisconsin Ave., Suite 400
Milwaukee, WI 53203
414-297-3941
Fax: 414-297-1377

Wyoming
Beth Hink
U.S. Small Business Administration
100 E. B St., Room 4001
Casper, WY 82602-2839
307-261-6500
Fax: 307-261-6535

60 Places
To Get A Little Help
From Your Friends

Sometimes you just need someone to show you the way.

The **Women's Demonstration Program** has 60 sites across the country where women are trained and counseled in the skills necessary to launch their own business. These sites get money from the government to offer financial, management, marketing and technical assistance to current and potential women business owners.

To locate the nearest Women's Business Ownership Representative, contact your local Small Business Administration Office, or Office of Women's Business Ownership, U.S. Small Business Administration, 409 3rd St., SW, Washington, DC 20416; 202-205-6673; 800-8-ASK-SBA; {www.sba.gov}.

Women's Business Centers

Sherrye Henry, Assistant Administrator
Ellen Thrasher, Deputy Director
Sally Murrell, Senior Program Director, Women's Business Centers
Harriet Fredman, Program Analyst

Organizational Profile

The U. S. Small Business Administration (SBA) is charged with promoting public policies that assist businesses to succeed in a competitive marketplace, especially business owners who have been historically under-served or excluded. Since women are starting businesses at twice the rate of all business, addressing the special needs of women's business ownership is essential to the overall economic well-being of the nation.

The SBA Office of Women's Business Ownership (OWBO) is the only federal agency with a mission to foster the growth of women's business ownership. The office promotes the growth of these businesses through programs that address business training and technical assistance, access to credit and capital, access to marketing opportunities including federal contracts, and research and information to develop a profile of women business owners in the United States.

Women's Business Centers

Each Women's Business Center (WBC) must provide assistance and/or training in: finance, management, marketing, procurement and specialized topics such as home-based businesses and corporate executive downsizing. Each WBC tailors programs to their constituencies' needs.

Alabama

Women's Business Assistance Center (WBAC)
Kathryn Cariglino, Director
1301 Azalea Road, Suite 201A
Mobile, AL 36693   334-660-2725
Mailing Address: P. O. Box 6021   800-378-7461
Mobile, AL 36660   Fax: 334-660-8854
E-mail: wbac@ceebic.org

Website: http://ceebic.org/~wbac
The Women's Business Assistance Center (WBAC) is located in the Center for
Entrepreneurial Excellence. This is a former school campus which was
purchased and renovated by the City of Mobile and Mobile County. It is now a
business incubator and training center. The Director of the WBAC is also
owner of the Women's Yellow Pages of the Gulf Coast. The WBAC provides
training seminars and one-on-one counseling for the South Alabama and
Northwest Florida area.

Alaska
WOMEN$ Fund, A Program of the YWCA of Anchorage
Kathryn J. Maieli, Program Director
Sharon Richards, YWCA Executive Director
245 West Fifth Avenue
P. O. Box 102059   907-274-1524
Anchorage, AK 99510-2059   Fax: 907-272-3146
E-mail: a net@alaska.net
WOMEN$ Fund was established in 1995 as a program of the YWCA and fully
implemented in Spring 1996. WOMEN$ Fund is a microenterprise training and
microlending program for women entrepreneurs in Anchorage, Alaska.
Consistent with the National YWCA's mission to empower women and girls
and to eliminate racism, the programs of the YWCA of Anchorage promote
independence, knowledge and self esteem especially for low-income and
minority women. WOMEN$ Fund mission is to secure financial independence
for women through the provision of capital and technical assistance. By
providing training classes in entrepreneurship, technical assistance, individual
mentoring and seed money for women-owned small businesses, WOMEN$
Fund seeks to empower low/moderate-income single-parent and minority
women in Anchorage and surrounding Alaska communities for economic self-
sufficiency.

Arizona
Self-Employment Loan Fund, Inc. (SELF)
201 North Central Avenue, Suite CC10   602-340-8834
Phoenix, AZ 85073-1000   Fax: 602-340-8953
E-mail: self-employment@juno.com
Self-Employment Loan Fund, Inc. (SELF) is a private non-profit organization
that provides training, technical assistance, and loan access to low-income
individuals, primarily women and minorities, who are starting or expanding
small businesses. The training sessions are ten to fourteen weeks in length and
the outcome is a completed business plan. Upon the completion of the business
plan, participants are eligible for SELF's peer lending process, called
Borrower's Circles. These circles of three to eight individuals provide an
avenue for support, debt repayment, and continuing business education. SELF

serves all of Maricopa County and will, with the OWBO grant, be providing its services in Graham and Gila counties. The population of Maricopa County is urban and comprises over half of the state's population; Graham and Gila counties are rural areas with high unemployment and few opportunities for nascent entrepreneurs. In its three years of operation, SELF has served over 350 individuals through the training program and loaned $83,000 to 60 borrowers. SELF serves an ethnically diverse population: 51% African-American, 29% Caucasians 16% Hispanic, and 4% Other.

California
Women's Enterprise Development Corporation (WEDC)
Phil Borden, Executive Director
100 West Broadway, Suite 500   562-983-3747
Long Beach, CA 90802   Fax: 562-983-3750
E-mail: wedcl@aol.com
WEDC, previously known as California AWED, began in 1989 with SBA funding to assist the growing number of women business owners in Los Angeles. Their core programs consist of two long-term training modules: *Starting Your Own Business* for beginning businesses and *Managing Your Own Business* for women who have been in business at least one year with gross receipts over $50,000. Courses are marketed in six languages: Chinese, English, Japanese, Khmer, Korean and Spanish.

Women's Initiative for Self Employment (WI)
Barbara Johnson, Executive Director
450 Mission Street, Suite 402   415-247-9473
San Francisco, CA 94105   Fax: 415-247-9471
E-mail: womensinitsf@igc.ape.org
Oakland Site: wioakland@igc.apc.org
Spanish Site: wialas@igc.apc.org
Women's Initiative (WI) provides business
training and technical assistance in English and
Spanish to low-income women in the San Francisco

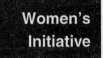
Women's Initiative

Bay Area. The English language program consists of a two-week business assessment workshop, a fourteen-week business skills workshop and a four-week workshop on writing a business plan. The Spanish language program parallels the English but is in a modular format. WI also offers business support services including one-on-one consultations, peer networking and support groups, and special seminars.

ONABEN — A Native American Business Network
Patrick Borunda, Director
520 Southwest 6th Avenue, Suite 930   503-243-5015

Portland, OR 97204   Fax: 503-243-5028
E-mail: borunda@onaben.org
Website: http://www.onaben.org
ONABEN — A Native American Business Network, is a non-profit public
benefit corporation created by Northwest Indian Tribes to increase the number
and profitability of private enterprises owned by Native Americans. ONABEN
offers training, individual counseling, assisted access to markets and facilitated
access to capital for its clients. Each of the ten tribes hosting an ONABEN
Service Center pays annual dues of $2,500 plus 40% of the cost of operating
their site. The sites, located on reservations in Oregon, Washington and
California, deliver services to all citizens regardless of tribal affiliation. Some
have up to 40% of users coming from the surrounding non-Native community.

WEST Company - Ukiah Office
Sheilah Rogers, Executive Director
367 North State Street, Suite 201   707-468-3553
Ukiah, CA 95482   Fax: 707-468-3555
E-mail: westco@pacific.net

WEST Company - Fort Bragg Once
Cinnamon Sky, Technology Manager
Carol Steele, Loan Fund Manager
306 East Redwood Avenue, Suite 2   707-964-7571
Fort Bragg, CA 95437   Fax: 707-964-7576
E-mail: westcofb@mcn.org
WEST Company serves micro-enterprise owners in rural Northern California,
targeting low-income women and minorities. WEST Company provides
business planning and management assistance at any stage of business
ownership from feasibility through expansion. Services include business plan
training, individual consulting, access to capital through individual and peer
loans, business network formation, and assistance with business applications
using technology.

Colorado
Mi Casa Resource Center for Women, Inc.
Barbara DesMarteau, Executive Director
571 Galapago Street   303-573-1302
Denver, CO 80204   Fax: 303-595-0422
E-mail: micasa@sni.net
Website: http://www.sni.net/micasa

Mi Casa Career Development and Business Center for Women
Gayle Warner, Director of Program Development

700 Knox Court   303-573-0333
Denver, CO 80204   Fax: 303-607-0872
E-mail: micasa@sni.net
Website: http://www.sni.net/micasa
Mi Casa Resource Center for Women, Inc., a non-profit organization founded
in 1976, provides quality employment and education services that promote
economic independence for low income, predominantly Latina women and
youth. Mi Casa accomplishes its mission through a number of programs and
services in its Career Development and Leadership Center, the Business Center
for Women and Youth Services. Services include educational counseling, job
readiness and job search training, life skills development, job placement, non-
traditional and computer skills training. Entrepreneurial training is provided
through either the Evening Entrepreneurial Training Program or Project
Success. Individuals are trained on how to start a business and develop business
plans with micro-loans available to program graduates. Youth development,
drop-out prevention, leadership training and responsible decision making is
provided through two youth programs — *Mi Carrera* (My Career) and *Fenix*
(teen pregnancy, AIDS and STD prevention program).

Connecticut
Women Business Development Center (WBDC)
Fran Pastore, Director of Training and Programs
2001 West Main Street, Suite 140   203-353-1750
Stamford, CT 06902   Fax: 203-353-1084
E-mail: wbdc@ferg.lib.ct.us

AWED Connecticut's programs follow the AWED model,
offering *Start Your Own Business* and *Managing Your Own
Business* training seminars. AWED provides individual
seminars and workshops. They have received a technical
assistance grant through SBA's micro-loan program to provide loan
packaging assistance to clients.

District of Columbia
National Women's Business Center
Paula Moore, Director
1250 24th Street, N.W. Suite 350   202-466-0544
Washington, D.C. 20037   Fax: 202-466-0581
E-mail: wbc@patriot.net
Website: http://www.womenconnect.com/womensbusinesscenter
The National Women's Business Center has one location in downtown D.C.
and a second location at the SBA District Office, co-located with the Small
Business Development Center sub-center to maximize the exposure to and
utilization of business training and counseling with several SBA resource

partners. The Center offers the following menu of programs: *Introduction to Business Ownership*; *Up and Running*; *Managing a Business with Accountability*; *Doing Business with the Government*; *The Business Council*; *The Roundtable*; *The Business Laboratory*; and *The Bottom Line.*

Florida

Women's Business Development Center (WBDC)

Christine Kurtz-White, Director	305-348-3951
10555 West Flagler Street, Room 2612	305-348-3903
Miami, FL 33174	Fax: 305-348-2931
E-mail: kurtzc@fiu.edu	Director
palustre@fiu.edu	Office Manager
rojasm@fiu.edu	Financial Consultant

The Center provides quality business education, technical assistance and access to capital for women, minorities, low- and moderate-income individuals who are starting or growing their own businesses. Business education programs incorporate both traditional and non-traditional methods of learning. In classroom settings, business owners and professionals teach participants about entrepreneurship, market research, financial analysis and business planning. Non-traditional programs include one-on-one business counseling, a Mentor/Protege program, business specialty workshops and networking forums. The Center also assists clients with preparation of loan packages and will present loans to financial institutions. The Center has been designated an intermediary for the SBA Women's Prequalification Loan Program and has a satellite office in downtown Miami at the SBA's Business Resource Center. Social skills training for women on welfare has been initiated and will be offered with dual goals of enhancing employability as well as providing the first step to self-employment.

> Business owners and professionals teach participants about entrepreneurship, market research, financial analysis and business planning

Women's Business Assistance Center (WBAC)

Kathryn Cariglino, Director	
1301 Azalea Road, Suite 201A	
Mobile, AL 36693	334-660-2725
Mailing Address: P. O. Box 6021	800-378-7461
Mobile, AL 36660	Fax: 334-660-8854
E-mail: wbac@ceebic.org	

Website: http://ceebic.org/~wbac

The Women's Business Assistance Center (WBAC) is located in the Center for Entrepreneurial Excellence. This is a former school campus which was purchased and renovated by the City of Mobile and Mobile County. It is now a business incubator and training center. The Director of the WBAC is also owner of the Women's Yellow Pages of the Gulf Coast. The WBAC provides training seminars and one-on-one counseling for the South Alabama and Northwest Florida area.

Georgia
Women's Economic Development Agency (WEDA)
Joyce Edwards, Chairperson for Board
675 Ponce de Leon Avenue   404-853-7680
Atlanta, GA 30308   Fax: 404-853-7677
The WEDA program is geared for individuals who are planning, expanding or strengthening a business. It is a 21-seminar series for women business owners, lasting two-and-one-half hours each week. This program was condensed in 1995 to a five-hour program. WEDA also provides mentoring and one-on-one counseling. The majority of clients are African-American women; however, it is open to all individuals. Topics covered in the training program include marketing, business planning, accounting and finance, contract negotiation, and domestic and international procurement.

Illinois
Women's Business Development Center (WBDC)
Hedy Ratner and Carol Dougal, Co-Directors
Linda Darragh, Project Director, Ext. 22
8 South Michigan Avenue, Suite 400   312-853-3477
Chicago, IL 60603   Fax: 312-853-0145
E-mail: wbdc@aol.com
Founded in 1986, the WBDC serves women business owners in the greater Chicago area, and advocates for women business owners nationwide. The WBDC has assisted in the establishment of Demonstration sites since 1989 in Illinois, Ohio, Florida, Pennsylvania and Massachusetts. The WBDC provides a variety of entrepreneurial training courses and seminars: one-on-one counseling; financial assistance and loan packaging for micro-loans, the SBA Prequalification Loan Program and other SBA and government loan programs including the mentor/protege program; WBE certification and private and public sector procurement; annual conference and Women's Buyers Mart; and extensive advocacy and policy development for women's economic and business development issues.

Louisiana
Women Entrepreneurs for Economic Development Inc. (WEED)
Paula Peete, Executive Director
Cynthia Beaulieu, Director of Training

1683 North Claiborne Avenue, Suite 101   504-947-8522
New Orleans, LA 70116   Fax: 504-947-8885
E-mail: webc@bellsouth.net
Women Entrepreneurs for Economic
Development, Inc. (WEED) was founded in 1989
by three business women. Since their inception,
WEED has assisted hundreds of women to
become economically self-sufficient. They assist
women in the Orleans Parish area of New Orleans.

Southeast Louisiana Black Chamber of Commerce (SLBCC)
Women's Business Center
Laverne Kilgore, Director
2245 Peters Road, Suite 200   504-365-3866
Harvey, LA 70058   Fax: 504-365-3890
E-mail: wbc200@bellsouth.net
Website: http://www.gnofn.org/~slbcc/wbc
The Women's Business Center is a program that was developed by the
Southeast Louisiana Black Chamber of Commerce (SLBCC) to assist women
in Jefferson Parish, but serves nine other parishes including: Orleans, St.
Bernard, St. Tammany, St. James, St. John the Baptist, St. Charles,
Tangipahoa, Plaquemines and Washington. The Center is located in JEDCO
West, an incubator program in Harvey, Louisiana. Many of the clients served
through the Center have started their own businesses. The Center also provides
training, counseling and mentoring to aid and encourage the growth and
development of small businesses, owned and controlled by women.

Maine
Coastal Enterprises Inc. (CEI)
Women's Business Development Program (WBDP)
Ronald Phillips, President
Ellen Golden, Senior Project Manager
P. O. Box 268   207-882-7552
Wiscasset, ME 04578   Fax: 207-882-7308
E-mail: efg@ceimaine.org
Website: http://www.ceimaine.org

Coastal Enterprises Inc. (CEI)
Women's Business Development Program (WBDP)
Janet Roderick, Women's Business Counselor
Betsy Tipper, Telecommunications Business Counselor
7 North Chestnut Street   207-621-0245
Augusta, ME 04330   Fax: 207-622-9739

E-mail: jmr@ceimaine.org
E-mail: eat@ceimaine.org
Website: http://www.ceimaine.org
Coastal Enterprises, Inc. (CEI) is a private non-profit community development corporation that provides financing and technical assistance to Maine businesses that provide income, ownership or employment opportunities to low income people. The Women's Business Development Project (WBDP) emerged from CEI's experience in assessing the needs of women business owners, and providing women business owners with training, technical assistance, financing and advocacy. Statewide in scope, the project targets assistance to women who have started their businesses. Project participants benefit from CEI's capacity to provide access to capital through its SBA Microloan Program, the SBA Women's Pre-Qualification Loan Program and other resources.

Maryland

Women Entrepreneurs of Baltimore, Inc. (WEB)
Amanda Crook Zinn, Chief Executive Officer
28 East Ostend Street   410-727-4921
Baltimore, MD 21230   Fax: 410-727-4989
Women Entrepreneurs of Baltimore, Inc. (WEB), a 501c(3) organization, is an entrepreneurial training program designed to help economically disadvantaged women become self-sufficient through business development. The main components of the WEB program are: an intensive three-month Business Skills Training course; Mentoring; Financing Strategy Development; Community Networking; Resource Sharing; and Professional Business Consultation.

Massachusetts

Center for Women & Enterprise Inc.
Andrea Silbert, Director
45 Bromfield Street, 6th Floor   617-423-3001, ext. 222
Boston, MA 02108   Fax: 617-423-2444
E-mail: info@cweboston.org
asilbert@cweboston.org
The Center for Women & Enterprise, Inc. (CWE) is a non-profit educational organization whose mission is to empower women to become economically self-sufficient and prosperous through entrepreneurship. The first center of its kind in Massachusetts, CWE provides courses, workshops, round tables, one-on-one consulting, and loan packaging assistance to women who seek to start and/or grow their own businesses. While services are open to everyone, scholarships target low-income women.

Michigan
Women's Initiative for Self-Employment (WISE)
c/o Center for Empowerment and Economic Development (CEED)
Michelle Richards, Executive Director
2002 Hogback Road, Suite 12   313-677-1400
Ann Arbor, MI 48105   Fax: 313-677-1465
E-mail: mrichards@miceed.org
The Women's Initiative for Self-Employment (WISE) Program began in 1987
as a means to provide low-income women with the tools and resources to begin
and expand businesses. The WISE Program provides a comprehensive package
of business training, personal development workshops, credit counseling, start-
up and expansion financing, business counseling, peer group support, and
mentoring. The creation and expansion of businesses is only one goal of this
program. The WISE Program was also designed to fight poverty, increase
incomes, raise self-esteem, stabilize families, develop skills and spark a process
of community renewal.

Grand Rapids Opportunities for Women (GROW)
Inger Giuffrida, Executive Director
Vicki Hudson, Marketing and Business Services Director
25 Sheldon SE, Suite 210   616-458-3404
Grand Rapids, MI 49503   Fax: 616-458-6557
E-mail: grow@voyager.net
Grand Rapids Opportunities for Women (GROW) is a non-profit economic
development organization which provides women from diverse backgrounds —
many of whom are facing social or economic barriers — with opportunities to
develop the skills and acquire the knowledge needed to achieve financial
independence. Focusing on small businesses, GROW provides entrepreneurial
training needed to start a small business as well as the follow-up services
needed to sustain and expand a business. Since starting a business often affects
all aspects of a woman's life, GROW is committed to providing group and
individual support for both business and personal development. GROW's
economic development programming has three components: Business
Readiness Assessment, Entrepreneurial Training/Business Plan Development,
and Follow-Up Services. GROW offers a 15-week course, "Minding Your Own
Business," which covers accounting, bookkeeping, taxes, marketing, financial
analysis, sales techniques, promotion, inventory, conflict management, trade
shows, business writing, public speaking, and market research. Follow-Up
Services include Business Circles, Up Close Seminars, a Marketing Fund,
Technical Assistance, Networking Opportunities and the FMB Bank/GROW
Step Loan and Savings Program.

Minnesota
Women in New Development (WIND)
(A Division of Bi-County Community Action Programs, Inc.)
Susan Hoosier, WIND Coordinator
2715 15th Street NW
P. O. Box 579   218-751-4631
Bemidji, MN 56601   Fax: 218-751-8452
E-mail: bicap@northernnet.com

Since 1969, WIND has served the small business
communities of Beltrami and Cass Counties in
rural northwestern Minnesota. In 1995, WIND
received funding to establish new sites in
Hubbard and East Polk County. Services were
also extended into Clearwater County. WIND
provides technical assistance to new and existing
businesses. Delivery of services is provided through one-on-one counseling,
classroom training (using a variety of workshop formats), an annual regional
Women's Business Conference, and through several networking organizations
which have been formed in Beltrami and Hubbard counties. In addition, WIND
also provides training services to eight additional counties in northwestern
Minnesota in collaboration with the Northwest Minnesota Foundation.

Mississippi
Women's Economic Entrepreneurial Project (MWEEP)
Jo Thompson, Director   601-741-3342
106 West Green Street   Fax: 601-741-2195
Mound Bayou, MS 38762   Fax: 601-335-3060
E-mail: jthompson@tecinfo.com

MWEEP Grant Recipient:
National Council of Negro Women
Christine Toney, Executive Director
Lucenia Dunn, Director of Programs
633 Pennsylvania Avenue, NW   202-737-0120
Washington, D.C. 20004   Fax: 202-737-0476
E-mail:ncnwmsbc@tecinfo.com
dirmsbc@tecinfo.com, carmicle@tecinfo.com
Website: http://www.ncnw.com

The National Council of Negro Women (NCNW) established economic
entrepreneurial centers in Mound Bayou and Ruleville in Bolivar County,
Mississippi. This area has been designated as a rural Enterprise Zone by the
government. THE NCNW works closely with key officials and staff persons
administering this revitalization effort to leverage SBA funding and avoid any
duplication of effort.

Missouri

NAWBO - St. Louis
(National Association of Women's Business Owners - St. Louis)
Irina Bronstein, Executive Director
7165 Delmar, Suite 204
St. Louis, MO 63130
E-mail: nawbostl@ibm.net

314-863-0046
Fax: 314-863-2079

This site is part of the St. Louis chapter of the National Association of Women
Business Owners (NAWBO). They offer one-on-one counseling, mentoring,
monthly educational and networking meetings, referrals to women-owned
businesses and an educational program. This program is called SUCCESS
Savvy and consists of a series of classes to help women start and grow a
successful business. Course topics include: *Do I Really Want To Be In
Business*, *Writing a Business Plan*, *Basic Accounting for Your Business*,
Writing a Marketing Plan, and *When and How to Use Professionals*. The
program also includes a SMART BUSINESS conference with seminars
designed to educate women in the various stages of business ownership.

Montana

Women's Capital Fund
Kris Bakula, Executive Director
Lisa Gentri, Business Development Specialist
302 North Last Chance Gulch, Suite 400
P. O. Box 271
Helena, MT 59624
E-mail: mwcf@ixi.net

406-443-3144
Fax: 406-442-1789

The Montana Women's Capital Fund OWBO grant activities target 12 counties
extending from the Helena area north to the Canadian border encompassing
30,403 square miles. They are one of five North American affiliates of
Women's World Banking. Their targeted area is very rural and, for that reason,
they offer training classes in four strategically located areas: Lewistown, Great
Falls, Browning and Helena.

Montana Community Development Corporation
Rosalie S. Cates, Executive Director
127 North Higgins
Missoula, MT 59802
E-mail: mcdc@montana.com

406-543-3550
Fax: 406-721-4584

Montana Community Development Corporation (MCDC) business workshops
cover basic or advanced business concepts. Business owners learn from
experienced trainers in a relaxed interactive setting. The training uses real-
world information, featuring local business owners as speakers. Trainers
emphasize practical problem-solving that most business owners can carry out

independently. MCDC's marketing alliances provide a network of similar businesses to work together on efforts which include market research, promotion, distribution and advertising. Business alliances they have developed include tourism, child care, and the arts.

Nevada
Nevada Self-Employment Trust (NSET)
Gerry Alcasas, Executive Director
116 E. 7th Street, Suite 3   702-841-1420
Carson City, NV 89704   Fax: 702-841-2221
E-mail: nemployl98@aol.com

Virginia Hardman, NSET Project Manager (OWBO)
1600 East Desert Inn Road, Suite 209E   702-734-3555
Las Vegas, NV 89109   Fax: 702-734-3530
E-mail: nemploy300@aol.com
The Nevada Self-Employment Trust (NSET) is a non-profit micro-enterprise development program. NSET's mission is to enhance the economic self-sufficiency of low- and moderate-income individuals by developing their entrepreneurial skills through training, technical assistance, and access to credit. These programs are designed to economically empower clients by providing the most comprehensive entrepreneurial services. NSET's programs provide women and men with business skills as well as life skills. Since its inception in 1991, NSET has served over 1200 women and men. Programs are available in Reno and Las Vegas.

New Hampshire
Women's Business Center, Inc.
Racheal Stuart, Executive Director
150 Greenleaf Avenue, Unit 4   603-430-2892
Portsmouth, NH 03801   Fax: 603-430-3706
E-mail: wbc.inc@rscs.com
The Women's Business Center, Inc. is a collaborative organization designed to encourage and support women in all phases of enterprise development. They provide access to educational programs, financing alternatives, technical assistance, advocacy and a network of mentors, peer advisors and business and professional consultants. By encouraging women in their business ventures, WBC fosters economic development. WBC aims to address the needs of women business owners through several targeted programs: Seminars for Women Entrepreneurs; WBC Newsletter; Monthly

> By encouraging women in their business ventures, WBC fosters economic development.

Peer Advisory Meetings; Internet for Small Business Workshops; and The
Entrepreneur's Network.

New Jersey
New Jersey NAWBO Ezcel
Harriet Scooler, Project Director
225 Hamilton Street   732-560-9607
Bound Brook, NJ 08805-2042   Fax: 732-560-9687
E-mail: njawbo@bellatlantic.net
Website: http://www.injersey.com/Clients/NJAWBO
The New Jersey National Association of Women Business Owners manages
this EXCEL training and counseling program. The training programs are in
three stages: Stage I: Thinking About Starting a Business — Are You an
Entrepreneur; Stage II: Creating or Assessing Your Business Plan — Start
Right, Build Right; Stage III: Looking to Grow Your Business — Grow Smart.
They offer training seminars throughout the state.

New Mexico
Women's Economic Self-Sufficiency Team (WESST Corp.)
Agnes Noonan, Executive Director
414 Silver Southwest   505-241-4760 - Main Number
Albuquerque, NM 87102   505-241-4753 - Office Manager
E-mail: wesst@swcp.com   505-241-4758 - Director
agnes@swcp.com - Agnes Noonan's E-mail   Fax: 505-241-4766

WESST Corp. - Farmington, NM
Joretta Clement, Regional Manager
500 West Main   505-325-0678
Farmington, NM 87401   Fax: 505-325-0695
E-mail: 4business@acrnet.com

WESST Corp. - Las Cruces, NM
Jennifer Craig, Regional Manager
691 South Telshor   505-522-3707
Las Cruces, NM 88001   Fax: 505-522-4414
E-mail: jencraig@zianet.com

WESST Corp. - Roswell, NM
Roberta Ahlness, Regional Manager
200 West First, Suite 324   505-624-9850
Roswell, NM 88201   Fax: 505-622-4196
E-mail: wesst@rt66.com

WESST Corp. - Santa Fe, NM
Marisa Del Rio, Regional Manager
418 Cerrillos Road, Suite 26   505-988-5284
Santa Fe, NM 87501   Fax: 505-988-5221
E-mail: sfwesst@swcp.com

WESST Corp. - Taos, NM
Dawn Redpath, Regional Manager
Box 5007 NDCBU   505-758-3099
Taos, NM 87571   Fax: 505-751-1575
E-mail: redpath@laplaza.org
The Women's Economic Self-Sufficiency Team (WESST Corp.) was
incorporated in 1988 to assist low-income and minority women throughout
New Mexico. This project focuses on the area of Las Cruces and Farmington,
New Mexico, with program services provided to women in Dona, Ana, Luna,
Otero and Sierra counties, with limited outreach to El Paso, Texas by the end of
the second project year. WESST Corp. is a micro-lender under SBA's microloan program. Counseling and mentoring are offered through professional
volunteers including attorneys, accountants, insurance agents and benefits
counselors.

New York
American Woman's Economic Development Corporation (AWED)
Suzanne Tufts, President and CEO
71 Vanderbilt Avenue, Suite 320   212-692-9100
New York, NY 10169   Fax: 212-692-9296
Founded in 1976, the American Woman's Economic Development Corporation is the premier national not-for-profit organization committed to helping entrepreneurial women start and
grow their own businesses. Based in New York City,
AWED also has offices in Southern California, Connecticut
and Washington, D.C. Since its inception, AWED has
served over 100,000 women through formal course
instructions, one-to-one business counseling, seminars,
special events and peer group support. AWED's goals is to
increase the start-up, survival and expansion rates of small businesses.

Women's Venture Fund, Inc.
Maria Semidei-Otero, President
155 East 42nd Street, Suite 316   212-972-1146
New York, NY 10017   Fax: 212-972-1167
The Women's Venture Fund, Inc., is based on a radically simple idea:
empowering women, particularly low-income women, to create new businesses

by making micro-loans available to them, and then ensuring their success through our mentoring and training component. The Fund makes micro-loans to entrepreneurial women who cannot get funding through conventional sources. These women have great ideas, but desperately need small loans, business planning, and the moral support it takes to develop a business into reality. By addressing their credit and training needs, the Fund enhances the ability of women to grow their businesses over time.

North Dakota
Women's Business Institute (WBI)
Penny Retzer, Director
320 North Fifth Street, Suite 203
P. O. Box 2043   701-235-6488
Fargo, ND 58107-2043   Fax: 701-235-8284
E-mail: wbinstitute@corpcomm.net
Website: http://www.rrtrade.org/women/wbi
The Women's Business Institute serves North Dakota entrepreneurs statewide. Information and counseling services are available through a toll-free Entrepreneur's Hotline. Training seminars focus on management, marketing, financing, government contracting and entrepreneurial self confidence. Topics have included Meet the Lenders, Communication Styles, Women & Investing — Taking Charge of Your Financial Future, I Resolve to Take Care of Me, How to Get Published, Retail Display, Power Networking, Analyzing Company Information Using Spreadsheets, I'm Your Manager, Not Your Mother, Redirecting Conflict to Opportunity, and many others. Group mentoring is available through Business Success Teams. They offer a statewide business conference and a region-wide Women's Showcase which includes a trade show, seminars, main stage of activity and celebrity entertainment. They are also in the beginning stages of developing a kitchen incubator.

Ohio
Ohio Women's Business Resource Network (OWBRN)
Mary Ann McClure, Director   614-466-2682
77 South High Street, 28th Floor   800-848-1300, ext. 62682
Columbus, OH 43215-6108   Fax: 614-466-0829
E-mail: owbrn@eurekanet.com

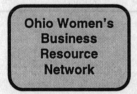

The Ohio Women's Business Resource Network (OWBRN) is a statewide effort to assist women business owners. Their mission is to promote successful women's entrepreneurship. This umbrella network promotes information sharing, technical assistance and education among participating member organizations. OWBRN seeks to provide consistent baseline services to women across the state.

The following eight centers are members of the statewide network:

Women's Organization for Mentoring, Entrepreneurship & Networking (WOMEN) & Wowmen's Network Inc.
Carrie Herman, Acting Executive Director   330-379-9280
526 South Main Street, Suite 235   330-379-2772
Akron. OH 44311-1058   Fax: 330-379-9283
E-mail: cherman@womennet.org
Website: http://www.womenmet.org
WOMEN provides training and counseling for start-up and existing small businesses. WOMEN also provides mentoring opportunities for expanding businesses.

Women's Business Resource Program of Southeastern Ohio
Debra McBride, Project Director
Ohio University
20 East Circle Drive, Suite 155
Technology and Enterprise Building   740-593-1797
Athens, OH 45701   Fax: 740-593-1795
E-mail: aa428@seorf.ohiou.edu
The Women's Business Resource Program of Southeastern Ohio supports women-owned businesses through a variety of services that focus on expanding networking opportunities, including support groups, monthly networking luncheons, business classes and an annual Women in Business Trade Fair. WBRP serves a seven-county area of southeast Ohio.

Pyramid Career Services
Mary Ellen Hess, Executive Director
Elaine Sherer, MBA Program Manager
2400 Cleveland Avenue North   330-453-3767
Canton, OH 44709   Fax: 330-453-6079
E-mail: pyramid@ezo.net
The Micro-Business Assistance program offers business plan development and one-on-one counseling for new and existing small businesses. Resources include technical and marketing assistance, micro loans, computer and internet training.

Women Entrepreneurs Inc.
Lyn Marsteller, Director
Sandy Evers, Program Director
Bartlett Building
36 East 4th Street, Suite 925
Cincinnati, OH 45202

or
P.O. Box 2662   513-684-0700
Cincinnati. OH 45201   Fax: 513-665-2452
E-mail: wei@eos.net
Women Entrepreneurs Inc. (WEI) is a networking and membership
organization for women business owners. They primarily provide specific
seminars for growing and expanding businesses. They are also an SBA microloan technical assistance recipient. WEI provides loan packaging services and
works with a variety of local lending institutions.

Glenville Development Corporation Micro-Enterprise Program
Rosalind Brewster, Micro-Enterprise Development Officer
540 East 105th Street   216-851-8724
Cleveland, OH 44108   Fax: 216-851-8941
Glenville Development Corporation provides long-term training to low-
through moderate-income women to assist them in personal and business
development. This is part of a community development corporation, which
provides a number of services to low income individuals.

Greater Columbus Women's Business Development Center
Linda Steward, Program Director
Cari Uhl, Project Coordinator   614-225-6081
37 North High Street   614-225-6082
Columbus, OH 43215-3065   Fax: 614-469-8250
E-mail: linda_steward@columbus.org
Website: http://www.columbus.org/busi/sbdc/index.htm
The Women's Business Initiative offers training for start-ups and existing
women business owners. They specialize in procurement, certification, and
international trade issues. They also offer the Women's Network for
Entrepreneurial Training (WNET) mentoring program.

Women's Development Center
Evelyn France, Executive Director
42101 Griswold Road   440-324-3688
Elyria, OH 44035   Fax: 440-324-3689
The Women's Development Center provides a long-term training program. This
program focuses first on personal development and then on entrepreneurship.
They target primarily low-income women. The Center assists women with
packaging their loans.

Women's Entrepreneurial Network
Linda Fayerweather, Director   419-867-8046
5555 Airport Highway, Suite 210   419-897-0528

Toledo, OH 43615   Fax: 419-867-8167
E-mail: lindafay@primenet.com
The Northwest Ohio Women's Entrepreneurial Network sponsors training for
start-up businesses and seminars for existing women business owners. They are
developing an "Expert Team Review" program which allows women-owned
businesses to meet with a panel of successful women business owners to
discuss problems with their business plans.

Oklahoma
Women's Business Center
Working Women's Money University (WWMU)
Lori Smith, Director   405-232-8257
234 Quadrum Drive   405-842-1196
Oklahoma City, OK 73108   Fax: 405-947-5388
E-mail: carol@wbc.okc.org
The Women's Business Center is an "entrepreneurial training
camp" where our team of small business supporters are
committed to help those who want to help themselves and
their businesses. We offer a complete one-stop resource
toolbox. Entrepreneur-led educational experiences
empower our clients with knowledge; developing every
aspect of their small business skills. We create
opportunities to build business-support networks
and connect our community's entrepreneurs with one
another. Through our alliance with the Small Business
Administration and the First National Bank of
Bethany, we provide access to capital for those small
business owners in our programs seeking financing. Our monthly programs
include: Connections -Building Business Networks; Quest for Capital; Intro to
the Internet and Entrepreneur 101. Bi-monthly programs offered are: Camp
Cash Flow and Jungle Marketing. Each Fall and Spring semester, we offer
Premier FastTrac I and Premier FastTrac II.

Oregon
Southern Oregon Women's Access to Credit (SOWAC)
Mary O'Kief, Director
33 North Central, Suite 209   541-779-3992
Medford, OR 97501   Fax: 541-779-5195
E-mail: sowac@cdsnet.net
Website: http://sowac@cdsnet.net
Founded in 1990, SOWAC provides business training, mentoring and financing
services for women and men with barriers. From 1993 through mid-1997,
SOWAC enrolled 260 students in its training program and helped in the startup

or expansion or over 65 businesses in Jackson and Josephine counties. In 1996-97, SOWAC also piloted its services to low-income Hispanic entrepreneurs and very rural entrepreneurs. Training graduates may apply to SOWAC's Mentor Program to receive assistance from an experienced person who volunteers expertise over a six month period, and/or for a SOWAC business loan of up to $25,000. SOWAC is funded by the SBA Office of Women Business Ownership, private foundations, client fees interest income and local contributions.

ONABEN — A Native American Business Network
Patrick Borunda, Director
520 Southwest 6th Avenue, Suite 930   503-243-5015
Portland, OR 97204   Fax: 503-243-5028
E-mail: borunda@onaben.org
Website: http://www.onaben.org
ONABEN - A Native American Business Network, is a non-profit public benefit corporation created by Northwest Indian Tribes to increase the number and profitability of private enterprises owned by Native Americans. ONABEN offers training, individual counseling, assisted access to markets and facilitated access to capital for its clients. Each of the ten tribes hosting an ONABEN Service Center pays annual dues of $2,500 plus 40% of the cost of operating their site. The sites, located on reservations in Oregon, Washington and California, deliver services to all citizens regardless of tribal affiliation. Some have up to 40% of users coming from the surrounding non-Native community.

Pennsylvania
Women's Business Development Center (WBDC)
Geri Swift, President
1315 Walnut Street, Suite 1116   215-790-9232
Philadelphia, PA 19107-4711   Fax: 215-790-9231
E-mail: wbdc@erols.com
The Women's Business Development Center (WBDC) is dedicated to the economic empowerment of women. The Center enables women to launch new businesses and to more successfully run their existing businesses. WBDC offers start-up, emerging and established entrepreneurs a unique continuum of supportive services including: Premier FastTrac I & II, comprehensive course work culminating in the development of a viable business plan for each entrepreneur; Individualized Business Consulting in management, marketing, and financial matters; Loan Packaging; Procurement and Certification Assistance. By offering a full range of services and utilizing the expertise of successful women business owners to deliver its programs, the Women's Business Development Center will be the Greater Philadelphia Region's focal point for women's economic empowerment opportunities.

Puerto Rico
Women's Business Institute (WBI)
Universidad Del Sagrado Corazon
(The University of the Sacred Heart)
Professor Hylsa Silva, Director
Center for Women's Entrepreneurial
    Development
P. O. Box 12383
San Juan, PR 00914-0383
E-mail: caring@caribe.net

787-728-1515, ext. 1-1471#
787-727-6545
Fax: 787-727-5519
787-727-1296
787-727-1692

The Women's Business Institute (WBI) at the University of the Sacred Heart, Center for Women's Entrepreneurial Development (CWED) offers technical assistance to women interested in establishing a business. It also provides women business owners a place to expose and share ideas, objectives and experiences. The WBI will contribute to the social and economic development of women through training on empowerment and business ownership as an alternative to attain economic independence.

South Carolina
Center for Women Entrepreneurs
Columbia College of South Carolina
Susan Davis, Project Director
Ms. Sam McKee, Director of Grants
1301 Columbia College Drive
Columbia, SC 29203
E-mail: susdavis@colacoll.edu
E-mail: smckee@colacoll.edu
Website: www.colacoll.com

803-786-3582 - Susan Davis
803-786-3177 - Sam McKee

Fax: 803-786-3804 - Center

Women's Business Institute

The mission of the Center for Women Entrepreneurs at Columbia College of South Carolina is to expand economic opportunities for women by advancing entrepreneurship and providing resources to assist in successful business start-ups, maintenance of growth, and exploration of new business opportunities. Services include individual consultations, management and technical assistance, annual women's conference, round table luncheon series, resource guides, seminars and workshops, and internships. The focus on communications through the Online Women's Business Center will enable the project to serve not only mature women ready to start businesses and women already in business, but young female entrepreneurs in high schools. As local support for this project can attest, the Center for Women Entrepreneurs is an active advocate of collaborative ventures among resources that support women entrepreneurs.

South Dakota

Watertown Area Career Learning Center
The Entrepreneur Network for Women (ENW)
Pat Helgeland, Director of ENW
Becky Doerr, Business Specialist for ENW
Kay Tschakert, Career Specialist/Financial Officer
100 South Maple
P. O. Box 81   605-882-5080
Watertown, SD 57201-0081   Fax: 605-882-5069
E-mail: network4women@basec.net
Website: http://www.network4women.com
The Entrepreneur's Network for Women (ENW) is a statewide program that
serves South Dakota entrepreneurs. The program's services include toll-free
telephone counseling, training seminars in management, marketing, financing,
government contracting and entrepreneurial confidence. Networking sessions, a
group mentoring program, and Business Success Teams are offered at many
locations in the state. ENW publishes a quarterly newsletter and holds an
annual spring conference. ENW is a division of the Watertown Area Career
Learning Center, which has assisted single parents, displaced homemakers,
dislocated workers and economically disadvantaged persons since the late
1980s. ENW works in cooperation with the Women's Business Institute in
North Dakota.

Tennessee

The National Assn. for Women Business Owners - Nashville Chapter (NAWBO)
Janice S. Thomas, Executive Director
P. O. Box 292283   615-248-3474
Nashville, TN 37229-2283   Fax: 615-256-2706
The Nashville Chapter of the National Association of Women Business Owners
(NAWBO) is a membership-based organization that informs, empowers and
promotes women business owners and invites its members to impact the social,
political and economic communities. Nashville NAWBO was the first chapter
chartered in Tennessee and provided assistance to establish chapters in
Chattanooga, Memphis and Tri-Cities, thus creating a statewide partnership of
women business owners. The Tennessee NAWBO Chapters are affiliated with
the national NAWBO association which includes 60 chapters throughout the
United States. NAWBO is a member of *Les Femmes Chefs D'Entreprises
Mondiales*, an international association of Women Business owners. In concert
with its educational foundation, the Nashville Foundation for Women Business
Owners (NFWBO), Nashville NAWBO has established the first, SBA-funded
women's business center in Tennessee. Located in Nashville, The Women's
Resource Center will offer on-site business counseling services, training
programs and technical assistance to women business owners in Middle

Tennessee, which includes 21 counties. Through the consortium of sister NAWBO Chapters and our corporate partnership with Bell South and the Tennessee Economic Development Center, the Women's Resource Center will be able to provide training programs statewide through satellite, two-way interactive video conferences and the internet.

Texas

Texas Center for Women's Business Enterprise (TxCWBE)
Susan Spencer, Executive Director and Contract Administrator
Michele Pettes, Senior Advisor/Trainer
Joy Williamson, Training Assistant
Two Commodore Plaza, 13th Floor
206 East 9th Street, Suite 13.140
Austin, TX 78701   512-472-8522
Mailing Address: P.O. Box 340219   888-352-2525
Austin, TX 78734-0219   Fax: 512-472-8513
E-mail: txcwbe@onr.com
Website: http://www.onr.com/CWE
The Texas Center for Women's Business Enterprise (TxCWBE) is a public/private initiative dedicated to the entrepreneurial success of Texas women. TxCWBE assists women who are starting or expanding business in Texas. Conveniently located in the capital city, TxCWBE has served Texas women for over six years. In 1996, Texas ranked 2nd out of the 50 states with 552,000 women-owned businesses, employing over 1 million people and generating $129.6 billion in sales. Providing current training for today's businesses, the TxCWBE has assisted over 1000 women-owned businesses and has assisted in the development of over $13 million in bank loans. The Texas Center for Women's Business Enterprise prepares a new generation of entrepreneurial women for business success dealing with topics including: certification information, internet training for small businesses, business plans, loan assistance referral program, women's construction network, and consortium and contributing partners.

North Texas Women's Business Development Center Inc. (NTWBDC)
Brenda Williams, Technical Counseling and Programs
Bill J. Priest Institute for Economic Development
1402 Corinth Street, Suite 1536   214-428-1177
Dallas, TX 75215-2111   Fax: 214-428-4633
E-mail: women@onramp.net
The North Texas Women's Business Development Center, Inc. (NTWBDC) is a collective effort of the National Association of Women Business Owners (NAWBO), the Greater Dallas Chamber of Commerce Women's Business Issues Division, the North Texas Women's Business Council, and the Bill Priest

Institute for Economic Development. One area of NTWBDC focus is women's government contracting opportunities in addition to long-term training, counseling and mentoring.

North Texas Women's Business Development Center Inc. (NTWBDC)
Online Women's Business Center
Paula Aryanpur, Project Director
Bill J. Priest Institute for Economic Development
1402 Corinth Street, Suite 209   214-565-0447
Dallas. TX 75215-2111   Fax: 214-565-7883
E-mail: virtual@onramp.net
Website: http://www.onlinewbc.org

The Online Women's Business Center (OWBC) is an internet site that provides information, training, and opportunities for online networking to women business owners wherever they might be at any time of the day. OWBC was developed on behalf of the U.S. Small Business Administration's (SBA) Office of Women's Business Ownership (OWBO) and several corporate sponsors who joined forces in a unique public/private partnership. This "virtual" women's business center works in unison with, and as an extension of, more than 54 Women's Business Centers (WBC) throughout the United States that have contributed actively to its creation. The combined efforts of the WBC and OWBO create unlimited possibilities for reaching women who want instant access to information, personal guidance and insight into business management skills, particularly if they do not have a WBC nearby or if their current employment prevents them from visiting a WBC during operating hours.

Women's Economic Self-Sufficiency Team
(WESST Corp. - Las Cruces, New Mexico)
Jennifer Craig, Regional Manager
691 South Telshor   505-522-3707
Las Cruces, NM 88001   Fax: 505-522 4414
E-mail: jencraig@zianet.com
The Women's Economic Self-Sufficiency Team (WESST Corp.) was incorporated in 1988 to assist low-income and minority women throughout New Mexico. This project focuses on the area of Las Cruces and Farmington, New Mexico, with program services provided to women in Dona, Ana, Luna, Otero and Sierra counties with limited outreach to El Paso, Texas by the end of the second project year. WESST Corp. is a micro-lender under SBA's micro-loan program. Counseling and mentoring are offered through professional

volunteers including attorneys, accountants, insurance agents and benefits counselors.

Utah
Womens Business Center at the Chamber
Salt Lake Area Chamber of Commerce
Ramona Rudert, Director
175 East 400 South, Suite 600   801-328-5051
Salt Lake City, UT 84111   Fax: 801-328-5098
E-mail: ramona@slachamber.com
Website: www.slachamber.com
The Women's Business Center at the
Chamber supports the success of
women business owners throughout
Utah with counseling, training and
loan packaging assistance. With more
than 30 committees and task forces,

Our onsite high-tech center offers access to the internet and all types of business software.

the Chamber provides unique networking opportunities for clients as well as a full service export assistance program. Our onsite high-tech center offers access to the internet and all types of business software. Women business owners can access help with marketing, management, finance and procurement. There is a modest fee for some services, but scholarships and specialized training are available for socially or economically disadvantaged women.

Washington
ONABEN - A Native American Business Network
Patrick Borunda, Director
520 Southwest 6th Avenue, Suite 930   503-243-5015
Portland, OR 97204   Fax: 503-243-5028
E-mail: borunda@onaben.org
Website: http://www.onaben.org

ONABEN - A Native American Business Network
Sonya Tetnowski, OWBO Coordinator
3201 Broadway, Suite C   425-339-6226
Everett, WA 98201   Fax: 425-339-9171
E-mail: Sonya@onaben.org
Website: http://www.onaben.org
ONABEN - A Native American Business Network, is a non-profit public benefit corporation created by Northwest Indian Tribes to increase the number and profitability of private enterprises owned by Native Americans. ONABEN offers training, individual counseling, assisted access to markets and facilitated access to capital for its clients. Each of the ten tribes hosting an ONABEN

Service Center pays annual dues of $2,500 plus 40% of the cost of operating their site. The sites, located on reservations in Oregon, Washington and California, deliver services to all citizens regardless of tribal affiliation. Some have up to 40% of users coming from the surrounding non-Native community.

West Virginia
Center for Economic Options, Inc.
Pam Curry, Executive Director
601 Delaware Avenue   304-345-1298
Charleston, WV 25302   Fax: 304-342-0641
E-mail: econoptns@citynet.net
The Center for Economic Options is a non-profit, statewide, community-based organization that promotes opportunities to develop the economic capacity of West Virginia's rural citizens, particularly women, and communities. The Center creates alternative approaches to economic development, such as networks of home-based business entrepreneurs, and works with communities to help build support for small and microbusinesses.

Wisconsin
Wisconsin Women's Business Initiative Corporation (WWBIC)
Wendy K. Werkmeister, President
Jeraldine K. Johnson, Vice President   414-372-2070
1915 North Dr. Martin Luther King Jr. Dr.   Fax: 414-372-2083
Milwaukee, WI 53212   414-372-1202
E-mail: wwbic@execpc.com
Website: http://www.execpc.com/wwbic

WWBIC - Madison Office
Marian Walluks, Local Contact
16 North Carroll Street, 7th Floor   608-257-7409
Madison, WI 53703   Fax: 608-257-7429
E-mail: wwbic@execpc.com
Website: http://www.execpc.com/wwbic
The Wisconsin Women's Business Initiative Corporation (WWBIC) has served over 2500 individuals with more than 65 business start-ups and over 100 business expansions since it began in 1989 as a Demonstration site. Hundreds of jobs were created by WWBIC's efforts. WWBIC is an economic development corporation providing business education training and technical assistance. It is also the state's largest micro-lender under SBA's micro-loan program. WWBIC has expanded its operations to an additional site in Madison, Wisconsin and provides on-going training in the Milwaukee, Madison, Green Bay and Racine/Kenosha areas.

Women Pre-Qualified Loans Cut Down On Banker Stress

Need help filling out your loan application package? The Women's Pre-Qualification Pilot Loan Program was developed to promote the Small Business Administration's business loan programs to current and prospective women small business owners. It also provides specialized support and assistance with the agency's loan application process.

This program uses non-profit organizations as intermediaries to assist prospective women borrowers in developing a viable loan application package. The program focuses on the applicant's character, credit, experience, and reliability — not just her assets.

Eligible businesses must be at least 51 percent owned, operated and managed by women. The loan guarantee is for $250,000 or less. The application can be submitted directly to the Small Business Administration for expedited consideration of a loan pre-qualification.

Currently this program is available in 16 states. For more information on this program, you may contact your local

Small Business Administration Office, or Office of Women's Business Ownership, U.S. Small Business Administration, 409 3rd St., SW, Washington, DC 20416; 202-205-6673; 800-8-ASK-SBA; {www.sba.gov}.

Local Sites

California
U.S. Small Business
Administration
2719 N. Air Fresno Dr.
Suite 107
Fresno, CA 93727
209-487-5791

**U.S. Small
Business
Administration
{www.sba.gov}**

U.S. Small Business
Administration
455 Market St., 6th Floor
San Francisco, CA 94105
415-744-6771

Colorado
U.S. Small Business
Administration
721 19th St., Suite 426
Denver, CO 80202
303-844-3461
(Program is offered statewide in
Colorado)

Illinois
U.S. Small Business
Administration
500 West Madison St.
Suite 1250
Chicago, IL 60661
312-353-5429

Kentucky
U.S. Small Business
Administration
600 Dr. Martin Luther King, Jr. Pl.
Room 188
Louisville, KY 40202
502-582-5971

Louisiana
U.S. Small Business
Administration
365 Canal St.
Suite 2250
New Orleans, LA 70130
504-589-6685

Maine
U.S. Small Business
Administration
Federal Bldg.
40 Western Ave.
Room 512
Augusta, ME 04330
207-622-8242

Massachusetts
U.S. Small Business
Administration
10 Causeway St.
2nd Floor, Room 565
Boston, MA 02222
617-565-5580

Missouri
U.S. Small Business
Administration
815 Olive St., Suite 242
St. Louis, MO 63101
314-539-6600

Montana
U.S. Small Business
Administration
301 S. Park, Room 334
Helena, MT 59626
406-441-1081

New Mexico
U.S. Small Business
Administration
625 Silver St., SW
Suite 320
Albuquerque, NM 87102
505-766-1870

New York
U.S. Small Business
Administration
111 West Huron St.
Room 1311
Buffalo, NY 14202
716-551-4517

North Carolina
U.S. Small Business
Administration
200 North College St.
Suite A2015

Charlotte, NC 28202
704-344-6563

Ohio
U.S. Small Business
Administration
2 Nationwide Plaza
Suite 1400
Columbus, OH 43215
614-469-6860

Oregon
U.S. Small Business
Administration
1515 SW 5th Ave.
Suite 1050
Portland, OR 97207
503-326-2683

Pennsylvania
U.S. Small Business
Administration
475 Allendale Rd.
Suite 201
King of Prussia, PA 19406
610-962-3800

Utah
U.S. Small Business
Administration
125 South State St.
Salt Lake City, UT 84138
801-524-5800

Liaison Outreach

If you need help learning about Transportation Department programs, services, and contracts, then the *Liaison Outreach Services Program* is for you. It is designed

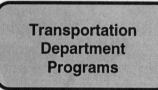

to increase participation by women and minorities in transportation procurement and funds trade and service association. They have women's business advocates that work with small women and minority-owned firms to increase their awareness of contracting opportunities and financial assistance programs.

To learn more about these programs, contact National Information Clearinghouse, U.S. Department of Transportation, 400 7th St., SW, Room 9414, Washington, DC 20590; 800-532-1169; {http://osdbuweb.dot.gov}.

Liaison Outreach Services Program Regional Offices

Bruce Young-Candelaria
Hispanic-American Chamber of
Commerce
67 Broad St.
Boston, MA 02109
617-261-4222
888-775-5677
E-mail: haccatbos@
compuserve.com
States: ME, NH, VT, MA, CT, RI,
NY, NJ, DE, PA, Puerto Rico, US
Virgin Islands

Enrique Carrillo
Latin Chamber of Commerce
2350 Coral Way
Suite 301
Miami, FL 33145
305-860-0780
800-448-2585
E-mail: ems@emservices. com
States: NC, SC, GA, AL, FL, MS,
TN, KY, VA, WV, MD,
Washington, DC

Charles King, Jr.
Arkansas Regional Minority
Supplier Development Council
300 Spring Bldg., Suite 415
Little Rock, AK 72203
501-374-7026
E-mail:
armsdc@swbell.net
States: OK, LA, AK,
NM

Richard Pierce
Susan Savage
American Indian
Science and
Engineering Society
5661 Airport Blvd.
Boulder, CO 80301
303-939-0023
800-250-3111
E-mail: aises@spot.
colorado.edu
States: CO, WY, MT, ND, SD,
UT

Karen Novo
Arizona Hispanic Chamber of
Commerce
2400 N. Central Ave.
Suite 303
Phoenix, AZ 85004
602-252-1101
800-742-8269
E-mail: ahcc@uswest.net
States: NV, AZ, HI, Guam,
American Samoa

Jean Conyers
Metropolitan Chamber of
Commerce
400 N. Saginaw St.
Suite 101A
Flint, MI 48502

810-235-5514
800-672-5516
E-mail: metro@tir.com
States: MI, MN, IA, IN, OH, WI,
IL, MO, KS, NE

Barbara Burton
Texas Association of Minority
Business Enterprises
P.O. Box 6206
Austin, TX 78741
512-322-0177
800-322-0447
E-mail: tambe@io-cpm
States: TX

Dolly Small
Women Construction Owners and
Executives
1140 140th Ave., NE, Suite A-2
Bellevue, WA 98005
206-957-4566
888-957-5677
E-mail: wcoelosp@ix.
netcom.com
States: WA, OR, ID, AK

Get Yourself Covered

The U.S. Department of Transportation has
a Bonding Assistance Program that
offers certified minority, women-owned
and disadvantaged business enterprises
an opportunity to obtain bid, payment
and performance bonds
for transportation-
related projects. The
Program provides an
80% guarantee
against losses on
contracts up to
$1,000,000. They will even help you fill out the
application package.

For more information on the Bonding Assistance Program,
contact National Information Clearinghouse, U.S.
Department of Transportation, 400 7th St., SW, Room
9414, Washington, DC 20590; 800-532-1169;
{http://osdbuweb.dot.gov}.

U.S. Department of Transportation
Bonding Program Agents

Bob Hrehor	Burton Harris
BDH Associates	Security Bond Assoc., Inc.
620 Hillcrest Rd., Suite 400	10131 SW 40th St.
Atlanta, GA 30247	Miami, FL 33165
770-564-2999	305-552-5414
Fax: 770-564-9327	Fax: 305-226-7876

Bob Stimpson
Alexander and Alexander
251 N. Illinois, Suite 1500
Indianapolis, IN 46204
317-237-2402
Fax: 317-237-2461

Jim Olsen
JR Olsen Bonds
22900 Ventura Blvd.
Suite 360
Woodland Hills, CA 91364
818-224-4855
Fax: 818-224-4857

James Axon
L. Robert Desanctis
10 Walnut Hill Park
Woodburn, MA 01801
617-935-8480
617-933-5645

Wayne McCartha
McCartha, Cobb
1407 Calhoun St.
Columbia, SC 29201
803-799-3474
Fax: 803-799-3711
(serves NC and SC)

Richard Jaffee
Jaffee Bonds and Ins.
809 Second St.
Santa Rosa, CA 95402
707-546-4910
Fax: 707-546-4931

John Abrams
Surety Services of America
6136 Campus Ln.
Cincinnati, OH 45230
513-688-0800
Fax: 513-688-0300

Frank Lech
O'Leary Kientz
2133 Luray Ave.
Cincinnati, OH 45206
513-872-5700
Fax: 513-872-5716

Don Wasoba
Surety Associates
4236 Lindell Blvd.
St. Louis, MO 63108
314-534-5545
Fax: 314-534-0991

Jim Damiano
Agent's Bond Connection
17774 Preston Blvd.
Dallas, TX 75252
972-250-0771
Fax: 972-250-3469

Pat Moore
Frank Jones Insurance
1000 Central Parkway N
Suite 225
San Antonio, TX 78232
210-496-6773
Fax: 210-496-6744

Mary Faure
Surety Insurance Services of the
Northwest, Inc.
155 NE 100th, Suite 303
Seattle, WA 98125
206-527-6624
Fax: 206-527-4358

Mary Ann Skinner
Skinner Bonding
O123 SW Hamilton
Portland, OR 97201
503-226-6444
Fax: 503-226-6534

Ila Delman
Universal Surety Agency, Inc.
4711 West Gold Rd.
Suite 700

Skokie, IL 60076
847-933-1200
Fax: 847-674-9774
(serving IL and MI)

Get 10% Of State Road Work

The U.S. Department of Transportation (DOT) has had in effect for more than 14 years a policy of assisting businesses owned and controlled by minorities and women in participating in contracting opportunities. The goal is to ensure that at least 10% of the funds authorized for contracts go to *Disadvantaged Business Enterprises (DBE).*

State and local transportation agencies that receive U.S. Department of Transportation Federal financial assistance must have goals for the participation of disadvantaged entrepreneurs and certify the eligibility of these firms to participate in DOT-assisted contracts.

For more information about Disadvantaged Business Enterprises, and to learn how you can be certified as a DBE and get state and local transportation contracts, contact National Information Clearinghouse, U.S. Department of

Transportation, 400 7th St., SW, Room 9414, Washington, DC 20590; 800-532-1169; {http://osdbuweb.dot.gov}.

State Disadvantaged Business Enterprise Contacts

Alabama
Mr. Ronald Green
Chief, Bureau of Human
Resources
Alabama Department of
Transportation
1409 Coliseum Blvd.
Montgomery, AL 36130
334-242-6336
800-247-3618

Alaska
Ms. Kay Rollison
DBE Manager
Alaska DOT and DBE Office
P.O. Box 196900
Anchorage, AK 99519
907-762-4260

Arizona
Ms. Lisa Wormington
Administrator
Office of Affirmative Action
Arizona DOT
1739 W. Jackson, Room 118
Phoenix, AZ 85007
602-255-7761

Arkansas
Mr. Dan Flowers, Director
Arkansas State Highway and
Transportation Department
P.O. Box 2261
Little Rock, AR 72203
501-569-2262

California
Ms. Algerine McCray
Chief, Office of Civil Rights
CALTRANS
1120 N St., Room 2545
Sacramento, CA 95814
916-227-9784

Connecticut
Ms. Margo Kilbon
Director
Bureau of Finance and
Administration
Connecticut DOT
Contract Compliance Unit
P.O. Box 31746
Newington, CT 06131
203-594-3067

Colorado
Guillermo Vidal
Executive Director
Colorado Department of
Transportation
4201 East Arkansas Ave.
Denver, CO 80222
303-757-9205

Delaware
Ms. Bobbi Hettel-Minner
DOT EEO Liaison Officer
Delaware DOT
P.O. Box 778
Dover, DE 19903
302-739-5716

District of Columbia
Mr. Jerry Carter
Chief, Office of Contract
Administration
District of Columbia Department
of Public Works
2000 14th St., NW, 5th Floor
Washington, DC 20009
202-939-8072

Florida
Mr. Howard Jemison
DE Certification
Florida DOT
Minority Programs Office
3717 Apalachee Parkway
Suite G
Tallahassee, FL 32311
850-921-7370

Georgia
Mr. Robert Bradley
EEO Administrator
Charles French
Contract Compliance Officer
Georgia DOT
No. 2 Capitol Square
Room 262
Atlanta, GA 30334
404-656-5323

Hawaii
Mr. Daniel Iyo
Business Management Officer
Hawaii DOT
869 Punchbowl St.
Honolulu, HI 96813
808-587-2133

Idaho
Kintu Nnambia
Chief, Civil Rights Manager
Ms. Heidi Gordon

Civil Rights Affirmative Action
Officer
State of Idaho ITD
P.O. Box 7129
Boise, ID 83707
208-334-8845

Illinois
Ms. R. Beverly Peters
Bureau Chief
Bureau of Small Business
Enterprise
Illinois DOT
2300 South Dirksen Parkway,
Room 319
Springfield, IL 62764
217-785-5947

Indiana
Mr. George Roney
Supportive Services Director
Indiana Government Center North
100 North Senate Ave.
Room 855
Indianapolis, IN 46204
317-233-3563

Iowa
Mr. Roger Bierbaum
Contract Engineer
Iowa DOT
800 Lincoln Way
Ames, IA 50010
515-239-1414

Kansas
Ms. Sandra Greenwell
DBE Liaison Officer
Kansas DOT
Docking Office Building
915 Harrison
Topeka, KS 66612
913-296-7916

Kentucky
Mr. Ronald Derricks
DBE Liaison Officer
Kentucky Transportation Cabinet
State Office Building
Room 904
501 High St.
Frankfort, KY 40622
502-564-3601

Louisiana
Ms. Frances Gilson
Compliance Programs Director
Louisiana DOT and Development
P.O. Box 94245
Baton Rouge, LA 70804
504-379-1382

Maine
Ms. Jane Gilbert
Director
Office of Equal Opportunity
Employee Relations
Maine DOT
Transportation Building
SHS-16
Augusta, ME 04333
207-287-3576

Maryland
Ms. Ruth Roberts Hendricks
Maryland DOT
P.O. Box 8755 #10 Elm Rd.
BWI Airport, MD 21240
410-859-7325

Massachusetts
Ms. Patricia O'Brien
Office of Civil Rights
Massachusetts Highway
Department
10 Park Plaza
Room 5453

Boston, MA 02116
617-973-7823

Disadvantaged Business Enterprises

Michigan
Mr. Charles Ford, Administrator
Mr. Robert Anderson
Assistance Administrator
Office of Equal Opportunity
Michigan DOT
P.O. Box 30050
Lansing, MI 48909
517-373-6732

Minnesota
Ms. Dawn Thompson
Marketing Specialist
Minnesota DOT, EEO Contract
Management
395 John Ireland Blvd.
Room 207
St. Paul, MN 55155
651-282-2633

Mississippi
Mr. Jim Smith
DBE Coordinator
Mississippi Department of
Transportation
Contract Administration Division
P.O. Box 1850
Jackson, MS 39215
601-359-7700

Missouri
Sharon Taegel
EEEO Administrator
Missouri Highway and
Transportation Dept.
P.O. Box 270
State Highway Building
Jefferson City, MO 65102
573-751-2859

Montana
Sam Prestipino
Chief, Civil Rights Bureau
Department of Transportation
P.O. Box 201001
Helena, MT 59620
406-444-6333

Nebraska
Ms. Laura Wood
Minority Business Officer
Nebraska Department of
Roads/Construction
Division/MBO
Central Office Building
Room 105
1500 Highway 2
P.O. Box 94759
Lincoln, NE 68509
402-479-4531

Nevada
Mr. Fred Skivington, Manger
Nevada DOT
1263 South Stewart St.
Carson City, NV 89712
702-888-7497

New Hampshire
Ms. Sandra Drouin, Supervisor
Labor Compliance Administrator
New Hampshire DOT
P.O. Box 483

Concord, NH 03302
603-271-6611

New Jersey
Ms. Linda Errico
DBE Liaison Officer
New Jersey DOT
1035 Parkway Ave., CN600
Trenton, NJ 08625
609-530-3872

New Mexico
Mr. Bill Jaramillo
DBE & EEO Liaison Officer
New Mexico State Highway &
Transportation Department
1120 Cerrillos Rd.
P.O. Box 1149
Santa Fe, NM 87504
505-827-1775

New York
Tracey Long, Director
Office of EEO Development &
Compliance
New York State DOT
1220 Washington Ave.
State Campus, Building 4
Room G16
Albany, NY 12232
518-457-1134

North Carolina
Delano Rackard
Director of Civil Rights Division
North Carolina DOT
P.O. Box 25201
Raleigh, NC 27611
919-733-2300

North Dakota
Ms. Deborah Igoe
Civil Rights Officer

North Dakota DOT
608 East Boulevard Ave.
Bismarck, ND 58505
701-328-2899

Ohio
Mr. Mark Kelsy
Office Administrator
Office of Contracts
Ohio DOT
25 South Front St.
Room 708
Columbus, OH 43215
614-782-8498

Oklahoma
Mr. Paul Adams
Oklahoma DOT
200 NE 21st St.
Oklahoma City, OK 73105
405-521-3957

Oregon
Ms. Lynn Todd
Manager
DBE/EEO/ESB
Oregon DOT
Transportation Department
112 Transportation Building
Salem, OR 97310
503-986-3290

Pennsylvania
Mr. Robert Wonderlend
Deputy Secretary for
Administration
Pennsylvania DOT
1220 Transportation and Safety
Bldg.
Commonwealth and Forster St.
Harrisburg, PA 17120
717-787-5628

Puerto Rico
Mr. Carlos Guilbe
Director, Office of Civil Rights
DOT and Public Works
Highway and Transportation
Authority
P.O. Box 42007
San Juan, Puerto Rico 00940
809-722-2625

Rhode Island
Mr. William Ankner
Chief, Civil Rights Office
Rhode Island DOT
2 Capitol Hill, Room 109
Providence, RI 02903
401-277-3260

South Carolina
Mr. B.F. Byrd, Director of
Compliance
South Carolina DOT
P.O. Box 191
Columbia, SC 29202
803-737-1372

South Dakota
Mr. Dennis Hull
Civil Rights Officer
South Dakota DOT
700 East Broadway
Pierre, SD 57501
605-773-4085

Tennessee
Mr. Raymond White
Contract Compliance Director
Tennessee DOT
James K. Polk Bldg.
Suite 400
505 Deaderick St.
Nashville, TN 37243
615-741-3681

Texas
Mr. Efrem Casarez
DBE Program Director
R.D. Brown, DBE Certification
Texas Department of
Transportation
Dewitt C. Greer State Highway
Bldg.
123 E. 11th St.
Austin, TX 78701
512-463-8870

Departments of Transportation

Utah
Mr. Charles Larson
Civil Rights Manager
Utah DOT
4501 South 2700 West
Salt Lake City, UT 84119
801-965-4208

Vermont
Mr. Carroll Witham
Compliance Officer
Vermont Agency of
Transportation
133 State St.
Montpelier, VT 05633
802-828-2644

Virginia
Mr. Peter Kolakowski
Assistance Commissioner for
Administration

Virginia DOT
1401 East Broad St.
Room 309
Richmond, VA 23219
804-786-9950

Washington
Brenda Richardson, Director
Washington State DOT
Transportation Building 7314
Olympia, WA 98504
360-705-7085

West Virginia
Mr. Jesse Haynes
State Capitol Complex
Director EEO Division
West Virginia Division of
Highways
Bldg. 5, Room 925
1900 Kanawha Blvd. East
Charleston, WV 25305
304-558-3862

Wisconsin
Mr. Eugene Johnson
Director DBE Program
Wisconsin DOT
4802 Sheboygan Ave.
Room 451
P.O. Box 7916
Madison, WI 53707
608-267-9527

Wyoming
Ms. Nora Lyon
DBE Program Analyst
Wyoming DOT
P.O. Box 1708
Cheyenne, WY 82003
307-777-4457

Think you don't have the money to start a business? *A*
Guide to Business
Credit for Women,
Minorities, and
Small Business is a
free publication that
describes the
various credit
opportunities for
industrious
entrepreneurs.

Don't let the lack of funds hold you back. Contact
Publications Services, MS-127, Board of Governors,
Federal Reserve System, Washington, DC 20551; 202-
452-3244; {www.bog.frb.fed.us}.

Help Selling

The Federal government can be overwhelming at times, but
one good contract could get your business off and running.
Women Business Owners: Selling to the Federal
Government is designed to help women business owners
by providing them with information about marketing their
goods and services to the federal government.

This invaluable sourcebook includes information on the basics of government contracting, including invitations for bids, requests for proposals, unsolicited proposals, types of contracts, and general contract provisions and clauses. Also included is a listing of federal agency resources for doing business with the federal government.

The cost of the publication is $3.25. To order, contact Superintendent of Documents, U.S. Government Printing Office, P.O. Box 371954, Pittsburgh, PA 15250; 202-512-1800; {www.gpo.gov}.

Free Help Finding Guardian Angels

Look no more. The Investment Division of the U.S. Small Business Administration licenses, regulates, and funds close to 300 Small Business Investment Companies (SBIC) nationwide, which supply equity investment to qualifying small businesses.

A free *Directory of Small Business Investment Companies* is available which lists names, addresses, telephone numbers and investment policies of SBICs. Contact Investment Division, U.S. Small Business Administration, 409 Third St., SW, Washington, DC 20416; 202-205-6510; {www.sba.gov}.

Your Business Handbook

Learn the basics by reading *For Women: Managing Your Own Business, A Resource and Information Handbook.* While specifically directed at women entrepreneurs, this direct, easy-to-read volume contains pertinent information necessary for anyone going into business.

Prepared at the Wharton Entrepreneurial Center, this text familiarizes the reader with the basics of running a successful business, including financial planning, marketing, insurance, personnel management, accounting, international operations, and much more.

The cost of the publication is $13.00. To order, contact Superintendent of Documents, U.S. Government Printing Office, P.O. Box 371954, Pittsburgh, PA 15250; 202-512-1800; {www.gpo.gov}.

Mom's Home Office

Starting a home-based business is often an economic necessity, because of the cost of childcare, the desire to be home with the kids and more. *The Business Plan for Home-Based Business* ($2) is a publication of the U.S. Small Business Administration (SBA) and provides a comprehensive approach to developing a business plan for just such a venture. Once you've got your plan, all the rest you need is courage.

★ *Selling By Mail Order* ($2) provides basic information on how to run a successful mail order business and includes information on product selection, pricing, testing, and writing effective advertisements.

★ *Child Day-Care Services* ($3) provides an overview of the industry, including models of day-care operations.

★ *How To Get Started with a Small Business Computer* ($2) helps you forecast your computer needs, evaluate the alternatives and select the right computer system for your business.

To obtain a directory and order form, write SBA Resource Directory, MC 7110, 409 3rd St., SW, Washington, DC 20416; 202-205-6666; {www.sba.gov}.

No Money – No Problem

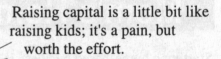

Raising capital is a little bit like raising kids; it's a pain, but worth the effort.

How To Raise Money for a Small Business is a free fact sheet outlining the basics of raising money, where to find it, borrow it, types of business loans, how to write a loan proposal, and U.S. Small Business

Administration (SBA) financial programs (you'll have to do the kids yourself).

For your free copy, contact Marketing and Customer Service, U.S. Small Business Administration, 409 3rd St., SW, Washington, DC 20416; 202-205-6744; 800-8-ASK-SBA; {www.sba.gov}.

Be Your Own
FINANCIAL MANAGER

Just make sure you know what you are doing.

The Small Business Administration (SBA) has a series of publications dealing with financial management, designed to educate you on budgeting, money management issues, and record keeping. Some of the titles include:

* ***ABCs of Borrowing*** ($2) tells you what lenders look for and what to expect when borrowing money for your small business.

SBA Resource Directory

* ***Understanding Cash Flow*** ($2) shows how to plan for the movement of cash through the business and thus plan for future requirements.
* ***Financing for Small Business*** ($2) helps you learn how, when, and where to find capital for business needs and includes step-by-step instructions.

✳ *Budgeting in a Small Service Firm* ($2) shows how to set up and keep sound financial records, and to use journals, ledgers, and charts to increase profits.

✳ *Pricing Your Products and Services Profitably* ($2) discusses how to price your products profitably, plus various pricing techniques and when to use them.

First, The Idea

Inventors are idea people. To help them become business people, the U.S. Small Business Administration (SBA) has several publications on what step two needs to be.

● *Ideas Into Dollars* ($2) identifies the main challenges in product development and provides a list of resources to help inventors.

● *Avoiding Patent, Trademark and Copyright Problems* ($2) shows how to avoid infringing the rights of others and the importance of protecting yours.

● *Creative Selling: The Competitive Edge* ($2) explains how to use creative selling techniques to increase profits.

To obtain a directory and order form, write SBA Resource Directory, MC 7110, 409 3rd St., SW, Washington, DC 20416; 202-205-6666; {www.sba.gov}.

To obtain a directory and order form, write SBA Resource Directory, MC 7110, 409 3rd St., SW, Washington, DC 20416; 202-205-6666; {www.sba.gov}.

MBA
Without The Degree

Your business is up and running, so keep it headed in a good direction with a little help from the Small Business Administration (SBA). They have publications on management and planning that can help you look at the decisions you need to make. Some of the publications include the following:

❏ *Checklist for Going Into Business* ($2) highlights the important factors you should know in reaching a decision to start your own business.

❏ *Problems in Managing a Family-Owned Business* ($2) offers suggestions on how to overcome the difficulties in making a family-owned business successful.

❏ *Planning and Goal Setting for Small Business* ($2) helps you learn proven management techniques to help you plan for success.

❏ *Developing a Strategic Plan* ($2) helps you develop an action plan for your small business.

❐ *Business Plan for Small Service Firms* ($2) outlines the key points to be included in the business plan of a small service firm.

To obtain a directory and order form, write SBA Resource Directory, MC 7110, 409 3rd St., SW, Washington, DC 20416; 202-205-6666; {www.sba.gov}.

MORE THAN RUNNING THE CASH REGISTER

Good employees are worth more than gold. Learn how to find and hire the right employees.

✔ *Employees: How To Find and Pay Them* ($2) gives you some guidelines for your personnel search.

✔ *Human Resource Management for Growing Businesses* ($3) uncovers the characteristics of an effective personnel system and training program. Learn how these functions come together to build employee trust and productivity.

To obtain a directory and order form, write SBA Resource Directory, MC 7110, 409 3rd St., SW, Washington, DC 20416; 202-205-6666; {www.sba.gov}.

Cheap Ways to
Spread the Word

Think about getting out the word using bulk mail discounts offered by the U.S. Postal Service. You can find out about using this and other postal discounts by getting free copies of: *Small Business Guide to Advertising with Direct Mail*; *Postal Business Companion*; *International Direct Marketing Guide*; and *Third Class Mail Preparation*.

There are 85 Postal Business Centers across the country set up to provide business building information at no cost to customers. Contact the U.S. Postal Service, Advertising Mail, 475 L'Enfant Plaza, SW, Room 5540, Washington, DC 20260; {www.usps.gov}.

A Business On The Web?

Scam artists selling fraudulent Internet-related business opportunities are trying to cash in on the Internet's potential.

Don't let them fool you. Although the Internet has vast commercial possibilities, not every entrepreneur who buys into an Internet "opportunity" will automatically find a pot of gold at the end of the rainbow.

Two free publications from the Federal Trade Commission that deal with this topic include *'Net Based Business Opportunities* and *Online Scams*. You will learn how to avoid scams, and become a more computer savvy consumer.

For your copies, contact Correspondence Branch, Federal Trade Commission, Washington, DC 20580; 202-326-2222; {www.ftc.gov}.

Business Credit

As a business owner, or a person planning to start a business, you may need to borrow money to get started or to help your business develop or expand. If so, you should know about a law that protects you against illegal discrimination in business credit.

In the free publication, *Getting Business Credit*, you can learn about the Equal Credit Opportunity Act and how the law can protect you. For your copy, contact Correspondence Branch, Federal Trade Commission, Washington, DC 20580; 202-326-2222; {www.ftc.gov}.

The Credit Process

Looking for money can be a stumbling block for businesses. *The Credit Process: A Guide for Small Business Owners* is a 26-page booklet written for small business owners seeking financing for the first time.

It covers sources and types of financing, preparation of a business plan and loan application, funding resources, and action to take if a loan is denied. It also contains an especially useful and comprehensive glossary of finance terms, agencies, and fair lending regulations.

For your free copy, contact The Federal Reserve Bank of New York, Public Information Department, 33 Liberty St., New York, NY 10045; 212-720-6134; {www.ny.frb.org}.

Business Research

The National Foundation for Women Business Owners is a non-profit research organization that can provide information on businesses owned by women. They conduct extensive research on the number of women-owned businesses, types of businesses run by women, and current trends. You can discover the number of home-based businesses run by women, how women compete internationally, types of benefits offered by women-owned businesses, and more.

For more information, contact National Foundation for Women Business Owners, 1100 Wayne Ave., Suite 830, Silver Spring, MD 20910; 301-495-4975; {www.nfwb.org}.

2,000 Productivity Specialists Offer *Free* Analysis

Lorrie Browing got help to find the best way to move her homemade beef jerky business out of her kitchen and into a real facility. A Texas wood products company turned their $35,000 loss disposing of sawdust into a $15,000 profit by selling it as animal bedding for horse stable floors.

The U.S. Department of Commerce has established 70 not-for-profit centers that will analyze your program and help you determine the best way to solve your problem. The analysis is free but there is a charge for follow up work.

 They have been established to help small and medium size manufacturers increase their potential for success. They can help companies cope with a changing environment, decrease manufacturing costs or discover ways to use new technology.

To identify your local center, contact Manufacturing Extension Partnership, National Institute of Standards and Technology, Gaithersburg, MD 20899; 800-637-4634; {www.mep.nist.gov}.

U.S. Department of Commerce Centers

Alabama
Alabama Technology Network
One Perimeter Park South
Suite 486 North Tower
Birmingham, AL 35243
205-968-3455
Fax: 205-969-2228
www.atn.org

Alaska
Industry Network Corporation-
Alaska
1155 University Blvd., SE
Albuquerque, NM 87106
505-843-4250
800-716-6462
Fax: 505-843-4255
www.mfg-inc.com

Arizona
Industry Network Corporation-
Arizona
1155 University Blvd., SE
Albuquerque, NM 87106
505-843-4250
800-716-6462
Fax: 505-843-4255
www.mfg-inc.com

Arkansas
Arkansas Manufacturing
Extension Network
100 Main St., Suite 450
Little Rock, AR 72201
501-324-9006
Fax: 501-324-9012
www.tecnet.org/amen

California
California Manufacturing
Technology Center
13430 Hawthorne Blvd.
Hawthorne, CA 90250

310-263-3060
Fax: 310-676-8630
www.cmtc.com

Corporation for Manufacturing
Excellence
48001 Fremont Blvd.
Freemont, CA 94538
510-249-1480
Fax: 510-249-1499
www.manex.org

San Diego Manufacturing
Extension Center, Inc.
9663 Tierra Grande St., Suite 204
San Diego, CA 92126
619-530-4890 ext. 1201
619-530-4898
www.sanmec.org

Colorado
Mid-America Manufacturing
Technology Center
10561 Barkley, Suite 602
Overland Park, KS 66212
913-649-4333
800-653-4333
Fax: 913-649-4498
www.mamtc.com

Connecticut
Connecticut State Technology
Extension Program
185 Main St., Suite 408
New Britian, CT 06051
860-832-4600
Fax: 860-832-4620
www.connstep.org

Delaware
Delaware Manufacturing
Extension Partnership
Delaware Technology Park

One Innovation Way, Suite 301
Newark, DE 19711
302-452-2520
Fax: 302-452-1101
www.delmep.org

Technology Centers

Florida
Florida Manufacturing
Technology Center
390 North Orange Ave.
Suite 1300
Orlando, FL 32801
407-316-4633
Fax: 407-316-4586
www.fmtx.org

Georgia
Georgia Manufacturing Extension
Partnership
Georgia Institute of Technology
223 O'Keefe Bldg.
Atlanta, GA 30332
404-894-8989
Fax: 404-894-8194
www.edi.gatech.edu

Hawaii
Industry Network Corporation-
Hawaii
1155 University Blvd., SE
Albuquerque, NM 87106
505-843-4250
800-716-6462
Fax: 505-843-4255
www.mfg-inc.com

Idaho
Idaho TechHelp
Boise State University

1910 University Dr.
Boise, ID 83725
208-426-3689
888-IDTEXHLP
Fax: 208-426-3877
www.techhelp.org

Illinois
Chicago Manufacturing Center
3333 West Arthington
Chicago, IL 60624
773-265-2020
Fax: 773-265-8336
www.cmcusa.org

Illinois Manufacturing Extension
Center
404 Jobst Hall
Bradley University
Peoria, IL 61625
309-677-4632
Fax: 309-677-3289
www.imex1.org

Indiana
Indiana Business Modernization
and Technology Corporation
One North Capitol Ave., Suite 925
Indianapolis, IN 46204
317-635-3058
800-877-5182
Fax: 317-231-7095
www.bmtadvantage.org

Iowa
Iowa Manufacturing Technology
Center
Des Moines Area Community
College
ATC Bldg., 3E
2006 S. Ankeny Blvd.
Ankeny, IA 50021
515-965-7125

Fax: 515-965-7050
www.tecnet.org/iowamtc

Kansas
Mid-America Manufacturing
Technology Center
10561 Barkley, Suite 602
Overland Park, KS 66212
913-649-4333
800-653-4333
Fax: 913-649-4498
www.mamtc.com

Kentucky
Kentucky Technology Service
167 W. Main St., Suite 500
Lexington, KY 40507
606-252-7801
Fax: 606-252-7900

Louisiana
Louisiana Manufacturing
Extension Partnership of
Louisiana
P.O. Box 44172
241 E. Lewis St.
Lafayette, LA 70504
318-482-6767
Fax: 318-262-5472
http://lpc.usl.edu/mepol

Maine
Maine Manufacturing Extension
Partnership
87 Winthrop St.
Augusta, ME 04330
207-623-0680
Fax: 207-623-0779
www.mainemep.org

Maryland
Maryland Technology Extension
Service

University of Maryland
Engineering Research Center
Potomac Bldg. 092, Room 2104
College Park, MD 20742
301-405-3883
301-403-4105
www.erc.umd.edu

Manufacturing Partnerships

Massachusetts
Massachusetts Manufacturing
Partnership
Corporation for Business, Work
and Learning
The Schrafft Center
529 Main St.
Boston, MA 02129
617-727-8158
800-667-6347
Fax: 617-242-7660
www.mmpmfg.org

Michigan
Michigan Manufacturing
Technology Center
P.O. Box 1485
2901 Hubbard Rd.
Ann Arbor, MI 48106
734-769-4472
800-292-4484
Fax: 734-213-3405
www.iri.org/mmtc

National Metal Finishing
Resource Center
National Center for Manufacturing
Sciences
3025 Boardwalk Dr.

Ann Arbor, MI 48108
313-995-4911
Fax: 313-995-1150
www.nmfrc.org

Minnesota Technology, Inc.
111 Third Ave., South, Suite 400
Minneapolis, MN 5540
612-338-7722
Fax: 612-339-5214
www.minnesotatechnology.org

Mississippi
Mississippi Polymer Institute and
Pilot Manufacturing Extension
Center
P.O. Box 10003
Hattiesburg, MS 39406
601-266-4607
Fax: 601-266-5635
www.psrc.usm.edu/MPI

Mississippi Technology Extension
Partnership
Bldg. 1103, Suite 146K
Stennis Space Center, MS 39529
228-688-3535
800-746-4699
Fax: 228-688-1426
www.technet.org/mtep

Missouri
Mid-America Manufacturing
Technology Center
800 W. 14th St., Suite 111
Rolla, MO 65401
573-364-8570
800-956-2682
Fax: 573-364-6323
www.tecnet.org/mamtc

Mid-America Manufacturing
Technology Center

10561 Barkley, Suite 602
Overland Park, KS 66212
913-649-4333
800-653-4333
Fax: 913-649-4498
www.mamtc.com

Montana
Montana Manufacturing Extension
Center
313 Roberts Hall
Montana State University
Bozeman, MT 59717
406-994-3812
Fax: 406-994-3391
www.coe.montana.edu/mmec

Nebraska
Nebraska Manufacturing
Extension Partnership
301 Centennial Mall South
4th Floor
Lincoln, NE 68509
402-471-3755
Fax: 402-471-4374
http://nics.ded.state.ne.us

Nevada
Industry Network Corporation-
Nevada
1155 University Blvd., SE
Albuquerque, NM 87106
505-843-4250
800-716-6462
Fax: 505-843-4255
www.mfg-inc.com

New Hampshire
Manufacturing Extension
Partnership of New Hampshire
Millyard Technology Park
25 Pine Street Extension
Nashua, NH 03060

603-594-1188
Fax: 603-594-9146
www.nhmep.org

New Jersey
New Jersey Manufacturing
Extension Partnership
New Jersey Institute of
Technology
University Heights
GITC Suite 3200
Newark, NJ 07102
973-642-7099
Fax: 973-596-6056
www.njmep.org

New Mexico
Industry Network Corporation-
New Mexico
1155 University Blvd., SE
Albuquerque, NM 87106
505-843-4250
800-716-6462
Fax: 505-843-4255
www.mfg-inc.com

New York
New York Manufacturing
Extension Partnership
New York Science and
Technology Foundation
99 Washington Ave., Suite 1730
Albany, NY 12210
518-486-7384
Fax: 518-473-6876

New York Manufacturing
Extension Partnership
Hudson Valley Technology
Development Center
33 Westage Business Center
Suite 130
Fishkill, NY 12524

914-896-6934
Fax: 914-896-706
www.hvtdc.org

New York Manufacturing
Extension Partnership
Alliance for Manufacturing and
Technology
61 Court St., 6th Floor
Binghamton, NY 13901
607-774-0022
Fax: 607-774-0026
http://amt-mep.org

New York Manufacturing
Extension Partnership
Industrial Technology Assistance
Corporation
253 Broadway, Room 302
New York, NY 10007
212-240-6920
Fax: 212-240-6879
www.itac.org

New York Manufacturing
Extension Partnership
Western New York Technology
Development Center
1576 Sweet Home Rd.
Amherst, NY 14228
716-636-3626
Fax: 716-636-3630
www.wnytdc.org

New York Manufacturing
Extension Partnership
High Technology of Rochester
Five United Way
Rochester, NY 14604
716-327-7930
Fax: 716-327-7931
www.monroe.edu/rochproj/
htr.html

New York Manufacturing
Extension Partnership
Center for Economic Growth
One Key Corporation Plaza
Suite 600
Albany, NY 12207
518-465-8975
Fax: 518-465-6681

New York Manufacturing
Extension Partnership
Central New York Technology
Development Organization
1201 E. Fayette St.
Syracuse, NY 13201
315-425-5144
Fax: 315-475-8460
www.cnytdor.org

New York Manufacturing
Extension Partnership
CI-TEC
Box 8561, Peyton Hall
Potsdam, NY 13699
315-268-3778
Fax: 315-268-4432
www.northnet.org.citec/

New York Manufacturing
Extension Partnership
Long Island Forum for
Technology
P.O. Box 170
Farmingdale, NY 11735
516-755-3321
Fax: 516-755-9264
www.lift.org

New York Manufacturing
Extension Partnership
Mohawk Valley Applied
Technology Commission
207 Genessee St., Room 1604

Utica, NY 13501
315-793-8050
Fax: 315-793-8057
www.borg.com/~mvatc

New York Manufacturing
Extension Partnership
National Center for Printing,
Publishing and Imaging
Rochester Institute of Technology
111 Lomb Memorial Dr.
Rochester, NY 14623
716-475-2100
Fax: 716-475-5250

North Carolina
North Carolina Manufacturing
Extension Partnership
900 Capability Dr.
Raleigh, NC 27695
919-515-5408
Fax: 919-515-8585
www.les.ncsu.edu

North Dakota
North Dakota Manufacturing
Technology Partnership
Institute for Business and Industry
Development
NDSU- Hastings Hall
P.O. Box 5256
Fargo, ND 58105
701-231-1001
Fax: 701-231-1007
www.growingnd.com/
man_part_prog.htm

Ohio
Great Lakes Manufacturing
Technology Center
Prospect Park Bldg.
4600 Prospect Ave.
Cleveland, OH 44103

216-432-5300
Fax: 216-432-5510
www.camp.org

Plastics Technology Development
Center
GLMTC Manufacturing Outreach
Program
Prospect Park Bldg.
4600 Prospect Ave.
Cleveland, OH 44103
216-432-5340
Fax: 216-432-2900
http://ptdc01.bd.psu.edu

Miami Valley Manufacturing
Extension Center
1111 Edison Dr.
Cincinnati, OH 45216
513-948-2000
800-345-4482
Fax: 513-948-2109
http://iams.org/mvmec/
mvmec.htm

Lake Erie Manufacturing
Extension Partnership
1700 N. Westwood Ave.
Toledo, OH 43607
419-534-3705
Fax: 419-531-8465
www.eisc.org

Oklahoma
Oklahoma Alliance for
Manufacturing Excellence
525 S. Main St., Suite 210
Tulsa, OK 74105
918-592-0722
Fax: 918-592-1417
www.okalliance.com

Oregon
Oregon Manufacturing Extension
Partnership

29353 Town Center, Loop East
Wilsonville, OR 97070
503-650-7350
800-MEP-4MFG
Fax: 503-682-4494
www.omep.org

Resource
Centers

Pennsylvania
North/East Pennsylvania
Manufacturing Extension
Partnership
125 Goodman Dr.
Bethlehem, PA 18015
610-758-5599
800-343-6732
Fax: 610-758-4716

Northeastern Pennsylvania
Industrial Resource Center
75 Young St.
Wilkes Barre, PA 18706
717-819-8966
800-654-8960
Fax: 717-819-8931

Manufacturers' Resource Center
125 Goodman Dr.
Bethlehem, PA 18015
610-758-5599
800-343-6732
Fax: 610-758-4716

Mid-Pennsylvania Manufacturing
Extension Partnership
MANTEC Inc.

The Manufacturers' Technology
Center
227 W. Market St.
P.O. Box 5046
York, PA 17405
717-843-5054
888-843-5054
Fax: 717-854-0087
www.mantec.org

Industrial Modernization Center
Farm Complex
RR #5
Box 220-62A
Montoursville, PA 17754
717-368-8361
800-326-9467
Fax: 717-368-8452
www.imcpa.com

Southwestern Pennsylvania
Industrial Resource Center
200 Technology Dr.
Pittsburgh, PA 15219
412-687-0200
Fax: 412-687-5232

Northwest Pennsylvania Industrial
Resource Center
Uniflow Center
1525 East Lake Rd.
Erie, PA 16511
814-456-6299
Fax: 814-459-6058

Delaware Valley Industrial
Resource Center
2905 Southhampton Rd.
Philadelphia, PA 19154
215-464-8550
Fax: 215-464-8570
www.technet.org/dvirc

Plastics Technology Development
Center
C/o Penn State-Erie
Behrend College
Station Rd.
Erie, PA 16563
814-898-6132
Fax: 814-898-6006
http://ptdc01.bd.psu.edu

Rhode Island
Rhode Island Manufacturing
Extension Services
229 Waterman St.
Providence, RI 02906
401-621-5710
Fax: 401-621-5702
www.rimes.org

South Carolina
South Carolina Manufacturing
Extension Partnership
1136 Washington St., Suite 300
Columbia, SC 29201
803-252-6976
Fax: 803-254-8512
www.scmep.org

South Dakota
South Dakota Manufacturing
Extension Partnership Center
Governor's Office of Economic
Development
711 E. Wells Ave.
Pierre, SD 57501
605-773-5653
Fax: 605-773-3256

Tennessee
Tennessee Manufacturing
Extension Partnership
University of Tennessee Center
for Industrial Services

226 Capitol Blvd., Suite 606
Nashville, TN 37219
615-532-8657
Fax: 615-532-4937
www.cis.utk.edu

Texas
Texas Manufacturing Assistance
Center
1700 Congress Ave., Suite 200
Austin, TX 78701
512-936-0234
800-488-TMAC
512-936-0433
www.tmac.org

Utah
Utah Manufacturing Extension
Partnership
UT MEP at UVSC
800 W. 1200 S.
Orem, UT 84058
801-764-7221
Fax: 801-764-7222
www.mep.org

Vermont
Vermont Manufacturing Extension
Center
Vermont Technical College
P.O. Box 520
Randolph Center, VT 05061
802-728-1432
Fax: 802-728-1456
www.vmec.org

Virginia
Virginia's A.L. Philpott
Manufacturing Extension
Partnership
P.O. Box 5311
645 Patriot Ave.
Martinsville, VA 24112

540-666-8890
Fax: 540-666-8892
www.vpmep.org

Washington
Washington Manufacturing
Services
2333 Seaway Blvd.
Everett, WA 98271
425-267-0173
800-637-4634
Fax: 425-267-0175
www.tecnet.org/wms

West Virginia
West Virginia Manufacturing
Extension Partnership
P.O. Box 6070
Morgantown, WV 26506
304-293-3800 Ext. 810
Fax: 304-293-6751

Wisconsin
Northwest Wisconsin
Manufacturing Outreach Center
University of Wisconsin- Stout
278 Jarvis Hall
Menomonie, WI 54751
715-232-2397
Fax: 715-232-1105
http://nwmoc.uwstout.edu

Wisconsin Manufacturing
Extension Partnership
2601 Crossroads Dr., Suite 145
Madison, WI 53718
608-240-1740
Fax: 608-240-1744
www.mep.org

Wyoming
Mid-America Manufacturing
Technology Center

10561 Barkley, Suite 602
Overland Park, KS 66212
913-649-4333
800-653-4333
Fax: 913-649-4498
www.mamtc.com

National
National Center for Printing,
Publishing and Imaging
Rochester Institute of Technology
111 Lomb Memorial Dr.
Rochester, NY 14623

716-475-2100
Fax: 716-475-5250

National Metal Finishing
Resource Center
National Center for Manufacturing
Sciences
3025 Boardwalk Dr.
Ann Arbor, MI 48108
313-995-4911
Fax: 313-995-1150
www.nmfrc.org

Commissions, Committees, and Councils On the Status of Women

Because women so often put the needs of others before their own, they are oftentimes reluctant to seek help for themselves. Feelings of guilt, low self-esteem, depression, anger, and stress often accompany the changes that can occur during a woman's life — changes like divorce, separation, job termination or change, abuse, or sexual harassment. Never before have there been more options for women seeking help, whether it is in learning new career skills or finding a support group of other women coping with life's ups and downs that affect all of us at one time or another.

In almost every state, there are Women's Commissions and similar groups that provide direction or assistance to women.

Missions and programs vary, but these groups all share the goal of working toward eliminating the inequities that affect women at home and in the workplace. Some commissions are simply advocacy groups, bringing attention to issues that affect women and working to bring about legislative changes that would improve situations that women face. Others provide information and referrals to help women get ahead — some even provide direct services to help women get the training, education, and financial help they need to succeed.

Through research, education, legislative action and special projects, the commissions are a strong voice for women's rights. Areas of interest and support include, but are not limited to:

♦ Child support laws
♦ Advancement in non-traditional jobs
♦ Sexual harassment
♦ Child care and dependent care programs
♦ Violence against women
♦ Housing
♦ Insurance
♦ Credit
♦ Legal rights
♦ Education
♦ Employment
♦ Economic equity
♦ Appointment of qualified women for all positions of government

Some also provide other services such as:

- ◆ Referrals and information on women's issues
- ◆ Seminars
- ◆ Workshops and/or workshop leaders
- ◆ Conferences
- ◆ Speakers bureaus
- ◆ Public forums
- ◆ Publications
- ◆ Audio-visual libraries
- ◆ Resource directories

Please don't hesitate to call your local commission. The people who work there are caring and very willing to help with just about any kind of problem. If you do not see a commission listed for your state, call the Governor's office to see if one has been established — or ask them for guidance with your problem.

Check the following list for the commission nearest you.

U.S. Department of Labor
Women's Bureau
Women's Bureau
U.S. Department of Labor
200 Constitution Ave., NW, S3311
Washington, DC 20210
800-827-5335
202-219-6631
www.dol.gov/dol/wb

National Association of
Commissions for Women
(NACW)
Patricia Hendel, President NACW
127 Parkway South
New London, CT 06320
860-442-1054
Fax: 860-442-1054

Carrolena M. Key
Assistant to the President
NACW National Office
8630 Fenton St., Suite 934
Silver Spring, MD 20910
800-338-9267
301-585-8101
Fax: 301-585-3445
E-mail: nacw2@nacw.org
www.nacw.org

Alabama
Alabama Women's Commission
P.O. Box 1277
Tuscaloosa, AL 35403
205-345-7668
Jean Boutwell, elected Secretary

Bab F. Hart, Chair
www.alawomenscommission.org

Alaska
Anchorage Women's Commission
P.O. Box 196650
Anchorage, AK 99519-6650
907-343-6310
Fax: 907-343-6730
www.ci.anchorage.ak.us

Arizona
Phoenix Women's Commission
Equal Opportunity Department
251 West Washington, 7th Floor
Phoenix, AZ 85003-6211
602-261-8242
Fax: 602-256-3389

Tucson Women's Commission
240 North Court Ave.
Tucson, AZ 85701
520-624-8318
Fax: 520-624-5599
E-mail: tctwc@starnet.com
Neema Caughran, Executive
Director
Louisa Hernandez, Chair

Arkansas
Closed 96-99

California
California Commission on the
Status of Women
1303 J St., Suite 400
Sacramento, CA 95814-2900
916-445-3173
Fax: 916-322-9466
E-mail: csw@sna.com
www.statusofwomen.ca.gov
Eileen Padberg, Chair

Colorado
Denver Women's Commission
303 West Colfax, Suite 1600
Denver, CO 80204
303-640-5826
Fax: 303-640-4627
www.denvergov.org/
Marilyn Ferran, Chair

Fort Collins City Commission on
the Status of Women
c/o Human Resources, City of Ft.
Collins
P.O. Box 580
Fort Collins, CO 80522
970-221-6871
970-224-6050
www.ci.fort-collins.co.us
Laurie Fonken-Joseph, Chair

Connecticut
Connecticut Permanent
Commission of the Status of
Women
18-20 Trinity St.
Hartford, CT 06106
860-240-8300
Fax: 860-240-8314
E-mail: pcsw@po.state.ct.us
www.cga.state.ct.us/pcswl/
Leslie Brett, Ph.D, Executive
Director
Barbara DeBaptiste, Chair

Delaware
Delaware Commission for Women
4425 N. Market St.
Wilmington, DE 19802
302-761-8005
Fax: 302-761-6652
E-mail: cgomez@state.de.us
Romona S. Fullman, Esq., Director

District of Columbia
Women's Bureau
U.S. Department of Labor
200 Constitution Ave., NW
Washington, DC 20210
800-827-5335
202-219-6631
Fax: 202-219-5529
www.dol.gov/dol.wb
Delores L. Crockett, Acting
Director
Lillian M. Long, Chair

Florida
Florida Commission on the Status
of Women
Office of the Attorney General, The
Capitol
Tallahassee, FL 32399-1050
850-414-3300
Fax: 850-921-4131
E-mail: Michele-Manning@
oag.state.fl.us
http://legal.firn.edu/units/fcsw
Kate Gooderham, Chair
Susan Gilbert, Vice Chair

Georgia
GA State Commission of Women
148 International Blvd., NE
Atlanta, GA 30303
404-657-9260
Fax: 404-657-2963
E-mail: gawomen@manspring.com
www.manspring.com/~gawomen
Nellie Duke, Chair
Juliana McConnell, Vice Chair

Hawaii
Hawaii State Commission on the
Status of Women
235 S. Beretaniast, Suite 401
Honolulu, HI 96813
808-586-5757
Fax: 808-586-5756
E-mail: hscsw@pixi.com
www.state.hi.us/hscsw
Alicynttikida Tasaka, Executive
Director

Idaho
Idaho Commission on the Women's
Program
P.O. Box 83720
Boise, ID 83720-0036
208-334-4673
Fax: 208-334-4646
E_mail: ehurlbudt@
women.state.id.us
www.state.id.us/women
Linda Hurlbudt, Director
Cindy Agidius, Chair

Illinois
Governor's Commission on the
Status of Women
100 W. Randolph, Suite 16-100
Chicago, IL 60601
312-814-5743
Fax: 312-814-3823
Ellen Solomon, Executive Director

Indiana
Indiana State Commission for
Women
100 N. Senate Ave., N103
Indianapolis, IN 46204
317-233-6303
Fax: 317-232-6580
E-mail: icw@state.in.us
www.state.in.us/icw

Iowa

Iowa Commission on the Status of
Women
Lucas State Office Building
Des Moines, IA 50319
515-281-4461
Fax: 515-242-6119
E-mail: icsw@compuserve.com
www.state.ia.us/dhr/sw
Charlotte Nelson, Executive
Director
Kathryn Burt, Chair

Kansas

Wichita Commission on the Status
of Women
Human Services Dept., 2nd Floor
455 North Main St.
Wichita, KS 67202
316-268-4691
Fax: 316-268-4219
Shirley Mast, Contact Person

Kentucky

Kentucky Commission on Women
614A Shelby St.
Frankfort, KY 40601
502-564-6643
Fax: 502-564-2315
E-mail: gpotter@mail.state.ky.us
www.state.ky.us/agencies/
women/index.html
Genie Potter, Executive Director

Louisiana

LA Office of Women's Services
1885 Woodale Blvd., 9th Floor
Baton Rouge, LA 70806
225-922-0960
Fax: 225-922-0959
E-mail: owsbradm@ows.state.la.us
www.ows.state.la.us/
Vera Clay, Executive Director

Maine

Abolished

Maryland

Maryland Commission for Women
311 West Saratoga St., Room 232
Baltimore, MD 21201
410-767-7137
Fax: 410-333-0079
E-mail: lsajardo@dhr.state.md.us
www.dhr.state.md.us/mcw/
index.html
Dr. Carl A. Silberg, Executive
Director
Dr. Fran V. Tracy-Mumsford, Chair

Massachusetts

Massachusetts Governor's Advisory
Committee on Women's Issues
Statehouse Governor's Office,
Room 360
Boston, MA 02133
617-727-3600
Fax: 617-727-9725
Jennifer Davis Carey, Contact
Joanne Thompson, Chair

Michigan

Michigan Women's Commission
741 N. Cedar St., Suite 102
Lansing, MI 48913
517-334-8622
Fax: 517-334-8641
www.mdcr.com
Patti Garrett, Chair

Minnesota

Minnesota Commission on the
Economic Status of Women
85 State Office Building
St. Paul, MN 55155
651-296-8590
Fax: 651-297-3697

E-mail: lcesw@commissions.
leg.state.mn.us
www.commissions.leg.state.mn.us/
Aviva Breen, Executive Director
Becky Lourey, Chair

Mississippi
Inactive

Missouri
Missouri Women's Council
P.O. Box 1684
Jefferson City, MO 65102
573-751-0810
Fax: 573-751-8835
E-mail: wcouncil@mail.state.mo.us
www.womenscouncil.org
Sue P. McDaniel, Executive
Director
Deborah Borchers-Ausmus, Chair

Montana
Interdepartmental Coordinating
Committee for Women (ICCW)
P.O. Box 1728
Helena, MT 59624
406-444-1520
E-mail: jbranscum@state.mt.us
www.mdt.state.mt.us/iccw
Jean Branscum, Chair
Jeanne Wolf, Vice Chair

Nebraska
Nebraska Commission on the Status
of Women
301 Centennial Mall South
Box 94985
Lincoln, NE 65809

402-471-2039
Fax: 402-471-5655
E-mail: ncswmail@mail.state.ne.us
www.ncsw.org
Toni Gray, Executive Director

Nevada
Nevada Women's Fund
201 W. Liberty
Reno, NV 89501
775-786-2335

New Hampshire
New Hampshire Commission on
the Status of Women
State House Annex, Room 334
25 Capitol St.
Concord, NH 03301-6312
603-271-2660
Fax: 603-271-2361
E-mail: kfrey@admin.state.nh.us
www.state.nh.us/csw
Katheryn Frey, Executive Director
Molly Kelly, Chair

New Jersey
New Jersey Dept. of Community
Affairs
Division of Women
101 South Broad St. CN 808
Trenton, NJ 08625-0801
609-292-8840
Fax: 609-633-6821
Elizabeth L. Cox

New Mexico
New Mexico Commission on the
Status of Women
2401 12th St. NW
Albuquerque, NM 87104-2302
505-841-8920
Fax: 505-841-8926
E-mail: rdakota@nm.us.
campuscwix.net

Yolanda Garcia, Info. Officer
Darlene B. Herrera, Vice Chair

New York
New York State Division for
Women
633 Third Ave.
New York, NY 10017
212-681-4547
Fax: 212-681-7626
E-mail: women@women.
state.ny.us
www.women.state.ny.us
Elaine Wingate Conway, Director

North Carolina
North Carolina Council for Women
526 North Wilmington St.
Raleigh, NC 27604-1199
919-733-2455
Fax: 919-733-2464
www.doa.state.nc.us/doa/
cfw/cfw.htm
Juanita Bryant, Executive Director
Jane Carver, Chair

North Dakota
North Dakota Governor's
Commission on the Status of
Women
600 East Boulevard
Bismarck, ND 58501-0250
701-328-5300
Fax: 701-328-5320
Carol Reed, Chairman

Ohio
Ohio Women's Commission
77 S. High St., 24th Floor
Columbus, OH 43266-0920
614-466-5580
Fax: 614-466-5434

Sally Farran Bulford, Executive
Director
Dr. Suzanne Crawford, Chair

Oklahoma
Oklahoma Governor's Commission
on the Status of Women
101 State Capitol Bldg.
2300 North Lincoln Blvd.
Oklahoma City, OK 73105-4897
918-492-4492
Fax: 918-492-4472
Claudia Tarrington, Chair
Kathi Goebel, Senior Vice Chair

Lawton Mayor's Commission on
the Status of Women
102 SW 5th St.
Lawton, OK 73501
405-581-3260
Janet Childress, Chair
Emma Crowder, Vice Chair

Tulsa Mayor's Commission on the
Status of Women
c/o Department of Human Rights
200 Civic Center
Tulsa, OK 74103
918-582-0558
918-592-7818

Oregon
Oregon Commission for Women
Portland State University
Smith Center, Room M315
Portland, OR 97207
503-725-5889
Tracy Davis, Contact

Pennsylvania
Pennsylvania Commission for
Women
Finance Building, Room 205

Harrisburg, PA 17120
888-615-7477
Fax: 717-772-0653
E-mail: lesbn@oa.state.pa.us
Loida Esbri, Executive Director

Puerto Rico
Puerto Rico Commission for
Women's Affairs
Office of the Governor
Commonwealth of Puerto Rico
P.O. Box 11382
Fernandez Juncos Station
Santurce, PR 00910
787-722-2907
Fax: 787-723-3611
E-mail: egavilan@prtc.net
Enid M. Gavilan, Executive
Director

Rhode Island
Rhode Island Advisory
Commission on Women
260 W. Exchange St., Suite 4
Providence, RI 02093
401-222-6105
E-mail: tayers@doa.state.ri.us
Toby Ayers, Ph.D., Director
James M. Anthony, Chair

South Carolina
Governor's Office Commission on
Women

1205 Pendleton St., Suite 306
Columbia, SC 29201
803-734-1609
Fax: 803-734-0241
Rebecca Collier, Executive Director

South Dakota
Abolished

Tennessee
Abolished

Texas
Texas Governor's Commission for
Women
P.O. Box 12428
Austin, TX 78711
512-463-1782
512-475-2615
Fax: 512-463-1832
www.governor.state.tx.us/women/
Ashley Horton, Executive Director

Utah
Utah Governor's Commission for
Women and Families
1160 State Office Bldg.
Salt Lake City, UT 84114
801-538-1736
Fax: 801-538-3027
E-mail: women&families@
gov.state.ut.us
www.governor.state.ut.us/women/
Michael Neider, Chair

Vermont
Vermont Governor's Commission
on the Status of Women
126 State St.
Drawer 33
Montpelier, VT 05602
802-828-2851
Fax: 802-828-2930

E-mail: info@women.state.vt.us
www.state.vt.us/wom
Judith Sutphen, Executive Director

Virginia
Alexandria Council on the Status of
Women
110 North Royal St., Suite 201
Alexandria, VA 22314
703-838-5030
Fax: 703-838-4976
http://ci.alexandria.va.us/
alexandria.html
Norma Gattsek, Executive Director
Tara Hardiman, Chair

Arlington Commission on the
Status of Women
2100 Clarendon Blvd., Suite 310
Arlington, VA 22201
703-228-3257
Fax: 703-228-3295
E-mail: publicaffairs@co.
arlington.va.us
www.co.arlington.va.us/cmo
Katherine Hoffman

Fairfax City Commission for
Women
10455 Armstrong St.
Fairfax, VA 22030
703-385-7894
Fax: 703-385-7811
www.ci.fairfax.va.us
Louise Armitage, Director

Fairfax County Commission for
Women
12000 Government Center Pkwy.,
Suite 318
Fairfax, VA 22035
703-324-5720
Fax: 703-324-3959

TTY: 703-222-3504
Leia Francisco, Executive Director

Richmond Mayor's Committee on
the Concerns of Women
City Hall
900 East Marshall St., Room 302
Richmond, VA 23219
804-646-5987
Nancy Ownes, Admin. Assistant
Caroline Adams, Chair

Washington
Seattle Women's Commission
c/o Seattle Office for Civil Rights
700 Third Ave, Suite 250
Seattle WA 98104
206-684-4500
Fax: 206-684-0332
E-mail: diane.pina@ci.seattle.wa.us
www.ci.seattle.wa.us/seattle/
civil/swc.htm

West Virginia
West Virginia Women's
Commission
Building 6, Room 637
Capitol Complex
Charleston, WV 25305
304-558-0070
Fax: 304-558-5767
E-mail: vrobinson@wvdhhr.org
www.state.wv.us/womenscom
Joyce M. Stover, Acting Executive
Director
Sally Riley, Chair

Wisconsin
Wisconsin Women's Council
16 North Carroll St., Suite 720
Madison, WI 53703
608-266-2219
Fax: 608-261-2432

E-mail: Katie.Mnuk@wwc.
state.wi.us
http://wwc.state.wi.us
Katie Mnuk, Executive Director

Wyoming
Wyoming State Government
Commission for Women

c/o Department of Employment
Herschler Building
122 West 25th St.
Cheyenne, WY 82002
307-777-7671
http://wydoe.state.wy.us
Amy McClure, Chair

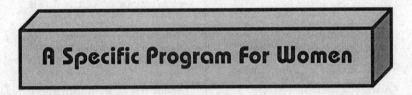

A Specific Program For Women

The Department of Defense (DoD) has developed the
**Women-Owned Small Business Program
(WOSB).** Annually, the DoD awards nearly $2 billion in
prime contracts and $2.4 billion in subcontracts to WOSB
 concerns. All DoD
subcontracting plans
are required to
have a separate
goal for awards to
Women-Owned Small
Businesses (WOSBs), and the DoD considers the extent of
participation by small business concerns when awarding
contracts.

Although DoD has neither the legislative authority to
restrict competition to WOSB concerns, nor the authority to
make awards to WOSB concerns at other than fair-market
price, the focus of the DoD WOSB program is the
provision of effective outreach, training and technical

assistance in order to increase the accessibility of WOSB concerns to DoD procurement opportunities.

The Office of Small and Disadvantaged Business Utilization operates in a policy capacity. They do not see individual requirements or procurements. Each branch of service

> ## Office of Small and Disadvantaged Business Utilization

(Army, Navy, Air Force) has designated a Women-Owned Small Business (WOSB) Advocate and you are encouraged to contact them directly. Those are the primary points of contact for the Department of Defense.

For more information on policy only, contact Office of the Secretary of Defense, Office of Small and Disadvantaged Business Utilization, Janet Koch, DoD WOB Program Manager, 1777 N. Kent Street, Suite 9100, Arlington, VA 22209; 703-588-8618; {E-mail: kochjk@acq.osd.mil}.

The Department of Defense has created a website with a "Procurement" feature that offers a step-by-step approach to the DoD marketplace and is quite comprehensive. For more information, visit {www.acq.osd.mil/sadbu/wosb}.

For more information on procurement training and opportunities, contact:

1. *Department of the Army* Office of Small and Disadvantaged Business Utilization; 106 Army

Pentagon, Washington, DC 20310-0106; 703-693-6115
(SADBU); 703-697-2868 (Small Business Office);
{E-mail: sadbu@hqda.army.mil};
{www.hqda.army.mil/sadbu}.

2. ***Department of the Navy*** Small and Disadvantaged
   Business Utilization (SADBU), Washington Navy
   Yard, 720 Kennon Street, SE, Room 207, Washington,
   DC 20374-5015; 202-685-6485; Fax: 202-685-6485;
   {E-mail: Sadbu@Hq.Navy.Mil};
   {www.hq.navy.mil/sadbu}.

3. ***Department of the United States Air Force***, Office of
   Small and Disadvantaged Business Utilization
   (SAF/SB), 1060 Air Force Pentagon, Washington, DC
   20330-1060; 703-697-1950; Fax: 703-614-9266; {E-
   mail: schlottj@af.pentagon.mil};
   {www.selltoairforce.org}.

Over 100 Government Grants For Your Business

One of the biggest frustrations we hear is from people looking for *FREE MONEY* from the government for their business. By free money, they usually mean grants or other programs where they don't have to pay back the money they receive.

Many people will contact the Small Business Administration asking about free money programs and will be told that there is no such thing. Well, they are right and wrong. They are right, because the Small Business Administration does not offer grants. They specialize in loans and loan guarantees. But, they are wrong because there are dozens of other government organizations that do offer grants to businesses.

The real good stuff in life is never the most plentiful and always takes extra effort and sometimes ingenuity to uncover it.

The following is a list of a number of national and local government organizations which offer grants or other forms of money you don't have to pay back, like venture capital.

> **The real good stuff in life is never the most plentiful and always takes extra effort and sometimes ingenuity to uncover it.**

It is in no way a complete list because programs always come and go in our fast changing society. But it certainly does offer you an idea of the opportunities that are out there waiting, and it dispels the myth that there are no government grants for business. Just ask Paul Newman when you see him. He received government grant money from the U.S. Department of Agriculture to help sell his salad dressing overseas.

$1 BILLION
TO WORK ON IDEAS

The Small Business Innovation Research (SBIR) Program is a highly competitive program that encourages small businesses to explore their technological potential and provides the incentive to profit from its commercialization.

Each year, ten federal departments and agencies are required to reserve a portion of their research and development funds to award to small businesses. SBIR funds the critical start-up and development stages and it encourages the commercialization of the technology, product, or service. There are three phases to the program: start-up, development, and marketplace.

To learn more about how to apply and about the various agencies involved, contact Office of Technology, U.S. Small Business Administration, 409 Third St., SW, Washington, DC 20416; 202-205-6450; {www.sba.gov/SBIR/ sbir.html}.

Technology Assistance

The Small Business Technology Transfer (STTR) Program is a highly competitive program that reserves a specific percentage of federal research and development funding for awarding to small business and nonprofit research institution partners.

Small business has long been where innovation and innovators thrive, and nonprofit research laboratories are instrumental in developing high-tech innovations. STTR combines the strengths of both entities by introducing entrepreneurial skills to hi-tech research efforts. There are specific requirements that must be met.

To learn more about how to apply and the various agencies involved, contact Office of Technology, U.S. Small Business Administration, 409 Third St., SW, Washington, DC 20416; 202-205-6450; {www.sba.gov/SBIR/ sbir.html}.

Invention Assistance

Do you have a plan to develop a company based on your energy-saving invention or innovation? Have you been searching for financial and technical support to bring your idea to market? The U.S. Department of Energy's Inventions and Innovation Program can help.

This program provides financial assistance for establishing technical performance and conducting early development of innovative ideas and inventions. Ideas that have a significant energy savings impact and future commercial market potential are chosen for financial support through a competitive solicitation process. In addition to financial assistance, this program offers technical guidance and commercialization support to successful applicants.

For more information, contact U.S. Department of Energy, Golden Field Office, Inventions and Innovation Program, 1617 Cole Blvd., 17-3, Golden, CO 80401; 303-275-4744; {www.oit.doe.gov/Access/inventions/inventions.html}.

ฦurt By Jmports?

The Economic Development Administration of the U.S. Department of Commerce funds the *Trade Adjustment Assistance Program*. If your company is affected by import competition, you may file a petition for certification of impact. If your firm is certified, you may then apply for technical assistance in diagnosing your problems, and assessing your opportunities. Once approved, your firm can apply for technical assistance to implement the recovery strategy. The average grant is for over $700,000.

For more information, contact Economic Development Administration, U.S. Department of Commerce, 14th and Constitution Ave., NW, Room 7804, Washington, DC 20230; 202-482-5081; {www.doc.gov/eda}.

$50,000,000
For Air Service

The Airline Deregulation Act gave airlines almost total freedom to determine which markets to serve domestically and what fares to charge for that service. The Essential Air Service Program was put into place to guarantee that small communities that were served by certificated air carriers before deregulation maintain a minimal level of scheduled air service.

The Department of Transportation currently subsidizes commuter airlines to serve approximately 100 rural communities across the country that otherwise would not receive any scheduled air service.

For more information, contact Office of Aviation Analysis, Office of the Assistant Secretary, U.S. Department of Transportation, 400 7th St., SW, Washington, DC 20590; 202-366-1053; {http://ostpxweb.dot.gov/aviation}.

Sell Overseas

The *Foreign Market Development Cooperator Program* is designed to develop, maintain, and expand long-term export markets for U.S. agricultural products. The program has fostered a trade promotion partnership between the U.S. Department of Agriculture (USDA) and U.S. agricultural producers and processors who are represented by nonprofit commodity or trade associations called cooperators.

The USDA and the cooperators pool their technical and financial resources to conduct market development activities outside the United States. Trade organizations compete for funds on the basis of the following allocation criteria: past export performance, past demand expansion performance, future demand expansion goals, and contribution levels. Projects include market research, trade servicing and more.

For more information, contact the Foreign Agriculture Service, Marketing Operations Staff, Stop Code 1042, U.S. Department of Agriculture, Washington, DC 20250; 202-720-4327; {www.fas.usda.gov}.

Venture Capital

The Small Business Investment Company (SBIC) programs are privately organized and privately managed investment firms that are licensed by the Small Business Administration. With their own capital and with funds borrowed at favorable rates through the federal government, SBICs provide venture capital to small independent businesses, both new and already established.

A major incentive for the SBICs to invest in small businesses is the chance to share in the success of the small business if it grows and prospers. Small businesses qualifying for assistance from the SBIC program are able to receive equity capital, long-term loans, and expert management assistance.

For more information on SBICs or for a Directory of Small Business Investment Companies, contact Investment Division, U.S. Small Business Administration, 409 Third St., SW, Washington, DC 20416; 202-205-6510; {www.sba.gov/INV}.

Advanced Technology Money

Not-yet-possible technologies are the domain of the National Institute of Standards and Technology's **Advanced Technology Program (ATP).**

The ATP is a unique partnership between government and private industry to accelerate the development of high-risk technologies that promise significant commercial payoffs and widespread benefits for the economy. ATP projects focus on the technology needs of the U.S. industry. The ATP does not fund product

Information USA, Inc.

development. It supports enabling technologies that are essential to the development of new products, processes, and services across diverse application areas. There are strict cost-sharing rules and peer-review competitions.

For more information on how to apply for funding, contact Advanced Technology Program, National Institute of Standards and Technology, A407 Administration Building, Gaithersburg, MD 20899; 800-ATP-FUND (287-3863); {www.atp.nist.gov}.

$425,000
To Save Energy

The U.S. Department of Energy sponsors an innovative, cost-sharing program to promote energy efficiency, clean production, and economic competitiveness in industry. The grant program, known as NICE3 (National Industrial Competitiveness through Energy, Environment, and Economics), provides funding to state and industry partnerships for projects that develop and demonstrate advances in energy efficiency and clean production technologies. The overall goal of NICE3 is to improve industry energy efficiency, reduce industry's costs, and promote clean production.

Grants support innovative technology deployment that can significantly conserve energy and energy-intensive feedstocks, reduce industrial wastes, prevent pollution, and improve industrial cost competitiveness.

For more information, contact U.S. Department of Energy, Office of Industrial Technologies, Golden Field Office, 1617 Cole Blvd., 17-3, Golden, CO 80401; 303-275-4728; {www.oit.doe.gov/Access/nice3/basicbody.html}.

Grants To
North Dakota Women

The North Dakota Women's Business Program was designed to provide counseling and technical assistance for women entrepreneurs, as well as administer the women's incentive grant program. This office can certify women-owned businesses for federal and state contracting purposes and more.

Contact North Dakota Women's Business Program, 418 East Broadway, Suite 25, Bismarck, ND 58501; 701-258-2251; {www.growingnd.com}.

North Dakota Venture Capital

The Technology Transfer, Inc invests financial resources in North Dakota companies and inventors. Individuals or companies with marketable ideas for products or manufacturing processes may use TTI funds to evaluate the product or process to find out if it has any commercial potential. They may also use TTI funds for expenses such as market research, prototyping, product testing, patenting, test marketing, and business plan development. The maximum amount allowed is $100,000.

For more information, contact Technology Transfer, Inc., 1833 East Bismarck Expressway, Bismarck, ND 58504; 701-328-5300; {www.growingnd.com}.

$100,000 to $300,000
in Massachusetts Venture Capital

The Venture Capital Fund provides debt and, occasionally, equity financing to established businesses to enable them to expand or retain employment for local residents.

Financing is provided for firms that are unable to meet all of their capital needs in the traditional markets. Funds are available for working capital, expansion, or acquisition costs. The preferred investment range is $100,000 to $300,000 with the Community Development Fund Corporation providing up to one third of the total financing. Interest rates are fixed for the term of the loan.

For more information, contact Massachusetts Office of Business Development, One Ashburton Place, Room 2101, Boston, MA 02108; 617-727-3206; 800-5-CAPITAL; {www.magnet.state.me.us/mobd/venture.htm}.

80% DISCOUNT
on Energy Consultants

Today, businesses need innovative ways to cut costs, and one way to cut costs is to conserve energy. Companies that are energy efficient have more money for capital improvements, wages, and jobs.

The Massachusetts Division of Energy Resources (EAS), through its Energy Advisor Service provides the technical assistance companies need to cut energy costs. EAS utilizes engineers from the private sector who provide flexible and comprehensive energy efficient analyses of manufacturing processes and facilities. The service is customized to meet the needs of individual companies. EAS is partly subsided through federal dollars so customers only pay approximately 12% of the overall cost.

For more information, contact Massachusetts Office of Business Development, One Ashburton Place, Room 2101, Boston, MA 02108; 617-727-3206; 800-5-CAPITAL; {www.magnet.state.me.us/ mobd/energy.htm}.

GRANTS TO TRAIN EMPLOYEES

The Set-Aside for Economic Development is designed to provide matching job training funds to companies that are either relocating to Rhode Island or expanding present operations in the state. The funds are used for the training of new employees through either customized training programs or on the job training. The Set-Aside may also be used to upgrade and/or retrain existing employees in order to develop increased business and long term employment.

For more information, contact Rhode Island Economic Development Corporation, One West Exchange St., Providence, RI 02903; 401-222-2890; {www.riedc.com/growth/jobs/ job_programs.htm}.

$25,000 To Upgrade Employees Skills

The **Competitiveness Improvement Program** allows an employer to upgrade the skills of existing employees, thus improving the productivity of the business.

The program awards matching grants of up to $25,000 per company through a competitive proposal process. Businesses are urged to work through trade associations and local colleges and universities to increase the effectiveness of the training programs.

For more information, contact Rhode Island Economic Development Corporation, One West Exchange St., Providence, RI 02903; 401-222-2890; {www.riedc.com/growth/jobs/job_programs.htm}.

$5,000 To Learn New Technology

Rapid changes require rapid and effective responses. To meet your organizational needs, the Rhode Island Economic Development Corporation can afford you the opportunity to increase your overall productivity.

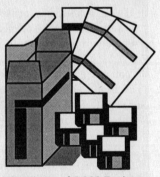

The intent of the **Project Upgrade** funds is to upgrade skills of currently employed workers who are being impacted by technological or organizational changes in the workplace. A maximum $5,000 Project Upgrade grant can be obligated to each eligible company.

For more information, contact Rhode Island Economic Development Corporation, One West Exchange St., Providence, RI 02903; 401-222-2890; {www.riedc.com/growth/jobs/job_programs.htm}.

$500,000 VENTURE CAPITAL FROM NEW YORK

High tech entrepreneurs, companies with technologies ready for market, and leading-edge enterprises each have different needs for investment capital. New York State has the seed and growth capital that will enable your high tech business to grow.

The *Small Business Technology Investment Fund Program (STBIF)* is a source of early-stage debt and equity funding for high tech companies. Initial investments can come to as much as $300,000 and later stage investments can go up to $500,000. New York State is banking on a strong high tech future.

$2,250 For Every Job

If your business is located in one of Connecticut's 17 enterprise zone locations, then you may be eligible for a variety of benefits and tax incentives.

You can earn $750 for each new full-time position that is created as a direct result of business expansion or renovation project. If 50% of the new hires are residents of the enterprise zone, the job grant increases to $2,250.

For more information, contact Department of Economic and Community Development, 505 Hudson St., Hartford, CT 06106; 860-270-8143; {www.state.ct.us/ecd/entzone/index.htm}.

Ben Franklin Seed Venture

The Ben Franklin Seed Venture Program was set up to encourage the development of technology based businesses in Pennsylvania. The Program provides product development and working capital to early-stage venture companies. The money is not to be used for general business operating expenses, and the amount is negotiable.

For more information, contact Department of Community and Economic Development, 494 Forum Bldg., Harrisburg, PA 17120; 727-787-7120; 800-379-7448; {www.dced.state. pa.us/PA_Exec/DCED/business/f.bfseed.htm}.

For more information, contact New York State Science and Technology Foundation, 99 Washington Ave., Suite 1731, Albany, NY 12210; 518-473-9741; {www.empire.state.ny.us/stf/sbtif.htm}.

Money For Job Training

Pennsylvanian companies can take advantage of the *Opportunity Grant Program*. This Program provides grant funds to create or preserve jobs within the Commonwealth.

Funds may be used for job training, infrastructure improvements, land and building improvements, machinery and equipment, working capital and environmental assessment and redemption. A 4 to 1 private to public match is required.

For more information, contact Department of Community and Economic Development, 494 Forum Bldg., Harrisburg, PA 17120; 727-787-7120; 800-379-7448; {www.dced.state.pa.us/PA_Exec/ DCED/business/f.opportunity.htm}.

Keep Jobs In
PENNSYLVANIA

The *Customized Job Training Program* provides grants to businesses in need of training assistance for new hires, retraining efforts, and upgrading employees in an effort to retain and create jobs in Pennsylvania.

Grants are available of up to 100% of the eligible costs for new job creations; 70% for job retention; and 25% for upgrade training. Money can be used for instructional costs, supplies, consumable materials, contracted services, and relevant travel costs for instructors.

For more information, contact Department of Community and Economic Development, 494 Forum Bldg., Harrisburg, PA 17120; 717-787-7120; 800-379-7448; {www.dced.state.pa.us/PA_Exec/DCED/business/3-ch-work.htm}.

Clean Up Assistance

Pennsylvania companies involved in the reuse of former industrial land may be eligible for the **Industrial Sites Reuse Program**. Grants and low interest loan financing are provided to perform environmental site assessment and remediation work at former industrial sites. This program provides grants and loans of up to $200,000 for environmental assessment and up to $1 million for remediation. A 25% match is required for grant and loan projects. The interest rate for loans is 2%.

For more information, contact Department of Community and
Economic Development, 494 Forum Bldg., Harrisburg, PA 17120;
717-787-7120; 800-379-7448; {www.dced.state.pa.us/PA_Exec/
DCED/business/3-ch-grants.htm}.

Convert Gas Vehicles to Alternative Fuels

In an effort to improve Pennsylvania air
quality and reduce the
consumption of imported oil, the
Office of Pollution Prevention
and Compliance Assistance

developed the *Alternative Fuels Incentive Grant Fund.*

Money can be used to increase the use of alternative fuel vehicles and
develop a refueling infrastructure in Pennsylvania. Applicants may
request a grant to cover a percentage of their costs to convert an
existing gasoline vehicle that meets certain age and mileage restrictions
to operate on alternative fuel, as well to purchase and install a refueling
or recharging facility.

$3 Million A Year In Grants To Coal Mine Operators

Have a coal mine and need to clean up your mess? The government
wants to help. The Office of Surface Mining Reclamation and
Enforcement of the U.S. Department of the Interior offers $3 million a
year to help small coal mine operators protect the environment from
negative effects of coal mining operations. For more information
contact Office of Surface Mining Reclamation and Enforcement, U.S.
Department of the Interior, 1951 Constitution Ave., NW, Washington,
DC 20240; 202-208-2651.

For more information, contact Department of Environment Protection, Office of Pollution Prevention and Compliance Assistance, 400 Market St., 15th Floor, RCSOB, P.O. Box 8772, Harrisburg, PA 17105; 717-772-8912; {www.dep.state.pa.us/dep/deputate/pollprev/Information/AFIG/AFIG_Guidelines.htm}.

Venture Capital for Low-Income Entrepreneurs

Maryland's *Equity Participation Investment Program* provides investments in technology-based businesses and business acquisitions that will be owned 70% or more by disabled, socially, or economically disadvantaged persons. The amount of money available ranges from $100,000 to $3 million and can be used to purchase machinery and equipment, inventory, working capital, real estate acquisitions, and more.

For more information, contact Maryland Department of Business and Economic Development, Division of Marketing, 217 E. Redwood St., Baltimore, MD 21202; 410-767-6555; 800-811-0051; {www.mdbusiness.state.md.us/Finance/msbdfa.html}.

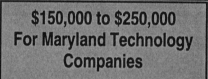

$150,000 to $250,000 For Maryland Technology Companies

The Enterprise Investment Program provides technology-driven companies in Maryland with equity capital. There is a matching funds component. Money given will require equity or limited interest in the company.

For more information, contact Maryland Department of Business and Economic Development, Division of Marketing, 217 E. Redwood St., Baltimore, MD 21202; 410-767-6555; 800-811-0051; {www.mdbusiness.state.md.us/Finance/inv_fin.html}.

POLLUTION CONTROL GRANTS FROM VIRGINIA

The Virginia Department of Environmental Quality has partnered with others to offer $10,000 pollution prevention grants.

The **Pollution Prevention Grants Program** is designed to encourage the implementation of pollution prevention techniques in businesses and governments throughout Virginia. It is an effort to support industrially significant pollution prevention programs that reduce the production waste and to help contribute to the bottom line of Virginia's manufacturers and businesses.

For more information, contact Virginia Department of Environmental Quality, 629 E. Main St., Richmond, VA 23219; 804-698-4545; 800-592-5482; {www/deq/state/va/us/opp/opp.html}.

Grants To Promote Virginia's Horse Industry

The Virginia Horse Industry Board is offering grants to groups or individuals who wish to develop projects that will benefit Virginia's horse industry. The Board will look at efforts that address the promotion and economic development of the horse industry, including areas of education, research, and marketing. A majority of the funding goes to non-profit groups.

For more information, contact Virginia Horse Industry Board, c/o Virginia Department of Agriculture & Consumer Services, 100 Bank St., Room 1004, Richmond, VA 23219; 804-786-5842; {www.state.va.us/~vdacs/vdacs.htm}.

$150,000 to $2 Million in Delaware Venture Capital

VENTURE CAPITAL

Venture capital is needed for both technology-based and non-technology oriented companies to get them up and running. In order to help these companies grow, the State of Delaware has joined as a partner in three venture capital funds. Each one funds businesses at various stages of development, but their investment focus varies.

For more information on the funds, contact Delaware Economic Development Office, 99 Kings Highway, Dover, DE 19901; 302-739-4271; {www.state.de.us/dedo/finance/dvp.htm}.

$50,000 For Delaware Inventors

The Small Business Innovation Research (SBIR) grant program is a federal government program designed to encourage small business to explore their technological potential and provides the incentive to profit from its commercialization.

SBIR funds the critical start-up and development stages. Phase I provides awards up to $100,000 for six months support for the exploration of technical merit or feasibility of an idea or technology. Delaware businesses that receive Phase I support are eligible for a bridge grant of up to $50,000 if they submit a Phase II proposal.

For more information, contact Delaware Economic Development Office, 99 Kings Highway, Dover, DE 19901; 302-739-4271; {www.state.de.us/dedo/finance/sbir.htm}.

Money For Development And Marketing In Delaware

Companies based in Delaware may be eligible for the **Delaware Innovation Fund** that "provides financial and technical assistance to businesses which have the potential to launch innovative products and processes into national markets, to create new jobs, and to make a significant contribution to the economic diversity and the technology base of Delaware's communities."

Money can be used to establish patents, develop business plans, and begin the commercialization process. A match is required for investments, but sweat equity is considered.

For more information, contact Delaware Innovation Fund, 100 West 10th St., Suite 413, Wilmington, DE 19801; 302-777-1616; {www.state.de.us/dedo/finance/innovatn.htm}.

$20,000 To Reduce Waste
In North Carolina

The North Carolina Division of Pollution Prevention and Environmental Assistance challenges North Carolina's industries and businesses to identify and apply pollution prevention techniques. To help meet this challenge, financial assistance in the form of matching grants up to $20,000 is offered to industries, businesses, and trade associations.

The *Challenge Grants* program is designed to help industries and businesses develop and implement innovative programs that will eliminate, prevent, and/or reduce the generation of wastewater, air emissions, and solid and hazardous waste.

Up To $250,000
In Venture Capital From North Carolina

The Innovation Research Fund is a venture capital investment fund created to provide flexible financing for new and existing businesses across North Carolina. The goal is to stimulate the state's economy through new business development and job creation. Competition for the fund is intense.

For more information, contact North Carolina Technological Development Authority, Inc., 2 Davis Dr., P.O. Box 13169, Research Triangle Park, NC 27709; 919-990-8558; {www.nctda.org/ven_capital/irf.html}.

For more information, contact North Carolina Division of Pollution Prevention and Environmental Assistance, P.O. Box 29560, Raleigh, NC 27626; 919-715-6500; 800-763-0136; {http://owr.ehnr.state. nc.us/grants/index.htm}.

$25,000 to Reduce Wood Waste

North Carolina is offering funding that will help reduce the flow of wood byproducts to disposal facilities. Examples of eligible projects include: equipment purchase to establish or expand wood waste processing, marketing, or end-use; establishing cooperative processing between several facilities using stationary or mobile equipment; using wood for reuse or as manufacturing feedstock; and developing or encouraging other end-use applications of wood byproducts.

$25,000 To $250,000 For Florida Technology

Enterprise Florida offers the Technology Investment Fund that makes venture capital available to Florida technology-oriented companies. The goal is to bring these technologies to market. This is a co-investment in the company. The amount of funding available ranges from $25,000 to $250,000 depending upon a number of factors.

For more information, contact Enterprise Florida, 390 N. Orange Ave., Suite 1300, Orlando, FL 32801; 407-316-4600; {www. floridabusiness.com/capital/ tifund.html}.

For more information, contact North Carolina Division of Pollution Prevention and Environmental Assistance, P.O. Box 29560, Raleigh, NC 27626; 919-715-6516; 800-763-0136; {http://owr.ehnr.state.nc.us/grants/index.htm}.

$500,000 From Tennessee Venture Alliance Capital Fund

The Venture Alliance Capital fund is designed to make equity investments in ideas for new products and services which create new companies in the Tennessee Valley. Venture Alliance LLC provides a world class management team which explores ideas for new companies and provides marketing and financial assistance in partnership with entrepreneurs.

For more information, contact TVA Economic Development, 400 W. Summit Hill Dr., Knoxville, TN 37902; 423-632-3405; {www.tva.gov/econdev/econhome.htm}.

$35 million From Cypress Equity Fund

The Cypress Equity Fund of Florida provides venture capital to Florida businesses and currently has over $35 million available. It was begun "to improve the availability of venture capital for Florida growth companies."

To learn how to apply for funds, contact Enterprise Florida, 390 N. Orange Ave., Suite 1300, Orlando, FL 32801; 407-316-4600; {www.floridabusiness.com/capital/cypress.html}.

$5,000 To Train Employees In Tennessee

The Tennessee Department of Labor operates a grant program for companies desiring to upgrade their employee safety programs. The goal of this program is to fund the education and training of employees in safe employment practices and to promote the development of employer-sponsored health and safety programs in the employer's own business.

Information USA, Inc.

For more information, contact Tennessee Department of Labor, Occupational Safety and Health Grant Program, Gateway Plaza 2nd Floor, 710 James Robertson Parkway, Nashville, TN 37243; 800-332-2667; 615-741-2582; {www.state.tn.us/ecd/smbus/ichpt6.htm}.

$3 Million To Growing Tennessee Businesses

Commerce Capital LP is a Small Business Investment Company that has equity funds for rapidly growing small business operating capital needs in the Tennessee Valley. These investments are made in both debt and equity financing for companies in health care, manufacturing, environmental services, communications and information systems.

For more information, contact TVA Economic Development, 400 W. Summit Hill Dr., Knoxville, TN 37902; 423-632-3405; {www.tva.gov/econdev/econhome.htm}.

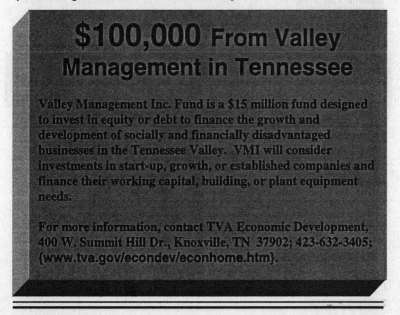

$100,000 From Valley Management in Tennessee

Valley Management Inc. Fund is a $15 million fund designed to invest in equity or debt to finance the growth and development of socially and financially disadvantaged businesses in the Tennessee Valley. VMI will consider investments in start-up, growth, or established companies and finance their working capital, building, or plant equipment needs.

For more information, contact TVA Economic Development, 400 W. Summit Hill Dr., Knoxville, TN 37902; 423-632-3405; {www.tva.gov/econdev/econhome.htm}.

Money To Train
Kentucky Employees

 The Bluegrass State Skills Corporation (BSSC) works with business and industry and Kentucky's educational institutions to establish a program of skills training. The BSSC provides funding support for the training of workers of Kentucky's new and expanding industries, and for skills upgrade and occupational upgrade training of workers of existing industries. There is a matching funds requirement.

For more grant information, contact Bluegrass State Skills Corporation, Capital Plaza Tower, 21st Floor, 500 Mero St., Frankfort, KY 40601; 502-564-2021; {www.state.ky.us/edc/bss.htm}.

$250,000 To Train Ohio Employees

The Ohio Industrial Training Program is designed to provide financial assistance and resources for customized training involving employees of new and expanding Ohio manufacturing businesses. Financial assistance is on a reimbursement basis for a portion of training expenses incurred, including instructor costs, materials, special needs, and more.

For more information, contact Ohio Industrial Training Program, Ohio Department of Development, 77 South High St., 28th Floor, Columbus, OH 43215; 614-466-4155; {www.odod.ohio.gov}.

Grants and Help For Ohio Business

The *Business Development Account 412* helps Ohio businesses prosper through technical assistance programs and customized assistance resources. It provides assistance with up-to-date information on sites, buildings, labor, markets, taxes, and financing. It helps companies seek state, local, or private financing and coordinates tax incentive programs and assists companies' infrastructure needs.

For more information, contact Office of Business Development, Ohio Department of Development, 77 South High St., 28th Floor, Columbus, OH 43215; 614-466-4155; {www.odod.ohio.gov}.

Money To Recycle Tires

The Ohio Department of Development has loans and grants available to scrap tire recyclers who locate or expand in Ohio and who demonstrate that they will create new/reuse scrap tire products. $2 million is available for qualifying loans and grants.

For more information, contact Economic Development Division, Ohio Department of Development, 77 S. High St., P.O. Box 1001, Columbus, OH 43215; 614-644-8201; {www.odod.ohio.gov/factbook/edd20.htm}.

Venture Capital For West Virginia

West Virginia Capital Company administers a program that provides for debt and equity venture capital investment to small businesses in West Virginia.

For more information, contact West Virginia Economic Development Authority, 1018 Kanawha Blvd., Suite 501, Charleston, WV 25301; 304-558-3650; {www.wvdo.org/business/financing.htm}.

$10,000 For Alternative Fuel In Indiana

The *Alternative Energy Systems Program* provides grants to businesses to fund eligible alternative-fuel technologies and infrastructure development. Eligible technologies include alternative fuels, landfill methane outreach, agricultural applications, geothermal heat pumps, wood waste boilers, and solar repair and service. The maximum amount available per project is $10,000 and matching funds are required.

Contact Indiana Department of Commerce, Energy Policy Division, Alternative Energy Program, One North Capital, Suite 700, Indianapolis, IN 46204; 317-232-8940; {www.state.in.us/doc/indiresidents/startbiz/grant.htm}.

GRANTS TO IMPROVE ENERGY EFFICIENCY

The National Industrial Competitiveness Through Energy, Environment and Economics Grant is a federal grant with possible state matching money to improve energy efficiency, promote a cleaner production process and improve the competitiveness of industry. Those eligible include manufacturers in industrial glass, metals, chemicals, forest

products, petroleum, steel, and aluminum. The maximum grant is
$400,000 and a 55% match is required.

Contact Indiana Department of Commerce, Energy Policy Division,
Alternative Energy Program, One North Capital, Suite 700,
Indianapolis, IN 46204; 317-232-8940; {www.state.in.us/doc/
indiresidents/startbiz/grant.htm}.

$5,000 TO GO
OVERSEAS

The Trade Show Assistance Program provides financial assistance to
Indiana manufacturers by reimbursing a portion of the costs incurred
while exhibiting their products at overseas trade shows. Reimbursement includes 100% of exhibit space rental or $5,000 whichever is less.

Eligible companies may use this program one time per fiscal year and
may not use the grant for the same show in two consecutive years.
Applicants must be ready to export, have available manufacturing
capacity for export and have basic export knowledge.

$40,000 To Use Used Tires

The Tire Recycling Market Development Program provides
grants to businesses involved in production of a product that
uses scrap tires as a feedstock. The Recycled Tire Product
Marketing Grants can go up to $20,000 and the Recycled Tire
Product Procurement Grants can go up to $40,000 with a 50%
match being required.

For more information, contact Indiana Department of
Commerce, Energy Policy Division, Recycling Programs, One
N. Capital, Suite 700, Indianapolis, IN 46204; 317-232-8940;
{www.state.in.us/doc/indiresidents/startbiz/grant.htm}.

For more information, contact Indiana Department of Commerce, International Trade Division, One North Capital, Suite 700, Indianapolis, IN 46204; 317-232-8845; {www.state.in.us/doc/indiresidents/startbiz/grant.htm}.

MONEY FOR MINORITY-OWNED BUSINESSES

LYNX Capital Corporation is a privately owned company established to link capital to minority business opportunities. The fund provides subordinated debt to minority-owned businesses in Marion and surrounding counties. Capital can be provided in the form of equity or debt. The minimum project amount is $75,000.

For more information, contact Cambridge Capital Management Corporation, 8440 Woodfield Crossing, Suite 315, Indianapolis, IN 46240, 317-469-3925; {www.state.in.us/doc/indiresidents/startbiz/minority.htm}.

Up To $200,000 For Job Training

Training 2000 is a grant program that provides financial assistance to Indiana manufacturing companies and distribution centers to train or retrain employees. Eligible uses include instructional costs, instructor wages, tuition, and training materials. Businesses need to submit a two-year training plan with the application.

For more information, contact Indiana Department of Commerce, Business Development Division, One North Capital, Suite 700, Indianapolis, IN 46204; 317-232-8888; {www.state.in.us/doc/indiresidents/startbiz/job.htm}.

$1.6 For Illinois Job Training

The *Industrial Training Program (ITP)* assists companies in meeting their employee training needs. There are two ways employers can access state training funds available through ITP.

One way is for individual employers to apply for grant funds to assist with training the employees. The second way is through the *Multi-Company Training Project* that allows companies with common employee training needs to join together.

Help To Improve Productivity

The mission of the Manufacturing Extension Partnership of Illinois is to improve the productivity and competitiveness of small manufacturing firms located in Illinois. They help companies develop affordable realistic plans for growth and competitiveness. An onsite team provides an objective analysis, identifying your company's strengths, weaknesses, opportunities and threats.

For more information, contact Illinois Manufacturing Extension Center, 403 Jobst Hall, Bradley University, Peoria, IL 61625; 800-MEPI-MFG.

For more information, contact Office of Industrial Training, Department of Commerce and Community Affairs, 620 Adams St., Springfield, IL 62701; 217-785-6284; {www.commerce.state.il.us}.

Used Tire Grants

The Used Tire Recovery Unit's mission is to develop self-sustaining markets for used and waste tires. The program offers funding in the form of grants and loans for projects which reuse, recycle, or recover energy from used tires.

For more information, contact Used Tire Recovery Unit, Bureau of
Energy and Recycling, Illinois Department of Commerce and
Community Affairs, 620 Adams St., Springfield, IL 62701; 217-785-
3999; {www.commerce.state.il.us}.

USE RECYCLED MATERIALS

The *Market Development Program* provides funding assistance
in the form of loans and grants for the purchase or conversion of
equipment to manufacture products from recycled products, and
procurement and end-use testing of recycled content products.

For more information, contact Resource Development Section, Bureau
of Energy and Recycling, Illinois Department of Commerce and
Community Affairs, 620 Adams St., Springfield, IL 62701; 217-785-
2006; {www.commerce.state.il.us}.

Grants to Recycle
Solid Waste

The mission of the Recycling Industry
Modernization (RIM) Program is to
divert materials from the solid waste
stream and improve the
competitiveness of Illinois
manufacturing firms, through
modernization. RIM projects increase
the use of recycled materials and/or
promote solid waste source reduction.
Grants are available to fund
modernization assessments and
implementation projects.

For more information, contact Bureau of Energy and Recycling, Illinois Department of Commerce and Community Affairs, 620 Adams St., Springfield, IL 62701; 217-785-2638; {www.commerce.state.il.us}.

$1,000
JOB TRAINING GRANTS

The Economic Development Job Training program is a major feature of Michigan's economic development incentive package. While the employer matches 25% of the state assistance, under this program employers customize training programs to meet their needs; training funds are channeled through Michigan's expansive educational network; and grants average $500- $1,000 per employee.

For more information, contact Michigan Jobs Commission, 201 N. Washington Square, Lansing, MI 48913; 517-373-9808; {www.state.mi.us/mjc}.

Grants For Environmental Cleanup In Wisconsin

Brownfields are potential business sites, but currently pose a danger due to environmental problems. The Brownfields Grant Program provides grants to persons or businesses for environmental remediation activities where the owner is unknown, cannot be located, or cannot meet the cleanup costs.

For more information, contact the Department of Commerce, 201 W. Washington Ave., Madison, WI 53707; 608-266-3494; 800-HELP-BUS; {www.commerce.state.wi.us}.

$10,000 FOR EVERY NEW JOB CREATED

The goal of the *Commerce/ DVR Job Creation Program* is to increase employment opportunities for Division of Vocational Rehabilitation (DVR) clients by providing equipment grants, technical assistance grants, customized technical assistance and other assistance to companies that will hire persons with disabilities.

Companies interested in applying should contact Wisconsin Department of Commerce, Bureau of Minority Business Development, Job Creation Program, 101 W. Pleasant St., Suite 100A, Milwaukee, WI 53212; 414-220-5360; {www.commerce.state.wi.us}.

Get 50% of Training Costs

The *Customized Labor Training Fund* provides training grants to businesses that are implementing new technology or production processes.

The goal is to help Wisconsin manufacturers maintain a workforce that is on the cutting edge of technological innovation. The program can provide up to 50% of the cost of customized training that is not available from the Wisconsin Technical College System.

For more information, contact the Department of Commerce, 201 W. Washington Ave., Madison, WI 53707; 608-266-1018; 800-HELP-BUS; {www.commerce.state.wi.us}.

$30,000
To Start A Rural Business

The Rural Economic Development Program Early Planning Grant Program's goal is to stimulate the start up and expansion of small businesses in communities throughout Wisconsin.

The program provides grants to rural entrepreneurs and small businesses so that they may obtain the professional services necessary to determine the feasibility of a proposed start-up or expansion. It makes individual awards up to $15,000 for feasibility studies and other professional assistance to rural businesses with fewer than 50 employees.

Grants For Entrepreneurs With Disabilities

The Business Development Initiative offers individual grants of up to $15,000 for planning and managerial assistance to entrepreneurs with severe disabilities, or to rehabilitation facilities of businesses that hire persons with severe disabilities.

For more information, contact the Department of Commerce, 201 W. Washington Ave., Madison, WI 53707; 608-266-8381; 800-HELP-BUS; {www.commerce.state.wi.us}.

For more information, contact the Department of Commerce, 201 W. Washington Ave., Madison, WI 53707; 608-266-1018; 800-HELP-BUS; {www.commerce.state.wi.us}.

Minority Enterprise Grants

The Minority Business Early Planning Grant Program offers individual grants for planning and managerial assistance to minority entrepreneurs and business owners. Grants are to be used to hire professional consultants for feasibility studies, business and management planning, marketing assistance and planning, and/or financial statements and loan packaging. Grants are up to $15,000 with a 25% match being required.

For more information, contact the Department of Commerce, 201 W. Washington Ave., Madison, WI 53707; 608-267-9550; 800-HELP-BUS; {www.commerce.state.wi.us}.

Grants for Recycling Businesses

The Recycling Market Development Board, attached to the Wisconsin Department of Commerce, identifies markets for recycled materials, and awards loans and grants to companies and organizations committed to manufacturing products from recycled materials.

For more information, contact the Department of Commerce, 201 W. Washington Ave., Madison, WI 53707; 608-2667-9548; 800-HELP-BUS; {www.commerce.state.wi.us}.

Recycle Wisconsin

The Recycling Early Planning Grant Program encourages the creation and expansion of businesses that will undertake the production of goods from recycled materials, or increase the use of recycled materials. Funds may be issued for up to 75% of eligible project costs to a maximum of $15,000.

For more information, contact the Department of Commerce, 201 W. Washington Ave., Madison, WI 53707; 608-267-9548; 800-HELP-BUS; {www.commerce.state.wi.us}.

Wood Utilization Grants

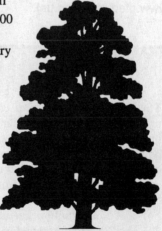

The Lake States Wood Utilization Grant Program awards up to $100,000 to universities, private and federal laboratories, and forest products industry businesses located in Wisconsin to develop value-added products from manufacturing by-products and other wood waste; to provide economical solutions to environmental protection; or to improve the use of available timber resources. Applicants must provide 25% of the project cost in cash or in-kind.

For more information, contact the Department of Commerce, 201 W. Washington Ave., Madison, WI 53707; 608-266-1018; 800-HELP-BUS; {www.commerce.state.wi.us}.

$4,000 For Technical Assistance

The *Microenterprise Assistance Grants* help start-up
entrepreneurs and expanding businesses receive
technical assistance and, in some cases, financial
support through selected nonprofit business
development organizations.

Technical assistance may include assisting
business owners in evaluating their abilities
and/or needs of their business; making
knowledgeable choices about their
business operations; developing new
management or operations skills; and underwriting expenses related to
the implementation of their business plans.

For more information, contact Minnesota Department of Trade and
Economic Development, 500 Metro Square, 121 7th Place East, St.
Paul, MN 55101; 651-297-1170; 800-657-3858;
{www.dted.state.mn.us}.

$5,000 for Foreign Travel

The Wisconsin Trade Project Program offers individual
matching grants up to 45,000 to help small export-ready firms
participate in international trade shows. The business covers
its own travel and lodging expenses. Eligible activities include
translation and preparation of promotional materials, booth or
exhibit space rentals, and entry fees.

For more information, contact the Department of Commerce,
201 W. Washington Ave., Madison, WI 53707; 608-266-0393;
800-HELP-BUS; {www.commerce.state.wi.us}.

Recycle Missouri

The Missouri Market Development Program assists recycling throughout Missouri by focusing economic development efforts on businesses and projects that use materials recovered from solid waste in manufacturing operations and other end-uses.

They can help identify what financial and business development assistance is available to you through a variety of resources and connect you with collection systems, processors, and manufacturers using recovered materials. Maximum amount of financial assistance is $75,000.

For more information, contact Missouri Market Development Program, Environmental Improvement and Energy Resources Authority, P.O. Box 744, Jefferson City, MO 65102; 573-526-0744; {www.ecodev. state.mo.us/cd/finance/programs/ momarket.htm}.

Grants To Train Arkansas Employees

The primary purpose of the **Existing Workforce Training Program (EWTP)** is to provide financial assistance to Arkansas manufacturing industries for upgrading the skills of their existing workforce.

EWTP will pay a portion of the costs of the approved training program. Financial assistance will range from 20 percent to 70 percent depending upon a series of scoring criteria.

To learn more, contact the Arkansas Economic Development Commission, 1 State Capitol Mall, Little Rock, AR 72201; 501-682-7323; {www.aedc.state. ar.us}.

Smart Texas Jobs

Smart Jobs is a business incentive program designed to help Texas companies become more competitive. Smart Jobs provides grants to employers for customized training. The employer decides what training is needed for the work force and who will provide the training. There is an employer match component.

For more information, contact Texas Department of Economic Development, Smart Jobs Fund, P.O. Box 12728; Austin, TX 78711; 800-888-0511; {www.tded.state.tx.us/commerce/bizsrv/annual/spage1.htm}.

Quality Oklahoma Jobs

The innovative Oklahoma **Quality Jobs Program** allows qualifying businesses that are creating new quality jobs to receive a special incentive to locate or expand in Oklahoma.

The program provides quarterly cash payments of up to 5 percent of new taxable payroll directly to a qualifying company, for up to ten years. There are requirements such as payroll amount, health insurance coverage, workweek, and more.

For more information, contact Office of Business Recruitment, Oklahoma Department of

Commerce, P.O. Box 26980, Oklahoma City, OK 73126; 800-588-5959; 415-815-5213; {www.odoc.state.ok.us}.

Money For Small Businesses

The Oklahoma small employer *Quality Jobs Program* allows qualifying small businesses that are creating a minimum of ten new direct jobs within one year of the date of application to receive a special incentive to locate or expand in Oklahoma.

The program provides annual cash payments of 5% of taxable payroll for new employees to a qualifying company for up to five years. There are requirements that must be met including health insurance coverage, hours worked, and more.

Louisiana Venture Capital

The Louisiana Economic Development Corporation administers several programs for small Louisiana businesses, including four venture capital programs.

The Programs include Venture Capital Match Program, Minority Venture Capital Match Program, Venture Capital Co-Investment Program, and BIDCO Investment Program. All require different types of matching funds, and support a variety of business ventures.

For more information, contact Louisiana Department of Economic Development, P.O. Box 94185, Baton Rouge, LA 70804; 225-342-300; {www.lded.state.la.us/new/financing.htm}.

For more information, contact Office of Business Recruitment, Oklahoma Department of Commerce, P.O. Box 26980, Oklahoma City, OK 73126; 800-588-5959; 415-815-5213; {www.odoc.state.ok.us}.

IOWA JOB TRAINING

The Iowa *Industrial New Jobs Training Program* provides funds to train new employees of eligible Iowa businesses. Eligible businesses may be new to Iowa, expanding their Iowa work force, or relocating to the state.

Two Companies Get Training

Iowa's Business Consortia Training Project consists of two or more businesses located in the same community college district and who will participate in the same training project. A consortia project is eligible for up to $50,000 in program assistance with a 25% cash match being required for projects costing $5,000 or more. No match is required for projects costing less that $5,000.

For more information, contact Iowa Department of Economic Development, Workforce Development, 200 East Grand Ave., Des Moines, IA 50309; 515-242-4878; {www.state. ia.us/government/ided/ workforce/IJTP.htm}.

Employees qualifying for training services must be in a newly created position and pay Iowa withholding tax. Job training services are defined as any training needed to enhance the performance of a business' new employees. Services include vocational and skill assessment testing, adult basic education, job-related training, cost of company, college, or contracted trainer or training services, and more.

The program is administered and operated by Iowa's 15 community colleges. Each college works with eligible businesses to assess training needs, determine funds availability, and provide training.

For more information, contact Iowa Department of Economic Development, Workforce Development, 200 East Grand Ave., Des Moines, IA 50309; 515-242-4878; {www.state.ia.us/government/ided/workforce/IJTP.htm}.

Forgivable Loans For Training

The *Community Economic Betterment Account* program provides financial assistance to businesses creating new job opportunities or retaining existing jobs. Assistance may be provided to encourage new business start-ups, expansion or retention of existing businesses, or recruitment of out-of-state businesses into Iowa. Assistance may be in the form of loans and/or forgivable loans.

For more information, contact Iowa Department of Economic Development, Workforce Development, 200 East Grand Ave., Des Moines, IA 50309; 515-242-4878; {www.smart.state.ia.us/financial.htm}.

NEW SKILLS DEVELOPMENT

The Iowa *Innovative Skills Development Program* promotes the development of new, creative and innovative approaches that address Iowa's current and future work force needs.

Program services are prioritized in support of projects that concentrate on skill development for new or emerging technologies as well as enhancement of technological skills for our current work force. Allowable program costs include purchase or development of training curricula and materials, cost of assessment, recruitment, outreach, tuition, vocational and skill assessment, adult basic education, and more.

For more information, contact Iowa Department of Economic
Development, Workforce Development, 200 East Grand Ave., Des
Moines, IA 50309; 515-242-4878; {www.state.ia.us/government/
ided/workforce/IJTP.htm}.

Business Network

The Iowa Community College Business Network Training Project
consists of five or more businesses located in two or more community
college districts with at least two community colleges sponsoring the
training project.

A community college business network training project is eligible for
up to $50,000 in program assistance per participating community
college. A 25% cash match from the participating businesses is
required for consortia projects costing $45,000 or more. Projects
costing less than $45,000 do not require a cash match.

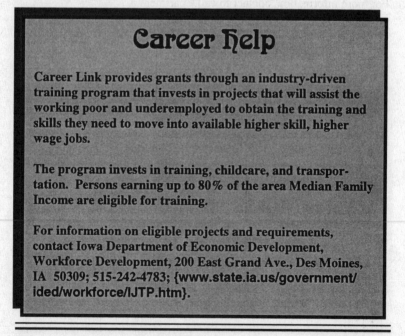

Career Help

Career Link provides grants through an industry-driven
training program that invests in projects that will assist the
working poor and underemployed to obtain the training and
skills they need to move into available higher skill, higher
wage jobs.

The program invests in training, childcare, and transportation. Persons earning up to 80% of the area Median Family
Income are eligible for training.

For information on eligible projects and requirements,
contact Iowa Department of Economic Development,
Workforce Development, 200 East Grand Ave., Des Moines,
IA 50309; 515-242-4783; {www.state.ia.us/government/
ided/workforce/IJTP.htm}.

For more information, contact Iowa Department of Economic Development, Workforce Development, 200 East Grand Ave., Des Moines, IA 50309; 515-242-4878; {www.state.ia.us/government/ided/workforce/IJTP.htm}.

Entrepreneurs With Disabilities

The *Entrepreneurs With Disabilities Program* provides technical and/or financial assistance to qualified individuals with disabilities seeking self-sufficiency by establishing, maintaining, expanding, or acquiring a small business.

Program services include technical assistance such as business plan development, accounting, legal services, and financial assistance for the purpose of purchasing business equipment, supplies, inventory, rent and more. Financial assistance shall not exceed $15,000.

For more information, contact Iowa Department of Economic Development, Workforce Development, 200 East Grand Ave., Des Moines, IA 50309; 515-242-4878; {www.smart.state.ia.us/financial.htm}.

New Agricultural Products

Value-Added Products and Processes Financial Assistance Program funds projects utilizing Iowa's wealth of agricultural commodities. Awards are based on project feasibility, utilization of Iowa commodities, and new or innovative products and processes.

For more information, contact Iowa Department of Economic Development, Workforce Development, 200 East Grand Ave., Des Moines, IA 50309; 515-242-4878; {www.smart.state.ia.us/financial.htm}.

Iowa Venture Capital

The Iowa Capital Corporation is a for-profit venture capital corporation. The corporation provides financing for a broad range of business capital needs in the form of equity participation, loans with stock purchase warrants, or royalties. It is tailored to the particular business situation. The average investment is $250,000.

For more information, contact Iowa Department of Economic Development, Workforce Development, 200 East Grand Ave., Des Moines, IA 50309; 515-242-4878; {www.smart.state.ia.us/ financial.htm}.

KANSAS JOB TRAINING GRANTS

The *High Performance Incentive Program* promotes the establishment and expansion of high performance industry in the state. The program provides incentives to qualified firms to provide training to employees to upgrade existing employee job skills and offers a sales tax exemption and substantial tax credits in connection with capital investment.

For more information, contact High Performance Incentive Program, Business Development Division, Kansas Department of Commerce and Housing, 700 SW Harrison, 13th Floor, Topeka, KS 66603; 785-296-5298; {www.kansascommerce.com}.

$125,000 In Kansas Venture Capital

The Kansas Applied Research Matching Fund awards grants to academic/business partnerships to offset the cost of financing research that leads to new or enhanced products. Matching funds are required to develop products that can be commercialized.

For more information, contact Kansas Technology Enterprise Corporation, 214 SW 6th Ave., Suite 100, Topeka, KS 66603; 785-296-5862; {www.ktec.com/armf/armf.htm}.

Venture Capital For Kansas Businesses

The Innovation and Commercialization Corporations (ICCs) seek entrepreneurs and scientists who are in need of help, to aid in commercializing high-tech products in the development stage.

The ICCs aid clients in preparing quality business plans to attract venture capital as well as assistance in preparing competitive ARMF proposals. ICCs help client corporations find affordable business incubator space nearby, so that they can take clients "on-board" and provide constant support.

The ICCs also each operate a pre-seed capital fund, which empowers start-up businesses to commercialize new technology. The type of aid available differs slightly between the three corporations.

For more information, contact one of the following:

Kansas Innovation Corporation, 1617 St. Andrews Dr., Lawrence, KS 66047; 785-832-2110; {www.kic.com}.

Mid-America Commercialization Corp., 1500 Hayes Dr., Manhattan, KS 66502, 785-532-3900; {www.ktec.com/macc/macc-home.html}.

Wichita Technology Corporation, 1845 N. Fairmont, NIAR Bldg., Wichita, KS 67260; 316-978-3690; {www.wichitatechnology.com}.

A Tourist Attraction

The Attraction Development Grant Program provides financial assistant to both public and private entities to develop new tourist attractions or to enhance existing ones. Funding is available for up to 40% of a project.

Contact Kansas Department of Commerce and Housing, Travel and Tourism Division, 700 SW Harrison, Suite 1300, Topeka, KS 66603; 785-296-2009; {www.kansascommerce.com}.

Grants For Businesses In Rural Kansas

The Rural Economic Development Loan and Grant Program provides zero-interest loans and grants to projects with the purpose of promoting rural economic development and job creation. For more information, contact Kansas Electric Power Cooperative, Inc., P.O. Box 4877, Topeka, KS 66604; 785-273-7010; {www.kepco.org}.

KANSAS VENTURE CAPITAL

Instituted to increase the availability of risk capital in Kansas, the venture capital and seed capital programs make use of income tax credits to encourage investment in venture and seed capital pools as a source of early stage financing for small businesses. Businesses demonstrating strong growth potential but lacking the financial strength to obtain conventional financing are the most likely candidates for risk capital funding.

The Business Development Division has in operation and continues to develop a network of venture capital resources to assist qualified small

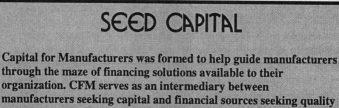

SEED CAPITAL

Capital for Manufacturers was formed to help guide manufacturers through the maze of financing solutions available to their organization. CFM serves as an intermediary between manufacturers seeking capital and financial sources seeking quality investment opportunities. Contact CFM, 10561 Barkley, Suite 600, Overland Park, KS 66212; 913-967-2000; {www.ktec.com}.

businesses in locating potential sources of venture capital financing. Contact Business Development Division, Kansas Department of Commerce and Housing, 700 SW Harrison, Suite 1300, Topeka, KS 66603-3712; 785-296-5298; {www.kansascommerce.com}.

$1,000
For Your Kansas Invention

The Invention Development Assistance program is designed to help inventors in the beginning stages with marketing their inventions to increase market-driven products and processes that can be commercialized in Kansas. Assistance is limited to matching grants of up to $1,000 per invention. For more information, contact Kansas Technology Enterprise Corporation, 112 W. 6th, Suite 400, Topeka, KS 66603; 785-296-5272; {www.ktec.com}.

$5,000 To Prepare Grant Proposals

The Small Business Innovation Research (SBIR) Matching Grants assist businesses in preparing federal SBIR/STTR grant proposals and to increase the number and quality being submitted by Kansas small businesses that will meet the research and development needs of the federal government. Reimbursement assistance is up to $5,000 in preparing a quality proposal, review of the draft proposal prior to submission, and assistance in locating resources.

For more information, contact Kansas Technology Enterprise Corporation, 112 W. 6th, Suite 400, Topeka, KS 66603; 785-296-3686; {www.ktec.com}.

$3,500 For Trade Shows

The Kansas Trade Show Assistance Program provides Kansas companies with financial assistance to target new markets. Companies who receive approval can be reimbursed for up to 50% of the show related expenses to attend trade shows.

To apply, contact Trade Development Division, Kansas Department of Commerce and Housing, 700 SW Harrison St., Suite 1300, Topeka, KS 66603; 785-296-4027; {www.kansascommerce.com}.

New Mexico Job Training

The New Mexico Industrial Development Training Program provides funds for classroom or on-the-job training to prepare New Mexico residents for employment. Training may be tailored to the needs of the business and is usually provided in one of three ways: classroom in nature and provided by a public education institution facility; training conducted at the business facility; and on-the-job and/or classroom training. Trainees must be guaranteed full-time employment upon

Grants For Employee Training

The Workforce Development Program funds industry/ education partnerships to deliver customized training programs and short-term, job-specific training. It includes new employee training, retraining current employees to adapt to change in the industry, and the upgrading of skills of current employees.

For more information, contact Governor's Office of Economic Development, 711 E. Wells Ave., Pierre, SD 57501; 605-773-5032; 800-872-6190; {www.state.sd.us/state/executive/dol/jtpa/wdp.htm}.

successful completion of training. Trainees wages are reimbursed to the company at 50% during hours of training.

For more information, contact New Mexico Economic Development Department, Development Division, 1100 St. Francis Dr., Santa Fe, NM 87503; 505-827-0323; {www.edd.state.nm.us}.

WASHINGTON JOB SKILLS

The *Job Skills Program* brings together employers or industries who have specific training needs with educational institutions that can provide customized employee training. Through matching grants, the Job Skills Program funds industry-education partnerships in which customized training materials are developed and short-term, job-specific training is delivered.

For more information, contact Workforce Training and Education Coordinating Board, Building 17 Airdustrial Park, Olympia, WA 98504; 360-753-5662; {www.wa.gov/tb/index.html}.

Oregon Employee Training

The Oregon Economic Development Department can help customize training programs for new and expanding companies. If two or more businesses within one of Oregon's "Key Industries" work together to develop a customized workforce training program through Oregon's community colleges, they may be eligible for a grant supporting part of the cost of the training. Employers must provide dollar-for-dollar matching funds or in-kind services. Training may include literacy courses, customized skills training and other programs leading to the hiring and retention of those completing training.

For workforce development assistance, contact Oregon Economic Development Department, 775 Summer St., NE, Salem, OR 97310; 502-986-0209; {www.econ.state.or.us}.

Oregon Venture Capital

Equity-based capital is available for Oregon businesses through the **Oregon Resource and Technology Development Fund.** Areas of focus include: biological and biomedical services, high technology, and natural resource industries. Funds are available to eligible companies for seed capital, applied research, and technical information.

For more information, contact Oregon Resource and Technology Development Fund, 4370 NE Halsey, Suite 233, Portland, OR 97213; 503-282-4462; {www.econ.state.or.us/ECONPG.HTM}.

More Colorado Money

The Colorado Institute for Research in Biotechnology sponsors seed-research grants designed to stimulate interactions between academic and industrial scientists. For more information on the program, contact University of Colorado, Department of Chemical Engineering, Campus Box 424, Boulder, CO 80309; 303-492-7314; {www.medmarket.com}.

TRAIN COLORADO EMPLOYEES

The *Colorado FIRST Program* is to encourage quality economic development by providing training assistance as an incentive for the location of new or expanding firms in Colorado. Companies can utilize innovative approaches to training. Training programs are not designed to assist companies with normal, on-going training requirements. Companies should provide a health plan for their employees.

To learn more, contact Office of Business Development, 162 Broadway, Suite 1710, Denver, CO 80202; 303-892-3840; {www.state.co.us/gov_dir/obd/cofirst.htm}.

Child Care Money

Alaska offers the Child Care Grant program that provides a small business subsidy for child care centers and licensed homes. Grantees must use the money for the long-term benefit of the child care facility and the children in care. Most child care facilities use these funds for staff salaries and benefits, goods relating to health, safety and nutrition, and age appropriate equipment, supplies and activities for the children.

For more information, contact Child Care Programs Coordinator, Division of Community and Rural Development, Department of Community and Regional Affairs, 333 West Fourth Ave., Suite 220, Anchorage, AK 99501; 907-269-4529; {www.comregaf.state.ak.us/dcrd_ccg.htm}.

Agriculture Marketing Grants

North Dakota agricultural products or by-products can get a helping hand from the *Agricultural Products Utilization Commission*. Funds are available for the development or implementation of a sound marketing plan for the promotion of these products. The products should be new to the area of should be an expansion of a use or uses of existing products.

For more information on requirements, contact North Dakota Agricultural Products Utilization Commission, 1833 East Bismarck Expressway, Bismarck, ND 58505; 701-328-5350; {www.growingnd.com/broshure.html#marketing}.

$25,000 To Develop Business Plans And Patents

The **Delaware Innovation Fund** provides financial and technical

assistance to Delaware-based business that have the potential to launch innovative products and processes into national markets, to create new jobs, and to make a contribution to the economic diversity of Delaware.

Demonstration Funding provides $25,000 to aid in establishing patents, business plans, and proof of concept issues. *Commercialization Funding* goes up to $250,000 to be used to begin the commercialization process of early-stage businesses.

For more information, contact Delaware Innovation Fund, 100 W. 10th St., Suite 413, Wilmington, DE 19801; 302-777-1616; {www.delawareinnovationfund.com}.

GRANTS TO NATIVE AMERICAN BUSINESSES

North Dakota's Native American Program provides Native American individuals, businesses, and tribal governments access to technical support and financial assistance. This program provides equity gap grants, as well as provides access to the Native American set-aside of the North Dakota Development Fund.

For more information, contact Economic Development and Finance Department, 1833 E. Bismarck Expressway, Bismarck, ND 58504; 701-328-5300; {www.growingnd.com/nabdp.html}.

Information USA, Inc.

Utah's Short Term Intensive Training Grants Cover New Employees

Utah's Short Term Intensive Training (STIT) Grant programs are customized and designed to meet full-time job openings. Programs are usually less than one year in length and are designed to meet the specific training needs of a company. Although employees must pay tuition to participate, STIT can provide qualified employees from which a company can hire. STIT gives the option of training at 50-70% discount of normal training costs.

For more information, contact Department of Community and Economic Development, 324 South State St., Suite 500, Salt Lake City, UT 84111; 801-538-8700; {www.dced.state.ut.us/NATIONAL/incentiv.htm}.

$2,000 For Employee Training In Idaho

The Workforce Development Training Fund provides funding to companies to help them train new employees, or provide skills upgrade training of current workers. Projects must emphasize job skill training. The maximum amount allowed per trainee is $2,000.

For more information on funding criteria and guidelines contact Idaho Department of Labor, 31 Main St., Boise, ID 83735; 208-334-6298; {www.idoc.state.id.us/pages/businesspage.html}.

$100,000 To Move Your Business To Utah

The State of Utah has an Industrial Assistance Fund that can be used for relocation costs. This incentive loan can be repaid as Utah jobs created. For more information about eligibility and requirements contact Department of Community and Economic Development, 324 South State St., Suite 500, Salt Lake City, UT 84111; 801-538-8700; {www.dced.state.ut.us/NATIONAL/incentiv.htm}.

Grants To Colorado Businesses Hurt By Defense Cutbacks

The *Office of Statewide Defense Initiatives* has been able to provide small incentive grants to a number of small and medium sized Colorado businesses. These grants are to be used for the conversion of defense or energy technologies to commercial applications and must be used as leverage dollars to obtain other funding.

For more information on requirements and eligibility, contact Colorado Office of Statewide Defense Initiatives, 1625 Broadway, Suite 1710, Denver, CO 80202; 303-892-3868; {www.state.co.us/gov_dir/oed/sdi/overview.html#business}.

Colorado Venture Capital

The Colorado Capital Alliance helps locate seed money and early stage capital. It matches private investors with entrepreneurs. For more information, contact Colorado Capital Alliance, Inc., P.O. Box 19169, Boulder, CO 80308; 303-499-9646; {www.angelcapital.org}.

State Money and Help
For Your Business

Who Can Use State Money?

All states require that funds be used solely by state residents.
But that shouldn't
limit you to
exploring
possibilities only
in the state in
which you
currently reside. If
you reside in Maine,
but Massachusetts agrees to
give you $100,000 to start your
own business, it would be worth
your while to consider moving to Massachusetts. Shop
around for the best deal.

Types Of State Money And Help Available

Each state has different kinds and amounts of money and
assistance programs available, but these sources of financial
and counseling help are constantly being changed. What may
not be available this year may very well be available next.
Therefore, in the course of your exploration, you might want
to check in with the people who operate the business
"hotlines" to discover if anything new has been added to the
states' offerings.

Described below are the major kinds of programs that are offered by most of the states.

Information

Hotlines or One-Stop Shops are available in many states through a toll-

free number that hooks you up with someone who will either tell you what you need to know or refer you to someone who can. These hotlines are invaluable -- offering information on everything from business permit regulations to obscure financing programs. Most states also offer some kind of booklet that tells you to how to start-up a business in that state. Ask for it. It will probably be free.

Small Business Advocates operate in all fifty states and are part of a national organization (the National Association of State Small Business Advocates) devoted to helping small business people function efficiently with their state governments. They are a good source for help in cutting through bureaucratic red tape.

Funding Programs

Free Money can come in the form of grants, and works the same as free money from the federal government. You do not have to pay it back.

Loans from state governments work in the same way as those from the federal government -- they are given directly to entrepreneurs. Loans are usually at interest rates below the rates charged at commercial institutions and are also set aside for those companies, which have trouble getting a loan elsewhere. This makes them an ideal source for riskier kinds of ventures.

Loan Guarantees are similar to those offered by the federal government. For this program, the state government will go to the bank with you and co-sign your loan. This, too, is ideal for high-risk ventures that normally would not get a loan.

Interest Subsidies On Loans is a unique concept not used by the federal government. In this case, the state will subsidize the interest rate you are charged by a bank. For example, if the bank gives you a loan for $50,000 at 10 percent per year interest, your interest payments will be $5,000 per year. With an interest subsidy you might have to pay only $2,500 since the state will pay the other half. This is like getting the loan at 5 percent instead of 10 percent.

Industrial Revenue Bonds Or General Obligation Bonds are a type of financing that can be used to purchase only fixed assets, such as a factory or equipment. In the case of Industrial Revenue Bonds the state will raise money from the general public to buy your equipment. Because the state acts as the middleman, the people who lend you the money do not have to pay federal taxes on the interest they charge you. As a result, you get the money cheaper because they get a tax break. If the state issues General Obligation Bonds to buy your equipment, the arrangement will be similar to that for an Industrial Revenue Bond except that the state promises to repay the loan if you cannot.

Matching Grants supplement and abet federal grant programs. These kinds of grants could make an under-capitalized project go forward. Awards usually hinge on the usefulness of the project to its surrounding locality.

Loans To Agricultural Businesses are offered in states with large rural, farming populations. They are available solely to farmers and/or agribusiness entrepreneurs.

Loans To Exporters are available in some states as a kind of gap financing to cover the expenses involved in fulfilling a contract.

Energy Conservation Loans are made to small businesses to finance the installation of energy-saving equipment or devices.

Special Regional Loans are ear-marked for specific areas in a state that may have been hard hit economically or suffer from under-development. If you live in one of these regions, you may be eligible for special funds.

High Tech Loans help fledgling companies develop or introduce new products into the marketplace.

Loans To Inventors help the entrepreneur develop or market new products.

Local Government Loans are used for start-up and expansion of businesses within the designated locality.

Childcare Facilities Loans help businesses establish on-site daycare facilities.

Loans To Women And/Or Minorities are available in almost every state from funds specifically reserved for economically disadvantaged groups.

Many federally funded programs are administered by state governments. Among them are the following programs:

The SBA 7(A) Guaranteed and *Direct Loan* program can guarantee up to 90 percent of a loan made through a private lender (up to $750,000), or make direct loans of up to $150,000.

The SBA 504 establishes Certified Development Companies whose debentures are guaranteed by the SBA. Equity participation of the borrower must be at least 10 percent, private financing 60 percent and CDC participation at a maximum of 40 percent, up to $750,000.

Small Business Innovative Research Grants (SBIR) award between $20,000 to $50,000 to entrepreneurs to support six months of research on a technical innovation. They are then eligible for up to $500,000 to develop the innovation.

Small Business Investment Companies (SBIC) license, regulate and provide financial assistance in the form of equity financing, long-term loans, and management services.

Community Development Block Grants are available to cities and counties for the commercial rehabilitation of existing buildings or structures used for business, commercial, or industrial purposes. Grants of up to $500,000 can be made. Every $15,000 of grant funds invested must create at least one full-time job, and at least 51 percent of the jobs created must be for low and moderate income families.

Farmers Home Administration (FmHA) Emergency Disaster Loans are available in counties where natural disaster has substantially affected farming, ranching or aquaculture production.

FmHA Farm Loan Guarantees are made to family farmers and ranchers to enable them to obtain funds from private lenders. Funds must be used for farm ownership, improvements, and operating purposes.

FmHA Farm Operating Loans to meet operating expenses, finance recreational and nonagricultural enterprises, to add to family income, and to pay for mandated safety and pollution control changes are available at variable interest rates. Limits are $200,000 for an insured farm operating loan and $400,000 for a guaranteed loan.

FmHA Farm Ownership Loans can be used for a wide range of farm improvement projects. Limits are $200,000 for an insured loan and $300,000 for a guaranteed loan.

FmHA Soil And Water Loans must be used by individual farmers and ranchers to develop, conserve, and properly use their land and water resources and to help abate pollution. Interest rates are variable; each loan must be secured by real estate.

FmHA Youth Project Loans enable young people to borrow for income-producing projects sponsored by a school or 4H club.

Assistance Programs

Management Training is offered by many states in subjects ranging from bookkeeping to energy conservation.

Business Consulting is offered on almost any subject. Small Business Development Centers are the best source for this kind of assistance.

Market Studies to help you sell your goods or services within or outside the state are offered by many states. They all also have State Data Centers which not only collect demographic and other information about markets within the state, but also have access to federal data which can pinpoint national markets. Many states also provide the services of graduate business students at local universities to do the legwork and analysis for you.

Business Site Selection is done by specialists in every state who will identify the best place to locate a business.

Licensing, Regulation, And Permits information is available from most states through "one-stop shop" centers by calling a toll-free number. There you'll get help in finding your way through the confusion of registering a new business.

Employee Training Programs offer on-site training and continuing education opportunities.

Research And Development assistance for entrepreneurs is a form of assistance that is rapidly increasing as more and more states try to attract high technology-related companies. Many states are even setting up clearing houses so that small businesses can have one place to turn to find expertise throughout a statewide university system.

Procurement Programs have been established in some states to help you sell products to state, federal, and local governments.

Export Assistance is offered to identify overseas markets. Some states even have overseas offices to drum up business prospects for you.

Assistance In Finding Funding is offered in every state, particularly through regional Small Business Development Centers. They will not only identify funding sources in the state and federal governments but will also lead you through the complicated application process.

Special Help For Minorities And Women is available in almost every state to help boost the participation of women and minorities in small business ventures. They offer special funding  programs and, often, one-on-one counseling to assure a start-up success.

Venture Capital Networking is achieved through computer databases that hook up entrepreneurs and venture capitalists. This service is usually free of charge. In fact, the demand for small business investment opportunities is so great that some states require the investor to pay to be listed.

Inventors Associations have been established to encourage and assist inventors in developing and patenting their products.

Annual Governors' Conferences give small business people the chance to air their problems with representatives from state agencies and the legislature.

Small Business Development Centers (SBDCs), funded jointly by the federal and state governments, are usually associated with the state university system. SBDCs are a godsend to small business people. They will not only help you figure out if your business project is feasible, but also help you draw up a sensible business plan, apply for funding, and check in with you frequency once your business is up and running to make sure it stays that way.

Tourism programs are prominent in states whose revenues are heavily dependent on the tourist trade. They are specifically aimed at businesses in the tourist industries.

Small Business Institutes at local colleges use senior level business students as consultants to help develop business plans or plan expansions.

Technology Assistance Centers help high tech companies and entrepreneurs establish new businesses and plan business expansions.

On-Site Energy Audits are offered free of charge by many states to help control energy costs and improve energy efficiency for small businesses. Some states also conduct workshops to encourage energy conservation measures.

Minority Business Development Centers offer a wide range of services from initial counseling on how to start a business to more complex issues of planning and growth.

Business Information Centers (BICs) provide the latest in high-tech hardware, software, and telecommunications to help small businesses get started. BIC is a place where business owners and aspiring business owners can go to use hardware/software, hard copy books, and publications to plan their business, expand an existing business, or venture into new business areas. Also, on-site counseling is available.

Alabama

Alabama Development Office
401 Adams Avenue
Montgomery, AL 36104-4340
800-248-0033
334-242-0400
Fax: 334-242-0415
www.ado.state.al.us

Alabama Department of Revenue
P.O. Box 327001
Montgomery, AL 36132-7001
334-242-1170
alaweb.asc.edu

Business Assistance

Alabama Development Office: A one-stop source for
business support and incentives that will tailor
programs to meet individual companies'
needs.

Economic Development Association: Members
exchange information and ideas and
participate in courses and other
professional development seminars.
Technology Assistance Program: Assists with technology-oriented problems,
maintains a database containing information about technical assistance
available from federal sources and from other sources throughout the State
of Alabama. Contact: Alabama Technology Assistance Program,
University of Alabama at Birmingham, 1717 11th Ave. South, Suite 419,
Birmingham, AL 35294; 205-934-7260.
Department of Agriculture and Industry: Supplies both information and
technical support to farmers, businesses and consumers. Contact:
Department of Agriculture and Industry, P.O. Box 3336, Montgomery, AL
36109; 334-240-7171.
Alabama Industrial Development Training: Offers recruiting, assessing and
training potential employees; developing and producing training materials,
and locating facilities; and, delivering customized services. Contact:
Alabama Industrial Develoment and Training, One Technology Court,
Montgomery, AL 36116; 334-242-4158.
Alabama Answers: Comprehensive handbook on doing business in Alabama.

Business Financing

Industrial Revenue Bonds: Financing available for land, buildings and
 equipment.
Economic Development Loan Program: Loans for the purchase of land,
 buildings, machinery and equipment for new and expanding businesses.
Revolving Loan Funds: Gap financing for land, buildings, equipment,
 renovation and working capital for companies creating jobs.
Business Loan Guarantee Program: Provides funding for the acquisitions of
 fixed assets or working capital for companies creating or retaining jobs in
 economically distressed areas.
Guaranteed Business and Industrial Loan Program: Companies located in
 communities under 50,000 can receive guaranteed long-term loans for real
 estate improvements.
Rural Economic Development Loan and Grant Program: Offered through the
 Rural Electrification Administration for project feasibility studies, start-up
 costs and incubator projects.
Venture Capital Funds: Small companies may receive equity capital and long-
 term loans.
Local and Regional Development Organizations: More than 100 throughout
 the state assist in securing loan assistance.
Section 108 Loan Guarantee: Provides communities with an efficient source
 of financing for economic development and large-scale physical
 development projects.
Tennessee Valley Authority's Economic Development Loan Fund: Multi-
 million dollar revolving loan program that provides financing for new
 industrial plants, plant expansions, plant retention, and infrastructure
 development such as speculative industrial buildings and industrial parks.

Tax Incentives

No inventory tax for businesses.
Corporate income tax limited to five percent.
Income Tax Capital Credit: If a business entity invests in a qualifying project
 that meets certain requirements and is approved by the Alabama
 Department of Revenue, the company may receive an annual credit
 against its income tax liability generated from the qualifying project. The
 capital credit is equivalent to 5% of the capital costs of the qualifying
 project, and can be utilized for a period of 20 years beginning during the
 year the project is placed in service.
Net Operating Loss Carryforward: Corporate income tax law provides for a
 15-year carryforward of net operating losses. In computing net income, a
 corporation is allowed a deduction for the sum of the net operating losses

which are carried forward. Each net operating loss may be carried forward and deducted only during the 15 consecutive year period immediately following the year in which it arose.

Pollution Control Equipment Deduction: All amounts invested in pollution control equipment/materials acquired or constructed in Alabama primarily for the control, reduction, or elimination of air or water pollution are deducted directly from the income apportioned to Alabama.

Enterprise Zone Credit: The corporate income tax enterprise zone credit is offered to help encourage economic growth to areas in Alabama that are considered economically depressed. To qualify for this credit, a business must meet detailed requirements concerning site location and employee qualifications.

Educational Tax Credit: An employer could qualify to receive a credit of 20% of the actual cost of an employer sponsored educational program that enhances basic skills of employees up to and including the twelfth grade functional level.

Foreign Corporation Deduction for Manufacturing Facilities: Alabama law contains several provisions to allow foreign corporations to significantly reduce or almost eliminate their corporate franchise tax liability.

Assessed Value fixed by Alabama Constitution: Amendment 373 of the Constitution provides that business property will be assessed at 20% of its fair market value. That is, for property with a fair market value of $1,000,000, the assessed value would be $200,000 ($1,000,000 x 20%). The combined state and local millage rate would then be applied to the assessed value.

Low Millage Rates: Section 214 of the Constitution limits the state millage rate on both real and personal property to 6.5 mills. This rate is equivalent to a tax of $6.50 for every $1000 of assessed value. However, both cities and counties may levy millage rates in addition to the state's 6.5 mills. These local rates vary but the average rate for any one locality is 43 mills, including the state's 6.5 mills. For business property with a fair market value of $1,000,000 the average property tax would be only $8,600 ($1,000,000 x 20% x .043).

Tax Incentive Reform Act: Allows qualified industries to receive abatements of non-educational ad valorem taxes for new businesses locating to Alabama, and for expansions of existing facilities in Alabama.

Inventory and Raw Materials Exemption: All stocks of goods, wares, and merchandise held for resale, as well as raw materials, are statutorily exempt from ad valorem taxes.

Corporate Shares Tax Deductions: Domestic corporations (incorporated in Alabama) are responsible for the payment of corporate shares tax. This tax is actually an ad valorem tax on the assessed value of capital stock of the corporation. The shares tax is calculated like any other ad valorem tax. There are several deductions from the value of shares that can be considered as tax incentives for Alabama domestic corporations.

Exports

International Trade Center: Services offered include foreign market research, strategic planning and consulting, implementation recommendations, training seminars and general information. Contact: Alabama International Trade Center, University of Alabama, Box 870396, Tuscaloosa, AL 35287; 205-348-7621.

Alabama Development Office: Offers trade promotion services to Alabama manufacturers, including:

- Participation in overseas catalog shows, trade shows, and trade missions
- Opportunities to meet one-on-one with foreign buyers visiting Alabama
- Listing in the *Alabama International Trade Directory*, a publication that is disseminated worldwide
- *Public/Private Grant Program*: Designed to assist Alabama companies in expanding export activities through participation in foreign trade shows and missions
- *Representative Offices*: Germany, Japan, and South Korea

Women and Minorities

Office of Minority Business Enterprise: Assists minorities in achieving effective and equitable participation in the American free enterprise system and in overcoming social and economic disadvantages that have limited their participation in the past. Management and technical assistance is provided to minority firms on request. Contact: Office of Minority Business Enterprise, 401 Adams Ave., Montgomery, AL 36130; 334-242-2224; 800-447-4191.

Alaska

Alaska Department of Commerce and Economic Development
P.O. Box 110800
Juneau, AK 98111
907-465-2017
800-478-LOAN
Fax: 907-465-3767
www.commerce.state.ak.us

Business Assistance

Division of Trade and Development: Has information on
assistance programs, licensing requirements,
taxation, labor laws, financial assistance
programs and state sources of information.
They have a Small Business Advocate that
provides assistance in cutting red tape and has
information and expertise in dealing with state,
federal and local agencies

Small Business Advocate

*Alaska Product Preference, Forest Product Preference, and The Alaska
Recycled Product Preference Programs*: These programs provide
incentives for Alaska businesses responding to bids or proposals for state
contracts by giving preferential consideration. The Alaska Product
Preference Program and the Alaska Forest Product Preference Program
can provide a cost preference of up to 7%, while the Recycled Product
Preference Program offers a 5% preference.
For these programs, contact Division of Trade & Development, 3601 C Street,
Suite 700, Anchorage, AK 99503; 907-269-8121; {www.commerce.state.ak.us/
trade/econ/prodpref.htm}.
Buy Alaska: The Buy Alaska Program's mission is to assist businesses,
consumers, and government entities in finding competitive Alaskan
sources for goods and services with the goal of keeping more dollars in
Alaska. The Buy Alaska Program offers the free service of researching
buying needs and "matching" buyers with sellers. Businesses and
consumers seeking to buy competitively-priced goods and services can get
help from Buy Alaska in identifying local Alaskan vendors and providers
from which to make their purchases. For these programs, contact Buy
Alaska, University of Alaska, Small Business Development Center, 430
W. 7th Avenue, Suite 110, Anchorage, AK 99501; 907-274-7232; 800-
478-7232; {www.alaskanet.com/buyalaska}.

Business Financing

Sustainable Development Program: The program's primary function is to provide (grant) seed money to entities that propose viable sustainable development projects that are community based and supported. The program is not intended to fund pure research. The maximum funding available for any one project is $50,000. But, it's anticipated that most applicants will receive less, thereby allowing the program to fund between six to twelve sustainable development projects. This program is not intended to provide the sole or majority funding of a project. The program will continue funding projects for as long as money is available.

Alaska Science and Technology Foundation Grants (ASTF): Major individual grants of over $2,000 and group grants are both available under this program. Projects that provide economic development, direct benefits and utilize end user participation are considered ideal. ASTF typically requires a financial match equal to the amount they contribute and technology projects that develop a product or process are required to repay ASTF funds through revenue, license fees or profit from sales of the product. For this program, contact Alaska Science and Technology Foundation, 4500 Diplomacy Drive, Suite 515, Anchorage, AK 99506; 907-272-4333; {pprc.pnl.gov/pprc/rfp/astf.html}.

Alaska Growth Capital: This is a commercial financial institution, licensed and regulated by the State of Alaska. It is not regulated as a bank, but rather as a Business and Industrial Development Corporation (BIDCO). BIDCOs do not accept deposits and do not provide consumer lending. BIDCOs focus exclusively on financing businesses. For more information, contact Alaska Growth Capital, 201 Arctic Slope Avenue, Suite 100, Anchorage, AK 99518; 907-349-4904; 888-315-4904; {www.akgrowth.com}.

Power Project Fund: Provides loans to local utilities, local governments or independent power producers for the development or upgrade of electric power facilities, including conservation, bulk fuel storage and waste energy conservation, or potable water supply projects. Loan term is related to the life of the project. For more information, contact Department of Community and Regional Affairs, Division of Energy, 333 West 4th Avenue, Suite 220, Anchorage, AK 99501-2341; 907-269-4625; {www.comregaf.state.ak.us/doehome.htm}.

The Polaris Fund: The purpose of the Polaris Fund is to finance young companies with potential to achieve profitable sales by providing equity capital. Ideal companies should have an experienced management team, an innovative, distinctive product with a $100-$500 million growing market and a well-defined channel for sales. Polaris investments are usually in the $100,000 to $500,000 range, and favor companies that align Polaris closely with management. For more information, contact Jim

Yarmon, c/o Yarmon Investments, 840 K Street, #201, Anchorage, AK 99501; 907-276-4466.

Business Incentive Program: Under this program companies will be reimbursed (rather than be paid up front) for designated portions of relocation costs, site development costs, special employee training not covered by other programs, and special analysis of sites in Alaska. The program was passed into law in April 1998 and is limited to $3 million annually. Contact: Bill Paulick, Division of Trade & Development, P.O. Box 110804, Juneau, AK 99811-0804; 907-465-3961; {E-mail: Bill_Paulick@commerce.state.ak.us}.

Small Business Economic Development Revolving Loan Fund: This program was established in 1987 in conjunction with the U.S. Department of Commerce, Economic Development Administration (EDA). The purpose of the program is to provide private sector employment in the areas designated by EDA. The maximum loan amount is $300,000. Applicants are required to obtain additional private, non-public financing of approximately twice the amount requested. The interest rate of prime minus 4 points is set by the Loan Administration Board consisting of three members from the existing divisional loan committee and two members from the private sector. The board is responsible for setting loan policy and for making all major loan decisions. For more information, contact Alaska Department of Commerce and Economic Development, Division of Investments, P.O. Box 34159, Juneau, AK 99803; 907-465-2510; {www.commerce.state.ak.us/investments/}.

Commercial Fishing Revolving Loan Fund: Commercial fishing loans are available for various purposes at prime plus two percent (up to a maximum of 10.5%) for a 15-year term. All loans must be secured by adequate collateral. Contact: Alaska Department of Commerce and Economic Development, Division of Investments, P.O. Box 34159, Juneau, AK 99803; 907-465-2510; {www.commerce.state. ak.us/investments/}.

Development Finance: Alaska Industrial Development and Export Authority (AIDEA) may own and operate projects that provide infrastructure support for resource development and bring economic benefits to Alaska. To qualify a project must be endorsed by the local government where the project will be sited and be economically feasible. Contact: Alaska Industrial Development and Export Authority, 480 West Tudor, Anchorage, AK 99503; 907-269-3000; Fax: 907-269-3044; {www.alaska.net/~aidea}.

Tax Incentives

Work Opportunity Tax Credit (WOTC): Offers employers tax credits as an
incentive to hire people from seven target groups including Alaska
Temporary Assistance Program (ATAP) and Aid for Families with
Dependent Children (AFDC) recipients, food stamp recipients, veterans,
vocational rehabilitation recipients, ex-felons, and high risk youth. The
credit amount is 40% of up to $6,000 in qualified first year wages with a
maximum credit of $2,400.

Welfare-to-Work Tax Credit (W2W): The W2W tax credit is available for
hiring long-term ATAP and AFDC clients. The W2W tax credit is 35% of
the first $10,000 in wages paid the first year, and 50% of the first $10,000
paid for the second year. The maximum tax credit is $3,500 the first year
and $5,000 the second year for a total of $8,500.

For information on these programs, contact Alaska Employment Service,
WOTC Coordinator, P.O. Box 25509, Juneau, AK 99802; 907-465-5925;
{www.state.ak.us/local/akpages/LABOR/offices/win_of.htm}.

Exploration Incentive: Up to $20 million in qualifying costs can be credited
against future state corporate income tax, mining license tax and
production royalties. Geophysical and geochemical surveys, trenching,
bulk sampling, drilling, metallurgical testing and underground exploration
are included as qualifying costs. Unused credit can be retained for 15
years and may be assigned to successors in interest. For more
information, contact Department of Natural Resources, Division of
Mining, 3601 C Street, Suite 884, Anchorage, AK 99503; 907-269-8600;
{www.dnr.state.ak.us}.

Depreciable Property: 18% of the federal income tax credit for investment in
specified depreciable property can be applied to Alaska state corporate
income tax. Each tax year, as the property is put into use in the state, up to
$20 million of qualified investments may be claimed with the exception of
the unlimited credit allowed on pollution control facilities. Contact:
Alaska Department of Revenue, Income & Excise Audit Division, P.O.
Box 110420, Juneau, AK 99811-0420; 907-465-2320;
{www.revenue.state.ak.us/index.htm}.

Exports

Division of Trade and Development: Trade representatives help to promote
Alaska products and services by providing information and access to
markets, acting as liaisons between domestic and foreign markets, and
promoting investment in Alaska's natural resources. Contact: Division of

Trade & Development, 3601 C Street, Suite 700, Anchorage AK 99503; 907-269-8121; {www.commerce.state.ak.us/trade/econ/prodpref.htm}.

Alaska Industrial Development Export Authority (AIDEA): AIDEA assists businesses through two programs:

1. *Loan Participation*: New or existing projects can receive long term financing or the refinancing of existing loans. Eligible projects include commercial facilities such as office buildings, warehouses, retail establishments, hotels, and manufacturing facilities. AIDEA participation may total up to 80% of a commercial lending institution loan with a maximum of $10 million.

2. *Business and Export Assistance*: This loan guarantee program provides financial institutions with up to an 80% guarantee on the principal of a loan. AIDEA's added support can make project financing, refinancing, and working capital guarantees up to $1 million available to borrowers who might not otherwise find commercial financing.

Accelerated Amortization Program: Under this program, AIDEA may allow the financial institution to amortize its portion of the loan using an accelerated amortization schedule if the project can support the increased debt service, and if the shortened schedule is necessary for the bank's participation. Borrowers may obtain such financing for manufacturing facilities, real estate and equipment under the Loan Participation Program. Contact: Alaska Industrial Development and Export Authority, 480 West Tudor, Anchorage, AK 99503; 907-269-3000; Fax: 907-269-3044; {www.alaska.net/~aidea}.

Arizona

Department of Commerce
3800 N. Central, Suite 1650
Phoenix, AZ 85012
602-280-1480
800-542-5684
Fax: 620-280-1339
www.commerce.state.az.us/fr_abc.shtml

Business Assistance

Arizona Business Connection: A resource center for information, referrals and advice for every stage of small business development. Representatives are available to answer questions and provide a free custom packet.

Small Business Advocate: Works with chambers of commerce and other groups to develop policies and programs that will address fundamental statewide issues of concern to all small businesses.

- Develops customized packets of information and licenses required for small business start-up, expansion, and relocation.
- Provides the booklet *Guide To Establishing and Operating a Business In Arizona* which includes an extensive directory and resources for referrals and networking opportunities.
- Provides coordination and publicity for programs and services that assist minority and women business owners, and assists state agencies in certification of minority and women owned businesses.
- Conducts seminars to help local companies procure goods and services from qualified firms.
- Assists entrepreneurs in resolving matters involving state government offices.
- The High Technology Division aids and assists the growth of high technology companies in Arizona.

The Community Planning Staff: Provides technical assistance on development-related issues, such as community-strategic planning, land-use planning, design review, zoning and infrastructure development, and financing. Provides direct assistance to rural communities in organizing an economic development program or effort, and evaluating community resources. Provides assistance with downtown revitalization projects. Provides support for rural community tourism development efforts. This program helps organizations responsible for retention and expansion develop a program to retain and encourage expansion of existing businesses. The program places significant emphasis on creating a business environment for stable, successful companies. It also provides resources to aid in the design and implementation of a locally defined and community-based Business Retention and Expansion program. It provides assistance with designing, implementing and monitoring cost-effective energy conservation projects in residential, commercial and industrial buildings throughout the state.

Arizona's Work Force Recruitment and Job Training Program: Provides job training assistance to businesses creating net new jobs in Arizona. The program is designed to provide companies with a well equipped work force while ensuring maximum leverage of state and federal training funds.

Business Financing

Strategic Finance Division: Offers a wide range of loan and grant programs which provide economic development resources for companies relocating to or expanding in Arizona including the following:

Commerce & Economic Development Commission (CEDC): A low-interest rate loan program funded by proceeds from the Arizona Lottery. The CEDC's activities include:

- *Direct Assistance To Arizona Business*: to provide expansion capital to existing companies.
- *Technology Sector Capital*: financing that supports the development and growth of high-tech industries.
- *Intermediary Participation Program*: partnerships with other groups that provide economic development loans.
- A *CEDC loan* can be used to purchase fixed assets. A grant component tied to specific wage levels may also be available. In general, projects are weighted based on job creation, the presence of other investors and projected tax revenues. Final loan approval is determined by a six-member commission appointed by the Governor of Arizona. Attractive terms and a fixed interest rate are available.

Revolving Energy Loans for Arizona (RELA): A loan fund to promote and assist energy-related projects and companies. Arizona non-profit entities, political subdivisions or companies that purchase energy-conserving products for use in their own facilities are eligible. In addition, manufacturers of energy-conserving products may apply. Loan requests may range from $10,000 to $500,000 up to a maximum of 60% of total project costs. The RELA program offers a 5% interest rate and variable terms depending on energy payback. Projects have varied in size from window tinting and light fixture replacement to major equipment retrofits of air conditioning systems and solar heaters.

Economic Strength Projects (ESP) offers grants for road construction. This is a very competitive program based on the economic impact of applicant projects in the community in which it will be located. Applications are submitted by a town, city or county.

Loan fund to promote and assist energy-related projects and companies.

50/50 matching grants to schools and hospitals to improve the energy efficiency of their buildings.

Grants for road construction.

Technical and financial assistance to local and tribal governments with the development of public infrastructure projects.

Tax Incentives

Tax credits and technical assistance for low-income housing development.

The Enterprise Zones Program: Offers income tax credits and property tax reclassification for eligible companies meeting employment and industry requirements. Benefits are based on net new job creation, employment of economically disadvantaged or dislocated workers and location in an enterprise zone.

Exports

The Arizona Department of Commerce provides export counseling, access to federal documents assisting with market research, contact facilitation, access to Arizona State offices in several foreign cities, publications including *Arizona International Business Resource Guide*.

Women and Minorities

Minority/Women-Owned Business Enterprises Office: Acts as a resource and advocate for women and minority small businesses. Services include: a statewide directory of women/minority-owned businesses, Professional Women's conference sponsorship, newsletter containing calendar of events and relevant articles, marketing to state agencies and businesses, and certification seminars.

Arkansas

Arkansas Economic Development Commission
1 State Capitol Mall
Little Rock, AR 72201
501-682-1121
Fax: 501-682-7341
www.aedc.state.ar.us

Business Assistance

Existing Workforce Training Program (EWTP): Provides financial assistance
to Arkansas manufacturing industries for upgrading the skills of their
existing workforce. Secondary objectives are to build the capacity within
their state-supported institutions to supply the
ongoing training needs of Arkansas industries and

to increase industry participation in the state's
School-to-Work initiative.
ScrapMatch: A program designed to help Arkansas
manufacturers find markets for their industrial scrap
materials, thereby lowering the cost of doing
business. ScrapMatch uses an electronic data
management system to match industrial waste generators with secondary
material markets.

Industrial Waste Minimization Program and Resource Recovery: Reduction,
reuse, and recycling of industrial waste is the Industrial Waste
Minimization Program's focus. By-product and surplus asset marketing
assistance are also provided. The program provides on-site waste
reduction audits and technical assistance to industry.

Environmental Permitting Services: The Arkansas Department of
Environmental Quality works in a pro-business manner with companies
looking to locate or expand operations in Arkansas. The agency
recognizes the need for business growth in Arkansas while maintaining
their state's positive environmental quality. Contact: Arkansas
Department of Environmental Quality, 8001 National Dr., Little Rock, AR
72219; 501-682-0821.

Customized Training Incentive Program: Provides intensive pre-employment
training for Arkansas workers to meet the increasing technical
employment needs of the state's new and expanding businesses.
Additionally, financial assistance to manufacturing industries for
upgrading the skills of their existing workforce is also available.

Business Financing

Bond Guaranty Programs: For companies that have a financial history but are unable to sell industrial revenue bonds to the public, the Arkansas Economic Development Commission (AEDC) can assure bond holders of repayment by guaranteeing up to $4 million of a bond issue. The state's guaranty allows the bonds to be sold at a higher credit rating, therefore lowering the effective interest rate for the company. The AEDC charges a 5% fee for guaranteeing issues of this type.

Arkansas Capital Corporation: A privately-owned, nonprofit organization established in 1957 to serve as an alternative source of financing for companies in Arkansas. Its main goal is to improve the economic climate in the state by providing long-term, fixed-rate loans to Arkansas companies. As a preferred lender for the Small Business Administration, ACC makes loans to existing operations and business start-ups for everything from new construction and equipment to working capital. ACC loans may be used in combination with bank loans, municipal bond issues, or other sources of financing. Contact: Arkansas Capital Corporation, 225 S. Pulaski St., Little Rock, AR 72201; 501-374-9247; {www.arcap.com}.

ASTA Investment Fund: The Arkansas Science and Technology Authority (ASTA) administers a special Investment Fund of $2.8 million which can provide seed capital for new and developing technology-based companies through loans, royalty agreements, and limited stock purchases. Contact: Arkansas Science and Technology Authority, 100 Main St., Suite 450, Little Rock, AR 72201; 501-324-9006.

Economic Development District Revolving Funds: Several planning and development districts in Arkansas have revolving loan funds for economic development purposes. The loans are limited to $100,000 per business, must involve specific levels of job creation, and must be matched by a bank loan.

Create Rebate Program: Companies hiring specified net new full-time permanent employees within 24 months after completion of an approved expansion and/or new location project can be eligible to receive a financial incentive to be used for a specific purpose. This incentive ranges from 3.9% to 5% in areas with an unemployment rate in excess of 10%, or more than 3% above the state's average unemployment rate for the preceding calendar year.

Industrial Revenue Bonds: Provide manufacturers with below-market financing. Interest on tax exempt issues is normally 80% of prime, but this may vary depending on terms of the issue. For real estate loans, 15 years is the most common term. The primary goal of this financing program is to enable manufacturers to purchase land, buildings, and equipment to expand their operations.

Tax Incentives

Arkansas Economic Development Act (AEDA): To utilize the AEDA program, companies must sign a financial agreement prior to construction outlining the terms of the incentives and stipulations. There are two basic incentives provided: A state corporate income tax credit up to 100% of the total amount of annual debt service paid to the lender financing a project; Refund of sales and use taxes on construction materials, machinery, and equipment associated with a project during the period specified by the financial agreement.

Advantage Arkansas Program: A job tax credit program for qualifying new and expanding companies which provides corporate income tax credits and sales and use tax refunds to companies locating or expanding in Arkansas.

Corporate Income Tax Credit: Provides a credit on corporate income tax equal to the average hourly wage of each new worker times a multiplier of 100, with a $2,000 cap per employee. The multiplier increases to 200 when a company locates in a county where the unemployment rate is at least 10% or 3% above the state average for the preceding calendar year.

InvestArk Tax Credit: Available to industries established in Arkansas for 2 years or longer investing $5 million or more in plant or equipment. A credit against the manufacturer's state sales and use tax liability of 7% of the total project cost, not to exceed 50% of the total sales and use tax liability in a single year, is allowed.

Free Port Law: No tax on goods in transit or raw materials and finished goods destined for out-of-state sales; no sales tax on manufacturing equipment, pollution control facilities, or raw materials; no property tax on textile mills.

Day Care Facility Incentive Program: Companies can receive a sales and use tax refund on the initial cost of construction materials and furnishings purchased to build and equip an approved child care facility. Additionally, a corporate income tax credit of 3.9% of the total annual payroll of the workers employed exclusively to provide childcare service, or a $5,000 income tax credit for the first year the business provides its employees with a day care facility is also available.

Tourism Development: Provides state sales tax credits up to 10% of approved project costs for the creation or expansion of eligible tourist attractions exceeding $500,000, and 25% of project costs exceeding $1,000,000.

Recycling Equipment Tax Credit: Allows taxpayers to receive a tax credit for the purchase of equipment used exclusively for reduction, reuse, or recycling of solid waste material for commercial purposes, whether or not for profit, and the cost of installation of such equipment by outside contractors. The amount of the credit shall equal 30% of the cost of eligible equipment and installation costs.

Motion Picture Incentive Act: Qualifying motion picture production companies spending in excess of $500,000 within six months, or $1 million within 12 months may receive a refund of state sales and use taxes paid on qualified expenditures incurred in conjunction with a film, telefilm, music video, documentary, episodic television show, or commercial advertisement.

Biotechnology Development and Training Act: Offers three different income tax credits to taxpayers furthering biotechnical business development. The first credit is a 5% income tax credit applied to costs to build and equip eligible biotechnical facilities. The second credit allows a 30% income tax credit both for eligible employee training costs and for contract with state-supported institutions for higher education to conduct qualified cooperative research projects. The third credit allows an income tax credit for qualified research in biotechnology, including but not limited to the cost of purchasing, licensing, developing, or protecting intellectual property. This credit is equal to 20% of the amount the cost of qualified research exceeds the cost of such resource in the base year.

Enterprise Zone Program: Corporate income tax credits and sales tax refund.

Sales and Use Tax Exemptions: For many manufacturing materials, equipment, and machinery; and, air and water pollution control equipment.

Exports

The *Arkansas Economic Development Commission's (AEDC)* international offices assist Arkansas companies in exporting their products and services by arranging personalized meetings with potential distributors, sales representatives or end users in the countries targeted for AEDC's export promotion efforts. In addition to this service, they also offer the following:

- Market research
- Assisting companies exhibiting in international trade fairs
- Planning and coordinating trade missions
- Obtaining trade leads
- Representing and/or advising companies on export transactions
- Accompanying company representatives on export sales trips
- Promoting companies in meetings with prospective buyers

California

California Trade and Commerce Agency
801 K St., Suite 1700
Sacramento, CA 95814
916-322-1394
www.state.ca.us/s/business

California's business resources are many and varied with many local and regional programs. The following is not all-inclusive:

Business Assistance

Office of Small Business: Offers workshops, seminars, individual counseling, and publications for those interested in small businesses. They have information and expertise in dealing with state, federal, and local agencies.

Business Financing

The Loan Guarantee Program: Assists small businesses that cannot qualify for bank loans. Normally, 80% of the loan amount, with the guaranteed portion of the loan not exceeding $350,000 is offered. Microloans, up to $25,000, are fully guaranteed.

Energy Technology Export Program: The California Energy Commission assists California companies through several energy export programs. For more information, contact California Energy Commission, Energy Technology Export Program, 1516 Ninth St., MS-45, Sacramento, CA 95814; 916-654-4528; {www.energy.ca.gov}.

Fishing Vessel: Direct loans to finance commercial fishing vessel equipment and modifications that result in fuel savings. Loans are from $10,000 to $25,000.

Hazardous Waste: Direct loans to finance equipment or a production practice that reduces waste or lessens hazardous properties. The minimum loan is $20,000. The maximum loan is $150,000.

Bond Guarantees: Access to surety bonds that allow greater participation by small and emerging contractors in state public works contracts. Maximum is $350,000 liability per contract.

Small Corporate Offering Registration Network: Raise up to $1 million by issuing shares directly to investors through a state-registered public offering.

Sudden and Severe Economic Dislocation (SSED): The California Trade and Commerce Agency provides gap financing to businesses in areas of the state affected by plant and military base closures, defense downsizing, industry layoffs, presidentially declared disasters and other economic problems which have contributed to job loss in California.

Old Growth Diversification Revolving Loan Fund: The California Trade and Commerce Agency provides low cost capital to businesses that create jobs in targeted timber-dependent areas. Businesses may borrow from $25,000 to $100,000 at a reduced interest rate to purchase machinery and equipment or for working capital.

The California Capital Access Program: The California Pollution Control Financing Authority (CPCFA) provides a form of loan portfolio insurance which provides up to 100% coverage on certain loan defaults, encouraging banks and other financial institutions to make loans to small businesses that fall just outside of most banks' conventional underwriting standards. The maximum loan amount is $2.5 million. The maximum premium CPCFA will pay is $100,000 (per loan). Contact: California Pollution Control Financing Authority, Attention: SBAF Program Manager, 915 Capitol Mall, Room 466, Sacramento, CA 95814; 916-654-5610.

California Industrial Development Financing Advisory Commission (CEDFAC): The Treasurer's office assists California manufacturing businesses in funding capital expenditures for acquisitions or expansions. Allows a business to borrow funds at competitive rates through the issuance of tax-exempt bonds enhanced by a letter of credit. The maximum face amount of an IDB bond issue is $10 million per applicant per public jurisdiction. Contact: California Industrial Development Financing Advisory Commission, 915 Capitol Mall, Sacramento, CA 95814; 916-653-3843.

Tax Incentives

Manufacturers operating in California are eligible for a 6% manufacturers' investment credit (MIC). This credit is generally unlimited.

Provides "new" or start up companies the option of a 5% partial sales or use tax exemption on all qualifying manufacturing property purchased or leased generally during the company's first three years of operation.

Research tax credits allow companies to receive a credit of 11% for qualifying research expenses (research done in-house) and 24% for basic research payments (payments to an outside company), making it the highest in the nation.

Net Operating Loss Carryover: Allows businesses that experience a loss for the year to carry this loss forward to the next year in order to offset income in the following year.

Enterprise Zone Program: Encourages business development in 39 designated areas through numerous special zone incentives.

Local Agency Military Base Recovery Area: Designations which are similar to enterprise zones allowing communities to extend the aforementioned California tax credits to companies locating in a LAMBRA zone.

Child Care Tax Credit: For employers who pay or incur costs for the start up of a child care program or construction of an on-site child care facility are eligible for a credit against state income taxes equal to 30% of its costs, up to a maximum of $50,000 in one year. Excess credits may be carried over to succeeding years.

Exports

International Trade and Investment: Acts as a catalyst to create jobs in California through vigorous and sustained promotion of exports to global markets and foreign investment into the Golden State. They have offices in California and ten foreign locations. They offer promotion of California products and companies abroad through the Office of Export Development, current information on foreign market opportunities, the Special American Business Internship Training Program, and assistance with attracting foreign investment through the California Office of Foreign Investment. They also provide exporting financial assistance for going global through several economic development programs provided by the California Export Finance Office, a division of California's Trade and Commerce Agency. The maximum guarantee amount is $750,000. That is 90% of an $833,000 loan.

Women and Minorities

Child Care and Development Facilities Loan Guarantee Fund and Child Care and Development Facilities Direct Loan Fund: Together, these funds support the California Child Care Facilities Finance Program. The Department of Housing and Community Development will deposit $3.1 million from the Child Care and Development Facilities Loan Guarantee Fund into the Small Business Expansion Fund. Corporations can issue guarantees against this fund as long  as the transaction adheres to the following HCD rules: The loan must be used for creating new child care spaces or preserving spaces that would otherwise be lost; the projects must fit into the HCD priority categories. A direct loan may not exceed 20% of the total project cost if the same facility is also utilizing a guaranteed loan. In no case can a direct loan exceed 50% of the project cost. Home-based child care will be financed by non-profit microlenders. Both small businesses and non-profit organizations will be eligible for either guarantees and/or direct loans.

Colorado

Office of Economic Development
1625 Broadway, Suite 1710
Denver, CO 80202
303-892-3840
Fax: 303-892-3848
TDD: 800-659-2656
www.state.co.us

Business Assistance

Office of Economic Development: The Office of
Economic Development (OED) works with
companies starting, expanding or relocating in
Colorado. OED offers a wide range of services to
assist new and existing businesses of every size.

Marketing Colorado: Marketing activities are
conducted nationwide to promote sectors of the
Colorado economy which are growing and provide high
quality jobs. Marketing activities include attendance at selected trade
shows, company visits, cooperative marketing with local enterprise zones
and community economic development councils and industry research.
Colorado Facts is published annually by OBD and includes statistics and
comparisons of key indicators to evaluate Colorado's economic climate
and to provide information of special interest to the business community.

Job Training: Colorado First and Existing Industries Job Training Programs
assists employers with customized job training. Assistance is provided to
new and existing businesses to retrain workers and improve their
workplace skills. The goal of the Colorado First program is to assist
companies in training employees to fill newly created full-time permanent
quality jobs.

Business Financing

Revolving Loan Fund Programs (RLFs): Administered locally in 15
geographic regions covering the rural areas of the state. RLFs have
considerable flexibility to make small loans of two or three thousand
dollars up to $100,000. Applicants can be existing or startup businesses.

Larger Business Loans: Between $100,000 and $250,000 are provided by
OBD through the Community Development Block Grant Business Loans

Program when the local government is willing to assume the risk on the loan in order to create or retain jobs. Larger loans may be considered on a case by case basis.

Economic Development Commission: Will provide interest rate write-downs, low interest rate loans or subsidies to companies interested in relocating to or expanding in Colorado.

Private Activity Bonds (PABs): Provide a tax-exempt financing vehicle for facilities and equipment used in the manufacture or production of tangible personal property.

Tax Incentives

Investment Tax Credits: The Colorado Tax Equity Act, signed into law during the 1987 legislative session, reinstates the Colorado Investment Tax Credit, up to $1,000 per year, for tax years beginning on or after January 1, 1998, based on 10% of what the Federal Investment Tax Credit would have been had such credit not been restricted by the Tax Reform Act of 1986. Excess credits may be carried forward up to three years.

Enterprise Zone Tax Credits: Enterprise Zones are geographic areas designated to promote economic development. Sixteen such zones have been designated in Colorado. They cover most rural areas of the state with the exception of the ski area/resort counties. There are also urban zones designated to attract investment and jobs to selected areas. Enterprise Zones offer the following advantages to businesses locating or expanding within their boundaries:

- A $500 credit for each new full-time employee working within the Zone.
- Double job tax credit for agricultural processing.
- $200 job tax credit for employer health insurance.
- Local government incentives.
- 3% investment tax credit for businesses making investments in equipment used exclusively in an Enterprise Zone.
- Exemption from state sales and use taxes for manufacturing equipment.
- Income tax credit of up to 3% for expenditures on research and development activities (as defined in federal tax laws) in an Enterprise Zone.
- A credit of 25% of qualified expenditures up to $50,000 to rehabilitate buildings which are at least 20 years old which have been vacant at least two years.
- A 25% tax credit for private contributions to local zone administrators for qualifying projects or programs within zones.

- A 10% tax credit for employer expenditures for qualified job training and school-to-work programs.

Sales Tax Exemptions: For purchases over $500 on machinery and machine tools purchased for use in manufacturing; Purchases of electricity, coal, gas, or fuel oil for use in processing, manufacturing, and all industrial uses; Sale of tangible personal property for testing, modification, inspection, or similar types of activities in Colorado; Interstate long distance telephone charges.

Local Governments: May provide incentive payments or property tax credits based on the amount of increased property taxes for qualifying new business activity in their jurisdictions.

Exports

Colorado International Trade Office (ITO): Responsible for assisting Colorado companies with all aspects of exporting, including counseling, protocol, leading trade missions, and conducting trade shows abroad. By promoting Colorado exports and attracting foreign investment, the ITO helps to build Colorado's identity as an international business center, encouraging foreign buyers to look to Colorado for products and services. The ITO is open to the public and most services are rendered at no cost.

Women and Minorities

Women's Business Office: Strives to keep the women entrepreneurs of Colorado informed about pertinent issues through all modes of communication.

Office of Economic Development Minority Business Office: Acts as a clearinghouse to disseminate information to the minority business community. Promotes economic development for minority businesses in cooperation with the state economic development activities. Establishes networks between majority and minority business sectors. Promotes minority participation in state procurement. Assists Colorado in achieving its Minority Procurement Goals of 17%. Works with the Minority Business Advisory Council and the minority community in promoting minority business development.

Connecticut

Economic Resource Center
Connecticut Department of Economic and Community Development
805 Brooks St., Bldg. 4
Rocky Hill, CT 06067-3405
860-571-7136
800-392-2122
Fax: 860-571-7150
www.cerc.com

Business Assistance

One Stop Centers: Authorized to enable businesses to obtain many necessary
permits and licenses in one location.
Connecticut Economic Resource Center (CERC): A non-profit private-sector
organization formed and managed through a
unique partnership of

utility/telecommunication companies and
state government. The CERC coordinates
Connecticut's business-to-business
marketing and recruitment efforts on behalf
of the state. As a one-stop gateway to the state's
programs and services for business, the CERC helps businesses obtain
quick and accurate information in the areas of financing, export assistance,
licensing, manufacturing programs, job training, utility,
telecommunications and real estate help, all at no cost.
Business Resource Index: The Connecticut Economic Resource Center's
website {www.cerc.com}offers a large and comprehensive database of
programs and services for businesses. The database contains information
from the public and private sectors on federal, state and local levels
including license and permit information. The *Business Resource Index* is
divided into three major sections, each of which can be searched
individually or collectively. The sections include *Resources By Agency,*
Licensing, and *Helpful Fact Sheets*. Available business resources are often
divided by city or region. Listings are extensive. To illustrate, a search
with the keyword "Small Business" yielded 119 documents including
loans, technical assistance, consulting services, grants, and economic
development assistance among others. As an example, the Entrepreneurial
Loan Program offers loans up to $100,000 insured by the Connecticut
Development Authority, for the benefit of start-up and early stage business
anywhere in Connecticut. The website also features a real estate search

engine enabling the user to input parameters such as size of building and
desired location to aid with business site selection.

Technology Extension Program: Provides direct technical assistance to small
and mid-sized manufacturing firms.

Institute for Industrial and Engineering Technology: Offers assistance with
process improvement, technical training, procurement, human resources,
business incubators, and others.

SiteFinder: A comprehensive computer database of available commercial and
industrial properties.

Demographic and Economic Analysis: Services include industry profiles,
competitive intelligence, regional analysis, survey research, bench
marking and evaluation.

Business Financing

Entrepreneurial Loan Program: Provides up to $1000,000 in start-up and
expansion financing. 75% of past loans were made to women and
minority owners.

URBANK: Loans up to $500,000 for any small business enterprise in targeted
communities that are unable to obtain conventional financing.

Business Loans: Up to $10 million for medium size enterprises.

Junior Participation Loans: Up to $5 million to assist the lender in meeting
the company's total borrowing requirements.

Inducement Loans: Up to $10 million at below market interest rates restricted
to significant competitive business retention or recruitment.

Industrial Revenue Bonds: Low rate, tax exempt financing for manufacturers,
utilities, certain non-profits and others.

Environmental Assistance Revolving Loan Fund: Provides loans, lines of
credit or loan guarantees for Clean Air Act compliance and pollution
prevention.

Job Training Finance Program: Pays up to 25% of the cost of improving
skills of manufacturing workers.

Custom Job Training Program: Department of Labor will pay up to 50% for
eligible training expenses.

For all the above loan programs, contact Connecticut Development Authority,
999 West St., Rocky Hill, CT 06067; 860-258-7800.

Manufacturing Assistance Fund: Program includes loans, defense
diversification project funding, tax credits and funding for new machinery
and equipment.

Naugatuck Valley Loan Fund: Fund can be used to purchase land or buildings,
construction, renovation, rehabilitation, and/or the purchase and
installation of machinery and equipment. Maximum loan is $200,000.

Connecticut Programs Fund: Program provides venture capital, including minority-focused venture capital, mezzanine financing and funds for restructuring.

For the above loan programs, contact Department of Economic and Community Development, 249 Thomaston Ave., Waterbury, CT 06702; 203-596-8862.

Community Economic Development Fund: Provides financing for a wide range of projects in certain targeted investment and public investment communities throughout the state.

Regional Revolving Loan Funds: Provide supplemental financing to stimulate job growth and business activity.

Community-Based Development Organizations: Local economic development organizations offering financing on varying conditions and terms.

For the above loan programs, contact Community Economic Development Fund, 50-G Weston St., Hartford, CT 06120; 800-656-4613; 860-249-3800.

Connecticut Venture Group: A non-profit membership organization that brings entrepreneurs and investors together.

Innovations Technology Financing: Offers a wide range of support from research assistance to financing for product development and marketing.

For the above loan programs, contact Connecticut Venture Group, 891 Post Rd., Suite F, Fairfield, CT 06430; 203-333-3284.

Product Development and Product Marketing Financing: Recipients of funding frequently gain the credibility that they need to leverage investment capital from more traditional, private sources. Typical investments range from $50,000 to $1,000,000.

Yankee Ingenuity Initiative Funding: Provides funding for collaborative research between businesses and colleges.

Technology Partnership: Invests $50,000 to $500,000 in businesses pursuing funding through federal research and development programs.

For more information regarding the loan programs listed above, contact Connecticut Innovations Technology Fiancing, 999 West St., Rocky Hill, CT 06067; 860-563-5851; {www.ctinnovations.com}.

Tax Incentives

Corporate Income Tax Credits:
- 50% for financial institutions constructing new facilities and adding new employees.
- 5% annual credit for fixed capital investment in tangible personal property.

- 4% annual credit for investments in human capital, employee training, childcare, and donations to higher education for technology training.
- 10% credit for increased investment in machinery and equipment for companies with 250 or fewer full-time permanent employees.
- Research and development credits.
- 100% credit for property taxes paid on data processing hardware, peripheral equipment and software.
- 25% credit for an increase in grant to institutions of higher learning for R&D related to technology advancement.
- 100% credit for investment over 10 years in an investment fund creating insurance related facilities and jobs.
- Other credits for low-income housing, contributions to neighborhood assistance programs, and alternative employee transportation.

Corporate Income Tax Exemptions:
All insurance companies, passive investment companies, and financial services companies.
- Property Taxes: 100% exemption for newly installed machinery and equipment, inventories, unbundled software, new commercial motor vehicles.
- Sales Tax: 100% exemption on newly acquired and installed machinery and equipment, inventories, unbundled software and commercial motor vehicles.
- Enterprise Zones and Targeted Investment Communities: 40 - 80% real and personal property tax exemptions, 25% corporate business tax credits for firms conducting research & development, 15 - 100% corporate business tax credits depending on industry and jobs created, $750 - $2,250 grants for each new job created for eligible companies.
- Department of Labor: Tax credits up to $4,800 are available for qualified apprenticeships in the manufacturing and construction trades.

Exports

Access International: Program designed to put businesses in touch with resources to support exporting efforts including consultants, suppliers, services and support.

Women and Minorities

Procurement Program: Set-Aside Program requires state agencies and political subdivisions to set aside 25% of their budget for construction, housing rehabilitation and the purchasing of supplies. These services are awarded to certified small business contractors, minority businesses, enterprises, non-profit corporations and individuals with a disability. 25% of this amount is to be awarded to certified minority owned firms.

Minority Supplier Development Council: A non-profit organization whose mission is to foster business relationships between corporations and certified minority businesses. Services include training seminars, matchmaking activities, bid notifications, networking functions and a large trade expo.

For these programs, contact Minority and Small Business Contractors Set-Aside Program, Department of Economic and Community Development, 505 Hudson St., Hartford, CT 06106, Attn: Set Aside Unit; 860-270-8025; {www.state.ct.us/ecd/setaside}.

Delaware

Delaware Economic Development Office
John S. Riley
99 Kings Highway
P.O. Box 1401
Dover, DE 19903
302-739-4271
Fax: 302-739-5749
www.state.de.us/dedo/index.htm

Business Assistance

Delaware Economic Development Office: Offers referrals to appropriate state
agencies and other organizations. Free tabloid,
Small Business Start-Up Guide is available.
Provides support for new businesses and
coordinates the efforts of organizations statewide
that assist small businesses.

Delaware Economic Development Office

Workforce Development Section: Works to ensure
the availability of a skilled, multilevel workforce
for new and existing Delaware businesses. Helps
employers obtain, upgrade and retain suitable
workers, by helping Delawareans gain the education and training to get
and keep quality jobs and steady employment.
Business Research Section: Collects, analyzes and distributes statistical data
on the state's economy and business climate and develops research
regarding the economic vitality of the State of Delaware
Delaware Tourism Office: Assists the tourism industry.
The State Data Center: Provides economic and demographic data for
Delaware.
Business Calendar: Maintained by the Delaware State Chamber of Commerce
(DSCC), it is the state's central location for listing business-related events.
Advanced Technology Centers (ATCs): Public/private partnerships designed to
bolster Delaware's technology base and to create and retain quality high-
tech jobs. The State of Delaware has committed $11 million to date in
grants to establish five Centers. Funding for the program comes from the
state's 21st Century Fund. Amounts are not available without a specific
inquiry. For more information, contact Delaware Economic Development
Office, 820 French St., Wilmington, DE 19801; 302-577-8477.
Green Industries Initiative: Targets specific businesses for receipt of financial
and technical assistance to further the goals of Governor Castle's

Executive Order #82 and Delaware's Pollution Prevention Program. The State of Delaware provides corporate income tax credits and/or gross receipts tax reductions for existing Delaware firms and those choosing Delaware as a location for new operations. The type of financial assistance is dependent upon the category under which assistance is requested.

Business Financing

Industrial Revenue Bonds: Statewide financial assistance to new or expanding businesses through the issuance of bonds (IRBs). The maximum for IRBs issued annually in Delaware is $150 million.

Economic Development Loan Program: Assists Delaware businesses to finance projects when 100% financing cannot be obtained through a bank. The program does require 70% bank financing. The remaining 30% is financed through the program up to a maximum of $450,000. In most cases the interest rate for monies loaned through the Economic Development Loan Program is 60% of the prime lending interest rate.

The Delaware Access Program: Designed to give banks a flexible and extremely non-bureaucratic tool to make business loans that are somewhat riskier than a conventional bank loan, in a manner consistent with safety and soundness. It is designed to use a small amount of public resources to generate a large amount of private bank financing, thus providing access to bank financing for many Delaware businesses that might otherwise not be able to obtain such access. The program sets minimum and maximum limits for the borrower's payment. At a minimum, it must be at least 1-1/2% of the loan amount. The maximum is 3-1/2% . (The premium payment, and other up-front expenses, may be financed as part of the loan.)

Small Business Innovation Research (SBIR): Bridge grant assistance to encourage Delaware businesses to participate in the federal Small Business Innovation Research (SBIR) grant program. The SBIR program requires that 1.25% of all federal research dollars be made available to small businesses. Phase I awardees are granted up to $100,000 by the federal government.

The Delaware Innovation Fund: Assists in the initial capitalization of pre-seed and seed stage enterprises within the State of Delaware. The Fund provides financial and technical assistance to Delaware based businesses which have the potential to launch innovative products and processes into national markets, to create new jobs, and to make a significant contribution to the economic diversity and the technology base of Delaware's communities.

Demonstration Funding: Limited one-time availability, provides $10,000 to
$25,000 to aid in establishing patents, business plans and proof of concept
issues.

Commercialization Funding: Ranging from $25,000 to $250,000, this funding
is used to begin the commercialization process of early-stage businesses
and may be available in multiple years.

Venture Capital Funds: Three funds — Anthem Capital, L.P., Triad Investors
Corporation, and Blue Rock Capital — have the ability to fund a variety of
seed stage, early stage, and later stage companies in both technology-
related and non-technology fields. The investment focus of each fund
varies. Investments can range from $150,000 for seed stage companies up
to $2,000,000 or more for later stage companies.

City of Wilmington: Projects located within the city limits of Wilmington may
also apply for financing through the Wilmington Economic Development
Corporation (WEDCO). Financing programs offered include SBA Section
504 Loans, Revolving Loan Funds, and other special purpose financing.
Contact: Wilmington Economic Development Corporation, 605A Market
St., Wilmington, DE 19801; 302-571-9088.

Sussex County: Operates an Industrial Revenue Bond program with a cap of
$15 million each year for industrial projects in the County. Project review
requires a letter of commitment for placement of the bond before a project
recommendation is made by the Industrial Revenue Bond Review
Committee to Sussex County Council (political jurisdiction). The
Industrial Revenue Bond process may require as little as five weeks from
inception to bond closing. Contact: Sussex County Office of Economic
Development, P.O. Box 589, 9 S. Dupont Hwy., Georgetown, DE 19947;
302-855-7770.

Tax Incentives

Bank Franchise Tax Credits: For taxable years beginning after December 31,
1996, credits against bank franchise taxes are available to qualifying firms.
Credits are $400 per year for each new qualifying employee in excess of
50 new employees and are for a period of ten years.

Export Trading Company Exemption: Delaware exporters who qualify as an
Export Trading Company can receive exemption from Delaware income
and mercantile taxes.

Targeted Area Tax Incentives: Firms which qualify for targeted industry
credits and are located in one of the targeted areas, qualify for corporate
income tax credits of $650 for each new employee and $650 for each new
$100,000 investment.

Retention and Expansion Tax Credits: Corporate income tax credits and gross
receipts tax reductions are available to qualifying manufacturers and
wholesalers planning new facilities or large expansions. The maximum

annual credit cannot exceed $500,000. Gross receipts tax reductions are limited to a maximum total credit of $500,000 over the ten-year life.

Green Industries Tax Credits: Manufacturers that reduce their chemical waste, as reported under the Toxics Release Inventory, by 20% or their other wastes by 50%, are granted a $400 corporate income tax credit for each 10% reduction.

Public Utility Tax Rebates for Industrial Users: Industrial firms meeting the criteria for targeted industries tax credits are eligible for a rebate of 50% of the Public Utilities Tax imposed on new or increased consumption of gas and electricity for five years.

Property Tax Incentives: The cities of Wilmington, Newark, Dover and the counties of New Castle and Kent offer a variety of property tax incentives for new construction, renovation, and property improvements. Amounts vary.

Exports

The International Trade Section: A one-stop resource for exporter assistance and international trade information in Delaware. Contact the International Trade Section, Delaware Economic Development Office, 820 French St., Carvel State Office Bldg., 10th Floor, Wilmington, DE 19801; 302-577-8477.

District of Columbia

Office of Economic Development
441 4th St., NW, Suite 1140
Washington, DC 20001
202-727-6365
www.dchomepage.net

Business Assistance

Welcome To Washington D.C. Online: A useful website with
links to business & finance opportunities in the district.
Certifies business as *local business development* for
purposes of procurement from the District of
Columbia government.
Transferable Development Rights: Permits businesses
to purchase the right to develop at higher
densities in designated TDR "receiving zones."
Contact Local Business Development, 441 4th St.,
NW, Suite 970N, Washington, DC 20001; 202-724-1385.

Business Location Assistance:
D.C. Chamber of Commerce, 1301 Pennsylvania Ave., NW, Suite 309,
Washington, DC 20004; 202-347-7201; {www.dcchamber.org};
D.C. Building Industry Association, 5100 Wisconsin Ave., NW, Suite
301, Washington, DC 20016; 202-966-8665;
{www.reji.com/associations/dcbia}.

Business Financing

Enterprise Zone: Eligible for up to $15 million per business in tax exempt
bonds for businesses within an Enterprise Zone; $20,000 of additional
expensing of business equipment.
Bond Financing and General Information: Contact D.C. Revenue Bond
Program, 441 4th St., NW, Suite 360, Washington, DC 20001; 202-727-
6055; 202-727-2778; {www.dccfo.com/dcbons.htm}.

Tax Incentives

Enterprise Zones: Consists of 65 census tracts with 20% and higher poverty
rate. Benefits include:
• *Tax-Exempt Bond Financing*: Up to 15 million.

- *Federal Capital Gains Exemption*: Requires 80% of the business' total gross income be derived from a business or trade conducted within the enterprise zone.
- *Employment Tax Credit*: Up to $3,000 for each employee at the EZ facility who is also a D.C. resident.
- *Special Expensing Allowance*: $20,000 available for business equipment and depreciable property purchase by EZ businesses.

Public Schools Tax Credit: Available for contributions to school rehabilitation and repair, the provision of school equipment, materials and teacher training and the advancement of innovative K-12 programs.

Work Opportunity Tax Credits: $2,400 first time work opportunity tax credit for each worker in the first year of employment.

Welfare-To-Work Tax Credit: $8,500 welfare to work one-time tax credit for employees certified by D.C. DOES.

Exports

The DC Office of International Business: OIB was created to support the District of Columbia's development and expansion of local business through international trade and joint-venture partnerships, and to attract outside investment to the District of Columbia. Programs offered include:

- *International Trade Counseling and Technical Program*: OIB offers counseling and assistance on all aspects of international business to firms, organizations and residents of the District of Columbia.
- *Resource Center for International Trade Information*: Offers country market profiles, current export licensing regulations, information on trade and financing, a comprehensive database of trade resources and a directory of Washington-based international firms.
- *Trade and Investment Program*: Offers a database of local, small and medium sized businesses, using criteria and categories useful for the analysis of the local market; match making potential for local small business, and investment needs; facilitates trade and investment leads; identifies overseas markets for local goods and services; supports trade and investment missions; hosts foreign buying delegations; works in tandem with its sister agencies in devising strategies and marketing activities to attract foreign investment and business entities to the District of Columbia; establishes regular and close relationships with the diplomatic community, chambers of commerce and other regional and state agencies to identify export and investment opportunities for local and area businesses.

- *OIB Seminar Series*: Provides hands-on training through an eight week course designed to provide concise, nuts-and-bolts instructions on how to conduct import, export, and joint venture transactions. Topics cover every aspect of international trade with emphasis on small business involvement. Upon successful completion of the course, participants receive a "Certificate of Achievement."
- *OIB Internship Program*: OIB offers a high school and college internship program that provides local youth with on-the-job training, skill development and an orientation to international trade.

Women and Minorities

Minority Business Opportunity Commission: Promotes equal opportunity in all aspects of District life and fosters minority business development through:
- *Business Marketing Directory*: listing of Local, Small, Disadvantaged and Minority Business Enterprises.
- *Minority Business Certification Program*
- *Technical Assistance Program*: Aids minority business enterprises through workshops, contracting conferences, referrals and the MBOC Directory to bid and compete on District Government contracts.
- *Bonding Assistance Program*: Establishes a financial assurance pool to serve as limited collateral for surety bonds on public construction projects awarded by the DC government.

For these programs, contact D.C. Department of Human Rights and Local Business Development, DC Department of Human Rights and Minority Business Development, 441 4th Street, NW, Suite 970, Washington, DC 20001; 202-724-1385; Fax: 202-724-3786.

Florida

Florida Economic Development Council
502 East Jefferson Street
Tallahassee, FL 32301
805-222-3000
Fax: 850-222-3019

Enterprise Florida
390 North Orange Avenue, Suite 1300
Orlando, FL 32801
407-316-4600
Fax: 407-316-4599
www.floridabusiness.com

Business Assistance

Enterprise Florida: Offers information and
referral services for current and potential
small business owners. Also serves as
ombudsman to small businesses to help resolve
problems being experienced with state
agencies. They sponsor workshops and
business forums and an annual Small Business
Development Workshop that brings together local,
state, and federal agency representatives. Distributes and
publishes the *Florida New Business Guide
Checklist* for small businesses.

Innovation and Commercialization Centers:
Sponsored by Enterprise Florida, Technology
Development Corporation provides services and assistance
designed to help entrepreneurs and emerging technology-based companies
grow, launch new products and succeed in the marketplace. Services
include business planning, market development, technology access,
commercialization assistance, financial expertise and additional services.

- *Vendor Bid System*: An online computer service allowing searches
  for state bids that fit a particular business.
- *Quick Response Training*: Up to 18 months of employee training for
  businesses that produce exportable goods or services, create new jobs
  and employ Florida workers who require customized entry-level
  skills training.

- **Info-bid**: Helps businesses locate bid opportunities to sell to federal, state and local government agencies, as well as some commercial firms.

Business Financing

Enterprise Bonds: Tax-exempt Industrial Development Bonds (IDBs). These bonds provide a cost-effective means for qualified manufacturers, processors and nonprofit organizations to access public and private bond markets, particularly for small fixed asset investment projects with limited access to those markets. Minimum loan size is $500,000. Maximum loan size is $2,000,000 unless a larger amount is strongly supported by local economic development officials.

The Economic Development Transportation Fund: Commonly referred to as the "Road Fund," provides funding to units of local government for the elimination of transportation problems that adversely impact a specific company's location or expansion decision. Up to $2,000,000 may be provided to a local government to implement the improvements.

Florida Energy Loan Program: Provides low interest loans for energy conservation measures (ECM) to encourage eligible Florida businesses to reduce energy consumption while increasing energy efficiency. Maximum to $75,000; Minimum of $1,500.

The Florida Recycling Loan Program: Provides funding for machinery and equipment for manufacturing, processing, or conversion systems utilizing materials which have been or will be recycled; collection systems are not eligible. Direct Loans — Maximum to $200,000; minimum of $20,000. Maximum amount for leveraged loans will be $200,000, or 40% of total eligible costs, whichever is less.

Florida Export Finance Corporation: Makes available pre- and post-shipment working capital to small and medium size Florida exporters. Programs include state-supported direct loans and guarantees as well as packaging services that provide access to EXIM Bank and SBA export finance and working capital guaranty programs. Direct loans for the lesser of 90% of the product cost or $50,000. Loan guarantees for the lesser of 90% of a loan provided by a lender or $500,000. No minimum size.

Community Development Corporation Support and Assistance Program: Provides funds to local community development corporations, which in turn make loans to private businesses for the establishment of new businesses; provide financial assistance to existing businesses; or purchase equity interest in businesses located within a service area.

Rural Revolving Loan Program: Designed to provide gap funding for economic development projects in rural counties. Loan size to $200,000 or 10% of the project being assisted, whichever is less.

Florida Venture Finance Directory: Acts as a "wholesaler" in providing information to assist in the guidance of financing searches, Capital Development developed and published *The Florida Venture Finance Directory*. The *Directory* serves as an effective tool for economic development organizations (primary distributors) to assist local businesses in their fund raising efforts.

Venture Capital Network Development: Financial support, within budget limitations, is provided to a limited number of venture capital conferences at which Florida entrepreneurs have opportunity to present their ventures to members of the venture capital community. Enterprise Florida also is specifically interested in supporting initiatives leading to increased participation of private individual investors in Florida business ventures.

The Technology Investment Fund: Makes co-investments with Florida companies in promising technology-related projects with near-term commercial potential. Investments fall within a range of $25,000 to $250,000, depending upon the project's scope, commercial potential, matching funds, leveraged funds, the number and quality of other proposals received and the amount of funding requested in the highest ranked proposals.

Cypress Equity Fund: A $35.5 million venture capital "fund of funds" organized to facilitate investment in the venture capital asset class by Florida financial institutions, and to provide a platform to showcase Florida to the national venture capital community.

Tax Incentives

No corporate income tax on limited partnerships, individuals, estates, and private trusts.

No state personal income tax.

No inventory tax.

No collected or assessed property tax at the state level.

No sales tax on groceries, prescription medicines, household fuels, and most services.

No sales tax on "Boiler Fuels" used at a fixed Florida location in an industrial manufacturing, processing, production or compounding process.

No sales and use tax on goods manufactured or produced in the state for resale for export outside the state.

The Qualified Target Industry Tax Refund Program: A tool available to Florida communities to encourage quality job growth in targeted high value-added businesses. The program provides tax refunds to pre-approved applicants of up to $5,000 per new job created ($7,500 in an enterprise zone).

Enterprise Zone Program: Offers financial incentives to businesses to encourage private investment as well as employment opportunities for residents of 30 designated Enterprise Zones. Tax incentives are available to all types of businesses located within a designated zone which employ zone residents, rehabilitate real property or purchase business equipment to be used in the zone. Tax credits, sales tax exemptions and refunds are also available.

Exports

Enterprise Florida offers on-staff multi-language capabilities and are prepared to help businesses open and operate companies in Florida or to engage in trade. A sophisticated and experienced network of financial, trade, transportation, and commercial services, including freight forwarders and the largest number of customs brokers and insurers in the United States, supports the global marketing efforts of the state's business community. A statewide network of world trade centers, bi-national chambers of commerce, and international business associations also can assist companies wishing to explore international business opportunities.

Women and Minorities

Minority Business Development Centers: Offers existing and potential minority entrepreneurs a wide range of free services, from initial counseling on how to start a business to the more complex issues of planning and growth.
Minority Business Advocacy and Assistance Office: Responsible for certifying minority business enterprises to do business with state agencies.
Office of Minority Business Development: Develops statewide initiative to help minority and women-owned businesses prosper in Florida and the global marketplace. Advocates for minority economic development and provides assistance to minority businesses and organizations. Contact: Office of Minority Business Development, 2801 Ponce de Leon Blvd., Suite 700, Coral Gables, FL 33134; 305-569-2654.

Black Business Investment Board: Oversees the state's investment in black business investment corporations, which provide technical assistance and loans to black-owned businesses. For more information, contact Florida Black Business Investment Board, 1711 S. Gadsen St., Tallahassee, Fl 32301; 850-487-4850.

Black Business Investment Corporations: Provides loans, loan guarantees, joint ventures, limited partnerships or any combination thereof. For more information, contact Florida Black Business Investment Board, 1711 S. Gadsen St., Tallahassee, Fl 32301; 850-487-4850.

Black Business Venture Corporation: A vehicle for initiating business acquisitions and engaging in real estate development. Serves a twofold purpose: to provide real and/or commercial office space for Black businesses; and to address the larger community needs such as local employment and retail centers.

Florida Contractors' Cooperative Surety Bond Support and Management Development Program: Assists the African American contractor in developing a relationship with a surety company that is equipped to meet long-term bonding needs of the business.

Georgia

Office of Economic Development
60 Executive Park South, NE, Suite 250
Atlanta, GA 30329-2231
404-679-4940
Fax: 800-736-1155
www.dca.state.ga.us

Business Assistance

Georgia Department of Community Affairs (DCA):
Responsible for state administration of many incentive
programs as well as providing technical assistance
in the area of economic development to local
governments, development authorities, and
private for-profit entities. Provides information
on financing programs and other services
offered by the state government.

DCA maintains a highly skilled and extremely
dedicated graphics and editorial staff to ensure that the information it
gathers is effectively digested and promptly disseminated. Some of the
department's many publications include:
1. *Small Business Resource Guide*: Manual for small business owners
    with useful instruction, organization addresses and telephone
    numbers and resources.
2. *Georgia's Communities-Planning, Growing, Achieving*: Publication
    contains information about various federal, state, and local financing
    programs that benefit businesses located in Georgia.
3. *Economic Development Financing Packet*
4. *Regional Development Center Listing*: List of Georgia's 16 RDCs
    with addresses and telephone numbers.

One-Stop Environmental Permitting: Georgia offers one-stop environmental
permitting through its Department of Natural Resources, Environmental
Protection Division. The state has the full authority of the U.S.
Environmental Protection Agency (EPA) to issue permits that meet
Federal standards, thus allowing a single permit to meet all requirements.

Emissions Credit Banking and Trading System: Companies can buy, sell or
trade credits received for reducing the amount of pollutants it emits
beyond those required by Federal regulations. These credits can be used at

a later time to offset requirements on pollution created by the company's new growth, or could be sold or traded to another company.

Industrial Revenue Bonds: Taxable and tax-exempt industrial revenue bond financing is available through the state or local development authorities at competitive, below-prime rates.

Supplier Choice Power: Georgia companies with electricity demands of 900 kilowatts or higher may choose among competing suppliers, taking advantage of a competitive market. This cost-saving option has been available to Georgia consumers long before deregulation of the industry was even contemplated.

Georgia Secretary of State: First Stop Business Information Center provides the small business owner and the prospective entrepreneur with a central point of information and contacts for state regulatory requirements for opening a business. Contact: Georgia Secretary of State, 214 State Capitol, Atlanta, GA 30334; 404-656-2881; Fax: 404-656-0513; {www.sos.state.ga.us}.

Business Financing

The Employee Incentive Program: A financing program that may be used in conjunction with traditional private financing to carry out economic development projects which will result in employment of moderate and low income persons. Amounts not available.

The Entrepreneurial Development Loan Fund (EDLF): A loan program to facilitate economic development, particularly in targeted Atlanta Project cluster areas by making credit available to small businesses located within those areas, particularly businesses owned by minorities and women. Typically, loans range from a low of $25,000 to a maximum of $100,000; however, smaller amounts and larger amounts may be considered.

Community Home Investment Program (CHIP): Created by the National  Affordable Housing Act of 1990, the Home Investment Partnerships (HOME) Program is the first federally funded block grant designed to address state and local affordable housing concerns with a maximum amount awarded per local government applicant of $200,000.

Lead Safe Homes Demonstration Program: Exists for the purpose of reducing lead-based paint hazards in approximately 475 homes occupied by low and moderate income persons. There is no set amount that each applicant can receive.

Immediate Threat and Danger Program: Funds community development, having a particular urgency because existing conditions pose a serious and immediate threat to the health or welfare of the community. The maximum amount an applicant may receive is $20,000, which shall not exceed half of total project cost.

Local Development Fund: A state funded grant program that provides local governments with matching funds for community improvement projects. The maximum grant amount is $10,000 for single community projects and $20,000 for multi-community projects.

Appalachian Regional Commission (ARC): An economic development program providing matching grant funds to eligible applicants for projects that will benefit the entire 35-county area of Appalachian Georgia.

Appalachian Region Business Development Revolving Loan Fund: A $2.2 million pool that can be used in the Appalachian Region for loans to projects that create or save jobs. The maximum loan amount is $200,000 per qualifying business, or 50% of total project cost, whichever is less. There is no maximum project cost and no minimum loan amount.

Regional Assistance Program (RAP): Grants are available on a competitive basis to local governments, development authorities, and regional development centers for regional industrial parks and similar facilities, regional water and sewer treatment facilities, regional transportation and communication facilities, regional marketing and recruitment programs, and other projects important to regional economic development. Grants will be available up to $250,000 per multi-county or regional economic development implementation project with no minimum match required.

Research and Development Tax Credit: Companies are eligible for a tax credit on research expenses for research conducted within Georgia for any business or headquarters of any such business engaged in manufacturing, warehousing and distribution, processing, telecommunications, tourism, and research and development industries. The credit is 10% of the additional research expense over the base amount and may be carried forward ten years, but may not exceed 50% of the business' net tax liability in any one year.

Small Business Growth Companies Tax Credit: Tax credit is granted for any business or headquarters of any such business engaged in manufacturing, warehousing and distribution, processing, telecommunications, tourism, and research and development industries having a state net taxable income which is 20% or more above that of the preceding year if its net taxable income in each of the two preceding years was also 20% or more. The credit applies to companies whose total tax liability does not exceed $1.5 million.

The Business Improvement Loan Fund (BILF) Program: Designed to encourage the revitalization of targeted business districts in Atlanta, and to support commercial/ industrial development in other eligible areas. Direct loans and loan participation up to $50,000 are available to businesses that are not able to obtain a market rate loan.

The Phoenix Fund: A program created to assist small and medium-sized businesses providing loan amounts from $10,000-$100,000 for construction or renovation of privately-owned commercial buildings, equipment purchases needed to operate a business, and, in some cases, working capital. Contact: Atlanta Development Authority, 230 Peachtree St., Suite 100, Atlanta, GA 30303; 404-568-7000.

Atlanta Export Assistance Center: Provides marketing assistance, a resource center and financial assistance. The professional counseling services

provided by EAC counselors are free of charge. Most market research and trade information is furnished at no cost to the client. Contact: Export Assistance Center, 285 Peachtree Center Ave., Suite 200, Atlanta, GA 30303; 404-657-1964.

The Georgia Procurement Assistance Center: Assists firms in their efforts to do business with the federal government. The Center helps firms solicit bids and locate procurement opportunities with the Department of Defense and area military facilities seeking certain goods and services. Although assistance is given upon request to any firm, the majority of clients are small and disadvantaged businesses. Contact Georgia Tech Economic Development Institute, 208 O'Keefe Bldg., Atlanta, GA 30332; 404-894-6121.

Business Retention and Expansion Process: Provides a process for local governments, chambers and/or development authorities to survey existing industries and identify the perceptions and potential problems of private sector firms concerning issues like future plans, international trade, labor and manpower, local government services, energy requirements, and community linkages.

Surety Bond Guarantee Program: Enables small contractors to obtain the surety bonds necessary to compete for government and non-government contracts.

Tax Incentives

Georgia Employment Tax Credit Program: A tax credit on Georgia income taxes for eligible businesses that create new jobs in counties or "less-developed" census tract areas.

Job Tax Credit: Companies engaged in manufacturing, warehousing and distribution, processing, telecommunications, tourism or research and development that create 25 or more jobs may receive between a $500 and

$2,500-per-job tax credit. Companies that locate in industrial enterprise zones are required to create 10 new jobs to be eligible for this tax credit.

Investment Tax Credit: Taxpayers operating an existing manufacturing or telecommunications facility or telecommunications support facility in Georgia for three years may obtain a 1% credit against their income tax liability when they invest $50,000. That credit increases to 3% for recycling, pollution control and defense conversion activities.

Industrial Enterprise Zones: The City of Atlanta, as authorized under a special provision of Georgia law, has designated two industrial parks as industrial enterprise zones. Companies in both the Atlanta and Southside industrial parks receive 100% freeport on all three classes of inventory and may receive real property tax reduction for up to 25 years. All buildings constructed in these enterprise zones are exempted from local property taxes at levels that begin at 100%. These exemptions decrease in increments of 20% every five years. New businesses in both parks are eligible for a $2,500-per job tax credit for a payroll of ten or more persons.

The Atlanta Empowerment Zone: Businesses which locate in the federally designated City of Atlanta Empowerment Zone and employ residents from this zone are eligible for various federal and state tax incentives, job training benefits and other assistance. A local executive board decides and manages the allocation of federal funds that are channeled through the State of Georgia.

Commercial Enterprise Zone: City of Atlanta offers a commercial enterprise zone designation for office employers applying in portions of the city including the central business district. Substantial property tax relief is possible.

Tax Exemptions

Computer Software: Taxable software includes canned prewritten software and canned software modified for specific applications. All other software is exempt.

Electricity Exemption: Electricity purchased that interacts directly with a product being manufactured is exempt from sales taxes when the total cost of the electricity makes up 50% or more of all the materials used in making the product.

Goods Delivered Out of State: Exemptions are provided for the sale of tangible personal property manufactured or assembled in Georgia for export when delivery is taken outside Georgia; aircraft, watercraft, motor vehicles and other transportation equipment mailed, manufactured or assembled in Georgia, when sold by the manufacturer or assembler by the purchaser within Georgia for the sole purpose of removing the property from this state under its own power when the equipment does not lend itself more reasonably to removal by other means.

Manufacturing Machinery: Tax exemptions are provided for machinery used directly in the manufacture of tangible personal property under two conditions: (1) the machinery is bought to replace or upgrade machinery in an existing manufacturing plant, and (2) the machinery is incorporated as additional machinery for the first time into an existing manufacturing plant. Machinery used directly in the remanufacture of aircraft engines, parts and components on a factory basis may also be exempt from sales and use tax.

Atlanta Economic Development Corporation

Primary Material Handling: Primary material handling equipment purchased for direct use in storage, handling and movement of tangible personal property in a new or expanding warehouse or distribution facility is exempted from sales and use tax when such new facility or expansion is valued at $5 million or more and does not engage in direct retail sales.

Transportation: Exemptions are provided on and for charges made for the transportation of tangible personal property including, but not limited to, charges for accessorial services such as refrigeration, switching, storage and demurrage made in connection with interstate and intrastate transportation of the property.

Exports

The *Atlanta Export Assistance Center* offers the following resources: Marketing Assistance, Resource Center, Financial Assistance, The Atlanta Export Assistance Center combines the export promotion and finance resources of the following eight agencies: U.S. Department of Commerce, U.S. Small Business Administration, The Georgia Department of Agriculture, The Georgia Department of Industry, Trade & Tourism, The Georgia Housing and Finance Authority, Georgia's Institute of Technology's Center for International Standards and Quality, and the Service Corps of Retired Executives.

The *Atlanta Region* houses consulates, trade offices, and Chambers of Commerce for 44 countries. These organizations provide assistance with foreign exporting, importing and investing.

International Trade Data Network (ITDN): A not-for-profit data multiplier, GDITT provides the business community with the timely, detailed market intelligence needed to be competitive in the global arena.

For these programs, contact Atlanta Regional Export Assistance Center, 285 Peachtree Center Avenue,, Suite 200, Atlanta, GA 30303; 404-657-1900; Fax: 404-657-1970.

Women and Minorities

Georgia Minority Subcontractors Tax Credit: Provides for an income tax adjustment on the State Tax Return, to any company which subcontracts with a minority-owned firm to furnish goods, property or services to the State of Georgia. The law allows a corporation, partnership, or individual, in computing Georgia taxable income, to subtract from federal taxable income or federal adjusted gross income, 10% of the amount of qualified payments to minority subcontractors. For more information, contact Small and Minority Business Program, 200 Piedmont Ave., Suite 1304, West Floyd Bldg., Atlanta, GA 30334; 404-656-6315; 800-495-0053.

Atlanta Economic Development Corporation (AEDC): Provides financial and technical assistance to small minority and female owned businesses to expand and/or relocate in the city. In cooperation with local financial institutions and government agencies, it provides a variety of financial aids for business development projects that have corresponding public benefits.

Minority Small Business Resource Organizations: These organizations provide a variety of technical counseling and financial assistance to minority small businesses:

1. *Atlanta Business League*, PO Box 92363, Atlanta, GA 30314; 404-584-8126
2. *Atlanta Public Schools*, Contract Compliance Office, 1631 LaFrance Street, NE, Atlanta, GA 30307;404-371-7129
3. *Business Development Center – NAACP*, 2034 Metropolitan Parkway, SW, Atlanta, GA 30315; 404-768-5755
4. *Department of Commerce*, Minority Business Development Agency (MBDA), Summit Building, Room 1715, 401 West Peachtree Street, NW, Atlanta, GA 30308; 404-730-3300
5. *Small Business Administration*, Minority Small Business Division, 1720 Peachtree Road, NW, Suite 606, Atlanta, GA 30309; 404-347-7416.

Hawaii

Department of Business, Economic Development and Tourism
P.O. Box 2359
Honolulu, HI 96804
No. 1 Capitol District Bldg.
250 S. Hotel Street
Honolulu, HI 96813
808-586-2593
Fax: 808-586-2589
www.hawaii.gov/dbedt/index.html

Business Assistance

Business Resource Center: Assists both new and existing businesses with
information on government permit and license requirements, government
procurement, sources of alternative financing, marketing,
preparing a business plan, and available
entrepreneurship training programs. Access to
statistical, economic and marketing information, as
well as information and services available from other
government sources. Contact Business Resource
Center, Department of Business, Economic
Development and Tourism, No. 1 Capitol District
Bldg., 250 S. Hotel St., 4th Floor, EWA Wing, Honolulu,
HI 96813; 808-586-2423.
Small Business Information Service: Responsible for providing
referrals and information on government licenses, permits and
procurement, funding source, and entrepreneurship training.
Business Services Division: Helps new and existing businesses
with direct business loans, community development projects, information
programs, licensing and permit information and referral, and business
advocacy.
Business Action Center: Provides Hawaii's entrepreneurs with the information,
business forms, licenses and permits they need to make their small
business dreams a reality. Contact: Business Action Center, State
Department of Business, Economic Development and Tourism, 1130 N.
Nimitz Hwy., Suite A-254, Honolulu, HI 96817; 808-586-2545.
Financial Assistance Branch: Administers loan programs.
Business Resource Center: Accurate timely statistical and economic
information for Hawaii. Access to information and services available from
other government sources in the State of Hawaii, nationally and

internationally. 15,000 titles relating to business, government and economic development in the State of Hawaii with an emphasis on statistical information.

Pacific Business Center Program University of Hawaii at Manoa: The Pacific Business Center matches faculty, students, and facilities at the University of Hawaii at Manoa with requests for assistance from businesses and community development organizations in Hawaii and the U.S. territories in the Pacific Islands. Consultation with program staff is free of charge, and after that clients may be assessed a modest consulting fee to pay faculty and students working on individual projects. Contact: Pacific Business Center, College of Business Administration, University of Hawaii at Manoa, 2404 Maile Way, 4th Floor, Honolulu, HI 96822; 808-956-6286.

Alu Like, Inc. offers a wide range of office support services and technical assistance to all individuals regardless of race. The organization  charges a nominal fee, and has several sites. Contact: Alu Like, Business Development Center, 1120 Maunakea St., Suite 271, Honolulu, HI 96817; 808-542-1225.

University of Hawaii Office of Technology Transfer & Economic Development (OTTED) works to involve the University of Hawaii system in economic development support activities for the state. OTTED is responsible for patenting and licensing technologies developed at the University, for funding University-based R&D projects and the development of unique computer applications, and for matching University-based technical, educational and business development resources with the needs of the community.

Hawaii Island Economic Development Board: HIEDB's mission is to facilitate federal resource programs and implement appropriate economic development projects. HIEDB provides valuable information and contacts for area businesses and industries, as well as key liaison to federal, state, county and private sector resources in financing, business planning, permitting, legal advice and other business services. Contact Hawaii Island Economic Development Board, Box 103-281, Hilo, HI 96720; 808-966-5416; Fax: 808-966-6792.

Opportunity Hawaii: Offers information of strategic business advantages to locating Hi-Tech industries in Hawaii. Contact High Technology Development Corporation, 2800 Woodlawn Dr., Suite 10, Honolulu, HI 96822; 888-677-4292; {www.hawaii.htdc.org}.

Employment and Training Fund Program: Business-specific training, upgrade training, new occupational skills training, management skills training, and other similar activities are available to both employers and individuals.

High Technology Development Corporation: Promotes the growth of commercial high-technology industry and assists in promoting hi-tech products and software. Contact High Technology Development Corporation, 2800 Woodlawn Dr., Suite 10, Honolulu, HI 96822; 888-677-4292; {www.hawaii.htdc.org}.

Business Financing

Innovation Loan Program: Controls loans up to $100,000 to start-up companies with innovative projects.

Hawaii Department Of Agriculture Loan Programs:
1. The Agricultural Loan Program is intended to provide financing to "Qualified Farmers" and "New Farmers" engaged in agricultural production of food, feed and fiber. Loans can be made to qualifying sole proprietorships, corporations, partnerships and cooperatives. In addition, qualifying corporations and cooperatives can obtain funding for enterprises engaged in marketing, purchasing, processing and for those who provide certain farm business services.
2. Aquaculture Loan Program: Aquaculture means the production of aquatic plant and animal life in a controlled salt, brackish, or freshwater environment situated on real property. Loans can be made to "Qualified Aquaculturists" organized as sole proprietorships, corporations, cooperatives and partnerships.

For these, contact Department of Agriculture, Agricultural Loan Division, P.O. Box 22159, Honolulu, HI 96823; 808-973-9460; 808-468-4644, ext. 39460.

Hawaii Small Business Innovation Research Grant Program: Its purpose is to expand science and technology-based economic development in Hawaii, increase revenues and quality job opportunities in the State.
1. Federal SBIR Program: Phase I awards determine the feasibility of a new technology and are valued up to $100,000. Phase II awards are a continuation of successful Phase I efforts. Phase II awards typically involve developing a prototype and are valued up to $750,000
2. Hawaii SBIR Matching Grant Program: To encourage Hawaii companies to participate in the program, the High Technology Development Corporation provides a matching grant of up to $25,000 to Hawaii companies that receive Phase I awards

The Rural Economic Transition Assistance: Hawaii (RETA-H) Program provides a limited "window of opportunity" to existing and potential entrepreneurs who would like to take part in the transition of Hawaii's agricultural economy from sugar caned-based monoculture to diversified agriculture and are willing to support the Program's goals. Any individuals, especially displaced sugar workers, and community and agricultural associations with an entrepreneurial spirit, are invited to determine if their ideas are eligible for RETA-H funds. These funds are only available for establishing or expanding businesses which produce, process and/or service agricultural products where funds will ultimately go to establishing former sugar workers as business owners and which will speed the transition toward a diversified agriculture in Hawaii. Most grants are in the range of $50,000 - $200,000.

State of Hawaii Government: May finance exports through its Department of Business, Economic Development & Tourism's Hawaii Capital Loan Program (HCLP). The loan program's objective is to provide standard commercial loans to small businesses unable to get financing from private lenders. With an average loan award amount of $250,000 (maximum $1 million) for terms of up to 20 years, HCLP is available to all SBA- defined small businesses with two bank turndowns. The interest rate is set at a very attractive prime rate minus 1%, which is not to exceed 7.5%.

Hawaii Strategic Development Corporation (HSDC) is a state agency created in 1990 to promote economic development and diversification in conjunction with private enterprise. HSDC has established four venture funds, some of which have new funds in formation. Keo Kea Hawaii is typical of the four funds, which are:

- Keo Kea Hawaii LP (KKH) is a Hawaii Based venture capital limited partnership that invests in start-up, emerging and established companies located in the state of Hawaii with an emphasis on high technology. KKH will purchase up to a maximum of 50% of the limited partnership units offered by each Venture Company, while the other units are purchased by third parties who are not directly involved with the Venture Partnership or the project, nor otherwise directly affiliated with the Venture Partnership or its general partner(s). KKH's maximum commitment is $50,000 per investment and may assist in identifying other investment partners when requested.
- HMS Investments, L. P.
- Hawaii Venture Fund, L. P.
- Tangent Growth Hawaii, L. P.: Mezzanine and Later Stage Fund

Contact: Hawaii Strategic Development Corporation, No. 1 Capitol District Building, 250 South Hotel Street, Suite 503, P.O. Box 2359, Honolulu, HI 96804; 808-587-3829; Fax: 808-587-3832.

Tax Incentives

Hawaii has only two levels of government taxation: state and local.
No personal property tax.
No tax on inventories, furniture, equipment or machinery.

Credit against taxes paid on the purchase of capital goods, machinery, and
　　equipment.
No state tax on goods manufactured for export.
No stock transfer tax: All security exchange transactions are exempt from
　　general excise tax, as an incentive to financial institutions.
No unincorporated business tax.
Banks and financial institutions pay only one business tax.
Manufactured products or those produced for export are exempt from the
　　general excise tax, including custom computer software.
Manufacturers, wholesalers, processors, millers, refiners, packer and canners
　　are taxed on 0.5% of gross proceeds.
Insurance solicitors and agents are taxed at .15 percent.
Contractors are taxed 4% of gross proceeds. All sales of retails goods and
　　services are taxed at 4% of gross income.
Purchase of depreciable and tangible property is allowed with a refundable tax
　　credit against excise and use taxes.
General excise tax exemptions are in effect for air pollution control facilities,
　　certain scientific contracts with the United State, ships used in
　　international trade and commerce, sugar and pineapple manufacturers, and
　　sales of tangible personal property to the federal government.
Enterprise Zones (EZ) Program: A joint state-county effort intended to
　　stimulate--via tax and other incentives--certain types of business activity,
　　job preservation, and job creation in areas where they are most appropriate
　　or most needed. Incentives include 100% exemption from the General
　　Excise Tax (GET) and Use Tax every year. Contractors are also exempt
　　from GET on construction done within an EZ for an EZ-qualified
　　business. An 80% reduction of state income tax the first year. (This
　　reduction goes down 10% each year for 6 more years.) An additional
　　income tax reduction equal to 80% of annual Unemployment Insurance
　　premiums the first year. (This reduction goes down 10% each year for 6
　　more years.)

Exports

*U.S. Department of Commerce-Commercial Service (Honolulu District
　　office):* The trade specialist at the Honolulu District office assists U.S.
　　companies seeking to expand into export markets. The Honolulu District
　　office provides companies with trade leads, foreign market research, and
　　information on trade events, seminars, and conferences.
Foreign Trade Zones: Ports designated for duty-free entry of goods.
　　Merchandise may be stored, displayed, or used for manufacturing within
　　the zone and re-exported without duties being paid. Contact: Foreign
　　Trade Zone #9, 521 Ala Moana, Pier 2, Honolulu, HI 96813; 808-586-
　　2507.

Local Chambers of Commerce: Provide exporters with copies of and instructions for completing a general Certificate of Origin. This certificate is a notarized statement authenticating the country of origin of an export good.

Consulate Generals in Hawaii: Various consulate generals in Hawaii offer limited trade counseling and a few have trade libraries.

Thai Trade Representative Office: Focuses primarily on the promotion of Thailand products in Hawaii.

Women and Minorities

The Honolulu Minority Business Development Center: The objectives of the Honolulu Minority Business Development Center are to 1) promote the creation and/or expansion of viable and competitive minority-owned businesses, 2) increase contracting opportunities from public and private sources for minority-owned businesses, and 3) provide management and technical assistance to qualified minority individuals and firms in the areas of planning, finance, construction assistance, and general management to improve the overall performance, profit, and net worth of minority firms.

Idaho

Idaho Department of Commerce
700 West State Street
P.O. Box 83720
Boise, ID 83720-0093
208-334-2470
Fax: 208-334-2631
www.idoc.state.id.us/pages/businesspage.html

Business Assistance

Economic Development Division: This office can provide information and
expertise in dealing with state, federal, and local agencies. They also
have information on financing programs and other services offered by
the state government.

   Idaho Business Network (IBN): Operated by the Idaho
   Department of Commerce to help Idaho companies bid on federal,
   state and large corporation contracts.

   • *Opportunity Notices*: Every day bid notices on
      federal, state and private contracts are entered into the
      Idaho Business Network computer. These bidding
      opportunities are matched with the capabilities of Idaho
      businesses participating in the IBN. When a match
      occurs the client company is notified with a printed or e-
      mail version "opportunity notice" alerting them to the
      opportunity and providing information needed to obtain
      the bid package.

   • *Military and Federal Standards*: Federal bid packages
   often reference military and federal specifications by name or number
   without providing the actual documents. The Idaho Business
   Network maintains a CD-ROM library of all military and federal
   standards and specifications. Printed copies of required specifications
   and standards are provided at no charge to businesses participating in
   the IBN.

   • *Federal Acquisition Regulations (F.A.R.)*: Contains the rules and
   regulations used by federal agencies to purchase products and
   services. Bid packages often refer to F.A.R. clauses by name or
   number without providing the text of the document. The IBN
   maintains the F.A.R. on CD-ROM, and provides printed copies of
   needed clauses to participating companies at no charge.

- *Trade Missions*: All IBN clients are welcome to attend periodic trade missions to visit large corporations, military sites, and other government agencies. Businesses attending the trade missions have the opportunity to meet with buyers to market their products and services.

- *Workshops and Seminars*: The IBN holds workshops statewide on topics such as selling to Mountain Home Air Force Base, selling to the INEEL, how to package for the military, quality assurance, etc.

- *The Governor's Business Opportunity Conference*: Annually, the IBN hosts the Governor's Business Opportunity Conference with over 60 large private corporations and government agencies sending buyers to meet with representatives of Idaho businesses. Concurrent training workshops are also held during the conference on a wide range of topics, such as introduction to procurement and marketing strategies for small businesses.

- *Electronic Bulletin Board*: Provides computer and modem access to all bid notices obtained by the IBN for the most current ten days.

- *CAGE Code*: All companies wishing to do business with the U.S. Department of Defense must have an identification number known as a Commercial and Government Entity Code, or CAGE Code. Companies applying for a CAGE Code must be sponsored by a government agency. The Idaho Business Network provides CAGE Code application forms and sponsors participating Idaho business applications

- *New Industry Training Program*: Provides customized job training for new and expanding industries.

- *Work Force Training*: Funds are available to provide skilled workers for specific economic opportunities and industrial expansion initiatives.

Business Financing

Revenue Allocation Finance Areas: Any city in Idaho can have established urban renewal areas. New facilities located within designated revenue allocation area boundaries may qualify for tax exempt bonds. Tax revenues from increases in property value within the urban renewal area are dedicated to servicing the bonds. Also known as Tax Increment Financing, these funds can be used to pay for infrastructure development costs of a project.

Industrial Revenue Bonds: Idaho cities and counties are able to form public corporations for the purpose of issuing industrial revenue bonds (IRBs). The IRB program provides for loans of up to $10 million, at tax-exempt interest rates, to finance the improvement or purchase of land, buildings, and machinery or equipment used in manufacturing, production, processing, or assembly.

Rural Economic and Community Development Administration: Offers guarantees up to 90% of loans between $500,000 and $10 million made to small businesses located in areas not within the boundaries of a city of 50,000 or more. Loan proceeds can be used for the purchase, development or improvement of land, buildings and equipment, or a start-up and working capital.

Tax Incentives

Idaho's Investment Tax Credit: Equal to 3% of qualified investment (not to exceed more than 45% of a given year's tax liability) and may be carried forward for seven years.

Nonbusiness-Related Contributions: Corporations are allowed credit for certain nonbusiness-related contributions, e.g., education and rehabilitation. Net operating loss carrybacks are limited to $100,000 per tax year. The $100,000 loss limit may be carried back three years and if it is not absorbed by the income in those three years, the rest of the loss may be carried forward 15 years. Instead of carrying a loss back, a taxpayer may choose to carry the loss forward for up to 15 years or until it has been completely absorbed.

Property Tax Exemptions: Include inventories, livestock, stored property in transit, pollution control facilities, household belongings, clothing, and properly licensed motor or recreational vehicles. Statewide, tax rates vary generally from 0.8 to 2.8 percent, with an average of 1.7 percent.

Excluded from a 5% sales tax: Utilities, motor fuels (which are taxed separately), and tangible personal property used for production activities involved in manufacturing, farming, processing, mining, and fabricating.

Mining Claims: Non-patented mining claims are exempt from property taxation.

Exports

The Idaho Department of Commerce's Division of International Business: Provides a variety of services and assistance to all Idaho firms interested in doing business overseas, with special programs for small- and medium-sized firms.

Idaho International Business Development Center (IIBDC): Seeks to coordinate efforts statewide to promote Idaho in the global marketplace. The division, in partnership with the Boise Branch Office of the U.S. Department of Commerce, maintains regular contact with importers, distributors, wholesalers, and retailers in foreign countries and can supply market data and information on foreign packaging, labeling requirements, language barriers, consumer preferences, and other trade factors.

Idaho Department of Agriculture: Offers a broad range of assistance to Idaho companies which export Idaho agricultural commodities and processed and specialty food products. The Department of Agriculture sponsors many special agricultural trade events and participates with the Department of Commerce in joint seminars, workshops, and trade shows.

Illinois

Department of Commerce and Community Affairs
620 E. Adams
Springfield, IL 62602
217-782-7500
Fax: 217-524-3701
www.commerce.state.il.us

100 West Randolph St.
Suite 3-400
Chicago, IL 60601
312-814-7179
Fax: 312-814-2370

Business Assistance

Department of Commerce and Community Affairs: Provides information, assistance and advocacy to facilitate and advance the economic

development process in partnership with Illinois' communities, businesses, and their network of public and private sector providers.

Small Business Division: Responsible for an environment that supports small business success resulting in increased employment opportunities and prosperous communities throughout Illinois. Provides advocacy, business assistance, training and information resources to help entrepreneurs, small companies and their partners enhance their competitiveness in a global economy. Serves customers through a dynamic, integrated small business assistance delivery system that matches the diversity of their customers' current and future needs.

Business Association Directory: Includes organization mission, location and member information.

Workforce Development & Manufacturing Technology Assistance: Provides programs to assist manufacturers to improve employee job skills and manufacturing efficiency. Labor-Management programs are also available.

First Stop Business Information Center: Provides individuals with comprehensive information on state business permits and licenses, business startup assistance, regulatory guidance, demographic and census data. Guides them through permitting, licensing and regulatory processes. Phone: 800-252-2923.

Procurement Technical Assistance Centers (PTAC): Provide one-on-one
counseling, technical information, marketing assistance and training to
existing Illinois businesses that are interested in selling their products
and/or services to local, state or federal government agencies. The services
are offered through PTACs located at community colleges, universities,
chambers of commerce and business development organizations.

Small Business Innovation Research Centers (SBIRC): Provide counseling,
technical information and training to Illinois entrepreneurs and small
businesses interested in pursuing research and development opportunities
available to them through various federal and state programs. These
programs provide small businesses with a means of developing new and
marketable technologies and innovations and also for enhancing existing
products and services.

Business Financing

*Participation Loan Program, Development Corporation Participation Loan
Program, Minority, Women and Disabled Participation Loan Program*:
Through these loan participation programs, the Illinois Department of
Commerce and Community Affairs (DCCA) helps small businesses obtain
financing through Illinois banks, development corporations, and lending
institutions for business start-up, expansion, modernization and
competitiveness improvement. Generally, the Department may provide
subordinated small business loans up to 25% of the total amount of a
project, but not less than $10,000 or more than $750,000.

Title IX Revolving Loan Fund: Provides low-cost supplemental financing to
small and medium-sized manufacturers located in areas declared eligible
for assistance. Proceeds may be used for the acquisition of land,
buildings, machinery and equipment, building construction or renovations,
and leasehold improvements.

Rural Development Loan Program: Assists businesses in communities with
populations less than 25,000. Proceeds may be used to purchase land,
construct or renovate buildings and purchase machinery and equipment.

Farm Development Authority Programs: 85% guarantee for loans by local
lenders; up to $300,000 for farm owners. Proceeds may be used for land
acquisition, building construction and improvements and the purchase of
machinery and equipment.

State Treasurer's Economic Program: Provides companies with access to
affordable capital to expand their operations and retain or create jobs in
the state. For each permanent full-time job that is created or retained, the
Treasurer can deposit $25,000 at well below market rates into the
borrower's financial institution. That institution will then lend the money
at below prevailing interest rates to the borrower.

Enterprise Zone Financing Program: Designed to encourage businesses to locate within an Illinois Enterprise Zone. DCCA may participate in an eligible loan for no less than $10,000, nor more than $750,000. In no case shall the amount of DCCA's subordinated participation exceed 25% of the total project. Ineligible uses of funds are debt refinancing and contingency funding.

Development Corporation Participation Loan Program: Provides financial assistance through a Development Corporation to small businesses that provide jobs to workers in the region served by the Development Corporation. The state will participate in loans up to 2% of the total amount of a project but not less than $10,000 nor more than $750,000.

Capital Access Program (CAP): Designed to encourage lending institutions to make loans to businesses that do not qualify for conventional financing. CAP is based on a portfolio insurance concept where the borrower and DCCA each contribute a percentage of the loan amount into a reserve fund located at the lender's bank. This reserve fund enables the financial institution to make loans beyond its conventional risk threshold and is available to draw upon to recover losses on loans made under the program.

Technology Venture Investment Program (TVIP): Provides investment capital for young or growing Illinois businesses in cooperation with private investment companies or investors. Program investments will be used for businesses seeking funding for any new process, technique, product or technical device commercially exploitable by Illinois businesses in fields such as health care and biomedical products, information and telecommunications, computing and electronic equipment, manufacturing technology, materials, transportation and aerospace, geoscience, financial and service industries, and agriculture and biotechnology. Program funds shall be used for such costs including, but not limited to, research and development costs, acquisition of assets, working capital, purchase or lease of machinery and/or equipment, and the acquisition and/or improvement or rehabilitation of land and buildings.

Affordable Financing of Public Infrastructure Program: Provides financial assistance to or on behalf of local governments, public entities, medical facilities and public health clinics.

Community Services Block Grant Loan Program: Provides long-term, fixed-rate financing to new or expanding businesses that create jobs and employment opportunities for low-income individuals.

Industrial Training Program: Assists companies in training new workers or upgrading the skills of their existing workers. Grants may be awarded to individual companies, multi-company efforts and intermediary organizations offering multi-company training.

Prairie State 2000 Programs: Businesses that need to retrain employees may utilize these funds. Loans are available to cover 100% of direct training costs. Grants covering 50% of those costs are also available.

Industrial Revenue Bonds: IDFA issues tax-exempt bonds on behalf of manufacturing companies to finance the acquisition of fixed assets such as land, buildings and equipment. Proceeds may also be used for new construction or renovation.

Tax Incentives

No personal income taxes.
Retirement income is not taxed.
Enterprise Zones: Incentives for businesses within a designated Enterprise Zone include:
- Sales tax exemption on building materials to be used in an Enterprise Zone.
- Sales tax exemption on purchases of tangible personal property to be used in the manufacturing or
- Assembly process or in the operation of a pollution control facility within an Enterprise Zone.
- Tax exemption on gas, electricity and the Illinois Commerce Commission's administrative charge is available to business located in Enterprise Zones.
- Tax credit of 0.5% is allowed a taxpayer who invest in qualified property in a Zone.
- Dividend Income Deduction for individual, corporations, trust, and estates are not taxed on dividend income from corporation doing substantially all their business in a Zone.
- Jobs tax credit allows a business a $500 credit on Illinois income tax for each job created in the Zone for which a certified eligible worker is hired.
- Financial institutions are not taxed on the interest received on loans for development within a Zone.
- Businesses may deduct double the value of a cash or in-kind contribution to an approved project of a designated Zone organization form taxable income.

Corporate Income Tax: Corporate income is taxed at 7.3% which includes a 4.8% state income tax and a 2.5% personal property replacement tax.
Incentives include:
- The 2.5% replacement tax may be deducted from the 4.8% state income tax.
- After 2000, apportionment will be based on sales alone.

Tax Credits include:
- 0.5% credit for investment in mining, manufacturing or retailing, plus an additional 0.5% if employment increases over 1%; a 1/6% training expense tax credit; and a 6.5% Research and Development credit.
- There are no local corporate income taxes in Illinois.

Sales Tax Exemptions: Purchases of manufacturing machinery as well as
replacement parts and computers used to control manufacturing
machinery; purchases of farm machinery; pollution controls, building
materials to be used in an Enterprise Zone; and materials consumed in the
manufacturing process in Enterprise Zones. Purchases or manufacturing
machinery receive a credit equal to 50% of what the taxes would have
been if the manufacturing machinery was taxable, making it possible for
the manufacturers to use this credit to offset any other sales tax liability
they incur. Food and drugs are taxed at the reduced rate of 1%.

Property Tax Exemptions: All property other than real estate is exempt from
the property tax. Taxing bodies within Enterprise Zones may abate
property taxes without a dollar limit for the life of the zone.

Exports

International Trade Centers/NAFTA Opportunity Centers (ITC/NOC):
Provide information, counseling and training to existing, new-to-export
Illinois companies interested in pursuing international trade opportunities.
The NOCs provide specialized assistance to those firms seeking to take
advantage of the trade opportunities in Mexico and Canada made possible
by the North American Free Trade Agreement.

Foreign Trade Zones: Offering low-cost production and warehousing facilities
for imported and export-bound products.

Women and Minorities

*Business Enterprise Program for Minorities, Females, and Persons with
Disabilities (BEP)*: Promotes the economic development of businesses
owned by minorities, females, and persons with disabilities.
The Business Enterprise for Minorities, Females, and Persons with
Disabilities Act is designed to encourage state agencies to purchase
needed goods and services from businesses owned and controlled by
members of minority groups, women, and/or persons with disabilities.

Surety Bond Guaranty Program: Designed to provide Illinois' small, minority
and women contractors technical assistance, help them receive experience
in the industry and assist in obtaining bid, performance and payment
bonds for government, public utility and private contracts.

Minority, Women and Disabled Participation Loan Program: (See Business
Financing above) Additional information: The Minority, Women and
Disabled Participation Loan Program guidelines differ, in that the program
funding may not exceed 50% of the project, subject to a maximum of
$50,000.

Indiana

Indiana Department of Commerce
One North Capitol, Suite 700
Indianapolis, IN 46204
317-232-8888
800-463-8081
317-233-5123 Fax
www.ai.org/bdev/index.html

Business Assistance

Indiana Department of Commerce: This office can provide
information and expertise in dealing with state, federal,
and local agencies. They also have information on
financing programs and other services offered by
the state government.

Technical & Marketing Assistance

Quality Initiative: Provides quality-awareness
education, assessments and information to
companies attempting to implement or improve
quality-management programs.

Energy Policy Division Services: A wide range of
assistance in energy efficiency, alternative
energy and recycling market development programs.

Enterprise Advisory Group: Counsels emerging and mature businesses.

Government Marketing Assistance Group: Helps companies that wish to sell
to federal, state or local governments.

Indiana Micro-Electronics Center (IMC): Assists businesses in using
Application Specific Integrated Circuits (ASICs). Contact: Indiana
Business Modernization and Technology corporation, One N. Capitol
Ave., Suite 925, Indianapolis, IN 46204; 317-635-3058.

The Indiana Quality Initiative: Quality-awareness education, assessments and
information. Contact: Indiana Business Modernization and Technology
corporation, One N. Capitol Ave., Suite 925, Indianapolis, IN 46204; 317-
635-3058.

International Trade Services: Assistance to Indiana companies in export
development in order to increase the sale of Indiana products worldwide.

Office of Regulatory Ombudsman: Acts as a mediator, expediter and problem-
solver in areas affecting business.

Government Marketing Assistance Group: Provides counseling to businesses
interested in obtaining federal or state government contracts.

Regional Manufacturing Extension Centers (RMEC): Helps small and
medium-sized businesses assess and solve problems related to technology,
training, marketing and financing. Contact: Indiana Business
Modernization and Technology corporation, One N. Capitol Ave., Suite
925, Indianapolis, IN 46204; 317-635-3058.

Trade Show Assistance Program (TSAP): Provides reimbursement for a
portion of the costs incurred while companies exhibit their products at
overseas trade shows.

Resources

Indiana Development Finance Authority (IDFA): Helps Indiana businesses
obtain financial assistance through loan guaranty programs, tax-exempt
private activity bonds for industrial development, Ex-Im Bank loan
guarantees, insurance and direct loans for export products and flexible
lending through case reserve accounts. Contact: Indiana Development
Finance Authority, One N. Capitol, Suite 320, Indianapolis, IN 46204;
317-233-4332.

Indiana Small Business Development (ISBD) Corporation: Offers
conferences and workshops, one-on-one counseling and up-to-date
information on new market opportunities. The ISBD Corp. also identifies
contracting opportunities with the government, assists growth-oriented
companies in approaching new market opportunities and serves as a
statewide advocate for contracting and marketing with Indiana's women-
and minority-owned businesses. Contact: Indiana Small Business
Development Corp., One N. Capitol, Suite 1275, Indianapolis, IN 46204;
317-264-2820.

Indiana Economic Development Association (IEDA): Provides continuity to a
statewide community development effort. The organization has two
objectives: (1) to utilize the knowledge and resources of the association to
make economic development activities in the state more effective, and (2)
to cooperate and interact with all state and local organizations engaged in
promoting the economic welfare of Indiana. Contact: Indiana Economic
Development Association, One N. Capitol, Indianapolis, IN 46204; 317-
573-2900.

Indiana Economic Development Council (IEDC): Helps to shape long-term
state goals, strategies and policies on economic development matters
through non-partisan planning, evaluation, policy development and
coordination. The role of the IEDC includes providing independent
performance reviews and recommendations relating to governmental
budgets and the economic development support systems of public and
private entities, both state and local. Contact: Indiana Economic

Development Council, One N. Capitol, Suite 425, Indianapolis, IN 46204; 317-631-0871.

Business Financing

Loans

Product Development/Commercialization Funding: Provides loans for businesses in need of financing to support research and development projects, or to support commercialization of new technology. Loan amounts vary.

Capital Access Program (CAP): Helps financial institutions lend money to Indiana businesses that don't qualify for loans under conventional lending policies. CAP loans may be of any amount

Certified Development Companies (CDC): Long-term, fixed-rate financing for a business's fixed-asset needs. CDC provides up to 40% of the cost with a commercial bank financing 50% of the total cost. The CDC portion is limited to $750,000. Minimum project cost is $125,000. Contact: Indiana Statewide Certified Development Corp., 8440 Woodfield Crossing, Suite 315, Indianapolis, IN 46240; 317-469-6166.

Hoosier Development Fund: Loans for small to medium-sized businesses. Loans range from $250,000 to several million dollars.

Indiana Community Business Credit Corporation (ICBCC): Loans for small to medium-sized businesses that exceed banks' customary limits. Loan amounts range from $100,000 to $750,000, and must be at least matched by a participating lender. Minimum project is $200,000. Contact Indiana Community Business Credit Corp., 8440 Woodfield Crossing, Suite 315, Indianapolis, IN 46240; 317-469-9704.

Industrial Development Infrastructure Program (IDIP): Supplemental financing for infrastructure projects in support of job creation/retention for low- to moderate-income persons. Amounts determined based on project needs. The program is designed to supplement local funding sources.

Industrial Development Loan Fund: Revolving loans for industrial growth. Loans up to $1 million are available.

Industrial Energy Efficiency Fund: The Energy Policy Division provides loans for improving energy efficiency in industrial processes. The maximum amount available per applicant is $250,000 or 50% of the total eligible project costs, whichever is less.

Loan Guaranty Programs: Financing for land or building acquisition or improvements, structures, machinery, equipment, facilities and working capital. Loan guaranties are available up to $2 million.

Product Development/Commercialization Funding: Loans for research and development or to support commercialization of new technology. Loan amounts are determined by the Business Modernization and Technology

Corporation (BMT) and the business. Leveraging of outside funds is encouraged in the loan consideration.

Recycling Promotion and Assistance Fund: Loans to enhance the development of markets for recyclable materials.

Small Business Investment Company Program: Long-term and/or venture capital for small firms.

Strategic Development Fund (SDF): Loans or grants for not-for-profits and cities, towns and counties whose purpose is to promote industrial/business development. Generally $100,000 to $500,000, but can vary depending on the particular SBIC.

Trade Finance Program Financing: Assistance for companies exporting internationally. Amounts: Varies with programs.

Grants

Industrial Energy Efficiency Audits: The Energy Policy Division provides grant to manufacturers to study energy use in their facilities and

recommend ways to reduce energy use and energy costs. Maximum amount available per applicant is $5,000.

Alternative Energy Systems Program: The Energy Policy Division offers grants to businesses to fund eligible alternative-fuel technologies and infrastructure development. The maximum amount available per project is $10,000.

Community Development Action Grant (CDAG): Grants to help organizations whose missions include economic development to expand administrative capacity and program development by offsetting miscellaneous expenses. In the case of organizations serving at least two counties, the amount of the grant may not exceed one dollar for every one dollar raised by the organization. The maximum grant award for organizations serving two or more counties may not exceed $75,000. Contact: Community Development Division, Indiana Department of Commerce, One N. Capitol, Suite 600, Indianapolis, IN 46204; 317-232-8911; 800-824-2476.

Industrial Development Grant Fund: Grants for non-profits and local units of government for off-site infrastructure projects in support of new business development. The grant amount is determined based on project needs. However, the program is designed to supplement local funding sources

National Industrial Competitiveness Through Energy, Environment and Economics Grant: The Energy Policy Division has information about Federal grants, with possible state matching funds, to improve energy efficiency, promote a cleaner production process and improve the competitiveness of industry. The maximum amount of federal grant available per applicant is $400,000.

Strategic Development Fund (SDF): Grants or loans for not-for-profits and cities, towns and counties whose purpose is to promote industrial/business development. Grant or loan funds may not exceed 50% of the cost of the project. The maximum grant amount is $250,000. The maximum grant and loan combination may not exceed $500,000.

Tire Recycling Market Development Program: The Energy Policy Division has grants to businesses involved in the production of a product that uses scrap tires as a feedstock. Recycled Tire Product Marketing grants up to $20,000. Recycled Tire Product Procurement grants up to $40,000.

Scrap Tire Market Development Research and Prototype Grant Program: Provides grant to support research on new products or machinery for handling scrap tire recycling. Grant range from $5,000 to $50,000.

Tire-Derived Fuel Testing Grant Program: Provides grants to develop fuel uses for scrap tires. Amount based on project needs.

Trade Show Assistance Program (TSAP): Provides reimbursement for a portion of the costs incurred while companies exhibit their products at overseas trade shows. Reimbursement includes 100% of exhibit space rental or $5,000, whichever is less.

Training 2000: Grants for reimbursement of eligible training costs. Up to 50% of eligible training costs. Awards for retraining have a maximum ceiling of $200,000. For companies seeking to become QS-9000 certified, up to 75% of QS-9000 related costs may be reimbursed.

Bonds

Tax-Exempt Bonds: Provide fixed-asset financing at competitive rates. Limits vary according to the type of project. Most manufacturing facilities are limited to $10 million. Contact: Indiana Development Finance Authority, One N. Capitol, Suite 320, Indianapolis, IN 46204; 317-233-4332.

Tax Increment Financing (TIF): Allows use of TIF revenues for purpose of developing an area. Amounts: Depends on the new property taxes generated as a result of development in the TIF allocation area.

Tax Incentives

Indiana Corporate Income Tax: Taxpayers eligible for state corporate income tax credits apply the value first against gross tax liability, then against corporate adjusted gross tax liability and finally against supplemental net liability. Some credits may be applied against future tax liabilities if the amount of current credit exceeds taxes due.

College and University Contribution Credit: A credit for contributions to Indiana colleges and universities. Limited to the lesser of: (a) $1,000; (b) 50% of the contribution; or (c) 10% of the adjusted gross income tax.

Neighborhood Assistance Credit: Credit to corporate or individual taxpayers contributing to neighborhood organizations or who engage in activities to upgrade disadvantaged areas. Up to 50% of the amount invested, not to exceed $25,000 in any taxable year.

Drug and Alcohol Abuse Credit: Maximum credit is $6,250 for corporations with more than 1,000 employees, and $3,750 for corporations with fewer than 1,000 employees.

Research Expense Credit: Credit to any corporate taxpayer entitled to the Federal Research Expense Credit who incurs qualified Indiana research expenses.

Teacher Summer Employment Credit: Credit to persons who hire a public school teacher during the summer in a position that is relevant to a teaching-shortage area in which the teacher is certified. Limited to the lesser of: (a) $2,500; or (b) 50% of the compensation paid.

Enterprise Zone Employment Expense Credit: A taxpayer who conducts business in an enterprise zone is entitled to a maximum credit of $1,500 for each employee who is an enterprise zone resident and who is employed primarily by the taxpayer.

Enterprise Zone Loan Interest Credit: A credit equal to 5% of the lender interest income from qualified loans made in an enterprise zone.

Enterprise Zone Investment Cost Credit: Credit to individual taxpayers against state tax liability equal to a percentage times the price of qualified investment in an enterprise zone business.

Industrial Recovery Tax Credit: Credit for qualifying investments to rehabilitate vacant industrial facilities ("dinosaurs") that are at least 20 years old and at least 300,000 square feet in size.

Personal Computer Tax Credit: Credit for donations of computer units to the "Buddy-Up with Education Program." A credit of $125 per computer unit is allowed.

Twenty-First Century Scholars Program Support Fund Credit: Credit for contributions to the fund. A maximum credit of the lesser of (a) $1,000; (b) 50% of the contribution made; or (c) 10% of the adjusted gross income tax is available.

Maternity Home Credit: Credit for maternity-home owners who provide a temporary residence for a pregnant woman (women).

Prison Credit: Credit for investments in Indiana prisons to create jobs for prisoners. The amount is limited to 50% of the inventory in a qualified project plus 25% of the wages paid to the inmates. The maximum credit a taxpayer may claim is $100,000 per year.

Property Tax Abatement: Property tax abatement in Indiana is authorized under Indiana Code 6-1.1-12.1 in the form of deductions from assessed valuation. Any property owner in a locally designated Economic

Revitalization Area (ERA) who makes improvements to the real property or installs new manufacturing equipment is eligible for property tax abatement. Land does not qualify for abatement. Used manufacturing equipment can also qualify as long as such equipment is new to the state of Indiana. Equipment not used in direct production, such as office equipment, does not qualify for abatement.

Real-Property Abatement Calculation: Real-property abatement is a declining percentage of the increase in assessed value of the improvement based on one of the three following time periods and percentages as determined by the local governing body.

Enterprise Zones: The purpose of the enterprise zone program in the state of Indiana is to stimulate local community and business

redevelopment in distressed areas. An enterprise zone may consist of up to three contiguous square miles. There are 18 enterprise zones in Indiana. In order to stimulate reinvestment and create jobs within the zones, businesses located within an enterprise zone are eligible for certain tax benefits. These tax benefits include:

- A credit equal to 100% of property-tax liability on inventory.
- Exemption from Indiana Gross Income Tax on the increase in receipts from the base year.
- State Investment Cost Credit (up to 30% of purchase price) for individuals purchasing an ownership interest in an enterprise zone business.
- State Loan Interest Credit on lender interest income (5%) from qualified loans made in an enterprise zone.
- State Employment Expense Credit based on wages paid to qualified zone-resident employees. The credit is the lesser of 10% of the increase in wages paid over the base year, or $1,500 per qualified employee.
- Tax deduction to qualified zone-resident employees equal to the lesser of 50% of their adjusted gross income or $7,500.

Interstate Inventory Tax Exemption: Indiana has a modest inventory tax with a number of deductions available, including the Interstate Inventory Tax Exemption. Finished goods awaiting shipment to out-of-state destinations are usually exempt from the inventory tax. In most instances, a taxpayer may determine the exemption by applying the percentage of that location's total shipments, which went out of state during the previous year.

Industrial Recovery Site (Dinosaur Building): Much like the dinosaurs, many large buildings that were once used for mills, foundries and large manufacturers are obsolete for today's new production methods and technologies. Because of this, these buildings now stand vacant. This program offers special tax benefits to offset the cost of adaptive reuse. Tax benefits are available for 10 years from date of project approval and include the following:

Investment Tax Credit: A credit against the cost of remodeling, repair or betterment of the building or complex of buildings.

Local Option Inventory Tax Credit: A municipality or county has the option of awarding an Inventory Tax Credit to tenants of "dinosaur" buildings.

Maritime Opportunity District: A geographical territory designated at Indiana ports by the Indiana Port Commission. Companies located in a designated district are eligible for tax benefits through the authority of the commission.

Tax Increment Financing (TIF): provides for the temporary allocation to redevelopment or economic districts of increased tax proceeds in an allocation area generated by increases in assessed value. Thus, TIF permits cities, towns or counties to use increased tax revenues stimulated by redevelopment or economic development to pay for the capital improvements needed to induce the redevelopment or economic development. Bond amounts are determined by the size of the project and the amount of the increment available.

Economic Development for a Growing Economy (EDGE): Provides tax credits based on payroll. Individual income tax withholdings for the company's employees can be credited against the company's corporate income tax. Excess withholdings shall be refunded to the company.

Exports

International Trade Services Program: The driving force behind the International Trade Services Program is a group of individuals whose job title is international trade specialist. Many of these people have lived and worked overseas and are proficient with foreign languages. They understand the cultural differences that must be overcome for successful exporting. And they are dedicated to helping Indiana companies -- at no cost -- in the following areas: export assistance, export documentation, foreign buyer visits to Indiana, overseas trade show identification, financial assistance, attendance at overseas trade shows, enrollment of employees in export-related classes/seminars, developing international markets, identification and selection of foreign agents, representatives and distributors, representation of companies at foreign trade shows, provision of economic and political information on other nations.

The Trade Finance Program (TFP): Provides Indiana manufacturers with the tools for export finance. On behalf of Indiana manufacturers and lending institutions, trained representatives at the Indiana Department of Commerce process applications Ex-Im Bank guarantees, loans and export credit insurance. The TFP helps exporters face the challenges of expanding their existing market by becoming more competitive in terms of price, performance, service and delivery by enabling Indiana's exporters to: get paid upon shipment, offer extended credit terms to minimize risk, offer foreign buyers better payment terms.

Available programs
- 90% working-capital loan guarantees, and may be used to purchase finished products, materials, services and labor to produce goods for export.
- Medium- & long-term export guarantees and loans.
- Guarantees provide repayment protection. Loans provide competitive, fixed-rate financing for U.S. export sales.
- Export credit insurance: Protects exporters against political and commercial risk.

Trade Show Assistance Program: Helps small and medium-sized companies realize their full export potential by participating in international trade shows and exhibitions. Financial assistance is available for qualified Indiana exporters who need a little help getting to their trade show of choice. The program also reimburses firms up to $5,000 for booth rental costs at overseas trade shows.

Foreign Trade Zones: Offer great financial incentives for conducting import/export business in the state.

Foreign Trade Zone or Free Trade Zone: An enclosed, secure area that is located outside U.S. Customs territory. A company located within a Foreign Trade Zone does not pay duties or personal property taxes on goods stored within the zone. Foreign and domestic goods may enter a zone to be stored, processed, distributed, manufactured, assembled or exhibited. Benefits to companies located in a Foreign Trade Zone include the following:
- Duty is deferred on imported goods admitted to the zone, thus improving cash flow for the company.
- No U.S. duty is assessed when exporting goods from the zone.
- Processing goods within the zone can eliminate or lower tariffs.
- Duties can be avoided on defective or damaged goods by inspecting and testing imported goods within a zone.
- Savings may be realized in transport insurance.
- Inventory stored in a Foreign Trade Zone is exempt from local property tax.

Contact International Trade Division, Indiana Department of Commerce, One North Capitol, Suite 700, Indianapolis, IN 46204; 317-233-3762.

Women and Minorities

LYNX: A privately owned company established to link capital to minority business opportunities. The fund provides subordinated debt to minority-owned businesses in Marion and surrounding counties. Capital can be provided in the form of equity or debt. Minimum project amount is $75,000. Contact Cambridge Capital Management Corporation, 8440 Woodfield Crossing, Suite 315, Indianapolis, IN 46240; 317-469-3925.

Women and Minorities in Business Group (WMBG): Eligibility: Indiana businesses owned by women and/or minorities. Services/Uses: Counsels emerging and mature businesses. Client needs are determined, evaluated and advised at no cost. Services include: workshops and seminars, direct counseling, information clearinghouse and referral source, general information, including statistics regarding women- and minority-owned businesses, administers Minority Outreach Resource Executive (MORE) Program in six regions. Contact Indiana Small Business Development Corporation (ISBD Corp.), One N. Capital Ave., Suite 1275, Indianapolis, IN 46204; 317-264-2820; 888-ISDB-244; {www.isbdcorp.org/index.htm}.

Minority Outreach Resource Executives (MORE): Extension of WMBG services in Gary, South Bend, Fort Wayne, Indianapolis, Evansville and Jeffersonville. Contact: Indiana Small Business Development Corporation (ISBD Corp.), One N. Capital Ave., Suite 1275, Indianapolis, IN 46204; 317-264-2820; 888-ISDB-244; {www.isbdcorp.org/index.htm}.

Iowa

Department of Economic Development
200 East Grand Ave.
Des Moines, IA 50309-1827
515-242-4700
800-245-IOWA
Fax: 515-242-4809
TTY: 800-735-2942
www.state.ia.us/ided

Business Assistance

Workforce Development Fund: Programs under this fund provide training for new and existing employees and include: Jobs Training, Business Network Training, Targeted Industries Training, Innovative Skills Development.

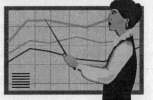

Professional Site Location/Expansion Services, Resources, and Confidential Consultation for Growing Companies: Provides expanding companies with many valuable and unique services, with the end goal of streamlining the site location process. Iowa Department of Economic Development (IDED) confidential services include:

- Working on a confidential basis with companies to determine expansion project needs
- Providing data and information on available buildings, sites and communities
- Coordinating community/site visits
- Packaging appropriate financial assistance and job training programs
- Serving as a liaison with state environmental permitting officials
- IDED Incorporates Information and Technology Into Team Approach

Multimedia Economic Development Information Access system (I-MEDIA): Working in partnership with local economic development groups and utilities, IDED maintains a comprehensive statewide database of community data, available buildings and industrial sites.

Center for Industrial Research and Service: Assists companies with management, production, marketing, engineering, finance, and technology problems and/or contact with resource people, organizations, and agencies

that can help provide solutions, and operates as an industrial arm of
University Extension, Iowa State University. Contact: Center for Industrial
Research and Service, ISU Research Park, 2501 N. Loop Park, Suite 500,
Ames, IA 50010; 515-294-3420; {www.ciras.iast.edu}.

Cooperative Services: Provides free technical assistance to help rural residents
form new cooperative ventures and improve operations of existing
cooperatives. Contact: USDA-Rural Development, 873 Federal Bldg., 210
Walnut St., Des Moines, IA 50309; 515-284-4714.

Manufacturing Technology Center: A resource for small and mid-sized
manufacturers. Helps identify problems and resources, conducts formal
needs assessments, and develops strategic plans. Also assists with
modernizing facilities, upgrading processes, and improving work force
capabilities through the use of effective training and skill development.
Contact: Iowa Manufacturing Technology Center, Advanced Technology
Center, Building 3E, 2006 S. Ankeny Blvd., Ankeny, IA 50021; 515-965-
7125; {www.tecnet.org/iowamtc}.

Procurement Outreach Center: Helps businesses successfully compete for
federal government contracts.

Regulatory Assistance Programs: Provide assistance with environmental
permitting, regulations, and compliance with the EPA Clean Air Act.

University of Northern Iowa/Market Development Program: Provides
customized market research, analysis, and strategic planning services to
existing businesses, primarily manufacturers. Contact: University of
Northern Iowa, College of Business Administration, The Business
Building, Suite 5, Cedar Falls, IA 50614; 319-273-2886.

Virtual Management Assistance Program: Maintains and monitors a
comprehensive, confidential, database system designed to act as a
clearinghouse to foster business-to-business connections by connecting
entrepreneurs with prospective management consultants and/or strategic
alliance partners.

Business Financing

New Jobs Training Program: Provides training funds for companies creating
new jobs, including assistance with screening, skills assessment, testing
and custom-designed training and other training programs. Companies
can be reimbursed up to 50% of new employees' salaries and fringe
benefits during the training period.

Community Economic Betterment Account (CEBA): Provides financial
assistance to companies that create new employment opportunities and/or
retain existing jobs, and make new capital investment in Iowa. The
amount of funding is based, in part, on the number of jobs to be
created/retained. Funds are provided in the form of loans and forgivable

loans. The CEBA program can provide assistance up to $1 million. As an alternative, non-traditional, short-term float loans or interim loans greater than $1 million may be available. The funding level for start-up companies varied depending upon employee wage rates. Assistance through CEBA's "Venture Project" component is provided as an "equity-like" investment, with a maximum award of $100,000.

Economic Development Set-Aside Program (EDSA): Provides financial assistance to companies that create new employment opportunities and/or retain existing jobs, and make new capital investment in Iowa. The amount of funding is based, in part, on the number of jobs to be created/retained. Funds are provided in the form of loans and forgivable loans. The EDSA program can provide assistance up to $500,000.

Entrepreneurs with Disabilities Program: Provides technical and financial assistance to individuals with disabilities who are seeking self-sufficiency by establishing, maintaining, expanding, or acquiring a small business.

Self Employment Loan Program: Offers low-interest loans to low-income entrepreneurs of new or expanding small businesses. Maximum amount is $10,000 with a 5% simple interest rate.

Value-Added Products and Processes Financial Assistance Program (VAAPFAP): Seeks to increase the innovative utilization of Iowa's agricultural commodities. It accomplishes this by investing in the development of new agri-products and new processing technologies. The program includes two components:
- Innovative Products and Processes encourages the processing of agricultural commodities into higher-value products not commonly produced in Iowa, or utilizing a process not commonly used in Iowa to produce new and innovative products from agricultural commodities.
- Renewable Fuels and Co-Products encourages the production of renewable fuels, such as soy diesel and ethanol, and co-products for livestock feed.
  Any single project may apply for up to $900,000 in assistance. Financial assistance is provided in the form of loans and forgivable loans. Generally, assistance of $100,000 or less is provided as a forgivable loan, while larger awards are usually a combination of loans and forgivable loans, with the forgivable portion decreasing as the award size increases.

Small Business Loan Program and Economic Development Loan Program: Provides financing to new and expanding businesses through the sale of tax-exempt bonds. The maximum loan is $10 million.

Link Investments for Tomorrow (LIFT): Assists with rural small business transfer, and horticulture and alternative agricultural crops. Contact: Treasurer of State's Office, Capitol Bldg., 1st Floor, Des Moines, IA 50309; 515-281-3287.

USDA Business and Industrial Loan Guarantee Program: Provides guarantees on loans up to $10 million or more made by private lenders for start-up or expansion purposes to for-profit or non-profit businesses or investors of any size.

Iowa Capital Corporation (ICC): A for-profit venture capital corporation established with funds provided by the state of Iowa and equity investments by Iowa financial institutions, insurance companies and electric utilities. The corporation's primary purpose is to provide an attractive risk-adjusted rate of return on investment to the corporation's shareholders and advance economic development in Iowa. The corporation provides financing for a broad range of business capital needs. Financing may be in the form of equity participation, loans with stock purchase warrants, royalties, etc. and is tailored to the particular business situation. Investments generally range from $50,000 to $1 million, with the average expected to be approximately $250,000.

Rail Economic Development Program: The Iowa Department of Transportation provides funds for construction or rehabilitation of rail spurs to serve new or existing industries. The rail project must be a key to the creation or retention of jobs.

Revitalize Iowa's Sound Economy (RISE)

Revitalize Iowa's Sound Economy (RISE): Administered by the Iowa Department of Transportation for expenditures on city, county and state highways to help attract new development or to support growth with existing developments. Projects are evaluated on economic potential and impact. Funding may be used in conjunction with other sources of federal, state, local and private financing for the purpose of improving area highways and specific access to roads.

Public Facilities Set-Aside Program: Administered by the Iowa Department of Economic Development, provides financial assistance to cities and counties to provide infrastructure improvements for businesses which require such improvements in order to create new job opportunities. The form of assistance is limited to grants to cities under 50,000 population and counties for the provision of or improvements to sanitary sewer systems, water systems, streets and roads, storm sewers, rail lines and airports. Assistance is limited to two-thirds of the total cost of the improvements needed. The emphasis of this program is to increase the productive capacity of the state. Priority will be given to projects that will create manufacturing jobs, add value to Iowa resources and/or export out-of-state.

Tax Increment Financing (TIF): City councils or county boards of supervisors may use the property taxes resulting from the increase in taxable valuation due to construction of new industrial or commercial facilities to provide economic development incentives to a business or industry. Tax increment financing may be used to pay the cost of public improvements and utilities which will serve the new private development, to finance direct grants or loans to a company, or to provide a local match for federal or state economic development assistance programs. TIF does not increase a company's property taxes, but it allocates virtually all of the taxes, which are paid back to the city or county, where they may be spent to benefit the company.

Seed Capital Corporation: Invests in start-up companies that are bringing new products or processes to the marketplace. Generally takes the form of royalty agreements or equity participation.

Venture Capital Resource Fund: A for-profit corporation whose mission is to stimulate economic development and provide an attractive rate of return to shareholders by investing in businesses with significant growth potential.

Tax Incentives

New Jobs and Income Program (NJIP): Provides a package of tax credits and exemptions to businesses making a capital investment of at least $10.38 million and creating 50 or more jobs meeting wage and benefit targets. Qualifying businesses participating in NJIP receive substantial benefits, including:

- A 3% withholding tax credit applied to the company's job training fund, essentially doubling the training funds otherwise available.
- An investment tax credit of up to 10% for use against Iowa's corporate income tax. The credit, based on machinery, equipment, buildings, and improvements, can be carried forward for seven years.
- A 13% research and development activity corporate tax credit may be carried forward or refunded.
- A refund will be paid for Iowa sales, service or use taxes paid to contractors or subcontractors during the construction phase of the project.
- Foreign-owned companies may receive exemptions from land ownership restrictions.
- The local government involved may elect to exempt property tax the improvements to land and buildings for a period not to exceed 20 years. These exemptions can cover all or a portion of the value added by the improvements.

Enterprise Zones: Manufacturers and other businesses expanding or locating in new or existing facilities and creating new jobs in economically distressed areas of Iowa have a new incentive to do so. Businesses expanding or locating in an Enterprise Zone can receive the following benefits:

- Property tax exemptions on all or part of the costs of improvements to land and buildings for up to 10 years.
- An investment tax credit of up to 10% on corporate income taxes for investments on machinery and equipment, new buildings, and improvements to existing buildings.
- Refunds of sales, services, or use taxes paid to contractors or subcontractors during construction.
- A 13% research and development activities credit (refundable) on corporate income taxes.
- Supplemental new jobs training withholding credit of 11/2% of the gross wages. This credit is in addition to, and not in lieu of, the withholding credit of 11/2% authorized for the Iowa New Jobs Training Program.

Supplemental New Jobs Credit From Withholding: This program is designed to create high-quality jobs by doubling the withholding credit for companies participating in the Iowa New Jobs Training Program. Starting wages must be at least the county average or regional average wage, whichever is lower. Eligibility for the credit is based on a one-time determination by the community college of the starting wage.

New Jobs Tax Credit: Businesses entering into an agreement under the state's training program, and which increase workforce by at least 10 percent, may qualify for this credit to their Iowa corporate income tax. This credit is equal to 6% of the state unemployment insurance taxable wage base. The tax credit can be carried forward up to 10 years.

Exempt Sales and Services: 911 surcharge, advertising, aircraft sales, rental and services, agriculture, containers, coupon books and gift certificates, educational, religious or charitable activities, finance charges, food, freight charges, fuel, government entities, green houses, hospitals, industrial machinery and equipment design and installation, industrial machinery, equipment computers, replace parts, insulin, interstate commerce, lease and rental, medical, mobile homes, newspapers, nonprofit organizations, prescription drugs, printers and publishers, prizes, processing, railroads, repair, resale, resales of property connected with a service, transportation, vehicles, vehicle manufacturing.

Exports

Export Trade Assistance Program: Promotes international trade though financial assistance for increased participation in overseas trade shows and trade missions.

Women and Minorities

Targeted Small Business Financial Assistance Program (TSBFAP):
Designed to assist in the creation and expansion of Iowa small businesses that have an annual gross sales of $3 million and are at least 51% owned, operated and managed by women, minorities or persons with a disability. The business must be certified as a "Targeted Small Business" by the Iowa Department of Inspections and Appeals before applying for or receiving TSB funds. Awards may be obtained in one of the following forms of assistance:

- Low-interest loans - Loans of up to $25,000 may be provided at interest rates of 0-5 percent, to be repaid in monthly installments over a five- to seven-year period. The first installment can be deferred for three months for a start-up business and one month for an existing business.
- Loan guarantees are available up to $40,000. Loan guarantees can cover up to 75% of a loan obtained from a bank or other conventional lender. The interest rate is at the discretion of the lender.
- In limited cases, equity grants - to be used to leverage other financing (SBA or conventional) - are available in amounts of up to $25,000.
- TSB funds may be used to purchase equipment, acquire inventory, provide operating capital or to leverage additional funding.

Self-Employment Loan Program (SELP): This program is designed to assist in the creation and expansion of businesses owned, operated and managed by women, minorities, or persons with a disability. To qualify for a SELP loan, applicants must have an annualized family income that does not exceed current income guidelines for the program. An applicant is automatically eligible for SELP if he or she is receiving Family Investment Plan (FIP) assistance or other general assistance such as disability benefits. The applicant can also qualify for SELP funds if determined eligible under the Job Training Partnership Act, or is certified as having a disability under standards established by the Iowa Department of Education, Division of Vocational Rehabilitation Services. SELP loans of up to $10,000 are available. The interest rate is 5 percent, and the loan is to be repaid in monthly installments over a five-year period. The first installment can be deferred for three months for a start-up business and one month for an existing business.

Entrepreneurs With Disabilities (EWD): Helps qualified individuals with disabilities establish, acquire, maintain or expand a small business by providing technical and financial assistance. To be eligible for the program, applicants must be active clients of the Iowa Department of Education Division of Vocational Rehabilitation Services or the Iowa Department for the Blind. Technical Assistance grants of up to $10,000

may be used to pay for any specific business-related consulting service such as developing a feasibility study or business plan, or accounting and legal services. Financial Assistance grants of up to $10,000 may be used to purchase equipment, supplies, rent or other start-up, expansion or acquisition costs identified in an approved business plan. Total financial assistance provided to an individual may not exceed 50% (maximum of $10,000) of the financial package. EWD financial assistance must be fully matched by funding from other sources.

Institute of Social and Economic Development: Focuses on minorities, women, persons with disabilities and low-income individuals. Encourages self-sufficiency through the growth of small business and self-employment opportunities, and provides services for any person who wants to start or expand a business employing up to five employees, including the owner(s). Contact Institute of Social and Economic Development, 1901 Broadway, Suite 313, Iowa City, IA 52240; 319-338-2331; Fax: 319-338-5824.

Kansas

Department of Commerce and Housing
700 SW Harrison Street, Suite 1300
Topeka, KS 66603-3712
785-296-5298
Fax: 785-296-3490
TTY: 785-296-3487
www.kansascommerce.com

Business Assistance

First-Stop Clearinghouse: A one-stop Clearinghouse for general information.
It also provides the necessary state applications required by agencies
which license, regulate and tax business, and furnishes
information about starting or expanding a business.

From the Land of Kansas Trademark Program: Offers
marketing opportunities for Kansas produced
food, arts, crafts, and plants.

Agricultural Value Added Center: Identifies new
technologies and assists companies in
commercialization efforts. Both food/feed
and industrial related projects are potential
candidates for assistance.

Kansas Match: Promotes economic growth in the state
by matching Kansas manufacturers who are currently
buying products from outside Kansas with Kansas
suppliers of those same products. The benefit to the
buyer includes reductions in freight,
warehousing, and communication costs.

Business First: Drawing from the existing KDOC&H business retention and
expansion instrument, this new survey software program assists
communities of any size in establishing a customized local retention and
expansion program.

Business Retention & Expansion Program: Offered to Kansas communities
and counties who wish to sustain existing industry, support its
modernization and competitiveness, foster its expansion and provide an
environment that encourages new industry creation and recruitment. The
Department works with community leaders and volunteers to conduct on-
site surveys of local businesses. The information gathered is then analyzed
and the results are used to solve immediate short-term problems, as well as
to develop long-term local retention and expansion strategies.

Partnership Fund: Provides financial assistance to Kansas cities and counties by making low-interest loans for infrastructure projects needed to encourage and assist in the creation of new jobs either through the relocation of new businesses or the expansion of existing businesses.

Industrial Training Program (KIT): Provides training assistance primarily to manufacturing, distribution and regional or national service firms in the process of adding five or more new jobs to a new or existing Kansas facility. KIT will pay the negotiated cost of pre-employment, on-the-job and classroom training expenses that include instructor salaries, travel expenses, minor equipment, training aids, supplies and materials, and curriculum planning and development.

Industrial Retraining Program (KIR): Provides retraining assistance to employees of restructuring industries who are likely to be displaced because of obsolete or inadequate job skills and knowledge.

Publications

The Kansas Department of Commerce & Housing (KDOC&H) distributes a variety of publications to help Kansas residents, businesses and visitors find the information needed about their state. Here are a few:

Data Book: The information found in the *Data Book* gives a good idea of what Kansas has to offer new and expanding businesses. The book is filled with information about the Kansas economy, labor and workforce training. It briefly describes taxes and incentives for new and expanding businesses. It also includes sections on finance, technology and education, markets and transportation, and the environment.

The Kansas Aerospace Directory: A complete resource for aircraft production, parts, equipment, research and development, etc. *Directory* includes a wide range of aviation products and companies.

Kansas Agribusiness Directory: A complete resource for agriculture-related business, the *Kansas Agribusiness Directory* offers assistance in contacting any firm or business as well as finding specialized products or services.

Steps to Success: A Guide to Starting a Business in Kansas: Created to give entrepreneurs and small business owners all the information needed on licenses, forms, rules and regulations required by State agencies. It discusses the aspects of business development including finance, incentives and taxation. Plus, it has referrals to programs such as Small Business Development Centers, development companies, the Kansas Technology Enterprise Corporation, Inc. and the Small Business Administration.

Business Financing

Venture Capital & Seed Capital Programs: Instituted to increase the availability of risk capital in Kansas. These programs make use of income tax credits to encourage investment in venture and seed capital pools as a source of early stage financing for small businesses. Businesses demonstrating strong growth potential but lacking the financial strength to obtain conventional financing are the most likely candidates for risk capital funding. The Business Development Division has in operation and continues to develop a network of venture capital resources to assist qualified small businesses in locating potential sources of venture capital financing.

INVESTMENTS IN MAJOR PROJECTS AND COMPREHENSIVE TRAINING (IMPACT)

Economic Opportunity Initiatives Fund (KEOIF): A funding mechanism to address the creation/retention of jobs presented by unique opportunities or emergencies. The fund has a higher level of flexibility than do many of the other state financing programs and allows the State to participate as a funding source when other options have been exhausted.

Existing Industry Expansion Program (KEIEP): Performance based, with a focus on the expansion/ retention of jobs that are associated with the activities of existing firms.

Investments In Major Projects And Comprehensive Training (IMPACT): A funding mechanism designed to respond to the training and capital requirements of major business expansions and locations in the state. SKILL (State of Kansas Investments in Lifelong Learning) funds may be used to pay for expenses related to training a new work force. MPI (Major Project Investment) funds may be used for other expenses related to the project such as the purchase or relocation of equipment, labor recruitment, or building costs. Individual bond size may not exceed 90% of the withholding taxes received from the new jobs over a 10-year period.

Network of Certified Development Companies: Provides financial packaging services to businesses, utilizing state, Small Business Administration, and private financial sources. The state provides supplemental funding to these organizations in recognition of the service they provide.

Private Activity Bonds (PABs): Tax-exempt bonds (IRBs) for facility and equipment financing for qualifying manufacturers and processors. The reduced financing costs generated through these bonds are passed through to the company.

Training Equipment Grants: Provide area technical schools and community colleges an opportunity to acquire instructional equipment to train or retrain Kansas workers.

Kansas Job Training Partnership Act (JTPA): Primarily targeted toward economically disadvantaged workers, dislocated workers, and workers facing severe barriers to employment. JTPA can reimburse a company for up to 50% of the employee's wages during training. JTPA may be used together with the KIT or IMPACT programs.

Tax Incentives

Enterprise Zone Act: Establishes a non-metropolitan regional business incentive program and provides for business expansion and development incentives on a statewide basis. Businesses throughout the state may be eligible for 1) a Sales Tax Exemption on the personal property, materials, and services associated with the project; 2) a Job Creation Tax Credit; and 3) an Investment Tax Credit. Tax credits may be used to offset up to 100% of the business' annual Kansas income tax liability. Unused credits may be carried forward indefinitely.

High Performance Incentive Program (HPIP): Provides incentives to qualified companies which make significant investment in employee training and pay higher than average wages. Incentives include 1) a Sales Tax Exemption; 2) a potentially substantial Training Tax Credit; 3) a generous Investment Tax Credit; and 4) priority consideration for other business assistance programs. Tax credits may be used to offset 100% of the business' annual Kansas income tax liability. Unused credits may be carried forward and must be used within a 10-year time frame.

Tax Exemptions In Connection With The Usage Of Industrial Revenue Bonds: Property financed with the proceeds of an IRB issue can be exempt from property taxation for a period of 10 years. In addition, the cost of building materials and permanently installed equipment are exempt from state and local taxes.

Property Tax Exemptions: Can be made available by the governing body of a city or county for up to ten years. The exemptions apply to land, building, machinery and equipment for new or expanding businesses.

Sales Tax Exemption On Manufacturing Machinery & Equipment: Manufacturing machinery and equipment used directly and primarily for the purposes of manufacturing, assembling, processing, finishing, storing, warehousing, or distributing articles of tangible personal property intended for resale are exempt from sales tax.

Research & Development Tax Credits: May be claimed at 6.5% of the amount which exceeds the business' average R&D expenditures during the preceding three years. A maximum of 25% of the total credits may be used in any given year and unused credits may be carried forward indefinitely.

Child Day Care Tax Credits: Available to businesses that pay for, or provide, child day care services to their employees. The credit is 30% of the annual cost of providing the service, not to exceed $30,000 total credit. A credit of up to 50%, not to exceed $45,000, may be earned during the first year on the costs of establishing a child day care facility. Multiple taxpayers may work together to establish such a facility.

Venture Capital Tax Credit: Designed to encourage cash investments in certified Kansas venture capital companies. Tax credit is equal to 25% of the taxpayer's cash investment in a venture capital firm in the year in which the investment is made.

Local Seed Capital Pool Tax: Designed to encourage cash investments in certified local seed capital pools. Credit is equal to 25% of the taxpayer's cash investment.

Job Expansion And Investment Tax Credit Act Of 1976: Allows an income tax credit for a period of 10 years, up to 50% of a business' Kansas income tax liability. The Job Expansion Tax Credit is $100 for each qualified business facility employee. The Investment Tax Credit is $100 for each $100,000 in qualified investment.

Economic Development Tax Abatement Assistance Program: Provides technical application assistance as well as consulting services to companies and communities applying for economic development and/or industrial revenue bond (IRB) tax exemptions. The Assistance Program serves as liaison between the applicant and the Board of Tax Appeals to ensure quality service and enhance approval success.

Exports

Export Loan Guarantee Program: Allows financial institutions to provide working capital loans to help Kansas companies pay for costs associated with an export transaction. The guarantee protects the financial institution against exporter non-performance risk. In addition to significantly reducing a lender's risk on an export loan, expertise available through the Kansas Export Finance Program can assist a lender in the area of international trade.

Kansas Export Financing Program: Allows the state to enter into agreements with Kansas exporters and financial institutions, and other public and private agencies to provide guarantees, insurance, reinsurance, and coinsurance for commercial pre-export and post-export credit risks.

Kansas Trade Show Assistance Program: Allows a Kansas company to receive a reimbursement of up to 50% of their international trade show expenses to a maximum of $3,500 per show and $7,000 per state fiscal year.

Foreign Trade Zones: Provide a duty-free and quota-free entry point for foreign goods into specific areas under customs' supervision for an unlimited period of time.

Kansas International Trade Resource Directory: A complete resource for anyone needing assistance in exporting goods to foreign countries and to other states. The guide offers a comprehensive listing of government agencies. It lists the state's six regent universities and the international trade services and information provided by each. It also lists international law firms, bankers, consultants and freight forwarders/ customhouse brokers. Also, it lists foreign consulates, U.S. Embassies, international telephone country and city codes, metric conversion tables and a complete glossary of terms used in international trade.

Women and Minorities

Office of Minority & Women Business Development: Promotes and assists in the development of minority-owned and women-owned businesses in Kansas. The program provides assistance in procurement and contracting, financing resources, business planning, and identification of business opportunities. A directory of minority-owned and women-owned businesses in Kansas is published annually.

Single Source Certification Program: Responsible for certifying minority-and-women-owned businesses as small disadvantaged businesses for non-highway related firms.

Kentucky

Kentucky Cabinet for Economic Development
2300 Capital Plaza Tower
500 Mero Street
Frankfort, KY 40601
502-564-7670
800-626-2930
www.thinkkentucky.com

Business Assistance

Kentucky Cabinet for Economic Development: The Cabinet is the primary state agency responsible for creating new jobs and new investment in the state.

- Job Recruitment, Placement And Training: Provides a package of time-and cost-saving employee recruiting and placement services to Kentucky employers, at no cost to either employers or employees.
- Industrial Location Assistance: Provides a comprehensive package of assistance to large manufacturing, services, and administrative facilities, both before and after their location in Kentucky.

Business Information Clearinghouse: Provides new and existing businesses a centralized information source on business regulations, licenses, permits, and other business assistance programs. Call 800-626-2250.

Business Financing

Kentucky Economic Development Finance Authority (KEDFA): Provides business loans to supplement other financing. KEDFA provides loan funds at below market interest rates. The loans are available for fixed asset financing (land, buildings, and equipment) for business startup, locations, and expansions that create new jobs in Kentucky or have a significant impact on the economic growth of a community. The loans must be used to finance projects in agribusiness, tourism, industrial ventures, or the service industry. KEDFA may participate in the financing of qualified projects with a secured loan for up to $10,000 per new job created, not to exceed 25% of a project's fixed asset cost. The maximum loan amount is $500,000 and the minimum is $25,000. Small businesses with projects of less than $100,000 may receive loans on fixed assets for up to 45% of the project costs if enough jobs are created. Interest rates are fixed for the life of the loan, and are determined by the length of the loan term.

KEDFA Direct Loan Program: Offers a loan program to work in conjunction with private financing. The program is designed to allow businesses to obtain the long term financing needed to encourage growth. Maximum loan amount is $500,000. Minimum amount is $25,000.

Commonwealth Small Business Development Corporation (CSBDC): Works with state and local economic development organizations, banks, and the SBA to achieve community economic development through job creation and retention by providing long-term fixed asset financing to small business concerns. The CSBDC can lend a maximum of 40% of project cost or $750,000 per project (in certain circumstances $1,000,000).

Linked Deposit Program: Provides loans up to $50,000 for small business and agribusiness. Credit decisions are the responsibility of the lender making the loan. The state will purchase certificates of deposit from participating lenders through the State Investment Commission, at the New York Prime interest rate less four percent, but never less than 2%.

Local Financial Assistance: Several local governments and area development districts offer loans and other financial incentives for economic development projects. The levels and terms of financial assistance provided generally are negotiable, and are based upon the availability of funds, jobs created, economic viability of the project, and other locally determined criteria.

Bluegrass State Skills Corporation (BSSC): An independent dejure corporation within the Cabinet for Economic Development, provides grants for customized skills training of workers for new, expanding and existing industries in Kentucky.

Industrial Revenue Bonds (IRB): Can be used to finance manufacturing projects and their warehousing areas, major transportation and communication facilities, most health care facilities, and mineral extraction and processing projects.

Utility Incentive Rates: Electric and gas utility companies regulated by the Kentucky Public Service Commission (excluding municipal systems) can offer economic incentive rates for certain large industrial and commercial customers.

Kentucky Investment Fund (Venture Capital): Encourages venture capital investment by certifying privately operated venture funds, thereby entitling their investors to tax credits equal to 0% of their capital contributions to the fund.

Kentucky Tourism Development Act: Provides financial incentives to qualifying tourism projects. Tourism projects are defined as a cultural or historical site, recreation or entertainment facility, or area of natural phenomenon or scenic beauty.

Local Government Economic Development Fund: Grants are made to eligible counties for specific project that enable the counties to provide infrastructure to incoming and expanding business and industry.

Job Development Incentive Grant Program: Grants are made to eligible counties from their coal severance accounts for the purpose of encouraging job development. The grant amount cannot exceed $5,000 per job created.

Tax Incentives

Kentucky Industrial Development Act (KIDA): Investments in new and expanding manufacturing projects may qualify for tax credits. Companies that create at least 15 new full-time jobs and invest at least $500,000 in projects approved under KIDA may receive state income tax credits for up to 100% of annual debt service costs (principal and interest) for up to 10 years on land, buildings, site development, building fixtures and equipment used in a project, or the company may collect a job assessment fee of 2% of the gross wages of each employee whose job is created by the approved project and who is subject to Kentucky income taxes.

Kentucky Rural Economic Development Act (KREDA): Larger tax credits are available for new and expanding manufacturing projects that create at least 15 new full time jobs in counties with unemployment rates higher than the state average in each of the five preceding calendar years and invest at least $500,000.

Kentucky Jobs Development Act (KJDA): Service and technology related companies that invest in new and expanded non-manufacturing, non-retail projects that provide at least 75% of their services to users located outside of Kentucky, and that create new jobs for at least 25 full-time Kentucky residents may qualify for tax credits.

Kentucky Industrial Revitalization Act (KIRA): Investments in the rehabilitation of manufacturing operations that are in imminent danger of permanently closing or that have closed temporarily may qualify for tax credits. Companies that save or create 25 jobs in projects approved under KIRA may receive state income tax credits and job assessment fees for up to 10 years limited to 50% of the costs of the rehabilitation or construction of buildings and the reoutfitting or purchasing of machinery and equipment.

Other Income Tax Credit:
- A credit of $100 is allowed for each unemployed person hired for at least 180 consecutive days.
- Credits are allowed for up to 50% of the installed costs of equipment used exclusively to recycle or compost business or consumer wastes (excluding secondary and demolition wastes) and machinery used exclusively to manufacture products substantially from recycled waste materials.
- A credit is allowed for up to 4.5% of the value of Kentucky coal (excluding transportation costs) used for industrial heating or processing.

Kentucky Enterprise Zone Program: State and local tax incentives are offered to businesses located or locating in zones, and some regulations are eased to make development in the area more attractive. A zone remains in effect for 20 years after the date of designation.

Tourism Sales Tax Credit: Approved new or expanding tourism attractions will be eligible for a sales tax credit against sales tax generated by visitors to the attraction.

Property Tax Exemptions: Manufacturing machinery, pollution control facilities, raw materials and work in process, tangible personal property in foreign trade zones.

Favorable Tax Treatments: Available for finished goods in a transit status, private leasehold interest in property owned and financed by a governmental unit through industrial revenue bonds.

Sales Tax Exemptions: Machinery for new and expanded industry, raw materials, supplies used directly in manufacturing, industrial tools, energy and energy-producing fuels used in manufacturing, industrial processing, mining or refining, pollution control equipment and facilities, fee processor or contract manufacturers that do not take title to the tangible personal property that is incorporated into a manufactured product for raw materials, supplies and industrial tools directly used in the manufacturing process, containers, packaging and wrapping materials, equipment used to collect, separate, compress, bale, shred or handle waste materials for recycling, customized computer programs, gross receipts from the sales of newspaper inserts or catalogs purchased for storage, use, or other consumption outside this state, motor fuels for highway use, motor vehicles, trailers, and semi-trailers registered for highway use, locomotives, rolling stock, supplies, and fuels used by railroad in interstate commerce, air carriers, parts and supplies used for interstate passenger or freight services, marine vessels, and supplies, farm machinery, livestock, feed, seed, fertilizer, motion picture production companies.

Exports

Kentucky International Trade Office: The Office offers the following services:
- Export Consulting
- Export Marketing
- Education and Training
- Overseas Offices
- International Trade Directory
- Kentucky Export Guide

Louisiana

Department of Economic Development
P.O. Box 94185
Baton Rouge, LA 70804
225-342-6000
225-342-5388
www.lded.state.la.us

Business Assistance

Economically Disadvantaged Business Development Division:
Division was created to assist businesses owned by
economically disadvantaged individuals. It offers
Development Assistance Program where a preliminary
assessment analysis of a business is conducted;
Mentor-Protégé Program; Recognition Program; Small
Business Bonding Program; and more. Contact:
Division for Economically Disadvantaged Business
Development, 339 Florida Blvd., Suite 212, P.O. Box 44153, Baton
Rouge, LA 70804; 225-342-5373.

Quality jobs: Provides an annual refundable credit of up to 5% of payroll for a
period of up to 10 years for qualifying companies.

Cost-free training: Louisiana's QuickStart Training Program utilizes the state's
vocational-technical institutes to provide cost-free pre-employment
training customized to a company's requirements. The Jobs Training
Partnership Act Program can help a company find trainees and will also
pay a portion of their wages while they are in training.

Workforce development and training: Develops and provides customized pre-
employment and workforce upgrade training to existing and prospective
Louisiana businesses.

Business Matchmakers: Seeks to pair small and medium-sized suppliers in the
state with larger companies which are currently making purchases out of
state.

Business Financing

Small Business Loan Program: Provides loan guarantees and participations to
banks in order to facilitate capital accessibility for businesses. Guarantees
may range up to 75% of the loan amount, not to exceed a maximum of
$1.5 million. Loan participations of up to 40% are also available.

Applicants must have a business plan and a bank that is willing to fund the loan.

Business Linked Deposit Program: Provides for a 1% to 4% interest rate reduction on a maximum of $200,000 for a maximum of 2 to 5 years on term loans that are funded by banks to Louisiana businesses. Job creation, statistical area employment, and cash flow requirements for underwriting are all criteria, which will effect the percentage and term of the linked deposit.

Micro Loan Program: Provides loan guarantees and participations to banks that fund loans ranging from $5,000 to $50,000 to Louisiana small businesses.

Contract Loan Program: Intended to provide a loan participation and guarantee to a bank for government contract loans. These loans are intended to help businesses finance working capital for contracts with local, state, or federal government agencies. Loans may range from $5000 to $1,000,000 and must be for terms of one year or less.

Exim Bank City/State Program: LEDC has a relationship with the U.S. Export-Import Bank in Washington, DC Under this program, LEDC facilitates export working capital loans for small Louisiana businesses.

Venture Capital Match Program

Venture Capital Match Program: Provides for a match investment for Louisiana venture capital funds. The fund must have at least $5 million of private investment for which LEDC may provide $5 million.

Venture Capital Co-Investment Program: Provides for a co-investment in a Louisiana business of up to 1/4 of the round of investment, but not more than $500,000, with any qualified venture capital fund with at least $7.5 million in private capital. The venture capital fund may be from outside of Louisiana.

BIDCO Investment Program: Provides for a match or co-investment in certified BIDCOs. BIDCOs are state-chartered, non-depository alternative financing sources for small businesses. BIDCOs frequently provide equity and subordinated debt financing to new and growing companies, as well as to companies requiring turnaround assistance. A BIDCO must have at least $2 million in private capital. LEDC may match the investment $1.00 for $2.00 of private capital up to $2.5 million. Co-investments are considered on a project by project basis and cannot exceed 33% of the total investment.

Specialty BIDCO Investment Program: Provides for a match or co-investment in certified Specialty BIDCOs. Specialty BIDCOs are BIDCOs established with a particular focus on assisting disadvantaged businesses and businesses located in impoverished and economically disadvantaged areas. The BIDCO must have at least $250,000 in private capital. LEDC may match the investment $1.00 for every $1.00 of private capital up to $2.5 million. Co-investments are considered on a project by project basis and cannot exceed 50% of the total investment.

Small Business Bonding Assistance Program: The primary goal of this program is to aid certified Economically Disadvantaged Businesses (EDBs) in acquiring quality bid, performance, and payment bonds at reasonable rates from surety companies. EDBs receive help reaching required bonding capacity for specific projects. Contractors often do not reach these levels on their own due to balance sheet deficiencies and a lack of adequate managerial and technical skills. After certification by the Division and accreditation by LCAI, contractors are eligible to receive bond guarantee assistance to be used as collateral when seeking bonds. The Division will issue a letter of credit to the surety for an amount up to 25% of the base contract amount or $200,000.

Economic Development Award: Provides financial incentives in the form of linked deposit loans, loan guarantees and grants to industrial or business development projects that promote economic development and that require state assistance for basic infrastructure development.

All of the above financing programs are available through Louisiana Economic Development Corporation, P.O. Box 44153, Baton Rouge, LA 70804; 225-342-5675.

Tax Incentives

Industrial property tax exemption: Exempts any manufacturing establishment entering Louisiana or any manufacturing establishment expanding its existing Louisiana facility from state, parish, and local property taxes for a period of up to ten years.

Enterprise zone: Provides a tax credit of $2,500 for each net new job created in specially designated areas. Also provides for a rebate of state sales/use taxes on building materials and operating equipment. Local sales/use taxes may also be rebated. Credits can be used to satisfy state corporate income and franchise tax obligations.

Restoration tax abatement: Encourages restoration of buildings in special districts by abating Ad Valorem taxes on improvements to the structure for up to ten years

Inventory tax credit: Provides tax credits against state corporate income and franchise tax obligations for the full amount of inventory taxes paid. When credits are in excess of tax obligations, a cash refund is made.

Exports

Freeport law: Cargoes in transit are exempt from taxation as long as they are kept intact within their smallest original shipping container. Most manufacturers can bring raw materials into the state without paying taxes on them until they are placed in the manufacturing process.

Foreign trade zones: Louisiana's six Foreign Trade Zones (FTZ) make it possible to import materials and components into the U.S. without paying duties until they enter the U.S. market. Goods shipped out of the country from FTZs are duty-free. Contact: International Trade Division, 101 France St., Baton Rouge, LA 70802; 225-342-4320.

Women and Minorities

Minority Venture Capital Match Program: Provides for a match investment for qualified minority venture capital funds. The fund must have at least $250,000 of private investment for which LEDC may invest $1.00 for every $2.00 of private capital up to $5 million.

Maine

Office of Business Development
Department of Economic and Community Development
59 State House Station
Augusta, ME 04333
207-287-3153
Fax: 207-287-5701
TTY: 207-287-2656
www.econdevmaine.com

Business Assistance

Small Business Energy Conservation Program: This program provides small
businesses with free energy audits, conservation recommendations and
low-interest loans for the purpose of energy conservation.

Business Answers: Maine's toll-free business information hotline provides
rapid responses to questions about doing business in Maine. Call 800-872-
3838.

One-Stop Business License Center: This
central clearinghouse for state regulatory
information helps simplify the process of
complying with state business regulations.
Callers may request business license and permit
applications, as well as information on state
regulations.

Business Answers/Small Business Advocate: Serves as a central clearinghouse
of information regarding business assistance programs and services
available to state businesses. Also helps small businesses resolve
problems they may be experiencing with state regulatory agencies.

Plus 1 Campaign: This program represents Maine's long-term strategy to foster
small business growth and remove barriers to business development.
Among the program's initiatives are the $5-million Small Enterprise
Growth Fund and the $6-million Agricultural Marketing Loan Fund
administered by FAME. In addition, financing packages for hardware and
software acquisitions which help businesses go online are available under
the Plus 1 Computer Loan Program. For more information, visit the Plus 1
Web site at {www.mainebusiness.com/ plus1}.

Maine Products Marketing Program: Provides marketing assistance to
producers of Maine-made consumer goods. Members of the program
promote their message of Maine quality through the use of product tags
and labels, literature and package design, which carry the unified theme,

"Maine Made America's Best." The program also publishes the "Maine Made" Buyer's Guide, which is sent to more than 25,000 wholesale buyers.

Apprenticeship Program: Maine's Apprenticeship Program provides customized training and instruction so workers can obtain professional credentials. Many of Maine's larger firms have taken advantage of this innovative workforce development program, which will underwrite 50% of apprenticeship-related tuition for new and existing employees. For more information contact Kenneth L. Hardt, Maine Apprenticeship Program, Maine Department of Labor, 55 State House Station, Augusta, ME 04333-0055; 207-624-6390; Fax: 207-624-6499; E-mail: {k.skip.hardt@state.me.us}.

School-to-Work Initiatives: This public-private partnership is designed to provide Maine industry with a competitive workforce. The program employs three strategies to train Maine youth. These include:

SCHOOL-TO-WORK INITIATIVES

- Maine Career Advantage: a nationally recognized two-year combination of business internship and integrated academics, including one free year at the technical college level.
- Registered Pre-Apprenticeship: four years of employer-driven high school academics, coupled with two summers of on-the-job training. This culminates in permanent employment and a Registered Apprenticeship upon high school graduation.
- Tech Prep: sequential, industry-driven academic and technical training beginning in eleventh grade and progressing through completion of Certificate, Associate and/or Bachelor Degrees.

For more information contact Susan Brown, Center for Career Development, Maine Technical College System, SMVTC, Fort Road, South Portland, ME 04106; 207-767-5210 ext. 111; Fax: 207-767-5210; E-mail: {susan@ccd.mtcs.tec.me.us}; {www.mtcs.tec.me.us}.

Maine Quality Centers Program. This is an economic development initiative of the Maine Technical College System, which provides new and expanding businesses with a trained and ready workforce. New or expanding firms creating at least eight new full-time jobs with benefits may be eligible to receive state financing for 100% of pre-hire classroom training. For a packet of information and application contact Michael M. Aube, Director, Maine Quality Centers, Maine Technical College System, 323 State Street, Augusta, ME 04330; 207-287-1070; Fax: 207-287-1037; E-mail: {MMAube@syst.mtcs.tec.me.us}; {www.mtcs.tec.me.us}.

Governor's Training Initiative: This program reimburses training costs when they are required for business expansion, retention or unique upgrading issues. Businesses that meet eligibility requirements may receive reimbursements for on-the-job training, competitive retooling, specialized recruitment, workplace literacy, high-performance skills or customized technical training. For an application contact Bureau of Employment Services, Maine Department of Labor, 16 State House Station, Augusta, ME 04333-0016; 207-624-6490; Fax: 207-624-6499; E-mail: {caroline.p.morgan@state.me.us}; {www.state.me.us/dolbes/labor.htm}.

Safety Education and Training: At no cost to a company, Maine's Bureau of Labor Standards provides customized health and safety training, site evaluation and technical support. Priority is given to small and mid-sized employers and large employers with documented health and safety problems. For more information contact Alan Hinsey, Director, Bureau of Labor Standards, Maine Department of Labor, 45 State House Station, Augusta, ME 04333-0045; 207-624-6400; Fax: 207-624-6449; E-mail: {alan.c.hinsey@state.me.us}.

Business Financing

The Finance Authority of Maine (FAME) is Maine's business finance agency. FAME supports start-up and expanding businesses by working closely with Maine banks to improve access to capital. FAME offers a wide array of programs, ranging from traditional loan guarantees for small and large businesses to tax credits for investments in dynamic manufacturing or export-related firms. FAME has also established taxable and tax-exempt bond financing programs that provide loans to creditworthy firms at very favorable rates and terms.

- *The Commercial Loan Insurance Program*: This program provides large business borrowers, who would otherwise have problems securing conventional loans, with access to capital. FAME can insure up to 90% of a commercial loan, not to exceed $7 million, for most types of business projects. There is a $2.5-million limitation on recreational projects; additional limitations and restrictions apply.
- *Major Business Expansion Program*: Any business proposing to expand or locate in Maine and whose borrowing needs fall in the $5,000,000 to $25,000,000 range is eligible for tax-exempt or taxable bond financing for up to 100% of project's cost.
- *Economic Recovery Loan Program*: Designed as a supplemental financial resource to help small businesses access the capital required to become more productive and more competitive. Maximum request is $200,000 for businesses seeking last-resort financial assistance.
- *Agricultural Marketing Loan Fund Program*: Helps natural resource based industries by providing a source of subordinated debt for eligible projects and borrowers. Maximum loan size is $25,000 for any person or

organization in the business of growing or
harvesting plants, raising animals, growing or
obtaining plant or animal byproducts,
aquaculture or engaged in the
producing, processing, storing,
packaging or marketing of a product
from such business.

- *Small Enterprise Growth
  Program*: Provides financing for
  small companies that demonstrate
  a potential for high growth and public benefit. Financing is limited to a
  maximum of $150,000 per loan and borrower must be engaged in at least
  one of the following: Marine Science, Biotechnology, Manufacturing,
  Exporting, Software Development, Environmental Sciences, Value Added
  Natural Resource and/or other enterprises that the Board determines will
  further the purposes and intent of the program.
- *Marine Technology Investment Fund*: Provides investment in businesses
  with technology that can lead to product or process innovation. Targets
  funding for the next step required to bring a promising idea from the
  bench to commercialization.
- *Tax Increment Financing (TIF) Districts*: Municipalities can use Tax
  Increment Financing as an economic development incentive within their
  community. The program enables a municipality to designate a TIF
  District in which new or expanding businesses can receive financial
  support based on the new property tax revenues generated by their project.
  The municipality may choose to fund a portion of the project
  improvements or to return a percentage of the tax revenues to the company
  to offset the costs of development.
- *Business Assistance Program*: Provides a grant to a local government to
  either loan or grant up to $400,000 to businesses to finance fixed assets
  including capital equipment, commercial or industrial buildings, fixtures
  or property improvements.
- *Development Fund Loan Program*: Can provide up to $200,000 or gap
  financing for up to 40% of a business' development activities.
- *Investment Banking Service*: FAME helps borrowers seeking large
  amounts of capital for major commercial projects find and secure
  financing alternatives.
- *Occupational Safety Loan Program*: In cooperation with the Maine
  Department of Labor, FAME administers a program to provide direct
  loans to businesses making workplace safety improvements.
- *Plus l Computer Loan Program*: This program provides lenders with loan
  insurance on an expedited basis for small businesses that need to borrow
  money to acquire and install computer equipment and software. For more

information on this program, visit the Plus 1 Web site at
{www.mainebusiness.com/plus1}.

- *Rapid Response Guarantee*: FAME's Rapid Response Guarantee
  provides lenders with loan insurance on an expedited basis for small
  business loans that meet certain minimum credit standards.
- *Regional Economic Development Revolving Loan Program*: This
  program distributes $10 million to community, regional or statewide
  public-sector or non-profit entities that, in turn, loan the funds to eligible
  small business borrowers.
- *Small Business and Veterans' Small Business Loan Insurance Program*:
  This program is designed to help small businesses that cannot obtain
  conventional commercial financing. FAME can insure up to 90% of a
  small business loan, to a maximum insurance exposure of $1 million. If
  the borrower is an eligible wartime veteran, the authority may insure up to
  100% of a loan of $75,000 or less, and up to 90% of a loan up to a
  maximum exposure of $1.1 million.
- *Small Enterprise Growth Fund*: This program was created to provide
  Maine entrepreneurs with access to "patient" sources of venture capital.
  The Fund targets the needs of entrepreneurs with financial requirements of
  between $10,000 and $300,000.
- *Bond Financing Programs*: FAME, using its authority to issue taxable
  and tax-exempt bonds, provides reduced-rate financing to large projects.
  Under the SMART-E Bond Programs, FAME issues tax-exempt bonds for
  manufacturing projects, which must meet eligibility requirements
  established under the Internal Revenue Code. The SMART Bond Program
  and Major Business Expansion Program offer reduced interest rates by
  using FAME's guarantee authority to put the strength of the State of
  Maine's credit rating behind financing for larger projects.

For information on the above programs, contact Finance Authority of Maine,
83 Western Ave., P.O. Box 949, Augusta, ME 04332; 207-623-3263.

Tax Incentives

Business Equipment Property Tax Reimbursement Program: Program
reimbursed, for up to 12 years, all local property taxes paid on eligible
business property.

Employee-Assisted Day Care Credit: Provides an income tax credit of up to
$5,000. The credit is limited to the lesser of $5,000, 20% of the cost
incurred or $100 for each child of an employee enrolled on a full-time
basis or for each full-time equivalent throughout the tax year.

Employer Provided Long-term Care Benefits Credit: Provides an income tax
credit equal to the lesser of $5,000, 20% of the cost incurred or $100 per
employee covered by a long-term care policy as part of a benefits package.

Employment Tax Increment Financing (ETIF): This program returns between 30 and 50% of new employees' income withholding tax to companies who add new workers. To qualify, employees must be paid a wage equal to or above the per capita wage in their labor market area, and be provided group health insurance and access to an ERISA qualified retirement program. The company must also demonstrate that ETIF funding is an essential component of the expansion project's financing.

High-Technology Investment Tax Credit: Offers businesses engaged in high-tech activities that purchase and use eligible equipment a credit amount equal to the adjusted basis of equipment place in service less any lease payments received during the taxable year.

Jobs and Investment Tax Credit: This program helps businesses with an income tax credit on equipment and facilities that generate new jobs. The program provides a 10% credit against Maine income taxes for investment in most types of personal property that generates at least 100 new jobs within two years, as long as the investment is at least $5 million for the taxable year. The credit amount is tied to  the federal investment tax credit and is limited to $500,000 per year with carry-forwards available for seven years.

Research and Development Tax Credit: Maine's R&D tax credit provides an income tax credit for qualifying research and development activities. The program is based on definitions within the Internal Revenue Code; therefore, Maine's Bureau of Taxation recommends a careful study of Section 41 of the Code. In general, qualified research expenses include in-house and contract research related to discovering information that is technological in nature and is intended for use in developing a new or improved business.

Custom Computer Programming Sales Tax Credit Program: Exempts from sales tax the purchase of custom computer programming.

Biotechnology Sales Tax Exemption: Exempts sales tax of purchase of machinery, equipment, instruments and supplies used by any biotechnology company directly and primarily in a biotechnology application.

Manufacturing Sales Tax Exemptions: Sales of machinery and equipment used by any manufacturing company directly and primarily in the production of tangible personal property is eligible for a sales tax exemption.

Partial Clean Fuel Vehicle Sales Tax Exemption: Businesses that sell clean fuel vehicles to the general public are eligible for an exemption amount based on a portion of the sales or lease price of a clean fuel vehicle.

Research and Development Sales Tax Exemption: Sales of machinery and
equipment used by the purchaser directly and exclusively in research and
development by any business is eligible for a sales tax exemption.

Fuel and Electricity Sales Tax Exemption: Program exempts any business
from sales tax 95% of the sales price of all fuel and electricity purchased
for use at the manufacturing facility.

Business Property Tax Reimbursement Program: Maine reimburses what
companies pay in local property taxes on facilities built after April 1,
1995. Taxes on this property may be reimbursed by the state for a
maximum of 12 years. The definition of qualified business property for
this program is broad and specified by law.

Maine Seed Capital Tax Credit Program: FAME authorizes state income tax
credits to investors in an amount equal to 30% of the cash equity they
provide to eligible Maine businesses.

For more information, contact Maine Revenue Services, 24 State House
Station, Augusta, ME 04333; 207-287-2336.

Exports

Maine offers businesses and organizations international assistance through the
Maine International Trade Center. The Trade Center's mission is to expand
Maine's economy through increased international trade in goods and services
and related activities such as:

- Trade missions
- Training programs in international trade
- Conferences, such as a major Trade Day event
- Publications, including the Trade Center newsletter
- Special member-only programs and one-on-one counseling and
technical service assistance
- Comprehensive international library resources

For more information on the Maine International Trade Center, including
membership information, contact Perry Newman, Trade Director, Maine
International Trade Center, 511 Congress Street, Portland, ME 04101; 207-541-
7400; Fax: 207-541-7420; E-mail: {newman@ mitc.com}; {www.mitc.com}.

Export Financing Services: Working Capital Insurance from FAME provides
additional security to lenders and encourages greater lending activity for
international business ventures. Export Credit Umbrella Insurance,
provided by the Export-Import Bank of the United States (Eximbank) and
administered by FAME, reduces international credit risk and allows an
exporter to offer credit terms to foreign buyers in a competitive market.

Maryland

Department of Business and Economic Development
217 East Redwood St.
Baltimore, MD 21202
410-767-6300
800-811-0051
Fax: 410-333-6792
TDD/TTY: 410-333-6926
www.mdbusiness.state.md.us

Business Assistance

Department of Business and Economic Development (DBED): This office can provide information and expertise in dealing with state, federal, and local agencies. They also have information on financing programs and other services offered by the state government.

Workforce Resources: Maryland offers several training and grants for training programs to meet a variety of workforce needs. The following are two of their many programs:
1. Maryland Job Service: Provides recruitment and screening services based on the specifications of a company at no costs. It maintains a state/ nationwide data bank of job seekers and acts as the state's labor exchange agent to match qualified workers with available employment opportunities.
   Industrial Training Program: Provides incentive grants for the development and training of new employees in firms locating or expanding their workforce in Maryland. MITP reimburses companies for up to 100% of the direct costs associated with training programs customized to the work process.
2. Partnership for Workforce Quality: Targets training grants to manufacturing firms with 500 or fewer employees to upgrade skills for new technologies.

Regional Response Resources: Coordinates services designed to improve the quality, productivity and competitiveness of a business and help develop new and innovative products and processes.

Engineering Assistance: Provides a gateway for companies to access the expertise of the University of Maryland faculty, staff and resource of the University's Engineering Resource center.

Technology Support: Helps companies diversify into new markets. In addition, the office: provides technical assistance to firms seeking to commercialize new technologies; facilitates collaboration between businesses and universities and federal laboratories; and oversees the Strategic Assistance Fund, which provides matching funds to support the cost of private sector consultants to aid in both strategic plan development and new market strategies.

Regulatory and Permitting Assistance: The Office of Business Advocacy assists businesses in navigating through the processes and regulations of local, state and federal government. The Office provides ombudsman service to businesses and acts an information source and liaison on behalf of the business community.

Business Financing

Investment Financing Programs: Provide for direct investment in technology-driven Maryland-based companies through three programs. All three provide a novel alternative to grants, direct loans or credit enhancements available through other State financing programs. All three involve the use of private sector capital, including venture capital, on a co-investment basis, and while having an underlying economic development agenda, are capital gains and return-on-investment driven.

Challenge Investment Program: Provides emerging or early "seed" stage, technology-driven companies with a capital formation capability of $100,000 through a direct investment of $50,000 from the Challenge Program, which facilitates a required 1:1, $50,000 co-investor match. A return on investment is potentially achieved through a repayment of up to $100,000 over a ten year period for DBED's original $50,000 investment, based on a contingent stream of royalty payments. The contingency is based in turn on the achievement of certain revenue and capital structure thresholds by the company during that time period. The Challenge Program invests $500,000 annually, in two "rounds" of five $50,000 investments, about six months apart.

Enterprise Investment Fund: An investment financing tool that enables DBED to make direct equity investments in "second -stage" technology driven companies located in the state. Investments range from $150,000 to $250,000 per entity. Investment decisions are based on the potential for return on investment, as well as the promotion of broad-based economic development and job creation initiatives.

Maryland Venture Capital Trust: Administered by DBED through the Division of Financing Programs and the Investment Financing Group. As a "Fund of Funds", the trust has invested a total of $19,100,000 directly in eight separate, private sector venture capital funds. The source of this funding from the State, from the Maryland Retirement System, and from the Baltimore Retirement System. In the aggregate, these eight venture capital funds seek to make direct investments of at least $19,100,000 on a pro-rata basis, in Maryland-based, technology-driven companies. The Enterprise Investment Fund will work closely with these eight venture capital funds in attempting to facilitate its co-investment requirements.

Community Financing Group (CFG): Consists of programs that support the effort of local jurisdictions to create jobs and enhance their communities. These innovative programs have been very successful in revitalizing downtown areas, creating attractive business areas, developing industrial sites, creating attractive business locations, and in general, improving the State's industrial and commercial base.

Community Financing Group

The Four CFG programs include the Maryland Industrial Land ACT (MILA), the Maryland Industrial and Commercial Redevelopment Fund (MICRF), the Community Development Block Grant for Economic Development (CDBG-ED), and the Economic Development Opportunities Program Fund (Sunny Day). Each has unique attributes that allow effective and timely support of the needs and priorities of Maryland's local jurisdictions.

- *Maryland Industrial Land ACT (MILA)*: MILA loans provide a financial resource in cases where the need to develop industrial sites is not fully met by the private sector. Loans are made to counties or municipalities at below market interest rates and are secured by the full faith and credit of the borrowing government. The Act authorizes loans for acquisition of industrial land, development of industrial parks, improvement to infrastructure of potential industrial sites, construction of shell buildings for industrial use, installation of utilities, and rehabilitation of existing buildings for business incubators.

- *Maryland Industrial & Commercial Redevelopment Fund (MICRF)*: MICRF financing is intended to encourage private investment to facilitate industrial and commercial development or redevelopment. Loans are made to counties or municipalities who can then re-loan the proceeds to an eligible end user.

- *Sunny Day Fund*: Created to allow the State to take advantage of extraordinary economic development opportunities where assistance from other sources are constrained by program design, timing or available resources. The fund has been an extremely valuable tool in both business retention and recruiting. Maryland has taken advantage of opportunities with rapid and creative proposals that have assisted in the establishment of several high-profile private sector enterprises, including prized technology and research companies.

Maryland Industrial Development Financing Authority (MIDFA): Available to industrial/commercial businesses except certain retail establishments. Normal project range is $35,000 to $5 million. Insured up to lower of 80% of loan or $1 million. The amount of insurance varies with each loan and is determined after discussing the lender's needs. Typically, MIDFA insures from 20% to 50% of the loan.

Tax Exempt Program: Available to manufacturers or 501(c)(3) non-profit organizations. Normal project range is $1 million to $10 million. May insure up to 100% of bond. Normal policy: financing not to exceed 90% or real estate value or 75% of equipment cost. The actual amount of insurance generally varies with each project.

Taxable Bond Program: Available to industrial/ commercial businesses with certain exceptions. Normal project range is $1 million or more. Insurance level varies with each project but is limited to $5 million. May be insured up to 100% of bond amount. Approved Uses of Funds: To finance fixed assets.

Seafood & Aquaculture Loan Fund: Available to individuals or businesses involved in seafood processing or aquaculture. Normal Project Range: $20,000 to $800,000. Maximum Program Participation: The lesser of $250,000 or 80% of the total investment needed.

Energy Financing: Eligible applicants are businesses seeking to conserve energy, to co-generate energy, to produce fuels and other energy sources, and to recycle material. Normal Project Range: $800,000 to $160 million. Maximum Program Participation: 80% to 90% of value not exceeding 100% of cost.

Contract Financing Program: Eligible applicants are businesses owned 70% or more by socially and economically disadvantaged persons. Normal Project Range: Up to $500,000. Maximum Program Participation: Direct up to $500,000. Loan guarantee up to 90% not to exceed a maximum participation of $500,000. Approved Uses of Funds: Working capital required to begin, continue and complete government or public utility contracts. Acquisition of machinery or equipment to perform contracts. Interest Rates: For guaranteed loans, maximum rate is prime plus 2% . For direct loans, maximum is 15% .

Long Term Guaranty Program: Eligible applicants are businesses owned 70% or more by socially and economically disadvantaged persons. Must have 18 successive months of experience in the trade or business for which financing is sought. Normal Project Range: $50,000 to $1 million.

Maximum Program Participation: Loan guarantees may not exceed the lesser of 80% of the loan or $600,000.

Surety Bond Program: Eligible applicants are independently owned small businesses generally employing fewer than 500 full-time employees or those with gross annual sales of less than $50 million. Normal Project Range: Guaranty Program - None. Direct Bonding Program - Up to $750,000. Maximum Program Participation: Guaranty Program - Guarantees up to 90% of face value of the bond not to exceed a total exposure of $900,000. Direct Bonding Program - Can directly issue bonds not to exceed $750,000. Approved Uses of Funds: Guaranty Program - Guarantees reimbursement of losses on a bid, payment or performance bond required in connection with projects where the majority of funds are from government or a regulated public utility. Direct Bonding Program - Issues bid, payment or performance bonds on projects where the majority of funds are from government or a regulated public utility.

Equity Participation Investment Program - Technology Component & Business Acquisition Component: Eligible applicants are technology based businesses and business acquisitions which will be owned 70% or more by disabled, socially or economically disadvantaged persons. Normal Project Range: $100,000 to $3 million. Maximum Program Participation: The lesser of $250,000 or 80% of the total investment needed.

Equity Participation Investment Program - Franchise Component: Eligible applicants are franchises that are or will be owned 70% or more by disabled, socially or economically  disadvantaged persons. Must have at least 10% of total project cost in owner's equity. Normal Project Range: $50,000 to $1.5 million. Maximum Program Participation: Equity investments or loans up to 45% of initial investment or $100,000, whichever is less.

Challenge Investment Program: Eligible applicants are technology-driven companies, with principal activity located in Maryland; applicants must have complete business plan as a minimum requirement. Size of Investment: $50,000.

Enterprise Investment Program: Eligible applicants are technology-driven companies, with principal activity located in Maryland; applicants must have complete business plan as a minimum requirement. Size of Investment: $150,000 to $250,000.

Defense Adjustment Loan Fund (DALF): The primary purposes of this program are: (1) to stimulate and support the development of defense and non-defense enterprises in Maryland that have the potential to create employment in areas hurt by defense downsizing; and (2) to support the diversification of Maryland defense companies. On average, DALF intends to create or retain one job for every $35,000 loaned. The fund will lend capital to companies with growth potential for working capital, product development, technology commercialization, or manufacturing modernization. Preference will be given to loans that will catalyze investment or loans from other sources. Loans as small as $25,000 are permitted, but it is expected that loans will average $100,000 to $250,000. Committed funds may be released by DALF against the achievement of specified milestones.

Neighborhood Business Development Program (NBDP): Initiative to help stimulate Maryland's established, older communities, NBDP provides flexible, gap financing (up to 50% of total project cost) for many small businesses starting up or expanding in targeted urban, suburban or rural revitalization areas throughout the State. Terms and conditions are established on an individual basis. Financing ranging from $25,000 to $500,000, up to 50% of total project cost, where other funds clearly are unavailable. Contact Maryland Department of Housing and Community Development, Neighborhood Business Development Program, Revitalization Center, 1201 W. Pratt Street, Suite D, Baltimore, MD 21223; 410-514-7288; Fax: 410-685-8270; {www.dhcd.state.md.us}.

Tax Incentives

No unitary tax on profits.
No income tax on foreign dividends.
No gross receipts tax on manufacturers.
No corporate franchise tax.
No separate school taxes.

Job Creation Tax Credits: ncome tax credits granted to businesses for the creation of jobs. Credit granted will be the lesser of $1,000 or 2 1/2% of a year's wages for each qualifying permanent job.

Employment of Individual with Disabilities Tax Credit: Includes tax credits for wages paid and for child care or transportation expenses for qualifying individuals with disabilities.

Employment Opportunity Tax Credit: Includes credits for wages and child care or transportation expenses for qualifying employees who were recipients of state benefits from the "Aid to Families with Dependent Children" program immediately prior to employment.

Neighborhood and Community Assistance Program Tax Credit: Provides tax credits for business contributions to approved, non-profit Neighborhood and Community Assistance Programs.

Property Tax Exemptions and Credits: Maryland does not impose a personal property tax on business. For those jurisdictions that do tax personal property, exemptions and credits available include the following: machinery, equipment, materials and supplies use in manufacturing or research; manufacturing inventory; commercial inventory for warehousing and distribution; custom computer software.

Enterprise Zones Tax Credits:

1. Property Tax Credits: Ten year credit against local property taxes on a portion of real property improvements. Credit is 80% the first five years, and decreases 10% annually thereafter to 30% in the tenth and last year.

2. Income Tax Credits: One to three year credits for wages paid to new employees in the zone. The general credit is a one-time $500 credit per new workers. For economically disadvantaged employees, the credit increases to a total of $3,000 per worker distributed over three years.

3. Priority access to Maryland's financing programs.

Empowerment Zone Incentives: Firms locating in the federally designated Empowerment Zone in Baltimore, one of six in the nation, may be eligible for state enterprise zone incentives including: income tax credits for job creation; property tax credits for real property improvements. Businesses in the Zone may also qualify for potential federal incentives such as: wage tax credits; increased depreciation on equipment; tax exempt bond financing; employment development incentives.

Brownfields Tax Incentives: The counties, Baltimore City or incorporated municipalities may elect to grant a five-year credit equal to 50% of real property taxes attributable to the increase in the assessment resulting from cleanup and improvement of a qualified Brownfields site. The Brownfields real property credit may be expanded as follows: localities may grant an additional credit of up to 20%; localities may extend the credit by an additional five years if the site is in a state-designated enterprise zone; a credit will also apply against state real property taxes for the same percentage and duration.

Sales Tax Exemptions: The following are major business-oriented exemptions from the Maryland Sales and Use tax. Local jurisdictions do not impose a sales tax:

1. Sales of capital manufacturing machinery and equipment, including equipment used for testing finished products; assembling, processing or refining; in the generation of electricity; or used to produce or repair production equipment.

2. Sales of noncapitalized manufacturing machinery and equipment; safety and quality control equipment use on a production activity site;

and equipment used to move a finished product on the production site.

3. Sales of tangible personal property consumed directly in manufacturing, testing of finished products, assembling, processing or refining, or in the generation of electricity.

4. Sales of fuels used in manufacturing, except those used to cool, heat and light the manufacturing facility.

5. Sales for resale and sales of tangible personal property to be incorporated in other tangible personal property manufactured for resale. In addition, there is an exemption for sales of computer programs reproduced for sale or incorporated in whole or in part into another computer program intended for sale.

6. Sales of customized computer software.

7. Sales of equipment and equipment used or consumed in research and development, to include testing of finished products.

8. Sales of aircraft, vessels, railroad rolling stock, and motor vehicles used principally in the movement of passengers or freight in interstate and foreign commerce.

9. Sales of certain end-item testing equipment used to perform a contract for the U.S. Department of Defense and transferred to the federal government.

Exports

Trade Financing Program: Eligible applicants are industrial/ commercial businesses which are engaged in the export and import of goods through Maryland ports and airport as well as service providers to the overseas market. Normal Project Range: $10,000 to $5 million. Maximum Program Participation: Insured up to lower of 90% of obligation or $1 million for export financing and 80% for all others. The actual amount of insurance generally varies with each transaction.

The State of Maryland's Office of International Business (OIB): Offers export assistance to small and medium-sized Maryland firms with internationally competitive products and services. OIB's international trade professionals provide Maryland companies with access to international market intelligence, targeted trade activities, financial assistance and high-level introductions to potential customers.

   • *Exporter's Hotline & Referral Service*: OIB marketing specialists deliver basic trade information to companies in all stages of the export process. The Exporter's Hotline handles inquiries concerning the exporting process, assistance offered to Maryland firms by international trade service providers, and data on Maryland's international business activity. The hotline's number is 410-767-6564.

Export Assistance Network: An alliance of international
business assistance centers, was developed by
the State of Maryland to facilitate the
transition of small and medium-sized
companies to the global marketplace. The
Network gives Maryland businesses
convenient access to foreign market reports,
profiles of the top industries for export, trade
leads and contacts, travel information, trade
statistics, and other information needed for entering
the global market. The five centers are:

★ World Trade Resource Center, Baltimore; 410-576-0022

★ Eastern Shore Export Assistance Center, Salisbury; 410-548-5353

★ Southern Maryland Export Assistance Center, La Plata; 301-934-2251

★ Suburban Maryland Export Assistance Center, Rockville; 301-217-2345

★ Western Maryland Export Assistance Center, Cumberland; 301-777-5867

Maryland's Trade Finance Program: Offers up to $1 million in loan insurance
per borrower for export and import financing. The trade finance office also
provides access to the export financing and foreign credit insurance
programs of the United States Export-Import Bank and the Overseas
Private Investment Corporation.

Sister State Relationships: Promotes business, educational and cultural
exchanges between Maryland and regions in Asia, Europe and Latin
America. This program, which is managed through alliances with the
World Trade Center Institute and the Maryland Business Center China,
facilitates high-level international contacts, meetings with visiting
delegations and networking with Maryland's international executives.
Maryland has active sister state relationships in Belgium, China, Japan,
Korea, Poland and Russia.

Foreign Offices & Representatives: Network of foreign offices and
representatives provide exporters with in-country resources and expertise
around the globe. These foreign offices in China, Japan, the Netherlands
and Taiwan -- and representatives in Argentina, Brazil, Chile, Israel and
Mexico -- deliver support in the following areas: agent/distributor searches
and business appointments; credit reports, competitor analysis and
regulatory information; marketing and logistical support at trade shows;
market research and analysis.

Export Credit Program: Businesses conducting substantial economic activity
in Maryland may submit proposals to receive export offset credits accrued
from state purchases.

Publications
- *Trade Secrets: The Export Answer Book*: This guide contains over 100 answers to the most commonly asked questions concerning international trade; provides contact information for export experts; and describes more than 300 current publications, software programs and other international trade resources. The book, produced by the Maryland Small Business Development Center, is distributed for free to Maryland businesses through the State's Export Assistance Network.
- *World View*: A collaborative effort of the State's international office and other international service providers, the World View newsletter covers exporting issues, events and other topics of interest to Maryland's international executives. *World View* is published bimonthly by the Office of International Business and distributed for free.

Women and Minorities

Day Care Facilities Guarantee Fund: Eligible applicants are individuals or business entities involved in the development or expansion of day care facilities for infants and children, the elderly, and disabled persons of all ages. Normal Project Range: Up to $1 million. Maximum Program Participation: Loan guarantee up to 80%.

Child Care Facilities Direct Loan Fund: Eligible applicants are individuals, business entities involved in the development of day care facilities for children, either center-based or home-based. Normal Project Range: Minimum $15,000. Maximum Program Participation: Maximum of 50% of fixed assets.

Child Care Special Loan Fund: Eligible applicants are individuals, business entities for expanding or improving child care facilities, meeting state and local licensing requirements and improving the quality of care. Normal Project Range: $1,000 to $10,000. Maximum Program Participation: Direct loans up to $10,000.

Massachusetts

Massachusetts Office of Business Development
10 Park Plaza, 3rd Floor
Boston, MA 02116
617-973-8600
800-5-CAPITAL
Fax: 617-973-8797
www.state.ma.us/mobd

Business Assistance

Massachusetts Office of Business Development (MOBD): Through five regional offices, they will advise and counsel businesses and individuals in utilizing federal, state, and local finance programs established to help businesses with their capital formation needs.

MASSACHUSETTS

Entrepreneurial Group: Provides funding, oversight, and, in some cases, the operation of a number of entrepreneurial training programs designed to help dislocated workers start their own businesses or consulting practices.

Achieving the Competitive Advantage Program: An intensive 10-week course designed to introduce entrepreneurs to strategic skills, methods, and models that are critical in planning and implementing a successful business plan. The classes provide training in the areas of business management, technology and financing, as well as such concepts as strategic partnerships, quality assurance and motivational vision.

One-Stop Business Centers: Offers a streamlined approach to economic development assistance. Offices located throughout the state are staffed with professionals who know about Massachusetts' programs and opportunities for businesses throughout the state's diverse regions.

Massachusetts Site Finder Service: Offers confidential, statewide searches for industrial land or buildings to fit defined specifications for expanding businesses. MOBD can also provide up-to-date Community Profiles of communities being considered as a business location. Information provided includes the local tax structure, local permitting requirements, and a demographic profile of area residents. For more information, contact Massachusetts Alliance for Economic Development, 800 Boylston St.,

Suite 1700, Boston, MA 02199; 617-247-7800; 800-872-8773;
{www.massecon.com}.

Economic Development Incentive Program (EDIP): To stimulate economic
development in distressed areas, attract new businesses, and encourage
existing businesses to expand in Massachusetts.

Business Finance Specialists: Assists companies with financing targeted to
urban and economically disadvantaged areas through the Community
Development Finance Corporation and other public funds.

One-Stop Permitting Program: For all construction-related, state-issued
permits. Project Managers act as advocates, assisting with identifying all
required permits and moving the application through the entire process.

Massachusetts Energy Advisor Service: Helps companies identify energy
efficiency opportunities in facilities and

manufacturing processes. The University
of Massachusetts and the Corporation
for Business, Work, and Learning
provide a similar service focusing on
smaller and medium-sized
manufacturing plants.

Economic Development Programs:
Designed to encourage businesses to
expand their operations, to move into the state, or to address specific
utility needs. Within a year, businesses will be able to shop around for
electricity, thereby creating competition among electric providers. This
new opportunity will position Massachusetts in a more competitive
environment regarding utility costs and will bring about lower commercial
and industrial rates.

Business Consulting and Municipal Loan Pools: Professional staff are
available at the municipal level who can offer business and technical
assistance, as well as valuable insights on the local business climate and
available local resources. Some municipalities also administer loan pools
that can provide businesses with low-interest financing.

Massachusetts Manufacturing Partnership (MMP): Helps plan and
implement a strategy for increased competitiveness, whether by adopting
new production technologies and management techniques, finding new
markets, or training a work force. Industry led regional offices are staffed
by Field Agents who will work with a company to create the best
combination of assistance.

The Commonwealth has resources to assist smaller and medium-sized
manufacturers to stay competitive and to ensure that their work force has the
skills necessary to be re-employed. Through the Corporation for Business,
Work, and Learning, the Commonwealth provides training and job search

services to unemployed workers, and offers consulting services and a loan
fund/loan guarantee program for turnarounds.

The New England Suppliers Institute (NESI): Helps manufacturing
companies become better suppliers to their larger customers by assisting
them to develop quality business relationships, implement continuous
improvement strategies, achieve supplier certification, and enhance
company-wide work force and management skills.

Massachusetts Manufacturing Network Program: Provides technical
assistance and funding to help them leverage resources, share information,
and accomplish tasks that they could not do on their own.

Office of Defense Adjustment Strategy: Provides information about federal
and state defense conversion programs. MOBD experts can discuss how
defense companies wishing to diversify into new commercial markets may
be eligible for federal grants.

Environmental Agency has an Office of Technical Assistance that has helped
many firms replace or reduce the use of toxic substances in production,
increasing productivity while lowering treatment and disposal costs.
Massachusetts' Energy Advisor Service helps companies reduce pollution
related to energy use while cutting their consumption and cost of energy.
The Industrial Extension Service has expertise in helping firms make
greater use of recycled materials.

Starting a Business in Massachusetts: A comprehensive guide for business
owners available from MOBD.

Business Financing

The Capital Access Program (CAP): Designed to assist small businesses
throughout the Commonwealth in obtaining loans to start, expand or
continue operating profitably. The program is designed to gain access to
capital where none currently exists. The state provides "cash collateral"
guarantees for banks willing to make loans to smaller, "less bankable"
businesses. Any person or business authorized to do business in
Massachusetts may borrow through CAP. There are no minimum loan
amounts.

The Emerging Technology Fund (ETF): A useful tool for economic growth
for technology based companies. Targeting the fields of biotechnology,
advanced materials, electronics, medical, telecommunications and
environmental technologies, the fund provides companies in these
industries with a greater opportunity to obtain debt financing. Loans can
be guaranteed for tenant build-out, construction or expansion of facilities
and equipment purchased for up to $1.5 million or 50% of the aggregate
debt, whichever is less. Loans are also provided for hard asset-owned

facilities and equipment, with a maximum amount of $2.5 million or 33 1/3% of the aggregate debt, whichever is less.

Equipment Lease/Purchase Program: The tax-exempt lease/purchase program provides manufacturers, non-profit institutions and environmental enterprises with a low-cost alternative for financing $300,000 or more in new equipment needs. By enabling leasing companies to furnish below-market, tax-exempt interest rates, the program offers companies sizable cost savings. Offers fixed interest rates approximately 70% of traditional leasing rates. 100% financing is available. Institutions must qualify as a 501(c)(3), not-for-profit entity and be located in Massachusetts. Potential borrowers include educational institutions, cultural institutions, long term care facilities, and other non-profits.

Tax-Exempt Industrial Development Bonds: Companies can borrow money via a tax-exempt Industrial Development Bond (IDB) to provide the lowest possible borrowing rates. Funds for an IDB can be used to purchase land, buildings and new equipment as well as to construct or renovate buildings. Based on the proposed project, the purchase of a new site, any new equipment needs and renovation or construction of facilities could be financed through an IDB. Should the project require a more flexible financing structure, the Massachusetts Development Finance Agency can work with the particular company to structure a taxable bond. Project size ranges from approximately $1.5 million to a federally imposed maximum of $10 million.

Tax Incentives

Investment Tax Credit: Massachusetts gives businesses a 3% Investment Tax Credit against the corporate excise tax for the construction of manufacturing facilities. The credit also applies to the purchase or lease of equipment. It is available to companies involved in manufacturing, research and development, agriculture or commercial fishing.

R&D Tax Credit: Massachusetts has permanent 10% and 15% R&D tax credits with a fifteen-year or indefinite carry-forward provision for companies investing in research and development. Companies are allowed to compute defense and non-defense R&D separately. This constitutes one of the highest R&D tax credits in the nation.

Economic Opportunity Areas: Qualified businesses operating within one of 36 Economic Target Areas are eligible for tax and financing incentives: A 5%

Investment Tax Credit for all businesses, not just manufacturing; A 10% Abandoned Building Tax Deduction (at least 75% vacant for at least 24 months); Local Property Tax Benefits (Special Tax Assessment or Tax Increment Financing); Priority status for state capital funding.

Economic Target Areas (ETA) are designated throughout Massachusetts. Within ETAs, Economic Opportunity Areas of particular economic need and priority are further defined. Businesses that undertake certified projects within Economic Opportunity Areas can qualify for additional investment incentives: 5% Investment Tax Credit for Certified Projects, 10% Abandoned Building Tax Deduction within designated areas, Municipal Tax Benefits (Tax Increment Financing or Special Assessments on Property Values), Priority for state capital funding.

Tax Increment Financing: Businesses may also benefit from the substantial property tax savings offered through Tax Increment Financing (TIF). TIF enables municipalities to enter into agreements with private companies to determine a baseline property value level at which taxes will be levied for a specified number of years.

Exports

Massachusetts Export Center: One-stop resource for international business. The Export Center is a cooperative effort of the Massachusetts Office of International Trade and Investment, the Massachusetts Port Authority, the Massachusetts Small Business Development Center, Mass Development and the Massachusetts Office of Business Development. Offers:

- One-on-one Export Counseling
- Export Workshops, Training Programs and Conferences
- Overseas Market Research, Statistics and Trade Leads
- International Marketing Activities, including Trade Missions and Exhibitions
- Network of International Offices
- Meetings with International Business Delegations
- Export Financing
- International Business Resource Library
- Bimonthly Newsletter on International Trade Opportunities

Contact the Massachusetts Export Center, Fish Pier West, Bldg., II, Boston, MA 02210; 617-478-4133; {www.state.ma.us/export}.

Assistance is also provided through the *Massachusetts Trade Office.* This office's home page provides information on upcoming trade missions and lists events and seminars about doing business in the global market. Contact

Massachusetts Trade Office, State Transportation Bldg., 10 Park Plaza, Boston, MA 02116; 617-367-1830; {www.state.ma.us/moiti}.

Women and Minorities

State Office of Minority and Women Business Assistance (SOMWBA): Certifies companies as minority or women-owned or controlled, and publishes a directory listing of verified firms. SOMWBA provides management and technical assistance seminars and workshops for minority and women entrepreneurs on a wide variety of business topics.

Minority Business Financing: A MOBD Business Finance Specialist can guide a company to several targeted financing programs including the Community Development Finance Corporation's Urban Initiative Fund, the Economic Development Fund and others.

Michigan

Michigan Jobs Commission
201 North Washington Square
Victor Office Center, 4th Floor
Lansing, MI 48913
517-373-9808
Fax: 517-335-0198
www.mjc.state.mi.us

Business Assistance

Michigan Business Ombudsman: Serves as a "one-stop" center for business permits. Acts as a mediator in resolving regulatory disputes between business and the various state departments and also provides consultation and referral services.

Michigan Works! is the state's workforce development resource agency. Offers workforce development services at 25 locations.

MiProSite: Lists more than 2,600 sites that can be searched based on client criteria for industrial site locations.

Economic Development Jobs Training: Provides financial assistance to companies that need to train or retrain workers to meet marketplace needs. Grant average: $2,000 per employee.

Business and Economic Services Team: Provides a broad variety of business and economic services to employers, entrepreneurs, and to those seeking to do business with the State of Michigan, which enable businesses to keep pace with civil rights and equal employment opportunity legal standards.

Customer Assistance: Provides a centralized intake unit in which economic development and workforce customers obtain services quickly and efficiently, and where individuals can receive information about starting a business in Michigan.

Economic Development Corporations: Provides a flexible tool to assist in job creation at the local level by acquiring, developing, and maintaining land, buildings, machinery, furnishings, and equipment necessary to complete a project plan.

Michigan Business Development: Assists existing companies with a wide array of business services which are customized to meet the specific needs of the business.

Michigan Business Strategies 2000: Provides affordable high quality management consulting services for small businesses seeking to position themselves for long-term growth. Businesses can receive expert consulting services in areas such as accounting, marketing, information systems, financial management, and internal operations.

Certified Industrial Park Program: Industrial park developers and communities have used this identification as a marketing tool to show prospective clients that they are prepared to accept the new client without delay. For more information, contact Michigan Economic Developers Association, P.O. Box 15096, Lansing, MI 48901; 517-241-0011.

Child Care Clearinghouse: Employers and organizations needing general information on employer-sponsored child care can obtain a resource kit which includes a series of fact sheets on topics related to workplace child care and information about a variety of tax issues. For more information, contact Michigan Child Care Clearinghouse, 201 N. Washington Square, Lansing, MI 48913; 517-373-9808; 800-377-2097.

Michigan Technical Assistance Center Network: Assists companies with government contracting and exporting.

Research Services: Detailed information concerning Michigan's economy and business climate. Information is also available regarding various industrial sectors critical to Michigan.

Employee Ownership Program: Provides information, technical assistance, and financing to enhance the establishment of employee-owned companies and Employee Stock Ownership Plans.

Business Financing

Alternative Investments Division: Invests in businesses with strong management that show a substantially above-average potential for growth, profitability, and equity appreciation. A typical initial investment is $5,000,000 and up. Contact: Michigan Department of Treasury, Alternative Investments Division, P.O. Box 15128, Lansing, MI 48901; 517-373-4330.

Capital Access Program: An extremely flexible and non-bureaucratic program designed to assist banks in making business loans that are somewhat riskier than conventional bank loans. The program utilizes a special loss reserve to assist banks in covering losses from a portfolio of loans that a bank makes under the program. The program is very broad based and can be used to finance most types of Michigan businesses. Due to premium payments that range from 3% to 7% of the amount borrowed [which are made to help fund the special loss reserve], loans under the program are generally more expensive than conventional bank loans. The key point is that, through the program, banks can provide access to bank financing for many businesses that otherwise might not qualify. Although there are no loan size limits, the average loan is approximately $53,000.

Business and Industrial Development Corporations (BIDCOs): Many sound businesses are unable to obtain growth capital because their finances are considered too risky for conventional bank lending, yet they cannot provide the high rates of return required by venture capitalists. BIDCOs are a new type of private institution designed to fill this growth capital gap. BIDCOs offer an array of financing options that can be structured flexibly to suit the needs of individual companies. In addition, they can provide management assistance to help businesses grow. As a privately owned and operated corporation, each BIDCO establishes its own criteria for the kinds of businesses it will finance and for the types of loans and investments it will make. BIDCOs do not normally finance start ups.

Industrial Development Revenue Bond Program (IDRB): Tax-exempt bonds issued on behalf of the borrower by the Michigan Strategic Fund and purchased by private investors. These loans can be made for manufacturing and not-for-profit corporation projects and solid waste facilities. Bond proceeds can only be used to acquire land, building and equipment. Working capital and inventory are not eligible for this type of financing. These bonds are generally used when financing of $1 million and higher is required.

Pollution Control Loans: Intended to provide loan guarantees to eligible small businesses for the financing of the planning, design, or installation of a pollution control facility. This facility must prevent, reduce, abate, or control any form of pollution, including recycling. SBA can guarantee up to $1,000,000 for Pollution  Control Loans to eligible businesses. The 7(a) Program interest rates and maturities apply and are negotiated with the lender.

Equipment and Real Property Purchases: Municipal Bonds provide streamlined tax-exempt, fixed interest rate financing well suited to equipment purchases. For more information, contact Michigan Municipal Bond Authority, Treasury Bldg., 3rd Floor, 430 West Allegan, Lansing, MI 48922; 517-373-1728.

Freight Economic Development Project Loans/Grants: Provides financial assistance to non-transportation companies which promote the development or expansion of new business and industries, by financing freight transportation infrastructure improvements needed to operate a new venture. For more information, contact Michigan Department of Transportation, Bureau of Urban and Public Transportation, Freight Services and Safety Division, 425 W. Ottawa, P.O. Box 30050, Lansing, MI 48909; 517-373-6494.

Industrial Development Revenue Bonds (IRBs): Provides healthy, profitable firms locating or expanding in Michigan with capital cost savings stemming from the difference between taxable and tax exempt interest rates. Maximum size of bonds is limited to: $1,000,000 free of any restriction on capital expenditures, or $10,000,000 subject to certain conditions.

Private Rail Loans: Privately owned railroad companies may receive capital loans up to 30% of the total project cost to improve or expand the privately owned infrastructure. For more information, contact Michigan Department of Transportation, Bureau of Urban and Public Transportation, Freight Services and Safety Division, P.O. Box 30050, Lansing, MI 48909; 517-373-6494.

Taxable Bond Program: Provides small and medium sized companies access to public capital markets normally available to larger companies.

Venture Capital Fund: Provides venture capital to growth-oriented firms ranging from $3 - $10 million.

Tax Incentives

Enterprise Zones: The program allows a designated community to provide a business and property tax abatement reducing property taxes approximately 50% on all new investment.

Tax-Free Renaissance Zones: 11 regions of the state designated as virtually tax free for any business or resident presently in or moving to a zone. The zones are designed to spur new jobs and investment. Each Renaissance Zone can be comprised of up to six smaller zones (sub zones) which are located throughout the community to give businesses more options on where to locate.

MEGA Jobs Tax Credit: Companies engaged in manufacturing, research and development, wholesale and trade, or office operations that are financially sound and that have financially sound proposed plans, are eligible to receive a tax credit against the Michigan Single Business Tax for a new location or expansion project and/or the amount of personal income tax attributable to new jobs being created.

Property Tax Abatements: Can be granted by the state and by local units of government. They reduce property tax on buildings, machinery and equipment by 50% for new facilities, 100% for existing.

Air Pollution Control Systems Tax Exemptions for Installation: Relieves a company of sales tax, property tax, and use taxes for air pollution control equipment.

Economic Growth Authority: Awards credits against the Single Business Tax to eligible companies for up to 20 years to promote high quality economic growth and job creation that otherwise would not occur without this program.

Registered Apprenticeship Tax Credit: Makes available a tax credit of up to $2,000 annually per apprentice to employers who, through registered apprenticeships, train young people while they are still in high school.

Work Opportunity Tax Credit: The tax credit is 35% of the first $6,000 in wages paid during the first year of employment for each eligible employee.

Exports

Export Working Capital Program (EWCP): The EWCP was designed to provide short-term working capital to exporters. It is a combined effort of the SBA and the Export-Import Bank. The two agencies have joined their working capital programs to offer a unified approach to the government's support of export financing.

International Trade Loan (ITL): This program provides short- and long-term financing to small businesses involved in exporting, as well as businesses adversely affected by import competition. The SBA can guarantee up to $1.25 million for a combination of fixed-asset financing and working capital. Loans for facilities or equipment can have maturities of up to 25 years. The working capital portion of a loan has a maximum maturity of three years. Interest rates are negotiated with the lender and can be up to 2.25% over the prime rate.

Export/Foreign Direct Investment Program: Promotes the export of Michigan-produced goods and services and attract investment in Michigan by foreign-based companies.

Women and Minorities

Minority And Women's Prequalification Loan and the Women's Pre-Qualification Loan Program: Use intermediaries to assist prospective minority and women borrowers in developing viable loan application packages and securing loans. The women's program uses only nonprofit organizations as intermediaries; the minority program uses for-profit intermediaries as well.

The Women Business Owner Advocacy Unit: Provides information to women business owners regarding government contracting, financing, legislation, and other business issues. It is establishing a statewide network to facilitate the sharing of information, resources, and business expertise, and more. Contact Women's Business Owner Advocate, Michigan Jobs Commission, 201 N. Washington Square, 1st Floor, Lansing, MI 48913; 517-335-1835; Fax: 517-373-9143.

Disadvantaged Business Enterprise Certification: Insures that firms owned and controlled by disadvantaged individuals, minorities, and women participate in federal-aid contracts and grant entered into and administered by MDOT.

Small Business Group: Promotes job creation and retention in small firms by fostering communication, coordination partnerships between the Michigan Jobs Commission and those public and private sector groups and organizations which advocate for and/or provide services to small companies and minority, women, and handicapped-owned businesses.

Minnesota

Department of Trade and Economic Development (MTED)
500 Metro Square Blvd.
121 7th Place East
St. Paul, MN 55101-2146
612-297-1291
800-657-3858
www.dted.state.mn.us

Business Assistance

Minnesota Small Business Assistance Office: Provides accurate, timely, and
comprehensive information and assistance to businesses in all
areas of start-up, operation, and expansion. They can also
provide referrals to other state agencies.

Business Development and Site Location Services: For
businesses interested in expanding or relocating
to a Minnesota site, it serves as a bridge
between government and the resources that
businesses are seeking. Business Development
Specialists act as liaisons between businesses
and state and local government to access
financial and technical resources. The program also serves as an important
information source, providing businesses with data on topics ranging from
the availability of buildings and property or the labor supply in a
particular location, to transportation or tax comparisons. The one-on-one
nature of this program provides businesses with assistance throughout
every phase of their expansion or location projects.

Computer and Electrical Components Industry Services: Exists to foster the
growth of jobs, revenues, and investment in Minnesota's computer and
electrical components industries. A specialist provides technical review of
projects, coordination of statistical analysis, overview of prospect
proposals, participation in development efforts with industry associations
and other agencies.

Healthcare and Medical Products Industry Services: Exists to seek business
investment and job growth in the healthcare industry while promoting
Minnesota companies' capabilities in this industry. A specialist provides
information to businesses on financial programs, suppliers, business
planning, trade opportunities, venture partners and other needed resources.
The specialist also works to attract direct investment in existing Minnesota

businesses with problems and opportunities involving sources, product development, marketing, financing, site selection, and by marketing Minnesota actively at industry gatherings.

Printing and Publishing Industry Services: Exists to foster the growth of jobs, revenues, and investment in Minnesota's printing and publishing industry. A specialist provides information on resources, markets, technologies, buildings and sites, transportation, and other issues, both in response to inquiries and by marketing Minnesota actively at industry gatherings.

Wood Products, Plastics, and Composites Industry Services: Exists to foster the growth of jobs and added value in Minnesota's wood processing and related businesses and to attract new industry consistent with environmental protection. A specialist represents the industry and the Department of Trade and Economic Development by reviewing projects, organizing statistical data, participating in development efforts with Department of Natural Resources, University of Minnesota, Minnesota Technology, Inc., National Resources Research Institute and other agencies, and by helping to coordinate demonstration projects like model homes. This position has evolved from a primary focus on wood products, to a wider interest in plastics and composite materials that are more frequently used in conjunction with wood.

A Guide to Starting a Business in Minnesota: Provides a current discussion of many of the major issues faced by persons planning to start a new business in Minnesota, including forms or organizations, business name filing, business licenses and permits, business plans, financing, employers' issues, business taxes and small business resources.

Business Financing

Minnesota Investment Fund: To create new and retain the highest quality jobs possible on a state wide basis with a focus on industrial manufacturing and technology related industries; to increase the local and state tax base and improve the economic vitality for all Minnesota citizens. Grants are awarded to local units of government who make loans to assist new expanding businesses. Maximum available: $500,000. Only one grant per state fiscal year can be awarded to a government unit.

Minnesota Job Skills Partnership Board: Awards grants for cooperative education and training projects between businesses and educational institutions.

Small Business Development Loan Program: Provides loans to industrial, manufacturing or agricultural processing businesses for land acquisition, building construction or renovation, machinery and equipment. Maximum available: $500,000 minimum up to a maximum of $6 million.

Rural Challenge Grant Program: Provides job opportunities for low-income
individuals, encourage private investment, and
promote economic development in rural areas of the
state. The Business and Community Development
Division has a partnership with each of six regional
organizations to provide low-interest loans to new or
expanding businesses in rural Minnesota. Eligible projects:
Up to 50% of start-up or expansion costs, including property acquisition,
site improvements, new construction, building renovation, purchase of
machinery and equipment, and working capital. Maximum available:
$100,000. Most loans will be smaller due to the high demand for funds
compared with the funds available.

Tourism Loan Program: Exists to provide low-interest financing to existing
tourism-related businesses providing overnight lodging. Additionally, the
program assists with the development of business plans. Businesses with
feasible business plans qualify to receive financing for up to half of all
eligible costs. Business owners meet with DTED staff to determine project
eligibility and receive counseling. Direct loans, or participation loans in
cooperation with financial institutions, can be made for up to 50% of total
project cost. The maximum state loan may not exceed 50% of the total
project cost, or $65,000, whichever is less. Maximum available Septic
System Loans: Participation Loans - State funds are used in conjunction
with loaned funds from financial institutions. Loans for septic system
replacement or upgrade are eligible for an additional $65,000. Direct
Loans - Only septic system projects of under $10,000 may receive a direct
loan. The borrower must fund 50% of the project with private financing.
The maximum direct loan is $5,000.

Certified Community Development Corporation: Certified CDCs may apply
for grant funds for several purposes: 1. specific economic development
projects within a designated area, 2 dissemination of information about, or
taking application for, programs operated by DTED, or 3 developing the
internal organizational capacity to engage in economic development
activities.

Capital Access Program: To encourage loans from private lending institutions
to businesses, particularly small-and medium sized-businesses, to foster
economic development. When loans are enrolled in the program by
participating lending institutions, the lender obtains additional financial
protection through a special fund created by the lender, borrower and the
State. The lender and borrower contribute between 3% and 7% of the loan
to the fund. The amount of funds contributed by the borrower/lender must
be equal; however, the funds contributed by the bank may be recovered
from the borrower as additional fees or through interest rates. If the
amount of all enrolled loans is less than $2,000,000, the State contribution

will be 150% of the borrower/lender contribution. The borrower/lender contribution can be financed as part of the loan.

Contamination Cleanup/Investigation Grant Program: The Department of Trade and Economic Development can award grants towards contamination investigations and the development of a Response Action Plan (RAP) or for the cleanup of contamination on sites which will be redeveloped. The contamination investigation grants will allow smaller, outstate communities to access sites believed to be contaminated which are typically not addressed due to limited financial resources. The Contamination Cleanup grants address the growing need for uncontaminated, developable land. In both cases, grants are awarded to those sites where there is serious, imminent private or public development potential.

Minnesota Pathways Program: Act as a catalyst between business and education in developing cooperative training projects that provide training, new jobs and career paths for individuals making the transition from public assistance to the workforce. Grants are awarded to educational institutions with businesses as partners. Maximum available: $200,000 of Pathway funds per grant can be awarded for a project.

Underground Petroleum Tank Replacement Program: Exists to provide low interest financing to small gasoline retailers for the replacement of an underground petroleum tank. Business owners submit an application on the approved form along with supporting documentation including third party cost estimates from a certified installer, prior year federal tax return, schedule of existing debt and proof of gasoline volume sold in the last calendar year. Loans can only be made to businesses that demonstrate an ability to pay the loan from business cash flow. The maximum loan in $10,000.

Exports

Minnesota Trade Office: Acts as an advocate for Minnesota businesses pursuing international markets and to promote, assist and enhance foreign direct investments that contribute to the growth of Minnesota's economy. Services provided for Minnesota companies include information on trade shows and trade missions; education and training; and financial assistance programs for Minnesota companies.

Services for International Companies: Resources, services and direct counseling for all companies interested in international trade.

Minnesota World Trade Center Corporation: An international business resource for Minnesota and the upper Midwest.

Minnesota Export Finance Authority: Assists with the financing of exports through four focus areas: working capital guarantees for purchase orders, receivable insurance for foreign buyers, ExIm bank, and agency liaison.

Women and Minorities

Microenterprise Assistance Grants: To assist Minnesota's small entrepreneurs successfully startup or expand their businesses and to support job creation in the state. Any type of business is eligible to receive assistance, especially nontraditional entrepreneurs such as women, members of minority, low-income individuals or persons currently on or recently removed from welfare assistance who are seeking work. Startup entrepreneurs and expanding businesses receive technical assistance and, in some cases, financial support through selected nonprofit business development organizations. Businesses are eligible for up to $4,000 of technical assistance through this program. Participating organizations are reimbursed by DTED for up to half of this amount for approved expenses they incur on behalf of the grant recipient. The participating organization provides the other matching amount.

Minnesota Job Skills Partnership Program: Acts as a catalyst between business and education in developing cooperative training projects that provide training for new jobs or retraining of existing employees. Grants are awarded to educational institutions with businesses as partners. Preference will be given to non-profit institutions, which serve economically disadvantaged people, minorities, or those who are victims of economic dislocation and to businesses located in rural areas. Maximum available: $400,000 of Partnership funds per grant can be awarded for a project.

Urban Initiative Loan Program: Exists to assist minority owned and operated businesses and others that will create jobs in low-income areas of the Twin Cities. Urban Initiative Board enters into partnerships with local nonprofit organizations, which provide loans and technical assistance to start-up and expanding businesses. Project must demonstrate potential to create jobs for low-income people, must be unable to obtain sufficient capital from traditional private lenders, and must be able to demonstrate the potential to succeed. Eligible projects: Start-up and expansion costs, including normal business expenses such as machinery and equipment, inventory and receivables, working capital, new construction, renovation, and site acquisition. Financing of existing debt is not permitted. Microenterprises, including retail businesses, may apply for up to $10,000 in state funds. Maximum available: The maximum total loan available through the Urban Initiative Program is $300,000. The state may contribute 50% of the loan up to $150,000.

Mississippi

Department of Economic and Community Development
P.O. Box 849
Jackson, MS 39205-0849
601-359-3040
800-340-3323
Fax: 601-359-4339
www.decd.state.ms.us

Business Assistance

Department of Economic and Community Development: This office can provide information and expertise in dealing with state, federal, and local agencies. They also have information on financing programs and other services offered by the state government.

- *Training*: Customized industrial training programs provided through the State Department of Education. Job Training Partnership Act assistance provided through the Mississippi Department of Economic and Community Development.
- *Site Finding*: The Mississippi Resource Center in Jackson offers an interactive video for site viewing and detailed data on video, computer disk, or hard copy for later study.
- *One-stop environmental permitting*.

Business Financing

Loan Guarantee Program: Provides guarantees to private lenders on loans made to small businesses allowing a small business to obtain a loan that may not otherwise be possible without the guarantee protection. The maximum guarantee is 75% of the total loan or $375,000, whichever is less.

Industrial Development Revenue Bond Program: Reduces the interest costs of financing projects for companies through the issuance of both taxable and tax-exempt bonds. Additionally, ad valorem and sales tax exemptions are granted in conjunction with this type of public financing. There is a $10 million cap.

Small Enterprise Development Program: Provides funds for manufacturing and processing companies to finance fixed assets. Although a company may qualify for more than one loan under this program, the aggregate amount loaned to any company cannot exceed $2 million.

Department of Economic and Community Development Finance Programs: Through the issuance of State General Obligation Bonds, low-interest loans are provided to counties or cities to finance improvements that complement investments by private companies.

Airport Revitalization Revolving Loan Program: Funds from the issuance of state bonds provide loans to airport authorities for the construction and/or improvement of airport facilities. Maximum loan amount is $500,000.

Port Revitalization Revolving Loan Program: Designed to make loans to port authorities for improvement of port facilities. Maximum is $500,000.

Agribusiness Enterprise Loan Program: Designed to encourage the extension of conventional financing by lending institutions by providing interest-free loans to agribusinesses. Maximum loan is 20% of the total project cost or $200,000, whichever is less. Proceeds may be used to finance buildings and equipment and for costs associated with the purchase of land.

Small Business Assistance Program: Established for the purpose of providing funds to establish revolving loan funds to assist in financing small businesses. Maximum is $100,000.

Energy Investment Program: Provides financial assistance to individuals, partnerships or corporations making energy conserving capital improvements or designing and developing energy conservation processes. This program offers low-interest loans of up to $300,000.

Local Industrial Development Revenue Bonds: Local political entities have the authority to issue tax-exempt and taxable industrial development revenue bonds to finance new or expanding industrial enterprises up to 100% of total project costs.

General Obligation Bonds: Local political entities have the authority to issue general obligation bonds for the purpose of acquiring sites and constructing facilities for lease to new or expanding industries.

Tax Incentives

Jobs Tax Credit: Provides a five-year tax credit to the company's state income tax bill for each new job created by a new or expanding business. Amounts: $2,000 per new job for less developed counties, $1,000 per new job for moderately developed counties, and $500 per new job for developed counties.

R&D Jobs Tax Credit: Provides a five-year credit of $500 per year for each net new R&D job created by new or expanding businesses.

Headquarter Jobs Tax Credit: Provides a five-year tax credit of $500 per year for each net new job created by the transfer of a national or regional headquarters to Mississippi.

Child/Dependent Care Income Tax Credit: An income tax credit of 50% of qualified expenses is offered to any employer providing child/dependent care for employees during working hours.

Basic Skills Training Tax Credit: Provides a tax credit to new or existing businesses that pay for certain basic skills training or retaining for their employees. Credit is equal to 25% of qualified expenses of the training.

Rural Economic Development Credits: Companies financing projects through the Small Enterprise Development or Industrial Revenue Bond Program may be eligible to receive credits on corporate income taxes.

Mississippi State Port Income Tax Credit: Provides an income tax credit to taxpayers who utilize the port facilities at state, county, and municipal ports in Mississippi. The taxpayer receives a credit in an amount equal to certain charges paid by the taxpayer of export cargo.

County Property Tax Exemptions: For new or expanding manufacturers, certain properties may be exempted from county property taxes, except school taxes, for up to ten years at the local option.

Local authorities may grant a fee in lieu of taxes, including school taxes, on projects over $100 million.

Free Port Warehouse Law: Exempts finished goods from property taxes, including school taxes.

No state property tax except school taxes.

Sales Tax Exemptions: No sales tax on purchases of raw materials, processing chemicals, or packaging materials. No sales tax on direct purchases of construction materials, machinery, and equipment for businesses that are financed through certain bonds or located in less developed counties.

Partial Sales Tax: 50% sales tax exemptions for purchases of construction materials, machinery and equipment in moderately developed and developed counties. A 1 1/2% sales tax on machinery and parts used directly in manufacturing and on industrial electricity, natural gas, and fuels.

Exports

Foreign Trade Zones (FTZ): A safe area where goods can be landed, stored, processed, and transhipped--all without incurring custom duties (import tax). Foreign trade zones can provide customers with manufacturing, assembling, packaging, and display facilities, all free of duties. They are considered outside the customs territory of the United States in reference to many factors relating to international trade.

Women and Minorities

Minority Business Enterprise Division (MBED): Provides assistance to businesses in those categories. The division acts as principal advocate on behalf of minority- and women-owned business enterprises and promotes legislation that will help them operate more effectively. Developing funding sources, including state funding, bonding resources, federal and local funds, and others is among the major aims of MBED. But identifying funding sources represents only one aspect of MBED's service to Mississippi's women- and minority-owned firms. The division also attempts to put those businesses in touch with potential customers; MBED maintains an outreach program designed to include them in contracting of goods and services and procurement of contracts. A regional and statewide network of workshops, seminars, and trade shows continually provide training to stimulate the role of entrepreneurship in Mississippi's economic development.

Minority Surety Bond Guaranty Program: Program enables minority contractors, not meeting the surety industry's standard underwriting criteria, to obtain bid and performance bonds on contracts with state agencies and political subdivisions. Maximum bond guarantee is 75% of contract bond amount, or $112,500, whichever is less.

Minority Business Enterprise Loan Program: Designed to provide loans to socially and economically disadvantaged minority-or women-owned small businesses. Loan proceeds may be used for all project costs associated with the establishment or expansion of a minority business, including the purchase of fixed assets or inventory or to provide working capital. The minimum loan is $2,000 and the maximum loan is $25,000. MBFC may fund up to 100% of a total project.

Missouri

Department of Economic Development (DED)
Truman Building, Room 720
P.O. Box 118
Jefferson City, MO 65102-0118
573-751-4962
800-523-1434
Fax: 573-526-2416
www.ecodev.state.mo.us

Business Assistance

First Stop Shop: Serves to link business owners and state government and
provides information on state rules, regulations, licenses, and permits.
Business Assistance Center: Provides information and technical
assistance to start-up and existing businesses on available state
and federal programs. Offers several useful publications.
Contact: 888-751-2863.
University Outreach and Extension: Programs
to help citizens apply university research
knowledge to solve individual and community
problems. Working with business owners and
managers on a one-to-one basis, B&I
specialists help entrepreneurs identify
problem areas and find solutions.
Workforce Development System: Integrates
previously fragmented employment and training programs into a
comprehensive workforce development system. Services benefit both job
seekers and employers through One-Stop Career Centers. Contact
Workforce Development Transition Team, P.O. Box 1928, Jefferson City,
MO 65102-1928; 573-751-7039; Fax: 573-751-0147.
Small Business Incubators: Buildings that have been divided into units of
space, which are then leased to new small businesses. In addition to low-
cost physical space, incubators can help clients with access to necessary
office machines, reception and secretarial services, furniture, conference
rooms and technical expertise in business management.
Innovation Centers: Provide a wide range of management and technical
assistance to businesses. These centers are familiar with up-to-date
business management and technology innovations and help businesses
apply these innovations to help increase profits.

Mid-America Trade Adjustment Assistance Center: Available to small and medium-sized manufacturers who have been hurt by foreign competition. Helps firms analyze their strengths and weaknesses, develop a strategy to offset foreign competition, pay for implementing this strategy with federal cost-share fund.

Regional Planning Commissions: Services provided include business assistance, development, education, job training programs, loan preparation request, community assistance, airport planning, environmental assessments, grant administration and writing, hazardous waste planning, housing programs, legislative activities, local emergency planning, research, rural assistance, solid waste management, transportation planning, water and sewer planning, workshop development.

Business Financing

Action Fund Program: The program provides a subordinate loan to certain types of for-profit companies that need funds for start-up or expansion and have exhausted other sources. The projected growth of the company, economic impact, the risk of failure, and the quality of management are critical factors for approval. DED must determine that the borrower has exhausted other funding sources and only the least amount needed to complete the project may be provided. In any event, an Action Fund Loan would be limited to the lower of: $750,000 per project; 30% of the total project cost; or $20,000 per new full-time year-round job.

Brownfield Redevelopment Program: The purpose of this program is to provide financial incentives for the redevelopment of commercial/industrial sites owned by a governmental agency that have been abandoned for at least three years due to contamination caused by hazardous substances. The program provides state tax credits for eligible remediation costs. DED may provide a loan or guarantee for other project costs, or a grant for public infrastructure. Also, tax credits may be provided to businesses that create jobs at the facility. The program provides Missouri state income tax credits for up to 100% of remediation costs. Guaranteed loans or direct loans to an owner or operator of the property are limited to $1 million. Grants to public entities are also available up to $100,000 or 50% for feasibility studies or other due diligence costs. Grants can also be issued up to $1 million for the improvement of public infrastructure for the project. The total of grants, loans or guarantees cannot exceed $1 million per project.

CDBG Loan Guarantee Program: The purpose of this program is to provide "gap" financing for new or expanding businesses that cannot access

complete funding for a project. "Gap" financing means other sources of financing (including bank loans and owner equity) have been maximized, and a gap exists in the total project cost. The Department of Economic Development (DED) will guarantee 50% to 80% of the principal balance (after liquidation of assets) of a loan made by a financial institution. DED must determine that the borrower has exhausted other funding sources and only the least amount needed to complete the project may be provided. The maximum funding available is based on the lower of: $400,000 per project or $20,000 per new full-time permanent job created or retained. Approval is based on the good character of the owners, sufficient cash flow, adequate management and reasonable collateral.

Certified Capital Companies (CAPCO): Purpose is to induce private investment into new or growing Missouri small businesses, which will result in the creation of new jobs and investment. DED has initiated the formation of private venture capital firms (CAPCOs). These firms have certain requirements to make equity investments in eligible businesses in Missouri. The amount a CAPCO may invest in one Missouri business depends on various factors, however the maximum amount is 15% of the CAPCO's certified capital. Funding decisions are made by each CAPCO based on their evaluation of the return on investment relative to the risk. CAPCO funds may be used for equity investments, unsecured loans or hybrid investments in eligible businesses. Typically, venture capitalists require a projected 25-40% annual ROI, depending on the risk.

Economic Development Administration Revolving Loan Funds: Designed to provide gap financing for start-up as well as existing business and industry in rural areas. The Revolving Loan Funds are administered by various agencies throughout the state and are available in cooperation with area financial institutions.

Industrial Development Bonds (IDBs): Developed by the US Congress and the Missouri General Assembly to facilitate the financing of business projects. The interest received by the bondholders may be exempt from federal and state income taxes, if the project is eligible.

Missouri Market Development Program: Financial assistance is targeted toward developing and expanding manufacturing capacity in the state by assisting businesses with the development, purchase and installation of specialized equipment needed to convert manufacturing facilities to utilize recovered materials. The maximum amount of financial assistance for any one project is $75,000.

Linked Deposit Program: The State Treasurer will provide a deposit of state funds to a lender selected by an approved company. The rate of deposit is lower than market rates, and the difference is passed on to the borrower as a lower interest rate on the loan.

Neighborhood Improvement Districts Program: General obligation bonds are issued to finance public improvements requested by benefiting property owners. The bonds are paid by special assessments to the property owners. The project should realistically be in excess of $150,000 due to the financing costs. The outstanding bonds cannot exceed 10% of the city or county's assessed valuation.

Urban Enterprise Loan Fund (UEL): A micro lending instrument established by the State of Missouri, Department of Economic Development and administered in Kansas City by the downtown Minority Development Corporation and in St. Louis by the St. Louis Development Corporation. The program is designed to assist Missouri residents with the creation, expansion, and retention of micro-enterprises. Eligible enterprises must be located - or aspire to locate- within the Federally designated Enhanced Enterprise Community and the State Enterprise Zone. One job must be created for every $20,000 in Urban Enterprise Loan proceeds invested. Loans from the State fund range from a minimum of $10,000 up to a maximum of $100,000. The Urban Enterprise Loan Fund also has a matching funds requirement and new job creation criteria.

Missouri First: The State Treasurer has reserved a portion of available linked deposit funds for small businesses. State funds are deposited with participating lending institutions at up to 3% below the one-year Treasury Bill rate, with the lender passing on this interest savings to the small business borrower. A company must have less than 25 employees, be headquartered in Missouri, and be operating for profit. Small Business MISSOURI FIRST Linked Deposit loans are available for working capital. The maximum loan amount is $100,000. Contact State Treasurer's Office, P.O. Box 210, Jefferson City, MO 65102-0210; 800-662-8257.

Market Development Loans for Recovered Materials: The Environmental Improvement and Energy Resources Authority funds activities that promote the development of markets for recovered materials. Loans of up to $75,000 are available to companies for equipment used in the production or manufacture of products made from recovered materials. After three years, if all contract obligations are met, the loan is forgiven and repayment is not required. Contact: Environmental Improvement and

Energy Resources Authority, P.O. Box 744, Jefferson City, MO 65102; 573-526-5555.

Financial Aid for Beginning Farmers: Beginning farmers can receive federally tax-exempt loans from commercial lenders at rates 20 to 30% below conventional rates through this program. A qualified borrower can borrow up to $250,000 to buy agricultural land, farm buildings, farm equipment and breeding livestock in Missouri. The borrower must be a Missouri resident, at least 18 years old and whose chief occupation must be farming or ranching after the loan is closed. The borrower's net worth must not exceed $150,000, and he or she must have adequate working capital and experience in the type of farming operation for which the loan is sought. A beginning farmer is one who has not previously owned more than 15% of the medium-sized farm in their county. Land cannot be purchased from a relative. For more information, contact Missouri Agricultural and Small Business Development Authority, Beginning Farmer Program, P.O. Box 630, Jefferson City, MO 65102; 573-751-2129.

Small Corporation Offering Registration (SCOR): Missouri's Small Corporate Offering Registration (SCOR) provides a process for entrepreneurs to register their securities. The SCOR process has been designed by state securities regulators to make it easier and less expensive for small companies to raise needed capital from Missouri residents. All securities registered through this process need to complete form U-7 available from the Secretary of State's Office. For more information, contact Securities Division, Secretary of State's Office, P.O. Box 1276, Jefferson City, MO 65102; 573-751-4136.

Working Capital, St. Louis: Working Capital is a micro-lending program
 which identifies small business people in the St. Louis area and makes available to them the commercial credit and business support which enables them to expand their business. Working Capital utilizes a peer-lending technique. At required monthly meetings borrowers receive continuing assistance in the marketing of their goods or services. The maximum first-time loan is $500 payable in four to six months; subsequent loans can have increased amounts (up to $5,000) and longer duration. Working Capital gives priority to individuals already in business to minimize loan risk; will consider applications from start-ups. Contact Working Capital, 3830 Washington, St. Louis, MO 63108; 314-531-4546.

Economic Council of St. Louis County: Services include Business Development Fund (BDF), Metropolitan St. Louis Loan Program,

Minority/ Disadvantaged Contractor Loan Guarantee, Recycling Market Development Loan Program, SBA 504 Loan Program and Minority & Women's Prequalified Loan Program. Economic Council of St. Louis County, 121 South Meramec St., St. Louis, MO 63105; 314-889-7663.

St. Charles County Economic Development Council: Program assists eligible companies with fixed asset and working capital needs; acts as the certified development company which packages SBA 504 loans. Contact St. Charles County Economic Development Council, 5988 Midrivers Mall Dr., St. Charles, MO 63304; 314-441-6880.

St. Louis Development Corporation:

1. St. Louis City Revolving Loan Fund: Provides direct, low interest, subordinated loans for working capital, machinery and equipment, purchasing land and buildings, renovation and constructing facilities and leasehold improvements. Business must be located in the City of St. Louis and be licensed to do business in the City. Must create one full-time job for every $10,000 of funds. Loans can provide up to 1/3 of the project cost to a maximum loan amount of $150,000.

    St. Louis Development Corporation

2. St. Louis Urban Enterprise Loan, St. Louis Development Corporation: Provides loans to businesses located within the Enterprise Community area or the Enterprise Zone within the City of St. Louis. Eligible borrowers must be for profit businesses with current employment of less than 100. Eligible program activities will include fixed asset or working capital needs. Eligible projects must retain existing or create new jobs (one job created for every $20,000 of funding). The UEL can lend up to 50% of the project costs to a maximum loan amount of $100,000.

3. LDC Micro Loan Program, St. Louis Development Corporation: Microloans are available to start-up companies or businesses less than one year old located within the City of St. Louis; one job, other than the owner's, must be created. Successful applicants must demonstrate a viable business plans and the inability to secure bank financing. Companies must show the ability to start or grow the business with a maximum loan amount of $25,000. Loans may be used to cover start-up costs, working capital and purchase of machinery and equipment.

Contact St. Louis Development Corporation, 1015 Locust St., #1200, St. Louis, MO 63101; 314-622-3400.

First Step Program, Kansas City: The First Step Fund (FSF) offers training in business basics such as record keeping, budgeting and marketing; assistance in completing a feasibility study for a business; opportunity to apply for loans of up to $2,500; and ongoing support group. FSF participants must be residents of Jackson, Clay or Platte counties in Missouri and must meet federal guidelines for low to moderate income. During a 10-week business training program, students work on a feasibility study for the proposed business. Potential borrowers receive continuing education at monthly meetings. Participants review each others' feasibility studies and approve loans. The maximum loan amount for first-time borrowers is $2,500 and $5,000 for second-time borrowers. Contact First Step Fund, 1080 Washington St., Kansas City, MO 64105; 816-474-5111, ext. 247; Fax: 816-472-4207.

Kansas City's Urban Enterprise Loan Fund, Kansas City: Fund is designed to assist with the creation, expansion and retention of small businesses located, or aspiring to locate, within the federally designated Enhanced Enterprise Community and the State Enterprise Zone. Eligible applicants include any Missouri resident with a for-profit business with gross annual revenues of less than $250,000 and less than 100 employees. Loan amounts can range from $10,000 to $100,000; matching funds are required as well as new job creation (minimum of one job per $20,000 borrowed). Contact First Business Bank, 800 West 47th St., Kansas City, MO 64112; 816-561-1000.

Community Development Corporation of Kansas City: Provides microloan business assistance to small businesses located in a five-county area; assists entrepreneurs whose credit needs are $25,000 and under. Contact Community Development Corporation of Kansas City, 2420 E. Linwood Blvd., Kansas City, MO 64109; 816-924-5800; Fax: 816-921-3350.

Thomas Hill Enterprise Center, Macon: The Thomas Hill Enterprise Center established a Revolving Loan Fund (RLF) to fill financing gaps not covered by conventional lenders. While certain restrictions exist, the RLF is designed to provide financing for businesses which cannot obtain adequate funds from conventional sources. Contact: Thomas Hill Enterprise Center, 1709 Prospect Dr., Suite B, Macon, MO 63552; 660-385-6550; 800-470-8625.

In$Dent Small Business Support: Peer lending program designed to assist low income residents of Dent County attain economic self-sufficiency by helping them start and/or maintain profitable businesses. All borrowers complete an approved business management training program and must be a member of a peer lending group. Loans will not be for more than $1,000 for any one group member. After the initial loan is repaid, members can apply for larger loans up to $2,000; each loan thereafter will have a ceiling of twice the previous loan, up to a maximum of $10,000. Contact: Bryan

Adcock, Child and Family Development Specialist, 112 E. 5th St., Jucicial Building, Suite 4, Salem, MO 65560; 573-729-3196.

CDBG Industrial Infrastructure Grant: This program assists local governments in the development of public infrastructure that allows industries to locate new facilities, expand existing facilities or prevent the relocation or closing of a facility. The use of this program is based on the local government exhausting their available resources. DED has targeted a 20% match by the community base upon the availability of unencumbered city or county funds.

Tax Incentives

Small Business Investment "Capital" Tax Credit: The state of Missouri, through the Small Business Investment Capital Tax Credit Program offers a 40% tax credit to eligible investors in qualified businesses. Eligible investors may not be principle owners in the business. Only unsecured investments are considered eligible. All businesses wishing to participate in the program must make application to the Department of Economic Development prior to accepting investments for which tax credits are to be issued.

Business Facility Tax Credit Program: State income tax credits are provided to the business based on the number of new jobs and amount of new investment created at the qualifying facility. The credits are provided each tax year for up to ten years after the project commences operations. The tax credits are earned each tax period for up to 10 years. The formula to earn the tax credits is based on:

- $100 (or $75 for a new MO company) for each new job created at the project.
- $100 (or $75 for a new MO company) per $100,000 of the new capital investment at the project.

Capital Tax Credit Program: The investors of an approved business will receive a 40% state income tax credit on the amount of their equity investment or, in the case of a qualified investment in a Missouri small business in a distressed community, may receive a 60% state income tax credit. The percentage of stock purchased by the investors is negotiated with the business. The minimum amount of tax credits allowed per investor is $1,500 ($3,750 investment). The maximum amount of tax credits allowed per investor is $100,000 ($250,000 investment).

Community Bank 50% Tax Credit: The purpose of this program is to induce investment into Community Banks, which then invest in new or growing businesses or real estate development, resulting in an expansion of the tax base, elimination of blight, reduction of reliance on public assistance and the creation of jobs. A contributor may obtain state tax credits based on 50% of investments or contributions in a Community Bank. The Community Bank then makes equity investments or loans to a business, or investment in real estate development within a target area. No more than $750,000 can be invested or loaned by the Community Bank for any one business (including any affiliated or subsidiary of the business) or real estate development.

Enterprise Zone Tax Benefits: State income tax credits are provided to the business based on the number of new jobs and amount of new investment created at the qualifying facility. The business may earn credits based on the facility's new jobs and investment, the number of zone residents and "special" employees hired and trained for the facility.

Historic Credit Tax Credit: The program provides state tax credits for 25% of eligible costs and expenses of the rehabilitation of an approved historic structure.

Infrastructure Tax Credit Program

- *Missouri Development Finance Board (MDFB):* Provides state tax credits to a contributor based on 50% of the contribution. The contributed funds are granted to a public entity to finance infrastructure needed to facilitate an approved project. Eligible contributors receive a tax credit of 50% of the contribution against Chapter 143 (excluding certain withholding taxes), 147, and 148 taxes. Contributions may be eligible for federal tax deductions also.

- *Distressed Communities Tax Credit Program*: Based on demographic requirements. Some entire cities qualify, and some areas qualify based on census block group demographics. The total maximum credit for all businesses already located within distressed communities shall be $750,000 for each calendar year.

- *Research Expense Tax Credit Program*: Purpose of the Research Expense Tax Credit Program is to induce existing businesses to increase their research efforts in Missouri by offering a tax credit. The amount of qualified research expenses for which tax credits shall apply, may not exceed 200% of the taxpayer's average qualified research expenses incurred during the three-year period immediately prior to the tax period the credits are being claimed. The aggregate of all tax credits authorized shall not exceed $10 million in any taxable year.

- *Seed Capital Tax Credit Program*: Purpose is to stimulate investment in new or young Missouri companies to fund the research, development and subsequent precommercialization phases of new, innovative products or services. Any person who makes a qualified contribution to a qualified fund shall be entitled to receive a tax credit equal to 50% of the amount of their contribution. This credit may be used to satisfy the state tax liability due within the year of the qualified investment, or in any of the ten tax years thereafter.

- *Small Business Incubator*: The purpose of the Small Business Incubator Tax Credit Program is to generate private funds to be used to establish a "protective business environment" (incubator) in which a number of small businesses can collectively operate to foster growth and development during their start-up period. The minimum tax credit is $1,500 per contributor. The maximum tax credit is $50,000 per contributor if made to a single incubator and $100,000 per contributor if made to multiple incubators. There is no maximum if the contribution is made to the Incubator Fund. The overall maximum amount of tax credits that can be issued under this program in any one calendar year is $500,000.

- *Tax Increment Financing Program*: A method to invent redevelopment of a project that otherwise would not occur. TIF redirects an approved portion of certain local taxes caused by the project to reduce project costs. The amount and length of the increment is negotiated by the TIF Commission based on the least amount to cause the project to occur. The "increment" may be up to 100% of the increased amount of real property taxes and 50% of local sales, utility and (in St. Louis and Kansas City) earnings taxed for a period of up to 23 years, as approved by the municipality.

- *Transportation Development Tax Credit Program*: A company (or individual) may be provided a state income tax credit for up to 50% of a contribution to a public entity for eligible activities. The project is needed to facilitate a business project or is a community development/public infrastructure improvement.

- *Wine and Grape Production*: To assist vineyards and wine producers with the purchase of needed equipment and materials by granting tax credits. A grape grower or wine producer is allowed a 25% state income tax credit on the amount of the purchase price of all new equipment and materials used directly in the growing of grapes or the production of wine in the state.

Exports

Missouri Office Of International Marketing: Services include: International Consulting Service, Competitive Analysis Reports, Trade Show Reports, Trade Exhibitions, Catalog Shows, Missouri International Office Assistance, Foreign Company Background Checks, Rep-Find Service, International Travel Program, Marketing Program, Trade Opportunity

Program, Foreign Trade Missions, Strategic Alliance Program, Export Finance Assistance, Made In Missouri Catalogs, Missouri Export Directory, Recognition Program.

Missouri's Export Finance Program: Missouri companies that need financial assistance exporting to foreign markets can use programs of the Export and Import Bank of the United States(Ex-Im Bank) and the Small Business Administration (SBA) through a joint project that provides local access for Missouri businesses. There are primarily two programs available, Working Capital Loan Guarantees and Export Credit Insurance. These programs are designed to help small and medium-sized businesses that have exporting potential but need funds or risk insurance to produce and market goods or services for export.

Export Credit Insurance: The state of Missouri offers assistance in obtaining export credit insurance through the Export/Import Bank of the US to take the risk out of selling to customers overseas. The Missouri program, which insures both commercial and political risks, guarantees an exporter that once his goods are shipped, he will be paid. Insured receivables can enhance an exporter's ability to obtain export financing and allow an exporter to offer more attractive credit terms to foreign buyers. For more information contact Missouri Export Finance Program, P.O. Box 118, Jefferson City, MO 65102-0118; 573-751-4855.

Women and Minorities

Missouri Women's Council: To help Missouri women achieve economic self-sufficiency by supporting education, training, and leadership opportunities. Each year the Missouri Women's Council reviews pilot program proposals across the state and selects projects to fund which promote training, employment, and support Missouri women in the work place.

Workplace Readiness for Women: This particular program provides skills for employment in manufacturing industries for women living in Camden, Laclede, and Pulaski Counties. Training includes classroom instruction, one-on-one instruction and tutoring, computer training and work experience assignments with private employers who agree to provide the necessary supervision and work experience to assist participants with skills development and transition into employment in the manufacturing industry. For more information on this program, please contact Trish Rogers, Central Ozarks Private Industry Council, 1202 Forum Drive, Rolla, MO 65401; 800-638-1401 ext. 153; Fax: 573-634-1865.

Workforce Preparation for Women: This program is currently served in two Missouri locations; Mineral Area College in Park Hills and Jefferson

College in Hillsboro. These programs focus on self-esteem, foundation skills and competencies as identified by an assessment process, and a workforce preparation plan developed by each student. Experts from education, business, and industry serve as speakers and consultants for the training sessions. Furthermore, the program matches each student with a mentor. For more information on this program, please contact Dr. Nancy Wegge, Consortium Director, Jefferson College, Hillsboro, MO 63050; 573-431-1951; Fax: 573-431-9397.

Capital for Entrepreneurs, Kansas City: Seed capital fund divided into three separate funds of $1 million each: Fund for Women, Fund for Hispanics, and Fund for African-Americans. Contact: Capital for Entrepreneurs, 4747 Troost Ave., Kansas City, MO 64110; 816-561-4646; Fax: 816-756-1530.

Office of Minority Business (OMB): Charged with the responsibility of identifying and developing support systems that assist the minority business community in gaining a foothold in the mainstream of Missouri's economy. This responsibility entails counseling minority small businesses on business start-up, retention, expansion, financing, and procurement; also including but not limited to providing ready access to information regarding current legislation and regulations that affects minority business. The staff of the Office of Minority Business can provide assistance with; administering technical and financial assistance programs; providing new and small businesses with management expertise; business development information; tying minority firms to national and global markets; connecting minority firms to the labor market; accessing research and technology; and other customized assistance.

Montana

Department of Commerce
1424 Ninth Ave.
P.O. Box 200505
Helena, MT 59620-0505
406-444-3814
800-221-8015 (in MT)
Fax: 406-444-1872
http://commerce.state.mt.us

Business Assistance

Economic Development Division: Offers a variety of programs aimed at assisting start-up and existing businesses with the technical and financial assistance necessary for their success. Works closely with other department divisions, state agencies, and federal and private programs, as well as local development groups, chambers and similar organizations.

Business Location Assistance: Provides prompt referrals of prospective

expanding or relocating firms to Montana communities meeting the company's physical, economic and/or demographic requirements; provides assistance to communities in working with recruitment prospects; works with individual communities or groups of communities and/or other organizations to design and implement proactive recruitment efforts to attract specific types of firms in industries targeted by the community; works with companies new to Montana to identify and utilize available technical assistance and resident suppliers of materials and services. If in-state demand for particular goods or services exists, the program will attempt to recruit one or more firms to fill that demand. Special services, including visa consulting and assistance, is available to investors from Canada or subsidiaries of international corporations. The program distributes prospects lists to Certified Community Lead organizations and appropriate Department of Commerce staff, unless otherwise requested and authorized by the prospective company.

The Census and Economic Information Center (CEIC): The official source of census data for Montana, the Center maintains a collection of documents and computer-retrievable files that address the economy and population of the state (historical as well as current), including special papers and annual, quarterly and monthly statistical reports from federal agencies and other Montana state agencies

Montana Health Facility Authority: Issues revenue bonds or notes to finance or refinance projects involving construction, renovation, or equipment purchases for public or private non-profit health care programs. The MHFA lends its bond proceeds to participating health care facilities at costs below those offered by commercial lending institutions, thereby substantially lowering the facilities' borrowing expenses. In some instances, however, the MHFA includes commercial lending institutions in the financing to provide credit enhancement or private placement for the bonds. The MHFA may issue its notes and bonds, which are not general obligations of the state, for a single entity or a pool of health care facilities. Eligible health facilities may include hospitals, clinics, nursing homes, centers for the developmentally disabled or a variety of other health facilities.

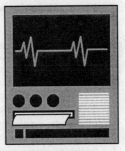

Montana Manufacturing Extension Center (MMEC): Improves the competitiveness of Montana manufacturers through direct, unbiased engineering and managerial assistance in partnership with public and private resources. MMEC field engineers help companies obtain the highest output from their people, equipment, and capital. They make "house calls" and provide free initial consultation. Their assistance includes, but is not limited to: productivity and quality audits, facility layouts, materials handling, ISO 9000 and quality assurance, benchmarking, managing growth, capacity planning, feasibility assessment, equipment justification, process design and improvement, cycle time reduction, production management, cost/benefit analysis, cost reduction, product costing, make/buy analysis, inventory analysis, supplier identification and relations, payroll incentive systems, materials requirements planning (MRP), and more. Contact: MMEC/ UTAP, 315 Roberts Hall, Montana State University-Bozeman, Bozeman, MT 59717; 406-994-3812.

University Technical Assistance Program: For more than 10 years, the University Technical Assistance Program (UTAP) has provided technical assistance to Montana manufacturers through engineering graduate students who work half-time during the academic year and full-time in the summers. It continues as an integral part of MMEC with the MMEC Bozeman field engineer serving as the UTAP supervisor. Undergraduates who have completed certain engineering course work may be hired as summer interns under the supervision of other field engineers. The UTAP staff engineers complete some projects and provide valuable support to the MMEC field engineers on other projects. Contact: MMEC/ UTAP, 315 Roberts Hall, Montana State University-Bozeman, Bozeman, MT 59717; 406-994-3812.

Business Financing

Microbusiness Finance: Montana "micro" business companies with fewer than 10 full-time equivalent employees and annual gross revenues under $500,000 can receive loans of up to $35,000 from the program's network of regional revolving loan funds lending directly to businesses. The loan program is designed to fund economically sound business projects that are unable to obtain commercial financing. Companies must provide a detailed written business plan and may be required to participate in business training classes. In addition to financing, borrowers receive technical assistance and consulting to help assure their success.

Job Investment Loans (JIL): This program is intended to provide funding for loans to Montana businesses as part of a financing package to permit business expansion, job creation and job retention. The program will provide a portion of the financing necessary to permit business expansion, job retention, and job creation. JIL monies will be used only in conjunction with equity and other debt financing in cases where other funding would not satisfy the total need and would not be available without this piece of additional financing.

Research and Development Financing: Montana Science and Technology Alliance provides $13.1 million in matching capital, from the Permanent Coal Tax Trust Fund, for research and development projects at Montana public universities.

Risk Capital Financing: The Montana Science and Technology Risk Capital Financing program may provide additional funding for current Montana companies. To receive MSTA financing, these businesses must meet the MSTA Board's investment criteria and have potential for achieving significant growth, benefiting the state's economy, and providing a substantial return on the board's investment. The MSTA structures all risk capital financing as loans. These loans may be convertible to company stock or would otherwise be structured to provide a risk-adjusted return on investment.

Growth Through Agriculture: Projects must embody innovative agricultural products or processes. Amounts: $50,000 in any one round, $150,000 to any one firm.

REA Loan and Grant Program: Provides zero-interest loans and grant to RE Act borrowers for relending to projects promoting rural economic development and job creation.

Seed Capital Program: provides funding for early-state entrepreneurial companies. The emphasis for funding is on technological companies but other companies can receive financing as well. The program may loan up to $350,000 in a single financing round, and up to a maximum of $750,000 to any one company over time.

Tax Incentives

New and Expanding Industry Tax Credit: Credit is equal to 1% of new wages paid by any corporation that is either brand new or has expanded its number of jobs by 30% or more.

Reclamation and Recycling Equipment Credit: Investment tax credit for businesses equal to 25% of the cost of property purchased to collect or process reclaimable material or to manufacture a product from reclaimed material.

Recycling Tax Credit: Income tax deduction for purchase of recycled material.

Wind Energy Generation Tax Credit: Income tax or license severance tax credit equal to 35% of the eligible costs for an investment of $5,000 or more in a commercial wind-powered energy generation system.

Small Business Investment Tax Credit: Corporation income, licenses, or coal severance tax credit for investment in a small business investment company. Credit is limited to 50% of the investment to a maximum credit of $250,000 for each taxpayer.

Research and Development Exemption: Exemption from the corporation income of license tax on the net income of a newly organized research and development firm during its first 5 years of operation.

Dependent Care Assistance Credit: A company can claim a credit for the amount paid or incurred during the taxable year for dependent care assistance actually provided to or on behalf of an employee.

Infrastructure Fees Credit: A nonrefundable tax credit is available against the corporation license tax or income tax for the portion of the fees that are charged to a specified new business for the use of the infrastructure that is built with loans.

Inventory Tax Exemption: Business inventories are exempt from property tax.

Property Tax Incentives for Selected Businesses: Reduction in property tax rates are available to: real and personal property used in the production of gasohol, machinery and equipment used in electrolytic reduction facilities (production of aluminum), market value on machinery and equipment

used in a maltiny barley facility, market value on machinery and
equipment used in a canola seed oil processing facility.

Property Tax Incentives for Specific Industries: Reduction in property tax
rates are available to: industries that manufacture, mill, mine, produce,
process, or fabricate materials; that convert materials unserviceable in
their natural state into commercial products or materials, engage in the
mechanical or chemical transformation of materials of substance into new
products, engage in the transportation, warehousing or distribution of
commercial products or materials, or if 50% or more of their annual gross
income comes from out of state sales. Additional property tax reductions
are available to: research and development firms, agricultural or timber
product processing plants, and property used in the production of motion
pictures or television commercials.

Local Option Property Tax Incentives: Property tax reduction is available to:
new and expanding industries, businesses making improvements,
machinery and equipment, business incubators, industrial parks, buildings
or land sold or donated to a local economic development organization, and
air and water pollution-control equipment.

Exports

Trade Program: Mission is to identify opportunities for worldwide and
domestic trade and to provide representation, information and technical
assistance. More specifically, the Trade Program provides: trade
consultation, Marketing/Country reports, trade leads, trade show
assistance, special promotions for Montana made products and services,
tourism promotion services in the Far East.

Made in Montana program: Works to elevate the status of Montana-made
products in the marketplace and to educate Montanans about the diversity
of products manufactured in their state.

Nebraska

Department of Economic Development
P.O. Box 94666
301 Centennial Mall South
Lincoln, NE 68509
402-471-3111
800-426-6505 (in NE)
Fax: 402-471-3365
TDD: 402-471-3441
www.ded.state.ne.us

Business Assistance

One-Stop Business Assistance Program: Provides
assistance on identifying, marketing and finance
information; business information and research,
regulations, licenses, fees, and other state
requirements for business operation.

Skilled Training Employment Program (STEP):
Offers a comprehensive, on-the-job training
program for new and expanding businesses.

Government Procurement Assistance: Helps create
additional markets.

Match Marketing: Assists with matching Nebraska buyers and suppliers.

Technical Assistance: Increases productivity and competitiveness.

Site Location Assistance: Includes facilitating access to programs.

Business Financing

Industrial Revenue Bonds (IRB): All Nebraska counties and municipalities, as
well as the Nebraska Investment Finance Authority, are authorized to
issue IRBs to finance land, buildings and equipment for industrial
projects. The rate of interest is normally lower than on most loans.

Nebraska Investment Finance Authority: Issues IRBs for land, building and
equipment for industrial enterprises, as well as provides financing for
housing.

Dollar and Energy Saving Loans: Energy saving loans are offered statewide
by the Nebraska Energy Office and the state's lending institutions. The
interest rate is 6% or less, but may be adjusted semi-annually.

Adjustments do not affect existing loans. Check with a lender or the Nebraska Energy Office for the current rate. Contact: Nebraska Energy Office, Box 95085, Lincoln, NE 68509; 402-471-2867.

Community Improvement Financing: This is Nebraska's version of Tax Increment Financing, a method of financing public improvements associated with a private development project in a blighted and substandard area by using the projected increase in the property tax revenue which will result from the private development.

Local Option Municipal Economic Development Act: Provides the ability for communities to add a sales or property tax for economic development projects.

Nebraska Energy Fund: Provides low-interest loans for energy efficiency improvements.

Nebraska Redevelopment Act: Authorizes Community Improvement Financing for real estate and equipment in a project that adds at least 500 new jobs and $50 million of new investment.

Adams County Central Community College: Total Loan Funds: $30,000 as of April 24, 1996. Sources: Private money. Loan Terms: Low interest rates, 3 year term, collateral required, payments put on amortization schedule, $10,000 maximum. Loan Eligibility: Serves the 25-county Central Community College area. Services: Counseling, CCC business courses, SCORE available. Contact Person: Jim Svoboda, Coordinator, P.O. Box 1054, Hastings, NE 68902-1024; 402-461-2461; 402-461-2506; Email: {svohbus@cccadm. gi.cccneb.edu}.

Mid-Nebraska Community Services: A caring, non-profit community action agency that provides resources to help people and communities in 27 counties grow within themselves for a better future. Total Loan Fund: $130,000. Contact Person: Robert E. Hobbs, Loan Coordinator, 16 West 11th Street, P.O. Box 2288, Kearney, NE 68848-2288; 308-865-5675; 308-865-5681.

Rural Business Development Fund, Small Enterprises Economic Development Project, Rural Economic and Community Development, State of Nebraska. LB144, private grants. Provides microenterprise loans, loan counseling, credit analysis, developing business plan and entrepreneurial training. Contact Person: Robert E. Hobbs, Loan Coordinator, 16 West 11th Street, P.O. Box 2288, Kearney, NE 68848-2288; 308-865-5675; 308-865-5681.

Northeast Nebraska Development District Business Loan Programs: Exists to promote and assist the growth and development of business and industrial concerns within Northeast Nebraska. Priority will be given to fixed asset financing (land, building, equipment); however, working capital can also be financed. Generally, loans will range from $10,000 to $100,000 (maximum). Contact: Northeast Nebraska Economic Development District, 111 S. 1st St., Norfolk, NE 68701; 402-379-1150; {www.nenedd.org}.

Tax Incentives

Employment and Investment Growth Act: With a $3 million investment in qualified property and addition of 30 full-time employees, a business qualifies for: direct refund of all sales and use taxes paid on purchases of qualified property; 5% tax credit on the amount of the total compensation paid to employees; 10% tax credit on total investment in qualified property, 5 and 10% tax credits applied to income tax liability or used to obtain refund of sales and use taxes paid on other purchases. With a $10 million investment in qualified property and addition of 100 full-time employees, a business qualifies for: all of the above plus up to a 15 year personal property tax exemption on newly acquired: turbine-powered aircraft, mainframe computers and peripheral components, equipment used directly in processing agricultural products. Investment in qualified property resulting in a net gain of $20 million with no increased employment qualifies a business for direct refund of all sales and use taxes paid on purchases of qualified property.

Employment Expansions and Investment Incentive Act: Provides tax credits for any business which increase investment by at least $75,000 and increase net employment by an average of two full-time positions during a taxable year. Credits of $1,500 per net new employee and $1,000 per $75,000 net new investment may be used to reduce a portion of the taxpayer's income tax liability or to obtain a refund of sales and use taxes paid.

Quality Jobs Act: Authorizes a wage benefit credit to new employees of approved companies that add at least 500 new jobs and $50 million in new investment or 250 new jobs and $100 million in new investment.

Enterprise Zones: Within these areas, tax credits are given for qualifying businesses which increase employment and make investments in the area.

For more information, contact Nebraska Department of Revenue, 301 Centennial Mall South, P.O. Box 94818, Lincoln, NE 68509; 402-471-2971; 800-742-7474.

Exports

Office of International Trade and Investment (OITI): Works with existing businesses to expand their international marketing efforts, as well as foster international manufacturing investments in the state.

Nevada

State of Nevada Commission on Economic Development
5151 South Carson St.
Carson City, NV 89710
775-687-4325
800-336-1600
Fax: 775-687-4450
www.state.nv.us/businessop

555 E. Washington Avenue
Suite 5400
Las Vegas, NV 89101
702-486-2700
Fax: 702-486-2701

Business Assistance

Commission on Economic Development: Publishes a pamphlet, *Business Assistance*. Acts as a clearinghouse for information and technical

assistance. Operates several business assistance programs and performs advertising and public relations activities on behalf of Nevada business. Maintains a computerized inventory of available manufacturing and warehousing buildings, land and corporate office space, and customized site selection. *Procurement Outreach Program*: Assists businesses in successfully tapping into this lucrative market by: introducing firms to federal agencies that purchase the products and services they sell; providing assistance to ensure that companies are prepared with all of the tools, knowledge and skills necessary to meet the federal government's specifications and standards, and properly complete bids; offering seminars, marketing fairs, mailing lists and direct assistance as well as the Automated Bidline which is a fax-on demand system allowing instant access to the latest bid and requests for proposal information.

Community Business Resource Center: A one-stop center for business information designed to enhance the economic self-sufficiency of low-and moderate-income individuals by developing their entrepreneurial skills. Services available include training, technical assistance and access to

credit. Contact Community Business Resource Center, 116 E. 7th St.,
Suite 3, Carson City, NV 89701; 800-337-4590.

Business Financing

Nevada Development Capital Corporation: A private development fund
   designed to finance growth opportunities for small, sound Nevada
   businesses which do not qualify for conventional financing. The
   financing provided by NDCC includes but is not limited to the following:
   working capital loans secured by primary or subordinated assets; loans
   secured by fixed assets with longer terms than could be provided by
   conventional lending sources; loans for the acquisition of a business or
   interest in a business; subordinated loans in cases where available bank
   financing is sufficient; loans to refinance existing debt in cases where
   existing terms present a hardship for the business. Most loans will
   probably be in the $50,000 to $150,000 range. Contact: Nevada State
   Development Corporation, 350 S. Center St., Suite 310, Reno, NV
   89501; 775-323-3625; 800-726-2494.
Nevada Self-Employment Trust: A start-up business may be eligible to borrow
   from $100 to $7,500 while existing companies may borrow a maximum of
   $25,000. Contact: Community Business Resource Center, 116 E. 7th St.,
   Suite 3, Carson City, NV 89701; 800-337-4590.
Venture Capital: A potential source of venture capital is the State Public
   Employees Retirement System that disperses funds through several
   venture capital pools.
Industrial Revenue Bonds: A special type of loan to qualified manufacturers
   who are buying land, building new facilities, refurbishing existing
   buildings and purchasing new equipment.
Rural Business Loans: Companies in rural Nevada have additional avenues for
   financial assistance designed to: lend money to small businesses in need
   of expansion or start-up financing; assist small businesses in obtaining gap
   financing to complete their business expansion projects; provide financing
   to small businesses which meet job creation requirements. Assistance is
   available through the Nevada Revolving Loan Fund, Rural Economic and
   Community Development Services, and Rural Nevada Development
   Corporation.
Train Employees Now: Grants to training providers up to 75% of the total
   eligible costs with a cap of $1,000 per trainee.
Business Assistance Program: Helps businesses understand environmental
   rules and explain the permitting process as well as identify sources of

financing for pollution control equipment and provide access to the latest information regarding environmental issues.

Tax Incentives

No Personal Income Tax

No Corporate Income Tax

No Franchise Tax on Income

No Unitary Tax

No Inventory Tax

No Inheritance, Estate, or Gift Tax

No Admissions or Chain Store Tax

Freeport: Protects shipments in transit from taxation and cuts the cost of doing business both domestically and internationally.

Sales and Use Tax Abatement: Partial sales/use tax exemption on machinery and equipment purchases.

Sales and Use Tax Deferral: Tax deferral on machinery and equipment purchases in excess of $100,000.

Business Tax Abatement: A 50% tax exemption determined on a case by case basis.

Personal Property Tax Abatement: 50% tax exemption for businesses operating in Nevada for 10 or more years.

Property Tax Abatement: 75% tax exemption on real and personal property for qualified recycling businesses.

Exports

Nevada's International Trade Program: Goal is to assist Nevada businesses to begin, or expand, exporting to international markets. Services include: Trade Missions, Export Seminars, Export Counseling, International Trade Database, Foreign Buyers Delegations, International Trade Directories.

Foreign Trade Zones: Two zones allow international importers duty-free storage and assembly of foreign products.

Export Financing: Assistance is available through private sector financial institution, the International Trade Program and the federal Export/Import Bank.

New Hampshire

State of New Hampshire
Department of Resources and Economic Development
172 Pembroke Road
P.O. Box 1856
Concord, NH 03302-1856
603-271-2341
800-204-5000 (in NH)
Fax: 603-271-6784
www.ded.state.nh.us/obid

Business Assistance

Office of Business and Industrial Development: Provides assistance and
publications designed to support and promote business
and industry in the state. Information in areas such as
licensing and permits, financial counseling, marketing, and
exporting, labor markets, and more.
Economic Development Data System: A comprehensive
database of all the communities and available industrial
properties within the state.
Business Visitation Program: Local volunteers visit
businesses to gather information about firms'
development issues, economic concerns and
opinions about their community as a place to do
business. Once aware of these issues, local,
state and federal programs can be accessed to assist
the firms. A referral network coordinates questions, issues and concerns.
Vendor Matching Program: A database that can be used to match a
prospective client's product needs with the appropriate New Hampshire
vendor of those products.
Procurement Technical Assistance Program: Provides the necessary tools to
be competitive in the federal marketplace through procurement
counseling; contract announcements; specifications and standards; and
support databases.
Industrial Research Center: Assistance in basic and applied research,
development and marketing through a matching grants program; hands-on
training in Design of Experiment methods; and helping inventors develop
patent and commercialize their ideas. Contact: New Hampshire Industrial

Research Center, University of New Hampshire, 222 Kingsbury Hall, Durham, NH 03824; 603-862-0123.

Job Training Council: Provides job training for citizens while helping businesses gain capable workers. Contact: New Hampshire Job Training, 64 Old Suncook Rd., Concord, NH 03301; 603-228-9500.

Manchester Manufacturing Management Center: Serves as a crucial link between the university and the manufacturing community through sponsorship of industry-specific programs, including seminars, symposia, expos, and internships. Contact: Manchester Manufacturing Management Center, 150 Dow St., Manchester, NH 03101; 603-625-0106.

Business Financing

Regional and Local Revolving Loan Funds: Many local and regional revolving loan funds exist throughout New Hampshire. These funds have been capitalized from a variety of services, many with federal monies. The administration of these funds is generally handled by a non-profit corporation, while the local funds most often are overseen by governing bodies with the help of a loan committee. The loans may be used in conjunction with other sources to leverage additional monies or independently finance the project.

Finance Clearinghouse: Offers companies assistance in obtaining financing. A complete listing of programs can be obtained through the clearinghouse.

Business Finance Authority: Has several loan programs designed to foster economic development and create employment with an emphasis on small business assistance.

1. Capital Access Program: Start-up businesses or business expansion are eligible for loans from $5,000 to $250,000 for business purposes.
2. Working Capital Line of Credit Guarantee: Up to $2,000,000 for business needing working capital line of credit.
3. Guarantee Asset Program: Provides assistance to capital intensive businesses.
4. Industrial Development Revenue Bond: Up to $10 million for any trade or business that is eligible for tax-exempt financing for acquisition of land, buildings and improvements, machinery and equipment.
5. Assistance to Local Development Organizations: Provides funding to municipalities and development organizations to assist in the promotion and development of New Hampshire businesses.

Contact: New Hampshire Business Finance Authority, Suite 101, 14 Dixon Ave., Concord, NH 03301; 603-271-2391.

Business Development Corporation: A non-profit company in the business of funding loans to small businesses that qualify. For more information, contact Business Development Corporation, 1001 Elm Street, Manchester, NH 03101; 603-623-5500; Fax: 603-623-3972.

Capital Consortium: A venture capital partnership that makes investments between $250,000 and $12,000,000 in high-potential companies. For more information, contact Business Development Corporation, 1001 Elm Street, Manchester, NH 03101; 603-623-5500; Fax: 603-623-3972.

Tax Incentives

No general sales or personal income tax

No tax on personal property or inventories

No property tax on machinery or equipment

No higher assessments or higher property tax rates for commercial or industrial real estate

Exports

International Trade Resource Center: A one-stop location when businesses, both current and potential exporters, can access the assistance and information necessary to effectively explore, develop and penetrate the foreign marketplace. Offers counseling, education and training seminars, automated trade leads, market research, marketing promotion, library and finance assistance.

New Hampshire Export Finance Program: To support export sales in providing working capital for the exporter to produce or buy a product for resale; provide political and/or commercial risk insurance in order to provide open account terms to foreign buyers; provide access to funding to qualified foreign buyers who need medium-term financing in order to purchase capital goods and services from New Hampshire Exporters. Rates and premiums arranged per sale or as needed. No dollar limit. Contact: New Hampshire Office of International Commerce, 17 New Hampshire Ave., Portsmouth, NH 03801; 603-334-6074.

Foreign Trade Zones: Provides economic incentives to companies doing business in foreign countries.

New Jersey

New Jersey Economic Development Authority
P.O. Box 990
Trenton, NJ 08625-0990
609-292-1800
www.njeda.com

Business Assistance

Division of Economic Development: Develops and administers comprehensive
marketing and support programs. Helps access public and
private services which address a broad array
of issues, ranging from financial, technical
and regulatory concerns to employee
training and site location.

Office of Account Management: Offers
assistance to existing companies to maintain
or expand operations.

Office of the Business Advocate and Business Information:
Assists businesses that are having difficulty navigating
through State regulations.

Entrepreneurial Training Institute: An eight week program is
offered to help new and aspiring entrepreneurs learn the basics of
operating a business.

Small Business Contracts: State law requires that at least 15% of the contracts
awarded by the State be given to small businesses. In the first half of
1998, these "set-aside contracts" amounted to more than $425 million.

Doing Business in New Jersey Guidebook: Provides information on starting
and operating a business in the state. Topics include requirements and
advice for starting a new business, information on tax and employee
regulations, state and federal financial information, franchising,
procurement opportunities, and exporting.

Selective Assistance Vendor Information Database: A computer database
designed especially to assist business owners that wish to do business with
the State of New Jersey and the private sector. SAVI-II matches buyers
and vendors for public and private contracting opportunities.

Department of Labor's Division of Field Support: New Jersey provides the
Business Resource Network, a coordinated interdepartmental resource to
identify and market programs available to employers through various New
Jersey agencies.

Department of Labor's Division of Workforce Development: The State provides matching customized training grants and technical assistance to upgrade the technical skills of incumbent workers.

Maritime Services: New Jersey offers several services to support businesses engaged in this enterprise. These include advice and assistance with permits and economic development issues, facilitation of dredging-related activities, and assistance in reducing or minimizing the creation of sediment.

Manufacturing Extension Partnership: Provides assistance to manufacturers in securing a wide variety of technical resources.

New Jersey Economic Development Authority's Trade Adjustment Assistance Center: Can provide technical assistance to manufacturers or certify manufacturers for eligibility for federal government assistance.

Real Estate Development Division: Businesses may be able to lease state-of-the-art, affordable laboratory, production, and research facilities in the Technology Centre of New Jersey. New high-technology businesses may be able to utilize inexpensive lab and office space at one of several technology business incubators throughout the state. These incubators typically offer administrative and consulting services to their tenants.

Technology Transfer Program: Businesses may be able to partner with an academic institution, facilitating the transfer of new technology from research to commercial application.

Technology Help Desk Hotline: Businesses may take advantage of a one-stop Technology Help Desk Hotline, 1-800-4321-TEC. The hotline offers answers to business and technology questions as well as financial advice, referrals to sources of commercialization assistance, help with research and development grant proposals, and advice on using a statewide and national network of business development resource organizations.

The New Jersey Economic Development Authority's Finance Finder: Helps match companies with appropriate finance programs administered by the NJEDA.

Technology Centre of New Jersey: State-of-the-art, affordable laboratory production and research facilities are available for emerging and advanced technology driven companies.

Consulting Assistance for Manufacturers Impacted By Imports: Manufacturers who can demonstrate that their employment and either sales or production have declined due to foreign competition of a like or similar product may be eligible for consulting assistance.

Business Financing

Bond Financing: Bonds are issued to provide long-term loans at attractive, below-market interest rates for real estate acquisitions, equipment, machinery, building construction, and renovations. Minimum loan size is approximately $1 million. Maximum tax-exempt bond amount for manufacturers is $10 million.

Statewide Loan Pool For Business: Loans from $50,000 up to $1 million for fixed assets and up to $500,000 for working capital are available to businesses that create or maintain jobs in a financially targeted municipality or represent a targeted industry such as manufacturing, industrial, or agricultural. Assistance usually will not exceed $35,000 per job created or maintained.

Business Employment Incentive Program (BEIP) Grant: Businesses creating at least 25 new jobs in designated urban areas, or 75 jobs elsewhere, may be eligible to receive a BEIP grant. These grants, which may last for up to 10 years, may be for up to 80% of the value of the income taxes withheld annually from the paychecks of new employees.

Loan Guarantees: Guarantees of conventional loans of up to $1 million for working capital and guarantees of conventional loans or bond issues for fixed assets of up to $1.5 million are available to credit worthy businesses that need additional security to obtain financing. Preference is given to businesses that are either job intensive, will create or maintain tax ratables, are located in an economically distressed area, or represent an important economic sector of the state and will contribute to New Jersey's growth and diversity.

Direct Loans: Loans are made for up to $500,000 for fixed assets and up to $250,000 for working capital for up to 10 years to businesses that are unable to get sufficient bank credit on their own or through the Statewide Loan Pool or with and EDA guarantee. Preference is given to job-intensive enterprises located in economically targeted areas or representing a targeted business sector.

New Jersey Seed Capital Program: Loans are made from $25,000 to $200,000 at a market rate of interest for working capital and fixed assets to technology businesses that have risked their own capital to develop new technologies and need additional funds to bring their products to market.

New Jersey Technology Funding Program: EDA participates with commercial banks to make term loans from $100,000 to $3 million for second stage technology enterprises.

Fund For Community Economic Development: Loans and loan guarantees are made to urban-based community organizations that in turn make loans to micro-enterprises and small businesses which may not qualify for traditional bank financing.

Urban Centers Small Loans: Loans ranging from $5,000 - $50,000 are available to existing retail and commercial businesses located in the commercial district of a targeted municipality.

Local Development Financing Fund: Loans ranging from $50,000 to $2 million may be made for fixed assets form commercial and industrial projects located in Urban Aid communities.

Hazardous Discharge Site Remediation Loan and Grant Program: Businesses may qualify for loans of up to $1 million for remediation activities due to a closure of operations or transfer of ownership.

Petroleum Underground Storage Tank Remediation Upgrade and Closure Program: Owners/operators may qualify for 100% of the eligible project costs.

Small Business Loans: Loans and loan guarantees administered by the New Jersey Economic Development Authority's Community Development and Small Business Lending Division.

The New Jersey Redevelopment Authority (NJRA): An independent state financing agency whose mission is to focus on investing in neighborhood-based redevelopment projects. NJRA offers low and no-interest loans, loan guarantees, equity investment and technical assistance to eligible businesses and municipalities. Contact: New Jersey Redevelopment Authority, 50 W. State St., P.O. Box 790, Trenton, NJ 08625; 609-292-3739; {www.state.nj.us/njra}.

New Jersey Economic Development Authority's Investment Banking Division: Loans may be available for the purchase of manufacturing equipment.

R&D Excellence Grant Program: Businesses may receive financial support for research and development in critical fields, such as healthcare (especially biomaterials, pharmaceuticals, and biotechnologies), software/information, and environmental and civil infrastructure technologies.

Very young technology enterprises may be eligible to receive seed-stage investments ranging from $50,000 to $1.5 million. Contact the managing partners of Early Stage Enterprises, LP, Mr. Ronald R. Hahn (e-mail rrhahn@aol.com) and Mr. James J. Millar (e-mail jimmillar@aol.com), or call ESE at 609-921-8896, Fax 609-921-8703. Such investments may also be available through the New Jersey Seed Capital Program.

Small Business Innovation Research Grants: Applicants for federal grants may receive technical consulting and bridge loans.

Edison Venture Fund: Provides funding assistance to high-technology companies in New Jersey. This private enterprise enjoys a close relationship with the State of New Jersey, having been selected through a competitive process to manage certain funds on behalf of the New Jersey Economic Development Authority. Contact: Edison Venture Fund, 1009 Lenox Dr. #4, Lawrenceville, NJ 08648; 609-896-1900; {www.edisonventure.com}.

New Jersey Redevelopment Authority and the New Jersey Economic Development Authority's Commercial Lending Division: Businesses and municipalities involved in urban redevelopment may be eligible for low- and no-interest loans, loan guarantees, equity investments, and technical assistance.

New Jersey Redevelopment Authority and the New Jersey Economic Development Authority's Community Development and Small Business Lending Division: Loans, loan guarantees, equity investments, and technical assistance may be available to finance investments in neighborhood-based redevelopment projects, small business lending, renovation, relocation, and/or real estate development in urban areas.

Business Relocation Assistance Grant: Provides grants to relocating companies that create a minimum of 25 new full-time jobs in New Jersey.

Tax Incentives

Urban Enterprise Zones: Provide significant incentives and benefits to qualified businesses located within their borders. Such benefits include sales tax to customers (3% instead of 6%), corporation tax credits for the hiring of certain employees, and subsidized unemployment insurance costs.

No net worth tax, no business personal property tax, no commercial rent or occupancy tax and no retail gross receipts tax.

Property Tax Abatements and Exemptions: Available for commercial and industrial properties in areas in need or redevelopment.

New Jobs Investment Tax Credit: Companies that make certain investments in new or expanded business facilities that are directly related to the creation of new jobs may be eligible for credits.

Manufacturing Equipment and Employment Investment Tax Credit: Certain investments made by companies for manufacturing equipment with a recovery life of four years or more are eligible for a credit.

Recognition of Subchapter S Status for Corporations: S corporations are provided a reduced corporation tax rate.

Research and Development Tax Credit for Corporation Business Tax: Businesses may be eligible for a credit for certain increased research expenditures in the state.

Exports

International Trade Services: Services include financing assistance, strategic advocacy in foreign markets, opportunities to network and receive information and advice regarding international commerce, and assistance in taking advantage of federal international trade programs and Foreign Trade Zones.

Export Financing: Up to a $1 million one-year revolving line of credit will be provided to finance confirmed foreign orders to assist businesses that want to enter the export market or expand export sales but are unable to do so because they cannot get the financing they need on their own.

Foreign Trade Zones: Within these zones, which are outside U.S. Customs territory, businesses may manufacture, assemble, package, process and exhibit merchandise with a substantial duty and cash flow savings.

Women and Minorities

New Jersey Department of Commerce and Economic Development
Division of Development for Small Businesses and Women and Minority Businesses
CN 835
Trenton, NJ 08625
609-292-3860
Fax: 609-292-9145

Services For Businesses Owned By Women And Minorities: Businesses owned by women and minorities play an important role in the New Jersey economy. New Jersey offers a number of services to help these businesses compete and overcome the special challenges they face. These services include financial assistance, advice and instructional materials, training and education, and certification necessary to receive certain contracts.

Set Aside Contracts: State law requires that 7% of the contracts awarded by the State be given to businesses owned by minorities, and 3% to businesses owned by women. In the first half of 1998, these "set-aside contracts" amounted to more than $180 million.

Women and minorities interested in establishing franchise businesses may receive investments from the Small Business Investment Company, which works in conjunction with the New Jersey Economic Development Authority's Commercial Lending Division.

Contractors Assistance Program: Small contracting businesses owned by women or minorities may receive training courses and consultations with experienced executives of large construction companies designed to make it easier to get performance bonds and successfully bid on major construction projects. This service is provided by the New Jersey Economic Development Authority's Community Development and Small Business Lending Division.

New Jersey Development Authority For Small Businesses, Minorities' And Women's Enterprises: This office offers women and minority-owned small businesses financial, marketing, procurement, technical and managerial assistance. Loans of up to $1 million can be made for real estate, fixed asset acquisition, and working capital. Guarantees to banks are also available for fixed asset acquisition and for working capital. To be eligible, a business must be certified as a small, minority-owned or women-owned enterprise. Most of the funds are targeted to enterprises located in Atlantic City or providing goods or services to customers in Atlantic City, including but not limited to the casinos. Limited monies are available for businesses located in other parts of the state.

New Mexico

Economic Development Department
Joseph M. Montoya Bldg.
1100 St. Francis Drive
Santa Fe, NM 87505-4147
505-827-0170
800-374-3061
Fax: 505-827-0407
www.edd.state.nm.us

Business Assistance

Technology Ventures Corporation: Promotes the commercialization of
technology. Offers technical, business and management assistance for its
clients. Contact: Technology Ventures Corporation, 1155 University
Blvd. SE, Albuquerque, NM 87106; 505-246-2882.

Technology: New Mexico offers a wide range of assistance for technology-
oriented companies such as research centers, partnerships with
universities, and facility use.

Business Financing

ACCION: A private non-profit organization that extend microloans to small
business entrepreneurs designed to help home-based and other self-
employed people grow to be self sufficient. Contact: ACCION New
Mexico, 219 Central NW, #620, Albuquerque, NM 87102; 505-243-8844.

Advanced Technology Program (ATP): Provides cost shared-funding to select
industries for high-risk research and development projects that have the
potential to launch important broad-based economic benefits to the U.S.
economy.

Airport Improvement Program (AIP): Supports the development and
improvement of airports in an effort to create a nationwide airport system
capable of supporting the nation's civil air travel.

Albuquerque Development Capital Program: Provides loan guarantees and
interest supplements for acquisition of real property, purchase of fixed
assets and/or working capital purposes. Contact: City of Albuquerque,
Economic Development Department, P.O. Box 1293, Albuquerque, NM
87103; 505-768-3270.

Business Participation Loans: The State Investment Council may invest a portion of the Severance Tax Permanent Fund in real property related business loans. There is a minimum of $500,000 and a maximum of $2 million.

Cibola Foundation Revolving Loan Fund: A variety of financial incentives offered to encourage economic development in Cibola County. Contact: Cibola Communities, Economic Development Foundation Inc., P.O. Box 277, Grants, NM 87020; 505-285-6604.

Community Development Loan Fund: Provides loans to businesses and organizations that have tangible benefits for low-income people. Typical loans are from $5,000 to $25,000. Contact: NM Community Development Loan Fund, P.O. Box 705, Albuquerque, NM 87103; 505-243-3196.

Community Foundation: Offers small grants, technical assistance, "capacity building" workshops, and serves as a convener around important issues for nonprofit organizations, communities and people throughout New Mexico, especially in rural areas.

FSA Farmer Programs: Guarantees loans made by agricultural lenders for

family farmers and ranchers for farm ownership, improvements and operating purposes. The FSA describes a family farm as one which a family can operate and manage itself. Guarantee of up to $300,000 for farm ownership, water and soil loans; and $400,000 for operating loans. The maximum guarantee is 90%.

Industrial Development Training Program: Provides funds for classroom or on-the-job training to prepare New Mexico residents for employment. Trainee wages are reimbursed to the company at 50% during hours of training; 65% in rural New Mexico. Instructional costs involving classroom training will be reimbursed to the educational institution at 100% of all costs outlined in the training contract.

Job Training Partnership Act (JTPA): A federally funded program intended to provide job training assistance to both eligible employees and employers. Employers can receive financial reimbursement of up to 50% of the costs associated with hiring and training JTPA eligible employees.

ilagro Fund: Programs designed to promote economic development opportunities for organizations which utilize natural resources, involve small scale growers or producers, strengthen traditional skills in agriculture and production, or defend land and water rights. Funds are available to facilitate problem identification, provide training in community organizing, and to improve business skills and production techniques.

North Central New Mexico Economic Development Revolving Loan Fund:
  Provides loans up to $100,000 to assist small businesses in the creation
  and/or saving of jobs in economically disadvantaged areas. Contact:
  North Central New Mexico Economic Development Revolving Loan
  Fund, P.O. Box 5115, Santa Fe, NM 87502; 505-827-7313.

RD Housing Preservation Grants: Grants to tribes, political subdivisions and
  other non-profit entities to enable them to rehabilitate housing owned and
  occupied by very-low and low-income rural persons.

RD Rural Business Enterprise Grant Program: The purpose of the program is
  to support the development of small and emerging private business
  enterprise in rural areas under 50,000 in population, or more and adjacent
  urbanized areas. Priority is given to applications for projects in rural
  communities of 25,000 in population and under.

RD Guaranteed Business and Industry Program: The purpose of the program
  is to improve, develop or finance business, industry and employment, and
  improve the economic and environmental climate in rural communities
  (under 50,000 population) and non-urbanized or non-urbanizing areas.
  This is achieved by bolstering the existing private credit structure through
  the guarantee of quality loans that will provide lasting community
  benefits.

Severance Tax Loan Program: New Mexico can purchase up to $20 million of
  bonds, notes, debentures or other evidence of indebtedness, excluding
  commercial paper, whose proceeds are used for the establishment or
  expansion of business outlets or ventures located in state.

Tax Incentives

Aerospace Research and Development Deduction: The Aerospace Research
  and Development tax deduction was implemented to facilitate the location
  of a spaceport in New Mexico.

Agriculture-Related Tax Deductions/Exemptions: Feed and fertilizer,
  warehousing, threshing, harvesting, growing, cultivating and processing
  agricultural products, agricultural products.

Compensating Tax Abatement: "Compensating tax" is an excise tax imposed
  for the privilege of using property in New Mexico. In New Mexico it is
  called gross receipts tax for purchases made within the state. For
  purchases made outside New Mexico and imported into the state, it is
  called compensating tax. Abatement of the state's portion of any sales,
  gross receipts, compensating or similar tax on machinery and equipment,
  and other movable personal property for an eligible facility. In New
  Mexico construction or rehabilitation of non-speculative office buildings,
  warehouses, manufacturing facilities, and service oriented facilities not

primarily engaged in the sale of goods or commodities at retail are eligible.

Enterprise Zones: The Enterprise Zone Act is designed to stimulate the creation of new jobs and to revitalize economically distressed areas. $50,000 tax credit to property owners for the rehabilitation of qualified business facilities, technical assistance, training reimbursement, and other benefits.

Filmmakers Gross Receipts Tax Incentive: Implemented to facilitate the filming of movies, television shows and commercials in New Mexico. A qualified production company may execute nontaxable transaction certificates with its suppliers for tangible personal property or services. The suppliers may then deduct their receipts from the gross receipts tax.

Historic Preservation Tax Credit Program: Offers a maximum tax credit of 20% of the substantial rehabilitation of historic buildings for commercial, industrial and rental residential purposes, and a 10% credit for substantial rehabilitation for non-residential purposes for structures built before 1936.

Indian Employment Credit: Provides for a tax credit to employers of Indians on Indian lands to encourage economic development. The maximum credit per employee is $4,000.

Low-income Housing Tax Credit Program (LIHTC): This program can be used for new construction and/or rehabilitation of rental units. The annual credit equals a fixed percentage of the project's total cost.

Modified Accelerated Cost Recovery System: Provides for a favorable deduction for property on Indian lands to encourage economic development. Capital outlays for depreciable business or income-producing property are recoverable through the depreciation deduction allowances. A business that acquires property for use in the business is entitled to deduct the cost of the property over time for the purposes of computing income tax liability.

Cultural Property Preservation Tax Credit: Property owners are eligible to receive a personal or corporate tax credit for restoring, rehabilitating or otherwise preserving cultural properties. Specifically, a tax credit is available where historic structures are certified as having received rehabilitation to preserve and enhance their historic character. Offers a maximum tax credit of 50% of the cost of restoration, rehabilitation or preservation up to $25,000.

Gross Receipts Tax Deduction: Equipment that goes into a plant financed with industrial revenue bonds is exempt for the gross receipts or compensating tax of 5%.

Interstate Telecommunications Gross Receipts Tax Exemption: This program exempts receipts from the provision of wide area telephone services (WATS) and private communications services from the interstate telecommunications gross receipts tax. Wide-area telephone service means a telephone service that entitles a subscriber to either make or receive large volumes of communications to or from persons in specified geographical areas.

Investment Tax Credit Program: Provides a general incentive for manufacturers to locate in New Mexico and to hire New Mexicans. Equipment is eligible if essential, used directly and exclusively in a manufacturing facility, and depreciated for federal income tax purposes. The creation of new, full time jobs is required to qualify for the credit. The credit allows the manufacturer to offset the amount of compensating tax paid on eligible equipment. The credit equals the amount of compensating tax actually paid, and may be applied against compensating tax, gross receipts tax or withholding tax due.

Preferential Tax Rate for Small Wineries and Breweries: Wine produced by a small winery carries a tax of 10 cents per liter on the first 80,000 liters; 20 cents on production over that level. The basic tax rate for wine is 45 cents per liter. Beer produced by a microbrewery is taxed at 25 cents per gallon. The basic tax rate for beer is 41 cents per gallon.

Property Tax Exemption: For industry financed with industrial revenue bonds, a local government may offer a real and personal property tax exemption of up to 30 years.

Targeted Jobs Tax Credit Program (TJTC): An employer may claim a tax credit equal to 40% of the first $6,000 in wages paid to the worker during the first year of employment for a maximum credit of $2,400 per employee. For economically disadvantaged summer youth, employers may claim a tax credit equal to 40% of the first $3,000 in wages for a maximum credit of $1,200 per employee.

Tax Increment Financing: At the beginning of a project, the valuation of the project properties is summed. As the project proceeds, these properties are developed or otherwise improved, increasing their valuations. The tax proceeds flowing from the increase in valuation may be diverted to finance the project. Tax increment financing in New Mexico is available only in a designated enterprise zone.

Taxpayer's Assistance Program (TAP): Enables home buyers to qualify for a larger mortgage because of reduced tax liabilities.

Property Tax Abatement: Land, buildings and equipment associated with an eligible project are exempt from ad valorem tax, generally to promote economic development.

Exports

Foreign Sales Corporations Tax Incentive Program: Regulations exempt
from taxation part of the profit earned on exports, which can be 15% of
the net income or 1.2% of gross receipts, whichever is greater.

Export-Import Bank (Eximbank) City/State Program: Assists exporters in
accessing federal loan guarantees and credit insurance through the Export/
Import Bank. Eximbank working capital loan guarantees may be used to
finance such pre-export activities as the purchase of raw materials,
finished products, labor and other services needed for processing export
orders. They may also be used to cover the cost of freight, port charges
and certain forms of overseas business development. Loan guarantees may
be used for a specific transaction or as a revolving line of credit. There are
no minimum or maximum amounts of funding.

Foreign Trade Zones: Merchandise in these zones is considered to be outside
U.S. Customs territory and is subject to duty only when it leave the zones
for consumption in the U.S. Market. New Mexico offers three such zones.

Export Financing Assistance: Often, even the most credit-worthy small and
medium-sized businesses find that commercial banks are reluctant to
approve their loan request for export financing. The New Mexico Export
Finance Team (NMEFT) exists to help such businesses finance their
export activities.

International Trade Division: Provides assistance to manufacturing,
agricultural and other production concerns in developing their worldwide
export capabilities. Services include:
- Export market development counseling
- Foreign trade shows and missions
- Foreign buying and reverse trade missions
- Identifying and disseminating overseas trade leads
- Attracting foreign businesses
- Developing, maintaining and using a database of potential domestic
  and international customers for New Mexico goods and services.

Women and Minorities

Administration for Native Americans (ANA) Grant: Provides financial
assistance through grants or contracts to further the three goals of the
ANA: governance, economic development and social development.
Technical assistance and training to develop, conduct and administer
projects. Funding to public or private agencies to assist local residents in
overcoming special obstacles to social and economic development.

Maximum Program Benefits: Up to 80% of program cost, however, no set maximum or minimum grant amount.

BankAmerica Foundation - Community Economic Development Initiative: A special grant program targeted toward nonprofit organizations supporting community economic development and the growth of minority businesses. Maximum Program Benefits: Up to $500,000 in cash grants.

Eagle Staff Fund: Seeks to support Native grassroots and tribal organizations that are working to create Native-controlled reservation economies. Promotes economic development through technical assistance and financial resources.

EDA District, Indian and Area Planning Program: Grant assistance to defray administrative expenses in support of the economic development planning efforts of Economic Development Districts, Redevelopment Areas and Indian tribes.

BIA Indian Loan Guarantee Fund: Guaranteed loans that are made by private lenders to eligible applicants for up to 90% of the unpaid principal and interest due. Funds may be used to finance Indian-owned commercial, industrial or business activities organized for profit, provided eligible Indian ownership constitutes at least 51% of the business. Loans must benefit the economy of an Indian reservation. Also, interest subsidies might be granted when the business is incurring losses. Individual guarantees are limited to $500,000; $5.5 million maximum for tribes or organizations.

Navajo Business and Industrial Development Fund: Provides loans or loan guarantees to qualified Navajo individuals or Navajo-owned businesses. The program is intended to foster the establishment of new businesses or the expansion of existing businesses within the Navajo Nation's territorial jurisdiction. Minimum loan is $10,000; maximum loan is $100,000. Loan not to exceed 90% of purchase price of assets, or 95% of value of permanent improvements on a reservation site.

Women's Economic Self-Sufficiency Team: Provides consulting, training and support programs as well as financial assistance (loans). For more information, contact WESST Corp., 414 Silver SW, Albuquerque, NM 87102; 505-848-4760; Fax: 505-241-4766.

New York

Empire State Development
One Commerce Plaza
Albany, NY 12245
518-474-7756
800-STATE-NY
www.empire.state.ny.us

633 Third Ave.
New York, NY 10017
212-803-3100

Business Assistance

Small Business Division: Offers fast, up-to-date information on the State's

economic development programs and can help in making contact with appropriate agencies in such areas as financing, job training, technical assistance, etc.

Small Business Advocacy Program: Reviews regulations affecting small business, maintains liaison with small business groups, assists business owners in the regulatory process, assists in expediting innovative business programs and projects, develops and presents workshops, seminars, conferences, and other training programs.

Technical Advisory Services; Provides free, confidential technical assistance concerning compliance to federal and state air quality requirements for small businesses.

Small Business Stationary Source Technical And Environmental Compliance Assistance Program: Provides technical assistance and advocacy services to eligible businesses in achieving environmental regulatory compliance.

Business Ombudsmen Services: Counseling and problem solving assistance to resolve complaints from small businesses concerning interactions with government authorities available to businesses employing 100 or less that are not dominant in their fields.

Entrepreneurial Assistance Program: Referrals of recipients to ESD funded assistance provides classroom instruction and individual counseling, business plan development for minorities, women, dislocated workers, public assistance recipients, public housing recipients and those seeking to start a new business or who have owned a business for five years or less.

Agricultural Business Development Assistance: Technical assistance to help locate public and private funding for food processors and agricultural producers. Contact: New York State Department of Agriculture and Markets, The Winners Circle, Albany, NY 12235; 518-457-7076.

Agricultural Ombudsman Services: Helps agricultural businesses communicate with regulatory agencies.

Food & Agricultural Industry Marketing Assistance: Marketing assistance for agricultural industries including trade shows, information distribution, and export financing.

America's Job Bank: Employers may list job openings in a statewide and national computer network.

Apprentice Training Program: Provides on-the-job training for more than 250 skilled occupations. Contact: Apprentice Training Program, Room 223, Bldg. 12, State Office Campus, Albany, NY 12240; 518-457-6820.

Business Development Office: Industrial and manufacturing companies are targeted for a variety of services.

New York State Contract Reporter: Provides listings of contracts made available for bidding by New York State agencies, public benefit corporations, and its public authorities.

Procurement Assistance: Provides technical assistance to businesses seeking to compete for contracts valued at $1,000,000 or more from the state.

Workforce Training: Empire State Development offers financial support and technical resources to companies to offset the cost of employee training.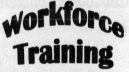

High Technology Program: The Science and Technology Foundation maintains a mission to create and administer programs that promote scientific and technical education, industrially relevant research and development, manufacturing modernization and the capitalization of high-tech companies. Contact: New York State Science and Technology Foundation, 99 Washington Ave., Suite 1731, Albany, NY 12210; 518-473-9741.

Recycling Assistance: New York State has one of the largest concentrations of recycling companies in the world. Works with companies to demonstrate that, in addition to being an important environmental activity, recycling makes good business sense. To this end, they diagnose the research and development, capital, and marketing needs of recycling companies and tailor-make a package of technical and financial assistance. Identifies new markets and assist companies retooling to reach those markets. Assists companies to implement waste prevention practices.

Technical Assistance: New York State has developed a host of business-friendly products ranging from understanding the federal Clean Air Act and its impact on small business to ownership transition plans that can help a company grow and prosper. A hotline (800-STATE NY) puts business people directly in touch with a business ombudsman. The experts staffing this hotline are ready to answer questions. In addition, they serve as advocates for business.

Ownership Transition Services: Technical assistance.

Rural Employment Program: Recruits workers for farm, landscaping and food processing industries. Contact: Rural Employment Program, Room 282, Bldg. 12, State Office Campus, Albany, NY 12240; 518-457-6798.

Technology Development Organizations; Provides assistance to technology based companies competing for state and federal research and development grant programs, business plan review and development, management, marketing and financial packaging assistance, venture capital assistance, information systems development, technology business development training, incubator facility management and technology transfer services. Contact: Industrial Technology Programs, New York State Science and Technology Foundation, 99 Washington Ave., Suite 1730, Albany, NY 12210; 518-473-9746.

Advanced Controls for Efficiency Program (ACE): Applied research, product design, demonstration and testing, and product commercialization for individuals or enterprises with an innovative, energy-related product.

Business Financing

Financial Services: Companies that plan to locate, expand or modernize their facilities in New York State are eligible for financial assistance. Generally, this assistance supports the acquisition of land and buildings or machinery and equipment. It also can help fund construction or renovation of buildings or the infrastructure and working capital required for the establishment or expansion of an eligible company.

Funds may be available through:

- direct loans to business for a portion of the cost of the project;
- interest rate subsidies to reduce the cost of borrowing from private or public sector financial institutions, in the form of a grant or linked deposit with the lending institution;
- loan guarantees for working capital assistance;
- assistance in the form of a loan and grant combination for a portion of the cost of an infrastructure project.

Economic Development Fund:

1. *Industrial Effectiveness Program*: Direct technical assistance for identifying, developing and implementing improved management and

production process and grants to pay the cost of feasibility studies up to $60,000.

2. *Employee Training Assistance*: Offers skills training grant from $15,000 to $25,000.

3. *Commercial Area Development*: Loans, loan guarantees, and grants to improve commercial buildings, commercial strips, downtown areas, and business districts from $75,000 to $100,000.

4. *General Development*: Loans and loan guarantees for manufacturers, non-retail service firms, headquarters facilities of retail firms, retail firms in distressed areas, and businesses developing tourist attractions from $75,000 to $2,000,000.

5. *Infrastructure Development*: Loans and grants for businesses located in distressed areas or a business that develops a tourist attraction from $25,000 to $2,000,000 for construction or renovation of basic systems and facilities.

6. *Capital Access*: For small and medium size businesses including minority and women-owned businesses and day care centers, financing from $100,000 to $300,000.

7. *General Development Financing*: Loans and loan guarantees for manufacturing, non-retail service firms, retail headquarters, retail firms located in distressed areas and businesses which develop recreational, cultural or historical facilities for tourist attractions. Amounts are determined case-by-case.

8. *Competitiveness Improvement Services - Global Export Marketing Service*: Grants up to $5,000 for consulting services to assess organizational and product readiness for exporting. Grants up to $25,000 for an individual business or up to $50,000 for a business or industry group to create market development plans.

Industrial Waste Minimization Program:
Technical assistance and grants up to $50,000 to assist, develop, and demonstrate energy-efficient methods to reduce, reuse, or recycle industrial wastes at the point of generation. Contact: NYS Energy Research and Development Authority, Corporate Plaza West, 286 Washington Ave. Extension, Albany, NY 12203; 518-862-1090, ext. 3206.

Environmental Finance Corporation: Grants for resource recovery facilities, solid waste disposal facilities, hazardous waste treatment facilities, Brownfields redevelopment, water supply and management facilities and sewage treatment works.

Recycling Investment Program: Technical assistance funding up to $75,000, capital project funding up to $300,000, research, development and demonstration project funding up to $100,000 for firms seeking to improve productivity and competitiveness by reducing solid waste and using recovered materials.

Energy Products Center: Product development demonstration and commercialization costs for technology-related businesses.

Retail and Office Development Assistance: Loans up to $5,000,000 for projects that retain or create significant numbers of private sector jobs in economically distressed areas.

Jobs Now Program: Worker training grant up to $10,000.

Venture Capital Fund: High Tech entrepreneurs, companies with technologies ready for market, and leading-edge enterprises each have different needs for investment capital. New York State has the seed and growth capital that will enable a high tech business to grow. The Small Business Technology Investment Fund program (SBTIF) is a source of early-stage debt and equity funding for high tech companies. Initial investments range as much as $300,000 and later stage investment up to $500,000. New York State is banking on a strong high tech future.

Jobs Now Program

Transportation Capital Assistance Program: Loans up to $1,000,000 for small business enterprises and NYS-certified minority and women-owned business enterprises that have transportation-related construction contracts.

Commercial District Revolving Loans Trust Fund: Loans up to $15,000 for retail, professional or commercial service for profit businesses with 50 or fewer full-time employees.

Metropolitan Economic Revitalization Fund: Loans, capital access and linked deposits up to $5,000,000 for businesses and non-profits located in economically distressed area.

Regional Revolving Loan Trust Fund: Loans and loan guarantees up to $80,000 for businesses employing fewer than 100 people.

Small Business Technology Investment Fund: For small technology based companies, financing from $25,000 to $500,000 for seed or capital.

Job Development Authority: Loans to small and medium sized businesses in manufacturing and services from $50,000 to $1,500,000.

Jobs Now Program: Capital loans and grants to private businesses creating at least 300 new full time jobs not to exceed $10,000 per job.

Linked Deposit Program: Interest rate subsidies to a variety of businesses seeking to improve competitiveness and performance up to $1,000,000.

Commercial District Revolving Loan Trust Fund: Loans up to $20,000 to businesses with 50 or fewer employees.

Empowerment Zone Program: Triple tax exempt bond financing up to $3,000,000 per zone for a variety of businesses located within a zone.

Enterprise Communities: Triple tax exempt bond financing up to $3,000,000 per community.

Economic Development through Greater Energy Efficiency: Grants and technical support for detailed engineering studies of manufacturing operations up to $50,000. Capital financing for demonstrations for energy efficient process technology up to $250,000. Contact: NYS Energy Research and Development Authority, Corporate Plaza West, 286 Washington Ave. Extension, Albany, NY 12203; 518-262-1090, ext. 3257.

Centers for Advanced Technology: Financial and technical assistance for commercially relevant research, technology transfer to industry, start up of new companies to commercialize research results, and incubator space. Amounts are determined case-by-case.

Tax Incentives

Tax Benefits

General: New York State offers a host of tax credits to companies. For manufacturers and certain types of production operations, New York offers one of the most generous tax credits in the nation. If a company builds or expands, a new capital investment can yield up to 5% credit that can be carried-forward for 15 years. If employment increases in New York as a result of investments, a 5% tax credit could double over the following two years. To further encourage the state's strong high-technology base, they offer a credit against the corporate franchise/income tax for research and development efforts. Clean-up facilities for industrial waste or air pollution also can earn credits. At the same time, commercial and industrial plants and pollution control efforts can be eligible for partial relief from real property tax levied by counties, cities, towns, villages or school districts. They can also provide a list of taxes not imposed on New York State business. For example, there are no personal property taxes here, and they do not impose a sales tax on the purchase of production equipment.

Economic Development Zones: New York State has currently designated 52 economically distressed areas - certified as Economic Development Zones. They want to encourage the creation of jobs in these areas. In a zone they offer an investment tax credit of up to 19 percent. They can provide a tax break of up to 25% for new investors in these areas. They offer a host of

benefits to make doing business easier, ranging from discounts on electric
power to wage tax credits for new employees. They also have set aside
Zone Equivalent Areas for special tax credits.

Empowerment Zone Program: Wage tax credits for businesses in severely
distressed areas.

Exports

Empire State Development: International market experts help a company enter
and expand in the global economy. Offers a step-by-step analysis of a
company's capabilities and matches them with the demands of the
international marketplace. If a company has what the global marketplace
needs, they will work with that company to find the niche, the spot on the
globe where they can sell. Then, they will assist them in determining how
to reach those markets. They provide information about tariffs, industry
specifications and government regulations. They can put a company in
touch with representatives, distributors, agents and strategic allies to sell a
product or service abroad.

Industrial Development Agencies: IDA projects are exempt from local
property taxes and mortgage recording tax. Building materials and certain
purchases of capital equipment are exempt from State and local sales
taxes.

Pollution Control Facilities: Facilities are exempt from local real property
taxes and ad valorem levies.

Commercial and Industrial Facilities: Property tax exemptions of up to 50% .

Corporate Franchise Tax Allocation Percentage: Business corporations are
subject to tax only on the portion of their activities that are deemed to be
attributable to their activities in New York State.

Credits for Bank Corporation Tax: For corporations which service mortgages
acquired by the New York State Mortgage Agency, the credit is equal to
the amount paid for the special recording tax on mortgages recorded after
1/1/79.

- *Credits for Insurance Corporation Tax*: Credits for additional taxes
  of premiums written on premiums. Credit of up to 90% or retaliatory
  taxes paid to the state by New York domiciled or organized insurers.
- Credit equaling the amount paid in the special additional mortgage
  recording tax. Credit for a portion of the cost of assessments paid to
  the Life Insurance Company Guaranty Corporation up to $40 million
  or 40% of the total tax liability.

International Banking Facility: A deduction for the adjusted net income for
banking corporations that establish international banking facilities in New
York to accept deposits from and make loans to foreign customers.

Retail Enterprise Credit: Investment tax credit for rehabilitation expenditures of a retail facility.

Sales Tax Exemptions; Exemptions include machinery, utility services and fuels used in production, labor for installing and maintaining production equipment, anything becoming a component part of a product for sale and others.

Tax Credit for Pollution Control Expenditures: A credit of 5% for businesses constructing or improving industrial waste or air pollution control facilities.

Tax Credits Based on New Capital Investment: 5% of new capital invested in buildings used primarily in production by manufacturing, processing, assembling and certain other types of activities.

Tax Credits Based on Research and Development: 7 to 9% of qualified research and development tangible property against the corporate franchise tax.

Personal Property: New York imposes no ad valorem taxes on personal property.

Women and Minorities

Division of Minority and Women's Business Development: Administers, coordinates, and implements a statewide program to assist the development of M/WBE's and facilitate their access to state contracting opportunities. Through the process of certification, the agency is responsible for verifying minority and women-ownership and control of firms participating in the program.

Division of Minority and Women's Business Development Lending Program: Loans up to $7,000 from the Microenterprise Loan Fund and up to $50,000 from the Minority and Women Revolving Loan Trust Fund.

North Carolina

Department of Commerce
Commerce Finance Center
301 N. Wilmington St.
P.O. Box 29571
Raleigh, NC 27626-0571
919-733-4977
Fax: 919-715-9265
www.commerce.state.nc.us/commerce

Business Assistance

Retention and Expansion Programs: Professional assistance is provided for

all aspects of business including
environmental consultation, financing
alternative, human resources
consulting, marketing information,
energy process surveys and other
issues that impact business and industry.
Master License Application Program: Offers
the business applicant a streamlined approach to applying for required
business licenses.

Industrial Extension Service: Provides technical and industrial management
assistance, conducts applied research, advocates industrial use of
technology and modern managerial practices, as well as conducts
continuing education programs for business, industry, entrepreneurs,
engineers and local governments.

Biotechnology Center: Carries out a variety of programs and activities
strengthening North Carolina's biotechnology community.

MCNC: A private nonprofit corporation that supports advanced education,
research and technology programs to enhance North Carolina's technology
infrastructure and businesses. Contact: MCNC, 3201 Cornwallis Rd., P.O.
Box 12889, Research Triangle Park, NC 27709; 919-248-1800;
{www.mcnc.org}.

Industrial Training Program: State funded customized job training programs
for new and expanding industries that create 12 or more new jobs in a
community within one year.

Small Business and Technology Development Center: Organized as an inter-
institutional program of The University of North Carolina, the Small
Business and Technology Development Center (SBTDC) is the primary

organization through which the state of North Carolina provides counseling and technical assistance to the business community. SBTDC services are well-defined and designed to meet client needs. The primary focus is in-depth, one-on-one, confidential counseling. Assistance is provided, free of charge, to the small business owner or aspiring entrepreneur. As the only full service counseling resource statewide, the SBTDC helps with the myriad of tasks facing a business owner, including:

- assessing the feasibility of a business idea
- preparing a business plan
- finding sources of capital
- developing marketing strategies
- operations and human resource management

For more information, contact Small Business and Technology Development Center, 333 Fayetteville Street Mall, Suite 1150, Raleigh, NC 27601; 919-715-7272; 800-258-0862 (NC only); {www.sbtac.org}.

SBTDC Special Market Development Assistance:

- *Procurement Technical Assistance Program*: The SBTDC provides comprehensive assistance in selling goods and services to the federal government. Services include help in finding out about contracting opportunities, preparing bid and proposal packages, obtaining 8(a) certification, interpreting regulations, and resolving contract administration problems. An integral part of this program is PRO-BID, a computer-based bid matching service that provides accurate and timely information on procurement opportunities.

- *International Business Development*: North Carolina businesses are increasingly looking at exporting as a vehicle to increase sales and profits. The SBTDC helps successful domestic, new-to-export businesses to identify, target and then penetrate foreign markets. SBTDC counselors provide marketing research information, assist with market planning, and then identify implementation procedures.

- *The Technology Group*: Part of the SBTDC's mission is to help emerging businesses commercialize innovative new technologies, and to facilitate the transfer of technology developed within the small business and university communities. Technology Group services include assistance in maritime technology transfer, identifying markets for scientific discoveries, guiding the development of strategies to protect intellectual property and providing referrals to specialized organizations and resources.

- *Marine Trades Program*: The SBTDC's Marine Trades Program provides business development support to marine industry firms. Specific services include assistance in marketing marine products and services, complying with environmental regulations, and maintaining safe operations. The program also provides marine specific training, education and research.

Business Financing

Industrial Revenue Bonds: Revenue Bonds have a variety of names and purposes but essentially three basic types exist. These bonds whose proper name is Small Issue Industrial Development Bonds are referred to as Industrial Revenue Bond's (IRB's). The state's principal interest in these bonds is assisting new and expanding industry while insuring that North Carolinians get good jobs at good wages. The regulations governing bond issuance are a combination of federal regulations and North Carolina statutes. The amount each state may issue annually is designated by population. There are three types of bond issuances as follows:

- Tax Exempt - Because the income derived by the bondholder is not subject to federal income tax, the maximum bond amount is $10 million in any given jurisdiction. According to federal regulations, the $10 million total includes the bond amount and capital expenditures over a six-year period going both backwards and forwards three years. The maximum any company may have is $40 million nationwide outstanding at any given period.

- Taxable - They are not exempt from federal tax (they are however exempt from North Carolina tax). The essential difference is that the Taxable bond rate is slightly higher to the borrower and not being subject to the federal volume cap, may exceed $10 million in bond amount.

- Pollution Control/Solid Waste Disposal Bond - These bonds are subject to volume cap although there is no restriction on amount, and the interest on these bonds is federally tax exempt.

Economic Development Category: Projects may involve assistance for public facilities needed to serve the target business, or loans to the private business to fund items such as machinery and equipment, property acquisition or construction. Public facility projects may provide grants of up to 75% of the proposed facility costs, with a 25% cash match to be paid by the local government applicant.

Industrial Development Fund: Purpose is to provide an incentive for jobs creation in the State's most economically distressed counties, also identified as Tier 1, 2, and 3 areas. Funds for the renovation of manufacturing buildings and the acquisition of infrastructure are made available by the Department of Commerce to eligible counties or their local units of government, which apply for the funds on behalf of their existing or new manufacturing businesses. A commitment to create jobs is executed by the benefiting firm. The amount of funds available to participating firms is determined by multiplying the number of jobs committed to be created times $4,000.00, up to a maximum of $400,000.00 or the cost of the project, whichever is less. Of course, the availability of funds also applies.

Business Energy Improvement: Program provides loans between $100,000 and $500,000 to industrial and commercial businesses located or moving to North Carolina. Loans can be financed for up to seven years at interest rates equal to 50% of the average (high and low) T-bill rate for the past year or five percent, whichever is lower. Current rate is 5%, which is the maximum. Funds are provided from a pool of $2,500,000 designated for energy related capital improvement such as cogeneration, energy saving motors, boiler improvements and  low energy use lighting. A participating bank will process loans on a first-come-first-served based upon the date of receipt of a letter of credit.

Partnerships for Regional Economic Development: The counties of North Carolina have been organized into seven regional partnerships for economic development. North Carolina's regional partnerships will enable regions to compete effectively for new investment and to devise effective economic development strategies based on regional opportunities and advantages.

North Carolina SBTDC Small Business Innovation Research (SBIR): Program is a highly competitive three-phase award system which provides qualified small businesses with opportunities to propose innovative ideas that meet specific research and research and development needs of the Federal government. Phase I is a feasibility study to evaluate the proposed project's technical merit for which an awardee may receive a maximum of $100,000 for approximately six months. Phase II is the principal R&D effort which expands on the Phase I results. This two-year project may receive up to $750,000 in funding. Only Phase I awardees are eligible to compete for Phase II funds. Phase III is the commercialization of the Phase II results and moves the innovation from the laboratory to the marketplace. This requires use of private sector or other non-SBIR funding. Contact: Small Business and Technology Development Center, 333 Fayetteville Street Mall, Suite 1150, Raleigh, NC 27601; 919-715-7272; 800-258-0862 (in NC); {www.sbtac.org}.

North Carolina SBTDC Small Business Technology Transfer (STTR): STTR is much like that of the Small Business Innovation Research (SBIR) program. Its unique feature is its requirement that the small business work jointly with a non-profit research institution. A minimum of 40% of the work must be performed by the small business and a minimum of 30% by the non-profit research institution. Such institutions include Federally funded research and development centers (FFRDCs), universities, university affiliated hospitals, and other non-profits. Contact: Small Business and Technology Development Center, 333 Fayetteville Street Mall, Suite 1150, Raleigh, NC 27601; 919-715-7272; 800-258-0862 (in NC); {www.sbtac.org}.

Tax Incentives

Double-Weighted Sales Factor in Corporate Income Tax: Structured so a business in North Carolina that makes significant sales outside the state would be taxed at a lesser level than a comparable business that is located elsewhere but makes significant sales within North Carolina.

Inventory Tax Exemption: There is no local or state property tax on inventory held by manufacturers, wholesale and retail merchants or contractors.

Computer Software Tax Exemptions: There are no local or state sales taxes on custom computer programs. Additionally, there is no property tax on computer software.

Recycling Equipment: Equipment or facilities installed for the purpose of recycling solid waste or resource recovery from solid waste receives the same treatment under the tax laws as that given to pollution abatement equipment described below.

Pollution Abatement Equipment: Property used to reduce air or water pollution receives special treatment under the tax law if the Board of Environmental Management certifies that the property complies with the requirements of the Board.

OSHA Equipment: The cost of equipment and facilities mandated by the Occupational Safety and Health Act may be amortized over 60 months for income tax purposes.

Equipment to Reduce Hazardous Waste: Equipment and facilities acquired for the purpose of reducing the volume of hazardous waste generated may be amortized over a period of 60 months for income tax purposes.

Jobs Creation Tax Credit: Provides a tax credit for creating jobs based on the number of jobs created and the location of the business.

Investment Tax Credit: Available to eligible companies that invest in machinery and equipment and based on the amount of machinery purchased.

Worker Training Tax Credit: Up to a 50% credit against eligible training expenses if the firm provides training for 5 or more employees. Maximum credit is $1,000 per employee.

Research and Development Tax Credit: A line item tax credit taken by an eligible company.

Business Property Tax Credit: Equals 4.5% of tangible personal business property capitalized under the tax code, up to a maximum single-year credit of $4,500.

Central Administrative Office Tax Credit: Available to companies who have purchased or leased real property in North Carolina to be used as a central administrative office for the company. Maximum credit is $500,000.

Ports Authority Wharfage and Handling Charges: Both importers and exporters who use the North Carolina ports can apply and qualify for a tax credit up to 50% of the total state tax liability for each tax year.

Credit for Construction of Cogenerating Power Plants: Any corporation that constructs a cogenerating power plant in North Carolina is allowed a credit equal to 10% of the costs required to purchase and install the electrical or mechanical power generation equipment of that plant.

Credit for Conversion of Industrial Boiler to Wood Fuel; Any corporation that modifies or replaces an oil or gas-fired boiler or kiln and the associated fuel and residue-handling equipment used in the manufacturing process of a manufacturing business in North Carolina with a furnace capable of burning wood is permitted a credit equal to 15% of the installation and equipment costs resulting from such a conversion.

Credit for Construction of a Peat Facility: Any corporation that constructs a facility in North Carolina that uses peat as the feedstock for the productions of a commercially manufactured energy source to replace petroleum, natural gas or other nonrenewable energy sources is allowed a credit equal to 20% of the installation and equipment costs of construction.

Sales Tax Exemptions and Discounts: Available for industrial machinery and equipment; coal, coke and fuel oil used in manufacturing; electricity or piped natural gas used in connection with manufacturing; raw materials used for production, packaging, and shipping, as well as things bought for resale; motor vehicles; aircraft, boats, railway cars, and mobile offices; purchases of ingredients or component parts of manufactured products; packaging material that becomes a part of a manufactured product. Contact: NC Department of Revenue, Box 25000, Raleigh, NC 27640; 919-733-3991; {www.dor.state.nc.us/DOR/}.

Exports

Export Outreach Program: A series of workshops designed to walk a company through every facet of the export process. In cooperation with the North Carolina Community College Small Business Network, the International Trade Division has made this program available in seven regional centers across the state. The Export Outreach Program is a hard-core, intense program where commitment, preparation and action are instilled as the basis for successful exporting. North Carolina is the only state to offer such a program, which increases the quality and competitiveness of North Carolina products.

Trade Events Program: This program consists of Catalog Shows, Trade Fairs and Trade Mission in carefully selected markets worldwide. The Trade Events Calendar is updated periodically to inform North Carolina companies of these opportunities.

International Trade Division: Because North Carolina companies are prepared and committed prior to entering international markets, North Carolina is recognized in the major trading blocs of the world as one of the most aggressive international business development states in the United States. Senior Trade Specialists of the International Trade Division represent the three major trading blocks of the world: Europe/Africa/The Middle East, The Americas, Far East.

Women and Minorities

SBTDC Minority Business Enterprise Development: More businesses are being started by minorities than ever before. While minorities owned only 6% of North Carolina's small businesses in 1987, the number of minority-owned firms in the state jumped by 46% between 1982 and 1987 (U.S. Small Business Administration). Realizing the importance of North Carolina's minority-owned companies to future job creation and economic growth, the SBTDC is committed to providing responsive and effective support to minority business enterprises.

The SBTDC offers specialized market development assistance in the areas of government procurement, international business development, and new product and technology development. The SBTDC provides the strongest counseling resource for minority clients in the state. 25% of the 5,200 clients counseled each year are minority businesses. In addition to extensive business counseling, special focus training programs on topics such as "Equal Access to Credit" & "Minority, Women and Disadvantaged Business Enterprise Certification" are presented periodically across the state. Contact: Small Business and Technology Development Center, 333 Fayetteville Street Mall, Suite 1150, Raleigh, NC 27601; 919-715-7272; 800-258-0862 (in NC); {www.sbtdc.org}.

North Dakota

Department of Economic Development and Finance
1833 East Bismarck Expressway
Bismarck, ND 58504-6708
701-328-5300
Fax: 701-328-5320
TTY: 800-366-6888
www.growingnd.com

Business Assistance

Department of Economic Development and Finance (ED&F): This office can
provide information and expertise in dealing with state, federal, and local
agencies. They also have information on financing programs and other
services offered by the state government.

Technology Transfer, Inc.: Serves as a liaison
between ED&F, the North Dakota
University System and entrepreneurs
and manufacturers. The North Dakota
University System provides services
that help stimulate, produce and sell
new ideas. Services include outreach
programs designed to discover new
technology; design, licensing, and

patenting technical help; business development assistance; and production
engineering.

North Dakota Manufacturing Technology Partnership (MTP):
Approximately 400 targeted manufacturers in the state will be able to
receive direct assistance from dedicated manufacturing specialists
experienced in manufacturing and will be able to access other appropriate
assistance through managed referrals. Manufacturers can expect benefits
from improved manufacturing processes; enhanced management skills;
better business practices; research and development funding and technical
assistance; expanded market opportunities; defense conversion assistance;
new product development resources; better trained staff; intercompany
working relationships; increased revenue; and increased profit.

Community Economic Development Team: Guides communities through an
intensive community inventory, a public input phase, and an ongoing
process of business retention, new business start-up and recruitment.
Community Services Team helps communities and counties by:

- Helping them assess the level of local interest in economic development.
- Helping them understand and assess their strengths and weaknesses.
- Identifying an organization or group of people in the community who will coordinate local development.
- Helping citizens understand the process of economic development and their role in it.
- Helping to identify community leaders and financial resources available for economic development.

Research and Information Services: A broad program to strengthen economic development efforts statewide. Its major responsibilities are:

- Responding to requests from businesses seeking to grow and wish to learn more about opportunities in North Dakota.

  Research and Information Services

- Helping identify new economic development opportunities.
- Exploring ways to enhance the state's and community's climate for business growth and investment.
- Providing services that assist economic developers in conducting research, accessing and using information.
- Information Fulfillment System (IFS) which is customer driven and includes all of the systems and processes used by the Team to better manage the information needed to provide quality communications, responses and services to both external and internal clients.

Center for Innovation at University of North Dakota: Provides comprehensive, hands-on assistance for technology entrepreneurs, innovators, and manufacturers interested in starting up new ventures, commercializing new products, and licensing university technologies. Contact: Center for Innovation, UND Rural Technology Center, 4300 Dartmouth Dr., P.O. Box 8372, Grand Forks, ND 58202; 701-777-3132; {www.und.nodak.edu/dept/cibd/welcome.htm}.

Rural Technology Incubator: Located in the Center for Innovation, the Rural Technology Incubator is designed to provide a seedbed to help innovators and entrepreneurs grow their businesses. Their highly diversified staff assists startups by providing them with supportive, creative places in which to work as a team. Located next to the University of North Dakota campus, the Rural Technology Incubator offers university talent, technology, training, and technical assistance to help business startups develop and test-market new products, ideas, technologies, and ventures. Contact: Center for Innovation, UND Rural Technology Center, 4300

Dartmouth Dr., P.O. Box 8372, Grand Forks, ND 58202; 701-777-3132; {www.und.nodak.edu/dept/cibd/welcome.htm}.

Skills & Technology Training Center: Located in Fargo. A partnership between NDSU-Fargo, North Dakota State College of Science, and Wahpeton private sector leaders. Contact: Skills and Technology Training Center, 1305 19th Ave. North, Fargo, ND 58102; 701-231-6900; {www.sttc.nodak.edu}.

Job Services North Dakota: Has labor, employment, and other statistical information available. For more information, contact Job Services North Dakota, P.O. Box 5507, Bismarck, ND 58506; 800-732-9787; 701-328-2868; {www.state.nd.us/jsnd/lmi.htm}.

Publications:

North Dakota You Should See Us Now: Information on ND labor, infrastructure, taxes and quality of life targeted to primary sector site selectors.

North Dakota Tax Incentives for Business

Financing North Dakota's Future Brochure: Summary of ND commercial financing programs

Mini-Grants for Research & Development

Business Financing

The North Dakota Development Fund: Provides gap financing for primary sector businesses expanding or relocating in the state. Primary sector is defined as: "an individual, corporation, partnership or association which, through the employment of knowledge or labor, adds value to a product, process or service that results in the creation of new wealth." Primary sector businesses are typically considered to be manufacturing, food processing, and exported services. Types of investments include equity, debt, and other forms of innovative financing up to a limit of $300,000. One of the criteria for dollars invested is projected job creation within 24 months of funding.

Technology Transfer, Inc.: Provides leadership and funding to bring new technology developed in North Dakota to the marketplace. TTI is the only resource in North Dakota for high-risk research and development. A vital source for R&D funds, TTI invests financial resources in North Dakota companies and inventors. Individuals or companies with marketable ideas for products or manufacturing processes may use TTI funds to evaluate the product or process to find out if it has any commercial potential. They may also use TTI funds for expenses such as market research, prototyping, product testing, patenting, test marketing, and business plan development. The maximum amount allowed for each project is $100,000. TTI expects repayment through royalties if the product or process is successfully commercialized. Typically, royalties are based on gross sales, usually between 3 and 5 percent. TTI then reinvests these funds in other viable projects. If a funded project fails, TTI expects no repayment.

Agricultural Products Utilization Commission: Mission is to create new wealth and jobs through the development of new and expanded uses of North Dakota agricultural products. The commission accomplishes its mission through the administration of a grant program.

Basic and Applied Research Grants: This program centers on research efforts that focus on the uses and processing of agricultural products and by-products. Further, consideration is given to products which develop an expanded use of technology for the processing of these products.

Marketing & Utilization Grants: Funds from this category are used for the development or implementation of a sound marketing plan for the promotion of North Dakota agricultural products or by-products.

Cooperative Marketing Grants: This category encourages groups of agricultural producers to develop innovative marketing strategies.

Farm Diversification Grants: This category focuses on the diversification of a family farm to non-traditional crops, livestock or non-farm value-added processing of agricultural commodities. Traditional crops and livestock are generally defined as those for which the North Dakota Agricultural Statistics Service maintains records. The proposed project must have the potential to create additional income for the farm unit.

About The One Stop Capital Center: Located at the Bank of North Dakota, the One Stop Capital Center offers one-stop access to over twenty financing programs. Together, the five partners work with local financial institutions and economic developers to offer integrated financial packages. The One Stop Capital Center has loan officers available from each of the agencies who jointly work to streamline the financing process and provide timely service. Contact: Bank of North Dakota, 700 E. Main, 2nd Floor, P.O. Box 5509, Bismarck, ND 58506; 800-544-4674; {http://webhost.btigate.com/ ~onestop}.

Tax Incentives

No personal property tax including equipment, inventory, materials in process or accounts receivable.

Allows the entire amount of federal income tax liability to be deducted before calculating state corporate tax.

County Property Tax Exemptions: Any new or expanding business may be granted an exemption for up to five years. Other possible exemptions include: rehabilitation of buildings more than 25 years old; Geothermal, solar or wind energy systems.

Corporate Tax Credits: A primary sector business such as manufacturing, agricultural processing and back office operations such as telemarketing may qualify for a five-year income tax exemption. Other items that may qualify for corporate tax credits include: research expenditures within the state; seed capital investments; wages and salaries for new businesses.

Sales and Use Tax: New or expanding businesses qualify for an exemption on machinery, building materials and equipment used for manufacturing, processing or recycling. There is no sales tax on electricity, water or money when used for manufacturing purposes.

Exports

International Trade Program: Mission is to increase the number of jobs in North Dakota by helping companies expand their business into foreign markets. Staff counsels companies on export procedures, international marketing, banking and financing. They also provide referrals to translators, customs brokers, consultants and opportunities for participation in international trade show events. Offers a series of international business workshops, titled "Hands-On Training in International Business," to provide North Dakota businesses with the tools to target global markets and expand export opportunities.

Women and Minorities

Women's Business Program assists women:
- by providing counseling and technical assistance for women entrepreneurs
- by maintaining a database of women-owned businesses
- by administering the women's incentive grant program
- by certifying women-owned businesses for federal and state contracting
- by supporting the Women's Business Leadership Council
- by providing information and support through trade shows and conferences
- by serving as an information clearinghouse on economic development service providers.

For more information about Women's Business Program, contact Tara Holt, ND Women's Business Program, 418 East Broadway, Suite 25, Bismarck, ND 58501; 701-258-2251; Fax: 701-222-8071; {email: holt@btigate.com}; {www.growingnd.com/wbd_prog.html}.

Native American Program: Provides Native American individuals, businesses and tribal governments access to technical support and financial assistance. But perhaps more importantly, the NA Program advocates an improved business climate for Native American businesses and also encourages policies that address their needs. The program strives to educate all people about the unique aspects of Native American businesses. To know and understand each tribe's focus on economic development, the staff monitors the total economic development plan for each tribe. And in keeping with their philosophy that all true economic development takes place on the local level, the staff works to foster mutually beneficial relationships between Native American entrepreneurs and businesses and local development corporations and North Dakota's tribes. Finance: Provides equity gap grants to new reservation-based private businesses. Provides access to the Native American set-aside of the ND Development Fund. Assists in the development of new grant and equity participant capitol resources.

Publications:

North Dakota Women's Business Development Program Packets: Materials on programs, assistance providers and guides for ND women-owned businesses.

North Dakota Native American Program: Brochure Description of the program, services available and summary of the impact of Native American businesses in ND.

Native American Business Guide Booklet: Directory of ND Native American-owned businesses.

Grants for Native American Businesses: Booklet Directory of grants available for Native American-owned businesses.

Native American Equity Grant Program Brochure: Grant program providing "seed money" to federally recognized Indian organizations and individuals.

Ohio

Ohio Department of Development
P.O. Box 1001
Columbus, OH 43216-1001
614-466-5017
800-345-OHIO
Fax: 614-463-1540
www.odod.ohio.gov

Business Assistance

Small Business Innovation Research (SBIR) Technical Assistance Services:
Increases the number of research contracts won by Ohio companies from eleven participating federal agencies. Provides small businesses with direct, hands-on assistance in identifying research topics; guides businesses through the proposal writing process from design to review; and offers educational and technical services. Also helps companies prepare proposals for SBIR Phase I awards of up to $100,000 and Phase II awards up to $500,000.

Business Development Assistance: Assists domestic and foreign businesses with up-to-date information on sites, buildings, labor, markets, taxes and financing. Development specialists act as liaison between the companies and state/local agencies. Works to maintain and create Ohio jobs through retention and expansion of established businesses and attraction of new businesses; assists local community development organizations and acts as a liaison for communities when dealing with issues under local control.

Labor Market Information: Measurements of economic conditions. Local and national employment/labor-force data to aid in market research, business development and planning. Attracts new employers by identifying skilled workforce. Supplies free information on the training/education available to help workers meet business needs.

Ohio Data Users Center: Census and statistical data; demographic; economic; specific trade, industry and labor analyses. Develops and disseminates population estimates, projections. Provides tools for better coordinated decision-making in public/private sectors.

Ohio Procurement Technical Assistance: Free in-depth counseling, technical resources and historical contracting data, military specifications, financial guidance and advocacy services for federal procurement opportunities. Increases the federal dollars invested in Ohio; increase job and business market opportunities; increase awareness of procurement programs and opportunities.

One-Stop Business Permit Center: Supplies new entrepreneurs with information about licenses and permits required by the State of Ohio; directs callers to proper area for technical, financial and management resources; acts as advocate for licensing and permit problems.

Buy Ohio Program: Provides marketing consultation for Ohio-made products; assists with promotions, special events, and media coverage; develops buyer/seller relationships; disseminates program logo and materials. Builds consumer awareness and support for quality Ohio-made products; creates more business opportunities for Ohio companies; uses taxpayers' dollars efficiently; helps maintain jobs; develops state and local pride. No charge for consulting or start-up packet to all Ohio travel-related businesses and organizations.

Edison Technology Centers: Provides businesses with access to state-of-the-art applied research performed in-house or obtained through linkages with universities, federal laboratories and other institutions; education and training programs; plant site assessments; technical problem solving; conferences, seminars and other networking opportunities.

Edison Technology Incubators: Low-cost space that reduces operating costs during start-up phase for technology-based businesses; access to business, technical, and professional services, including legal, accounting, marketing, and financial counseling.

Federal Technology Transfer Program: "Gateway" organizations to resources of the federal laboratory system including intellectual property, engineering expertise, facilities, and equipment.

Labor Market Information: Measurements of economic conditions. Local and national employment/labor-force data to aid in market research, business development and planning.

Enterprise Ohio: Matches qualified workers to job opportunities; administers job training programs, including JTP Ohio, the Work Incentive Program and the Veterans Job Training Act.

Business Financing

166 Regional Loan Program: Land and building acquisition, expansion or renovation, and equipment purchase; industrial projects preferred. Up to 40% of total eligible fixed cost ($350,000 maximum); rate negotiable for 5-15 years; equity minimum 10%, bank minimum 25%. Ohio prevailing wage rate applies.

Child Day Care Loan Program (CDCGLP): Expansion of existing day care centers and start-up of new day care centers, thus providing employment and job training opportunities for employers and employees. Encourages new child care relationships between communities, businesses and government, as well as new approaches to child care services. $15,000 per project/ no minimum.

Community Development Corporation Program: Created for the purpose of meeting the needs of a defined low- and moderate-income neighborhood or community, or target area population. Funds may be used for housing, economic development or commercial revitalization projects. Competitive grants of up to $50,000, with at least 50% of the grant being used for project implementation costs. Requires at least 2:1 ratio of other funds. As much as $25,000 of grant may be used for project development (professional services planning and administration).

Direct Loan (166 Loan): Land and building acquisition, expansion or renovation, and equipment purchase; industrial projects preferred. Up to 30% of total eligible fixed cost ($1 million maximum, $350,000 minimum), two-thirds of prime fixed rate for 10-15 years; equity minimum 10%, bank minimum 25%. In distressed areas of the State, preferential rates and terms are available. However, the Director of Development may authorize a higher loan amount or modified terms that address a unique and demonstrated economic development need. Must show repayment and management capabilities; must create one job for every $15,000 received; Ohio prevailing wage rate applies.

Labor/Management Cooperation Program: Enhances relationship between labor and management through regular meetings, seminars, conferences, and work-site labor/management training programs. Creates a stable and positive work environment by nurturing cooperative labor/management relationships and by dispelling negative labor images. Matching grants support community-based area labor/management committees, regional centers for the advancement of labor-management cooperation, and an employee stock ownership assistance program.

Linked Deposit Program: Fixed assets, working capital and refinanced-debt for small businesses, creating or retaining jobs. A similar Agricultural Linked Deposit Program provides funds for Ohio farmers to help meet planning deadlines. 3% below current lending rate fixed for 2 years (possible 2-year extension); bank may then extend term at current rates. (All other sources of funds allowable.) The Agricultural Linked Deposit

Program provides up to $100,000 per farm at reduced rate, approximately 4% below borrower's current rate. Must have Ohio headquarters and no divisions out of state, create one job for every $15,000 to $25,000 received, have 150 or fewer employees, be organized for profit, and have bank loan from eligible state depository.

Ohio Enterprise Bond Fund: Land and building acquisition, construction, expansion or renovation, and equipment purchase for commercial or industrial projects between $1 million and $10 million in size. Long-term, fixed rate for up to 16 years; interest rate based on Standard & Poor's A-minus rating, for up to 90% of total project amount.

Revolving Loan Funds: Projects must create or retain jobs; 51% of all jobs  must be for persons from low- and moderate-income households; federal prevailing wage rates may apply; and an environmental review covering entire project must be performed. All CDBG guidelines must be met, including documentation of all project aspects. Loan ceiling determined locally or by availability. Available to user or developer, typically at 5% to 7% fixed; flexible term. Appropriate use of federal program income funds determines participation level of community. Projects must create and/or retain jobs and help develop, rehabilitate or revitalize a participating "small city" community. Financing is usually approved for fixed assets related to commercial, industrial or infrastructure.

Ohio Coal Development Program: Financial assistance for clean coal research and development projects. Advances promising technology into the commercial market. Installed technologies will result in cleaner air, better use of by-products, greater demand for Ohio coal and the jobs associated with its production and use. Strong potential also exists for the export of the technologies. For research: up to $75,000 or two-thirds of total project costs (TPC). Pilot and demonstration scale projects: up to $5 million or one-half of TPC for a pilot project, or one-third TPC for demonstration project. Funds can be issued in the form of a grant, loan, or loan guarantee.

Small Business Innovation Research Program (SBIR) Winners' Support System: Offers SBIR winners a wide range of services including: funding between federal Phase I and Phase II awards through the Bridge Grant Program; assistance in identifying potential partners or customers through the Winners' Portfolio; assistance in securing funding for commercialization through Phase III Funding conferences; and access to a network of public and private experts through a Mentor Network.

Scrap Tire Loan and Grant Program: Financing available to scrap tire recyclers who locate or expand in Ohio and who demonstrate that they will create new/reuse scrap tire products.

Defense Adjustment Program: Provides assistance to communities and technology-based companies impacted by economic losses because of company and military base drawdowns, realignments and closures.

Coal Development Program: Financial assistance for clean coal research and development projects.

Labor/Management Cooperation Program: Matching grant support community-based area labor/management committees, regional centers for the advancement of labor-management cooperation, and an employee stock ownership assistance program.

Industrial Training Program: Up to 50% funding for orientation, training, and management program; instructional materials, instructor training.

Tax Incentives

Community Reinvestment Areas: Local tax incentives for businesses that expand or locate in designated areas of Ohio. Up to 100% exemption of the improved real estate property tax valuation for up to 15 years. In some instances, local school board approval may be required. Business must undertake new real estate investment.

Enterprise Zones: Local and state tax incentives for businesses that expand or locate in designated areas of Ohio. Up to 75% exemption in incorporated areas and up to 60% in unincorporated areas of the improved real estate or new tangible personal property tax valuation for up to 10 years.

Ohio Manufacturing Machinery & Equipment Investment Tax Credit: A non-refundable corporate franchise or state income tax credit for a manufacturer that purchases new machinery and equipment that is located in Ohio and is used in the production or assembly of a manufactured good. The manufacturer shall receive a 7.5% tax credit on the increase of the investment that is in excess of the three-year annual average investment on machinery and equipment.

Ohio Job Creation Tax Credit: State and municipal tax incentives are available for businesses that expand or locate in Ohio. State guidelines regulate the type of business and project eligible for the incentive. A business can receive a tax credit or refund against its corporate franchise tax based on the state income withheld on new, full-time employees. The amount of the tax credit can be up to 75% for up to ten years. The tax credit can exceed 75% upon recommendation of the Director of ODOD when there is an extraordinary circumstance. Municipalities can provide a similar arrangement with their local employee income taxes.

Targeted Jobs Tax Credit Program: Offers employers a credit against their federal tax liability for hiring individuals from nine target groups. TJTC benefits job seekers from groups that traditionally have had difficulty in obtaining jobs. When hiring from most target groups, employers may claim a credit of 40% of first year wages (up to $6,000 per employee) for a maximum credit of $2,400 per employee.

Export Tax Credit: Credits of up to 10% from pre-tax profits that result from expanded export operations with a cap of $250,000 per year.

Technology Investment Tax Credit: Taxpayers who invest in small, research and development and technology-oriented firms may reduce their state taxes by up to 25% of the amount they invest.

Exports

International Trade Division: Assists Ohio companies to develop export markets worldwide. Ohio's trade staff in Columbus, Tokyo, Hong Kong, Toronto, Mexico City, Sao Paulo, Brussels, and Tel Aviv provide custom-tailored assistance in international marketing and export finance and lead Ohio companies on trade missions and to the world's leading trade shows. Services include:

- Export Counseling
- Trade Shows and Trade Missions
- Electronic Trade
- Export Finance
- Export Incentives
- Japan Trade Program

Women and Minorities

Minority Management and Technical Services: Provides assistance in management analysis, technical assistance, educational services and financial consulting. Supports overall growth and development of minority firms throughout the State. Counseling is provided at no charge.

Minority Contractor and Business Assistance Program: Provides management, technical, financial, and contract procurement assistance; loan, grant, bond packaging services. Networks with all levels of government, private businesses. Aids in economic growth and development of the minority community; increases awareness of local, state, and federal business assistance programs. Counseling is provided at no charge. Fees may be charged for some programs using federal funding.

Minority Contract Procurement Services: Assists primarily minority firms in procuring public and private sector contracts. Supports efforts of minority firms to obtain contract awards that will aid in sustaining and developing these firms. Counseling is provided at no charge.

Minority Business Bonding Program: Surety bonding assistance for state-certified minority businesses. Maximum bond pre-qualification of up to $1,000,000 per Minority Business. The bond premium for each bond issued will not exceed 2% of the face value of the bond.

Minority Direct Loan: Purchase or improvement of fixed assets for state-certified minority-owned businesses. Up to 40% of total project cost at 4.5% fixed for up to 10 years (maximum).

Ohio Mini-Loan Program: Fixed assets and equipment for small businesses. Start-up or existing business expansion. Projects of $100,000 or less. Up to 45% guarantee of an eligible bank loan. Interest rate of the State guarantee of the loan is currently 5.5%, and may be fixed for 10 years. Eligibility: Small business entrepreneurs with fewer than 25 employees, targeted 50% allocation to businesses owned by minorities and women.

Women's Business Resource Program: Assistance for start-up, expansion and management of businesses owned by women; assures equal access to state business assistance and lending programs; direction to purchase and procurement opportunities with government agencies. Researches legislation that may impact businesses owned by women. Increases start-ups and successes of women-owned businesses. No charge.

Oklahoma

Department of Commerce
900 North Stiles
P.O. Box 26980
Oklahoma City, OK 73126-0980
405-815-6552
800-879-6552.
Fax: 405-815-5199
www.locateok.com
www.odoc.state.ok.us/index.html

Business Assistance

Office of Business Recruitment: Provides comprehensive site location assistance to companies considering new investment in Oklahoma.

Business Development Division: Promotes growth by addressing the needs of existing and start-up businesses. Provides information and seminars directly to businesses. Offers business information and a referral network to assist companies through the maze of regulatory requirements and introduces local resource providers.
Site Location Planner: On CD-ROM and the web at {www.locateok.com}. Provides comprehensive site location data including available buildings, community information, state incentives, and statistical and other information.

Market Research:

- *National Trade Data Bank (NTDB)*-the U. S. Government's most comprehensive source of world trade data, consisting of more than 130 separate trade- and business-related programs (databases). NTDB offers one-stop-shopping for trade information from more than 20 federal sources.

- *The Economic Bulletin Board (EBB)* provides on-line trade leads, time-sensitive market information, and the latest statistical releases from a variety of federal agencies.

- *Country Commercial Guides (CCG)* present a comprehensive look at a particular country's commercial environment including economic, political, and market analysis.

- *Industry Sector Analyses (ISA)* are in-depth, structured reports on a broad range of industries regularly compiled by commercial specialists at U. S. embassies and consulates abroad.

Technology Partnerships: Testing of technologies developed by private business may be performed in partnership with research universities. Such institutions may devote resources such as laboratory usage and faculty time to a particular business's need in return for a portion of business's profits.

Business Financing

Oklahoma Finance Authorities: Provides permanent financing for real estate and equipment. Contact: Oklahoma Finance Authorities, 301 NW 63rd, Suite 225, Oklahoma City, OK 73116; 405-842-1145.

Small Business Linked Deposit Program: Provides below market interest rates for qualified small businesses and certified industrial parks through local financing sources. Contact Oklahoma State Treasurer's Office, 4545 N. Lincoln Blvd., #169, Oklahoma City, OK 73105; 405-522-4235.

Public Trust Financing: Oklahoma authorizes public trust financing for economic development purposes at the county and city level.

General Obligation Limited Tax Bonds: Revenue bonds are issued in association with a particular project.

Tax Increment Financing: Provides economic development in distressed areas for up to 25 years.

Sales Tax Financing: Oklahoma cities and counties are authorized, upon a vote of the people, to build facilities and provide other economic development benefits for businesses financed by sales tax collections.

Private Activity Bond Allocation: Generally allocations are on a first-come, first-served basis, with some size limitation.

Capital Investment Board: Facilitates investment in venture capital companies that focus on investing in quality Oklahoma companies. Contact: Oklahoma Capital Investment Board, 301 NW 63rd, Suite 520, Oklahoma City, OK 73116; 405-848-9456.

Capital Access Program: Provides a credit insurance reserve for Oklahoma banks through a fee-matching arrangement for loans enrolled in the program. Contact: Oklahoma Capital Investment Board, 301 NW 63rd, Suite 520, Oklahoma City, OK 73116; 405-848-9456.

Training for Industry: Assists qualifying businesses by paying for training for new employees.

Quality Jobs Program: Provides quarterly cash payments of up to 5% of new taxable payroll directly to a qualifying company, for up to ten years.

Small Employer Quality Jobs Program: Provides annual cash payments of 5% of taxable payroll for new employees to a qualifying company, for up to 5 years.

Enterprise Zones: The enterprise district management authorities created in some enterprise districts are empowered to establish venture capital loan programs and to solicit proposals from enterprises seeking to establish or expand facilities in the zones.

Tax Incentives

Ad Valorem Tax Exemptions: New and expanding qualifying manufacturers, research and development companies, certain computer services and data processing companies with significant out-of-state sales, aircraft repair and aircraft manufacturing may be eligible for ad valorem exemptions.

Exempt Inventory: Oklahoma's Freeport Law exempts goods, wares, and merchandise from taxation that come into Oklahoma from outside the state and leave the state within nine months.

Pollution Control: Pollution control equipment that has been certified by the DEQ is exempt from Ad Valorem taxation.

Sales Tax Exemptions: Exemptions are available in the following areas: machinery and equipment used in manufacturing; tangible personal property used in manufacturing including fuel and electric power; tangible personal property which becomes part of the finished product; packaging materials; items sold by the manufacturer and immediately transported out of state for exclusive use in another state; machinery, equipment, fuels and chemicals used directly or in treating hazardous industrial waste, tangible personal property used in design and warehousing and located on the manufacturing site.

Aircraft Maintenance Facilities: Sales tax exemption on aircraft and parts.

Telecommunications: Exemptions apply to various services as part of an inducement to contract for wireless telecommunications services.

Sales and Use Tax Refunds: Refunds of sales/use tax are available for purchase of data processing equipment, related peripherals and telephone or telecommunications services or equipment and for construction materials.

Income Tax Credits/Exclusions: Reduces tax liability for the taxpayer that invests in qualifying property and also hires new employees. The credit is doubled for companies that locate in state Enterprise Zones.

Technology Transfer Income Tax Exemption: The taxable income of any corporation is decreased for transfers of technology to qualified small businesses located in Oklahoma not to exceed 10% of the amount of gross proceeds received by such corporation as a result of the technology transfer.

New Products Development Income Tax Exemption: Royalties earned by an inventor on products developed and manufactured in Oklahoma are exempt from state income tax.

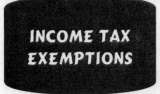

Agricultural Commodity Processing Facility Income Tax Exclusion: Owners of agricultural commodity processing facilities may exclude a portion from taxable income based on investment.

Income Tax Credit for Investment in Oklahoma Producer-Owned Agriculture Processing: An income tax credit of 30% of investment is available to agricultural producer investors in Oklahoma producer-owned agricultural processing ventures, cooperative, or marketing associations.

Income Tax Credit for Computer/Data Processing/ Research & Development Jobs: Credit is available for a net increase in the number of full-time employees engaged in computer services, date processing or R & D. The credit allowed is $500 per employee, up to 50 employees.

Insurance Premium Tax Credit: Insurance companies which locate or expand regional home offices in Oklahoma are eligible for special tax credits against the tax imposed in the Insurance Code ranging from 15% to 50% based on number of full-time employees.

Small Business Capital Formation Tax Credit: Authorizes an income tax credit of 20% of equity investment for investors in qualified businesses.

Qualified Venture Capital Company Tax Credit: Freely transferable tax credits for investors in qualified venture capital companies.

Recycling, Reuse and Source Reduction Incentive Act: Manufacturing and service industries may receive an income tax credit of up to 20% of investment cost for equipment and installation or processes used to recycle, reuse, or reduce the source of hazardous waste. Credits are limited $50,000.

Income Tax Exemption for Interest Paid on Bonds: Interest payment received as a result of bonds issued by non-profit corporations on behalf of towns, cities, or counties for housing purposes are not subject to state income tax.

Tax Incentives on Former Indian Reservation Lands:
1. Employee Credit: Businesses located on qualified areas of former Indian reservations are eligible for a tax credit based on the increase in qualifying annual wages paid to enrolled Indian tribal members or their spouses. The credit equal 20% of the increased wages.
2. Depreciation Incentive: Provides a shorter recovery period of approximately 40% for most non-residential depreciable property being used in an active trade or business.

Work Opportunity Tax Credit Program: A tax credit is available up to $2,400 for each new hire from a target group of individuals.

Welfare-to-Work Tax Credit: Available to employers who hire individuals certified and long-term assistance recipients. The credit is as much as $8,500 per new hire.

Investment/Jobs: Allows a five-year tax credit on the greater of (1%) per year of investment in qualified new depreciable property or a credit of $500 per year per new job, doubled in an Enterprise Zone.

Exports

International Trade and Investment Division: Provides diverse services including hands on assistance for companies wishing to learn more about exporting to promoting Oklahoma products at trade shows throughout the world. Also works closely with the international business community to develop top of mind awareness of Oklahoma's business climate advantages. Provide confidential, reliable site location assistance, site selection assistance, tax comparisons, and incentive projections.

International Market Insights (IMI): Commercial specialists also regularly report on specific foreign market conditions and upcoming opportunities for U. S. business.

Customized Market Analysis (CMA): Provides detailed information needed to make the most efficient and beneficial export marketing decisions. CMA will give an accurate assessment of how a product or service will sell in a given market.

Trade Opportunities Program (TOP): Up-to-the-minute sales leads from around the world are prescreened and transmitted every work day to commercial specialists in U. S. embassies and consulates abroad.

Agent/Distributor Service (ADS): Customized search needed to successfully launch an export marketing campaign. Provides pertinent information on up to six prequalified potential representatives per market.

International Company Profiles (ICP): Thorough, up-to-date background checks on potential clients.

Country Directories of International Contacts (CDIC): Provides the name and contact information of importers, agents, trade associations, government agencies, etc., on a country-by-country basis.

Trade Fair Certification: Selects events in the countries and industries with the best opportunities for U. S. exporters. Only major shows within a given industry are certified-those that have proven to be well-established, high-quality events.

Foreign Trade Zones: Businesses engaged in international trade within these zones benefit from special customs procedures.

Export Finance Program: Assistance is available through a relationship with the Export-Import Bank of the United States to facilitate export financing with working capital guarantees, credit insurance and foreign buyer financing.

Women and Minorities

Women-owned Business Certification Program: Established to facilitate contracting capabilities for women-owned businesses with public and private sector entities.

Minority Business: Provides a forum to network with banking organizations, utility companies, state agencies and other that can be valuable resources for a business. Each month several business owners are selected to give a brief presentation about their business.

Minority Business Development Centers: A vehicle for small minority-owned businesses that are seeking help in start-up information. The centers provide assistance in business plans, procurement assistance and works with the SBA in the certified lenders program and 8(a) certification.

Oklahoma Minority Supplier Development Council (OMSDC): The mission of the OMSDC is to assist corporations and public sector agencies in creating a business environment that promotes access and increased opportunities for minority-owned businesses. The Council also helps to promote, educate and develop minority-owned businesses.

Oklahoma Consortium for Minority Business Development, Inc.: Provides a forum whereby government/private agencies and organizations may coordinate functions and activities to increase overall effectiveness in advocating and supporting the minority business community.

Minority Assistance Program, Office of Central Services: Created to increase the level of Oklahoma minority business participation in state purchases. The State has designated a percentage of contract awards to properly certified minority vendors.

Native American: Almost two-thirds of Oklahoma is considered "former Indian reservation land." Businesses located in these lands before the end of the year 2003 receive accelerated depreciation rates on capital investment. Federal employment tax credits are also available to businesses in these areas that employ American Indians or spouses.

Oregon

Economic Development Department
775 Summer St., NE
Salem, OR 97310
503-986-0260
Fax: 503-581-5115
www.econ.state.or.us/javahome.htm

Business Assistance

Economic Development Department: This office can provide information and expertise in dealing with state, federal, and local agencies. They also have information on financing programs and other services offered by the state government.

Small Business Advocate: Entrepreneurs can find connections to a network of private sector advisers who can help them access capital.

 Inventors, entrepreneurs and mature companies can obtain information on how to access research and development federal grants, assessment of their technology concepts and innovative best practices from the technology transfer services supported by the department. All of Oregon's small and emerging businesses can benefit from the efforts of a public/private partnership to design and implement tools, incentives and policies that can make it easier to start and grow a company in Oregon. Small Business Advocate, Economic Development Department, 775 Summer St., NE, Salem, OR 97310; 503-986-0057.

Government Contract Acquisition Program (GCAP): Established to provide comprehensive information and assistance to Oregon small businesses desiring to compete in this market.

Impact: Provides business management, marketing and financing assistance to start-up, small businesses and existing business expansion.

Oregon Business Network: Helps Portland minority start-up businesses and established businesses in a group environment.

Oregon Downtown Development Association works to revitalize and maintain the heritage and economic health of Oregon's downtowns and older business districts.

Rural Development Initiatives: A non-profit corporation that builds the capacity of rural communities to make strategic decisions about their futures and to act on those decisions to ensure high quality of life and a vital economy.

Employment Department: Comprehensive source of qualified job applicants for new businesses in Oregon communities.

Industry Workforce Training: Provides grants to community colleges for the development and implementation of training programs for multiple firms within an industry. Employers must provide matching funds or in-kind services.

Business Financing

Capital Access Program: Offered through the Oregon Economic Development Department, is designed to increase the availability of loans to Oregon small businesses from banks. The program provides loan portfolio insurance so lenders may make loans that carry higher than conventional risks. Borrowers pay a fee of between 3% and 7% of the loan amount, which is matched by the department and contributed to a loan loss reserve account in an enrolled bank. The loans must be within soundness and safety requirements of federal and state banking regulations. A Capital Access Program loan is a private transaction between the borrower and lender. The Oregon Economic Development Department is not a party to loan negotiations or to the loan agreement. The department does not monitor the loan or require reporting from the borrower. Loan may be used for virtually any purpose, except to construct or purchase residential housing, to purchase real property that is not used for business operations of the borrower, or to refinance the principal balance of an existing loan.

Credit Enhancement Fund: Administered by the Oregon Economic Development Department, provides guarantees to enrolled banks to increase capital availability to small Oregon firms, helping them create jobs. The maximum guarantee for a loan is $500,000. The department has authority to guarantee up to $75 million of financial institution loans.

Entrepreneurial Development Loan Funds: Entrepreneurial businesses can receive loans of up to $25,000 through the Oregon Entrepreneurial Development Loan Fund.

Resource and Technology Development Fund: Equity-based capital is available for Oregon "basic-sector" businesses through the Oregon Resource and Technology Development Fund. Areas of focus include biological and biomedical services, high technology, and natural resource industries. For more information, contact Oregon Resource and Technology Development Fund, 4370 NE Halsey, Suite 233, Portland, OR 97213; 503-282-4462.

Oregon Enterprise Forum: Provides assistance to help companies that are in
transition by providing mentoring services.
For more information, contact Oregon
Enterprise Forum, 2611 S.W. Third
Ave., Suite 200, Portland, OR 97201;
503-222-2270.

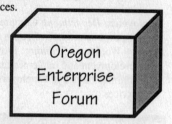

Rural Development: Offers loan guarantees
to banks to further business and
industrial development in rural areas
of the country. Loan guarantees may
be made in any rural area or communities with a population of 50,000 or
less. The maximum loan guarantee is $10 million. 10% equity is required.
Projects must comply with certain federal requirements. Loans may be for
land, facilities, equipment or working capital. Ineligible purposes include
agricultural production (other federal programs are available for this
purpose), hotels, motels, convention centers and tourist facilities. For
more information, contact Rural Development Services, Business and
Cooperative Programs, 101 SW Main, Suite 1410, Portland, OR 97204-
3222; 503-414-3366.

Subordinated and Direct Loans: Subordinated loans usually fill a gap in a
financing package, where commercial and private debt financing and
equity have been maximized and additional funds are required to complete
the financing transaction. Often these loans will "subordinate" or take a
lesser security interest in the assets being financed, which will allow the
senior lender first priority on project assets in the event of a default. The
subordinated loan is often secured with additional assets to help
collaterize its position. Direct loans and, in some limited cases, grants are
available to finance businesses when the project will further the public
objectives of the entity making the loan or grant.

Business Development Fund: Manufacturing, processing and regionally
significant tourism projects are eligible for the Oregon Business
Development Fund. The fund provides long-term, fixed rate financing for
land, buildings, equipment and machinery.

Local Revolving Loan Funds: Many local and regional development groups
and local governments throughout Oregon administer revolving loan funds
for small business financing. In most cases, funding has been provided by
the federal Department of Housing and Urban Development (HUD), the
federal Economic Development Administration (EDA), the U.S.
Department of Agriculture Rural Economic and Community Development
Administration (RECD) or the Oregon Economic Development
Department. Loan criteria may reflect some of the objectives of those
funding organizations or may have special requirements of those agencies.

Oregon Port Revolving Fund Loans: Provides long-term loans to ports at below-market interest rates. Individual loans may be made to a maximum of $700,000 per project. The total outstanding loan amount any individual port can have at any one time cannot exceed $2 million. Funding may be used for port development projects (infrastructure) or to assist port-related private business development projects. The 23 legally formed Port Districts are the only entities eligible for Port Revolving Fund loans. The variety of projects eligible is very broad. These include, but are not limited to, water-oriented facilities, industrial parks, airports and eligible commercial or industrial developments. Projects must be located within port district boundaries. For more information contact Ports Division, Oregon Economic Development Department, 775 Summer Street NE, Salem, OR 97310; 503-986-0143.

Industrial Development Revenue Bonds: The Economic Development Commission may issue industrial development revenue bonds for manufacturing and processing facilities in Oregon. Industrial development bonds can finance fixed assets only, along with some limited transaction costs. If a project qualifies the bonds can be issued on a tax-exempt basis which lowers the overall cost of financing. Revenue bonds are not direct obligations of the State of Oregon. The individual or corporation on whose behalf the bonds are issued is legally obligated to repay them. An eligible company may borrow up to $10 million through the Oregon Industrial Development Revenue Bond Program. Typically, the minimum bond is for $2 million.

Small Scale Energy Loan Program: The Small Scale Energy Loan Program (SELP), administered by the Oregon Department of Energy, finances energy conservation and renewable energy projects in Oregon, through the issuance of general obligation bonds. Bond proceeds can be loaned to finance eligible equipment costs, construction, certain design and consultation fees, some reserves, construction interest and most loan closing costs. Eligible costs are those incurred after loan approval. Land and working capital are normally not financed. Costs not part of the energy project also are not eligible. All Oregonians, Oregon businesses, nonprofit organizations, municipal corporations and state agencies can apply for loans. Eligible projects are those which conserve conventional energy, such as electricity and natural gas; or projects which produce renewable energy from geothermal or solar sources or from water, wind, biomass and some waste materials. For more information, contact Oregon

Department of Energy, 625 Marion Street NE, Salem, OR 97310; 503-373-1033; 800-221-8035 (in OR).

Regional Development: Cities, counties and other governmental entities also can obtain loans and grants to help pay for construction projects. The department uses grant and loan funds to support public works, safe drinking water and housing rehabilitation projects. The department also provides funding for community facilities projects to improve or build day care, senior centers, emergency shelters and family counseling facilities, among others.

Tax Incentives

Corporate Income Tax Credits: Oregon businesses may be eligible for a number of tax credits allowed under Oregon law. Some of these business-related tax credits include:
- pollution control tax credit,
- business energy tax credit,
- research tax credit,
- reclaimed plastics product tax credit,
- dependent child care tax credit, and
- donation of computers and scientific equipment in Oregon.

Enterprise Zone Program: Created as a business incentive to create new jobs by encouraging business investment in economically lagging areas of the state. Construction of new facilities in an enterprise zone entitles a business to a 100% property tax abatement for three to five years on a new plant and most of the equipment installed.

Construction in Progress Exemption: Under Oregon law, new facilities are exempt from property taxes for up to two years while they are under construction and not in use on July 1 of the taxing year. The Construction in Progress Exemption also applies to any machinery or equipment installed in the unoccupied facility on July 1. The exemption does not apply to land. For more information, contact the county assessor or Oregon Department of Revenue, Property Tax Division, Room 256, Revenue Building, Salem, OR 97310; 503-945-8290.

Strategic Investment Program: Provides property tax exemptions for significant projects that will benefit Oregon's key industries. Properties developed under this program are exempted from local property taxes for up to 15 years on assessed value in excess of $100 million. With local government approval, participating companies pay property taxes on the first $100 million in assessed value for the approved project. This base amount ($100 million) is increased by 6% per year. Participating companies also make a direct community service payment to the local government equal to 25% of the abated amount, not to exceed $2 million per year. After local government approval, the Oregon Economic Development Commission is authorized to determine that the project is eligible for the program and determine the maximum eligible cost of real and personal property for the project.

Exports

International Division of the Oregon Economic Development Department: The international arm of state government. It provides "export ready" Oregon companies assistance in export markets, assists the Governor's Office on protocol and other assignments, and works with public and private organizations to promote Oregon in the international business community. The Division is located at One World Trade Center, Suite 300, 121 SW Salmon, Portland, OR 97204; 503-229-5625; 800-448-7512.

Women and Minorities

Southern Oregon Women's Access to Credit: Offers a business development program for new and existing business owners in Jackson, Josephine and Klamath counties. Focuses on training, mentoring and financing. Contact SOWAC, 33 N. Central Avenue, Suite #209, Medford, OR 97501; 541-779-3992; Fax: 541-779-5195.

Association Of Minority Entrepreneurs: A non-profit, tax exempt organization formed to promote and develop entrepreneurship and economic development for ethnic minorities in the State of Oregon. OAME works as a partnership between ethnic minorities, entrepreneurs, education, government and established corporate business. OAME provides a core of services to start-up and/or existing minority businesses. These services include:

- Technical Assistance
- Access To Capital/Loan Fund
- Capability And Opportunity Matching (OAME's Marketing/Clearinghouse)
- Administrative Services
- Incubator With & Without Walls Development

Contact Oregon Association of Minority Entrepreneurs, 4134 N. Vancouver, Portland, OR 97217; 503-249-7744; Fax: 503-249-2027.

Native American Business Entrepreneurs Network: Created by Northwest Indian Tribes to increase the success of private businesses owned by Native Americans. ONABEN's approach consists of technical training, access to capital, (conditional on an on-going consulting relationship), access to markets and mentors. The program is organized to integrate community resources. It assists and encourages tribes to share business development resources amongst themselves and with non-Indian neighbors. The program works where no predecessor has succeeded because it approaches business ownership as an expression of Native Americans' common values; inter-generation and community awareness, mutual respect, non-destructive harvest. Contact: ONABEN, 520 SW 6th Ave., Suite 930, Portland, OR 97204; 800-854-8289; {www.onaben.org}.

Pennsylvania

Department of Community and Economic Development
433 Forum Building
Harrisburg, PA 17120
800-379-7448
www.dced.state.pa.us

Governor's Action Team
100 Pine Street, Suite 100
Harrisburg, PA 17101
717-787-8199
Fax: 717-772-5419
www.teampa.com

Business Assistance

Entrepreneurial Assistance Office: Established to ensure small business owners receive the support and assistance they require. The Entrepreneurial Assistance Office works to build an environment which encourages the creation, expansion and retention of small, women and minority owned businesses.

Small Business Resource Center: The single point of contact and hub of information for small businesses, answering state related and general business questions about licenses and permits. The Center has select state forms and applications available as well as other sources of information and technical assistance.

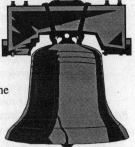

Environmental Business Advocate: Assists small businesses in complying with requirements of the Federal Clean Air Act and appropriate state regulations. Housed in the PA Department of Environmental Protection, (DEP), the EBA represents the interests of small businesses in matters affecting them with DCED and the U.S. Environmental Protection Agency.

Industrial Resource Centers: Assists companies in solving problems through the deployment of technologies.

Job Centers: Provide employers with a wide array of employment and training services.

Small Business Incubators: Sites where young businesses can start and grow. Offers businesses the opportunity to rent small units of space at a lower than market rate. Provides tenants with business development services that help to reduce costs and increase profits.

Business Financing

PA Industrial Development Authority: Low-interest financing through Industrial Development Corporations for land and building acquisitions, construction and renovation resulting in the creation or retention of jobs. Amounts: Loans up to $1 million (within Enterprise Zones, $1.5 million) no more than 30 to 40% of the total eligible project costs, advanced technology projects and those in an Act 47 or within an Enterprise Zone qualify for lower interest rates.

Machinery and Equipment Loan Fund: Low-interest loan financing to acquire and install new or used machinery and equipment or to upgrade existing machinery and equipment. Amounts: Loans up to $500,000 or 50% of the total eligible project costs, whichever is less.

Small Business First: Funding for small businesses including: low-interest loan financing to small businesses for land and building acquisition and construction; machinery and equipment purchases and working capital; financing to comply with environmental regulations; for businesses involved in municipal or commercial recycling; and for those impacted by defense conversion. Amounts: $200,000 or 50% of the total eligible project costs, whichever is less. Maximum loan amount is $100,000 for working capital.

PA Infrastructure Investment Authority (PennVEST): Low-interest loans for design, engineering and construction of publicly and privately owned drinking water distribution and treatment facilities, storm water conveyance and wastewater treatment systems. Amounts: Loans up to $11 million per project for one municipality, up to $20 million for more than one municipality, up to $350,000 for design and engineering, up to 100% of the total project costs.

PA Capital Access Program: Through participating banks, loan guarantees are provided to support a wide variety of business purposes. Amounts: Loan guarantees up to $500,000.

PA Economic Development Financing Authority: An issuer of tax-exempt and taxable bonds, both in pooled transactions and stand-alone transactions. Bond funds are loaned to businesses and can be used to finance land, building, equipment, working capital and refinances. Amounts: Loans no less them $400,000 and no more than $10 million for manufacturers, no upper limits for other projects, up to 100% of project costs.

Customized Job Training: Provides grants to businesses in need of training assistance for new hires, retraining efforts and upgrading employees in an effort to retain and create jobs in Pennsylvania. Amounts: Grants up to 100% of the eligible costs for new job creations, grants up to 70% of eligible costs for job retention, grants up to 25% of the eligible costs for upgrade training. Contact: Office of Workforce and Technology Development, 464 Forum Bldg., Harrisburg, PA 17120; 717-787-4117.

Job Training Partnership Act: Up to 50% of wage rate for employees while in training.

Opportunity Grant Program: Provides grant funds to create or preserve jobs within the Commonwealth. Funds may be used for job training, infrastructure improvements, land and building improvements, machinery and equipment, working capital and environmental assessment and redemption. Amounts: No minimum or maximum grant amount.

Infrastructure Development Program: Grant and low-interest loan financing for public and private infrastructure improvements. Amounts: Loans and grants up to $1.25 million, no more than 20% of the annual appropriation for a single municipality.

Industrial Sites Reuse Program: Grant and low-interest loan financing is provided to perform environmental site assessment and remediation work at former industrial sites. Amounts: Grants and loans up to $200,000 for environmental assessment, grants and loans up to $1 million for remediation.

Rail Freight Assistance: Grants to build or repair rail lines and spurs. Amounts: Grants up to $250,000 for maintenance, up to $100,000 for construction.

Enterprise Zone Program: Grants available for loans to businesses: Planning Grant up to $50,000; Basic Grant up to $50,000; Competitive Grant: up to $250,000.

Industrial Resource Center Network: Provides financial and technical assistance to manufacturers to improve their manufacturing operations.

Seed Venture Program: Provides product development and working capital to early-stage venture companies.

Small Business First Export Loan Program: Provides short-term loans to meet the pre and post-export financing needs of small businesses. Amounts: Pre-Export loans: Up to $350,000 or 50% of total eligible

project costs, whichever is less. Post-Export loans: Loans not to exceed
80% of the face amount of the contract.

Underground Storage Upgrade Loan: Loans to assist owners of regulated
storage tanks in upgrading their underground storage tank systems to meet
federal Environmental Protection Agency upgrade requirements.
Amounts: $500,000 or 75% of the total eligible project costs, whichever
is less.

Challenge Grant Program: Provides grants ranging from $5,000 to $100,000
for research and development, technology transfer, joint research and
development.

Tax Incentives

Job Creation Tax Credits: A $1,000-per-job tax credit to approved businesses
that agree to create jobs in the Commonwealth within three years.

Keystone Opportunity Zones: Zones in which businesses and residents will be
exempt from virtually all state and local taxes.

Manufacturing, processing and research and development activities are exempt
from the Capital Stock and Franchise Tax.

Pollution control devices are exempt from the Capital Stock and Franchise Tax.

Machinery and equipment used in manufacturing are exempt from the Sales
and Use Tax.

Computer services are exempt from the Sales and Use Tax.

Machinery and equipment, business inventories and personal property are
exempt from Pennsylvania's real property tax.

Improvements to property can be exempted from the real property tax for up to
ten years.

Capital gains are taxed at a rate of 2.8%.

Films: A sales tax exemption is available for most purchases made by
producers of full-length feature films.

Local Economic Revitalization Tax Assistance Act: Local municipalities,
school districts and counties can offer up to 100% abatements on property
taxes for up to 10 years.

Neighborhood Assistance Tax Credit: Up to 70% of the amount invested in
programs that help families or communities in impoverished areas.

Employment Incentive Payments Program: Provides credits to employers that
hire welfare recipients.

Enterprise Zone Credit Program: Allows corporations a tax credit of up to
20% on investments to rehabilitate or improve buildings or land in an
Enterprise Zone.

Exports

Headquartered in Harrisburg, the Office of International Business Development maintains offices around the world. The Office, together with the Team Pennsylvania Export Network Regions, supports Pennsylvania firms wishing to do business in the overseas market. The Office coordinates a range of trade development activities including:
- industry sector trade initiatives
- provision of market intelligence
- export financing programs
- in-country support for firms in association with the Commonwealth's overseas offices

Contact Office of International Business Development, 308 Forum Building, Harrisburg, PA 17120; 888-PA EXPORT.

Women and Minorities

PA Minority Business Development Authority: Low-interest loan financing to businesses which are owned and operated by minorities. Amounts: Manufacturing, industrial, high-tech, international trade or franchise companies with loans up to $500,000 (within Enterprise Zones, $750,000) or 75% of total eligible project costs, whichever is less, retail or commercial firms loans of up to $250,000 ($350,000 in Enterprise Zones).

Minority Business Development Agency: Provides minority entrepreneurs with management and technical assistance services to start, expand, or mange a business.

National Minority Supplies Development Council: A non-profit corporation chartered in 1972 to expand business opportunities for minority owned companies, to encourage mutually beneficial economic links between minority suppliers and the public and private sectors, and to help build a stronger, more equitable society by supporting and promoting minority business development.

Pennsylvania Minority Business Development Authority: Offers low interest loan financing to businesses that are owned and operated by minorities. Maximum loan amount is $500,000 or $750,000 depending on whether the business is located in a targeted area and the nature of the business.

50 Best Women in Business: Awards program recognizes and applauds the significant contributions Pennsylvania's women business owners and leaders make to their communities, to their families and to their work.

Minority Business Advocate: Encourages the development of minority-owned businesses as part of the overall economic development strategy of the Commonwealth. Serves as an advocate for minority owned business

owners in resolving issues with state agencies and interacting with other
government agencies.

Women's Business Advocate: Works to assist women businesses in the
development of their business, specifically assisting in resolving issues
with state agencies, exploring marketing options and identifying financing
strategies.

***Bureau of Contract Administration and Business Development (Formerly
the Minority and Women Business Enterprise Office)***: Benefits small,
minority and women businesses. Provides the necessary resources and
direction for business owners to compete for and participate in the state
contracting process. Furthermore, it is the statewide agency for
certification as a Minority Business Enterprise and Women Business
Enterprise.

Rhode Island

Economic Development Corporation
One West Exchange St.
Providence, RI 02903
401-222-2601
Fax: 401-222-2102
www.riedc.com

Business Assistance

Economic Development Corporation: This office can provide information and
expertise in dealing with state, federal, and local agencies. They also have
information on financing programs
and other services offered by the
state government.

Economic Development Set Aside:
The Set-Aside for
Economic Development is
designed to provide
matching job training funds

to companies that are either relocating to Rhode Island or expanding
present operations in the state. The funds are used for the training of new
employees through either customized training programs or on the job
training.

Customized Upgrade Training to Improve Productivity: This program allows
an employer to upgrade the skills of existing employees, thus improving
the productivity of the business. The program awards matching grants of
up to $25,000 per company through a competitive Request for Proposal
process. In some cases, the company will be a fast growing firm, while
others may be marginal with the training program becoming part of an
overall business strategy to improve competitiveness. Businesses are urged
to work through trade associations and local colleges and universities to
increase the effectiveness of the training programs.

Customized Training (new hires): This type of program involves occupational
skills with training provided either by the employer or by an outside
trainer. The training location can be the employer's worksite or at an
educational facility (or some combination). The employer makes the final
decision on program design, curriculum content, and trainee selection.

First Stop Business Center: Helps businesses deal with federal, state, and local
requirements and provides information and referral assistance. Contact

First Stop Business Center, 100 North Main St., Providence, RI 02903; 401-277-2185; Fax: 401-277-3890; {www.state.ri.us/bus/frststp.htm}.

Business Financing

Industrial Revenue Bonds: Industrial Revenue Bonds may be used to finance qualified commercial and industrial projects. The bonds offer a competitive interest rate and state sales tax exemption on building materials that may be significant for projects involving new construction. Financing is available through the Rhode Island Industrial Facilities Corporation and covers the entire project cost. The project and the credit of the user provides the security for the bonds which may be issued on the financial strength of the user when the user is appropriately rated. The bonds may also be issued with an enhancement letter of credit from a financial institution.

Tax-Exempt "Small Issue Bonds": Under the small-issue bond provisions of the Omnibus Budget Reconciliation Act of 1993, interest on certain bonds with face amounts of less than $10 million is excluded from income if at least 95% of the bonds' proceeds is used to finance manufacturing facilities. Industrial Revenue Bonds are tax-exempt obligations of the issuer, the interest on which is exempt from federal and state income tax. The interest rate on such obligations is normally below that available for conventional mortgages.

Bond and Mortgage Insurance Program: The Program reduces the capital necessary for new manufacturing facilities, renovation of manufacturing facilities, the purchase of new machinery and equipment in financing projects up to $5,000,000.

The Small Business Loan Fund: The SBLF provides eligible Small Business Fixed Asset Loans from $25,000 to a maximum of $150,000 and Working Capital Loans to a maximum of $30,000.

Ocean State Business Development Authority: Through the SBA 504 and 7A program the Authority can provide up to 90% financing on loan requests to $2,000,000 with a participating bank. Loan proceeds may be used to purchase land, renovate, or construct buildings and acquire new and used machinery and equipment.

Seafood Revolving Loan Fund: Eligible Applicants - R. I. Seafood Industry, Dollar Limit Per Project - Maximum: $150,000, Approved Use Of Funds - New equipment. Rehabilitation of existing fishing equipment. Funds to start up non-fishing businesses.

Samuel Slater Innovation Partnership Program: Designed to provide public-sector supporting funds on a matching, cost reimbursement basis to private-sector initiated activities designed to improve the competitiveness

of Rhode Island-based firms. It is designed to foster and support efforts by companies to increase their competitiveness through the development and/or better use of technology that directly and indirectly lead to an improved Rhode Island economy. By the nature of this program, the EPC is looking for creative, yet feasible, approaches to improving their industrial competitiveness through collaboration with institution of higher education and/or other firms or through the development of new technology-based businesses. A total of $1,375,000 in matching funds is available in the Innovation Partnership Program and will be awarded on a competitive, merit basis in three distinct grant programs:
- Industry-Higher Education Partnership Grants Available Funds: $750,000
- Multi-firm Collaboration Grants Available Funds: $500,000
- Technology Entrepreneur Seed Grants Available Funds: $125,000

Tax Incentives

No Income Tax for Insurance Carriers.

Passive Investment Tax Exemption: A corporation's investment income may be exempt from the Rhode Island income tax if it confines its activity to the maintenance and management of its passive intangible assets, maintains an office in Rhode Island, and employs at least five persons in Rhode Island.

Telecommunication Sales Tax Exemption: Regulated investment companies with at least 500 full-time equivalent employees are exempt from the sales and use tax imposed on toll-free terminating telecommunication service.

Insurance and Mutual Holding Companies: Rhode Island allows a mutual insurance company to create a mutual holding company, owned by the policy holders exactly as they now own the mutual company. This holding company, however, would then own the actual insurance company as a stockholder, while the insurance company itself could issue stock to raise capital. The process could be controlled by the mutual holding company, which means that policyholders would be protected from any dilution of control over the majority stockholder of the company. Policyholders ownership of the insurance subsidiary would be shared with other stockholders only to the extent that they choose to issue stock to raise capital for expansion.

Captive Insurance Companies: Rhode Island allows captive insurance companies to capitalize with a letter of credit or cash as in other states.

Insurance Company Retaliatory Tax Exemption: Foreign insurance companies are exempt from gross premiums retaliatory taxes in Rhode Island when their home jurisdiction does not impose a like tax.

Income Allocation Modification for Manufacturers of Medical Instruments and Supplies (SIC Code 384) and Drugs (SIC Code 283): A Rhode Island manufacturer of Medical Instruments and Supplies or Drugs registered and certified by the United States Food and Drug Administration with a place of business outside the state may modify the numerator in the allocation formula for the current tax year.

4% Credit for Equipment and Facilities Used in Manufacturing: Manufacturers may take a 4% tax credit for new tangible personal and other tangible property that is located in Rhode Island and is principally used by the taxpayer in the production of goods by manufacturing, processing, or assembling.

Research and Development Expense Credit: A special Rhode Island credit is allowed against the business corporation taxes and Rhode Island personal income tax for qualified research expenses. The credit is computed at 22.5% of the expense as defined in Section 41 of the Internal Revenue Code for companies increasing research and development expenditures, making Rhode Island the highest in the nation. The credit drops to 16.9% for R&D expenditures above the first $25,000 of credit. Unused credit may be carried forward for up to seven years.

Rhode Island Job Training Tax Credit: A special Rhode Island credit allows companies to receive a credit of $5,000 per employee against the business corporation taxes in any three year period against the cost of offering training and/or retraining to employees. This tax credit is critically important to existing Rhode Island employers, which formerly were not provided any tax incentives for the retraining of existing employees. With this tax credit, Rhode Island businesses will be able to reduce costs, be more efficient, and add to their competitiveness.

Rhode Island Employer's Apprenticeship Tax Credit: The annual credit allowed is 50% of the actual wages paid to the qualifying apprentice or $4,800, whichever is less. The credit applies to the following trades in the metal and plastic industries: machinist, toolmaker, modelmaker, gage maker, patternmaker, plastic process technician, tool & machine setter, diesinker, moldmaker, tool & die maker, machine tool repair.

Educational Assistance and Development Credit: A credit is 8% of the contribution in excess of $10,000 made to a Rhode Island institution of higher education and the contribution is to be for the establishment or maintenance of programs of scientific research or education. "Contributions" include the cost or other basis (for federal income tax purposes) in excess of $10,000 of tangible personal property excluding sale discounts and sale-gift arrangements concerning the purchase of equipment. Amounts of unused credit may be carried over for 5 years and documentation of the credit requires a written statement from the institution.

Adult Education Tax Credit: The Rhode Island Adult Education Tax Credit allows for both a worksite and nonworksite tax credit for vocational training or basic education of 50% of the costs incurred up to a maximum of $300 per employee and $5,000 per employer per calendar year.

Child and Adult Daycare Tax Credit: Credits are available against the business corporation tax, the bank excise tax, the insurance companies gross premiums tax and the personal income tax. These credits are computed at 30% of the amount of Rhode Island licensed daycare purchased and 30% of the cost to establish and/or operate a Rhode Island licensed daycare facility whether established and/or operated by the taxpayer alone or in conjunction with others. The maximum annual credit for purchased daycare is $30,000 per year and the amounts of unused credit may not be carried forward. For daycare facilities and rents/lease foregone, the maximum total credit is $30,000 per year and amounts of unused may be carried forward for 5 years.

Tax Incentives for Employers to hire unemployed Rhode Island Residents: The incentive of 40% of an eligible employee's first year wages up to a maximum of $2,400 may be used to reduce the gross Rhode Island income of businesses and individuals that employ and retain previously unemployed Rhode Island residents.

SBA Credit for Loan Grantee Fee: A small business may take a tax credit equal to any guaranty fee they pay to the United States Small Business Administration pursuant to obtaining SBA financing.

Rhode Island Enterprise Zone Program Tax Benefits: Rhode Island offers an Enterprise Zone Program developed to revitalize distressed urban areas in Rhode Island. The program provides an aggressive and comprehensive incentive package to businesses willing to relocate or expand into the designated Enterprise Zones.

Wage Differential Tax Credit: A qualified business having a minimum of 25% Enterprise workers may receive credits against the State business corporation or personal income tax of 50% of wages and salaries paid to qualified Enterprise workers in excess of the wages and salaries paid to those employees in the prior year. Enterprise Zone businesses must increase their employment by at least 5% to qualify for the Wage Differential Tax Credit.

Resident Business Owner Tax Modification: Business owners who operate a qualified business and who live in the same Enterprise Zone are eligible for a three year modification of $50,000 from their federal adjusted gross income when computing their state income tax liability and a $25,000 modification for years four and five.

Interest Income Tax Credit: Corporations or taxpayers that make new loans to qualified Enterprise Zone businesses are eligible to receive a 10% tax credit on interest earned from the loan. The maximum credit per taxpayer is $10,000 per year.

Donation Tax Credit: A taxpayer is eligible for a credit of 20% for any cash donation against the state tax imposed for donations to public supported improvement projects in the zone.

Tax Credit Available to Certified Mill Building Owner(s): A specialized investment tax credit equal to 10% of the cost of the substantial rehab. The rehab must occur within two years following certification.

Tax Credits Available to Lenders: A credit equal to 10% of the interest earned on loans to eligible businesses. Maximum of $10,000 per taxable year. A credit equal to 100% of the interest on loans made solely and exclusively for the purpose of substantial rehab of a Certified Building. Maximum of $20,000 per taxable year.

Tax Credits Available to Eligible Businesses: Eligible businesses must meet the requirements of Enterprise Zone year end certification. A credit equal to 100% of the wages paid to new employees with a maximum credit of $3,000 per new employee.

Alternative Transportation: 50% of the capital, labor, and equipment costs incurred by businesses for construction of or improvements to any filling station that provides alternative fuel or recharging of electric vehicles and 50% of the incremental costs incurred by a taxpayer for the purchase of alternative fueled motor vehicles or for the cost of converting vehicles into alternative fueled vehicles. The amount of either of the two credits may be transferred by one taxpayer to another if the transferee is a parent, subsidiary, affiliate, or is subject to common ownership, management, and control with the transferor. A taxpayer who has not transferred a credit and whose credit exceeds its tax liability may carry forward any unused portion of the credit to one or more of the succeeding five years.

Disabled Access Credit for Small Business: The expenses must be made to enable the small business to comply with federal or state laws protecting the rights of persons with disabilities. The credit is equal to 10% of the total amount expended during the tax year in Rhode Island, up to a maximum of $1,000, for removing architectural, communication, physical, or transportation barriers; providing qualified interpreters or other effective methods of delivering aurally delivered materials to persons with hearing impairments; providing readers, tapes, or other effective means of making visually delivered materials available to persons with visual impairments; providing job coaches or other effective means of supporting workers with severe impairments in competitive employment; providing specialized transportation services to employees or customers with mobility impairments; buying or modifying equipment for persons with disabilities; and providing similar services, modifications, material or equipment for persons with disabilities.

Sales and Use Tax Exemptions: Manufacturers' machinery and equipment is exempt; Manufacturers' machinery, equipment, replacement parts and computer software used in the manufacturing process are exempt.

Professional Services: Services such as those provided by physicians, attorneys, accountants, engineers, and others are exempt. However, the tax applies to any tangible personal property that may be sold at retail by such professionals (i.e.--opera glasses, field glasses, etc.).

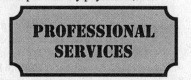

Occupational Services: Services such as provided by barbers, beauty parlors, bootblacks, cleaning and pressing shops, laundries, and similar service establishments are exempt. However, if delivery to the purchaser or his agent is consummated within, the tax applies to any tangible personal property that may be sold at retail by such establishments.

Sales in interstate commerce: A shipment by common carrier, United States mail, or delivery facilities not operated by the seller to a purchaser outside Rhode Island is not subject to the tax. If the purchaser takes delivery within the state, the tax applies.

Intangibles: Sales or transfers of intangible personal property such as stocks, bonds, accounts receivable, money, or insurance policies are exempt.

Pollution Control Equipment: Sales of air and water pollution control equipment for incorporation into or used and consumed directly in the operation of a facility or installation approved by the Rhode Island Director of Environmental Management are exempt.

Precious Metal: Sales of precious metal bullion are exempt.

Scientific Equipment: Sales of scientific equipment, computers, software and related items to a qualifying firm to be used predominantly by that firm for research and development purposes. The qualifying firm must furnish the vendor with a Rhode Island Research and Development Exemption Certificate.

Boat Sales: The sale of boats has been exempted from the state sales tax. Boats are also exempt from local property taxes.

Local Property Taxes: Intangible property is not taxed.

Inventory & Equipment Tax Exemption For Manufacturer: Manufacturers' machinery and equipment used in the production process and inventories of manufacturers in Rhode Island are exempt from property taxes.

Real Estate Property Tax Exemption/Stabilization: Any city or town in Rhode Island may exempt or stabilize the tax on real and personal property used for manufacturing, or commercial purposes, for a period not exceeding ten years. The incentive may not be used to encourage a firm to move from one municipality to another in Rhode Island.

Property Tax Exemption/Stabilization For Wholesaler's Inventory: Any city or town in Rhode Island may exempt or stabilize the tax on a wholesaler's inventory for a period of up to twenty five years. The incentive may not be used to encourage a firm to move from one municipality to another in Rhode Island.

Property Tax Exemption/Stabilization Office Equipment: Any city or town in Rhode Island may exempt or stabilize the tax on computers, telephone equipment and other office personal property for a period of up to twenty five years. The incentive may not be used to encourage a firm to move from one municipality to another in Rhode Island.

Energy Related Property Tax Exemptions: For local tax purposes, solar, wind, or cogeneration equipment shall not be assessed at more than the value of the conventional heating, cooling, or energy production capacity that would otherwise be necessary to install in the building.

Air and Water Pollution Control Equipment: Air and water pollution control equipment used to treat waste water and air contaminants produced as the result of industrial processing is exempt from local property taxes for ten years and may continue to remain exempt with municipal approval.

Hazardous Waste Equipment: Tangible personal property used for the recycling, recovery or reuse of "hazardous waste" generated by the same taxpayer on the same or adjacent property is exempt.

Capital Gains Reduction: Employees of qualified firms are exempt from paying Rhode Island Personal Income Tax on profits made from selling company stock. This law exempts current and former employees of qualified companies and their heirs from paying any state tax on capital gains resulting from the sale of stock or the purchase of stock options.

Estate and Gift Tax: An estate is required to file Rhode Island Estate Tax Form 100 with a $25 filing fee. There is no Estate Tax unless the gross value of the estate exceeds $600,000 and there is no surviving spouse.

Then, the Estate Tax due is an amount equal to the Federal Credit apportioned to Rhode Island.

Rhode Island has no *Gift Tax*.

Foreign Sales Corporation: Rhode Island Foreign Sales Corporations (FSC's) are exempt from the business corporation tax.

Exports

International Trade Partnership: As the official arm of state government, RIEDC is the principal liaison with foreign governments and hosts incoming trade delegations from other countries. As the entity charged with developing the state's economic agenda, RIEDC is the partner responsible for providing business services directly to companies. These services include: development and execution of trade shows and trade missions; customized export management training and general trade assistance to Rhode Island companies.

South Carolina

Department of Commerce
P.O. Box 927
Columbia, SC 29202
803-737-0400
877-751-1262
Fax: 803-737-0418
www.callsouthcarolina.com

Business Assistance

Department of Commerce: This office can provide information and expertise
in dealing with state, federal, and local agencies. They also have

information on financing programs and other
services offered by the state government.
Enterprise Development, Inc.: Develops
strategic initiatives and business resources for new
capital investments. Initiatives are in the
development of finances, technology and human
resources.

South Carolina Research Authority: A public, self-funded, non-profit
organization that works to attract and support technology-based
companies in South Carolina by: encouraging collaboration between
industry, government, and educational institutions; providing unique site
locations in specialized research parks; offering technology management
specialization. Contact: South Carolina Research Authority, P.O. Box
12025, Columbia, SC 29211; 803-799-4070; {www.scra.org}.

Business Financing

Industrial Revenue Bonds
Jobs-Economic Development Authority (JEDA)
Small Business Administration
Economic Development Administration
Farmers Home Administration
Carolina Capital Investment Corporation: A bank consortium administered by
JEDA to provide funding to small, growth oriented firms.
Taxable and Tax-Exempt Industrial Development Bonds: Bond for individual
company funding range from $1 million to $10 million.

Taxable Bond Financing Program: Assists commercial business and real estate development firms with affordable long-term debt financing. Proceeds may be used to fund the acquisition, construction or renovation of buildings and land, the purchase of new or used equipment, and for working capital purposes as well as the refinancing of existing debt.

Venture Capital Funding: Loans to businesses for innovative products or processes.

Tax Incentives

Jobs Tax Credit: Provides income tax credits for companies locating in or expanding current business in any county in South Carolina ranging from $1,500 to $4,500.

Child Care Credit: Payments made to licensed and/or registered child care facilities for the benefit of an employee are eligible for a credit against state corporate income tax not to exceed a maximum of $3,000 per employee.

Corporate Headquarters Credit: Firms establishing headquarters or expanding existing headquarters in South Carolina are eligible for credits to state corporate income taxes or corporate license fees.

Net Operating Loss: Net operating losses incurred may be carried forward for up to 15 years.

Credit for Former Military Employees: Offers a credit to state corporate income taxes of 10% of the first $10,000 of income per employee to firms hiring laid off defense workers.

Sales and Use Tax Exemptions: The following items are exempt for manufacturers from sales and use tax: production machinery and equipment; repair parts; materials which will become an integral part of the finished product; industrial electricity and fuels used in the manufacturing process; packaging materials.

Property Tax Exemptions: The following items are exempt from property tax: manufacturing inventory; intangible property; facilities or equipment of industrial plants designed for elimination, mitigation, prevention, treatment, abatement, or control of water, air, or noise pollution.

Other Corporate Income Tax Incentives:
- Tax credits for investments in infrastructure
- No unitary taxes on worldwide profits
- No wholesale sales taxes
- No value-added taxes
- No intangible taxes

- Five year moratorium on county ordinary property taxes for manufacturing, distribution, corporate headquarters and office facilities
- Opportunity for large investors to negotiate a fee in lieu of county property taxes

Enterprise Program: Offers tax advantages for new jobs to businesses located anywhere in the state.

Exports

Trade Development Program: Mission is twofold: to increase awareness among South Carolina companies of world market profitability and the valuable export resources available; and to promote South Carolina companies and products to prospective overseas importers, resulting in an increased international market share and direct sales for South Carolina companies.

- Hands-on trade services include such matters as answering export-related inquiries and extending referrals to other export assistance providers. In addition, they regularly co-host trade-related conferences and seminars.
- Promotional activities include assistance to and the recruitment of companies for participation in trade shows and trade missions overseas and the hosting of visiting international trade missions sourcing South Carolina products. These activities are accomplished through staff-organized meetings with South Carolina manufacturers.
- Technological capabilities allow the trade staff to provide the most efficient service through both targeted events scheduling, and the ability to disseminate the most current international sales leads and trade-related reports to South Carolina firms with the push of a button.
- Exporters Database & Directory allows the matching of South Carolina firms with overseas requests for products, and serves as a resource for storing useful promotional information on in-state exporters. South Carolina firms may request their addition to this database, which doubles as the trade programs' mailing list, by completing an Export Questionnaire available from their office.

Export Trade and Finance Program: Assistance through financial counseling, facilitating services and lending/guarantee program.

Foreign Trade Zones: Operating with an FTZ offers several cost benefits: possible reduction or elimination of customs duty, deferral of duty payment, efficiency gains of bypassing customs through direct delivery.

South Dakota

Governor's Office of Economic Development
711 East Wells Ave.
Pierre, SD 57501-3369
605-773-5032
800-872-6190
Fax: 605-773-3256
www.state.sd.us/goed

Business Assistance

Governor's Office of Economic Development: This office can provide
information and expertise in dealing with state, federal, and local agencies.
They also have information on financing programs and other services
offered by the state government

Workforce Development Program: Trains new employees, retrains current
employees, and upgrades current employee skills.

Business Financing

Economic Development Finance Authority: Allows enterprises to pool tax-
exempt or taxable development bonds for the purpose of constructing any
site, structure, facility, service or utility for the storage, distribution or
manufacturing of industrial or agricultural or nonagricultural products or
the purchase of machinery and equipment used in an industrial process.
Generally, the Authority will not consider loan requests for enterprises for
amounts less than $300,000 and will not pool projects unless the pool
volume is $1 million or more.

Revolving Economic Development and Initiative (REDI) Fund: Objective is
to create "primary jobs" in South Dakota. Primary jobs are defined as
"jobs that provide goods and services which shall be primarily exported
from the state, gain market shares from imports to the state or meet an
unmet need in the area resulting in the creation of new wealth in South
Dakota. Primary jobs are derived from businesses that bring new income
into an area, have a stimulative effect on other businesses or assist a
community in diversification and stabilization of its economy." All for-
profit businesses or business cooperatives are encouraged to apply,
whether they are business start-ups, expansions, or relocations from
outside South Dakota. The REDI Fund may provide up to 45% of the

total project cost and requires the applicant to secure the matching funds before applying to the Board of Economic Development for the REDI Fund, including a 10% minimum equity contribution.

Bond Financing: For capital intensive projects, offers a pooled or stand-alone tax-exempt or taxable development bond issue.

Tax Incentives

South Dakota is one of only two states with no corporate income tax, no personal income tax, no personal property tax and no business inventory tax.

Exports

International Trade Directory: Identifies South Dakota traders (i.e. exporters and importers) of manufactured products, agribusiness products, services and technologies. The directory also offers a list of various private companies and public agencies that are available to serve the special needs of South Dakota exporters and importers. Exporters Directory is available in hard copy upon request. Contact: Mr. Joop Bollen, South Dakota International Business Institute - NSU, 1200 S. Jay Street, Aberdeen, SD 57401-7198; 605-626-3149; Fax: 605-626-3004; {E-mail: bollenj@wolf.northern.edu}.

Foreign Direct Investment: For information on Foreign Direct Investment opportunities in South Dakota, contact one of the out-of-state development specialists at the Governor's Office of Economic Development.

Tennessee

Department of Economic and Community Development
Rachel Jackson Building, 8th Floor
320 Sixth Avenue North
Nashville, TN 37243-0405
615-741-1888
Fax: 615-741-7306
www.state.tn.us

Business Assistance

ACCE$$: The Nashville Area Chamber of Commerce, U.S. Small Business
Administration and area banks started a
financing program for small businesses.
ACCE$$ serves the small business loan
market, booking loans of $5000 and up.
The program enables entrepreneurs the
opportunity to present their business plans
orally to a panel of bank loan
officers. Panelists can qualify good
credit risks immediately, improving the presenter's chances of obtaining
an SBA guarantee. Regardless of the decision, small business owners
receive valuable outside appraisal of their business plans. Contact:
Nashville Area Chamber of Commerce, 161 Fourth Ave. N., Nashville,
TN 37219; 615-259-4755; {www.nashvillechamber.com}.

Self Help: There are two self help resource centers sponsored by Nations Bank
and 1st Tennessee. The centers offer information on starting a business;
preparing business plans; pro forma financial statements, small business
management.
* 1st Tennessee has sponsored a center at the Memphis Public Library,
Main Branch, 1850 Peabody, Memphis, TN 38104; 901-725-8877. It
is open library hours. Nations Bank operates their own Business
Resource Center at their West End Office in Nashville and Beale
Street Office in Memphis. Each center has a large business library,
plus PC-based access to national magazines and newspapers. They
offer videos, cassettes and slide presentations, as well as self-help
guides. Entrepreneurs do not have to be bank clients to use the
centers and can even schedule early evening appointments with bank
staff. Contact TN Small Business Center, 3401 West End Avenue,
Suite 110, Nashville, TN 37203-1069; 615-749-4088; 800- 342-8217

Ext. 4088; or Business Resource Center, 555 Beale Street, Memphis, TN 38103; 901-526-9300.

- The Tennessee Economic Development Center provides conference rooms equipped with video conferencing and multimedia capability. The demonstration room offers computers with internet access that is available for people wishing to conduct research related to business and economic development.

Manufacturing Services: Utilizes field representatives, each with extensive industrial experience and expertise, to work with Tennessee's existing industries as they strive to succeed in today's competitive marketplace. Through its Manufacturing Means Jobs Initiative the division seeks to provide businesses an environment in which to prosper and expand, creating new jobs in the process and adding strength to the state's economic growth.

Agricultural Extension Service: Assistance in areas such as research based agricultural practices, agribusiness management, small and home based businesses in a rural setting. The extension service can draw on the resources of the university for many areas of technical expertise in rural based businesses.

Consulting Services: There are several no fee consulting services available in Tennessee. Funded by federal, state, local and private sources; these services can aid business owners in a variety of ways. However, these services are in great demand. In order to maximize the effectiveness of the programs, new business owners should examine their situations to determine the most appropriate form of assistance.

For these services, contact Tennessee Economic Development Center, Bellsouth Building, 300 Commerce Street, Nashville, TN 37201-33011; 615-214-3003.

Industrial Extension:

1) University of Tennessee Center for Industrial Services
   CIS is a state wide industrial extension program dedicated to helping managers of Tennessee business and manufacturing firms find solutions to technical and managerial problems they face. CIS provides information and counseling services and strives to link resources of higher education with industrial needs. Contact UT Center for Industrial Services, Suite 401 Capitol Boulevard Building, Nashville, TN 37219-1804; 615-532-8657.

2) Tennessee Technological University Center for Manufacturing Research and Technology Utilization
   The Manufacturing Center was created to help improve the manufacturing productivity of state industry and to enhance instructional quality in

manufacturing-related areas. The Center seeks to assist industry not only in research and development, but also in integrating manufacturing processes with a systems approach. At any given time in the Manufacturing Center, over 30 separate, but complimentary projects may be in progress. Contact Tennessee Tech Manufacturing Center, College of Business Administration, TTU Box 5077, Cookeville, TN 38505; 615-372-6634; Fax: 423-372-6249.

Management Consulting: Service Corps of Retired Executives/Active Corps of Executives is a national volunteer organization of executives (both active and retired) who can provide both counseling and training to entrepreneurs and business owners. SCORE members come from many different industries and can contribute valuable expertise in either a single counseling session or in a long term no fee consulting relationship. Counseling is available to any business and can be profitably employed by stable businesses wishing to consider long range objectives and expansion plans. SCORE/ACE is also active in conducting seminars and workshops for those interested in starting new businesses.

Small Business Incubation Centers: Incubation centers offer a low cost way for entrepreneurs to start their businesses in an office/light manufacturing environment. Offering low cost rental rates per square foot, incubators also offer shared resources such as conference rooms, utility hook ups, office copiers, some telephone support. The most valuable commodity they offer is a shared environment in which business owners can discuss common problems and reach solutions.

Small Business Information Guide: A resource manual that assists start-up and existing small businesses with issues like state and federal business taxes, business regulations and government assisted funding programs.

Industrial Training Service: Helps recruit, screen and train new employees, provide job-specific training and overall workforce development. They partner with over 40 community colleges, and technical institutes and technology centers across the state.

Business Financing

Small And Minority Owned Telecommunications Business Assistance Program (Loan Guarantee): Designed to enhance and stimulate the growth, development and procurement opportunities for small, minority, and women owned businesses in the telecommunications industry in Tennessee.

Revolving Loan Funds: Available through nine community development corporations in Tennessee. The revolving loan fund combines funds secured from the Economic Development Administration and Farmer's

Home Administration with regional funding sources to provide new or
expanding businesses with financing at below market rates.

Tennessee Valley Authority Special Opportunity Counties Program: Designed
to provide capital to finance projects which support the recruitment of new
industry, the expansion of existing industry, the growth of small business,
and the creation of new companies in the Tennessee Valley.

a) The Economic Development Loan Fund (EDLF): $20 million per
    year revolving loan program targeted on low interest loans to
    established companies relocating or expanding their operations in the
    Tennessee Valley. Loans are made for buildings, plant equipment,
    infrastructure, or property based on the capital investment leveraged,
    the number of jobs created, power load generated and geographic
    diversity. TVA Economic Development staff market the program,
    manage the loan review process, and manage the loan portfolio.
    Primary Focus: Sustained Growth.

b) Special Opportunities County Fund: $15 million revolving loan
    program targeted on low interest loans for companies expanding or
    relocating in the Tennessee Valley's most economically
    distressed counties. Loans are made for buildings,
    plant equipment, infrastructure, or property based
    on the capital investment leveraged and the number
    of jobs created. TVA Economic Development staff
    market the program, manage the loan review process,
    and manage the loan portfolio. Primary Focus:
    Sustained Growth.

c) Valley Management Inc.: $15 million fund designed
    to invest in equity or debt to finance the growth and
    development of socially and financially disadvantaged businesses.
    VMI will consider investments in start-up, growth, or established
    companies and finance their working capital, building, or plant
    equipment needs. Businesses must be located in the Tennessee
    Valley. Those firms who meet VMI investment criteria can apply for
    $100,000 to $1,000,000 to support their business. TVA Economic
    Development staff market the VMI program and submit projects for
    review by VMI management. As the principle investor in VMI, TVA
    Economic Development management sit on the VMI board, review
    investment decision making processes and return on investment.
    Primary focus: Initial and sustained growth.

d) Commerce Capital LP. A Small Business Investment Company
    chartered by the Department of Commerce. Administration
    Commerce Capital's $5 million equity fund leverages up to $90
    million federal dollars for rapidly growing small business operating
    capital needs in the Tennessee Valley. These investments are made in

both debt and equity financing for companies in health care, manufacturing, environmental services, communications and information systems. Investments range from $500,000 to $3,000,000. TVA Economic Development staff market the SBIC program to valley businesses and submit the projects for review by the Commerce Capital General Partner. A TVA representative sits on the Commerce Capital board to review investment decisions and monitor return on investment. Primary Focus: Initial growth.

e) Venture Alliance Capital Fund: $4 million venture capital fund designed to make equity investments in ideas for new products and services which create new companies in the Tennessee Valley. Venture Alliance LLC provides a world class management team which explores ideas for new companies and provides marketing and financial assistance in partnership with entrepreneurs to recommend new ventures to the VACF board of governors. The VACF provides on average up to $500,000 in capital to launch the new business and position it for later stage venture capital investment from other sources. TVA Economic Development staff market the VACF and Venture Alliance LLC management team to entrepreneurs with ideas for viable businesses. Venture Alliance management builds business plans for projects with a defined market and recommends investments to VACF board of governors. A TVA representative sits on the VACF board of governors to review investment decisions and monitor return on investment. Primary Focus: Concept and start-up firms.

Contact: Tennessee Valley Authority, P.O. Box 292409, Nashville, TN 37229; 615-882-2051.

Tennessee Child Care Facilities Program: Assists child care providers by enabling them to upgrade facilities, create or expand the number of child care slots. The Program was established to accomplish two main goals: assist child care providers in attaining higher standards of safety and environment; increase the number of child care slots especially in rural and economically distressed areas. The program also assists companies and organizations wishing to establish day care centers for employees or groups of employees. The Program has three components:

- Guarantees to lenders up to $250,000 for new construction
- Direct loans to providers up to $10,000 for upgrade of facilities
- Direct loans to providers up to $25,000 for new or addition of slots

As of spring, 1998, the guarantee portfolio totaled $2.3 million, close to its cap for prudent risk. Direct loans are subject to funding on an annual basis from different sources. Maturities as well as interest rates vary based on uses of the loans.

Rural Electric Administration (REA), Rural Economic Development Revolving Loan Program For Rural Electric And Telephone Cooperatives: Designed to promote rural economic development and job creation by providing zero interest loans to REA borrowers. The program will fund up to $100,000 per project. The maximum term of the loan is ten years at zero interest rate with a two-year deferred payment. For more information, contact your local electric utility company.

Small Business Energy Loan Program: Designed to assist in the identification, installation, and incorporation of approved energy efficiency measures onto, or into, the existing Tennessee located facilities processes, and for operations of approved applicants. The Energy Division currently maintains a loan portfolio of $4,560,000 to 115 borrowers. Approved loan requests average $39,000.

Energy Loan Program

Rural Business & Cooperative Development Service Loan Guarantees: The U.S. Department of Agriculture, through the RBCDS (formerly Farmers Home Administration), guarantees term loans to non-farm businesses in rural areas; that is, localities with populations below 50,000 not adjacent to a city where densities exceed 100 persons per square mile. The Tennessee RBCDS currently maintains a loan portfolio in excess of $40,000,000 (in addition to their relending program with the Development Districts listed above) with 40 industrial borrowers. Approved loan requests average just over $1,000,000.

Small Business Investment Companies: Private investment and loan companies established to serve the small business market. They are funded with a combination of private and federal investment. SBICs assist only businesses below $6,000,000 in net worth and less than $2,000,000 in annual net income. They may prioritize investments in type (equity or loan); dollar amount, location or industry.

Occupational Safety And Health Grant: The goal of this program is to fund the education and training of employees in safe employment practices and conduct in the employer's own business for the employer's own employees; and promote the development of employer - sponsored health and safety programs in the employer's own business for the employer's own employees. Grants average in the $5000 range with some greater amounts. Contact Tennessee Department of Labor, Occupational Safety and Health Grant Program, Gateway Plaza, 2nd Floor, 710 James Robertson Parkway, Nashville, TN 37243; 800-332-2667.

Pollution Prevention Loan Program: Loans for the purchase of equipment and/or construction to complete pollution prevention activities at small and medium sized businesses.

Tax Incentives

Personal Income: Earned income is not taxed in Tennessee; however, certain dividend and interest income received by a Tennessee resident is taxable.

Energy Fuel and Water: Reduced sales tax on manufacturers' use of energy fuel and water at manufacturing site; tax-exempt if they have direct contact with product during manufacturing process.

Pollution Control Equipment: Exempt from sales tax.

Raw Materials: Exempt from sales tax.

Industrial Machinery: Exempt from sales tax.

Work-In-Progress: Exempt from property tax.

Finished Product Inventory: Exempt from property tax.

Investment Tax Credit: Manufacturers are allowed a tax credit of 1% of the cost of industrial machinery.

Franchise Tax Jobs Credit: Allows a $2,000 or $3,000 tax credit against franchise tax liability for each new full-time employee of qualified business that increases employment by 25 or more and meets required capital investment.

Manufacturers are allowed an investment tax credit of 1% on the purchase, installation and repairs of qualified industrial machinery.

Allows excise tax credit of 1% of purchase price of equipment associated with required capital investment of $500,000 by a distribution or warehouse facility.

Exports

Export Assistance: Five core agencies provide assistance to Tennessee firms interested in or already exporting products abroad. Tennessee Department of Economic and Community Development, International Development Group provides strategic counsel support and coordination for the expansion of Tennessee's non-agricultural business and export interests in selected international markets. Contact International Development Group, 8th Floor Rachel Jackson Building, 320 Sixth Avenue, N., 7th Floor, Nashville, TN 37243; 615-741-5870; Fax: 615-741-7306.

International Trade Centers: Export efforts focus on novice and new to exporting firms. Maintaining offices in Memphis and Knoxville, the ITC can offer one on one counseling at any SBDC office across the state. ITC counselors:

- Assists in evaluating a company's export potential.

- Assists in market research.
- Assists with market entry strategies.
- Advises on market opportunities.
- Advises on export practices.
- Advises on export procedures.
- In addition to counseling, ITC sponsors continuing education seminars and workshops across the state. Those firms interested in exporting for the first time should contact the Small Business Development Center nearest them for ITC assistance. Contact SBDC - International Trade Center, University of Memphis, Memphis, TN 38152; 901-678-4174; Fax: 901-678-4072; or SBDC - International Trade Center, 301 East Church Street, Knoxville, TN 37915; 423-637-4283; Fax: 423-523-2071.

Tennessee Department of Agriculture, Division of Marketing: Offers similar services as the Tennessee Export Office, however specifically catering to the Tennessee farmers and agri-business people in the state. Their services include:

- hosting foreign buyer visits from abroad
- participating in trade shows and sales missions to key agricultural market destinations
- identifying foreign import requirements and assistance in obtaining appropriate documentation
- conducting seminars highlighting agricultural exports
- disseminate trade leads and other trade information

Contact Tennessee Department of Agriculture, Division of Marketing, Ellington Agricultural Center, P.O. Box 40627, Nashville, TN 37204; 615-837-5160.

Foreign Trade Zones: Tennessee has five foreign trade zones with eight sub-zones.

Women and Minorities

Office of Minority Business Enterprise: Facilitates the resources needed in assisting minority businesses in growth and business development by identifying sources of capital; linking successful businesses with minority businesses which need help in areas like training, quality control, supplier development or financial management; providing education and training, specialized technical assistance and identification of procurement opportunities in the public and private sectors; and publishing the Minority and Women Business Directory profiling minority businesses and their capabilities for public and private organizations which use their services or products.

Purchasing Councils: Encourages mutually beneficial economic links between ethnic minority suppliers and major purchasers in the public and private sectors. Contact Tennessee Minority Purchasing Council, Metro Center, Plaza 1 Building, 220 Athens Way, Suite 105, Nashville, TN 37225; 615-259-4699; or Mid-South Minority Purchasing Council, 4111 West Park Loop, Memphis, TN 38124; 901-678-2388.

Minority Business Development Center: Provides management, marketing, and technical assistance to increase business opportunities for minority entrepreneurs. Each center provides accounting, administration, business planning, construction, and marketing information to minority firms. The MBDC also identifies minority firms for contract and subcontract opportunities with government agencies and the private sector.

Small and Minority-Owned Telecommunications Program: Provides loan guarantees, education and training, consulting and technical assistance to help small, minority-and/or women-owned telecommunications businesses grow.

Texas

Department of Economic Development
P.O. Box 12728
Austin, TX 78711
512-936-0260
800-888-0511
www.tded.state.tx.us

Business Assistance

Department of Economic Development: Provides business counseling for both new and established firms. Helps firms locate capital, state procurement opportunities, state certification programs for minority and women-owned businesses, and resources management and technical assistance. An Office of Business Permit Assistance serves as a clearinghouse for permit-related information throughout the state and refers applicants to appropriate agencies for permit and regulatory needs. Publications are available containing information and resources for start-up and existing businesses.

Office of Small Business Assistance: Charged with helping the state's small businesses become more globally competitive. The Office provides information and assistance to establish, operate and expand small and historically underutilized businesses (HUBS). In addition, the Office is charged with being the focal point for comments, suggestions and information regarding HUBS and small businesses to develop and suggest proposals for changes in state and federal policies in response to this information.

Texas Manufacturing Assistance Center: Works for all Texans by enabling small manufacturers to better compete in the international marketplace. It's a manufacturing brain trust with a single mission: To improve and expand manufacturing in Texas through free technical assistance to small business manufacturers. Contact: Texas Manufacturing Assistance Center, P.O. Box 12728, Austin, TX 78711; 800-488-TMAC.

General Service Commission: To facilitate the ordering needs of the State of Texas, the General Services Commission has established procedures for procuring goods and services. Contact: General Services Commission, P.O. Box 13047, Austin, TX 78711; 512-463-3416.

Economic Development Clearinghouse: A one-stop center for information about economic development programs and technical assistance offered by state and federal agencies, local governments and other organizations. The clearinghouse's website is {www.edinfo.state. tx.us}.

Texas Marketplace: Offers businesses access to the internet including free web page, daily posting of all major procurement opportunities with the State of Texas, electronic bulletin board for posting information about commodities for sale or to buy, and other resources and government procurement opportunities. Contact: Texas Marketplace, Texas Department of Economic Development, Internet Services Group, P.O. Box 12728, Austin, TX 78711; 512-936-0236; {www.texas-one.org}.

Business & Industry Data Center (BIDC): Provides one-stop access to data, information, and analyses on the Texas economy. Contact Business and Industry Data Center, P.O. Box 12728, Austin, TX 78711; 512-936-0550; {www.bidc.state.tx.us}.

Business Financing

Linked Deposit Program: Established to encourage lending to historically underutilized businesses, child-care providers, non-profit corporations, and/or small businesses located in distressed communities by providing lenders and borrowers a lower cost of capital. Minimum loan amount is $10,000; maximum loan amount is $250,000, fixed borrower loan rate.

Capital Fund Infrastructure Program: This economic development program is designed to provide financial resources to non-entitlement communities. Funds can be utilized for public infrastructure to assist a business, which commits to create and/or retain permanent jobs, primarily for low and moderate-income persons. This program encourages new business development and expansions located in non-entitlement communities. The minimum & maximum award is $50,000 & $750,000 inclusive of administration. The award may not exceed 50% of the total project cost.

Capital Fund Real Estate Development Program: This economic development program is designed to provide financial resources to non-entitlement communities. Funds can be utilized for real estate development to assist a business that commits to create and/or retain permanent jobs, primarily for low and moderate-income persons. The minimum and maximum award is $50,000 and $750,000 inclusive of administration. The award may not exceed 50% of the total project cost.

Capital Fund Main Street Improvements Program: The Texas Capital Fund Main Street Improvements Program is designed to foster and stimulate the development of small businesses by providing financial assistance to non-entitlement cities (designated by the Texas Historical Commission as a

Main Street City) for public improvements. This program encourages the elimination of slum or blighted areas. Minimum awards are $75,000. Maximum awards are $150,000. Matching funds must be provided.

Small Business Industrial Revenue Bond Program: Designed to provide tax-exempt financing to finance land and depreciable property for eligible industrial or manufacturing projects. The Development Corporation Act allows cities, counties, conservation and reclamation districts to form non-profit industrial development corporations or authorities on their behalf. Program objective is to issue taxable and tax-exempt bonds for eligible projects in cities, counties, conservation and reclamation districts. The industrial development corporation acts as a conduit through which all monies are channeled. Generally, all debt services on the bonds are paid by the business under the terms of a lease, sale, or loan agreement. As such, it does not constitute a debt or obligation of the governmental unit, the industrial development corporation, or the State of Texas.

Capital Access Fund: Established to increase the availability of financing for businesses and nonprofit organizations that face barriers in accessing capital . Through the use of the Capital Access Fund, businesses that might otherwise fall outside the guidelines of conventional lending may still have the opportunity to receive financing. The essential element of the program is a reserve account established at the lending institution to act as a credit enhancement, inducing the financial institution to make a loan. Use of proceeds may include working capital or the purchase, construction, or lease of capital assets, including buildings and equipment used by the business. There is no minimum or maximum loan amount, only a maximum amount that the state will provide to the financial institution's reserve fund.

Smart Jobs Fund: Provides grants to businesses to train their employees. Although a company is limited to $1.5 million per fiscal year, subject to certain limitations, the Fund recommends that applicants limit their applications to a maximum of $2,500 per trainee for small businesses and $1,200 per trainee for large businesses.

Leverage Fund: An economic development bank offering an added source of financing to communities that have passed the economic development sales tax. This program allows the community to make loans to local businesses for expansion or to recruit new industries.

Tax Incentives

Enterprise Zone Program: Designed to induce capital investment and create new permanent jobs into areas of economic distress. Qualified businesses located in an enterprise zone may qualify for a variety of local and state incentives including a refund of state sales and use taxes, franchise tax reductions, and state administered program priority.

Reinvestment Zones: Zones can be created for the purpose of granting local businesses ad valorem property tax abatements on a portion of the value of real and/or tangible personal property located in the zone. Special taxation entities having jurisdiction over a reinvestment zone may participate in executed abatement agreements.

Texas does not have statewide business tax incentives. These are handled at the city and/or county level in the city/county in which a business enterprise is based.

Exports

Office of Trade and International Relations (OTIR) helps Texas companies expand their business worldwide. By providing a forum for international business exchange through international trade missions, trade shows, seminars and in-bound buyers missions, OTIR gives Texas companies the opportunity to promote their products and services to international buyers and partners. OTIR also helps to connect companies with counseling and training available through the International Small Business Development Centers and works with entities such as the U.S. Department of Commerce, the Japan External Trade Organization, the Texas consular corps and its counterparts in the Mexican border states to ensure that Texas business interests are represented abroad. The State of Texas office in Mexico City is an invaluable resource for facilitating business between Texas and Mexico. Programs include:

- Trade Missions and Trade Shows
- Export Counseling
- Partnerships
- Trade Lead Distribution
- Texas International Center
- Research Publications

Utah

Business and Economic Development Division
324 South State St., Suite 500
Salt Lake City, UT 84111
801-538-8800
Fax: 801-538-8889
www.ce.ex.state.ut.us

Business Assistance

Business and Economic Development Division: Provides information on
regulations, sources of assistance, and other important information for
starting a business.

Custom Fit Training: Provides training for new or
expanding companies. A Custom Fit
representative will discuss with the
company the training needs anticipated
and then develop a specific customized
training plan to meet those needs. The
required training can take place at a
variety of locations including the
business or a local institution. Often training is
provided in both locations. The program can provide
instructors from the State's learning institutions, private sector, consultants
or instructors within the business. The program is designed to be flexible
to meet the specific needs of the company. Contact: Utah State Office of
Education, Applied Technology Division, 250 East 500 South, Salt Lake
City, UT 84111; 801-538-7867;
{www.usoe.k12.ut.us/ate/CF/custom.htm}.

Short Term Intensive Training (STIT): Programs are customized and designed
to meet full-time job openings. Programs are usually less than one year in
length and will be designed to meet the specific training needs of a
company while matching needs with people seeking employment.
Although potential employees must pay tuition to participate, STIT can
provide qualified employees from which a company can hire. STIT gives
the option of training at 50% - 70% discount of normal training costs.
Funding for this program is distributed to State Colleges.

Job Service: A computerized job matching system that quickly screens
applicants to ensure that they meet the qualifications set by a company.
Over 16,000 active applicants are presently registered with the Salt Lake
Office. Job Service personnel can save countless hours by taking all of

company applications and then referring only the most qualified applicants.

Centers of Excellence Program: Supports selected research programs at Utah's universities. Programs are selected based on leading edge research activities that have projected commercial value. The primary objective is to encourage the commercialization of leading edge technologies through licensing patented technologies and by creating new companies. The Centers of Excellence Program impacts Utah's economic development by the creation of jobs, the flow of licensing royalties, the expansion of the tax base, and the leveraged use of matching fund dollars to strengthen research and development at Utah's institutions of higher learning.

Utah Partners in Education: Facilitates business/ education/ government partnerships statewide. Purpose is to find ways in which those three entities can work together to meet common needs and thereby strengthen the economy of Utah. Contact: Utah Partners in Education, 324 South State St., Suite 500, Salt Lake City, UT 84111; 801-538-8628; {www.utahpartnership.utah.org}.

Utah Directory of Business and Industry: A listing of more than 9,800 individual employers sorted by Standard Industrial Classification (SIC), which is a standard method for classifying what businesses or other organizations do.

Environmental Permitting: One-stop shopping for the environmental permitting process through the Department of Environmental Quality.

Business Financing

Utah Ventures: a privately financed venture fund focusing on investments in the life sciences and information technology in Utah, other Intermountain states and California. Utah Ventures seeks to identify the best opportunities, secure subsequent coinvestments from other venture funds and corporate investors, and works with the entrepreneur to help build the business. Contact Utah Ventures, 423 Wakara Way Suite 206, Salt Lake City, UT 84108; 801-583-5922.

Revolving Loan Funds: In an effort to create jobs and improve the business climate of a community, some cities, counties, and Associations of Governments (geographical regions) will lend money to small businesses located in their areas. The amount available to a business goes from a few thousand dollars to over $100,000. Typically, the money is used for plant and equipment, working capital, inventory or accounts receivable financing. Rates are usually less than or equal to conventional lender financing, and the term for repayment may be either short (6 months) or extended (many years). This type of financing is often used in conjunction with other lender financing since most revolving loan programs will accept a second or third position on financed assets.

Microenterprise Loan Fund (UMLF) is a tax-exempt, nonprofit corporation. It provides a modestly secured form of financing up to $10,000, with terms up to five years, to owners of startup and existing firms who do not have access to traditional funding sources, especially those who are socially or economically disadvantaged. The interest rate is prime plus 3% fixed, and the business must be located in Salt Lake County. Contact: Utah Microenterprise Loan Fund, 3595 S. Main St., Salt Lake City, UT 84115; 801-269-8408.

The Utah Technology Finance Corporation is an independent corporation of the state that makes debt investments in Utah companies. UTFC leverages state and federal funds as a catalyst in capital formation for the creations, growth, and success of Utah Businesses. UTFC offers various types of debt financing through such programs as Early Technology Business Capital, Utah Rural Loan Program, MicroLoan Program, Utah Revolving Loan Fund, Bank Participation Loan Program, and Defense Conversion Loan Program. Contact Utah Technology Finance Corporation (UTFC), 177 East 100 South, Salt Lake City, UT 84111; 801-364-4346; Fax: 801-364-4361; {www.urfc.state.ut.us}.

Industrial Assistance Fund: Can be used for relocation costs. This incentive loan can be repaid as Utah jobs created meet the IAF requirements resulting in higher quality jobs, and as Utah purchases merit enough earned credits to convert the loan to a grant. Three basic programs exist: 1) rural Utah program with funding up to $100,000 for relocation expenses; 2) Corporate Funding which is dependent on the amount of Utah purchases and wages: 3) Targeted Industries which is primarily aimed at information technology, biomedical and aerospace.

Industrial Development Bonds (IDB's): A financing tool used by private sector developers for manufacturing facilities. The federal tax code places a limit of $10.0 million per project on IDB financing.

Tax Incentives

No inventory or worldwide unitary taxes.

New Equipment: An exemption of sales and use taxes are available for the purchase or lease of new equipment or machinery for manufacturing facilities.

Economic Development Area/Tax Increment Financing: Tax increment financing (TIF) is utilized in areas that have been targeted for economic development. Redevelopment areas are determined by local municipalities. Portions of the new property tax generated by new development projects are returned to project developers in the form of infrastructure development, land cost write down or other appropriate

means. Details of TIF are site specific. Development of a proposal is
relatively simple, yet the benefits can be great.

Enterprise Zones: The act passed by the Utah State Legislature provides tax
credits for manufacturing companies locating in rural areas that qualify for
assistance. A $750 tax credit is given for all new job created plus a credit
of $1,250 for jobs paying at least 125% of the average wage for the
industry. In addition, investment tax credits are available for all
investment in new plant and equipment as follows: 10% for first $100,000;
5% of next $250,000. Tax credits can be carried forward for 3 years.
Enterprise Zones benefits are only available in certain non-metro counties.

Special programs such as Affirmative Action, Targeted Job Tax Credits and
veterans programs are also available.

Exports

International Business Development Office: Programs offered include:
- Trade Representatives
- Country Information
- Market Research Reports
- Trade Lead Resource Center
- Foreign Business Directories
- Trade Shows and Exhibits

Women and Minorities

Offices of Ethnic Affairs: Recognizing that state government should be
responsive to all citizens, and wishing to promote cooperation and
understanding between government agencies and its ethnic citizens, these
offices were created:
- Office Of Asian Affairs
- Office Of Black Affairs
- Office Of Hispanic Affairs
- Office Of Polynesian Affairs
- Division of Indian Affairs

Minority and Women Owned Business Source Directory: Offered by the Utah
PTAC (Procurement Technical Assistance Center). The directory includes
approximately 850 companies, and is the most complete such listing
available. However, listings are voluntary, having been obtained through
surveys, and this is not to be construed as a comprehensive catalog. There
are some 4,400 minority-owned employers in the state, and 46,000 that are
women-owned.

Vermont

Department of Economic Development
National Life Building, Drawer 20
Montpelier, VT 05620-0501
802-828-3221
800-341-2211
Fax: 802-828-3258
www.thinkvermont.com

Business Assistance

Department of Economic Development: A one-stop shop ready to help with
businesses to support the economic growth of the state through job
creation and retention. Areas in which the Department can assist

Vermont businesses are entrepreneurs;
international trade; financing;
government contracts, marketing;
permits; site location; and training.
Regional Development Corporations:
Twelve RDCs serve every geographic region
of the state serving as satellites of the
Department of Economic Development, and
provide many of the same services. Their
primary function is to coordinate job and business development activities
within their geographic region.

Manufacturing Extension Center: Provides one-on-one support and services
through Field Engineers to small and mid-sized manufacturers. Their goal
is to assist Vermont manufacturers increase productivity, modernize
processes, and improve their competitiveness. Ongoing training
opportunities designed specifically for manufacturers are also offered.
Contact: Vermont Manufacturing Extension Center, VT Technical
College, P.O. Box 500, Randolph Center, VT 05061; 802-728-1432;
{www.vmec.org}.

Business Assistance Network: An accessible series of resources designed to
provide timely and pertinent information to businesses interested in
participating in new markets for their products or services, increasing
competitiveness, or building "teaming arrangements" with other
businesses. The information may be accessed through the Internet at
{www.state.vt.us}.

Micro Business Development Program: Promotes self-employment and
business expansion opportunities for low income Vermonters. Offers free,

one-to-one technical assistance and business development workshops for income eligible person.

Northeast Employment and Training Organization: Manages the Entrepreneurial Training Program which provides statewide small business management courses to enterprises of all sizes, including individuals interested in self-employment and micro businesses. Contact: Northeast Employment Training Organization, P.O. Box 186, 145 Railroad St., St. Johnsbury, VT 05819.

Government Marketing Assistance Center: Exists to design, implement, and maintain resources that promote economic expansion by providing assistance to Vermont businesses' which allow them to pursue and compete in the public procurement process and introduce them to new markets for their goods and/or services. The GMAC can provide a business with a customized search to receive Federal bid opportunities, including bids available through Electronic Data Interchange (EDI). A business must be registered to receive Federal Bids opportunities.

Vermont Business Registry: An on-line registry of businesses throughout Vermont involved in manufacturing, manufacturing support, product distribution, services, research and development, and construction.

Vermont Bid Opportunities: An electronic resource which provides businesses with a current listing of bid opportunities available through Vermont based federal, state and local governments and by the private sector purchasing organizations.

Business Calendar of Events: Lists business assistance seminars, training workshops, trade shows, etc., which are sponsored by various organizations.

The Vermonter's Guide to Doing Business: Provides information relating to public and private institutions that can assist local businesses on any aspect of successful business operation.

Department of Employment and Training: Offers a full range of workforce-related services and information through a network of 12 One-Stop Career Resource Centers.

Market Vermont Program: A cooperative effort among the Departments of Economic Development; Agriculture, food and Markets; Tourism and Marketing; Forest, Parks and Recreation; Fish and Wildlife; Historic Preservation; Vermont Life Magazine; Vermont Economic Progress Council; and Vermont Council on the Arts to identify and promote goods made, and services offered, in Vermont.

Agricultural Marketing: Provides resource for the promotion of various agricultural projects and works with commodity groups to improve market opportunities. Marketing representatives help with promotion, marketing, packaging, support publications, etc. Contact: Department of Agriculture, Development Division, 116 State St., Drawer 20, Montpelier, VT 05620; 802-828-2416.

Business Financing

Rural Economic Activity Loans: REAL loans are available to assist rural entrepreneurs who cannot obtain adequate financing from other sources on reasonable terms to establish or expand their business. These businesses must demonstrate the potential to significantly improve or retain employment opportunities. Loans up to $25,000 may be made to fund the cost of an eligible project, but cannot exceed 75% of total project costs. For loans greater than $25,000, funds may be provided for up to 40% of fixed asset project costs and/or 50% of working capital loan projects.

Small Business Development Corporation: A non-profit corporation offering loans between $2,500 and $50,000 to assist growing Vermont small businesses who cannot access conventional sources of credit. Funds may be used to finance the acquisition of fixed assets or for working capital with restrictions.

Job Start Program: Helps develop self-employment opportunities for low and moderate income Vermonters through loans used to start, strengthen or expand small businesses. Funds may be used to purchase equipment, inventory or for working capital.

Financial Access Program: Designed to enhance opportunities for small businesses to access commercial credit utilizing a pooled reserve concept. Loans must be in an amount up to and including $200,000 made to businesses with sales less than $5 million.

Mortgage Insurance Program: Designed to aid businesses by insuring loans made by commercial banks. Proceeds may be used to insure loans made for the acquisition of land, buildings, machinery and equipment or working capital, for use in an eligible facility. Maximum is $2 million per project.

Local Development Corporation Loans: Loans to nonprofit local development corporations are available through VEDA-s Subchapter 3 program. "Spec" buildings and incubators can provided low cost, flexible leased space for businesses which prefer not to own their own facility. Loan proceeds may be used for the purchase of land for industrial parks, industrial park planning and development, and the construction or improvement of speculative buildings or small business incubator facilities.

Industrial Revenue Bonds: Designed to aid businesses through VEDA's issuance of tax-exempt, low interest bonds to provide funds for the acquisition of land, buildings, and/or machinery and equipment for use in a manufacturing facility.

Direct Loan Program: Designed to finance the establishment or expansion of eligible facilities through the acquisition, construction and installation of fixed assets. Provides attractive variable rate loans to business for the purchase of land, the purchase or construction (including renovation) of buildings, and the purchase and installation of machinery and equipment for use in an eligible facility.

For above loans, contact Vermont Economic Development Authority, 58 E. State St., Montpelier, VT 05602; 802-828-5627; {www.veda.state.vt.us}.

Vermont Sustainable Jobs Fund: The goal of the fund is to develop and support projects throughout the State  leading to the creation or retention of quality jobs, and the protection and enhancement of Vermont's human and natural resources. Grants and technical assistance will be available for collaborative activity including the development of flexible manufacturing networks, business clusters, and networks. A specific area of focus will be adding value to agricultural products that use the natural resource of grass. Contact: Vermont Sustainable Jobs Fund, Inc., 58 E. State St., Montpelier, VT 05602; 802-828-5320.

Agricultural Facility and Debt Stabilization Loans: Provides loans and refinancing for family farms or agricultural facility operators.

Regional/Local Revolving Loan Funds: Existing through the state, the administration of these funds is generally a non-profit development corporation.

Business and Industrial Loan Guarantees: Designed to serve the credit needs of large rural businesses. Emphasis is placed on loan guarantees between $500,000 and $3 million, but may be issued up to $10 million.

Business and Industry Direct Loans: A limited amount of funding is available for direct business loans in designated areas of economic distress. The program is targeting loans in the $100,000 to $250,000 range.

Intermediary Relending Program: Designed to finance small and emerging business and community development projects in rural areas. Loans are made to qualified intermediaries who in turn relend to small businesses and community development organizations. Business or organizations borrowing from the intermediary must be located in a rural area. The maximum loan to an intermediary is $2 million and the maximum loan that the intermediary can relend for a project is $150,000.

Rural Business Enterprise Grant: Provides grants to public bodies and non-profit corporations for the benefit of small and emerging businesses.

Grant funds may be used to establish revolving loan funds, construct facilities, provide planning, or technical assistance.

Burlington Micro Loan Program: Available for asset financing, inventory financing, and working capital to businesses located in the City of Burlington. Typical loans range from $500 to $5,000.

Green Mountain Capital, L.P.: Established as a Small Business Investment Company to provide working capital loans to rapidly growing small businesses in Vermont. Companies that qualify will probably have achieved a level of sales in excess of $1 million dollars annually. GMC does not finance start-ups.

Vermont Venture Capital Fund, L.P.: A private enterprise that seeks to invest from $100,000 to $750,000 in high-quality opportunities that have outgrown seed capital resources and are either not ready for or have exceeded the limits of commercial bank lending resources.

Planning Grant for Suspected Contaminated Site: Available in an amount not to exceed $8,000 per site, for an initial assessment of a suspected contaminated site in a downtown district that otherwise qualifies under the Community Development Block Grant program.

Tax Incentives

Payroll Tax Credit: A firm may receive a credit against income tax liability equal to a percentage of its increased payroll costs.

Research and Development Tax Credit: A firm may receive a credit against income tax liability in the amount of 10% of qualified research and development expenditures.

Workforce Development Tax Credit: A firm may receive a credit against income tax liability in the amount of 10% of its qualified training, education and workforce development expenditures. A 20% credit may be taken for qualified training, education and workforce development expenditures for the benefit of welfare to work participants.

Small Business Investment Tax Credit: A firm may receive a credit against income tax liability in the amount equal to 5% to 10% of its investments within the state in excess of $150,000 in plants, facilities, and machinery and equipment.

Sales and Use Tax Exemptions:
1. Sales of electricity, oil, gas and other fuels used on site directly in the production of projects or services.
2. Sales of building materials within any three consecutive years in excess of $1 million in purchase value used in the construction, renovation or expansion of facilities that are used exclusively for the manufacture of tangible personal property for sales. The threshold for sales of building materials can be reduced to $250,000 for businesses that receive approval

from VEDC or are located in a designated downtown development district.

3. Machinery and equipment, including system-based software used directly in the production of products or services.

Construction In Progress Property Tax Exemption: A tax exemption for a period not to exceed two years is available for real property, excluding land, consisting of unoccupied new facilities, or unoccupied facilities under renovation or expansion that are less than 75% complete.

Brownfields Property Tax Exemption: Exempt from the statewide education property tax are real property consisting of the value of remediation expenditures incurred by a business for the construction of new, expanded or renovated facilities on contaminated property.

Rehabilitation Investment Tax Credit: A federal income tax credit is available for 20% of the costs of rehabilitating income-producing historic buildings.

Sprinkler System Rebate: A building owner who installs a complete automatic fire sprinkler system in an older or historic building that has been certified for one of the state building rehabilitation tax credits is eligible for a rebate for the cost of a sprinkler system, not to exceed $2,000.

Money Management Industry Tax Credit: An income tax credit of up to 75% for the money management industry that can be taken every year and is easy to understand and therefore claim.

Employee Training Tax Credit: An employer can claim up to $400 in tax credits per year for training qualified employees if the employer does business in a designated downtown district with the intent of providing permanent employment.

Credit For Income From Commercial Film Production: A credit shall be available against the tax imposed for that taxable year upon the taxable income received from a dramatic performance in a commercial film production during that taxable year. The credit shall be in the amount by which the Vermont tax on such income, without regard to this credit, exceeds the highest personal income tax rate in the taxpayer's state of residence, multiplied by the Vermont commercial film production income.

Exports

Vermont World Trade Office: Assists businesses wishing to export their products and services, to expand by developing sales in new markets, and by encouraging suitable foreign companies to establish operations within the state.

VEDA Export Financing: In addition to the Export Working Capital Guarantee Program, VEDA offers a number of other loan and insurance programs for Vermont's exporting community. This includes small business credit insurance, and environmental exports program, and export credit insurance short-term multi-buyer policy, and a medium-term single-buyer policy.

Export Tax Credit: A firm which makes sales outside of Vermont may take as a credit against their income tax liability, the difference between the income tax calculated under the existing state apportionment formula and the proposed formula which double weights the sales factor and disregards throwback provision. The incentive is favorable to exporters, encouraging Vermont businesses that export to declare a greater amount of taxable income.

Women and Minorities

Women's Small Business Program: Offers a continuum of services to women seeking to identify, start, stabilize and expand a small business. Services include: Getting Serious, a workshop to determine a business idea and whether business meets personal goals; Start-Up, a 15 week intensive course to develop a business plan and business management skills; Working Solution, topic specific workshops for micro-business owner; and a graduate association to foster ongoing networking and access to information. They also offer comprehensive skills training and the opportunity to connect with other women entrepreneurs. Grants and scholarships for training are available to income eligible women. Contact: Women's Small Business Program, Trinity College, 208 Colchester Ave., Burlington, VT 05401; 802-658-0337.

Virginia

Economic Development Partnership
P.O. Box 798
Richmond, VA 23206
804-371-8100
Fax: 804-371-8112
www2.yesvirginia.org/YesVA

Business Assistance

Economic Development Partnership: Helps new and expanding businesses by
answering questions about licensing, taxes, regulations, assistance
programs, etc. The office can also locate sources of
information in other state agencies, and it can
identify sources of help for business planning,
management, exporting, and financing.

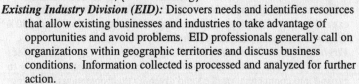

Virginia Department of Business Assistance: A
good starting point for new businesses to
learn about financial programs,
workshops, business planning and more.
Contact Virginia Department of
Business Assistance, P.O. Box 466,
Richmond, VA 23218; 804-371-8200;
Fax: 804-371-2142; {www.vdba.org}.

Existing Industry Division (EID): Discovers needs and identifies resources
that allow existing businesses and industries to take advantage of
opportunities and avoid problems. EID professionals generally call on
organizations within geographic territories and discuss business
conditions. Information collected is processed and analyzed for further
action.

Workforce Services Division (WFS): Works with new and existing businesses
and industries to recruit and train qualified workers at all skill levels for
newly created jobs. The programs addressing these efforts support State
and local Economic Development marketing efforts.

Workforce Services: Mission is to train and retrain Virginians for specific
employment opportunities. Offers consulting, video production for
training purposes, and funding.

Center for Innovative Technology: Exists to stimulate economic growth by
serving technology businesses. Services include: access to 11 technology
development centers; assistance with pursuing joint product development
with a Virginia university and provide co-funding for projects;

entrepreneurship programs designed to help early stage companies bring new products to market; assistance solving manufacturing production problems. Contact Center for Innovative Technology, 2214 Rock Hill Rd, Suite 600, Herndon, VA 20170; 800-383-2482.

Virginia's Business Development Network: Designed to provide management and technical assistance to small and medium-sized companies. Provides one-on-one counseling and group training on a variety of subjects and assists entrepreneurs with pre-business planning.

Business Financing

Virginia Small Business Financing Authority: Offers financing programs to provide businesses with access to capital needed for growth and expansion. Programs include:

1. *Industrial Development Bonds (IDBs) and the Umbrella IDB Program*: VSBFA issues tax-exempt and taxable revenue bonds (IDBs) statewide to provide creditworthy businesses with access to long term, fixed asset financing at favorable interest rates and terms. Tax-exempt IDBs may be used to finance new or expanding manufacturing facilities and exempt projects, such as solid waste disposal facilities. In addition, VSBFA offers an Umbrella IDB Program that provides a cost-effective means for businesses to sell their bonds in the public bond market, particularly for smaller projects with limited access to this market.

2. *Virginia Economic Development Revolving Loan Fund*: This fund provides loans of up to $700,000 to bridge the gap between private debt financing and private equity for projects that will result in job creation or retention. Funding is available for fixed asset financing to new and expanding manufacturing companies and other industries that derive 50% or more of their sales outside of Virginia.

3. *Virginia Defense Conversion Revolving Loan Fund*: This fund provides loans of up to $700,000 to assist defense dependent companies seeking to expand into commercial markets and diversify their operations. Funding is available for fixed assets and working capital.

4. *Loan Guarantee Program*: This program is designed to reduce the risk to banks in making loans thereby increasing the availability of short-term capital for small businesses. Under the program, VSBFA will guarantee up to $250,000 or 50%, whichever is less, of a bank loan. Typical borrowings include revolving lines of credit to finance accounts receivable and inventory, and short-term loans for working capital and fixed asset purchases, such as office or research equipment.

5. *Virginia Capital Access Program (VCAP):* VCAP provides a form of loan portfolio insurance for participating banks through special loan loss

reserve accounts which are funded by loan enrollment premiums paid by the bank/borrower and matched by the VSBFA. This allows the banks to exceed their normal risk thresholds for commercial loans of all types and, thereby, accommodate a broader array of loan requests from Virginia businesses.

6. *Export Financing*: Offers bank loans for export working capital, and continues to work in partnership with the Export-Import Bank of the United States.

7. *Child Day Care Financing Program*: VSBFA provides small direct loans to child day care providers for quality enhancement projects or to meet or maintain child care standards. Eligible loan uses include infant care equipment or equipment needed to care for children with special needs, playground improvements, vans, and upgrades or minor renovations to kitchens, bathrooms, and plumbing and electrical systems.

Contact: Virginia Small Business Financing Authority, P.O. Box 446, Richmond, VA 23218; 804-371-8254.

Financial Services Division (FSD): Identifies potential financial resources to meet the capital needs of Virginia business clients, and administers loan and guarantee programs designed to foster growth and private financing in Virginia business.

Governor's Opportunity Fund: Supports economic development projects that create new jobs and investment in accordance with criteria established by state legislation. Funds can be used for such things as site acquisition and development; transportation access; training; construction or build-out of publicly owned buildings; or grants or loans to Industrial Development Authorities.

Solar Photovoltaic Manufacturing Grants: Designed to encourage the product development and manufacture of a high technology, renewable energy source in Virginia. Any manufacturer who sells solar photovoltaic panels, manufactured in Virginia, is entitled to receive an annual grant of up to seventy-five cents per watt of the rated capacity of panel sold. Contact: Virginia Department of Mines, Minerals, and Energy, 202 N. Ninth St., Ninth Street Office Bldg., 8th Floor, Richmond, VA 23219; 804-692-3200.

Virginia Coalfield Economic Development Authority: Designed to enhance the economic base of specific areas. The Authority provides low interest loans or grants to qualified new or expanding industries through its financing program to be used for real estate purchases, construction or expansion of buildings, and the purchase of machinery and equipment. Contact: Virginia Coalfield Economic Development Authority/ The Virginia Southwest Promise, P.O. Box 1060, Lebanon, VA 24266; 540-889-0381.

Virginia Capital L.P.: A private venture capital firm. Investments that are attractive include ownership transactions and profitable, growing companies whose needs exceed senior bank debt capacity. Typical investments range between $500,000 and $1,500,000. Contact: Virginia Capital L.P., 9 South 12th St., Suite 400, Richmond, VA 23219; 804-648-4802.

Enterprise Zone Job Grants: Businesses creating new-full-time positions are eligible to receive grants of up to $500 per position ($1,000 if a zone resident fills a position). The maximum grant to any one firm is $100,000 a year for the three consecutive years in the grant period.

Tax Incentives

Major Business Facility Job Tax Credit: Qualified companies locating or expanding in Virginia receive a $1,000 corporate income tax credit for each new full-time job created over a threshold number of jobs

Recycling Equipment Tax Credit: An income tax credit is available to manufacturers for the purchase of certified machinery and equipment for processing recyclable materials. The credit is equal to 10% of the original total capitalized cost of the equipment.

Day Care Facility Investment Tax Credit: Corporations may claim a tax credit equal to 25% of all expenditures incurred in the construction, renovation, planning or acquisition of facilities for the purpose of providing day care for children of company employees. The maximum credit is $25,000.

Neighborhood Assistance Tax Credit: An income tax credit is provided for companies that make donations to neighborhood organizations conducting approved community assistance programs for impoverished people. The credit equals 45% of the total donation.

Clean Fuel Vehicle Job Creation Tax Credit: Businesses manufacturing or converting vehicles to operate on clean fuel and manufacturers of components for use in clean fuel vehicles are eligible to receive an income tax credit for each new full-time job created over and above the previous year's employment level. The credit is equal to $700 in the year the job is created, and in each of two succeeding years if the job is continued, for a maximum of $2,100 per job.

Clean Fuel Vehicle Tax Credit: An income tax credit is available to companies which purchase clean fuel vehicles or invest in related refueling facilities. The credit is equal to 10% of the IRS allowed deduction or credit for these purchases.

Worker Retraining Tax Credit: Employers are eligible to receive an income tax credit equal to 30% of all expenditures made by the employer for eligible worker retraining.

Property Tax Incentives: No property tax at the state level; real estate and tangible personal property are taxed at the local level. Virginia differs from most states in that its counties and cities are separate taxing entities. A company pays either county or city taxes, depending on its location. No tax on intangible property; manufacturers' inventory, manufacturers' furniture, fixtures, or corporate aircraft. Exemptions include: certified pollution control facilities and equipment; certified recycling equipment, rehabilitated commercial/industrial real estate; manufacturers' generating equipment; certified solar energy devices.

Sales and Use Tax Exemptions: Manufacturers' purchases used directly in production; items purchased for re-sale by distributors; certified pollution control equipment and facilities; custom computer software; purchases used in research and development; most film, video and audio production related purchases.

Enterprise Zones: Designed to stimulate business development in distressed urban and rural areas. Incentives include:

1. General Tax Credit: A 10 year tax credit is available against state income tax liability (80% first year and 60% in years two through ten) that results from business activity within an enterprise zone.

2. Refundable Real Property Improvement Tax Credit: A tax credit equal to 30% of qualified zone real property improvements is available to businesses that rehabilitate property or undertake new construction in an enterprise zone. The maximum credit within a five-year period is $125,000.

3. Investment Tax Credit For Large Qualified Zone Projects: Projects with an investment of at least $100 million and creating at least 200 jobs are eligible for a negotiated credit of up to 5% of total investment in real property, machinery and equipment.

Exports

Export Financing Assistance Program: VSBFA provides guarantees of up to the lesser of $750,000 or 90% of a bank loan for export working capital, and also works with the Export-Import Bank of the United States (Eximbank) and the U.S. Small Business Administration (SBA) to provide Virginia exporters with easier access to federal loan guarantees. In addition, VSBFA administers an Eximbank Export Credit Insurance Umbrella Policy to assist Virginia exporters in obtaining insurance on their foreign receivables.

International Market Planning: Designed to assist companies developing new export markets and increase sales. Offers international marketing research; current market analyses; specific strategies to access selected markets.

Women and Minorities

VWBE Certification Program: Helps Virginia's women-owned and operated companies certify themselves as WBE's to better compete in government and corporate procurement markets. In addition to being listed in the directory, certified companies will be registered in the WBE website, as well as in the Virginia Procurement Pipeline website. Certified WBE's also have the privilege of using the WBE seal on marketing materials and letterhead. They also receive information on other resources available to women-owned businesses regarding government contracting, management issues, and women's ownership. Contact: Women's Enterprise Program, P.O. Box 446, Richmond, VA 23218; 804-371-8200; {www.dba.state.va.us/SBDWBE.htm}.

Washington

Department of Community, Trade and Economic Development
906 Columbia St. SW
P.O. Box 48300
Olympia, WA 98504-8300
800-237-1233
access.wa.gov

Business Assistance

Business Assistance Center:
1. **The Business Assistance Center Hotline**: A statewide, toll-free information and referral service, provides information regarding state business licensing, registration, technical assistance, other state agencies or one-to-one business counseling. To contact a person from the Business Assistance Hotline, call 800-237-1233; 360-586-4840; TDD 360-586-4852.
2. **Education & Training**: Efforts are focused on providing practical application of economic development techniques along with providing a forum for practitioners for the interchange of economic development ideas. Contact Business Assistance Center, 2001 6th Ave., Suite 2600, Seattle, WA 98121; 800-237-1233; 360-664-9501.

One-Stop Licensing Center: A convenient, one-stop system that takes care of basic registration requirements and offers information about any additional licensing.

Business Retention & Expansion Program: Works with at-risk manufacturing and processing firms to reduce the number of business closures, layoffs and failures that result in significant job loss. State and local staff provide technical and problem solving assistance for these companies.

Job Skills Program: Provides grants for customized training projects. It requires at least 50% matching support from industry which may be in the form of donated or loaned equipment, instructional time contributed by company personnel, use of company facilities or training materials.

Loan Portfolio Management: Staff evaluate and process loan applications.

Business Investment Program: Support the creation of family wage jobs by providing technical assistance and consulting services to businesses considering expansion in the state.

Downtown Revitalization Service: Encourages partnerships between business and government that revitalize a community's economy, appearance and traditional business image.

Education and Training: Works in partnership with local Economic Development Councils to provide businesses and communities with practical application of economic development techniques.

Business Financing

Child Care Advantages: Provides businesses with financial and technical assistance to develop on-site or near-site child care facilities. Qualified businesses are eligible to receive direct loans, loan guarantees, or grants through the Facilities Fund to start or expand their child care facilities.

Coastal Revolving Loan Fund: This fund lends to public agencies and businesses in Jefferson, Clallam, Grays Harbor, Pacific and Wahkiakum counties. Borrowers must demonstrate job creation and private investment to qualify for loans up to $150,000. The program also provides technical assistance loans up to $50,000 for public agencies and $30,000 for businesses for feasibility studies and planning.

Industrial Revenue Bonds: Up to $10 million may be issued to finance a project. Taxable nonrecourse economic development bonds are also available through the Washington Economic Development Finance Authority.

Forest Projects Revolving Loan Fund: Provides financial assistance to small- and medium-sized forest projects companies. Loans up to $750,000 are available for secondary wood product companies and their suppliers.

Community Development Finance: Program is available to help business and industry secure long-term expansion loans. By combining private financial resources with federal and state lending assistance and local leadership, this program focuses on business expansion through community development activities.

Loan programs are available for real estate, new construction, renovation, major leasehold improvements, machinery, equipment, and working capital. Government financing for a start-up business is possible, but more difficult and requires a larger down payment by the business.

Community Economic Revitalization Board: Provides low-cost financing for public facilities improvement that are required for private development.

Tax Incentives

Sales/Use Tax Exemption On Machinery And Equipment: Manufacturers and processors for hire are not required to pay the sales or use tax on machinery and equipment used directly in manufacturing operations. In addition, charges made for labor and services for installing the machinery and equipment are not subject to the sales tax.

Distressed Area Sales/ Use Tax Deferral/Exemptions: Grants a waiver of sales/use tax for manufacturing, research and development, or computer-related businesses (excluding light and power businesses) locating in specific geographical areas. In certain other locations, the sales/use taxes on qualified construction and equipment costs are waived when all qualifications are met for a specified period of time.

Sales/Use Tax Waiver: The sales and/or use taxes for businesses located in distressed areas are waived when the project is certified as operationally complete and all purchases are verified as eligible by the Department of Revenue. No repayment is required.

Areas With Employment Requirements: Deferrals are also available for certain businesses who locate in specific distressed areas and meet the employment requirements. No repayment is required on the deferred sales/use tax for these businesses after the project is operationally complete.

Distressed Area Business And Occupation Tax Credit: A program for increasing employment provides a $1,000 credit against the B&O tax for each new employment position created and filled by certain businesses located in distressed areas. A distressed county is one with unemployment rates at 20% or above.

High Technology Sales/Use Tax Deferral/Exemption: Businesses in the following research and development technology categories may be eligible for a sales/use tax deferral/exemption, if they start new research and development or pilot scale manufacturing operations, or expand or diversify a current operation by expanding, renovating or equipping an existing facility anywhere in Washington.

High Technology Business And Occupation Tax Credit: An annual credit of up to $2 million is allowed for businesses that perform research and development in Washington in specified high technology categories and meet the minimum expense requirements. The credit cannot exceed the amount of the business and occupation tax due for that calendar year. The rate for the credit is: Nonprofit corporation or association: 515% (.00515) of the expenses. For profit businesses: 2.5% (.025) of the expenses.

Investment Tax Credits for Rehabilitation of Historic Structures: Office of Archaeology and Historic Preservation helps businesses apply for a 20% investment tax credit for the certified rehabilitation of historic structures.

Exports

International Trade Division: Works to expand future and existing export markets by distributing trade statistics, a bi-monthly newsletter, industry directories, organizing trade missions, participating in trade shows and managing state office in Europe, Japan, Taiwan, Tokyo, and Vladivostock.

Export Finance Assistance Center: Provides information and guidance on the repayment risk of financing aspects of export transactions.

Women and Minorities

Linked Deposit Loan Program: Allows minority or women-owned businesses with 50 or fewer employees to apply at participating banks for reduced rate loans.

DLF Minority and Women-Owned Business Loan: Loans can be available to assist certified minority and woman-owned businesses that are located in non-metropolitan areas.

Office of Minority and Women's Business Enterprises: Mission is to enhance the economic vitality of Washington State by creating an environment which mitigates the effects of race and gender discrimination in public contracting and promotes the economic development and growth of minority and women businesses. Certifies Women's business ventures and publishes a directory.

Minority & Women Business Development: Access resources and technical assistance to start or expand a business. MWBD provides entrepreneurial training, contract opportunities, bonding assistance, export assistance, and access to capital for start-ups or expanding businesses in the minority and women's business community.

West Virginia

West Virginia Development Office
1900 Kanawha Blvd., East
Charleston, WV 25305-0311
304-558-2234
800-982-3386
Fax: 304-558-0449
www.wvdo.org

Business Assistance

West Virginia Development Office: This office can provide information and
expertise in dealing with state, federal, and local agencies. They also have
information on financing programs and other
services offered by the state government.
Business Counseling: Confidential free service is
available to those exploring the option of
starting or purchasing a new business and to
current owners of small businesses.
Seminars and workshops: Small group training is
provided in areas such as starting a business
in West Virginia, the basics of business
planning, accounting and record keeping,
business management techniques, tax law, personnel management
techniques, quality customer service, etc. Most seminars and workshops
may be attended for a nominal fee.

Other services: Staff members are well networked to the business and banking
community and can make referrals to state, federal, and private agencies.
The staff can provide problem solving assistance, business plan assistance;
financial planning assistance; loan packaging assistance;
minority/woman/veterans business outreach; a minority-owned and
women-owned business directory; and an employee training program
called the Small Business Work Force Program. Most of these services are
free of charge. In addition, the SBDC is creating a customer learning
center which will allow the entrepreneur to use SBDC owned computers
to generate a business plan, devise and print corporate plans, learn about
the internet, and the use of Electronic Data Interchange (EDI) for the
purpose of electronic commerce.
Site Selection: Industrial specialists assist out-of-state companies, existing state
businesses and site location consultants with the identification of suitable
locations for their proposed operations utilizing a computerized inventory.

Small Business Work Force Program: Designed to serve businesses with
fewer than 20 employees that are established,
viable small businesses with demonstrable
growth potential. Training programs will be
developed based upon a comprehensive needs
analysis and the business plan.

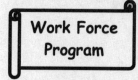

**Work Force
Program**

Regional Contracting Assistance Center: A
private non-profit corporation founded to create information and
assistance programs to help West Virginia businesses understand, adapt to,
and excel in the evolving business environment. Services include:

1. ***Bid Network*** which links local businesses, based on their product
    and/or service capabilities, to opportunities represented by internal,
    national, regional, and local purchasing requirements.
2. ***West Virginia Information Connection***: This business resource is a
    modem accessible series of five interactive databases on a 24-hour
    basis. Using the system, businesses can utilize a searchable
    electronic yellow pages of West Virginia businesses to locate sources
    of supply or in-state marketing leads. It also offers a bid board that
    displays contracts available through local government and private
    sector purchasing organizations; a directory of West Virginia
    industrial plants, sites, and office buildings; a demographic file
    providing information on West Virginia cities and counties; and a
    directory or resources available through government agencies and
    non-profit organizations. To access the WVIC: Modem Dial: 304-
    344-0685 (2400 bad) 304-344-0687 (1200 baud).
3. ***Information Exchange System***: A business-to-business information
    distribution network designed to allow West Virginians to send and
    receive electronic mail, distribute and collect marketing leads, and
    directly access the Information Connection. Through this program,
    West Virginians may also borrow computer modems that will allow
    them to electronically connect to information resources such as on-
    line services.
4. ***Quality From The Outset***: A direct in-plant technical assistance
    program aimed at helping businesses improve their quality,
    productivity, and competitiveness. The consulting service is offered
    at no charge.
5. ***Other Services***: Bid assistance; assistance with government contracts;
    market location assistance; access to a computer-assisted library of
    federal, military, and industry adopted standards and specifications as
    well as technical assistance to understand and comply with
    specifications and standards.

Robert C. Byrd Institute: A teaching factory to help small and medium-sized
manufacturing companies increase their competitiveness through the

adoption of world-class manufacturing technologies and modern management techniques. Contact Robert C. Byrd Institute, 1050 4th Avenue, Huntington, WV 25755; 304-696-6273.

Business Financing

Direct Loans: The WVEDA can provide up to 45% in financing fixed assets by providing low interest, direct loans to expanding state businesses and firms locating in West Virginia. Loan term is generally 15 years for real estate intensive projects and 5 to 10 years for equipment projects.

Indirect Loans: The WVEDA provides a loan insurance program and a capital access program through participating commercial banks to assist firms that cannot obtain conventional bank financing. The program insures up to 80% of a bank loan for a maximum loan term of four years.

Industrial Revenue Bonds: This provides for customized financing through the federal tax exempt industrial revenue bonds. $35 million of the state's bond allocation is reserved for small manufacturing projects.

Leveraged Technology Loan Insurance Program: This program expands the loan insurance coverage to 90% for those businesses involved in the development, commercialization, or use of technology- based products and processes.

West Virginia Capital Company Act: WVEDA administers a program that provides for debt and equity venture capital investment to small business. For the above loans, contact: West Virginia Economic Development Authority, 1018 Kanawha Blvd., East, Suite 501, Charleston, WV 25301; 304-558-3650.

Small Business Development Loans: This program provides capital to entrepreneurs for new or expanded small business with loans from $500 to $10,000. Please contact the West Virginia Small Business Development Center.

Jobs Investment Trust: A $10 million public venture capital fund that uses debt and equity investments to promote and expand the state's economy.

Training Grants: Up to $5,000 available exclusively to small businesses.

Governor's Guaranteed Work Force Program: Provides training funds to assist new employees in learning their jobs, as well as to improve and expand the skills of existing employees for companies moving to or expanding in West Virginia.

Tax Incentives

Super Tax Credit Program: Provides substantial tax credits for companies that create jobs in industries such as manufacturing, information processing, distribution, and destination tourism projects. A business that creates 50 jobs or more can offset up to 80% of its basic business tax liability over ten years with this credit. This innovative program is based on a formula calculated by using a job creation and a qualified investment factor. In addition, small businesses in industries previously mentioned may qualify for the credit by creating at least 10 jobs over three years.

Corporate Headquarters Relocation Credit: Available to corporations in particular industries that relocate their headquarters to West Virginia. If at least 15 jobs are created, the allowable credit is 10% of qualified investment. If the corporate headquarters relocation results in 50 or more new jobs, then the allowable credit is 50% of qualified investment. Qualified investment includes the reasonable and necessary expenses incurred by the corporation to move its headquarters to this state.

Small Business Credit: Small businesses also are eligible under the Super Tax Credit program. If ten new jobs are created, the small business is allowed 30% of it qualified investment as credit. For every job created over ten, but not over 50, the company is allowed an additional 1/2 of 1% of its qualified investment as credit.

West Virginia Capital Company Credit: Established to encourage the formation of venture capital in West Virginia. Investors in qualified capital companies are entitled to a state tax credit equal to 50% of their investment. Capital companies must have a capital base of at least $1 million but not greater than $4 million.

Warehouse
Freeport
Amendment

Warehouse Freeport Amendment: Allows goods in transit to an out-of-state destination to be exempt from local ad valorem property tax when "warehoused" in West Virginia. This exemption is specifically applicable to finished goods inventories.

Research and Development Project Credits: Manufacturers, producers of natural resources, generators of electric power and persons providing manufacturing services may qualify for the credit for research activities conducted within the state. The credit generally equals 10% of the qualified investment in depreciable personal property, wages and other expenses incurred for conducting a qualified research or development project.

Industrial Expansion and Revitalization Credit: Industrial expansion and revitalization investment by manufacturers within the state qualifies for a 10% tax credit pro-rated over a period of 10 years.

Wood Processing Tax Credit: This credit is available for new wood processing operations. The tax credit is $250 per year per full time employee for 10 years to new or expanding companies involved in the manufacture of value-added wood products. The finished product must be consumer ready.

Five For Ten Program: Provides a tax incentive to businesses that make qualified capital improvement of at least $50 million to an existing base of $100 million or more. It assesses the new capital addition at a salvage value of 5% for the first ten years.

Sales Tax Exemption: For materials and equipment used directly in manufacturing process.

Industrial Expansion or Revitalization Tax Credit: Available for manufacturers as a credit against the business franchise tax.

Major Project Appraisal: Available for expansions at facilities that have original investment of more than $ 100 million. This requires the property tax for capital improvements of more than $ 50 million be appraised at salvage value.

Exports

Office of International Development: Offers export counseling and trade promotion opportunities to West Virginia companies. Maintains overseas offices.

Business and Industry Development Division: The Industrial Development Division of the West Virginia Development Office, in cooperation with the Department of Commerce and SBA, cosponsors workshops in international marketing.

West Virginia Export Council: A non-profit export promotion organization committed to expanding West Virginia exports. The Council assists public sector organizations in planning, promoting, and implementing activities that assist international export efforts.

Center for International Programs: For information on this program, contact Dr. Will Edwards, Director, Marshall University, Huntington, WV 25755; 304-696-6265; Fax 304-696-6353.

Women and Minorities

Center for Economic Options: A non-profit statewide, community-based organization which promotes opportunities that develop the economic capacity of West Virginia's rural citizens and communities. Working with members of society who traditionally have been excluded from economic decision-making, the Center advocates equity in the workplace, coordinates alternative approaches for economic development, and works to impact the direction of public policy. The Center coordinates three strategies to accomplish these goals:

1. *Community Resources*: Coordinates a pool of facilitators and training specialists who provide technical assistance to individuals, organizations, and community groups in many areas including strategic planning,

business plan development, board development, and community assessments. The program also provides workshops and resource materials on community-based development.

2. ***Enterprise Development***: Promotes rural job creation through self-employment and links small-scale, sector-specific entrepreneurs in statewide production and marketing networks. The Center facilitates the development of these flexible networks and connects the business owners with information, resources, training opportunities, and markets.

3. ***Public Policy***: Researches and recommends policy in several areas including worker equity, enterprise development, sustainable development, work force training, and economic equity. Through the program, consultants on establishing equity in the workplace and meeting state and federal sex equity regulations are provided.

Contact: Center for Economic Options, 601 Delaware Ave., Charleston, WV 25302; 304-345-1298.

West Virginia Women's Commission: Offers women opportunities to learn to be advocates for themselves and to work with others to address systemic change. Projects include leadership and legislative conference like the Women's Town Meeting and Women's Day at the Legislature among others. Contact West Virginia Women's Commission, Building 6, Room 637, 1900 Kanawha Boulevard, East, Charleston, WV 25305; 304-558-0070; Fax: 304-558-3240.

Minority-owned and Women-owned Business Directory: Each year the West Virginia Small Business Development Center publishes a "Minority-owned and Women-owned Business Directory" This directory is distributed to public and private purchasing agents, Chambers of Commerce, Economic Development Authorities, legislators and many privately owned businesses including contractors and all of the listees. There is no cost for the directory nor is there a charge for being included. The only requirement is that the business be located in West Virginia, be a for profit company and be 51% owned by a minority or woman.

Wisconsin

Department of Commerce (COMMERCE)
201 W. Washington Avenue
Madison, WI 53707
Business Helpline: 800-HELP-BUSiness
Fax Request Hotline: 608-264-6154
Export Helpline: 800-XPORT-WIsconsin
www.commerce.state.wi.us

Business Assistance

Department of Commerce: The Wisconsin Department of Commerce is the
state's primary agency for delivery of integrated services to businesses.
Services include business financing, technical and managerial services to a
wide range of businesses.

Business Development Resources: The Area
Development Manager Program assists
business expansions, promotes business
retention, and helps local development
organizations in their respective territories. Area

development managers use their knowledge of federal,
state, and regional resources to provide a variety of information to
expanding or relocating firms. They also mobilize resources to help
struggling businesses.

Brownfields Initiative Technical Assistance Program: Provides information
and assistance related to brownfields redevelopment. The program can
assist in the identification and resolution of regulatory issues, and
electronically link prospective buyers with information on available
brownfield sites.

Business Development Assistance Center: Provides assistance to small
businesses. The office furnishes information on government regulations,
and refers businesses to appropriate resources. Call 800-HELP BUSiness.

Dairy 2020 Initiative: A state, business, and education partnership that works
to enhance the competitive edge of the Wisconsin dairy industry. Contact:
Dairy 2020 Program, P.O. Box 7970, Madison, WI 53707; 608-266-7370.

Assistance with Environmental Regulations and Permits is available to
manufacturers. COMMERCE can also expedite regulatory and permit
clearance and resolve delays and communications problems. Businesses
storing or handling flammable or combustible liquids can receive
compliance assistance.

Wisconsin Health Consultation Program: Provides free assistance to employers who request help to establish and maintain a safe and healthful workplace. Health Consultants will conduct an appraisal of physical work practices and environmental hazards, will perform an ergonomics analysis, review various aspects of the employers present occupational safety and health program, and will present occupational health related training.

Industrial Recycling Assistance Program: Conducts site visits and detailed assessments to help manufacturers find the best available solutions for waste management and waste reduction problems.

Manufacturing Assessment Center: Helps small and medium manufacturers improve quality and productivity through professional assessment of operations, systems, and layouts. The center maintains a list of related seminars available throughout the country, and can arrange plant tours of leading-edge manufacturers in the state. ***Plan Review Program*** provides plan review and consultation for structures, plumbing, elevators, HVAC, lighting, erosion control, and private onsite wastewater treatment systems. The services help designers, installers, and owners protect public safety and promote economic efficiency.

Plan Review Program

Recycling Technical Assistance Program: Helps companies switch to recycled feedstock or reduce waste generation.

Small Business Clean Air Assistance Program: Designed to help small businesses comply with standards established by the federal Clean Air Act.

Small Business Ombudsman: Provides information on government regulations and financing alternatives to small businesses, particularly entrepreneurs. Through its advocacy function, the office promotes special consideration for small businesses in Wisconsin administrative rules.

WiSCon Safety Consultation Program: Assesses current safety programs and suggests improvements; evaluates physical work practices; identifies available assistance; and provides training and education for managers and employees. The consultants do not issue citations, propose penalties, or report possible safety violations to the Occupational Safety and Health Administration.

Wisconsin TechSearch is the fee-based information outreach program of the Kurt F. Wendt Library. TechSearch offers document delivery and reference services to businesses and industry. On-line literature, patent and trademark searches are available. TechSearch provides access to the information resources of the Wendt Library, which contains outstanding collections in science and engineering, and is a US Patent and Trademark Depository Library and more than 40 libraries and information centers on the UW-Madison campus. For more information and a fee schedule, call 608-262-5913/5917 or E-mail {wtskfw@ doit.wisc.edu}.

UW-Madison Engineering Cooperative Education and Internship Program: Provides student engineering interns that can help companies undertake a variety of technical and engineering initiatives. Interns are paid commensurate with their educational level and previous experience. Advantages to the employer include developing a stronger, experienced workforce; identifying outstanding students for potential employment at graduation; evaluating an individual's performance prior to making a full-time commitment; and sharing new technology, research, and procedures.

Solid and Hazardous Waste Education Center: Provides technical assistance to businesses and communities on emissions reduction, pollution prevention, recycling, and solid waste management. The Center also offers grants that companies can use for hazardous waste reduction audits. UW-Green Bay Campus, 2420 Nicolet Dr., ES317, Green Bay, WI 54311; 920-465-2327.

Business Financing

Customized Labor Training Fund: Provides training grants to businesses that are implementing new technology or production processes. The program can provide up to 50% of the cost of customized training that is not available from the Wisconsin Technical College System.

Dairy 2020 Initiative: Awards grants and loans for business and feasibility planning to dairy producers and processors considering a modernization or expansion project.

Employee Ownership Assistance Loan Program: Can help a group of employees purchase a business by providing individual awards up to $25,000 for feasibility studies or professional assistance. The business under consideration must have expressed its intent to downsize or close.

Division of Vocational Rehabilitation Job Creation Program: Designed to increase employment opportunities for DVR clients by providing equipment grants, technical assistance grants, and customized assistance to companies that will hire persons with disabilities as part of a business expansion.

Major Economic Development Program: Offers low-interest loans for business development projects that create a significant economic impact.

Rural Economic Development Program: Makes individual awards up to $30,000 for feasibility studies and other professional assistance to rural businesses with fewer than 25 employees. Businesses and farms that have completed their feasibility evaluations are eligible for individual micro loans up to $25,000 for working capital and the purchase of equipment.

Technology Development Fund: Helps businesses finance Phase I product development research. Firms completing Phase I projects can receive Phase II product-commercialization funding.

Tax Incremental Financing: Helps cities in Wisconsin attract industrial and commercial growth in underdeveloped and blighted areas. A city or village can designate a specific area within its boundaries as a TIF district and develop a plan to improve its property values. Taxes generated by the increased property values pay for land acquisition or needed public works.

Brownfields Initiative: Provides grants to persons, businesses, local development organizations, and municipalities for environmental remediation activities for brownfield sites where the owner is unknown, cannot be located or cannot meet the cleanup costs.

BDI Micro Loan Program: Helps entrepreneurs with permanent disabilities and rehabilitation agencies finance business start-ups or expansions.

BDI Self-Employment Program: Helps severely disabled DVR clients start micro-businesses.

Industrial Revenue Bonds (IRBs): A means of financing the construction and equipping of manufacturing plants and a limited number of non-manufacturing facilities. The municipality is not responsible for debt service on IRBs, nor is it liable in the case of default. IRBs are also exempt from federal income tax.

Petroleum Environmental Clean-up Fund: Reimburses property owners for eligible clean-up costs related to discharges for petroleum tank systems.

Recycling Demonstration Grant Program: Helps businesses and local governing units fund waste reduction, reuse, and recycling pilot projects.

Recycling Early Planning Grant Program: Awards funds to new and expanding business plans, marketing assistance, and feasibility studies on the start-up or expansion of a recycling business.

Recycling Loan Program

Recycling Loan Program: Awards loans for the purchase of equipment to businesses and nonprofit organizations that make products from recycled waste, or make equipment necessary to manufacture these products.

Recycling Technology Assistance Program: Provides low cost loans to fund research and development of products or processes using recovered or recyclable materials. Eligible activities include product development and testing, process development and assessment, specialized research, and technical assistance.

Wisconsin Fund: Provides grants to help small commercial businesses rehabilitate or replace their privately owned sewage systems.

Wisconsin Housing and Economic Development Authority (WHEDA): Offers a program that buys down commercial interest rates, enabling Wisconsin lenders to offer short-term, below-market-rate loans to small, minority- or women-owned businesses. A loan guarantee program is available for firms ramping-up to meet contract demands; for firms in economically-distressed areas; and for tourism and agribusiness projects. The authority also operates a beginning farmer bond program.

Wood Utilization Program: Provides grants to the forest products industry, universities, laboratories, and industry-research partnerships for conducting research and development and in-plant trials that develop value-added products from manufacturing by-products and other wood residue; develop economical solutions for environmental protection; and improve the use of available timber resources.

Community-Based Economic Development Program: Awards grants to community-based organizations for development and business assistance projects and to municipalities for economic development planning. The program helps community-based organizations plan, build, and create business and technology-based incubators, and can also capitalize an incubator tenant revolving-loan program.

Tax Incentives

Development Zone Program: A tax benefit initiative designed to encourage private investment and to improve both the quality and quantity of employment opportunities. The program has $21 million in tax benefits available to assist businesses that meet certain requirements and are located or willing to locate in one of Wisconsin's 20 development zones.

Enterprise Development Zone Program: This program promotes a business start-up or expansion on a particular site in any area of the state that suffers from high unemployment, declining incomes and property values, and other indicators of economic distress. The program pays on performance. Tax credits can be taken only on income generated by business activity in the zone. The maximum amount of tax credits per zone is $3 million. Up to 50 sites can be designated around the state for projects that are not likely to occur or continue unless a zone is created. Types of Credits: A business in an enterprise development zone is eligible to earn the following tax credits:

1. The jobs credit: Equal to 40% of the first $6,000 in qualified wages for the first and second years of employment of a member of a "target group."
2. The sales tax credit: Equal to the amount of sales tax paid on building materials and equipment.
3. The location credit: Equal to 2.5% of the cost of acquiring, constructing, rehabilitating, remodeling or repairing real property.
4. The investment credit: Equal to 2.5% of the cost of depreciable tangible personal property.
5. The research credit: Equal to 5% of increased expenditures on research.

6. The child care credit: Equal to expenses incurred by an employer for child care provided to children of target group members. Up to $1,200 per year per child for two years.
7. The environmental remediation credit: Equal to 7.5% of cost of the remediation of contaminated land.

Wisconsin Small Business Innovative Research (SBIR) Support Program: Coordinates resources to help businesses pursue federal SBIR grants and contracts. The federal SBIR program provides Phase I awards of up to $100,000 for feasibility studies and Phase II awards of up to $750,000 for project development.

Exports

COMMERCE maintains International Offices in Frankfurt, Mexico City, Seoul, Toronto and Sao Paolo. They also contract with consultants in Hong Kong/China, Japan, Singapore and Southeast Asia, Chile, Peru, and Ecuador to provide export services to state firms. Participating in a variety of promotional activities, such as trade shows and Wisconsin product exhibits, the offices forward trade leads and set up business meetings between state firms and potential clients. Overseas firms interested in sites or investment in Wisconsin can contact the offices for assistance.

Wisconsin Trade Project Program: Can help small export-ready firms participate in international trade shows. The business covers its own travel and lodging expenses. COMMERCE can then provide up to $5,000 in reimbursements to a business for costs associated with attending a trade show, such as booth rental or product brochure translation.

Trade Shows and Trade Missions: Showcase Wisconsin firms and products to prospective international clients. The Department sponsors a Wisconsin-products booth at approximately 12 international trade fairs per year, and also arranges trade and reverse investment missions abroad, many of them led by the Governor.

Women and Minorities

Bureau of Minority Business Development
Department of Commerce
123 W. Washington Ave.
P.O. Box 7970
Madison, WI 53707
608-267-9550
badger.state.wi.us

Certifies companies to be eligible to participate in state's minority business bid preference. Company must be at least 51% owned, controlled, and managed by minority (being a woman is not considered a minority).

Certification to participate in the state's minority business purchasing and contracting program is available to minority vendors. Interested firms may apply through the department. They are then listed in the *Annual Directory of Minority-Owned Firms*.

Marketing Assistance of various kinds is offered to minority-owned firms. Certified minority vendors are listed in the department's database for access by the purchasing community. Minority-owned firms can receive help developing marketing plans. Each year, the department sponsors the Marketplace Trade Fair to encourage business contacts between minority vendors and state and corporate buyers.

American Indian Liaison: Provides advice, training, technical assistance, and economic development information to the Wisconsin tribes, tribal communities, and American Indian entrepreneurs, and serves as state economic development liaison.

Minority Business Development Fund Revolving Loan Fund (RLF) Program: Designed to help capitalize RLFs administered by American Indian tribal governing bodies or local development corporations that target their loans to minority-owned businesses. The corporation must be at least 51-percent controlled and actively managed by minority-group members, and demonstrate the expertise and commitment to promote minority business development in a specific geographic area.

Minority Business Development Fund: Offers low-interest loans for start-up, expansion or acquisition projects. To qualify for the fund, a business must be 51-percent controlled, owned, and actively managed by minority-group members, and the project must retain or increase employment.

Minority Business Early Planning Grant Program: Provides seed capital to minority entrepreneurs for feasibility studies, business plans, and marketing plans.

Wisconsin Women's Business Initiative Corporation (WWBIC): Offers micro loans to businesses owned by women, minorities, and low-income individuals. WWBIC also offers training and technical assistance.

Wyoming

Department of Commerce
2301 Central Ave.
Cheyenne, WY 82002
307-777-6303
Fax: 307-777-6005
http://commerce.state.wy.us

Business Assistance

Division of Economic and Community Development: This office can provide information and expertise in dealing with state, federal, and local agencies. They also have information on financing programs and other services offered by the state government.

Science, Technology and Energy Authority: Helps to improve the development of research capability, stimulate basic and applied technological research and facilitate commercialization of new products and processes.

Mid-America Manufacturing Technology Centers: A non-profit organization that assists small and medium-sized manufacturers in becoming more competitive, improve quality, boost sales and locate production resources.

Business Financing

The state offers a wide spectrum of public sector financial and technical assistance programs.

Wyoming Industrial Development Corporation: Matches resources in both private and public sectors that best fit the needs of business.

Workforce Training: Financial support is available for on-the-job training, classroom training, or a combination of both.

Relative Cost of Doing Business: RFA.com is an annually updated index that compares business costs in each state to the national average composed of unit labor costs, effective tax burden and energy costs. In 1998, Wyoming had the lowest costs of doing business all 50 states. Check out {www.rfa.com/free/cdb.asp}.

Tax Incentives

No personal income tax.
No corporate income tax.
No tax on intangible assets such as bank accounts, stocks, or bonds.
No tax on retirement income earned and received from another state.
No inventory tax.
No tax on goods-in-transit or made from out-of-state.

Federal Money Programs For Your Business

The following is a description of the federal funds available to small businesses, entrepreneurs, inventors, and researchers. This information is derived from the *Catalog of Federal Domestic Assistance*, which is published by the U.S. Government Printing Office in Washington, DC. The number next to the title description is the official reference for this federal program. Contact the office listed below the caption for further details. The following is a description of the terms used for the types of assistance available:

Loans: money lent by a federal agency for a specific period of time and with a reasonable expectation of repayment. Loans may or may not require payment of interest.

Loan Guarantees: programs in which federal agencies agree to pay back part or all of a loan to a private lender if the borrower defaults.

Grants: money given by federal agencies for a fixed period of time and which does not have to be repaid.

Direct Payments: funds provided by federal agencies to individuals, private firms, and institutions. The use of direct payments may be "specified" to perform a particular service or for "unrestricted" use.

Insurance: coverage under specific programs to assure reimbursement for losses sustained. Insurance may be provided by federal agencies or through insurance companies and may or may not require the payment of premiums.

Information USA, Inc.

Grants to Producers of Honey, Cotton, Rice, Soybeans, Canole, Flaxseed, Mustard Seed, Rapeseed, Safflower, Sunflower Seed, Feed Grains, Wheat, Rye, Peanuts, Tobacco, and Dairy Products

(10.051 Commodity Loans and Purchases)
U.S. Department of Agriculture
Farm Service Agency
Price Support Division
Stop 0512, 1400 Independence Ave., SW
Washington, DC 20250-0512
202-720-7641

Objectives: To improve and stabilize farm income, to assist in bringing about a better balance between supply and demand of the commodities, and to assist farmers in the orderly marketing of their crops. Types of assistance: direct payments with unrestricted use; direct loans. Estimate of annual funds available: Commodity purchases: $61,700,000 in 1998; Loans: $7,451,289,000.

Grants to Dairy Farmers Whose Milk Is Contaminated Because of Pesticides

(10.053 Dairy Indemnity Program)
U.S. Department of Agriculture
Farm Service Agency
1400 Independence Ave., SW
Washington, DC 20250-0512
202-720-7641

Objectives: To protect dairy farmers and manufacturers of dairy products who through no fault of their own, are directed to remove their milk or dairy products from commercial markets because of contamination from pesticides which have been approved for use by the federal government. Dairy farmers can also be indemnified because of contamination with chemicals or toxic substances, nuclear radiation or fallout. Types of assistance: direct payments with unrestricted use. Estimate of annual funds available: Direct payments: $450,000.

Grants to Producers of Corn, Sorghum, Barley, Oats, and Rye

(10.055 Production Flexibility Payments for Contract Commodities)
Philip W. Sronce
U.S. Department of Agriculture
Farm Service Agency

Economic and Policy Analysis Staff
Stop 0532, 1400 Independence Ave. SW
Washington, DC 20250-0532
202-720-4418
Objectives: To support farming certainty and flexibility while ensuring continued compliance with farm conservation and wetland protection requirements. Estimate of annual funds available: Contract Payments: $700,921,515.

Money to Run an Agriculture Related Business, Recreation Related Business or Teenage Business

(10.406 Farm Operating Loans)
Director, Loan Making Division
U.S. Department of Agriculture
Farm Service Agency
Ag Box 0522
Washington, DC 20250
202-720-1632
Objectives: To enable operators of not larger than family farms through the extension of credit and supervisory assistance, to make efficient use of their land, labor, and other resources, and to establish and maintain financially viable farming and ranching operations. Types of assistance: direct loans; guaranteed/insured loans. Estimate of annual funds available: Direct Loans: $500,000,000; Guaranteed Loans: $1,700,000,000.

Money to Farmers, Ranchers, and Aquaculture Businesses

(10.407 Farm Ownership Loans)
Director, Loan Making Division
U.S. Department of Agriculture
Farm Service Agency
Ag Box 0522
Washington, DC 20250
202-720-1632
Objectives: To assist eligible farmers, ranchers, and aquaculture operators, including farming cooperatives, corporations, partnerships, and joint operations, through the extension of credit and supervisory assistance to: Become owner-operators of not larger than family farms; make efficient use of the land, labor, and other resources; carry on sound and successful farming operations; and enable farm families to have a reasonable standard of living. Types of assistance: direct loans; guaranteed/ insured loans. Estimate of annual funds available: Direct Loans: $85,000,000; Guaranteed Loans: $425,031,000.

Loans to Family Farms That Can't Get Credit

(10.437 Interest Assistance Program)
FmHA County Supervisor in the county where the proposed farming operation
will be located, or
Director, Loan Making Division
U.S. Department of Agriculture
Farm Service Agency
Ag Box 0522
Washington, DC 20250
202-720-1632
Objectives: To aid not larger than family sized farms in obtaining credit when they
are temporarily unable to project a positive cash flow without a reduction in the
interest rate. Types of assistance: guaranteed/insured loans. Estimate of annual
funds available: Subsidized Guaranteed Loans: $200,000,000. (There have been
no funds authorized for Subsidized Farm Ownership Loans.)

Grants to Market Food Related Products Overseas

(10.600 Foreign Market Development Cooperation Program)
Deputy Administrator
Commodity and Marketing Programs
Foreign Agricultural Service
U.S. Department of Agriculture
Washington, DC 20250
202-720-4761

FAMILY FARMS

Objectives: To develop, maintain and expand long-term export markets for U.S.
agricultural products through cost-share assistance and the opportunity to work
closely with FAS and its overseas offices. Types of assistance: direct payments for
specified use (cooperative agreements). Estimate of annual funds available: Direct
payments: $27,500,000.

Grants to Sell Food Related Products Overseas

(10.601 Market Access Program)
Deputy Administrator
Commodity and Marketing Programs
Foreign Agricultural Service
U.S. Department of Agriculture
Washington DC 20250
202-720-4761
Objectives: To encourage the development, maintenance, and expansion of
commercial export markets for U.S. agricultural commodities through cost-share
assistance to eligible trade organizations that implement a foreign market

development program. Priority for assistance is provided for agricultural commodities or products in the case of an unfair trade practice. Funding of the program is accomplished through the issuance by the Commodity Credit Corporation (CCC) of a dollar check to reimburse participants for activities authorized by a specific project agreement. Types of assistance: direct payments for specified use (cooperative agreements). Estimate of annual funds available: Direct payments: $90,000,000.

Money to Local Communities Near National Forests to Help Businesses Grow or Expand

(10.670 National Forest-Dependent Rural Communities)
Deputy Chief
State and Private Forestry
Forest Service
U.S. Department of Agriculture
P.O. Box 96090
Washington, DC 20090-6090
202-205-1657
Objectives: Provide accelerated assistance to communities faced with acute economic problems associated with federal or private sector land management decisions and policies or that are located in or near a national forest and are economically dependent upon forest resources. Aid is extended to these communities to help them to diversify their economic base and to improve the economic, social, and environmental well-being of rural areas. Types of assistance: project grants; direct loans; use of property, facilities, and equipment; training. Estimate of annual funds available: $3,500,000.

Loans to Non-Profits to Lend Money to New Businesses

(10.767 Intermediary Relending Program)
Rural Business and Cooperative Development Service
Room 6321, South Agriculture Building
Washington, DC 20250-0700
202-690-4100
Objectives: To finance business facilities and community development. Types of assistance: direct loans. Estimate of annual funds available: Loans: $35,000,000.

Loans to Businesses in Small Towns

(10.768 Business and Industry Loans)
Administrator, Rural Business and Cooperative Development Service
U.S. Department of Agriculture
Washington, DC 20250-3201

202-690-4730
Fax: 202-690-4737
Objectives: To assist public, private, or cooperative organizations (profit or non-profit), Indian tribes or individuals in rural areas to obtain quality loans for the purpose of improving, developing or financing business, industry, and employment and improving the economic and environmental climate in rural communities including pollution abatement and control. Types of assistance: Direct loans; guaranteed/insured loans. Estimate of annual funds available: Direct Loans: $50,000,000; Guaranteed Loans: $1,000,000,000.

Grants to Non-Profits to Lend Money to New Businesses

(10.769 Rural Development Grants)
Director, Specialty Lenders Division
Rural Business-Cooperative Service
U.S. Department of Agriculture
Washington, DC 20250-3222
202-720-1400
Objectives: To facilitate the development of small and emerging private business, industry, and related employment for improving the economy in rural communities. Types of assistance: project grants. Estimate of annual funds available: Grants: $40,300,000.

Loans to Companies That Provide Electricity to Small Towns

(10.850 Rural Electrification Loans and Loan Guarantees)
Administrator, Rural Utilities Service
U.S. Department of Agriculture
Washington, DC 20250-1500
202-720-9540
Objectives: To assure that people in eligible rural areas have access to electric services comparable in reliability and quality to the rest of the Nation. Types of assistance: direct loans. Estimate of annual funds available: Direct Loans: $366,000,000; Guaranteed FFB: $700,000,000.

Loans to Companies That Provide Telephone Service to Small Towns

(10.851 Rural Telephone Loans and Loan Guarantees)
Assistant Administrator, Rural Utilities Services
U.S. Department of Agriculture
Washington, DC 20250
202-720-9554

Objectives: To assure that people in eligible rural areas have access to telecommunications services comparable in reliability and quality to the rest of the Nation. Types of assistance: Direct loans; guaranteed/insured loans. Estimate of annual funds available: Hardship Loans: $50,000,000; Cost of Money Loans: $300,000,000; FBB Treasury Loans: $120,000,000.

Extra Loans to Companies That Provide Telephone Service to Small Towns

(10.852 Rural Telephone Bank Loans)
Assistant Governor
Rural Telephone Bank
U.S. Department of Agriculture
Washington, DC 20250
202-720-9554
Objectives: To provide supplemental financing to extend and improve telecommunications services in rural areas. Types of assistance: direct loans. Estimate of annual funds available: Direct Loans: $175,000,000.

Grants and Loans to Telephone Companies That Then Provide Financing to Small Businesses

(10.854 Rural Economic Development Loans and Grants)
Director, Specialty Lenders Division
Rural Business-Cooperative Service
U.S. Department of Agriculture
Washington, DC 20250
202-720-1400
Objectives: To promote rural economic development and job creation projects, including funding for project feasibility studies, start-up costs, incubator projects, and other reasonable expenses for the purpose of fostering rural development. Types of assistance: direct loans; project grants. Estimate of annual funds available: Loans: $15,000,000; Grants: $11,000,000. (Note: Grants to establish Revolving Loan Fund Programs.)

Free Plants to Nurseries

(10.905 Plant Materials for Conservation)
Deputy Chief For Science and Technology
Natural Resources Conservation Service
U.S. Department of Agriculture
P.O. Box 2890
Washington, DC 20013
202-720-4630

Objectives: To assemble, evaluate, select, release, and introduce into commerce, and promote the use of new and improved plant materials for soil, water, and related resource conservation and environmental improvement programs. To develop technology for land management and restoration with plant materials. To transfer technology on plant materials. Types of assistance: provision of specialized services. Estimate of annual funds available: Salaries and expenses: $8,745,000.

Grants to Communities That Provide Money And Help to Small Business Incubators

(11.300 Economic Development Grants for Public Works and
Infrastructure Development)
David L. McIlwain, Director
Public Works Division
Economic Development Administration
Room H7326, Herbert C. Hoover Building
U.S. Department of Commerce
Washington, DC 20230
202-482-5265
Objectives: To promote long-term economic development and assist in the construction of public works and development facilities needed to initiate and encourage the creation or retention of permanent jobs in the private sector in areas experiencing substantial economic distress. Types of assistance: project grants. Estimate of annual funds available: Grants: $160,200,000.

Grants to Communities to Help Small Businesses Start or Expand

(11.302 Economic Development Support for Planning Organizations)
Luis F. Bueso, Director Planning Division
Economic Development Administration
Room H7319, Herbert C. Hoover Bldg.
Washington, DC 20230
202-482-3027
Fax: 202-482-0466
Objectives: To assist in providing administrative aid to multi-county Economic Development Districts, Redevelopment Areas and Indian Tribes to establish and maintain economic development planning and implementation capability and thereby promote effective utilization of resources in the creation of full-time permanent jobs for the unemployed and the underemployed in areas of high distress. Types of assistance: project grants. Estimate of annual funds available: Grants: $20,000,000.

Grants to Communities That Help Finance New or Old Businesses Due to New Military Base Closings

(11.307 Special Economic Development and Adjustment Assistance Program-Sudden and Severe Economic Dislocation (SSED) and Long-Term Economic Deterioration (LTED))
David F. Witschi, Director
Economic Adjustment Division
Economic Development Administration
Room H7327, Herbert C. Hoover Building
U.S. Department of Commerce
Washington DC 20230
202-482-2659
Objectives: To assist state and local areas develop and/or implement strategies designed to address structural economic adjustment problems resulting from sudden and severe economic dislocation such as plant closings, military base closures and defense contract cutbacks, and natural disasters (SSED), or from long-term economic deterioration in the area's economy (LTED). Types of assistance: project grants. Estimate of annual funds available: Grants: $175,393,116 (includes funds for economic adjustment, defense adjustment, disaster recovery and trade impacted areas).

Grants to Fishermen Hurt by Oil and Gas Drilling on the Outer Continental Shelf

(11.408 Fishermen's Contingency Fund)
Chief, Financial Services Division
National Marine Fisheries Service
1315 East West Highway
Silver Spring, MD 20910
301-713-2396
Objectives: To compensate U.S. commercial fishermen for damage/loss of fishing gear and 50 percent of resulting economic loss due to oil and gas related activities in any area of the Outer Continental Shelf. Types of assistance: direct payments with unrestricted use. Estimate of annual funds available: Direct payments: $500,000.

Grants to Develop New Technologies for Your Business

(11.612 Advanced Technology Program)
Dr. Lura Powell, Director
Advanced Technology Program
National Institute of Standards and Technology
Gaithersburg, MD 20899

301-975-5187
E-mail: {lura.powell@nist.gov}
To receive application kits:
ATP customer service staff
1-800-ATP-FUND
Objectives: To work in partnership with industry to foster the development and
broad dissemination of challenging, high-risk technologies that offer the potential
for significant, broad-based economic benefits for the nation. Types of assistance:
project grants (cooperative agreements). Estimate of annual funds available:
Cooperative Agreements: $209,931,000.

Grants to Organizations That Help Minorities Start Their Own Businesses

(11.800 Minority Business Development Centers)
Mr. Paul R. Webber, Acting Deputy Director
Room 5087, Minority Business Development Agency
U.S. Department of Commerce
14th and Constitution Avenue, NW
Washington, DC 20230
202-482-3237
Objectives: To provide business development services for a minimal fee to
minority firms and individuals interested in entering, expanding, or improving
their efforts in the marketplace. Minority business development center operators
provide a wide range of services to clients, from initial consultations to the
identification and resolution of specific business problems. Types of assistance:
project grants. Estimate of annual funds available: Grants: $6,900,000.

Grants to Organizations That Help American Indians Start Their Own Businesses

(11.801 Native American Program)
Mr. Joseph Hardy
Business Development
Specialist for the Office of Operations
Room 5079, Minority Business Development Agency
U.S. Department of Commerce
14th and Constitution Avenue, NW
Washington, DC 20230
202-482-6022
Objectives: To provide business development service to American Indians
interested in entering, expanding, or improving their efforts in the marketplace. To

help American Indian business development centers and American Indian business consultants to provide a wide range of services to American Indian clients, from initial consultation to the identification and resolution of specific business problems. Types of assistance: project grants. Estimate of annual funds available: Grants: $1,000,000.

Grants to Help Minority Businesses Enter New Markets

(11.802 Minority Business Development)
Mr. Paul R. Webber, Acting Deputy Director
Room 5055, Minority Business Development Agency
U.S. Department of Commerce
14th and Constitution Avenue, NW
Washington, DC 20230
202-482-3237
Objectives: The resource development activity provides for the indirect business assistance programs conducted by MBDA. These programs encourage minority business development by identifying and developing private markets and capital sources; expanding business information and business services through trade associations; promoting and supporting the mobilization of resources of federal agencies and state and local governments at the local level; and assisting minorities in entering new and growing markets. Types of assistance: project grants (cooperative agreements). Estimate of annual funds available: Cooperative Agreements/Contracts: $1,448,000.

Grants to Organizations That Will Help You Sell to the Department of Defense

(12.002 Procurement Technical Assistance For Business Firms)
Defense Logistics Agency
Office of Small and Disadvantaged Business Utilization (DDAS)
8725 John J. Kingman Rd., Suite 2533
Ft. Belvoir, VA 22060-6221
703-767-1650

Objectives: To increase assistance by the DoD for eligible entities furnishing PTA to business entities, and to assist eligible entities in the payment of the costs of establishing and carrying out new Procurement Technical Assistance (PTA) Programs and maintaining existing PTA Programs. Types of assistance: Cooperative agreements. Estimate of annual funds available: Cooperative Agreements: $12,000,000.

Loans to Start a Business on an Indian Reservation

(15.124 Indian Loans - Economic Development)
Orville Hood
Office of Economic Development
Bureau of Indian Affairs
1849 C Street, NW, MS-2061
Washington, DC 20240
202-208-5324
Objectives: To provide assistance to Federally Recognized Indian Tribal
Governments, Native American Organizations, and individual American Indians
in obtaining financing from private sources to promote business development
initiatives on or near Federally Recognized Indian Reservations. Types of
assistance: Guaranteed/ insured loans. Estimate of annual funds available:
Guaranteed Loans: $5,005,000.

Grants to Small Coal Mine Operators to Clean Up Their Mess

(15.250 Regulation of Surface Coal Mining and Surface Effects of Underground
Coal Mining)
Chief, Division of Regulatory Support
Office of Surface Mining Reclamation and Enforcement
U.S. Department of the Interior
1951 Constitution Ave., NW
Washington, DC 20240
202-208-2651
Objectives: To protect society and the environment from the adverse effects of
surface coal mining operations consistent with assuring the coal supply essential
to the Nation's energy requirements. Types of assistance: project grants; direct
payments for specified use. Estimate of annual funds available: $50,656,000.
(Includes all cooperative agreements and State Grants except SOAP grants.) Small
Operator Assistance: $3,800,000.

Money to Fishermen Who Have Their Boats Seized by a Foreign Government

(19.204 Fishermen's Guaranty Fund)
Mr. Stetson Tinkham
Office of Marine Conservation
Bureau of Oceans and International Environmental and Scientific Affairs
Room 5806, U.S. Department of State
Washington, DC 20520-7818
202-647-3941

Fax: 202-736-7350

Objectives: To provide for reimbursement of losses incurred as a result of the seizure of a U.S. commercial fishing vessel by a foreign country on the basis of rights or claims in territorial waters or on the high seas which are not recognized by the United States. Effective November 28, 1990, the United States acknowledges the authority of coastal states to manage highly migratory species, thus reducing the basis for valid claims under the Fishermen's Protective Act. Types of assistance: insurance. Estimate of annual funds available: Reimbursement of Losses: $500,000.

Grants to Build an Airport

(20.106 Airport Improvement Program)
Federal Aviation Administration
Office of Airport Planning and Programming
Airports Financial Assistance Division, APP-500
800 Independence Avenue, SW
Washington, DC 20591
202-267-3831
Objectives: To assist sponsors,
owners, or operators of public-use
airports in the development of a
nationwide system of airports

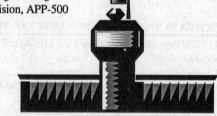

adequate to meet the needs of civil aeronautics. Types of assistance: project grants; advisory services and counseling. Estimate of annual funds available: Grants: $1,700,000,000.

Grants to Bus Companies

(20.509 Public Transportation for Nonurbanized Areas)
Federal Transit Administration
Office of Grants Management
Office of Capital and Formula Assistance
400 Seventh Street, SW
Washington, DC 20590
202-366-2053

Objectives: To improve, initiate, or continue public transportation service in nonurbanized areas by providing financial assistance for the operating and administrative expenses and for the acquisition, construction, and improvement of facilities and equipment. Also to provide technical assistance for rural transportation providers. Types of assistance: formula grants. Estimate of annual funds available: Grants: $203,164,311.

Grants to Become a Women-Owned Transportation Related Company

(20.511 Human Resource Programs)
Director, Office of Civil Rights
Federal Transit Administration
U.S. Department of Transportation
400 Seventh Street, SW, Room 7412
Washington, DC 20590
202-366-4018
Objectives: To provide financial assistance for national, regional and local initiatives that address human resource needs as they apply to public transportation activities. Such programs may include but are not limited to employment training programs; outreach programs to increase minority and female employment in public transportation activities; research on public transportation manpower and training needs; and training and assistance for minority business opportunities. This description is applicable only to projects awarded directly by the Federal Transit Administration (FTA) under the authority of Section 5314(a), the National component of the Transit Planning and Research Program. Types of assistance: project grants (cooperative agreements); dissemination of technical information. Estimate of annual funds available: Grants, Cooperative Agreements: $1,189,000.

Grants to U.S. Shipping Companies That Have to Pay Their Employees Higher Salaries Than Foreign Shipping Companies

(20.804 Operating Differential Subsidies)
Edmond J. Fitzgerald, Director
Office of Subsidy and Insurance
Maritime Administration
U.S. Department of Transportation
400 Seventh Street, SW
Washington, DC 20590
202-366-2400
Objectives: To promote development and maintenance of the U.S. Merchant Marine by granting financial aid to equalize cost of operating a U.S. flag ship with cost of operating a competitive foreign flag ship. Types of assistance: direct payments for specified use. Estimate of annual funds available: $51,030,000 in 1998.

Money for Airlines to Fly to Small Towns and Make a Profit

(20.901 Payments for Essential Air Services)
Director, Office of Aviation Analysis, X-50
U.S. Department of Transportation

400 Seventh Street, SW
Washington, DC 20590
202-366-1030
Objectives: To assure that air transportation is provided to eligible communities by subsidizing air carriers when necessary to provide service. Types of assistance: direct payments for specified use. Estimate of annual funds available: Direct payments to air carriers: $50,000,000.

Grants to Women-Owned Businesses to Help Get Contracts from the Department of Transportation

(20.903 Support Mechanisms for Disadvantaged Businesses)
Office of Small and Disadvantaged Business Utilization, S-40
Office of the Secretary
400 Seventh Street, SW
Washington, DC 20590
800-532-1169
Objectives: To develop support mechanisms, including liaison and assistance programs, that will provide outreach and technical assistance to small disadvantaged business enterprises (DBEs) to successfully compete on transportation-related contracts. Recipients will provide a communications link between the Department of Transportation; its grantees, recipients, contractors, subcontractors; and minority, women-owned and disadvantaged business enterprises (DBEs) in order to increase their participation in existing DOT programs and DOT funded projects. Types of assistance: project grants (cooperative agreements). Estimate of annual funds available: Cooperative Agreements: $1,100,000.

Loans to Start a Credit Union

(44.002 Community Development Revolving Loan Program for Credit Unions)
Ms. Joyce Jackson
Community Development Revolving Loan Program for Credit Unions
National Credit Union Administration
1775 Duke St.
Alexandria, VA 22314-3428
703-518-6610
Objectives: To support low-income credit unions in their efforts to: (1) stimulate economic development activities which result in increased income, ownership, and employment opportunities for low-income residents; and (2) provide basic financial and related services to residents of their communities. Types of assistance: direct loans. Estimate of annual funds available: Direct Loans: $2,400,000.

Money if Your Business Was Hurt by a Natural Disaster or Drought

(59.002 Economic Injury Disaster Loans)
Herbert Mitchell
Office of Disaster Assistance
Small Business Administration
409 3rd Street, SW
Washington, DC 20416
202-205-6734
E-mail: {disaster.assistance@sba.gov}
Objectives: To assist business concerns suffering economic injury as a result of
Presidential, Small Business Administration (SBA), and/or Secretary of
Agriculture declared disasters. Types of assistance: direct loans;
guaranteed/insured loans (including immediate participation loans). Estimate of
annual funds available: $901,000,000 (Includes funds for 59.002 and 59.008).

Money for Businesses Hurt by Physical Disaster or Drought

(59.008 Physical Disaster Loans)
Herbert Mitchell
Office of Disaster Assistance
Small Business Administration
409 3rd Street, SW
Washington, DC 20416
202-205-6734
Objectives: To provide loans to the victims of declared physical-type disasters for
uninsured losses. Types of assistance: direct loans; guaranteed/insured loans
(including immediate participation loans). Estimate of annual funds available:
Loans: $901,000,000 (Includes funds for 59.002 and 59.008).

Money to Start a Venture Capital Company

(59.011 Small Business Investment Companies)
Associate Administrator for Investment
Investment Division
Small Business Administration
409 Third Street, SW
Washington, DC 20416
202-205-6510
Objectives: To establish privately owned and managed investment companies,
which are licensed and regulated by the U.S. Small Business Administration; to
provide equity capital and long term loan funds to small businesses; and to
provide advisory services to small businesses. Types of assistance: direct loans;
guaranteed/ insured loans; advisory services and counseling. Estimate of annual
funds available: Loans: $1,526,119,000.

Up to $750,000 to Start Your Own Business

(59.012 Small Business Loans)
Director, Loan Policy and Procedures Branch
Small Business Administration
409 Third Street, SW
Washington, DC 20416
202-205-6570
Objectives: To provide guaranteed loans to small businesses which are unable to

obtain financing in the private credit marketplace, but can demonstrate an ability to repay loans granted. Guaranteed loans are made available to low-income business owners or businesses located in areas of high unemployment, non-profit sheltered workshops and other similar organizations which produce goods or services; to small businesses being established, acquired or owned by handicapped individuals; and to enable small businesses to manufacture, design, market, install, or service specific energy measures. The SBA's 7(a) lending authority includes: 1) the Low Documentation Loan Program (Low Doc); 2) the Cap Line Program; 3) FA$ TRAK Program, formerly the Small Loan Express; 4) the Women's Prequalification Program; and 5) Minority Prequalification Program. Types of assistance: guaranteed/insured loans (including immediate participation loans). Estimate of annual funds available: Loans: $10,000,000,000.

Help for Contractors and Others to Get Bonded to Obtain Contracts

(59.016 Bond Guarantees for Surety Companies)
Assistant Administrator Robert J. Moffitt
Office of Surety Guarantees
Small Business Administration
409 3rd Street, SW
Washington, DC 20416
202-205-6540
Objectives: To guarantee surety bonds issued by commercial surety companies for small contractors unable to obtain a bond without a guarantee. Guarantees are for up to 90 percent of the total amount of bond. Types of assistance: insurance (guaranteed surety bonds). Estimate of annual funds available: Guaranteed Surety Bonds: $1,672,000,000.

Money to Local Organizations to Finance Small Businesses

(59.041 Certified Development Company Loans [504 Loans])
Office of Loan Programs
Small Business Administration

409 3rd Street SW
Washington, DC 20416
202-205-6485
Objectives: To assist small business concerns by providing long-term fixed rate financing for fixed assets through the sale of debentures to private investors. Types of assistance: guaranteed/insured loans. Estimate of annual funds available: Guaranteed Loans: $3,000,000,000.

Grants to Local Organizations That Help Women Start Their Own Businesses

(59.043 Women's Business Ownership Assistance)
Harriet Fredman
Office of Women's Business Ownership
Small Business Administration
409 3rd Street, SW
Washington, DC 20416
202-205-6673
Objectives: To fund non-profit economic development organizations to assist, through training and counseling, small business concerns owned and controlled by women, and to remove, in so far as possible, the discriminatory barriers that are encountered by women in accessing capital and promoting their businesses. Types of assistance: project grants (cooperative agreements or contracts). Estimate of annual funds available: Cooperative Agreements: $9,000,000.

Grants to Local Organizations That Help Veterans Start Their Own Businesses

(59.044 Veterans Entrepreneurial Training and Counseling)
William Truitt
Office of Veteran Affairs
Small Business Administration
6th Floor, 409 3rd Street, SW
Washington, DC 20416
202-205-6773
Objectives: To design, develop, administer, and evaluate an entrepreneurial and procurement training and counseling program for U.S. veterans. Types of assistance: project grants (cooperative agreements). Estimate of annual funds available: Grants: $40,000.

Money to Local Organizations to Provide Micro-Loans

(59.046 Microloan Demonstration Program)
Small Business Administration
Office of Financial Assistance

Microenterprise Development Branch
409 Third Street SW, Eighth Floor
Washington, DC 20416
Mail Code 7881
202-205-6490

Objectives: To assist women, low-income, and minority entrepreneurs, business owners, and other individuals possessing the capability to operate successful business concerns and to assist small business concerns in areas suffering from lack of credit due to economic downturns. Under the program, the Small Business Administration (SBA) will make loans to private, non-profit and quasi-governmental organizations (intermediary lenders) who will use the loan funds to make short-term, fixed interest rate microloans in amounts up to $25,000 to start-up, newly established, and growing small business concerns. These microloans are to be used exclusively for working capital, inventory, supplies, furniture, fixtures, machinery, and/or equipment. In addition, the SBA will  make grants to participating intermediary lenders to provide marketing, management, and technical assistance to borrowers receiving microloans. In addition, the SBA will make grants to non-profit organizations, which are not intermediary lenders, to provide marketing, management, and technical assistance to low-income individuals seeking private sector financing for their businesses. Under the program, SBA will also provide training for intermediary lenders and non-lenders participating in the program. Types of assistance: formula grants; project grants; direct loans. Estimate of annual funds available: Direct Loans: $60,000,000; Loan Guarantees: $11,995,000; Formula Grants: $12,000,000.

Money for Disabled Veterans to Start New Businesses

(64.116 Vocational Rehabilitation for Disabled Veterans)
Veterans Benefits Administration
Vocational Rehabilitation and Counseling Service (28)
U.S. Department of Veterans Affairs
Washington, DC 20420
202-273-7413

Objectives: To provide all services and assistance necessary to enable service-disabled veterans and service persons hospitalized or receiving outpatient medical care services or treatment for a service-connected disability pending discharge to get and keep a suitable job. When employment is not reasonably feasible, the program can provide the needed services and assistance to help the individual learn skills to achieve maximum independence in daily living. Types of assistance: direct payments with unrestricted use; direct payments for specified use; direct loans; advisory services and counseling. Estimate of annual funds available: Direct payments: $402,907,000; Loan advances: $2,401,000.

Help for Retired Military to Start a Business

(64.123 Vocational Training for Certain Veterans Receiving VA Pension)
Veterans Benefits Administration
Vocational Rehabilitation and Counseling Service (28)
U.S. Department of Veterans Affairs
Washington, DC 20420
202-273-7413
Objectives: To assist new pension recipients to resume and maintain gainful employment by providing vocational training and other services. Types of assistance: direct payments for specified use; advisory services and counseling. Estimate of annual funds available: Direct Payments: $234,000 in 1998.

Money to Invest in Companies Overseas

(70.002 Foreign Investment Guaranties)
Information Officer
Overseas Private Investment Corporation
1100 New York Ave., NW
Washington, DC 20527
202-336-8799
Fax: 202-336-8700
E-mail: {OPIC@opic.gov}
www.opic.gov
Objectives: To provide financing for projects sponsored by eligible U.S. invesntors in friendly developing countries and emerging economies throughout the world, thereby assisting development goals and improving U.S. competitiveness, creating American jobs and increasing U.S. exports. Types of assistance: guaranteed/insured loans; direct loans. Estimate of annual funds available: $50,000,000 in subsidy obligations is expected to support $2,000,000,000 in loans and direct loans.

Insurance Against Your Business in Another Country Being Hurt by Foreign Politics

(70.003 Foreign Investment Insurance)
Information Officer
Overseas Private Investment Corporation
1100 New York Ave., NW

Washington, DC 20527
202-336-8799
Fax: 202-336-8700
E-mail: {OPIC@opic.gov}
www.opic.gov
Objectives: To insure investments of eligible U.S. investors in developing
countries and emerging markets, against the political risks of inconvertibility,
expropriation, and political violence. Special programs include insuring
contractors and exporters against arbitrary drawings of letters of credit posted as
bid, performance or advance payment guaranties, energy exploration and
development, and leasing operations. Types of assistance: insurance. Estimate of
annual funds available: Insurance Issued: $9,000,000,000.

Free Patent Rights to Government Discoverers of Energy Saving Ideas

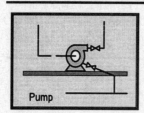

Pump

(81.003 Granting of Patent Licenses)
Robert J. Marchick
Office of the Assistant General Counsel for
Patents
U.S. Department of Energy
Washington, DC 20585
202-586-2802
Objectives: To encourage widespread utilization
of inventions covered by Department of Energy (DOE) owned patents. Types of
assistance: dissemination of technical information. Estimate of annual funds
available: (Salaries) Not identifiable.

Money to Work on an Energy-Related Invention

(81.036 Energy-Related Inventions)
Sandra Glatt
Office of Industrial Technologies (EE-23)
U.S. Department of Energy
1000 Independence Avenue, SW
Washington, DC 20585
202-586-3987

Objectives: To encourage innovation in developing non-nuclear energy
technology by providing assistance to individual and small business companies in
the development of promising energy-related inventions. Types of assistance:
project grants; use of property, facilities, and equipment; advisory services and
counseling; dissemination of technical information. Estimate of annual funds
available: Grants: $2,900,000.

Grants to Local Organizations That Help Women and Minorities Get Department of Energy Contracts

(81.082 Management and Technical Assistance for Minority Business
Enterprises)
Sterling Nichols
Office of Economic Impact and Diversity
U.S. Department of Energy
ED-1, Forrestal Building, Room 5B-110
Washington, DC 20585
202-586-8698
Objectives: (1) To support increased participation of minority, and women-owned
and operated business enterprises (MBE's); (2) to develop energy-related minority
business assistance programs and public/private partnerships to provide technical
assistance to MBE's; (3) to transfer applicable technology from national federal
laboratories to MBE's; and (4) to increase the Department of Energy's (DOE) high
technology research and development contracting activities. Types of assistance:
advisory services and counseling. Estimate of annual funds available: Contracts
and Grants: $480,000.

Grants to Develop Energy Saving Products

(81.086 Conservation Research and Development)
Energy Efficiency and Renewable Energy Programmatic Offices:
Office of Building Technology
State and Community Programs
Contact: Lynda Dancy
202-586-2300

Office of Transportation Technologies
Contact: Nancy Blackwell
202-586-6715

Office of Industrial Technologies
Contact: Beatrice Cunningham
202-586-0098

Office of Utility Technologies
Contact: Gloria Elliott
202-586-4142
Objectives: To conduct a balanced long-term research effort in the areas of
buildings, industry, and transportation. Grants will be offered to develop and
transfer to the non-federal sector various energy conservation technologies. Types
of assistance: project grants. Estimate of annual funds available: Grants: not

separately identified. (Note: Discretionary funds for grants are not specifically contained in the President's request for Energy Conservation Programs. However, the Department does issue grants if found to be appropriate as a result of unsolicited proposals that clearly are consistent with program objectives and are appropriate as grants in lieu of other contractual methods. Unsolicited proposals have received grants totalling approximately $2,000,000 to $2,500,000 over the past 5 years.)

Grants to Work on Solar Energy Products

(81.087 Renewable Energy Research and Development)
Energy Efficiency and Renewable Energy Programmatic Offices:
Office of Building Technology
State and Community Programs
Contact: Lynda Dancy
202-586-2300

Residential, Commercial and Institutional Buildings
Contact: Regina Washington
202-586-1660

Office of Industrial Technologies
Contact: Beatrice Cunningham
202-586-0098

Office of Transportation Technologies
Contact: Nancy Blackwell
202-586-6715

Office of Utility Technologies
Contact: Gloria Elliott
202-586-4142
Objectives: To conduct balanced research and development efforts in the following energy technologies; solar buildings, photovoltaics, solar thermal, biomass, alcohol fuels, urban waste, wind, and geothermal. Grants will be offered to develop and transfer to the nonfederal sector various renewable energy technologies. Types of assistance: project grants. Estimate of annual funds available: Grants: not separately identified. (Note: Discretionary funds for grants are not specifically contained in the President's request for Renewable Energy Research and Development Programs. However, the Department does issue grants if found to be appropriate as a result of unsolicited proposals that clearly are consistent with program objectives and are appropriate as grants in lieu of other

contractual methods. Unsolicited proposals have received grants totalling approximately $1,500,000 to $2,000,000 over the past 5 years.)

Grants to Develop Uses of Fossil Fuels

(81.089 Fossil Energy Research and Development)
Mary J. Roland
Fossil Energy Program, FE-122
U.S. Department of Energy
Germantown, MD 20545
301-903-3514
Objectives: The mission of the Fossil Energy (FE) Research and Development program is to promote the development and use of environmentally and economically superior technologies for supply, conversion, delivery and utilization of fossil fuels. These activities will involve cooperation with industry, DOE Laboratories, universities, and states. Success in this mission will benefit the Nation through lower energy costs, reduced environmental impact,  increased technology exports, and reduced dependence on insecure energy sources. Types of assistance: project grants; project grants (cooperative agreements). Estimate of annual funds available: Grants and cooperative agreements: $7,000,000.

Grants to Businesses That Employ People with Disabilities

(84.234 Projects with Industry)
Ms. Martha Muskie
Rehabilitation Services Administration
U.S. Department of Education
600 Independence Ave.
Washington, DC 20202
202-205-7320
Objectives: To create and expand job and career opportunities for individuals with disabilities in the competitive labor market, to provide appropriate placement resources by engaging private industry in training and placement. Types of assistance: project grants; project grants (cooperative agreements). Estimate of annual funds available: Grants: $22,071,000. (Note: This amount may change upon enactment of the Rehabilitation Act.)

Free Local Consultants To Start Or Grow Your Business

Small Business Development Centers (SBDCs) could be the best deal the government has to offer to entrepreneurs and inventors, and a lot of people don't even know about them! Where else in the world can you have access to a $150 an hour consultant for free? There are over 700 of these offices all over the country and they offer free (or very low cost) consulting services on most aspects of business including:

- ➡ how to write a business plan
- ➡ how to get financing
- ➡ how to protect your invention
- ➡ how to sell your idea
- ➡ how to license your product
- ➡ how to comply with the laws
- ➡ how to write a contract
- ➡ how to sell overseas
- ➡ how to get government contracts
- ➡ how to help you buy the right equipment

Information USA, Inc.

You don't even have to know how to spell
ENTREPRENEUR to contact these offices. They cater to
both the dreamer, who doesn't even know where to start, as
well as to the experienced small business that is trying to
grow to the next stage of development. In other words, the
complete novice or the experienced professional can find
help through these centers. Why spend money on a
consultant, a lawyer, an accountant, or one of those invention
companies when you can get it all for free at your local
SBDC?

Recently, I spoke with some entrepreneurs who used a
California SBDC and each of them had nothing but praise for
the services. A young man who dropped out of college to
start an executive cleaning
business said he received over
$8,000 worth of free legal
advice from the center and
said it was instrumental in
getting his business off the
ground. A woman who
worked in a bank started her
gourmet cookie business by
using the SBDC to help her
get the money and technical
assistance needed to get her

**Why spend money
on a consultant, a
lawyer, an
accountant, or one
of those invention
companies when
you can get it all for
free at your local
SBDC?**

venture up and running. And a man who was a gymnast
raved about how the SBDC helped him get his personal
trainer business off the ground. All kinds of businesses being
started, and all kinds of compliments for the SBDC's role in
assisting these entrepreneurs, in whatever they are
attempting. It sounds like a solid recommendation to me.

Can something that is free be so good? Of course it can. Because most of the people who work there are not volunteers, they are paid for by tax dollars. So it's really not free to us as a country, but it

is free to you as an entrepreneur. And if you don't believe me that the SBDCs are so good, would you take the word of Professor James J. Chrisman from the University of Calgary in Calgary, Alberta, Canada? He was commissioned to do an independent study of SBDCs and found that 82% of the people who used their services found them beneficial. And the businesses that used SBDCs had average growth rates of up to 400% greater than all the other businesses in their area. Not bad. Compare this to the Fortune 500 companies who use the most expensive consulting firms in the country and only experience growth rates of 5% or less. So, who says you get what you pay for?

To locate the nearest Small Business Development Center, contact your lead SBDC from the list below, contact the Small Business Administration Answer Desk at 800-8-ASK-SBA, or go online at {www.sba.gov/proghome.html}.

Lead Small Business Development Centers

Alabama
Alabama Small Business
Development Consortium
University of Alabama at
Birmingham
Medical Towers Building
1717 Eleventh Ave. South

Suite 419
Birmingham, AL 35294-4410
205-934-7260
Fax: 205-934-7645
E-mail: sandefur@uab.edu
www.asbdc.org

Alaska
Alaska Small Business
Development Center
University of Alaska Anchorage
430 W. Seventh Ave., Suite 110
Anchorage, AK 99501-3550
907-274-7232
Fax: 907-274-9524
E-mail: anjaf@uaa.alaska.edu

Arizona
Arizona Small Business
Development Center Network
Maricopa County Community
Colleges
Small Business Development Ctr.
2411 West 14th Street
Tempe, AZ 85281
602-731-8720
Fax: 602-230-7989
E-mail: york@maricopa.edu
www.dist.maricopa.edu/sbdc

Arkansas
Arkansas Small Business
Development Center
University of AR at Little Rock
Little Rock Technology Center
Building
100 South Main, Suite 401
Little Rock, AR 72201
501-324-9043
Fax: 501-324-9049
E-mail: jmnye@ualr.edu
www.ualr.edu/~sbdcdept

California
California Small Business
Development Center
California Trade and Commerce
Agency
801 K Street, Suite 1700
Sacramento, CA 95814

916-324-5068
800-303-6600
Fax: 916-322-5084
http://commerce.ca.gov/business/
small/starting/sb_sbdcl.html

Colorado
Colorado Small Business
Development Center
Office of Business Development
1625 Broadway, Suite 1710
Denver, CO 80202
303-892-3809
800-333-7798
Fax: 303-892-3848
E-mail: cec.ortiz@state.co.us
www.state.co.us/gov_dir/obd/
sbdc.htm

Connecticut
Connecticut Small Business
Development Center
University of Connecticut
School of Business Administration
2 Bourn Place, U-94
Storrs, CT 06269-5094
860-486-4135
Fax: 860-486-1576
E-mail: statedirector@ct.sbdc.
uconn.edu
www.sbdc.uconn.edu

Delaware
Delaware Small Business
Development Center
University of Delaware
102 MBNA America Hall
Newark, DE 19716-2711
302-831-1555
Fax: 302-831-1423
E-mail: clinton.tymes@mvs.
udel.edu
www.delawaresbdc.org

District Of Columbia
Howard University
Small Business Development Ctr.
2600 6th Street, NW, Room 125
Washington, DC 20059
202-806-1550
Fax: 202-806-1777
E-mail: husbdc@cldc.howard.edu
www.cldc.howard.edu/~husbdc

Florida
Florida Small Business
Development Center
University of West Florida
19 W. Garden St., Suite 302
Pensacola, FL 32514-5750
850-595-5480
800-644-SBDC
Fax: 850-595-5487
E-mail: fsbdc@uwf.edu
www.sbdc.uwf.edu

Georgia
Georgia Small Business
Development Center
University of Georgia
Chicopee Complex
1180 East Broad Street
Athens, GA 30602-5412
706-542-6762
Fax: 706-542-6776
E-mail:SBDCDIR@sbdc.uga.edu
www.sbdc.uga.edu

Hawaii
Hawaii Small Business
Development Center Network
University of Hawaii at Hilo
200 West Kawili Street

Hilo, HI 96720-4091
808-974-7515
Fax: 808-974-7683
E-mail: darrylm@interpac.net
www.hawaii-sbdc.org

Idaho
Idaho Small Business
Development Center
Boise State University
College of Business
1910 University Drive
Boise, ID 83725
208-385-1640
800-225-3815
Fax: 208-385-3877
E-mail: jhogge@bsu.idbsu.edu
www.idbsu.edu/isbdc

Illinois
Illinois Small Business
Development Center
Department of Commerce &
Community Affairs
620 East Adams Street, 3rd Floor
Springfield, IL 62701
217-524-5856
217-524-0171
Fax: 217-785-6328
www.commerce.state.il.us/dcca/m
enus/business/sbdc_hme.htm

Indiana
Small Business Development Ctr.
One North Capitol, Suite 1275
Indianapolis, IN 46204
317-264-2820
E-mail: sbdc@isbdcorp.org
www.isbdcorp/sbdc

Iowa
Iowa Small Business
Development Center
Iowa State University

College of Business
Administration
137 Lynn Avenue
Ames, IA 50014
515-292-6351
800-373-7232
Fax: 515-292-0020
E-mail: rmanning@iastate.edu
www.iowasbdc.org

Kansas
Fort Hays State University
Kansas Small Business
Development Center
214 SW 6th Street, Suite 205
Topeka, KS 66603
785-296-6514
Fax: 785-291-3261
E-mail: ksbdc@cjnetworks.com
www.pittstate.edu/bti/sbdc.htm

Kentucky
Kentucky Small Business
Development Center
University of Kentucky
Center for Entrepreneurship
225 College of Business and
Economics
Lexington, KY 40506-0034
http://gatton.gws.uky.edu/Kentucky
Business/ksbdc/ksbdc.htm

Louisiana
Louisiana Small Business
Development Center
Northeast Louisiana University
College of Business
Administration
Room 2-123
Monroe, LA 71209-6435
318-342-5506
Fax: 318-342-5510
E-mail: esc@alpha.nlu.edu

hhtp://leap.nlu.edu/html/lsbdc/
Nlu/nlu.htm

Maine
Small Business Development
Center
University of Southern Maine
15 Surrenden Street
Portland, ME 04103
(Mailing Address
96 Falmouth Street)
Portland, ME 04104-9300
207-780-4420
Fax: 207-780-4810
E-mail: msbdc@portland.
maine.edu
www.usm.maine.edu/~sbdc

Maryland
Maryland Small Business
Development Center
7100 Baltimore Avenue, Suite 401
College Park, MD 20740
301-403-8300
Fax: 301-403-8303
E-mail: sbdc@rhsmith.umd.edu
www.mbs.umd.edu/sbdc

Massachusetts
Massachusetts Small Business
Development Center
University of Massachusetts
Amherst
205 School of Management
Amherst, MA 01003-4935
413-545-6301
Fax: 413-545-1273
www.umassp.edu/msbdc/

Michigan
Michigan Small Business
Development Center
Wayne State University

2727 Second Avenue, Suite 107
Detroit, MI 48201
313-964-1798
Fax: 313-964-3648
Fax: 313-964-4164
E-mail: ron@misbdc.wayne.edu
http://bizserve.com/sbdc

Minnesota
Minnesota Small Business
Development Center
Minnesota Department of Trade
and Economic Development
500 Metro Square
121 Seventh Place East
St. Paul, MN 55101-2145
612-297-5770
Fax: 612-296-1290
E-mail: mary.kruger@dted.
state.mn.us
www.dted.state.mn.us

Mississippi
Mississippi Small Business
Development Center
University of Mississippi
216 Old Chemistry Building
University, MS 38677
601-232-5001
800-725-7232
Fax: 601-232-5650
E-mail: msbdc@olemiss.edu
www.olemiss.edu/depts/mssbdc

Missouri
Missouri Small Business
Development Center

University of Missouri
1205 University Ave., Suite 300
Columbia, MO 65211
573-882-0344
Fax: 573-884-4297
E-mail: summersm@missouri.edu
http://tiger.bpa.missouri.edu/Research/
Training/sbdc/homepage.htm

Montana
Montana Small Business
Development Center
Montana Department of
Commerce
1424 Ninth Avenue
Helena, MT 59620
406-444-4780
Fax: 406-444-1872
E-mail: rkloser@mt.gov
www.com.state.mt.us/economic/
sbdc.htm

Nebraska
Nebraska Small Business
Development Center
University of Nebraska at Omaha
60th & Dodge Streets
College of Business
Administration, Room 407
Omaha, NE 68182-0248
402-554-2521
Fax: 402-554-3473
E-mail: Bob_Bernier/CBA/UNO/
UNEBR@unomail.unomaha.edu

Nevada
Nevada Small Business
Development Center
University of Nevada, Reno
College of Business
Administration/032
Nazir Ansari Business Building
Room 411

Reno, NV 89557-0100
702-784-1717
Fax: 702-784-4337
E-mail: nsbdc@scf.unr.edu
www.scs.unr.edu/nsbdc

New Hampshire
New Hampshire Small Business
Development Center
University of New Hampshire
108 McConnell Hall
Durham, NH 03824-3593
603-862-2200
Fax: 603-862-4876
E-mail: gc@christa.unh.edu
www.NHSBDC.org

New Jersey
New Jersey Small Business
Development Center
Rutgers Graduate School of
Management
University Heights
49 Bleeker Street
Newark, NJ 07102-1993
973-353-1927
Fax: 973-353-1110
E-mail: bhopper@andromeda.
rutgers.edu
www.nj.com/njsbdc

New Mexico
New Mexico Small Business
Development Center
Santa Fe Community College
6401 Richards Avenue
P.O. Box 4187
Santa Fe, NM 87502-4187
505-438-1343
800-281-7232
Fax: 505-428-1469
www.nmsbdc.org

New York
New York Small Business
Development Centers
State University of New York
(SUNY)
SUNY Plaza, S523
Albany, NY 12246
518-443-5398
800-732-SBDC
Fax: 518-465-4992
E-mail: kingjl@cc.sunycentral.edu
www.smallbiz.suny.edu/
NYSBDC.HTM

North Carolina
North Carolina Small Business
Development Center
University of North Carolina
333 Fayetteville Street Mall,
#1150
Raleigh, NC 27601-1742
919-715-7272
800-2580-UNC
Fax: 919-715-7777
E-mail: sdaugherty@sbtdc.org
www.sbtdc.org

North Dakota
North Dakota Small Business
Development Center
University of North Dakota
College of Business & Public
Administration
118 Gamble Hall, UND
Box 7308
Grand Forks, ND 58202-7308
701-777-3700
800-445-7232
Fax: 701-777-3225
E-mail: kearns@prairie.nodak.edu
www.und.nodak.edu/dept/ndsbdc/
index.htm

Ohio

Ohio Small Business
Development Center
Department of Development
77 South High Street
28th Floor
Columbus, OH 43216-1001
614-466-2711
Fax: 614-466-0829
www.seorf.ohiou.edu/~xx02/

Oklahoma

Oklahoma Small Business
Development Center
Southeastern Oklahoma State
University
517 University
Station A, Box 2584
Durant, OK 74701
580-924-0277
800-522-6154
Fax: 580-920-7471
www.osbdc.org

Oregon

Oregon Small Business
Development Center
Lane Community College
44 West Broadway, Suite 501
Eugene, OR 97401-3021
541-726-2250
Fax: 541-345-6006
E-mail: cutlers@lanecc.edu
www.i2m.org/html

Pennsylvania

Pennsylvania Small Business
Development Center
University of Pennsylvania
The Wharton School
Vance Hall, 4th Floor
3733 Spruce Street
Philadelphia, PA 19104-6374

215-898-1219
Fax: 215-573-2135
E-mail: pasbdc@wharton.
upenn.edu
www.libertynet.org/pasbdc

Rhode Island

Bryant College
Small Business Development Ctr.
1150 Douglas Pike
Smithfield, RI 02197-1284
401-232-6111
Fax: 401-232-6933
E-mil: Admin@RISBDC.org
www.RISBDC.org

South Carolina

South Carolina Small Business
Development Center
University of South Carolina
College of Business
Administration
Hipp Building
1710 College Street
Columbia, SC 29208
803-777-4907
Fax: 803-777-4403
E-mail:lenti@darla.badm.sc.edu
http://sbdc.web.badmsc.edu

South Dakota

South Dakota Small Development
Center
University of South Dakota
School of Business
414 East Clark Street/
Patterson 115
Vermillion, SD 57069-2390
605-677-5287
Fax: 605-677-5427
E-mail: stracy@charlie.usd.edu
www.usd.edu/brbinfo/brb/sbdc/
index.htm

Tennessee
Tennessee Small Business
Development Center
University of Memphis
South Campus (Getwell Road)
Building #1
Memphis, TN 38152-0001
901-678-2500
Fax: 901-678-4072
E-mail:gmickle@cc.memphis.edu
www.tsbdc.memphis.edu

Texas
North Texas Small Business
Development Center
Dallas County Community
College
1402 Corinth Street
Dallas, TX 75215
214-860-5831
Fax: 214-860-5813
E-mail: daw1404@dcccd.edu
www.smbizsolutions.uh.edu

Utah
Small Business Development
Center
Salt Lake Community College
1623 South State Street
Salt Lake City, UT 84115
801-957-3480
Fax 801-957-3489
E-mail: FinnerMi@slcc.edu
www.slcc.edu/utahsbdc

Vermont
Vermont Small Business
Development Center
Vermont Technical College
Randolph Center, VT 05060
(Mailing Address: P.O. Box 422)
Randolph, VT 05060-0422
802-728-9101
800-464-SBDC

Fax: 802-728-3026
E-mail: dkelpins@vtc.vsc.edu
www.vtsbdc.org

Community Colleges

Virginia
Virginia Small Business
Development Center
Department of Economic
Development
901 East Byrd Street, Suite 1400
Richmond, VA 23219
804-371-8253
Fax: 804-225-3384
E-mail: rwilburn@dba.state.va.us
www.dba.state.va.us/SBDMain.
htm

Washington
Washington State Small Business
Development Center
Washington State University
College of Business and
Economics
501 Johnson Tower
P.O. Box 644851
Pullman, WA 99164-4851
509-335-1576
Fax: 509-335-0949
E-mail: riesenbe@wsu.edu
www.sbdc.wsu.edu/wsbdc.htm

West Virginia
West Virginia Small Business
Development Center
West Virginia Development
Office
950 Kanawha Boulevard
Charleston, WV 25301
304-558-2960

Free Local Consultants To Start or Grow Your Business

Fax: 304-558-0127
E-mail: palmeh@mail.wvnet.edu
www.state.wv.us/wvdev/sbdc/
sb_main.htm

Wisconsin
West Virginia Small Business
Development Center
West Virginia Development
Office
950 Kanawha Boulevard
Charleston, WV 25301
304-558-2960
Fax: 304-558-0127

E-mail: palmeh@mail.wvnet.edu
www.uwex.edu/sbdc

Wyoming
Wyoming Small Business
Development Center
University of Wyoming
P.O. Box 3922
Laramie, WY 82071-3922
307-766-3505
800-348-5194
Fax: 307-766-3406
E-mail: DDW@uwyo.edu
www.uwyo.edu/sbdc

Microenterprise Loans

A recent survey showed that
approximately 33% of the top 500 fastest
growing small businesses in the U.S.
started with less than $10,000. It doesn't
take much money to start a business in
today's information age and service
economy. We're no longer in the
manufacturing age, when you
needed a lot of money to start
a business because you needed
to buy an expensive plant and
costly equipment. Today, many businesses are started with
nothing more than a phone, a desk, and business cards.
Traditional government money programs required
entrepreneurs to ask for at least $50,000 to $100,000. Now
the government has set up Microenterprise Programs where
you can ask for just a little amount of money to make that big
change in your life.

A Growing Unknown Resource

These programs are continually growing. They seem so
successful that policy makers are finding new ways to help
them grow. But this growth and success seems to be causing
as many problems as the opportunities they are creating. On
one hand, the SBA programs recently increased the number
of banks that participate in its microloan program from 100 to
200 and also added a subcategory of lenders to include for
profit and nonprofit organizations. I read that programs like

the one at the U.S. Department of Housing and Urban Development fell short of quota by $1.5 billion because not enough people applied. This means that the poor bureaucrat administering the program couldn't give out all their money because not enough people applied. I even got a personal call from a local organization that had $50,000 of this money for someone to open up a bakery, and no one applied for it.

66% Chance of
Being a Microloan Winner

 Each year thousands of people will be getting microloans to start or expand their businesses. Although data is not available for every program, one of the major microloan lenders estimates that 66% of the people who apply for money, get it. Here are a few examples of recent recipients:

★ *$5,000* to Street Smart, Inc., a street-hockey equipment distributor in Southeastern Pennsylvania

★ *$25,000* to Med-Ex Medical Express, a courier service that specializes in the health care field

★ *$15,000* to Jeannette Saunders and Pamela Marshall of Sacramento, CA to start P&J Word Processing Service

Public Housing Entrepreneurs

Call yourself a handyman and get money to fix up your neighborhood. Money is set aside to give to public housing residents to modernize existing public housing projects. The money can also be used to provide residents with on-the-job training in construction and contractor related trades. It's called the Comprehensive Grant Program, and is available to Public Housing Agencies of 250 housing units or more, which includes 897 public housing agencies nationwide.

Contact your local Public Housing Authority for more information or you may contact U.S. Department of Housing and Urban Development, Deputy Director of Resident Initiatives, 451 Seventh Street, SW, Room 4112, Washington, DC 20410; 202-619-8201.

Money To Start A Business In A Small Town

The Intermediary Relending Program (IRP) is a rural development program administered by the Rural Business-Cooperative Service (RBS). The purpose is to provide loans for the establishment of new businesses, expansion of existing businesses, creation of new employment opportunities, saving of existing jobs, and funds to recipients for business facilities or community development projects in rural areas.

Loans are made to intermediaries who relend funds to recipients for business facilities or community development. You can borrow up to $150,000 with a maximum term of 30 years and an interest rate of one percent per annum.

Microenterprise Loans

For information, copies of regulations, and forms, contact any USDA, Rural Development State Office or write to the RBS National Office at USDA, Rural Business-Cooperative Service, 1400 Independence Avenue, SW, Room 5050 South Building, Washington, DC 20250; 202-720-1400.

Active/Approved IRP Loans

Alabama
Contact the USDA Rural
Development office closest to you

Alaska
Alaska Village Initiatives
1577 C Street #304
Anchorage, AK 99501
907-274-5400

Tanana Chiefs Conference
122 1st Avenue
Fairbanks, AK 99705
907-452-8251

Juneau Economic Development
Council
612 W. Willoughby Ave.
Suite A
Juneau, AK 99801-1732
907-463-3662

Arizona
Business Development Finance
Corporation (BDFC)
186 East Broadway Boulevard
Tucson, AZ 85701
520-722-5626

Northern Arizona Council of
Governments (NACOG)
119 East Aspen Avenue
Flagstaff, AZ 86001-5296
520-774-1895

PEEP Microbusiness
806 East 46th Street
Tucson, AZ 85713
520-622-3553

Arkansas
Arkansas Capital Relending
Corporation
225 South Pulaski Street
Little Rock, AR 72201
501-374-9247

Arkansas Development Finance
Authority
100 Main Street, Suite 200
Little Rock, AR 72201
501-682-5900

Arkansas Enterprise Group
708 Clinton Street, Suite 111
Arkadelphia, AR 71732
870-246-9739

Arkansas Land and Farm
Development Corporation
Rt. 2, Box 291
Brinkley, AR 72012
870-734-1140

Community Resource Group
38 West Trenton Boulevard
Fayetteville, AR 72701
501-443-2700
Fax: 501-443-5036

Delta Community Development
Corporation
335 West Broadway Street
Forrest City, AR 72335
870-633-9112

East Arkansas Planning and
Development District
P.O. Box 1403
Jonesboro, AR 72403
870-932-3957

Mississippi County AR Economic
Opportunity Commission
2513 Atlanta
Blytheville, AR 72315
870-532-2348

Southwest Arkansas Planning and
Development District
P.O. Box 767
Magnolia, AR 71753
870-234-4030

White River Planning and
Development District
P.O. Box 2396
Batesville, AR 72503
870-793-5233

California
Arcata Economic Development
Corporation
Aldergrove Industrial Park
100 Ericson Court, Suite 100
Arcarta, CA 95521
707-822-4616
Fax: 707-822-8982

CDC Small Business Finance
Corporation
1224 State Street, Suite C
El Centro, CA 92243

760-353-3095
Fax: 760-353-0305

California Capital Small Business
Development Corporation
926 J Street, Suite 1500
Sacramento, CA 95814
916-442-1729
Fax: 916-442-7852

Small Business Finance Corporation

California Coastal Rural
Development Corporation
221 Main Street, Suite 301
Salinas, CA 93901
831-424-1099
Fax: 831-424-1094
    Santa Cruz
    831-459-6095
    Fax: 831-459-6097

California Statewide Certified
Development Corporation
129 "C" Street
Davis, CA 95616
530-756-9310
Fax: 530-756-7519

Crown Economic Development
Corporation
1222 W. Lacey Blvd., Suite 101
Hanford, CA 93230
209-582-4326
209-582-7908

Del Norte Economic Development
Corporation
882 "H" Street

P.O. Box 728
Crescent City, CA 95531
707-464-2169
Fax: 707-464-3561

Lake County Business Outreach &
Response Team
4615 Work Right Circle, Suite B
Lakeport, CA 95453
707-262-1090
Fax: 707-262-1092

RURAL COMMUNITY
ASSISTANCE

Rural Community Assistance
Corporation
2125 19th Street, Suite 203
Sacramento, CA 95818
916-447-2854
Fax: 916-447-2878

SAFE-BIDCO
1626 Fourth Street
Santa Rosa, CA 95404
707-577-8621
Fax: 707-577-7348

Tri-Agency
P.O. Box 473
Crescent City, CA 95531
707-464-7288

Superior California EDD
737 Auditorium Drive, Suite A
Redding, CA 96001
530-225-2769

Tri-County Economic
Development Corporation

2540 Esplanade, Suite 7
Chico, CA 95973
530-893-8732
Fax: 530-893-0820

Valley Small Business
Development Corporation
3417 W. Shaw, Suite 100
Fresno, CA 93711
559-271-9030
Fax: 559-271-9078

Yuba-Sutter E.D.C.
422 Century Park Drive, Suite B
Yuba City, CA 95991
530-751-8555
Fax: 530-751-8515

Colorado
The Colorado Housing & Finance
Authority
1981 Blake Street
Denver, CO 80202
303-297-2432
800-877-CHFA
TDD: 303-297-7305

Mercy Housing, Inc.
601 East 18th Avenue #150
Denver, CO 80203
303-393-3908

Connecticut
Contact the USDA Rural
Development office closest to you

Delaware
Contact the USDA Rural
Development office closest to you

Florida
Jackson County Development
Council

P.O. Box 920
Moriama, FL 32447
850-526-4005

Community Equity Investments,
Inc.
302 North Barcelona Street
Pensacola, FL 32501
850-595-6234

Georgia
Central Savannah River Area
Rural Lending Authority, Inc.
2123 Wrightsboro Road
Augusta, GA 30914
706-737-1823

Coastal Area District
Development Authority
1313 New Castle Street, 2nd Floor
Brunswick, GA 31520
912-261-2500

Development Corporation of
Middle Georgia
600 Grand Building
651 Mulberry Street
Macon, GA 31201
912-751-6160

Georgia Mountains Regional
Economic Development
Corporation
1010 Ridge Road
Gainesville, GA 30501
404-536-3431

Middle Flint Area Development
Corporation
228 West Lamar
Americus, GA 31709
912-931-2909

South Georgia Area Resource
Development Agency, Inc.
327 West Savannah Avenue
Valdosta, GA 31601
912-333-5277

Fort Valley State University
Foundation
Rural Business Outreach Institute
10005 State University Drive
Fort Valley, GA 31030
912-825-6060

Hawaii
Lokahi Pacific
1935 Main Street, Suite 204
Wailuku, HI 96793
808-242-5761
Fax: 808-244-2057

Molokai Ranch Foundation
55 Merchant Street, Suite 2000
Honolulu, HI 96813
808-531-0158
Fax: 808-531-2279

Planning and Development

Idaho
Panhandle Area Council
Planning & Development
Association
11100 Airport Drive
10624 W. Executive Drive
Hayden Lake, ID 83835
Boise, ID 83713
208-772-0584
208-322-7033

East Central Idaho Planning and
Development
Southeast Idaho Council of
Governments
P.O. Box 330
310 N 2nd East
Rexburg, ID 83440
208-356-4524

P.O. Box 6079
Pocatello, ID 83205-6079
208-233-4032

Clearwater Economic
Development Association
1626 6th Avenue, North
Lewiston, ID 83501
208-746-0015

Illinois
South Central Illinois Regional
Planning and Development
Commission
120 Delmar Avenue, Suite A
Salem, IL 62881-2006
618-548-4234

City of Olney
300 South Whittle Avenue
Olney, IL 62450
618-395-7302

City of Flora
P.O. Box 249
151 North Sycamore Street
Flora, IL 62838
618-662-8313

Illinois Development Finance
Authority
150 Pleasant Hill Road
Box 46

Carbondale, IL 62901
618-453-5566

Indiana
City of Tell City
P.O. Box 515
City Hall Building
Tell City, IN 46586
812-547-5511

Iowa
Dubuque County
720 Central Avenue
Dubuque, IA 52001
319-589-4441

Albia Industrial Development
Corporation
6 South Main
Albia, IA 52531
515-932-7053

Upper Explore Land Regional
Planning Commission
134 West Green Street
P.O. Box 219
Postville, IA 52162
319-864-7551

Butler County Rural Electric
Cooperative
428 6th Street
Allison, IA 50602
319-267-2858

Cherokee Area Economic
Development Association
418 West Cedar Street
Cherokee, IA 51012-1340
712-225-5739

Humbolt County Development
Association

Courthouse Box 100
Dakota City, IA 50529-0100
515-332-5205

Newton Development Corporation
113 First Avenue West
Newton, IA 50208
800-792-1737

Wright County
P.O. Box 214
Clarion, IA 50525
515-532-6422

Sheldon Community Development
Corporation
P.O. Box 276
Sheldon, IA 51201
712-324-2813

Kansas
South Central Kansas Economic
Development District (SCKEDD)
151 North Volutsia
Wichita, KS 67214
316-683-4422

Great Plains Development Inc.
(GPDI)
100 Military Plaza
Dodge City, KS 67801
316-227-6406

Kentucky
Appalachian Investment
Corporation
431 Chestnut Street, Suite 7
Berea, KY 40403
606-986-2375

Buffalo Trace Area Development
District
327 West 2nd Street

P.O. Box 460
Maysville, KY 41056
606-564-6894

Barren River Area Development
District
177 Graham Avenue
P.O. Box 90005
Bowling Green, KY 42102-9005
502-781-2381
Fax: 502-842-0768

Harlan Revitalization Association,
Inc.
P.O. Box 1709
Harlan, KY 40831
606-573-7698

Kentucky Highlands Investment
Corporation
400 South Main Street
London, KY 47476
606-864-5175

Pennyrile Area Development
District
300 Hammond Drive
Hopkinsville, KY 42240
502-886-9484
Fax: 502-886-3211

Purchase Area Development
District
1002 Medical Drive
P.O. Box 588
Maysfield, KY 4206
502-247-7171
Fax: 502-247-9000

Louisiana
Evangeline Economic & Planning
District
P.O. Box 90070

Lafayette, LA 70509
318-233-3215

Coordinating & Development
Corporation
P.O. Box 37005
Shreveport, LA 71133-7005
318-632-2022

Dixie Electric Membership
Corporation
16262 Wax Road
Greenwell Springs, LA 70739
504-261-1221

Kisatchie-Delta Regional Planning
& Development
P.O. Box 12248
Alexandria, LA 71315-2248
318-487-5454

Macon Ridge Economic
Development Region
P.O. Drawer 746
Ferriday, LA 71334-0746
318-757-3033

Minden/South Webster Chamber
of Commerce
P.O. Box 819
Minden, LA 71058
318-377-4240

North Delta Regional Planning &
Development District
2115 Justice Street
Monroe, LA 71201
318-387-2572

Northeast Louisiana Delta
Community Development Center
P.O. Box 1149
Tallulah, LA 71282
318-574-0995

University Community
Development Corporation
7990 Scenic Highway
Baton Rouge, LA 70807
504-775-8146

Maine
Northern Maine Development
Commission
P.O. Box 779
Caribou, ME 04736
207-427-8736
800-427-8736
Fax: 207-493-3108

Growth Finance Corporation of
Oxford Hills
166 Main Street
South Paris, ME 04281
207-743-8830
Fax: 207-743-5917

Androscoggin Valley Council of
Governments
125 Manley Road
Auburn, ME 04210
207-783-9186
Fax: 207-783-5211

Lewiston-Auburn Economic
Growth Council

P.O. Box 1188
Lewiston, ME 04243-1188
207-784-0161
Fax: 207-786-4412

Finance Authority of Maine
P.O. Box 949
Augusta, ME 04333-0949
207-623-3263
Fax: 207-623-0095

Caribou Development
60 Sweden Street
Caribou, ME 04736-2320
207-493-4233
800-477-1082
Fax: 207-492-1362

Eastern Maine Development
Corporation
P.O. Box 2579
Bangor, ME 04402-2579
207-942-6389
Fax: 207-942-3548

Kennebec Valley Council of
Governments
17 Main Street
Fairfield, ME 04937-1119
207-453-4258
Fax: 207-453-4264

Beddeford-Saco Development
Corporation
110 Main Street
Suite 1202
Saco, ME 04072
207-282-1748
Fax: 207-282-3149

Coastal Enterprises, Inc.
P.O. Box 268
Wiscasset, ME 04578-0268

207-882-7552
Fax: 207-882-7308

Town of Lisbon
P.O. Box 8
Lisbon, ME 04525
207-353-3007

Massachusetts
Franklin County Community
Development Corporation
324 Wells Street
Greenfield, MA 01301
413-774-7404

Cape & Islands Community
Development, Inc.
480 Barnstable Road
Hyannis, MA 02601

Michigan
Cornerstone Alliance
38 West Wall Street
P.O. Box 428
Benton Harbor, MI 49203
616-925-6100

Coastal
Enterprises

First Rural Relending Co.
130 South Cedar Street
Manistique, MI 49854
906-753-2225

Fivecap, Inc.
302 North Main Street
Scottville, MI 49454
616-757-3785

Great Lakes Energy Cooperative
P.O. Box 70
Boyne City, MI 49712-0070
800-748-0121
616-582-6521

Community Development

Marquette County
417 A. Avenue
Gwinn, MI 498413
906-346-3137

Muskegon Heights
City of EDC
3635 South Carr Road
Fruitport, MI 49415
616-788-3700

Northern Initiatives Corporation
228 West Washington
Marquette, MI 49855
906-228-5571

Northern MI Foundation
P.O. Box 1569
Acme, MI 49610
616-938-4409
800-652-4326

Rural MI IRP Co.
121 E. Front St., Suite 201
Traverse City, MI 49783
616-941-5858

Minnesota
Benton County
531 Dewey Street
Foley, MN 56239
320-968-6254
Fax: 320-968-7626

Blooming Prairie EDA
City Hall
P.O. Box 68
Bloooming Prairie, MN 55911
507-583-7573
Fax: 507-583-4520

Caledonia Economic Development
Authority
231 East Main Street
P.O. Box 68
Caledonia, MN 55921
507-724-3632

Initiative Foundation
700 SSE First Avenue
Little Falls, MN 56345
320-632-9255
Fax: 320-632-9258

Community Development of
Morrison City, Inc.
107 SE 2nd Street
P.O. Box 356
Little Falls, MN 56345
320-632-5466

City of Crookston
124 North Broadway
Crookston, MN 56716
218-281-4503
Fax: 218-281-5609

Detroit Lakes Development
Authority
1025 Roosevelt Avenue
Detroit Lakes, MN 56501
218-847-5658

Development Corporation of
Austin (DCA)
1900 8th Avenue, NW
Austin, MN 55912
507-433-0345

East Central Regional
Development Commission
100 Park Street
Mora, MN 55051
320-679-4065
Fax: 320-679-4120

City of East Grand Forks
P.O. Box 373
East Grand Forks, MN 56721
218-773-8939

City of Fergus Falls
112 West Washington
P.O. Box 868
Fergus Falls, MN 56538-0868
218-739-2251

City of Fosston
220 East First Street
Fosston, MN 56542
218-435-1377
Fax: 218-435-1961

Housing & Redevelopment
Authority In and For the
City of Willmar
333 SW 6th Street
Willmar, MN 56201
320-235-8637

Lakefield Economic Development
Authority
City Hall
P.O. Box 900
Lakefield, MN 56150
507-662-5457
Fax: 507-662-5990

City of McIntosh
115 Broadway NW
McIntosh, MN 56553
218-563-3043
Fax: 218-563-3042

Meeker County Development
Corporation
325 North Sibley Avenue
Litchfield, MN 55355
320-693-5272
Fax: 320-693-5444

**NORTHWEST
MINNESOTA
FOUNDATION**

Midwest Minnesota Community
Development Corporation
P.O. Box 623
Washington Square Mall
Detroit Lakes, MN 56501-0623
218-847-3191
Fax: 218-847-3192

Minnesota's Community
Development Corporation
P.O. Box 509
Park Rapids, MN 56570
218-732-3677
Fax: 218-732-8985

Northland Foundation
610 Sellwood Building
202 West Superior Street
Duluth, MN 55802
218-723-4040

Northwest Minnesota Foundation
4225 Technology Drive NW
Bemidji, MN 56601
218-759-5057
Fax: 218-759-2328

City of Perham
125 Second Avenue NE
P.O. Box 130

Perham, MN 56573
218-346-9798
Fax: 218-346-9364

Prairieland Economic
Development Corporation
2401 Broadway Avenue, Suite 3
Slayton, MN 56172-1142
507-836-6656
Fax 507-836-8866

Red Lake Falls Development
Corporation
201 Second Street
P.O. Box 280
Red Lakes Falls, MN 56750
218-253-2143

Economic
Improvement

Red Wing Port Authority
433 West Third Street
Red Wing, MN 55066
612-388-4781

The Initiative Fund
540 West Hills Circle
P.O. Box 570
Owatonna, MN 55060
507-455-3215
Fax: 507-455-2098

Southwest Minnesota Foundation
P.O. Box 428
Hutchinson, MN 55355
320-587-4848
Fax: 320-587-3838

Stevens County Economic
Improvement Commission

507 Oregon Avenue
Morris, MN 56267
320-589-2609
Fax: 320-589-4814

West Central Minnesota Initiative
Fund
220 West Washington Ave.
Suite 205
Ferrous Falls, MN 56537
218-739-2239
Fax: 218-739-5381

Wheaton Economic Development
Authority
104 Ninth Street North
P.O. Box 868
Wheaton, MN 56296
320-563-4110

Mississippi
Northeast MS Planning &
Development District
P.O. Box 600
Booneville, MS 38829
601-728-6248

South Delta Planning &
Development District
P.O. Box 1776
Greenville, MS 38702
601-378-3831

Southwest MS Planning &
Development District
110 South Wall Street
Natchez, MS 39120
601-446-6044

Three Rivers Planning &
Development District
75 South Main
P.O. Drawer B

Pontotoc, MS 38863
601-489-2415

Missouri
Rural Missouri, Inc.
1014 Northeast Drive
Jefferson City, MO 65109
573-635-0136

Green Hills Rural Development,
Inc.
900 Main Street
Trenton, MO 64683
660-359-5086
N.W. Development Corporation
P.O. Box 565
Camron, MO 64429
816-632-2121

North Central Missouri Rural
Housing Development Corp.
P.O. Box 220
Mylan, MO 63556
660-265-4404

Knox County Community
Development Corporation
104 East Jackson Street
Edina, MO 63537-1335
816-397-2509

Montana
Bear Paw Development
Corporation
P.O. Box 1549
Harve, MT 59501
406-265-9226

Nebraska
Nebraska Economic Development
Corporation (NEDCO)
2631 "O" Street
Lincoln, NE 68510
402-475-2795

Southeast Nebraska Development
District (SENDD)
2631 "O" Street
Lincoln, NE 68510
402-475-2560

West Central Nebraska
Development District (WCNDD)
P.O. Box 599
Ogallala, NE 69153
308-284-6077

Nevada
Rural Nevada Development
Corporation (RNDC)
740 Park Avenue
Ely, NV 89301

New Hampshire
Belknap County Economic
Development Council
64 Court Street
Laconia, NH 03246
603-524-3057

Bear Paw
Development
Corporation

New Jersey
South Jersey Economic
Development District
18 N. East Avenue
Vineland, NJ 08360
856-794-8497

New Mexico
New Mexico Community
Development Loan Fund
700 4th Street SW
Albuquerque, NM 87102

505-243-3196
505-243-8803

New York
Adirondack Economic
Development Corporation
Trudeau Road
Saranac Lake, NY 12983
518-891-5523
Fax: 518-891-9820

COMCO Development
Corporation
572 S. Salina Street
Syracuse, NY 13202
315-470-1888

**Regional
Development
Corporation**

Lake Champlain-Lake George
Regional Development
Corporation
Amherst Street
Lake George, NY 12845
518-668-5773

Herkimer County Industrial
Development Agency
P.O. Box 390
4301 North Washington St.
Room 434
Herkimer, NY
315-867-1373

New York Job Development
Authority
605 3rd Avenue, 26th Floor
New York, NY 10158
518-474-7580

North Country Alliance Local
Development Corporation
317 Washington Street
Watertown, NY 13601
315-785-2593

REDEC Relending Corporation
145 Village Square
Painted Post, NY 14807
604-962-3021

Rural Opportunities, Inc.
400 East Avenue
Rochester, NY 14607
716-546-7180

Southern Tier Enterprise
Development Organization
465 Broad Street
Salamanca, NY 14779
716-945-5301

Tioga County Local Development
Corporation
County Building
56 Main Street
Owego, NY 13827
607-687-8255

Washington County Local
Development Corporation
Washington County Municipal
Center
383 Broadway
Fort Edward, NY 12828
518-746-2292

North Carolina
Dunn Area Committee of 100, Inc.
600 South Magnolia Avenue
Dunn, NC 28334
910-892-2884

Self Help Ventures Fund
301 West Main Street
Durham, NC 27701
919-956-4400

North Dakota
Lake Agassiz Regional
Development Corporation
417 Main Avenue
Fargo, ND 58018
701-239-5373

Lewis & Clark Regional
Development Council
400 E. Broadway Ave., Suite 418
Bismarck, ND 58501
701-255-4591

Roosevelt Custer Regional
Council
Pulver Hall
Dickinson, ND 58601
701-277-1241

Ohio
Ashtabula County 503
Corporation
36 West Walnut Street
Jefferson, OH 44047
216-576-3759

Enterprise Development
Corporation
900 East State Street
Suite 101
Athens, OH 45701
614-592-1188

Mahoning Valley Economic
Development Corporation
4319 Belmont Avenue
Youngstown, OH 44505
330-759-3668

Portage Area Development
Corporation
231 West Main Street
Ravenn, OH 44266
330-297-6400

Oklahoma
Central Oklahoma Economic
Development District
400 North Bell
P.O. Box 3398
Shawnee, OK 74802-3398
405-273-6410

Little Dixie
Community
Action

Little Dixie Community Action
Agency, Inc.
502 West Duke Street
Hugo, OK 74743
580-326-3351

Logan County Economic
Development Council
P.O. Box 995
Guthrie, OK 73044
405-282-0060

Miami Area Economic
Development Service
2 North Main, Suite 601
Miami, OK 74354
918-542-7751

Ozarks Corporation for Innovation
Development, Inc.
P.O. Box 1335
Durant, OK 74702-1335
580-924-5094

People's Electric Cooperative
1130 West Main Street
P.O. Box 429
Ada, OK 74820
580-332-3031

Rural Enterprises, Inc.
P.O. Box 1335
Durant, OK 74702
580-924-5094

South Western Oklahoma
Development Authority
P.O. Box 569
Fourth & Sooner Drive
Building 420
Burns Flat, OK 73624
580-562-4882

Cherokee Hills RC&D
1007 South Muskogee Avenue
Tahlequah, OK 74464-4733
918-456-2304

Choctaw Nation
Drawer 1210
16th and Locust
Durant, OK 74702-1210
580-924-8280

Adair County Indian Credit
Association
P.O. Box 602
Stilwell, OK 74960
918-696-3803

Cherokee Nation
P.O. Box 948
Tahlequah, OK 74465-0948
918-456-0671, ext. 2532

Oregon
Valley Development Initiatives
C/O Mid-Willamette Valley
Council of Governments
105 High Street, SE
Salem, OR 97301
503-588-6177

Oregon Cascades West Council of
Governments
P.O. Box 686
Albany, OR 97321
541-967-8551

Morrow Development Corporation
C/O Port of Morrow
P.O. Box 200
Boardman, OR 97818
541-481-7678

Curry Economic Development
Corporation
P.O. Box 848
Brookings, OR 97415
541-469-2218

Port of Bandon Economic
Development Fund
P.O. Box 1950
Bandon, OR 97411
541-347-9105

Central Oregon Intergovernmental
Council
2363 SW Glacier Place
Redmond, OR 97756
541-548-8163

Information USA, Inc.

CCD Business Development
Corporation
744 SE Rose Street
Roseburg, OR 97470
541-672-6728

**Council on
Economic
Development**

Southern Oregon Regional
Economic Development, Inc.
332 West Sixth Street
Medford, OR 97501-2711
541-773-8946

Greater Eastern Oregon
Development Corporation
P.O. Box 1041
Pendleton, OR 97801
541-276-6745

Lane Council of Governments
125 East 8th Avenue
Eugene, OR 97401
541-682-7450

Northeast Oregon Business
Development
101 NE First Street, Suite 100
Enterprise, OR 97828
541-426-3598

Columbia Pacific Economic
Development District of Oregon,
Inc.
P.O. Box 598
St. Helens, OR 97051
503-397-2888

Mid-Columbia Economic
Development District
400 East Scenic Drive, Suite 2420
The Kalles, OR 97058
541-296-6182 ext. 3208

Ida-Ore Planning & Development
Association
10624 West Executive Drive
Boise, ID 83713
208-322-7033

Shorebank Enterprise Group
P.O. Box 826
Ilwaco, WA 98624
360-642-4265

Pennsylvania
Northwest Pennsylvania Regional
Planning & Development
Commission
Biery Building, Suite 406
Franklin, PA 16323
814-437-3024
Fax: 814-432-3002

Northern Tier Regional Planning
Commission
507 Main Street
Towanda, PA 18848-9987
717-265-9103
Fax: 717-265-7585

SEDA-Council of Governments
R.R. 1, Box 372
Lewisburg, PA 17837
570-524-4491
Fax: 570-524-9190

Washington County Council on
Economic Development
100 West Beau Street, Suite #703
Courthouse Square

Washington, PA 15301
724-228-6949
Fax: 724-250-6502

Southern Alleghenies Planning
and Development Commission
541 58th Street
Altoona, PA 16602-1193
814-949-6500

North Central Pennsylvania
Regional Planning and
Development Commission
P.O. Box 488
Ridgway, PA 15853
814-772-6901

Economic Development Council
of North East Pennsylvania
1151 Oak Street
Pittston, PA 18640-3795
717-655-5581

Jefferson County Development
Council, Inc.
R.D. 5, Box 47
Brookville, PA 15825
814-849-3047

Rhode Island
None

South Carolina
Carolina Capital Investments
Corporation
1201 Main Street, Suite 1750
Columbia, SC 29201
803-737-0101

Catawba Regional Development
Corporation
P.O. Box 450
215 Hampton Street

Rock Hill, SC 29731
803-327-9044

Lake City Development
Corporation
P.O. Box 1329
202 Kelley Street
Lake City, SC 29560
843-394-5421, ext. 276

Lower Savannah Regional
Development Corporation
P.O. Box 850
2748 Wagener Road
Aiken, SC 29802
803-649-7981

Santee-Lynches Regional
Development Corporation
P.O. Drawer 1837
36 West Liberty Street
Sumter, SC 29151
803-775-7381

Williamsburg Enterprise
Community Commission, Inc.
P.O. Box 428
Kingstree, SC 29556
843-354-9070

South Dakota
Beadle and Spink Enterprise
Community
P.O. Box 68
Yale, SD 57386
605-599-2991
Fax: 605-599-2992

First District Development
Company
124 First Avenue NW
P.O. Box 1207
Watertown, SD 57201

605-886-7224
Fax: 605-882-5049

Grant County Development
Corporation
707 South 5th Street
Milbank, SD 57252
605-432-6851
Fax: 605-432-6258

Greater Huron Development
Corporation
375 Dakota Avenue South
Huron, SD 57350
605-352-0363
Fax: 605-352-9327

Northeast Council of
Governments
P.O. Box 1985
Aberdeen, SD 57402-1985
605-626-2595
Fax: 605-626-2975

Northeast South Dakota Economic
Corporation
414 3rd Avenue East
Sisseton, SD 57262
605-698-7654
Fax: 605-698-3038

Rural Electric Economic
Development, Inc.
121 SE 1st Street
P.O. Drawer E
Madison, SD 57042
605-256-4536
Fax: 605-256-8058

South Dakota Economic
Development Finance Authority
Governor's Office of Economic
Development

711 East Wells Avenue
Pierre, SD 57501-3369
605-773-5032
Fax: 605-773-3256

West River Foundation
P.O. Box 218
2885 Dickson Avenue
Sturgis, SD 57785
605-347-5837
Fax: 605-347-5223

Tennessee

Areawide Development
Corporation
5616 Kingston Pike
Knoxville, TN 37939-2806
423-588-7972

Caney Fork Electric Cooperative,
Inc.
920 Smithville Highway
P.O. Box 272
McMinnville, TN 37110

Cumberland Area Investment
Corporation
1225 South Willow Avenue
Cookeville, TN 38506-4194
931-432-4050

East Tennessee Enterprise
Partnership, Incorporated
P.O. Box 186
Carson Drive
Huntsville, TN 37756
423-663-2910

First Tennessee Economic
Development Corporation
207 North Bone Street, Suite 800
Johnson City, TN 37604-5699
423-928-0224

Mid-Cumberland Area
Development Corporation
501 Union Street, 6th Floor
Nashville, TN 37219-1705
615-862-8828

Northwest Tennessee Certified
Development Corporation
124 Weldon Drive
P.O. Box 963
Martin, TN 38237
901-587-4213

Seouachee Valley Electric
Cooperative
512 Cedar Avenue
South Pittsburg, TN 37380
423-837-8605

South Central Tennessee
Development District
815 South Main Street
Columbia, TN 38402-1346
615-381-2040

Southeast Local Development
Corporation
25 Cherokee Boulevard
Chattanooga, TN 37405
423-266-5781

Southwest Tennessee
Development District
27 Conrad Drive, Suite 150
Jackson, TN 38305
901-668-7112

Texas
Brownwood Industrial Foundation
P.O. Box 880
Brownwood, TX 76804
915-646-9535

Utah
Utah Technology Finance
Corporation
177 East 100 South
Salt Lake City, UT 84111
801-741-4200

Deseret Certified Development
Company
7050 Union Park Center
Suite 570
Midvale, UT 84047
801-566-1163
or
Central Utah Office at Evergreen
Square
907 South Orem Boulevard
Orem, UT
801-221-7772

Vermont
Addison County Economic
Development Corporation
RD4, Box 1309 A
Middlebury, VT 05753
802-388-7953

Connecticut River Valley
P.O. Box 246
White River Jct., VT 05001-0246
802-295-3710

Franklin County Industrial
2 North Main Street
St. Albans, VT 05478-1099
802-524-2194

Lamoille Economic Development
Corporation
P.O. Box 455
Morrisville, VT 05661
802-888-5640

Northern Community Investment
Corporation
20 Main Street
P.O. Box 904
St. Johnsbury, VT 05819
802-748-5101

Northeastern Vermont
Development Association
44 Main Street
P.O. Box 640
St. Johnsbury, VT 05819
802-748-5181

Rutland Economic Development
Corporation
256 North Main Street
Rutland, VT 05701
802-773-9147

Vermont 503 Corporation
56 East State Street
Montpelier, VT 05602
802-828-5474

Vermont Community Enterprise
Fund Inc.
7 Court Street
P.O. Box 827
Montpelier, VT 05602
802-223-1448

Vermont Small Business
Development Corporation
56 East State Street
Montpelier, VT 05602
802-828-5466

Virginia
Southeast Rural Community
Assistance Project Incorporated
P.O. Box 2868
Rolling Oak, VA 24001-2868
540-345-1184

Lake County Development
Corporation
P.O. Box 150
South Hill, VA 23970
804-447-7101

Mount Rogers Planning District
Commission
1021 Terrace Drive
Marion, VA 24354
540-783-5103

Hampton University Rural
Business Assistance Center
11916 Rolfe Highway
Furry, VA 23887
757-294-5176

Virginia Eastern Shore Economic
Development and Housing
Corporation
P.O. Box 814
Nassawadox, VA 23413

Washington
TRICO Economic Development
347 West Second, Suite A
Colville, WA 99114
509-684-8411

509-684-4571
Fax: 509-684-4788

Okanogan County Investment
Association
P.O. Box 741
Okanogan, WA 98840
509-826-5107

Columbia Regional Economic
Development Trust
P.O. Box 217
Richland, WA 99352
509-943-9187

Lending Network
P.O. Box 916
Chenghalis, WA 98532
360-748-0114
Fax: 360-748-1235

Cascadia Revolving Fund
119 First Ave. South
Suite 1000
Seattle, WA 98104
206-447-9226
Fax: 206-682-4804

Private Industry Council of
Snohomish County (PIC)
728-134th Street SW
Building A, Suite 211
Everett, WA 98204
425-743-9669
425-353-2025
TDD: 425-743-9669
Fax: 425-742-1177

Evergreen Community
Development Association
900 Fourth Avenue, Suite 2900
Seattle, WA 98164
800-878-6613

Shorebank Trading Group
P.O. Box 826
Ilwaco, WA 98624

West Virginia
The McDowell County Action
Network
P.O. Box 158
Wilcoe, WV 24895
304-448-2118

Mid-Ohio Valley Regional P&D
Council
P.O. Box 247
Parkersburg, WV 26102
304-422-4993

Mountain CAP of West Virginia,
Inc.
26 North Kanawha Street
Buckhannon, WV 26102
304-472-1500

West Virginia Economic &
Development Authority
Suite 501
1018 Kanawha Boulevard East
Charleston, WV 25301-2827
304-558-3650

Wisconsin
Northwest Wisconsin Business
Development Corporation
1400 S. River Street
Spooner WI 54801
715-635-2197

North Central Wisconsin
Development Corporation
407 Grant Street
Wausau, WI 54403
715-845-4208

Adams-Columbia Electric
Cooperative
401 E. Lake Street
P.O. Box 70
Friendship, WI 54934-0700
608-339-6945

Impact Acceptance Corporation
651 Garfield Street

Almena, WI 54805
705-357-3334

Wyoming
Frontier Certified Development
Company
232 East 2nd Street, Suite 300
Casper, WY 82601
307-234-5351

Rural Business Enterprise Grants

The Rural Business Enterprise Grant Program (RBEG) is administered by the Rural Business-Cooperative Service (RBS), and provides grant funds to a local or regional intermediary which, in turn, lends funds in a flexible manner to local businesses. Funds are designed to facilitate the development of small and emerging private business, industry, and related employment.

Money can be used for the acquisition and development of land, and the construction of buildings, plants, equipment, access streets and roads, parking areas, utility and service extensions, refinancing, fees, technical assistance, startup operating cost, working capital, providing financial assistance to a third party, production of television programs to provide information to rural residents; and to create, expand, and operate rural distance learning networks. Grant applications are available from any USDA Rural Development State Office.

For more information, contact the U.S. Department of Agriculture, Rural Business-Cooperative Service, 1400 Independence Avenue, SW, Room 5050 South Building, Washington, DC 20250; 202-720-1400.

U.S. Department Of Agriculture
Rural Development State Offices

Alabama
USDA Rural Development
Horace Horn
4121 Carmichael Road
Sterling Center, Suite 601
Montgomery, AL 36106-3683
334-279-3400
Fax: 334-279-3484

Alaska
USDA Rural Development
Dean R. Stewart
800 West Evergreen, Suite 201
Palmer, AK 99645
907-745-2176
Fax: 907-745-5398

Arizona
USDA Rural Development
Leonard Gradillas
3003 N. Central Ave., Suite 900
Phoenix, AZ 85012
602-280-8745
Fax: 602-280-8730

Arkansas
USDA Rural Development
Shirley Tucker
Federal Building, Room 346
700 Capitol Avenue
Little Rock, AR 72201
501-324-6284
Fax: 501-324-6346

California
USDA Rural Development
Charles Clendenin
430 G Street, Agency 4169
Davis, CA 95616
530-792-5800

Colorado
USDA Rural Development
Leroy W. Cruz
655 Parfet Street, Room E100
Lakewood, CO 80215
303-236-2801, ext. 131
Fax: 303-236-2854

Delaware/Maryland
USDA Rural Development
James E. Waters
5201 South DuPont Highway
P.O. Box 400
Camden, DE 19934
302-697-4324
TTY: 302-697-4303
Fax: 302-697-4388

Florida
USDA Rural Development
Joseph M. Mueller
4440 NW 25th Place
Gainesville, FL 32614-7010
352-338-3482
Fax: 352-338-3450

Georgia
USDA Rural Development
Howard W. Franklin
Federal Building
Athens, GA 30601
706-546-2154
Fax: 706-546-2135

Hawaii
USDA Rural Development
Joe Diego
Room 311, Federal Building
154 Waianuenue Avenue
Hilo, HI 96720
808-933-3019

Fax: 808-933-6901
TDD: 808-933-6902

Idaho
USDA Rural Development
Daryl G. Moser
9173 West Barnes Street, Suite A1
Boise, ID 83709
208-378-5623
Fax: 208-378-5643

Illinois
USDA Rural Development
Gerald Townsend
Illini Plaza, Suite 103
1817 South Neil Street
Champaign, IL 61820
217-398-5412 ext. 243
Fax: 217-398-5337

Indiana
USDA Rural Development
Joseph Steele
5975 Lakeside Boulevard
Indianapolis, IN 46278
317-290-3100
Fax: 317-290-3127

Iowa
USDA Rural Development
Randy Frescoln
210 Walnut Street, Room 873
Des Moines, IA 50309
515-284-4663
Fax: 515-284-4821

Kansas
USDA Rural Development
Donnis Williams
1200 SW Executive Drive
Box 4653
Topeka, KS 66604
785-271-2732

Kentucky
USDA Rural Development
Vernon Brown
771 Corporate Drive, Suite 200
Lexington, KY 40503
606-224-7336
Fax: 606-224-7344

Louisiana
USDA Rural Development
Judy Meche
3727 Government Street
Alexandria, LA 71302
318-473-7920
TYY/TDD: 318-473-7655/7697
Fax: 318-473-7920

RURAL DEVELOPMENT

Maine
USDA Rural Development
Dean Churchill or Michael Rollins
444 Stillwater Avenue, Suite 2
P.O. Box 405
Bangor, ME 04402-0405
207-990-9168

Massachusetts/Connecticut/ Rhode Island
USDA Rural Development
Daniel R. Beaudette
451 West Street
Amherst, MA 01002-2999
413-253-4340

Michigan
USDA Rural Development
Mae Locke
3001 Coolidge Road, Suite 200

East Lansing, MI 48823
517-324-5100
TDD: 517-337-6906
Fax: 517-324-5225

Minnesota
USDA Rural Development
Agribank Building
375 Jackson Street
St.Paul, MN 55101
651-602-7800
Fax: 651-602-7824

Mississippi
USDA Rural Development
Hershel F. Johnson
Suite 831, Federal Building
100 West Capital SF
Jackson, MS 39269
601-965-5460

Missouri
USDA Rural Development
Clark Thomas
601 Business Loop 70 West
Park Aid Center, Suite 225
Columbia, MO 65203
573-876-0925

Montana
USDA Rural Development
John D. Guthmiller
P.O. Box 850
Bozeman, MT 59771
406-585-2505
TDD: 406-585-0819
Fax: 406-585-2565

Nebraska
USDA Rural Development
Deborah D. Drbal
Room 152 Federal Building
100 Centennial Mall North

Lincoln, NE 68508
402-437-5558

Nevada
USDA Rural Development
Larry J. Smith
1390 South Curry Street
Carson City, NV 89703
775-887-1222 ext. 25
Fax: 775-887-1287

New Hampshire
USDA Rural Development
Rob McCarthy
10 Ferry St., Suite 218, Box 321
Concord, NH 03301
603-223-6037
602-223-6041

New Jersey
USDA Rural Development
Michael P. Kelsey
790 Woodlane Road
Mt. Holly, NJ 08060
609-265-3641
Fax: 609-265-3651
TDD: 609-265-3687

New Mexico
USDA Rural Development
Mike McDow
700 4th Street SW
Albuquerque, NM 87102
505-243-3196
505-243-8803

New York
USDA Rural Development
Lowell Gibson
The Galleries of Syracuse
441 South Salina Street
Suite 357, 5th Floor
Syracuse, NY 13202-2541

315-477-6425
Fax: 315-477-6448

North Carolina
USDA Rural Development
Dennis DeLong
4405 Bland Road, Suite 260
Raleigh, NC 27609
919-873-2046

North Dakota
USDA Rural Development
220 East Rosser Avenue
Bismarck, ND 58501
701-250-4791

Ohio
USDA Rural Development
Jennifer Sonnenberg
200 North High Street, Room 507
Columbus, OH 43215
614-469-5400

Oklahoma
USDA Rural Development
Susan Estes
100 USDA, Suite 108
Stillwater, OK 74074
405-742-1036
TTY/TDD: 405-742-1007
Fax: 405-742-1005

Oregon
USDA Rural Development
101 SW Main, Suite 1410
Portland, OR 97204-3222
503-414-3366
Fax: 503-414-3398

Pennsylvania
Eastern Pennsylvania
USDA Rural Development
R.D. #3 Box 27 F

Montrose, PA 18801-9548
570-278-3781 ext. 112

Western Pennsylvania
USDA Rural Development
P.O. Box 329
Meadowlands, PA 15347-0329
724-222-3060 ext. 112

South Carolina
USDA Rural Development
Strom Thurmond Federal Building
1835 Assembly St., Room 1007
Columbia, SC 29201
803-253-3651
Fax: 803-765-5910

South Dakota
USDA Rural Development
Robert R. Bothwell
200 4th Street SW
Federal Building, Room 210
Huron, SD 57350
605-352-1142

TEChNicAl AssisTANCE

Tennessee
USDA Rural Development
Lee Loveless
3322 West End Ave., Suite 300
Nashville, TN 37203
615-783-1341
800-342-3149
Fax: 615-783-1301

Texas
USDA Rural Development
Pat Liles

101 S. Main, Suite 102
Temple, TX 76501
254-742-9780

Utah
USDA Rural Development
Bonnie Carrig
125 State, Room 4431
P.O. Box 11350
Salt Lake City, UT 84147
801-524-4330

Vermont
USDA Rural Development
David Robinson
89 Main Street, 3rd Floor
City Center
Montpelier, VT 05602
802-828-6030

Virginia
USDA Rural Development
Culpeper Building
Suite 238, 1606 Santa Rosa Road
Richmond, VA 23229-5014
804-287-1557

Washington
USDA Rural Development
Jackie Gleason
1835 Black Lake Boulevard SW
Suite B
Olympia, WA 98512
360-704-7708
Fax: 360-704-7742

West Virginia
USDA Rural Development
75 High Street
Morgantown, WV 26505
304-291-4797

Wisconsin
USDA Rural Development
4949 Krischling Court
Stevens Point, WI 54481
715-345-7610

Wyoming
USDA Rural Development
P.O. Box 820
Casper, WY 82602-0820
307-261-6319

HELP THOSE HELP THEMSELVES

The Discretionary Grants Program's goal is to strengthen the American family, which includes improving access of youth living in low income families to needed support services, including employment training and other transition to work services, and improving the integration, coordination, and continuity of other health and human services funded services. The program areas focus on employment opportunities and self-sufficiency among low income individuals; however, they are not micro-enterprise oriented programs.

This program supports projects which provide employment and
ownership opportunities for low income
people through business, physical or
commercial development and which
generally improve the quality of the
economic and social environment of
low-income residents in
economically-depressed areas. The
emphases of projects must be on self-
help and mobilization of the community-at-large.

For application information, contact the U.S. Department of Health and
Human Services, Office of Community Services, 3701 L'Enfant
Promenade, SW, Fifth Floor, Washington, DC 20447; 202-401-9346.

FY 1998 Discretionary Grant Awards Issued by the Division of Community Discretionary Programs

Urban And Rural Community Economic Development

Alabama
Southeast Alabama Self-Help
P.O. Drawer 1080
Macon County, AL 36087
334-727-2340

Alaska
Alaska Village Initiative
1577 C Street, Suite 304
Anchorage, AK 99501
907-274-5400

California
Esperanza Community Housing
Corporation
2337 South Figueroa Street
Los Angeles, CA 90007
213-748-7285

LTSC CDC
231 East Third Street

Suite G106
Los Angeles, CA 90013
213-473-1684

Rural California Housing
Corporation
2125 19th Street
Suite 101
Sacramento, CA 95818
916-442-4731

South County Economic
Development Council
1200 A Street
National City, CA 91950
619-336-2474

The East LA Community Union
5400 East Olympic Boulevard
Los Angeles, CA 90059
323-721-1655

Watts Labor Community Action
Committee
10950 South Central Avenue
Los Angeles, CA 90059
213-629-3065

Bayview CDC
5100 Federal Blvd., 2nd Floor
San Diego, CA 92105
619-262-8403

Chinatown Service Center
767 North Hill Street, Suite 400
Los Angeles, CA 90012-2381
213-253-0880

Planada CDC
P.O. Box 882
Planada, CA 95365
202-382-1033

Connecticut
Hall Neighborhood House
52 George Pipkin's Way
Bridgeport, CT 06608
203-332-4323

District of Columbia
Anacostia Economic Development
Corporation
2019 Martin Luther King, Jr.
Avenue, SE
Washington, DC 20020
202-889-5100

Friendship House Association
619 D Street, SE
Washington, DC 20003
202-675-9050

Las Americas Ave. Development
Corporation
1868 Columbia Road, NW #705

Washington, DC 20009
202-265-9561

Peoples Involvement
2146 Georgia Avenue, NW
Washington, DC 20001
202-797-3900

Florida
Coconut Grove Local
Development Corporation
P.O. Box 33075
3672 Grand Avenue
Coconut Grove, FL 33133
305-446-3095

Tampa Hillsborough CDC
1207 E. Martin Luther King, Blvd.
Tampa, FL 33603
813-248-4232

West Perrine CDC
17623 Homestead Avenue
Miami, FL 33157
305-234-0803

Union Fidelity Development, Inc.
P.O. Box 2501
Belle Glade, FL 33430-7501
561-308-7954

Work America, Inc.
3050 Biscayne Blvd.
Suite 501
Miami, FL 33137
305-576-3333

Georgia
Reynolds Revitalization Corp.
P.O. Box 89092
Atlanta, GA 30312
404-525-4130

Hawaii
Hawaii County Economic
Opportunity Council
47 Rainbow Drive
Hilo, HI 96720
808-961-2681

Illinois
Bethel New Life, Inc.
367 North Karlov
Chicago, IL 60624
773-826-5540
Fax: 773-826-5728

Indiana
Near North Development Corp.
1800 N. Meridian St., Suite 100
Indianapolis, IN 46204
317-927-9881, ext. 25

Kentucky
Kentucky Highlands Investment
Corporation
P.O. Box 1738
London, KY 40743-1738
606-864-5175
Fax: 606-864-5194

Louisville Central Development
Corporation
1015 West Chestnut Street
Louisville, KY 40203
502-583-8821

Mountain Association for CMTY
Economic Development, Inc.
433 Chestnut Street
Berea, KY 40403
606-986-2373

Louisiana
New Orleans Center for
Successful Living, Inc.

1100 Morrison Road, Suite 105
New Orleans, LA 70127
504-242-6178

Maryland
Druid Height CDC
1821 McCulloh Street
Baltimore, MD 21217
410-523-1350

Massachusetts
East Boston CDC
72 Marginal Street
Boston, MA 02128
617-569-5590

Neighborhood Development
Corporation of Jamaica Plains
31 Germania Street
Jamaica Plains, MA 02130
617-522-2424, ext. 22

Neighborhood of Affordable
Housing, Inc.
22 Paris Street
East Boston, MA 02128
617-569-3356, ext. 211

Vietnamese American Initiative
for Development
1485 Dorchester Ave.
Suite 206
Dorchester, MA 02122
617-822-3717

Focus Hope

Michigan
Focus Hope
1335 Oakman Boulevard
Detroit, MI 48238
313-494-4170

Detroit Hispanic Development
Corporation
7752 W. Venor Hwy., Suite 103
Detroit, MI 48209
313-965-9513

Minnesota
American Indian Business
Development Corporation
1113 East Franklin Avenue
Minneapolis, MN 55404
612-870-7555

Midwest Minnesota Community
Economic Development Corp.
P.O. Box 623
803 Roosevelt Avenue, Suite 301
Detroit Lakes, MN 56501
218-847-3191

HELPING HANDS

Mississippi
West Jackson CDC
1060 John R. Lynch Street
Jackson, MS 39289
601-352-6993

Missouri
CDC of Kansas City
2420 E. Linwood Blvd., Suite 400
Kansas City, MO 64109
816-924-5800

Midtown CDC
3801 Blue Parkway
Kansas City, MO 64130
816-922-7660

Nebraska
Lincoln Action Program
2202 South 11th Street
Lincoln, NE 68502
402-471-4515

New Jersey
New Community Corporation
233 West Market Street
Newark, NJ 07103
973-623-2800

First Baptist CDC
630 Franklin Boulevard
Suite 102
Somerset, NJ 08873
732-249-0677

New Mexico
Helping Hands, Inc.
P.O. Box 708
Mora, NM 87732
505-387-2288

New York
Cypress Hills Local Development
Corporation
625 Jamaica Avenue
Brooklyn, NY 11208
718-647-8100

St. Nicholas Neighborhood
Preservation
11-29 Catherine Street
Brooklyn, NY 11211
718-388-5454

Audubon Partnership for
Economic Development LDC
5000 Broadway, Suite A
New York, NY 10034
212-544-2470

River City Development Corp.
7 Alphonsa Court
Salisbury Mills, NY 12577
914-691-6006

Westhab in Mount Vernon, Inc.
156 South 1st Avenue
Mount Vernon, NY 10550
914-345-2800

North Carolina
Rocky Mount/Edgecombe
Community Development
148 S. Washington St., Suite 103
Rocky Mount, NC 27801
252-442-5178

River City CDC
501 East Main Street
Elizabeth City, NC 27909
252-331-2925

Family and Community Enrich-
ment Development Center, Inc.
10 3rd Avenue, SE
Hickory, NC 28601
828-327-7217

Ohio
ShoreBank Enterprise Group, Inc.
540 East 105th Street
Cleveland, OH 44108
216-268-6104 or 6100

Oklahoma
Rural Enterprise of OK, Inc.
P.O. Box 1335
Durant, OK 74702
580-924-5094

Oregon
Neighborhood Pride Team
7453 SE 52nd Avenue

Portland, OR 97206
503-774-4880

Pennsylvania
Crispus Attucks CDC
605 South Duke Street
York, PA 17403
717-848-3610

Germantown Settlement
48 East Penn Street
Philadelphia, PA 19144
215-849-3104

Hill CDC
2015-17 Centre Avenue
Pittsburgh, PA 15219
412-765-1320

Impact Services, Corporation
124 East Indiana Street
Philadelphia, PA 19134
215-739-1600

Mount Washington CDC
307 Shiloh Street
Pittsburgh, PA 15211
414-481-3220

Renaissance Community
Development Corporation
1438 Warnock Street
Philadelphia, PA 19122
215-763-7500

The Cecil B. Moore Avenue CDC
1616 North Broad Street
Philadelphia, PA 19121
215-763-8996

Fayette County CAA, Inc.
137 North Beeson Avenue
Uniontown, PA 15401
724-437-6050

South Carolina

Historically Black Colleges and
Universities (HBCU) Urban and
Rural Community Economic
Development/Set-Aside
Benedict College
Center of Excellence for
Community Development
1600 Harden Street
Columbia, SC 29204
803-253-5077

Light of the World CDC
5228 Farrow Road
Columbia, SC 29203
803-757-6000

Marion County CDC
P.O. Box 683
1811 North 501 Bypass
Marion, SC 29571
843-423-9510

South Dakota

NorthEast South Dakota Energy
Conservation Corporation
414 3rd Avenue, East
Sisseton, SD 57262
605-698-7654

Tennessee

Inner City Development Corp.
801 1/2 Central Avenue
Chattanooga, TN 37403
423-267-5405

Texas

Fifth Ward Community
Redevelopment Corporation
P.O. Box 21502
4120 Lyons Avenue
Houston, TX 7726-1502
713-674-0175

Southern Dallas Development
Corporation
1402 Corinth Street
Dallas, TX 75215
214-428-7332

Pre-Developmental Set-Aside
American GI Forum Community
Housing and Development
Organization, Inc.
206 San Pedro, Suite 200
San Antonio, TX 78205
210-223-4088

El Puente CDC
2000 Texas Avenue
El Paso, TX 79901
915-533-9710

Vermont

Central Vermont CAA
36 Barre-Montpelar Road
Barre, VT 05641
802-479-1053

Virginia

Hampton CDC
Hampton University Business
Assistance Center
Hampton, VA 23658
804-727-5077

Washington

Metropolitan Development
Council
622 Tacoma Avenue South
Tacoma, WA 98402
253-597-6710

West Virginia

Lightstone CDC
HC 63, Box 73
Moyers, WV 26815

304-249-5200
Fax: 304-249-5310

Wisconsin
CAP Services, Inc.
5499 Highway 10 East
Stevens Point, WI 54481
715-345-5200

Impact Seven, Inc.
651 Garfield Street
Almena, WI 54805
715-357-3334

Hunger Task Force of Milwaukee
Inc.
811 East Vienna Avenue
Milwaukee, WI 53212
414-962-3111

Developmental Set-Asides

Action for a Better Community,
Inc.
550 East Main Street
Rochester, NY 14604
716-325-5116

Alianza Dominicana, Inc.
2410 Amsterdam Avenue
New York, NY 10033
212-740-1960

East Winston CDC
1225 East Fifth Street
Winston-Salem, NC 27101
336-723-1783

George Gervin Youth Center, Inc.
6903 Sunbelt Drive, South
San Antonio, TX 78218
210-804-1786

Northeast Louisiana Delta CDC
400 East Craig Street, Suite B
Tallulah, LA 71282
318-574-0995

Rio Grande CDC
P.O. Box 12791
Albuquerque, NM 87915
505-452-8525

West Angeles CDC
3045 Crenshaw Boulevard
Los Angeles, CA 90016
213-745-6945

Urban Administrative And Management Grantee Assistance/Set-Aside

Impact Seven, Inc.
651 Garfield Street
Almena, WI 54805
715-357-3334

Technical Assistance

National Congress for Community
Economic Development, Inc
11 Dupont Circle, NW
Washington, DC 20038
202-234-5009

Rural Community Facilities Development

Community Resource Group, Inc.
2423 East Robinson Avenue
Springdale, AR 72764
501-443-2700

Inter Tribal Council of AZ, Inc.
4205 North 7th Avenue
Suite 200

Phoenix, AZ 85013
602-248-0071

Midwest Assistance Program, Inc.
P.O. Box 81
New Prague, MN 56071
612-758-4334

Rural Community Assistance
Corporation
2125 19th Street, Suite 203
Sacramento, CA 95818
916-447-2854

Rural Housing Improvement, Inc.
218 Central Street

Winchendon, MA 01475
978-297-5300

SE Rural Community Assistance
Project, Inc.
P.O. Box 2868
145 Campbell Avenue SW
Roanoke, VA 24001-2868

WSOS Community Action
Commission, Inc
109 South Front Street
P.O. Box 590
Fremont, OH 43420
419-334-8911

Welfare Moms Can Start Their Own Business

If you're getting help from Temporary Assistance for Needy Families (TANF), you may be able to get free training on how to become an entrepreneur, along with money to help you become your own boss. The program is called Job Opportunities for Low-Income Individuals (JOLI) program, which seeks to enhance the capacity and self-sufficiency of participating individuals.

JOLI aims to help TANF recipients and others whose income falls below the federal poverty guidelines become self-sufficient by starting their own micro-enterprises or through employment in newly created permanent jobs. The program is designed to demonstrate and evaluate ways of creating new employment and business opportunities for certain low income individuals through the provision of technical and financial assistance to private employers in the community, self-employment/ micro-enterprise programs, and/or new business development programs. JOLI awards grants to nonprofit organizations to develop these projects.

For information on programs in your area or application information, contact U.S. Department of Health and Human Services, Office Community Services, 370 L'Enfant Promenade, SW Fifth Floor, Washington, DC 20447; 202-401-5282.

Job Opportunities For Low-Income Individuals

Arizona
Arizona Council For Economic Conversion
P.O. Box 4218
Tucson, AZ 85733
520-620-1241
Fax: 520-622-2235

California
Materials For The Future Foundation
P.O. Box 29091
San Francisco, CA 94129-0091
415-561-6530
Fax: 415-561-6474

Hawaii
Hawaii County Economic Opportunity Council
47 Rainbow Drive
Hilo, HI 96720
808-961-2681
Fax: 808-935-9213

Illinois
Shorebank Neighborhood Instate
5100 West Harrison
Chicago, IL 60644-5101
773-854-4360
Fax: 773-854-4380

Maine
Coastal Enterprises
Water Street
P.O. Box 268
Wiscasset, ME 04578
207-882-7552
Fax: 207-882-4455

Maryland
Women Entrepreneurs of Baltimore, Inc.
28 East Ostend Street
Baltimore, MD 21230
410-727-4921
Fax: 410-727-4989

Massachusetts
Jewish Vocational Services
105 Chauncy Street
Boston, MA 02111
617-451-8147
Fax: 617-451-9973

Michigan
Operation Helping Hand. Inc.
2250 14th Street
Detroit, MI 48216
313-961-1631
Fax: 313-961-1274

Missouri
The Youth and Family Center
2929 North 20th Street
St. Louis, MO 63107
314-231-1147
Fax: 314-436-9057

New York
Covenant House York/
Under 21. Inc.
460 West 41st Street

New York, NY 10036
212-613-0300
Fax: 212-947-2478

Pennsylvania
Washington County Council On
Economic Development
100 W. Beau St., Suite 703
Washington, PA 15301-4432
724-228-6816
Fax: 724-250-6502

GRANTS TO TOWNS THAT WILL LEND YOU BUSINESS MONEY

Cities can get grants that can be used to lend you money to start a small business. The Entitlement Grants is the largest component of the

Community Development Block Grant Program and provides annual grants to entitled cities (population 50,000) and counties (population 200, 000) to develop viable urban communities by providing decent housing and suitable living environments, and by expanding economic opportunities, principally for low and moderate income persons.

The program provides funds to carry out a wide range of community development activities directed toward neighborhood revitalization, economic development, improved community facilities and services, and micro-enterprise. Funds can be used to establish credit (direct loans and loan guarantees, revolving loan funds, and more) for the stabilization and expansion of micro-enterprise; provide technical assistance, advice, and business support services to owners of micro-enterprises; and provide general support to owners of micro-enterprises and organizations developing micro-enterprises.

To learn if your community received funds and the person to contact in your area for more information, contact Community Connections, Information Center, Office of Community Planning and Development, P.O. Box 7189, Gaithersburg, MD 20898-7189; 800-998-9999. You may also contact the HUD office nearest you (listed below).

HUD Offices

New England
Boston Region
Mary Lou Crane, Secretary's
Representative
HUD-Boston Office
10 Causeway Street, Room 375
Boston, MA 0222-1092
617-565-5236
Fax: 617-565-6558

Burlington Region
Temporarily Covered
HUD-Burlington Office
Room 244, Federal Building
11 Elmwood Avenue
P.O. Box 879
Burlington, VT 05402-0879
802-951-6290
Fax; 802-951-6298

Manchester Region
David B. Harrity, Senior
Builder/Coordinator
HUD-Manchester Office
Norris Cotton Federal Building
275 Chestnut Street
Manchester, NH 03103-2487
603-666-7682
Fax: 603-666-7667

Bangor Region
Loren W. Cole
Senior Community
Builder/Coordinator

HUD-Bangor Office
202 Harlow Street
Chase Building, Suite 101
P.O. Box 1384
Bangor, ME 04401-4925
207-945-04273
Fax: 207-945-0533

Rhode Island Region
Nancy D. Smith
Senior Community
Builder/Coordinator
HUD-Providence Office
10 Weybosset Street, 6th Floor
Providence, RI 02903-2808
401-528-5352
Fax: 401-528-5312

Hartford Region
Raymond A. Jordan
Senior Community
Builder/Coordinator
HUD-Hartford Office
One Corporate Center
Hartford, CT 06106-3220
860-240-4800 ext. 3100
Fax 860-240-4850

New York/New Jersey
New York Region
Bill deBlasio, Secretary's
Representative
HUD-New York Office
26 Federal Plaza

New York, NY 10278-0068
212-264-1161
Fax: 212-264-3068

Buffalo Region
Office Temporarily Covered
Michele E. Bernier, Community
Building
HUD-Buffalo Office
5th Floor, Lafayette Court
465 Main Street
Buffalo, NY 14203-1780
716-551-5733
Fax: 716-551-5752

Camden Region
Laura Pelzer
Senior Community
Builder/Coordinator
HUD-Camden Office
800 Hudson Square, 2nd Floor
Camden, NJ 08102-1156
609-757-5081
Fax: 609-757-5373

New Jersey Region
Diane Johnson, Senior
Community Builder/Coordinator
HUD-Newark Office
13th Floor, One Network Center
Newark, NJ 07102-5260
201-622-7900 ext. 3102
Fax: 201-645-2323

Midatlantic Area
Pennsylvania Region
Karen Miller, Secretary's
Representative
HUD-Philadelphia Office
The Wanamaker Building
Pennsylvania Square, E
Philadelphia, PA 19107-3380
215-656-0606
Fax: 215-656-3445

Charleston Region
Fred Roncaglione, Senior
Community Builder/Coordinator
HUD-Charleston Office
405 Capitol Street, Suite 708
Charleston, WV 25301-1795
304-347-7036 ext. 101
Fax: 304-347-7050

Pittsburgh Region
Richard M. Nemoytin
Senior Community
Builder/Coordinator
HUD- Pittsburgh Office
339 6th Avenue, 6th Floor
Pittsburgh, PA 15222-2515
412-644-5945
Fax: 412-644-4240

Richmond Office
MaryAnn Wilson, Senior
Community Builder/Coordinator
HUD-Richmond Office
The 3600 West Broad Street
Richmond, VA 23230-4920
804-278-4507 ext. 3208
Fax: 804-278-4603

District of Columbia Region
Lorraine Richardson, Community
Builder
HUD-Washington, DC Office
820 1st Street, NE, Suite 300
Washington, DC 2002-4205
202-275-9206 ext. 3075
Fax: 202-275-9212

Delaware Region
Diane Lello, Senior Community
Builder/Coordinator
HUD-Wilmington Office
824 Market Street, Suite 850
Wilmington, DE 19801-3016

302-573-6300
Fax: 302-573-6259

Maryland Region
Harold D. Young,
Senior Community
Builder/Coordinator
HUD-Baltimore Office, 5th Floor
10 South Howard Street
Baltimore, MD 21201-2505
410-962-2520, ext. 3474
Fax: 410-962-1849

Southeast Area
Atlanta Region
Davey Gibson
Secretary's Representative
HUD-Atlanta Office
Richard B. Russell Federal
Building
75 Spring Street, SW
Atlanta, GA 30303-3388
404-331-5136
Fax: 404-730-2365

Birmingham Region
Heagar Hill, Senior Community
Builder/Coordinator
HUD-Birmingham Office
Suite 300, Beacon Ridge Tower
Birmingham, AL 35209-3144
205-290-7630 ext. 1001
Fax: 205-290-7593

Caribbean Region
Michael A. Colon
Senior Community
Builder/Coordinator
HUD-Caribbean Office
159 Carlos E. Chardon Avenue
San Juan, PR 00918-1804
787-766-5202
Fax: 787-766-5995

Columbia Region
Office Temporarily Covered
David Ball, Community
Builder/Coordinator
HUD-Columbia Office
1835 Assembly Street
Columbia, SC 29201-24803
803-765-5592
Fax: 803-253-3043

Coral Gables Region
Jose Cintron, Senior Community
Builder/Coordinator
HUD-Coral Gables Office
1320 South Dixie Highway
Coral Gables, FL 33146-2911
605-662-4510
Fax: 305-662-4588

HUD Regional Offices

Greensboro Region
James E. Balckmon
Senior Community
Builder/Coordinator
2306 West Meadowview Road
Greensboro, NC 27407-3707
910-547-4001
Fax: 910-547-4120

Jackson Region
Patricia Hoban-Moore
Senior Community
Builder/Coordinator
HUD-Jackson Office
100 W. Capitol St., Room 910

Jackson, MS 39269-1096
601-965-4738
Fax: 601-965-4773

Jacksonville Region
James Walker, Senior Community
Builder/Coordinator
HUD-Jacksonville Office
301 West Bay Street, Suite 2200
Jacksonville, FL 32202-5121
904-232-2627
Fax: 904-232-3759

Knoxville Region
Mark Brezina
Senior Community
Builder/Coordinator
HUD-Knoxville Office
710 Locust Street, SW
Knoxville, TN 37902-2526
423-545-4384
Fax: 423-545-4569

Louisville Region
John Milchik, Senior Community
Builder/Coordinator
HUD-Louisville Office
601 West Broadway
P.O. Box 1044
Louisville, KY 40201-1044
502-585-6132
Fax: 502-582-6074

Memphis Region
Benjamin F. Davis
Senior Community
Builder/Coordinator
HUD-Memphis Office
One Memphis Place
200 Jefferson Avenue, Suite 1200
Memphis, TN 38103-2335
901-544-3367
Fax: 901-544-3697

Nashville Region
Brenda Cleaver, Senior
Community Builder/Coordinator
HUD-Nashville Office
251 Cumberland Bend Dr.
Suite 200
Nashville, TN 37228-1803
615-736-5213
Fax: 615-648-6310

Tampa Region
George A. Milburn, Jr.
Senior Community Builder
HUD-Tampa Office
501 East Polk Street, Suite 700
Tampa, FL 33602-3945
813-228-2504
Fax: 813-228-2431

Midwest Area
Chicago Region
Rosanna A. Marquez
Secretary's Representative
HUD-Chicago Office
Ralph Metcalfe Federal Building
77 West Jackson Boulevard
Chicago, IL 60604-5680
312-353-5680
Fax: 312-886-2729

Cincinnati Region
Louistine Tuck, Senior
Community Builder/Coordinator
HUD-Cincinnati Office
525 Vine Street
Cincinnati, OH 45202-3188
513-684-2967
Fax: 513-684-6224

Cleveland Region
Douglas W. Shelby, Senior
Community Builder/Coordinator
HUD-Cleveland Office

1350 Euclid Avenue, 5th Floor
Cleveland, OH 44115-1815
216-522-4065
Fax: 216-522-4067

Columbus Region
Office Temporarily Covered
Jack Brown, Economist
HUD-Columbus Office
200 North High Street
Columbus, OH 43215-2499
614-469-2540
Fax: 614-469-2432

Detroit Region
Regina P. Solomon
Senior Community
Builder/Coordinator
HUD-Detroit Office
477 Michigan Avenue
Detroit, MI 48226-2592
313-226-6241
Fax: 313-226-5611

Grand Rapids Region
Louis K. Berra
HUD-Grand Rapids Office
Trade Center Building
50 Louis Street, NW
Grand Rapids, MI 49503-2648
616-456-2103
Fax: 616-456-2191

Flint Region
Office Temporarily Covered by
Detroit
Senior Community
Builder/Coordinator
HUD-Flint Office
605 N. Saginaw St., Room 200
Flint, MI 48502-1953
517-766-5107
Fax: 517-766-5122

Indianapolis Region
William K. Fattic, Senior
Community Builder/Coordinator
HUD-Indianapolis Office
151 North Delaware Street
Indianapolis, IN 46204-2526
317-226-6322
Fax: 317-226-6317

Wisconsin State
Delbert Reynolds
Senior Community
Builder/Coordinator
HUD-Milwaukee Office
Henry S. Reuss Federal Plaza
310 W. Wisconsin Ave.
Room 1380
Milwaukee, WI 53203-2289
414-297-1495
Fax: 414-297-3947

Minneapolis Region
Thomas Feeney, Senior
Community Builder/Coordinator
HUD-Minneapolis Office
220 Second Street, South
Minneapolis, MN 554012195
612-370-3289
Fax: 612-370-3220

Springfield Region
Debbie Willis, Senior Community
Builder/Coordinator
HUD-Springfield Office
Temporarily Working out of
Chicago Office

Microenterprise Loans

Southwest
New Mexico State
Michael R. Griego, Acting State
Coordinator
HUD-Albuquerque Office
625 Truman Street, NE
Albuquerque, NM 87110-6472
505-262-6463 ext. 223
Fax: 505-262-6463

Dallas Area
C. Don Babers
Senior Community
Builder/Coordinator
HUD-Dallas Office
HUD-Room 860
525 Griffin Street
Dallas, TX 75202-5007
214-767-8300
Fax: 214-767-8973

Arkansas State Office
Richard L. Young
HUD-Little Rock Office
425 W. Capitol Ave., Suite 900
Little Rock, AR 72201-3488
501-324-5401
Fax: 501-324-5401

Lubbock Area Office
Miguel C. Rincon, JR
Senior Community
Builder/Coordinator
HUD-Lubbock Office
1205 Texas Avenue
Lubbock, TX 79401-4093
806-472-7265 ext. 3030
Fax: 806-472-7275

Texas State
Elizabeth K. Julian
Secretary's Representative
HUD-Ft. Worth Office

1600 Throckmorton
P.O. Box 2905
Ft. Worth, TX 76113-2905
817-978-9000
Fax: 817-978-9001

Louisiana State Office
Jason Gamlin, Senior Community
Builder/Coordinator
HUD-New Orleans Office
Hale Boggs Building
501 Magazine Street, 9th Floor
New Orleans, LA 70130-3099
504-589-7200
Fax: 504-589-6619

Oklahoma State Office
Margaret F. Milner
Senior Community
Builder/Coordinator
HUD-Oklahoma City Office
500 West Main Street, Suite 400
Oklahoma City, OK 73102-2233
405-553-7500
Fax: 405-553-7588

San Antonio Area Office
A. Cynthia Leon
Senior Community
Builder/Coordinator
HUD- San Antonio Office
800 Dolorosa Street
San Antonio, TX 78207-4563
210-475-6806
Fax: 210-472-6804

Shreveport Region
Martha Sakre
Senior Community Builder
401 Edwards Street, Room 1510
Shreveport, LA 71101-3289
318-676-3385
Fax: 318-676-3407

Tulsa Region
James Colgan, Senior Community
Builder/Coordinator
HUD-Tulsa Office
50 East 15th Street
Tulsa, OK 74119-4030
918-581-7496
Fax: 918-581-7440

Great Plains Area
Missouri State
Michael Tramontina, Secretary's
Representative
HUD-Kansas City Office
400 State Avenue, Room 200
Kansas City, KS 66106-2406
913-551-5462
Fax: 913-551-5469

Iowa State
William McNarney
Senior Community
Builder/Coordinator
HUD-Des Moines Office
210 Walnut Street, Room 239
Des Moines, IA 50309-2155
515-284-4573
Fax: 515-284-4743

St. Louis Region
Kenneth G. Lange
Senior Community
Builder/Coordinator
HUD-St. Louis Office
1222 Spruce Street, #3207
St. Louis, MO 63103-2836
314-539-6560

Nebraska State Office
Ernest Gratz
Senior Community
Builder/Coordinator
HUD-Omaha Office

10909 Mill Valley Road
Omaha, NE 68514-3955
402-492-3103
Fax: 402-492-3150

Community
Builder/
Coordinators

Rocky Mountain Area
Colorado State Region
Joseph A. Garcia
HUD-Denver Office
633 17th Street, FITN
Denver, CO 80202-3607
303-672-5440
Fax: 303-672-5004

Wyoming State
William Garrett, Senior
Community Builder/Coordinator
100 East B Street
P.O. Box 120
Casper, WY 82601
307-261-6254
Fax: 307-261-6245

North Dakota State Region
Office Temporarily Covered
Keith Elliot
HUD-Fargo Office
Federal Building
657 2nd Avenue, North
P.O. Box 2483
Fargo, ND 58102
701-239-5040
Fax: 701-239-5249

Microenterprise Loans

Montana State Region
Richard Brinck, Senior
Community Builder/Coordinator
HUD-Helena Office
301 South Park, Room 464
Helena, MT 59626-0095
406-441-1298
Fax: 406-441-1292

Utah State Region
Office Temporarily Covered
HUD-Salt Lake City Office
257 East 200 South, Room 550
Salt Lake City, UT 84111-2048
801-524-3323
Fax: 801-524-3439

South Dakota State Region
Sheryl Miller
Senior Community
Builder/Coordinator
2500 W. 49th St., Room-II-204
Sioux Falls, SD 57105
605-330-4226
Fax: 605-330-4428.

Pacific/Hawaii
California State Region
Arthur Agnos, Secretary's
Representative
HUD-San Francisco Office
450 Golden Gate Avenue
P.O. Box 36003
San Francisco, CA 94102-3448
415-436-6532
Fax: 415-436-6446

Fresno Region
Ann Marie Sudduth
Senior Community
Builder/Coordinator
HUD-Fresno Office
2135 Fresno Street, Suite 100

Fresno, CA 93721-1718
209-487-5032
Fax: 209-487-5191

Hawaii State Region
Gordon Y. Furutani
Senior Community Builder
HUD-Honolulu Office
Seven Waterfront Plaza
500 Ala Moana Boulevard, #500
Honolulu, HI 96813-4918
808-522-8175 ext. 256 or 259
Fax: 808-522-8194

Nevada State Region
Ken Lobene
Senior Community Builder
HUD-Las Vegas Office
333 North Rancho Drive
Atrium Building, Suite 700
Las Vegas, NV 89106-3714
702-388-6525
Fax: 702-388-6244

Arizona State Region
Terry Goddard, Senior
Community Builder/Coordinator
HUD-Phoenix Office
400 North 5th Street, Suite 1600
Phoenix, AZ 85004-2361
602-379-4434
Fax: 602-379-3985

Reno Region
Wayne Waite, Senior Community
Builder/Coordinator
HUD-Reno Office
1575 DeLucchi Lane
Suite 114
P.O. Box 30050
Reno, NV 89502-6581
702-784-5356
Fax: 702-784-5360

Sacramento Region
William L. Bolton
Senior Community
Builder/Coordinator
HUD-Sacramento Office
925 "L" Street, Suite 675
Sacramento, CA 95814-3702
916-498-5220 ext. 622
Fax: 916-498-5262

San Diego Region
Office Temporarily Covered
HUD-Santa Ana Office
3 Hutton Centre, Suite 500
Santa Ana, CA 98707-5764
714-957-7354
Fax: 714-957-1702

Los Angeles Region
Thomas Honore, Senior
Community Builder/Coordinator
HUD-Los Angeles Office
611 West 6th, Suite 800
Los Angeles, CA 90017
213-894-8007
Fax: 213-894-8096

Tucson Region
Sharon Atwell
Senior Community
Builder/Coordinator
HUD-Tucson Office
Security Pacific Bank Plaza
33 North Stone Ave., Suite 700
Tucson, AZ 85701-1467
602-670-5220
Fax: 602-670-6207

Northwest Alaska Area
Washington State Region
Bob Santos
Secretary's Representative
HUD-Seattle Office

909 First Avenue, Suite 200
Seattle, WA 98104-1000
206-220-5101
Fax: 206-220-5108

Alaska State Region
Arlene Patton, Senior Community
Builder/Coordinator
HUD-Anchorage Office
949 East 36th Avenue
Anchorage, AK 99508-4135
907-271-4170
Fax: 907-271-3667

Idaho State Region
Gary Gillespie, Senior Community
Builder/Coordinator
HUD-Boise Office
Plaza IV, Suite 220
800 Park Boulevard
Boise, ID 83712-7743
208-334-1900, ext. 3007
Fax: 208-334-9648

Oregon State Region
Thomas C. Cusack
Senior Community
Builder/Coordinator
HUD-Portland Office
400 SW 6th Avenue #700
Portland, OR 97204-1632
503-326-2561

Spokane Region
Rafael Metzget
Senior Community
Builder/Coordinator
HUD-Spokane Office
8th Floor East
West 601 1st Avenue
Spokane, WA 99204-0317
509-353-2510, ext. 3022
Fax: 509-353-2513

YOUR STATE CAN GET YOU MONEY

This is the second largest component of the Community Development Block Grant (CDBG) program and aids communities that do not qualify for assistance under the CDBG entitlement program. The grants assist communities in carrying out a wide range of community development activities directed toward neighborhood revitalization, economic development, and the provision of improved community facilities and services. Funds can also be used to provide assistance to public and private organizations, agencies, and other entities (including nonprofits and for profits to facilitate economic development in supporting micro-enterprise).

Funds can be used to establish credit (direct loans and loan guarantees, revolving loan funds, and more) for the stabilization and expansion of microenterprises; provide technical assistance, advice, and business support services to owners of micro-enterprises; and provide general support to owners of micro-enterprises and organizations developing micro-enterprises.

Up To $10,000 For Refugees

Refugees can receive technical assistance, training, or loans of up to $10,000 through a program called the Micro-Enterprise Development Project. The program allows states and public or private, nonprofit organizations and institutions to apply to receive grants to develop and administer micro-enterprise programs consisting of small-scale financing ($10,000) available through microloans to refugees. It also includes funding for technical assistance and support to these refugee entrepreneurs.

For information on organizations that were awarded grants, contact ORR/Division of Community Resettlement, 370 L'Enfant Promenade, SW Sixth Floor, Washington, DC 20447; 202-401-9246.

If you are an interested citizen, you should contact your local officials for more information. If your local government or state officials cannot answer your questions, you may wish to contact the HUD Field Office that services your area (look for the office closest to you from the list later in this chapter). Be aware that the state administers the program and determines which local projects receive funding.

You can also contact: Community Connections, Information Center, Office of Community Planning and Development, P.O. Box 7189, Gaithersburg, MD 20898-7189; 800-998-9999.

Government Regulations Say A Little-Bitsy Loan Is $25,000

The U.S. Small Business Administration's (SBA) *Microloan Program* was developed for those times when just a small loan can make the real difference between success and failure. Under this program, loans range from less than $100 to a maximum of $25,000.

SBA has made these funds available to nonprofit organizations for the purpose of lending to small businesses. These organizations can also provide intense management and technical assistance. A microloan must be repaid on the shortest term possible — no longer than six years, depending on the earnings of the business. The interest rates on these loans will be competitive and based on the cost of money to the intermediary lender.

This program is currently available in 44 states. To learn which nonprofit organizations in your area offer this program, contact U.S. Small Business Administration, 409 3rd St., SW, Suite 8300, Washington, DC 20416; 800-8-ASK-SBA; 202-205-6490; {www.sba.gov}.

U.S. Small Business Administration
Microloan Demonstration Program

Participating Intermediary Lenders and
Non-Lending Technical Assistance Providers

Intermediary Lenders

Alabama
Elmore Community Action
Committee, Inc.
1011 W. Tallassee
P.O. Drawer H
Wetumpka, AL 36092
334-567-4361
Fax: 334-567-0755
Exec.Director: Marion D. Dunlap
Service Area: Autauga, Elmore, and
Montgomery counties

Community Equity Investments,
Inc.
302 N. Barcelona St.
Pensacola, FL 32501
850-595-6234
Fax: 850-595-6264
E-mail: bigdanfla@aol.com
Executive Director: Dan Horvath
Microloan Contact: Elbert Jones
Service Area: Baldwin, Mobile,
Washington, Clarke, Monroe,
Escambia, Conecuh, Covington,
Geneva, Coffee, Dale, Henry, and
Houston counties

Arizona
Chicanos Por La Causa, Inc.
1112 E. Buckeye Rd.
Phoenix, AZ 85034-4043
602-252-0483
Fax: 602-252-0484
Executive Director: Pete Garcia

Microloan Contact: Frank Cano/
Frank Martinez
Service Area: Urban Maricopa and
Pima counties, Graham and Gila
counties (including Point of Pines
Reservation and the Southwestern
area of Fort Apache Reservation),
Coconino and Mohave counties
(including the Kaibab, Havasupai,
and Hualapai Reservations and
western portions of the Navajo and
Hopi Reservations), Yavapai and
LaPaz counties

PPEP Housing Dev. Co.
Micro Ind. Credit Rural Org.
802 E. 46th St.
Tucson, AZ 85713
520-622-3553
Fax: 602-622-1480
E-mail: ppep2@azstarnet.com
Exec. Director: Frank Ballesteros
Microloan Contact: Frank
Ballesteros
Service Area: Cochise, Santa Cruz,
Pinal, Yuma, rural Pima, and rural
Maricopa counties including the
Fort McDowell, Gila River,
Maricopa, Papago, Salt River, and
San Xavier Indian Reservations.

Arkansas
Arkansas Enterprise Group
2304 W. 29th St.
Pine Bluff, AR 71603

870-535-6233
Fax: 870-535-0741
E-mail: goodfaith@earthlink.net
Executive Director: Penny Penrose
Microloan Contact: Brian Kelley
Service Area: Southern and extreme
northeast areas of the state
including Arkansas, Ashley,
Bradley, Calhoun, Chicot, Clark,
Clay, Cleveland, Columbia,
Craighead, Dallas, Desha, Drew,
Garland, Grant, Greene,
Hempstead, Hot Spring, Howard,
Jefferson, Lafayette, Lawrence,
Lincoln, Little River, Lonoke,
Miller, Mississippi, Montgomery,
Nevada, Ouachita, Phillips, Pike,
Poinsett, Polk, Prairie, Pulaski,
Randolph, Saline, Sevier, and
Union counties

Delta Community Development
Corporation
335 Broadway
P.O. Box 852
Forrest City, AR 72336
870-633-9112
Fax: 870-633-9191
E-mail: aharvey@earle.crsc.
k12.as.us
Executive Director: Fred Lee
Microloan Contact: Pat Scott
Service Area: Cross, Crittenden,
Monroe, Lee, and St. Francis
counties

White River Planning and
Development District, Inc.
P.O. Box 2396
Batesville, AR 72503
870-793-5233
Fax: 870-793-4035
E-mail: wrpdd@mail.cei.net

Executive Director: Van C. Thomas
Microloan Contact: Ben Earls
Service Area: Cleburne, Fulton,
Independence, Izard, Jackson,
Sharp, Stone, Van Buren, White,
and Woodruff counties

California
Arcata Economic Development
Corporation
100 Ericson Court, Suite 100
Arcata, CA 95521
707-822-4616
Fax: 707-822-8982
E-mail: jerry@reninet.com
Executive Director: Jim Kimbrell
Microloan Contact: Jerry Aldorty
Service Area: Del Norte, Humboldt,
Lake, Mendocino, Siskiyou, and
Trinity counties

Microloans

California Coastal Rural
Development Corporation
221 Main St., Suite 300
P.O. Box 479
Salinas, CA 93901
408-424-1099
Fax: 408-424-1094
E-mail: martha/gonzalez@salinas.
ccmail.compuserve.com
Executive Director: Herb Aarons
Microloan Contact: Ginger
McNally
Service Area: Santa Cruz,
Monterey, San Benito, San Luis
Obispo, Santa Barbara, and Ventura

Southeast Asian Community Center
875 O'Farrell St.
San Francisco, CA 94109

415-885-2743
Fax: 415-885-3253
E-mail: akanksham@juno.com
Executive Director: Philip Tuong
Duy Nguyen
Microloan Contact: Victor Hsi
Service Area: Alameda, Contra
Costa, Marin, Merced, Sacramento,
San Francisco, San Joaquin, San
Mateo, Santa Clara, and Stanislaus
counties

Valley Small Business
Development Corporation
3417 W. Shaw, Suite 100
Fresno, CA 93711
209-271-9030
Fax: 209-271-9078
E-mail: valleysb@fia.net
Exec. Dir.: Michael E. Foley
Microloan Contact: Lee Takikawa/
Liz Fields
Service Area: Fresno, Kings, Kern,
Stanislaus, Madera, Mariposa,
Merced, Tuolumne, and Tulare
counties

Colorado
Colorado Enterprise Fund
1888 Sherman St. Suite 530
P.O. Box 2135
Denver, CO 80203
303-860-0242
Fax: 303-860-0409
Exec. Dir.: Cecilia H. Prinster
Microloan Contact: Laura Hanssen
Service Area: City of Denver, and
Adams, Arapahoe, Boulder,
Denver, and Jefferson counties

Region 10 LEAP, Inc.
P.O. Box 849
300 N. Cascade St., Suite 1

Montrose, CO 81401
970-249-2436
Fax: 970-249-2488
Executive Director: Leslie Jones
Microloan Contact: Bob Bolt
Service Area: West Central area
including Delta, Gunnison,
Hinsdale, Montrose, Ouray, and
San Miguel counties

Connecticut
New Haven Community Investment
Corp.
900 Chapel St., Suite 640
New Haven, CT 06510
203-776-6172
Fax: 203-776-6837
Exec. Dir.: Salvatore J. Brancati, Jr.
Microloan Contact: Mark
Cousineau
Service area: Statewide

Delaware
Wilmington Economic
Development Corporation
605-A Market Street Mall
Wilmington, DE 19801
302-571-9088
Fax: 302-652-5679
E-mail: wedco605@aol.com
Executive Director: Louise Eliason
Microloan Contact: Lynette Scott
Service Area: New Castle county,
in the cities of Wilmington,
Newark, New Castle, Middletown,
Odessa, and Townsend

District of Columbia
ARCH Development Corporation
1227 Good Hope Rd., SE
Washington, DC 20020
202-889-5023
Fax: 202-889-5035

Executive Director: Duane Gautier
Service Area: Portions of the
District of Columbia commonly
referred to as Adams Morgan,
Mount Pleasant, and Anacostia,
Congress Heights, Columbia
Heights, and 14th Street Corridor

H Street Development Corporation
501 H Street, NE
Washington, DC 20002
202-544-8353
Fax: 202-544-3051
E-mail: omhscdc@aol.com
Exec. Dir.: William Barrow
Microloan Contact: Yulonda Queen
Service Area: West-the Anacostia
River; East-7th Street, NW; North-
Benning Road to K Street; and
South-the Southeast/Southwest
Freeway: Servicing Capitol Hill, H
Street, NE, Lincoln Park, Mt.
Vernon Square, Judiciary Square,
Benning Road-West of the
Anacostia River, Union Station,
Stadium Armory, and Lower North
Capitol. Eastern border of North
Capitol to Rhode Island to 7th Street
NW; West-Anacostia River; North-
Eastern Avenue to North Capitol;
and Southeast/Southwest Freeway:
Servicing Eckington, Catholic
University, Michigan Park,
Edgewood, Brookland, Ft. Lincoln,
New York Avenue, Florida
Avenue, Brentwood-DC,
Woodridge, Trinidad, and NE
Rhode Island Avenue

Florida
Community Equity Investments,
Inc.
302 North Barcelona St.

Pensacola, FL 32501
850-595-6234
Fax: 850-595-6264
E-mail: bigdanfla@aol.com
Executive Director: Dan Horvath
Microloan Contact: Elbert Jones
Service Area: Florida Panhandle
including Bay, Calhoun, Escambia,
Gadsden, Gulf, Jackson, Holmes,
Liberty, Leon, Franklin, Wakulla,
Walton, Wasington, Okaloosa, and
Santa Rosa counties

United Gainesville Community
Dev. Corp., Inc.
505 NW 2nd Avenue
P.O. Box 2518
Gainesville, FL 32602
352-376-8891
Fax: 352-377-0288
E-mail: vian@ugcdc.org or
lyndah@ugcdc.org
Executive Director: Vian Guinyard
Microloan Contact: Bill Watson
Service Area: North Central section
including Alachua, Bradford,
Columbia, Dixie, Gichrist,
Hamilton, Jefferson, Lafayette,
Levy, Madison, Marion, Putman,
Suwanee, Taylor, and Union
counties

Georgia
Fulton County Development
Corp/GRASP Enterprises
55 Marietta St., NW, Suite 2000
Atlanta, GA 30303
404-659-5955
Fax: 404-880-9561
E-mail: tpscott@mindspring.com
Executive Director: Maurice
Coakley
Microloan Contact: Tim Scott

Service Area: Fulton, Dekalb, Cobb, Gwinnett, Fayette, Clayton, Henry, Douglas, and Rockdale counties

Small Business Assistance Corporation
111 E. Liberty St., Suite 100
P.O. Box 10516
Savannah, GA 31412-0716
912-232-4700
Fax: 912-232-0385
E-mail: sbac001@aol.com
Executive Director: Tony O'Reilly
Microloan Contact: Tony O'Reilly
Service Area: Chatham, Effingham, Bryan, Bulloch, and Liberty counties

Development Finance Authority

Hawaii
The Immigrant Center
720 N. King St.
Honolulu, HI 96817
808-845-3918
Fax: 808-842-1962
E-mail: myaing@aol.com
Exec. Dir.: Tin Myaing Thein
Microloan Contact: Michael Lord
Service Area: Island of O'ahu within the City and County of Honolulu, Hawaii, Maui, and Kauai

Idaho
Ida-Ore Planning and Development Association
10624 W. Executive Dr.

Boise, ID 83713
208-322-7033
Fax: 208-322-3569
Executive Director: Phillip Choate
Microloan Contact: Phillip Choate
Service Area: Payette, Washington, Adams, Valley, Gem, Boise, Elmore, Ada, Canyon and Owhyee counties

Panhandle Area Council
11100 Airport Dr.
Hayden, ID 83835-9743
208-772-0584
Fax: 208-772-6196
E-mail: pacbus@nidlink.com or ksmith@nidlink.com
Executive Director: James Deffenbaugh
Microloan Contact: Kurt Smith
Service Area: Northern Panhandle including Benewah, Bonner, Boundary, Kotenai, and Shoshone counties

Illinois
Greater Sterling Development Corporation
1741 Industrial Dr.
Sterling, IL 61081
815-625-5255
Fax: 815-625-5094
E-mail: jbaeza@essex1.com
Executive Director: Reid Nolte
Microloan Contact: Reid Nolte
Service Area: City of Sterling, Whiteside and Lee counties

Illinois Development Finance Authority
5310 Sears Tower
233 S. Wacker Dr., Suite 5310
Chicago, IL 60606

312-793-5586
Fax: 312-793-6347
Executive Director: Bobby
Wilkerson
Microloan Contact: Sharnell Curtis
Service Area: Statewide with the
exceptions of Peoria, Tazwell,
Woodford, Whiteside and Lee
counties, the City of Sterling, and
those portions of Chicago currently
served by WSEP

The Economic Development
Council for the Peoria Area
124 SW Adams St., Suite 300
Peoria, IL 61602
309-676-7500
Fax: 309-676-6638
E-mail: mfkuhns@juno.com
Executive Director: William
Browning
Microloan Contact: Michael Kuhns
Service Area: Peoria, Tazwell and
Woodford counties

Neighborhood Inst./Women's Self
Employment Project
20 N. Clark St., Suite 400
Chicago, IL 60602
312-606-8255
Fax: 312-606-9256
E-mail: hn1578@handsnet.org
Executive Director: Connie Evans
Microloan Contact: Connie Evans
Service Area: Portions of the City
of Chicago

Indiana
Eastside Community Investments
Inc.
26 North Arsenal Ave.
Indianapolis, IN 46201
317-637-7300

Fax: 317-637-7581
Executive Director: Dennis J. West
Service Area: City of Indianapolis

Metro Small Business Assistance
Corp.
306 Civic Center Complex
1 NW Martin Luther King, Jr. Blvd.
Evansville, IN 47708-1869
812-426-5857
Fax: 812-426-5384
E-mail: wildeman@evansville.net
Exec. Dir.: Michael Robling
Microloan Contact: Debra
Lutz/Diane Powless
Service Area: Vanderburgh, Posey,
Gibson, and Warrick counties

Iowa
Siouxland Economic Development
Corporation
428 Insurance Center
507 7th St.
P.O. Box 447
Sioux City, IA 51102
712-279-6286
Fax: 712-279-6920
E-mail: simpco@pionet.net
Executive Director: Ken Beekley
Microloan Contact: Billie Kwikkel
Service Area: Cherokee, Ida
Monona, Plymouth, Sioux, and
Woodbury counties

Kansas
South Central Kansas Economic
Dev. District, Inc.
151 N. Volutsia
Wichita, KS 67214
316-683-4422
Fax: 316-683-7326
Exec. Dir.: Jack Alumbaugh
Microloan Contact: Christie Henry

Service Area: Butler, Chautauqua, Cowley, Elk, Greenwood, Harper, Harvey, Kingman, Marion, McPherson, Reno, Rice, Sedgwick, and Sumner counties

Small Business Assistance

Center for Business Innovations, Inc.
4747 Troost Ave.
Kansas City, MO 64110
816-561-8567
Fax: 816-756-1530
E-mail: pmwheeler@kc-cbi.org
Executive Director: David Eltiste
Microloan Contact: Pratheba Mathews-Wheeler
Service Area: Wyandotte, Johnson, Douglas, and Leavenworth

Kentucky
Community Ventures Corporation
1450 N. Broadway
Lexington, KY 40505
606-231-0054
Fax: 606-231-0261
E-mail: cvccorp@worldnet.att.com
Executive Director: Kevin Smith
Microloan Contact: Tyrone Tyra/Mark Koller
Service Area: Anderson, Bourbon, Clark, Fayette, Harrison, Jessamine, Nicholas, Scott, and Woodford counties

Kentucky Highlands Investment Corporation
362 Whitley Rd.
P.O. Box 1738

London, KY 40743-1738
606-864-5175
Fax: 606-864-5194
E-mail: knicnet@aol.com
Executive Director: Jerry Rickett
Microloan Contact: Brenda McDaniel/Stephen Taylor
Service Area: Bell, Clay, Clinton, Harlan, Jackson, Knox, Laurel, McCreary, Pulaski, Rockcastle, Wayne, and Whitley counties

Louisville Central Development Corporation/Business Plus
1015 West Chestnut St.
Louisville, KY 40203
502-583-8821
Fax: 502-583-8824
E-mail: microlcdc@aol.com
Exec. Dir.: Sam Watkins Jr.
Microloan Contact: Cheri Davis Taylor
Service Area: Russell neighborhood of Louisville

Purchase Area Development District
1002 Medical Drive
P.O. Box 588
Mayfield, KY 42066
502-247-7171
Fax: 502-251-6110
E-mail: purradd@apex.net
Executive Director: Henry Hodges
Microloan Contact: Norma Reed-Drouin
Service Area: Ballard, Calloway, Carlisle, Fulton, Graves, Hickman, McCracken and Marshall counties

Maine
Coastal Enterprises, Inc.
P.O. Box 268

Water Street
Wiscasset, ME 04578
207-882-7552
Fax: 207-882-7308
E-mail: efg@cei.maine.org or
jgs@cei.maine.org
Executive Director: Ronald Phillips
Microloan Contact: Ellen Golden
Service Area: Statewide excluding
Aroostock, Piscataquis,
Washington, Oxford, Penobscot and
Hancock counties

Northern Maine Development
Commission
2 S. Main St.
P.O. Box 779
Caribou, ME 04736
207-498-8736
Fax: 207-493-3108
E-mail: julied@emdc.org
Executive Director: Robert Clark
Microloan Contact: Duane Walton
Service Area: Aroostook,
Piscataquis, Washington, Penobscot
and Hancock counties
> In consortium with
> Eastern Maine Development
> Corporation
> One Cumberland Pl., Suite 300
> Bangor, ME 04401
> 207-942-6389
> Fax: 207-942-3548
> E-mail: dmetzler@emdc.org
> Executive Director: David Cole
> Microloan Contact: Debbie
> Metzler
> Service Area: Hancock,
> Penobscot, Piscataquis, and
> Washington counties

Community Concepts, Inc.
35 Market Sq.

P.O. Box 278
South Paris, ME 04281
207-743-7716
Fax: 207-743-6513
E-mail: wriseman@community-
concepts.org
Executive Director: Charleen Chase
Microloan Contact: Walter Riseman
Service Area: Oxford county

Maryland
Council for Economic Business
Opportunity, Inc.
The Park Plaza
800 N. Charles St., Suite 300
Baltimore, MD 21201
410-576-2326
Fax: 410-576-2498
Executive Director: Larry J. Smith
Microloan Contact: Helene
McBride
Service Area: City of Baltimore and
Ann Arundel, Baltimore, Carroll,
Harford, and Howard counties

Massachusetts
Economic Development Industrial
Corp. of Lynn
37 Central Square, 3rd Floor
Lynn, MA 01901
617-581-9399
Fax: 617-581-9731
E-mail: msmalley@shore.net
Exec. Director: Peter M. DeVeau
Microloan Contact: Peter M.
DeVeau
Service Area: City of Lynn

Jewish Vocational Service, Inc.
105 Chauncy St., 6th Floor
Boston, MA 02111
617-451-8147
Fax: 617-451-9973

Microenterprise Loans

E-mail: jvsmicro@shore.net
Exec. Dir.: Barbara Rosenbaum
Microloan Contact: Paula Mannillo
Service Area: Greater Boston with
special emphasis on businesses in
the Boston Enterprise Zone/Boston
Empowerment Zone, and
businesses in Mattapan, Dorchester,
Roxbury, Hyde Park, and Jamaica
Plain

Jobs for Fall River, Inc.
One Government Center
Fall River, MA 02722
508-324-2620
Fax: 508-677-2840
E-mail: info@fallriver-ma.com
Executive Director: Kenneth Fiola
Microloan Contact: Stephen Parr
Service Area: City of Fall River

Springfield Business Development
Fund
1176 Main St.
Springfield, MA 01103
413-781-6900
Fax: 413-736-0650
E-mail: hcetc@javanet.com
Executive Director: Jim Krzytofik
Microloan Contact: James Asselin
Service Area: City of Springfield

Western Massachusetts Enterprise
Fund
308 Main St., Suite 2B
Greenfield, MA 01301
413-774-4033
Fax: 413-773-3562
E-mail: wmeflh@aol.com
Executive Director: Christopher
Sikes
Microloan Contact: Lorraine
Heidemann

Service Area: Berkshire, Franklin
counties, the towns of Chester and
Chicopes within Hampden county,
the towns of Athol, Petersham,
Phillipston and Royalston within
Worcester county, and the
following towns within Hampshire
county: Amherst, Chesterfield,
Cummington, Easthampton,
Goshen, Hadley, Huntington,
Middlefield, Northampton,
Plainfield, Westhampton,
Williamsburg and Worthington

Michigan
Ann Arbor Community
Development Corp.
2002 Hogback Rd., Suite 12
Ann Arbor, MI 48105
313-677-1400
Fax: 313-677-1465
E-mail: mrichards@miceed.org
Exec. Dir.: Michelle Richards
Microloan Contact: Tammy Jolley
Service Area: Washtenaw county

Detroit Economic Growth
Corporation
150 W. Jefferson, Suite 1000
Detroit, MI 48226
313-963-2940
Fax: 313-963-8839
E-mail: degc@aol.com
Executive Director: C. Beth
Duncombe
Microloan Contact: C. Beth
Duncombe
Service Area: City of Detroit

Community Capital and
Development Corp.
The Walter Reuther Center
711 N. Saginaw St., Suite 123

Flint, MI 48503
810-239-5847
Fax: 810-239-5575
E-mail: ccdc@bizserv.com
Executive Director: Bobby Wells
Microloan Contact: Bobby Wells
Service Area: Genesee county

Northern Initiatives Corp.
228 West Washington St.
Marquette, MI 49855
906-228-5571
Fax: 906-228-5572
E-mail: ni@northerninits.com
Executive Director: Dennis West
Microloan Contact: Roni
Montieth/Scott Sporte
Service Area: Upper Peninsula
including Alger, Baraga, Chippewa,
Delta, Dickinson, Gogebic,
Houghton, Iron, Keewenaw, Luce,
Macinac, Marquette, Menonimee,
Ontonagon, and Schoolcraft
counties

Minnesota
Northeast Entrepreneur Fund, Inc.
820 Ninth Street North
Virginia, MN 55792
218-749-4191
Fax: 218-741-4249
E-mail: nefva@northernnet.com
Executive Director: Mary Mathews
Microloan Contact: John
Damjanovich/Carla Tichy
Service Area: Koochiching, Itasca,
St. Louis, Aitkin, Carlton, Cook and
Lake counties

Women Venture
2324 University Ave.
St. Paul, MN 55112
651-646-3808
Fax: 651-291-2597

E-mail: womenven@minn.net
Executive Director: Kay
Gudmedstad
Microloan Contact: Cynthia
Paulson
Service Area: Cities of Minneapolis
and St. Paul, and Andra, Carver,
Chisago, Dakota, Hennepin, Isanti,
Ramsey, Scott, Washington, and
Wright counties

Minneapolis Consortium of
Community Developers
1808 Riverside Ave. S., Suite 206
Minneapolis, MN 55454-1035
612-371-9986
Fax: 612-673-0379
E-mail: reidk@cando.org or
lamberte@cando.org
Executive Director: Ed Lambert
Microloan Contact: Karen Reid
Service Area: Portions of the City
of Minneapolis

Northwest Minnesota Foundation
722 Paul Bunyan Dr., NW
Bemidji, MN 56601
218-759-2057
Fax: 218-759-2328
E-mail: nwmf@paulbunyan.net
Executive Director: Ruth Edevold
Microloan Contact: Steve
Schoeneck
Service Area: Beltrami, Clearwater,
Hubbard, Kittsson, Lake of the
Woods, Mahnomen, Marshall,
Norman, Pennington, Polk, Red
Lake, and Rousseau counties

Mississippi

Delta Foundation
819 Main St.
Greenville, MS 38701
601-335-5291
Fax: 601-335-5295
E-mail: deltafdn@tech.info.com
Executive Director: Harry Bowie
Microloan Contact: Lisa Tate
Service Area: Statewide excluding
Issaquena, Sharkey, Humphreys,
Madison, Leake, Kemper, Copiah,
Hinds, Rankin, Newton, Smith,
Jasper, Clarke, Jones, Wayne, and
Greene counties

Friends of Children of Mississippi,
Inc.
4880 McWillie Cr.
Jackson, MS 39206
601-362-1541
Fax: 601-362-1613
Executive Director: Marvin Hogan
Microloan Contact: Willie
Robinson
Service Area: Issaquena, Sharkey,
Humphreys, Madison, Leake,
Kemper, Copiah, Hinds, Rankin,
Newton, Smith, Jasper, Clarke,
Jones, Wayne, and Greene counties

Missouri

Center for Business Innovation, Inc.
4747 Troost Ave.
Kansas City, MO 64110
816-561-8567
Fax: 816-756-1530
E-mail: pmwheeler@kc-cbi.org
Executive Director: Dale Eltiste
Microloan Contact: Prathiba
Mathews-Wheeler
Service Area: Statewide

Montana

Capital Opportunities/District IX
HRDC, Inc.
321 E. Main St., Suite 300
Bozeman, MT 59715
406-587-4486
Fax: 406-585-3538
Executive Director: Charlie Hill
Service Area: Gallatin, Park and
Meagher counties

Montana Community Development
Corp.
127 N. Higgins Ave., 3rd Floor
Missoula, MT 59802
406-543-3550
Fax: 406-721-4584
E-mail: tswenson@montana.com
Executive Director: Rosalie Cates
Microloan Contact: Thomas
Swenson
Service Area: Lake, Mineral,
Missoula, Ravalli, and Sanders
counties

Nebraska

Rural Enterprise Assistance Project
Center for Rural Affairs
101 S. Tallman St.
P.O. Box 406
Walthill, NE 68067
402-846-5428
Fax: 402-846-5420
E-mail: hn1721@handset.org
Executive Director: Don Ralston
Microloan Contact: Rose Jaspersen
Service Area: Antelope, Banner,
Blaine, Boone, Box Butte, Boyd,
Brown, Burt, Cass, Cedar, Cherry,
Cheyenne, Colfax, Custer, Dawes,
Deuel, Dixon, Gage, Garden,
Garfield, Greeley, Holt, Jefferson,
Johnson, Keya Paha, Kimball,

Knox, Lancaster, Loup, McPherson, Morrill, Nance, Nemaha, Otoe, Pawnee, Pierce, Platte, Richardson, Rock, Saline, Saunders, Seward, Sheridan, Sioux, Scottsbluff, Thurston, Wayne, and Wheeler counties

West Central Nebraska
Development District, Inc.
201 East 2nd Street, Suite C
P.O. Box 599
Ogailala, NE 69153
308-284-6077
Fax: 308-284-6070
E-mail: wcndd@megavision.com
Executive Director: Ronald J. Radil
Microloan Contact: Ronald J. Radil
Service Area: Arthur, Chase, Dawson, Dundy, Frontier, Furnas, Gosper, Grant, Hayes, Hitchcock, Hooker, Keith, Lincoln, Logan, Perkins, Red Willow, and Thomas counties

Nevada
NWF /Nevada Self Employment
Trust
560 Mill St., Suite 260
Reno, NV 89502
702-786-2335
Fax: 702-786-8152
Executive Director: Janice Barbour
Service Area: Statewide

New Hampshire
Northern Community Investment
Corp.
c/o 20 Main St.
St. Johnsbury, VT 05819
802-748-5101
Fax: 802-748-1884
E-mail: terry@ncic.org

Exec. Dir.: Carl J. Garbelotti
Microloan Contact: Terry Hoffer
Service Area: Grafton, Carol and
Coos counties

New Jersey
Trenton Business Assistance Corp.
Division of Economic Development
P.O. Box 2451
Trenton, NJ 08608
609-396-8271
Fax: 609-396-8603
E-mail: ljanotalll@aol.com
Executive Director: Liz Janota
Microloan Contact: Liz Janota
Service Area: Portions of the City
of Trenton and Mercer County

Greater Newark Business
Development Consortium
One Newark Center, 22nd Floor
Newark, NJ 07102-5265
973-242-6237
Fax: 973-824-6587
Executive Director: David Means
Microloan Contact: David Means
Service Area: Bergen, Essex, Hudson, Middlesex, Monmouth, Morris, Passaic, and Somerset counties with the exception of the city of Jersey City

Union County Economic
Development Corp.
Liberty Hall Corporate Center
1085 Morris Ave., Suite 531
Union, NJ 07083
908-527-1166
Fax: 908-527-1207
E-mail: ucedc@worldnet.att.net
Executive Director: Maureen Tinen
Microloan Contact: Ellen McHenry
Service Area: Union county

Jersey City Economic Development
Corp.
601 Pavonia Ave.
Jersey City, NJ 07306
201-420-7755
Fax: 201-420-0306
Executive Director: Thomas Ahern
Microloan Contact: John Rogers
Service Area: City of Jersey City

New Mexico
Women's Economic Self
Sufficiency Team
414 Silver SW
Albuquerque, NM 87102-3239
505-241-4758
Fax: 505-241-4766
E-mail: agnes@swcp.com or
dbaca@swcp.com
Executive Director: Agnes Noonan
Microloan Contact: Debbie Baca
Service Area: Statewide

New York
Adirondack Economic
Development Corporation
Trudeau Road
P.O. Box 747
Saranac Lake, NY 12983
518-891-5523
Fax: 518-891-9820
E-mail: aedc@northnet.org
Executive Director: Ernest
Hohmeyer
Microloan Contact: Rod Garret
Service Area: Clinton, Essex,
Franklin, Fulton, Hamilton,
Herkimer, Jefferson, Lewis, Oneida,
Oswego, St. Lawrence, Saratoga,
Warren and Washington counties

Columbia Hudson Partnership
444 Warren St.

Hudson, NY 12534-2415
518-828-4718
Fax: 518-828-0901
E-mail: 76072.2771@
compuserve.com
Executive Director: Jim Callander
Microloan Contact: Jim Callander
Service Area: Columbia county

Manhattan Borough Development
Corp.
15 Park Row, Suite 510
New York, NY 10038
212-791-3660
Fax: 212-571-0873
Executive Director: Jeff Deasy
Microloan Contact: David Gale
Service Area: The borough of
Manhattan

Rural Opportunities Enterprise
Center, Inc.
339 East Avenue
Suite 401
Rochester, NY 14604
716-546-6325
Fax: 716-546-7337
E-mail: jdallis@frontiernet.com
Executive Director: Stuart Mitchell
Microloan Contact: Joan Dallis
Service Area: Allegheny,
Cattaraugua, Cayuga, Chatauqua,
Erie, Genessee, Livingston,
Niagara, Ontario, Orleans, Senece,
Steuben, Wayne, Wyoming and
Yates counties

North Carolina
Self-Help Ventures Fund
301 W. Main St.
P.O. Box 3619
Durham, NC 27701
919-956-4400

Fax: 919-956-4600
E-mail: bob@self-help.org
Executive Director: Martin
Eakes/Carolyn Walker
Microloan Contact: Bob Schall
Service Area: Statewide

W.A.M.Y. Community Action
152 Southgate Dr.
Box 2688
Boone, NC 28607
704-264-2421
Fax: 704-264-0952
E-mail: wamyloan@boone.net
Executive Director: Don Baucom
Microloan Contact: Lisa Avalos
Service Area: Watauga, Avery,
Mitchell, and Yancey counties

North Dakota
Lake Agassiz Regional Council
417 Main Ave.
Fargo, ND 58103
701-235-1197
Fax: 701-235-6706
Executive Director: Irvin Rustad
Microloan Contact: Sue Hartmann
Service Area: Statewide

Ohio
Enterprise Development
Corporation
9030 Hocking Hills Dr.
The Plains, OH 45780
740-797-9646
Fax: 740-797-9659
E-mail: edc@seorf.ohiou.edu
Executive Director: Karen Patton
Microloan Contact: Brian Martin
Service Area: Adams, Ashland,
Athens, Belmont, Brown, Carrol,
Columbiana, Coshocton, Gallia,
Guernsey, Harrison, Highland,

Holmes, Jackson, Jefferson, Knox,
Lawrence, Meigs, Monroe, Morgan,
Muskingum, Nocking, Noble,
Perry, Pike, Ross, Scioto,
Tuscarawas, Vinton and
Washington counties

Columbus Countywide
Development Corporation
941 Chatham Lane, Suite 300
Columbus, OH 43221-2416
614-645-6171
Fax: 614-645-8588
E-mail: ccdc@earthlink.net or
bshimp@earthlink.net
Executive Director: Mark Barbash
Microloan Contact: Brad
Shrimp/Andrea Patterson
Service Area: City of Columbus,
Franklin, Delaware, Fairfield, and
Licking counties

Hamilton County Development Co.,
Inc.
1776 Mentor Ave.
Cincinnati, OH 45212
513-631-8292
Fax: 513-631-4887
E-mail: hcbctr@aol.com
Executive Director: David Main
Microloan Contact: Patrick Longo
Service Area: City of Cincinnati,
Adams, Brown, Butler, Clermont,
Clinton, Highland, and Warren
counties

Women's Organization for
Mentoring, Entrepreneurship, and
Networking
526 S. Main St., Suite 235
Akron, OH 44311-1058
330-379-9280
Fax: 330-379-9283

E-mail: cherman@womennet.org
Executive Director: Carrie Herman
Microloan Contact: Catherine
Robertson
Service Area: Ashtabula,
Cuyahoga, Geauga, Lake, Lorain,
Mahoning, Medina, Portage, Stark,
Summit, Trumbull, Wayne

Oklahoma

Rural Enterprises, Inc.
422 Cessna Dr.
P.O. Box 1335
Durant, OK 74702
580-924-5094
Fax: 580-920-2745
E-mail: sherryh@ruralenterprises.
com
Executive Director: Tom Smith
Microloan Contact: Sherry Harlin
Service Area: Statewide

Tulsa Economic Development
Corporation
907 S. Detroit Ave., Suite 1001
Tulsa, OK 74120
918-585-8332
Fax: 918-585-2473
Executive Director: Frank McGrady
Microloan Contact: Frank McGrady
Service Area: Adair, Canadian,
Cherokee, Cleveland, Craig, Creek,
Delaware, Haskell, Hayes, Hughes,
Kay, Latimer, Leflore, Lincoln,
Logan, McIntosh, Muskogee,
Noble, Nowata, Okfuskee,
Oklahoma, Okmulgee, Osage,
Ottawa, Pawnee, Payne, Pittsburg,
Pottawatomie, Rogers, Seminole,

Sequoyah, Wagoner, Washington,
and Wayne counties including the
city of Tulsa

Oregon

Cascades West Financial Services,
Inc.
P.O. Box 686
Albany, OR 97321
541-924-8480
Fax: 541-967-4651
E-mail: dsearle@cwcog.or.us
Executive Director: Robert
Wisniewski
Microloan Contact: Diane Searle
Service Area: Benton, Clackamas,
Hood River, Jefferson, Lane,
Lincoln, Linn, Marion, Multnomah,
Polk, Tillamook, Wasco,
Washington, and Yamhill

Ida-Ore Planning and Development
Association, Inc.
10624 W. Executive Dr.
Boise, ID 83713
208-322-7033
Fax: 208-322-3569
Executive Director: Phillip Choate
Microloan Contact: Phillip Choate
Service Area: Harney and Malheur
counties

Pennsylvania

The Ben Franklin Tech. Center of
SE Pennsylvania
3624 Market St.
Philadelphia, PA 19104-2615
215-382-0380
Fax: 215-382-6050
E-mail: bftc@benfranklin.org or
irving@benfranklin.org
Executive Director: Rose Ann
Rosenthal

Microloan Contact: Irving Finley
Service Area: Bucks, Chester,
Delaware, Montgomery, and
Philadelphia counties

The Washington County Council on
Economic Development
100 W. Beau St., Suite 703
Washington, PA 15301-4432
724-228-6816
Fax: 724-250-6502
E-mail: dano@pulsenet.com
Executive Director: Malcolm
Morgan
Microloan Contact: Ed Collins/Jim
Fulton
Service Area: Southwestern area of
Pennsylvania including Greene,
Fayette, Washington, and
Westmoreland counties

York County Industrial
Development Corp.
160 Roosevelt Ave.
York, PA 17401
717-846-8879
Fax: 717-843-8837
E-mail: cyberctr@ycidc.org
Executive Director: David Carver
Microloan Contact: Jill Edwards
Service Area: York county

Puerto Rico
Economic Development
Corporation of San Juan
(COFECC)
1103 Rio Piedras
San Juan, PR 00926
787-756-5080
Fax: 787-753-8960
E-mail: cofecc@worldnet.att.net
Exec. Director: Jesus Rivera Viera

Microloan Contact: Milagros E.
Resto
Service Area: Territory wide

South Carolina
Charleston Citywide Local
Development Corporation
75 Calhoun St., 3rd Floor
Charleston, SC 29403
803-724-3796
Fax: 803-724-7354
E-mail: economicdev@
charleston.net
Executive Director: Sharon
Brennan
Microloan Contact: Michelle
Ingle/Dwayne Jubar
Service Area: City of Charleston

Santee-Lynches Regional
Development Corp.
P.O. Box 1837
Sumter, SC 29151
803-775-7381
Fax: 803-773-9903
Exec. Director: James Darby, Jr.
Microloan Contact: Linda Shipley
Service Area: Clarendon, Kershaw,
Lee and Sumter counties

South Dakota
Lakota Fund
P.O. Box 340
Kyle, SD 57752
605-455-2500
Fax: 605-455-2385
Exec. Director: Dani Not Help Him
Microloan Contact: Dani Not Help
Him
Service Area: Bennett county, Pine
Ridge Indian Reservation, and areas
of Shannon and Jackson counties
which are surrounded by Indian

Lands, and exclusive of Northern
Jackson county

NE South Dakota Economic
Corporation
414 Third Ave., East
Sisseton, SD 57262-1598
605-698-7654
Fax: 605-698-3038
E-mail: nesdcap@tnics.com
Executive Director: Robert Hull
Microloan Contact: Bruce
Austad/Robert Hull
Service Area: Beadle, Brown,
Buffalo, Campbell, Clark,
Codington, Day, Edmunds, Faulk,
Grant, Hand, Hyde, Jerauld,
Kingsbury, McPherson, Marshall,
Miner, Potter, Roberts, Sanborn,
Spink, and Walworth counties

Tennessee
South Central Tennessee
Development District
815 S. Main St.
P.O. Box 1346
Columbia, TN 38402
931-381-2040
Fax: 931-381-2053
E-mail: sctdd@sctdd.org
Exec. Director: Joe Max Williams
Microloan Contact: Doug Williams
Service Area: Bedford, Coffee,
Franklin, Giles, Hickman,
Lawrence, Lewis, Lincoln,
Marshall, Maury, Moore, Perry, and
Wayne counties

Texas
Business Resource Center Incubator
401 Franklin
Waco, TX 76708
254-754-8898

Fax: 254-756-0776
E-mail: brc@digilogix.com
Executive Director: Lu Billings
Microloan Contact: John Dosher
Service Area: Bell, Bosque,
Coryell, Falls, Hill, and McLennan
counties

Local Development Corporations

The Corporation for Economic
Development of Harris County
3100 Timmens Lane, Suite 222
Houston, TX 77027-5926
713-840-8804
Fax: 713-840-8806
E-mail: jfowler@hchcda.co.
harris.tx.us
Executive Director: Amos Brown
Microloan Contact: Janis Fowler
Service Area: Brazoria, Chambers,
Fort Bend, Galveston, Harris,
Liberty, Montgomery, and Waller
counties

San Antonio Local Development
Corporation
215 S. San Saba
San Antonio, TX 78207
210-207-8152
Fax: 210-207-8151
E-mail: operez@ci.sat.tx.us
Executive Director: Clinton Bolden
Microloan Contact: Oscar Perez
Service Area: Atascosa, Bandera,
Bexar, Comal, Frio, Gillespie,
Guadalupe, Karnes, Kendall, Kerr,
Medina, and Wilson counties

Southern Dallas Development
Corporation
1402 Corinth, Suite 1150
Dallas, TX 75215
214-428-7332
Fax: 214-426-6847
Executive Director: Charles English
Microloan Contact: Victore
Elmore/Theresa Lee
Service Area: Portions of the City
of Dallas

Utah
Utah Technology Finance
Corporation
177 East 100 South
Salt Lake City, UT 84111
801-741-4206
Fax: 801-741-4249
Microloan Contact: Scott
Stenburg/Steve Grizzell
Service Area: Statewide

Vermont
Economic Development Council of
Northern Vermont, Inc.
155 Lake St.
St. Albans, VT 05478
802-524-4546
Fax: 802-527-1081
E-mail: edcnv@together.net
Executive Director: Connie Stanley-
Little
Microloan Contact: Connie Stanley-
Little/William Farr
Service Area: Chittenden, Franklin,
Grand Isle, Lamoille, and
Washington counties

Northern Community Investments
Corporation
20 Main St.
P.O. Box 904

St. Johnsbury, VT 05819
802-748-5101
Fax: 802-748-1884
E-mail: terry@ncic.org
Executive Director: Paul Denton
Microloan Contact: Terry Hoffer
Service Area: Caledonia, Essex, and
Orleans counties

Virginia
Ethiopian Community
Development Council, Inc.
1038 S. Highland St.
Arlington, VA 22204
703-685-0510
Fax: 703-685-0529
E-mail: ecdcmicro@erols.com
Executive Director: Tschaye
Teferra
Microloan Contact: Caroline
Hayashi
Service Area: Prince William,
Arlington and Fairfax counties and
the cities of Alexandria and Falls
Church

Business Development Centre, Inc.
147 Mill Ridge Road
Lynchburg, VA 24502
804-582-6100
Fax: 804-582-6106
E-mail: catherine@bdc.com
Executive Director: Catherine
McFaden
Microloan Contact: Rich Stallings
Service Area: Amherst,
Appomattox, Bedford, Campell
counties, cities of Lynchburg and
Bedford, and the Town of Amherst

People Incorporated of Southwest
Virginia
1173 W. Main St.

Abingdon, VA 24210
540-623-9000
Fax: 540-628-2931
E-mail: businesstart@naxs.com
Executive Director: Robert G.
Goldsmith
Microloan Contact: Welthy Soni
Service Area: Buchanan,
Dickenson, Lee, Russell, Scott,
Washington, Wise counties and the
cities of Bristol and Norton

Washington
Snohomish County Private Industry
Council
917 134th St., SW, Suite A-10
Everett, WA 98204
425-743-9669
Fax: 425-742-1177
E-mail: snopic@fx.netcom.com
Executive Director: Emily Duncan
Microloan Contact: Eric Wogstad
Service Area: Adams, Chelan,
Douglas, Grant, King, Kitsap,
Kittitas, Klickitat, Okanogan,
Pierce, Skagit, Snohomish,
Whatcom, and Yakima counties

Tri-Cities Enterprise Association
2000 Logston Boulevard
Richland, WA 99352
509-946-4334
Fax: 509-946-2129
E-mail: cgamache@owt.com
Executive Director: Dallas E.
Breamer
Microloan Contact: Cris Gamache
Service Area: Benton and Franklin
counties

West Virginia
Ohio Valley Industrial and Business
Dev. Corp.

P.O. Box 1029
1140 Chapline St.
Wheeling, WV 26003
304-232-7722
Fax: 304-232-7727
E-mail: jkagler@hge.net
Executive Director: Terry Burkhart
Microloan Contact: Joanne Kagler
Service Area: Marshall, Ohio,
Wetzel, Brooke, Hancock, and
Tyler counties

The Washington County Council on
Economic Development
703 Courthouse Square
Washington, PA 15301
724-228-6816
Fax: 724-250-6502
E-mail: dano@pulsenet.com
Exec. Director: Malcolm L. Morgan
Service Area: Preston and
Monongalia counties

Wisconsin
Advocap, Inc.
19 W. 1st St.
P.O. Box 1108
Fond du Lac, WI 54936
920-922-7760
Fax: 920-922-7214
E-mail: tonyb@advocap.org
Executive Director: Richard
Schlimm
Microloan Contact: Mort Gazerwitz
Service Area: Fond du Lac, Green
Lake, and Winnebago counties

Impact Seven, Inc.
651 Garfield St. S
Almena, WI 54805-9900
715-357-3334
Fax: 715-357-6233
E-mail: impact@win.bright.net

Executive Director: William Bay
Microloan Contact: William Bay
Service Area: Statewide with the
exceptions of Fond du Lac, Green
Lake, Kenosha, Milwaukee,
Oasukee, Racine, Walworth,
Waukesha, Washington, and
Winnebago counties and inner city
Milwaukee

Wisconsin Women's Business
Initiative Corporation
1915 N. Dr. Martin Luther King Jr.
Dr.
Milwaukee, WI 53212
414-372-2070
Fax: 414-372-2083
E-mail: wwbic@execpc.com
Executive Director: Wendy
Werkmeister
Microloan Contact: Geraldine
Johnson
Service Area: Kenosha, Milwaukee,
Ozaukee, Racine, Walworth,
Washington and Waukesha counties

Technical Assistance Grant Recipients

Alaska
Juneau Economic Development
Council
612 W. Willoughby
Juneau, AK 99801-1724
907-463-3662
Fax: 907-463-3929
E-mail: jedc@ptialaska.net or
kflanders@ptialaska.net
Executive Director: Charles
Northrip
Microloan Contact: Kirk Flanders
Service Area: Through SBDCs, the
Alaska Panhandle

California
Women's Initiative for Self
Employment
450 Mission, Suite 402
San Francisco, CA 94105
415-247-9473
Fax: 415-247-9471
E-mail: womensinitsf@igc.apc.org
Executive Director: Barbara
Johnson
Microloan Contact: Corinne Florek
Service Area: defined sectors of San
Francisco Bay Area

Connecticut
American Woman's Economic
Development Corp.
Plaza West Office Centers
200 W. Main St., Suite 140
Stamford, CT 06902
203-326-7914
Executive Director: Fran Polak
Service Area: SW corner including
Ansonia, Beacon Falls, Bethel,
Bridgeport, Bridgewater,
Brookfield, Danbury, Darien,
Derby, Easton, Fairfield,
Greenwich, Milford, Monroe, New
Canaan, New Fairfield, New
Milford, Newtown, Norwalk,
Oxford, Redding, Ridgefield,
Seymour, Shelton, Sherman,
Stamford, Stratford, Trumbull,
Weston, Westport, and Wilton
counties

Florida
Lee County Employment and
Economic Dev. Corp.
2121 W. 1st St., Suite One
P.O. Box 2285
Fort Myers, FL 33901
941-337-2300

Fax: 941-337-4558
Executive Director: Roy Kennix
Microloan Contact: Roy Kennix
Service Area: Community
Redevelopment areas of Lee
County including Charleston Park,
Dunbar, Harlem Heights, North
Fort Myers, and State Road 80

Illinois
Women's Business Development
Center
8 South Michigan Ave., Suite 400
Chicago, IL 60603
312-853-3477
Fax: 312-853-0145
E-mail: wbdc@aol.com
Executive Director: Hedy Ratner
Microloan Contact: Carol Dougal
Service Area: Boone, Cook,
DeKalb, DuPage, Kane, Kankakee,
Kendall, Lake, McHenry, Will, and
Winnebago counties

Women's Organizations

Indiana
Hoosier Valley Economic
Development Corp.
1613 E. 8th
P.O. Box 843
Jeffersonville, IN 47130
812-288-6451
Fax: 812-284-8314
Executive Director: Robert Moore
Microloan Contact: Darnell Jackson
Service Area: Clark, Crawford,
Floyd, Harrison, Orange, Scott, and
Washington counties

Iowa
Institute for Social and Economic
Development
1901 Broadway, Suite 313
Iowa City, IA 52240
319-338-2331
Fax: 319-338-5824
E-mail: jfriedman@ised.org
Executive Director: Jason Friedman
Microloan Contact: Jason Friedman
Service Area: Statewide

Kansas
Great Plains Development, Inc.
100 Military Plaza, Suite 128
P.O. Box 1116
Dodge City, KS 67801
316-227-6406
Fax: 316-225-6051
Exec. Director: Patty Richardson
Microloan Contact: Patty
Richardson
Service Area: Statewide

Michigan
Cornerstone Alliance
38 W. Wall St.
P.O. Box 428
Benton Harbor, MI 49023-0428
616-925-6100
Fax: 616-925-4471
E-mail: gvaughn@
cstonealliance.org
Executive Director: Jeff Noel
Microloan Contact: Gregory
Vaughn
Service Area: Berrien County and
City of Benton Harbor

Minnesota
Neighborhood Development
Center, Inc.
651½ University Ave.

St. Paul, MN 55104
651-291-2480
Fax: 651-291-2597
E-mail: windndc@mtn.org
Executive Director: Mihailo Temali
Microloan Contact: Mara O'Neil
Service Area: Districts 3, 5, 6, 8, 9,
and 16 of the City of St. Paul

Missouri
Community Development
Corporation of Kansas City
2420 E. Linwood Blvd., Suite 400
Kansas City, MO 64130
816-924-5800
Fax: 816-921-3350
E-mail: cdckcl@aol.com
Exec. Director: Donald Maxwell
Microloan Contact: Terrance
Hendricks
Service Area: Cass, Clay, Platte,
Ray and Jackson counties

Montana
Montana Department of Commerce
SBDC Division
1424 9th Ave.
P.O. Box 200501
Helena, MT 59620-0501
406-444-4780
Fax: 406-444-1872
E-mail: Rkloser@mt.gov
Executive Director: Gene Marcille
Service Area: Through SBDCs,
Cascade, Chouteau, Fergus, Glacier,
Golden Valley, Judity Basin,
Musselshell, Petroleum, Pondera,
Teton, Toole, and Wheatland
counties, and the Blackfeet,
Flathead, and Fort Peck
Reservations, and the Crow, Fort
Belknap, Northern Cheyenne and
Rocky Boys Reservations and their
Trust Lands

Nebraska
Omaha Small Business Network,
Inc.
2505 N. 24th St.
Omaha, NE 68110
402-453-5336
Fax: 402-451-2876
E-mail: crodgers@ne.uswest.net
Executive Director: Sherrye
McGhee
Microloan Contact: Chris Rodgers
Service Area: Areas of the City of
Omaha known as the North Omaha
and South Omaha Target Areas

New Mexico
New Mexico Community
Development Loan Fund
P.O. Box 705
Albuquerque, NM 87103-0705
505-243-3196
Fax: 505-243-8803
Exec. Director: Vangie Gabaldon
Microloan Contact: Rockling Todea
Service Area: Statewide

New York
Brooklyn Economic Development
Corporation
30 Flatbush Ave., Suite 420
Brooklyn, NY 11217-1197
718-522-4600
Fax: 718-797-9286
E-mail: info@bedc.org or
mad@bedc.org
Exec. Director: Joan Bartolomeo

Microloan Contact: Madeline
Marquez
Service Area: The five boroughs of
New York City

North Carolina
North Carolina Rural Economic
Dev. Center, Inc.
4021 Carya Dr.
Raleigh, NC 27610
919-250-4314
Fax: 919-250-4325
E-mail: pblack@mindspring.com
Executive Director: Billy Ray Hall
Microloan Contact: Phil Black
Service Area: Statewide

Pennsylvania
Philadelphia Commercial
Development Corporation
1315 Walnut St., Suite 600
Philadelphia, PA 19107-4706
215-790-5006
Fax: 215-790-5016
Executive Director: Curtis Jones Jr.
Microloan Contact: Linda Karl
Service Area: Bucks, Montgomery,
Philadelphia, Chester, and Delaware
counties

Texas
Greater Corpus Christi Business
Alliance
1201 N. Shoreline
P.O. Box 640
Corpus Christi, TX 78403

512-881-1847
Fax: 512-882-4256
E-mail: rortiz@cctexas.org
Executive Director: Keith Arnold
Microloan Contact: Rudy Ortiz
Service Area: Nueces and San
Patricio counties

Vermont
Champlain Valley Office of
Economic Opportunity, Inc.
95 North Ave.
Burlington, VT 05401 or
P.O. Box 1603
Burlington, VT 05402
802-860-1417
Fax: 802-860-1387
E-mail: mbdp@together.net
Executive Director: Robert Kiss
Microloan Contact: Dale Lane
Service Area: Statewide

Virginia
Virginia Microbusiness
Development Plan
VA SBDC Network
P.O. Box 446
Richmond, VA 23218
804-786-8087
Fax: 804-225-3384
E-mail: lroberts@dba.state.va.us
Executive Director: Larry Roberts
Microloan Contact: Larry Roberts
Service Area: Through SBDCs,
statewide

Money & Help To Start A Business When You Have No Money

Unconventional Loan Programs

The following is a description of loan programs available to low and moderate income individuals, minorities, Native Americans, Hispanics, refugees, unemployed individuals, welfare recipients, youths, and low and moderate income individuals who don't qualify for credit through conventional methods.

Most of these programs allow individuals (depending on the situation) to roll closing costs and fees into the amount of the loan. So you actually go to the closing with NO money in your pocket.

The aim of these programs is to stimulate economic growth through small businesses or microenterprises. Helping individuals become self-sufficient is the main focus, and also to challenge conventional methods of providing credit. All of the programs hope to demonstrate that persons with limited incomes are responsible, will repay, and can become successful if given access to knowledge and resources.

Some programs are designed just for youths, (15-21 years old), to develop their own businesses, avoid drugs and crime, sharpen academic skills and form positive attitudes about themselves and their communities. This is accomplished by utilizing the leadership, communication, management and business skills they may have acquired through affiliation with the illegal drug trade and other street activities. Loan amounts can range from $50 to $2,000 with terms from six months to two years.

The following is a small sample of many success stories that we found:

ACCION NEW YORK

Susanna Rodriquez started making ceramic figurines for children's parties. Susanna is a former teacher's assistant who presently works in the kitchen of her small apartment. Her creations fill every free corner. She was constantly looking for ways to expand her business. One day she was in a store where the owner sold similar products. As they were comparing notes, the owner mentioned ACCION New York. After four loans as a result of working with that organization, Susanna's monthly revenue from her ceramics business has increased from $350 a month to $800 a month. In time, she hopes to open her own store. She feels that if it were not for ACCION, she would not be at the advanced stage of business that she is enjoying now.

Jeff Hess of Virginia had fished and hunted with his father since the age of five. He earned his associates degree in business and was working in an assembly plant for a moderate hourly wage, but wanted more. At the age of 24 he didn't see opportunity coming to call on him because he had no money and no credit. He and his wife, Cherylanna enrolled in the BusinessStart class at People, Inc. With this training, assistance in small business planning and a small loan, Jeff and Cherylanna were able to buy a bait shop in Honaker and turn it into Bucks and Bass, a full service hunting and fishing store. Located in prime hunting and fishing country, Bucks and Bass has nearly doubled its sales in its first year alone. Both Jeff and Cherylanna have left their jobs and run Bucks and Bass full time.

Loan Programs

Alabama
SBA Microloan Program
Birmingham Business Resource Center
110 12th Street North   205-250-6380
Birmingham, AL 35203   Fax: 205-250-6384
E-mail: bbrc@inlinenet.net
Generally this loan is open to any micro business, but it has mainly served minorities and women owned businesses. Attendance of monthly peer group meetings for technical assistance is required. The loan can be up to $7,500 with the interest rate at 10 to 13 percent. The term is determined by each case, but generally from 12 to 24 months. This is for the Jefferson County area.

Arizona
Borrowers' Circle
Self-Employment Loan Fund, Inc.   602-340-8834
201 North Central Avenue, Suite CC10   Fax: 602-340-8953
Phoenix, AZ 85703   TDD: 800-842-4681
E-mail: Self-Employment@Juno.com
SELF offers assistance for those just starting a small business or that have been operational for less than six months. They use a peer lending system with a group of graduates that review the loans. Initial loans are up to $1,000 with 12 months to repay. Subsequent loans can be up to $5,000 with as many as 24 months to repay. Funding is through the U.S. Small Business Administration's Office of Women's Business Ownership, the City of Phoenix, corporations, foundations and Arizona banks.

Small Business Loan
PEEP Microbusiness and Housing Development Corporation
1100 East Hao Way, Suite 209   520-806-9513
Tucson, AZ 85713   Fax: 520-806-9515
This loan targets minority women and low-income small business owners. It is
specific to the Rural Central and Southern Arizona areas. The loan is for $500
to $25,000 and the term is 60 months. It can be used for inventory, supplies,
equipment and fixed assets.

Arkansas
The Good Faith Fund (GFF) - Peer Group Loan Program
The Good Faith Fund (GFF)
2304 W. 29th Ave.   870-535-6233
Pine Bluff, AR 71603   Fax: 870-535-0741
GFF's peer-lending program is for new and emerging entrepreneurs and operates
much like a community based credit union, with GFF providing the loan capital.
Members join peer-lending groups, which consider and approve small business
loans for their fellow member entrepreneurs. First time borrowers are eligible to
borrow up to $1,200. In a "Stair-step" loan process, borrowers may secure loans of
up to $7,500. Loan representatives assist interested borrowers in preparing their
loan request, including cash flow projections indicating that the proposed loan use
will produce increased sales and ensuring that the loan payments will be
manageable. This Fund receives funding from private foundations, SBA Microloan
Demonstration Program, contributions, and earnings.

Micro Loan
Good Faith Fund
2304 West 29th Street
Pinebluff, AR 71603   870-535-6233
This loan is available to people in the Delta region that would like to start a
business. The amount of the loan is from $500 to $25,000. The interest rate
varies depending on the loan, from 9 1/2% to 12%. Repayment must not be
over 7 years.

California
Micro Enterprise Assistance Program of Orange County
Micro Enterprise Assistance Program of Orange County
18011 Skypark Circle, Suite E
Irvine, CA 92614   949-252-1380
Eligible applicants are women and ethnic minorities below the poverty level. This
program receives funding from banks and private organizations. The aim of this

program is to provide access to credit, training, and support so that low income individuals and their families may become self-sufficient. Loans are up to $1,500 with terms up to one year. The interest rate is prime rate plus 4%.

Self-Employment Loan Fund
Women's Economic Ventures of Santa Barbara
1136 E. Montecito St.   805-965-6073
Santa Barbara, CA 93103   Fax: 805-962-9622
This program is helping women create their own employment in a community that is currently losing jobs. Loans are from $1,000 to $25,000, with terms set by the loan officer. This fund receives funding from foundation grants, corporate and individual gifts, fees, and interest payments.

BUSINESS OPPORTUNITIES

Self-Employment Microenterprise Development (SEMED)
Economic and Employment Development Center (EEDC)
241 S. Figueroa St.
Los Angeles, CA 90012   213-617-3953
SEMED assists the Southeast Asian Community in Los Angeles and surrounding counties to attain self-sufficiency. Eligible applicants are refugees admitted to the U.S. within the last five years and currently living under the national poverty level. Loans are from $2,000 to $5,000 with the term at one year. Group Lending loans are from $2,000 to $5,000 with the term at one year and the interest rate at 9.3%. SEMED receives funding from the Office of Refugee Resettlement.

The West Company
The West Enterprise Center
367 N. State St., Suite 206   707-468-3553
Ukiah, CA 95482   Fax: 707-462-8945
This program has a comprehensive approach that combines human and economic development. The aim is to stimulate the growth of economic opportunity in Northern California. Particular emphasis is on small business, economic options for low income people, and employment in the community. Eligible applicants are low income women/minorities located in Mendocino County. Loans are from $200 to $5,000 with terms from 6 to 24 months. The interest rate is at 10%. West Company receives funding from foundations, banks, utilities, CAP agency, local, state, and federal government, and donations.

Revolving Loan Fund
Tri-County Economic Development Corporation
2540 Esplanade, Suite 7   530-893-8732
Chico, CA 95973   Fax: 530-893-0820

E-mail: tcedcloan@thegrid.net
http://tricountyedc.org
The goal of this loan is to stimulate economic growth in Chico. The loan can be used for working capital, machinery, equipment, and leasehold improvements. You can apply for $2,500 to $50,000. The amount of time allowed for repayment varies with each loan. The interest rate is Prime plus 2%, or as low as 7%. For every $10,000 borrowed, one job must be created.

City of Long Beach Microenterprise Loan

City of Long Beach Business Assistance Division
200 Pine Avenue, Suite 400   562-570-3822
Long Beach, CA 90802   562-570-3800
www.ci.long-beach.ca.us/bdc
The goal of the program is to assist in the development of new businesses, to help economic growth, and to create and retain jobs. It is available to low and moderate income small business owners who cannot get conventional funding. The existing or start-up business must be located in the City of Long Beach. Funds can be used for property acquisition, machinery, equipment and moveable fixtures and working capital. The loan amount is from $5,000 to $25,000 at a fixed rate.

Micro-Loan Program

Oakland Business Development Corporation
519 17th Street, Suite 100   510-763-4297
Oakland, CA 94612   Fax: 510-763-1273
E-mail: mike@obdc.com
www.obdc.com
This loan is for small businesses located within the Seven Community Development Districts of Oakland. It can be used for working capital, inventory purchases, expansions and renovations, and contract finishing. Initially from $1,000 to $10,000 can be borrowed. After that has been repaid, up to $20,000 can be requested. The maximum term is 5 years and the interest is Prime + 3%. Eligible businesses are those in operation for one year, but 25% of funds are available for start-ups.

Entrepreneurial Resource Center Loan

Entrepreneurial Resource Center
2555 Clovis Avenue
Clovis, CA 93612   559-650-5050
Loans are only available to graduates of the Entrepreneurial Training Program. Funds are available from $1,000 to $5,000. The term is from 12 to 36 months depending on the loan amount.

Micro Loan Fund
Start Up: An East Palo Alto Micro-Business Initiative
1935 University Avenue
East Palo Alto, CA 94303   650-321-2193
To take advantage of this loan, entrepreneurs must graduate from the Start-Up
Program. Up to $5,000 is available with a term of 5 years. Preferences are
given to the residents of Palo Alto.

The Los Angeles Community Development Bank Micro Loan Program
Community Financial Resource Center
4060 S. Figueroa Street   323-233-1900
Los Angeles, CA 90037   Fax: 323-235-1686
The goal of this loan is to create jobs and to promote a positive investment
environment in the Los Angeles Supplemental Empowerment Zone. It is
available to micro businesses, home-based businesses and recent start-ups.
Loans are from $1,000 to $25,000 and for those that have been turned down for
a conventional loan. The term is 3 to 5 years at 12% fixed interest rate.

Micro Loan Revolving Loan Fund
Economic and Employment Development Corporation
2411 Figueroa Street, Suite 240
Los Angeles, CA 90012   213-617-3953
This program is available to refugees in the service area that have not been
naturalized by the US. After completing a business
training program, the applicant can
submit a business plan and loan
application. The maximum loan
amount is $5,000. However, if a
husband and wife apply for the same
business, they could apply for $10,000. After the
original has been paid back, borrowers can apply for 2 to 3 more loans and can
double the loan amount. Technical assistance continues with the loan and the
business is monitored on a weekly basis.

Micro Loan Fund
Interfaith Service Bureau
2117 Cottage Way
Sacramento, CA 95828   916-568-5020
This group is available for refugees that are green card holders and low income
Americans. It is for those small businesses in the Sacramento area for start-up
and inventory costs. After completing the training program, you may apply for
a loan of up to $5,000. The maximum amount of time to repay the loan is 3
years. Funding is from private grants.

Women's Initiative Loan Fund
Women's Initiative For Self Employment
450 Mission Street, Suite 402
San Francisco, CA 94105   415-247-9473
Women's Initiative helps low-income women to learn the skills necessary to
successfully start and run their businesses. After completing the training
course, you can apply for a small loan. The initial loan amount is up to $1,000,
and after that, up to $10,000 can be sought. The staff will work with each
owner on a one-to-one basis for post loan assistance. Networking and access to
experts are also available.

Small Business Micro-Lending Program
Lenders for Community Development
111 West St. John St., Suite 710   408-297-9937
San Jose, CA 95113   Fax: 408-297-4599
This loan program targets women, minority, and low-income business owners,
and those businesses that are located in low-income areas. The business must
have been in operation for one year and located in Santa Clara or San Mateo
County. The loans range from $5,000 to $50,000 and can be used for working
capital, equipment, inventory, leasehold improvements, and business
acquisition.

Peer Lending Circles
West Company
306 East Redwood Ave., Suite 2
Ft. Bragg, CA 95437   707-964-7571
It is their mission to expand economic self-sufficiency and social well-being for
those people that have limited access to conventional resources. The Peer
Lending Circles have up to 6 members with at least 6 months of self-
employment or a complete business plan. The loan amount ranges from $250
to $5,000 and the members all sign the loan note. Technical assistance is part
of this program and must be continued for the term of the loan.

Colorado
Business Center for Women (BCW)
Mi Casa Resource Center for Women
571 Galapago St.   303-573-1302
Denver, CO 80204   Fax: 303-595-0422
This program assists women who are low income and Hispanic in achieving self-
sufficiency. It has assisted in startup businesses and helped existing businesses
expand. Loan amounts are up to a maximum of $500 for individual lending and
from $500 to $5,000 for group lending. Loan terms are up to one year for

individual lending; up to two years for group lending. The interest rate is at 8% for individual lending; prime rate plus 3% for group lending.

Project Success (PS)
Mi Casa Resource Center for Women
571 Galapago St.   303-573-1302
Denver, CO 80204   Fax: 303-595-0422
This program is available to women receiving welfare benefits in Denver County. The aim is to assist women who are low income and Hispanic in achieving self-sufficiency. Loans are at a maximum of $500 for individual lending and from $500 to $5,000 for group lending. Terms are up to one year for individual lending; up to two years for group lending. The interest rate is 8% for individual lending and at prime rate plus 3% for group lending.

Micro Loan
Credit for All, Inc.
2268 Birch Street
Denver, CO 80207   303-320-1955
This loan is geared towards low-income people to help them get out of poverty. Credit for All uses a pure lending model method. Five to seven small business owners approve and insure repayment of loans to peers. The first loan amount is for $500 and must be repaid in 4 months. After that, $1,000 is available and there are 8 months for repayment. If everything goes well with the first year of loans, up to $8,000 can be applied for in the second year, and so on for the following years. This is available for those within the service are of Credit for All.

Micro Loan
Colorado Capital Initiatives
1616 17th Street, Suite 371
Denver, CO 80202   303-628-5464
Basically, they provide loans to those people of good character who have difficulty obtaining conventional funding. With this program, there are 13 counties where each area makes up its own community group. Each group sets its own guidelines and standards that would best serve their region. From $500 to $30,000 is available for a loan with a maximum of 3 years for repayment. The interest rate is 1 or 2% over Prime, depending on the loan.

Small Business Loan
Colorado Enterprise Fund
1888 Sherman Street, Suite 530
Denver, CO 80203   303-860-0242
E-mail: microloans@coloradoenterprisefund.org

www.coloradoenterprisefund.org
This is available in the 10 county service are of Colorado Enterprise. It is for small businesses that need money for things like working capital and equipment. Up to $25,000 can be applied for with a term of up to 5 years. The interest rate is from 13.5% to 14.25%.

Community Enterprise Lending Initiative
Denver Small Business Development Center
1445 Market Street   303-620-8076
Denver, CO 80203   Fax: 303-514-3200
It is the mission of this program to provide counseling and loans to finance new

or expanding businesses that are located in low-income, multi-ethnic areas. Also, it is for those entrepreneurs that cannot get a conventional loan. An existing business must have been in operation for at least one year. The maximum loans are $2,000 for a start-up and $15,000 for an existing company. The goal is that after this program the borrowers will be able to get conventional funding.

El Valle Microloans
San Luis Valley Christian Community Services
P.O. Box 984
309 San Juan Avenue   719-589-5192
Alamosa, CO 81101   Fax: 719-589-4330
E-mail: ccs@slvccs.org
www.slv.org/ccs
SLVCCS wants to encourage economic development for disadvantaged individuals through support for existing and start-up business owners in the San Luis Valley. It is for those entrepreneurs that cannot get traditional bank loans. The loan amount is between $500 and $19,000 for a term of 3 years. They also have technical assistance, computer access, and network exposure.

Connecticut
Hartford Economic Development Corporation Loan Programs
Hartford Economic Development Corp.
15 Lewis St.   860-527-1301
Hartford, CT 06103   Fax: 860-727-9224
This Corporation receives funding from CDBG funds, membership fees, and dues. Their aim is to create and retain jobs and tax rateable property. This program is

available to AFDC recipients, low and moderate income individuals. Loans are from $1,500 to $20,000 with terms from 6 months to 7 years. The interest rate is 9%.

Trickle Up Grant
Action for Bridgeport Community Development
955 Connecticut Ave., Suite 1215   203-382-5440
Bridgeport, CT 06607   Fax: 203-382-5442
Over 75% of the recipients of this program either have no credit or bad credit history. Entrepreneurs are given $700 in conditional start-up capital in two installments. For the first $500, they must complete a Business Plan, agree to spend a minimum of 250 hours per person over a 3 month period, and save or reinvest at least 20% of the profits in the business. At the end of three months, and when all of the requirements have been met, they can receive the final $200. Most of the recipients work out of their homes.

Delaware
Capital Works Team Success Loans
First State Community Loan Fund and YWCA of New Castle County
100 West 10th Street, Suite 1005   302-652-6774
Wilmington, DE 19801   Fax: 302-656-1272
E-mail: fsclf@diamond.net.ude.edu
This program uses the peer group lending process. The group offers support, training, and loan reviews. It is available to those businesses that are located in Delaware. The loan amounts are from $500 to $6,000. The term is 4 months to 3 years at a 12% interest rate. The group will approve the business use of the funds.

District of Columbia
Youth Microloan Fund
The Entrepreneurial Development Institute
P.O. Box 65882
Washington, DC 20035-5882   202-882-8334
This fund was established to empower disadvantaged youth to develop their own businesses, avoid drugs and crime, sharpen academic skills, and form positive attitudes about themselves and their communities. Eligible applicants are minority youths ages 17 to 21 years old. There are three levels of financing: up to $1,000, $2,500, and $5,000. Young people must have a business plan and have successfully repaid each loan before advancing to the next level. Loans carry below market interest and must be repaid within one year.

Micro Loan Fund
East of the River Community Development Corporation
4800 Nannie Helen Burroughs
Washington, DC 20019

202-397-0685

This loan is available to people in the area who want to start a small business or one that has been in existence for 2 or more years. Up to $25,000 can be applied for at 12% interest. The amount of time allowed for repayment varies depending on the loan.

Florida
SBA Microenterprise Loan Fund
Community Equity Investments, Inc. (CEII)
302 North Barcelona Street
Pensacola, FL 32501
E-mail: ceii2234@aol.com
http://ceii.pensacola.com

850-595-6234
888-605-2505
Fax: 850-595-6234

CEII provides assistance to businesses in northwest Florida and southern Alabama to help create jobs in those areas. The program has loans available for up to $25,000 for existing or start-up small businesses. The loans must be paid back within 5 years. Normally these are available to those that have had problems qualifying for a conventional loan.

Micro Loan
Florence Villa Community Development Corporation
111 Avenue R NE
Winter Haven, FL 33881

941-299-3263
Fax: 941-299-8134

Available businesses are start-up and existing that are generally owned by low to moderate-income people. The money can be used for mainly equipment. A loan of $5,000 is the maximum at 6.5% interest. The term is up to 3 years. It is only for the Polk county area.

Working Capital Program
3000 Biscayne Blvd., Suite 101A
Miami, FL 33137
www.workingcapital.org

305-438-1407
Fax: 305-438-1411

Working Capital's loans are set up in steps with each amount having a different repayment time. They start off at $500 and go in steps up to $10,000, in some cases they will go as high as $20,000. There is a 16% interest rate for processing loans. Members also can also take advantage of the business programs and network with other business owners.

Georgia
Working Capital Program
52 W. Alton St.   404-688-6884
Atlanta, GA 30303   Fax: 404-688-4009
www.workingcapital.org
Working Capital's loans are set up in steps with each amount having a different repayment time. They start off at $500 and go in steps up to $10,000, in some cases they will go as high as $20,000. There is a 16% interest rate for processing loans. Members also can also take advantage of the business programs and network with other business owners.

Micro Loan Fund
Goodwill Industries of North Georgia
2201 Glenwood Avenue
Atlanta, GA 30316   404-486-8400
This fund primarily serves Decatur and metro Atlanta. It is for women business owners that have low to moderate income. It mostly funds existing businesses, but there are some startups also. A loan from $50 to $5,000 can be applied for after completion of the Business Now training program. The term of the loan is 12 months with an interest rate that is currently 10%.

Hawaii
Refugee Enterprise Development Project
Immigrant Center
720 N. King St.   808-845-3918
Honolulu, HI 96817   Fax: 808-842-1962
This program focuses on Vietnamese and Laotian low income or welfare recipients. The objective of this program is to advance economic self-sufficiency among recently arrived refugees by providing culturally sensitive lending and support programs for the startup or expansion of microenterprise in Hawaii. Loans are from $1,500 to $5,000 with terms from 6 months to two years. The interest rate is at prime rate plus 2%, 3%, or 4%.

RED Manini MicroLoan Fund
The Immigrant Center
720 North King Street   808-845-3918
Honolulu, HI 96817   Fax: 808-842-1962
E-mail; redmanini@hotmail.com
This loan fund provides small loans, support, and technical assistance in order to help business owners to turn their talents and personal resources into economic self-sufficiency. It is for start-up and growing small businesses and

to be used for inventory, supplies, furniture, fixtures, machinery, equipment, and working capital. The maximum loan is $25,000 for a maximum term of 6 years.

Idaho

JTPA Entrepreneurial Training
IDA-ORE Planning and Development Association
10624 West Executive Dr.   208-322-7033
Boise, ID 83704   Fax: 208-322-3569
JTPA receives funds from EDA revolving loan fund grant, EDA revolving loan fund interest, and JTPA training funds. Program is available to individual entrepreneurs who do not qualify for commercial credit, and who are located in rural southwest Idaho, Malheur and Harney counties. The primary motive is business and economic development in rural areas where jobs are few, and entrepreneurial activity may be the only option to support rural families. Loans are up to $10,000 with loan terms up to three years. The interest rate is at prime rate plus 5% or 12%.

Small Business Micro-Loan Program
Panhandle Area Council, Inc.
11100 Airport Drive
Hayden, ID 83835   208-772-0584
This loan is available in North Idaho to ensure growth and prosperity of the region's small businesses. Generally the loans are for businesses that have been operational for at least one year. Consideration will be given to start-up businesses. The minimum amount for a loan is $1,000 and the maximum is $25,000. The term is three to five years at a fixed interest rate. The loan can be used for the purchase or repair of equipment, purchase of inventory, and working capital.

Illinois

Community Enterprising Project
Uptown Center Hull House Association
4520 N. Beacon St.   312-561-3500
Chicago, IL 60640   Fax: 312-561-3507
Eligible applicants are low and moderate-income individuals located in Uptown, Edgewater, and Ravenswood areas. This project has assisted several new start up businesses, and others have been able to increase sales for businesses such as food industry and service businesses. Loans are from $1,000-$10,000 with terms from 1-2 years. Interest rate is at prime rate plus 6%. Receives funds from foundations, corporations, governments and individuals.

Peoria Area Micro Business Development Program
The Economic Development Council for The Peoria Area, Inc.
124 S. West Adams St., Suite 300   309-676-7500
Peoria, IL 61602   Fax: 309-676-7534
The Economic Development Council (EDC) is committed to assisting in the
development of small businesses and microbusinesses and helping them overcome
obstacles to growth. Eligible applicants are low and moderate-income existing or
startup businesses, minorities and females. Loans are from $500 to $25,000 with
terms from three to five years. The interest rate is from 5 to 12%. Receives funds
from SBA Microloan Demonstration program, City of Peoria, and county of
Peoria.

Self-Employment Loan Fund
Chicago Association of Neighborhood Development Organizations
123 W. Madison St., Suite 1100   312-372-2636
Chicago, IL 60602-4589   Fax: 312-372-2637
The aim of this Fund is the revitalization of all Chicago neighborhoods, retail and
industrial areas. It works with community based organizations to assist low and
moderate-income individuals start new business ventures. Loans are from $1,000
to $10,000 with a term of two years. Interest rate is at prime rate plus 6%. Closing
costs can be included in the loan amount.

Self-Employment Training Program
Project NOW - Community Action Committee
418 19th St., P.O. Box 3970   309-793-6388
Rock Island, IL 61201   Fax: 309-793-6352
Eligible applicants are low-income county residents in the counties of Rock Island,
Henry, and Mercer. Assists individuals interested in self-employment by providing
training, consulting services, support services and
assistance in identifying and accessing startup capital.
Loans are from $1,500 to $45,000 with terms from
two to four years. The interest rate is 5%.
Funding comes from the Illinois Department of
Commerce and Consumer Affairs.

WBDC Micro-Loan Program
Women's Business Development Center
8 S. Michigan Ave., Suite 400   312-853-3477
Chicago, IL 60603   Fax: 312-853-0145
This program has started a new initiative to strengthen the programs and services
for women, and worked as an advocate on access to financing through relationship
building with banks and regulators. The aim is to support women in their quest for
economic self-sufficiency through entrepreneurship. Loans are up to $5,000 with

terms up to one year. The interest rate is at 9%. This program receives funding from loans from various foundations and banks.

Women's Economic Venture Enterprise (WEVE)
YWCA
229 16th St.   309-788-9793
Rock Island, IL 61201   Fax: 309-788-9825
Women's Economic Venture Enterprise (WEVE) assists women in achieving economic self-sufficiency through business ownership. Eligible applicants are women of all races and income levels living in Scott County, Iowa, Rock Island County in Illinois, and Metropolitan Quad Counties. Loans are from $200 to $3,000, terms from three months to five years. Interest rate is 2% below prime rate. WEVE receives funding from Banks, SBA, foundations, individuals, program fees and corporations.

Women's Self-Employment Project (WSEP)
20 N. Clark St.   312-606-8255
Chicago, IL 60602   Fax: 312-606-9215
The Women's Self-Employment Project (WSEP) programs provide economic support and a chance for self-sufficiency to women who reside in some of Chicago's most disinvested communities. The goal of WSEP is to raise the income of low/moderate income women through a strategy of self-employment. Loans are from $100 to $10,000 with terms from four months to two years. The interest rate is at 15%. WSEP receives funding from SBA Microloan Demonstration, foundations, corporations, government contracts, individual donors, and consulting contracts.

Self-Employment Loan Fund
Chicago Association of Neighborhood
  Development Organizations (CANDO)
123 West Madison, Suite 1100
Chicago, IL 60602-4589   312-939-7171
This loan is generally available to low income business owners that are primarily women and minorities. It is for start-up and emerging businesses in Chicago. The loans for emerging businesses are $1,000 to $20,000 at 12.5% and repayable in 3 months to 2 years. A start-up company can apply for $1,000 to $15,000 at 10 to 12.5% interest for a term of 3 months to 2 years.

City of Rockford Microenterprise Investment Match Program
City of Rockford
Illinois Community Development Department
425 East State Street   815-987-5610
Rockford, IL 61104   Fax: 815-967-6933

---

www.ci.rockford.il.us
This program has been designed to strengthen new or young businesses owned
by low and moderate-income residents in the
City of Rockford. The City will provide up
to four times the amount of the business'
equity, or $10,000, whichever is less.
Equity can include cash, previously
purchased equipment, and "sweat-equity".
The term is 5 years, with 20% forgiven
each of the 5 years. The interest rate is 0%.
Fifty-one percent of the jobs must be for low

and moderate-income residents of the City. The applicant must graduate from
the training program or have a business education.

Special Initiative Funds
ACCION Chicago
3245 West 26th Street
Chicago, IL 60623   773-376-9004
This loan is geared towards African Americans, women owned businesses, and
geographic areas that are depressed. These loans are based on character as long
as there is a cash flow in the business. The loan amount is from $500 to
$25,000 with a term of 3 months to 24 months. This is for start-up and existing
businesses.

Micro Loan Program for Small Businesses
West Cook Community Development
1127 South Mannheim Road, Suite 1021   708-450-0100
Westchester, IL 60559   Fax: 708-450-0655
This program is for small businesses in Western Suburban Cook County that
have first been turned down by a bank for funding. It targets low to moderate-
income women and minorities. The loan amount is from $2,000 to $50,000
with a term of up to 5 years. For funding, money is pooled from loans received
from 20 area banks, and then in turn is loaned out from West Cook Community
Development.

Indiana
Eastside Community Fund
Eastside Community Investments (ECI)
26 N. Arsenal Ave.   317-637-7300
Indianapolis, IN 46220   Fax: 317-637-7581
The aim is to loan money and provide technical assistance to both startup and
existing small businesses. Preference is given to New Eastside residents or low

income individuals. Loans are from $150 -$25,000; terms from three months to five years. Interest rate is 10 to 12%. This fund receives funding from SBA, Mott Foundation, state loan money, and Partners for Common Good Loan Fund.

Rural Business Assistance Grant
City of Madison Micro Loan Program
P.O. Box 765
Versailles, IN 47042   812-689-5505
This loan is funded through the U.S. Department of Agriculture (USDA). It is available to start-up or growing businesses. A maximum of $25,000 can be applied to equipment and working capital. The amount of time allowed for pay back is generally 5 to 7 years, depending on the loan, and the loan committee can decide on an extension.

City of Madison Micro Loan Program
SE Indiana Regional Planning Commission
P.O. Box 765
Versailles, IN 47042   812-689-5505
This loan is for start-up or growing small businesses in the area. The maximum of a $25,000 loan can be used for equipment and working capital. The term varies with the loan amount. Funding is from the U.S. Department of Agriculture (USDA).

Iowa
SBA Microloan Demonstration Program
Siouxland Economic Development Corporation
428 Insurance Centre   712-279-6286
Sioux City, IA 51102   Fax: 712-279-6920
Eligible applicants are low and moderate-income individuals located in Woodbury,

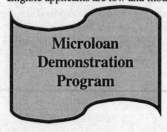

Plymouth, Cherokee, Ida and Monona counties. This program receives referrals from local banks and community development organizations and assist in funding non-bankable individuals. Loans are from $1,500 to $25,000 with terms from 1-6 years. Funding comes from SBA grant, SEDC cash match, and other SEDC operating surplus and revenue.

Small Enterprise Development
Institute for Social and Economic Development
1901 Broadway, Suite 313   319-338-2331

Iowa City, IA 52240   Fax: 319-338-5824
This program is focused on low income, ethnic minorities, and women. Receives
funds from foundations, corporations, civic and religious organizations, federal and
state grants and contracts, and private contributions. The aim is to facilitate the
empowerment of disadvantaged populations through the integration of social and
economic development strategies. Loans are from $500 to $23,000 with terms
from 6 months to five years. The interest rate is 5% for Institute's loans, and 8.5%
to 15% for bank loans.

SBA Microloan Program
Siouxland Economic Development Corporation (SEDC)
P.O. Box 447
Sioux City, IA 50102   712-279-6286
Small businesses in and around the 6 counties of Sioux City can apply for this
loan. The maximum amount is for $25,000 that is to be paid back in a
maximum of 6 years. The interest rate is 10%. Funding is from the Small
Business Association.

Kansas
SBA Micro-Loan
South Central Kansas Economic Development District
209 East William, Suite 300
Wichita, KS 67202-4012   316-262-7033
www.sckedd.org
The goal of this loan is to stimulate the economy within the 14 county service
area. A maximum of $25,000 is available for a term of 6 years. No funds may
be used for the purchase of real estate. Funds are from the Small Business
Association.

Kentucky
Bluegrass Microenterprise Program
Community Ventures Corporation
1450 N. Broadway
Lexington, KY 40505   606-231-0054
Upon joining the small business training program, you will have access to classes
designed to help with specific areas of self-employment and business ownership.
Classroom instruction is offered in business feasibility, management, marketing
and financial planning. Upon completion of an approved business plan, you may
be considered for inclusion in a small loan group, where loans of $500 to $2,500
are made to people operating or starting a small business.

Community Loan Fund
Human/Economic Appalachian Development Corp.
P.O. Box 504   606-986-8423
Berea, KY 40403   Fax: 606-986-1299
The Community Loan Fund is available to low income individuals and women
located in Central Appalachia. Fund has provided loans to new and existing
businesses in low-income communities including pilot program targeting welfare
recipients and community day care. The aim is to strengthen low-income
communities. Receives funds from permanent capital, investments, grants and
donations. Loans are from $100 to $25,000 with terms from one to five years. The
interest rate is from 8 to 12%.

Micro-Enterprise Loan Fund
Kentucky Highlands Investment Corporation
P.O. Box 1738
London, KY 40743   606-864-5175

The purpose of this fund is to encourage the
development of small businesses in counties
of Kentucky Highlands. Expansion and
start-up for profit businesses that meet the
Small Business Administration's size
standards are eligible. A maximum loan of
$25,000 can be used for working capital and equipment. Borrowers have up to
6 years to repay with a fixed interest rate based on the loan.

SBA Micro Loan Program
Community Ventures Corporation
1458 North Broadway   606-231-0054
Lexington, KY 40505   Fax: 606-231-0261
This loan is open to existing micro businesses in Central Kentucky, a 20 county
region. Its use is primarily for working capital and equipment. The maximum
amount of the loan is for $20,000. The term is determined by the loan.

Louisiana
Micro Loan Fund
Catholic Social Services
1220 Aycock Street
Houma, LA 70360   504-876-0490
The area covered by this loan is the Diocese of Houma-Thibodax. A start-up
business can borrow up to $1,500 and then borrow more after that loan has
been paid off on time. If the business is existing, it can borrow up to $2,000 for
the first loan, and more after that. The term is from 1 to 2 years.

Maine

Androscoggin Valley Council of Governments (AVCOG)
125 Manley Rd.   207-783-9186
Auburn, ME 04210   Fax: 207-783-5211
The primary goal of these programs is to stimulate business investment that results
in job creation and retention within the Androscoggin, Franklin, and Oxford
Counties. Loans are up to $150,000. Terms are for 3-5 years at prime rate plus 1%.
Eligible applicants are startups and existing businesses of all kinds.

Aroostook County Action Program, Inc. - Fleet Bank Set-Aside
P.O. Box 1116   207-764-3721
Presque Isle, ME 04769   Fax: 207-768-3040
This program is available to individuals who cannot obtain funding through
conventional loan programs. Program is for startup and existing micro businesses,
and to establish a link to conventional lending channels for each sustained
business. Loans are from $1,000 to $10,000. Terms are up to five years at prime
rate plus 2%.

Auburn Community Development Block Grant (CDBG) Microloan
Lewiston/Auburn Economic Growth Council
P.O. Box 1188
37 Park St.   207-784-0161
Lewiston, ME 04240   Fax: 207-786-4412
The Auburn Community Development Block Grant (CDBG) Microloan program
is available to startup and existing businesses, manufacturing, distribution, service,
non-retail, and low to moderate incomes.

Enterprise Fund
Coastal Enterprises Inc. (CEI)
P.O. Box 268
Wiscasset, ME 04578   207-882-7552
The aim of this fund is to help people with limited resources create their own jobs.
Women-owned and child care businesses are typical examples. Loans are from
$500 to $50,000. Rates are fixed market rate. Terms are up to 15 years. Funding is
from the Ford Foundation, Mott Foundation, state legislative appropriation,
Betterment Fund, U.S. Department of Health and Human Services, national
churches, Maine Department of Economic and Community Development.

Entrepreneurs With Disabilities Loan Fund
Newmarket Tech
P.O. Box 724   207-287-7370
Augusta, ME 04330   Fax: 207-287-3038
The Entrepreneurs With Disabilities Loan Fund is available to startup and existing
businesses, businesses that create jobs, manufacturing, and people with mental and

physical disabilities. Loans are from $500 to $2,000 and terms vary. Newmarket Tech also provides technical assistance.

Maine Centers for Women, Work and Community
46 University Dr.   207-621-3440
Augusta, ME 04330   Fax: 207-621-3429
This microloan is available to startup and existing businesses. Applicants must submit a written Business Plan to a committee. Loans are from $100 to $1,000. Eligible applicants are: family income below $20,000; displaced homemakers; single parents; and people in transition.

Working Capital Program
Western Mountains Alliance
P.O. Box 29   207-778-7274
Farmington, ME 04938   Fax: 207-778-7247
This loan is based on a peer-lending process. A potential applicant joins a business loan group of 4-10 business owners and applies directly to the group for loans. The group reviews and approves loans. All members must be current on their loans before any group member is eligible for another loan. Available to startup or businesses that projects to have a sustainable idea or product to sell or create. Loans are from $500-$5,000. Terms are four months to three years at 12%. Applicants must be a member of a peer lending group.

SBA Microloan Program
Eastern Maine Development Corporation
One Cumberland Place, Suite 300   207-942-6389
Bangor, ME 04401   800-339-6389
www.emdc.org
This loan is available only to counties in the area. Businesses that are starting up, expanding, or that need working capital can apply for up to $25,000. The loan includes post-loan technical support to help the owner in being successful. It must be paid back in up to 5 years.

Microloan Fund
Biddeford-Saco Area Economic Development Corporation
110 Main Street, Suite 1202   207-282-1748
Saco, ME 04072   Fax: 207-282-3149
E-mail: bsaedc@lamere.net
www.bsaedc.org
The loan is available to any small business in the area with emphasis on women and minorities. The maximum loan is for $25,000 at a fixed interest rate based on the market rate. One hundred percent financing is available up to $15,000. The terms of the loan vary depending on the use of the funds, but on an average

are from 5 to 10 years. The Corporation is certified by the Treasury
Department as CDFI.

New Ventures Loan Fund
Maine Centers for Women, Work, and Community
Stoddart House UMA
46 University Drive   207-621-3440
Augusta, ME 043303-9410   Fax: 207-621-3429
E-mail: wkrose@maine.edu

They established this fund to help women become
economically successful. In order to apply for funds,
women must graduate from New Ventures of Career/Life
Planning Training. The loan is for up to $500. The term
is from 3 months to one year. After that, borrowers are
eligible to apply for another loan. Either start-ups or
existing businesses that are low income and create
jobs are eligible in the state of Maine.

NMDC Microloan Program
Northern Maine Development Commission
302 Main Street   207-498-8736
P.O. Box 779   800-427-8736 (Maine only)
Caribou, ME 04736   Fax: 207-493-3108
The purpose of this loan is to provide capital to women, low-income and
minority small business owners that cannot get conventional loans. Money
may be used for the purchase of machinery and equipment, furniture and
fixtures, inventory, supplies and working capital. For loans of $7,500 and less,
the interest rate is 10%. Loans over $7,500 have an interest rate of 9%.
Applicants are eligible for technical assistance. Call first to be sure your
business falls within the guidelines of the Small Business Administration.

Commercial Lending Program
Perquis Community Action Program
P.O. Box 1162
Bangor, ME 04402   207-973-3500
The Commercial Lending Program offers gap financing. The applicants must
fall within the HUD guidelines for low income. One-third of the total amount
needed can be applied for, with the maximum loan of $35,000. The term is an
average of 5 to 7 years. It is available in Pennobscott and Piscataquis counties.

Androscoggin Valley Micro Loan Program
Androscoggin Valley Council of Governments
125 Manley Road
Auburn, ME 04210   207-783-9186

They call themselves the "Lender of last resorts". This loan can be used by
either start-up or existing businesses for things like working capital, equipment.
The loan amount is up to $40,000 with a maximum term of 7 years. Collateral,
cash flow and a business plan are required. It is available to those in the 3
county service area.

Aroostook County Action Micro Loan Program
Aroostook County Action Program Inc.
P.O. Box 1166
Presque Isle, ME 04769   207-768-3033
Business owners in the Aroostook County area that meet HUD's median
income guidelines can join this program. The maximum loan is $10,000 at
10% for a term of 10 years.

Maryland
Business Owners Startup Services (BOSS)
Council for Economic and Business Opportunities
800 N. Charles St., Suite 300   410-576-2326
Baltimore, MD 21201   Fax: 410-576-2498
www.cebo.com/
The aim of Business Owners Startup Services (BOSS) is to develop
microenterprises via training and funding and to maintain microenterprises through
technical assistance, support and funding. Eligible applicants are AFDC recipients,
and residents of Housing Authority of Baltimore County. Loans are from $5,000 to
$10,000, terms up to two years and interest rate is 10%. Receives funds from SBA,
CDBG funds, SEID Grant, state, city, county PI and Title III contracts, and a grant
from HUD.

Women Entrepreneurs of Baltimore, Inc. (WEB)
1118 Light St., Suite 202   410-727-4921
Baltimore, MD 21230   Fax: 410-727-4989
Women Entrepreneurs of Baltimore, Inc. (WEB) is a nonprofit organization, and
its clients must have a viable business idea and the entrepreneurial spirit to make
their business a success. WEB is committed to the economic empowerment of
neighborhood women and the revitalization of Baltimore's neighborhoods. The
development of microenterprise in Baltimore helps to revitalize these
neighborhoods by stopping the dollar drain. The owners serve as strong role
models and in some instances provide employment in their communities. Eligible
applicants are economically disadvantaged women in Baltimore City. Loans are up
to $500 with terms from three to six months. The interest rate is at 10%. WEB
receives funding from foundations and bank contributions.

Massachusetts
Hilltown Enterprise Fund
Hilltown Community Development Corp.
432 Main Rd. #A   413-296-4536
Chesterfield, MA 01012   Fax: 413-296-4020
This fund receives funding from state and federal grants, loans from individuals,
Western Massachusetts Enterprise Fund, and contributions. The aim is to promote
rural cooperation and to ensure the best quality of life for all Hilltown residents.
This is available to individuals with limited resources who wish to start or expand
a business. Loan amounts are from $500 to $10,000 with loan terms at three years.
The interest rate is 12%. For Hilltown residents only.

Microenterprise Development Program
Brightwood Development Corporation
2345 Main St.   413-734-2144
Springfield, MA 01107   Fax: 413-746-3934
This program's aim is to provide affordable housing and economic development to
low and moderate income Hispanics and Puerto Ricans. Program is presently
assisting eight new businesses to start in a low-income community. Loans are from
$500 to $15,000. Terms are from three to five years. The interest rate is at 10%.
Receives funds from the City of Springfield, Springfield Chamber of Commerce,
SBA, and HUD.

Microenterprise Training and Loan Program for Refugees
Jewish Vocational Service
105 Chauncy St., 6th Floor   617-451-8147
Boston, MA 02111   Fax: 617-451-9973
Program receives funds from the Office of Refugee Resettlement and the Jewish
Vocational Service. Provides refugees the opportunity to create their own jobs
within the communities in which they live. Vulnerable populations, such as the
disadvantaged and disabled, are the agency's priority. Loans are from $100 to
$5,000 with terms from six months to three years. The interest rate is at prime rate
plus 4%.

New Bedford Working Capital Network
Community Economic Development Center
166 William St.   508-999-9920
New Bedford, MA 02740   Fax: 508-990-0199
Eligible applicants are low and moderate income, racially and culturally diverse
individuals. Small loans provide needed resources to these individuals who would
not have funds to invest in their businesses. Loans are from $500 to $10,000 with
the interest rate at 12%. Funding comes from credit through Fleet Banks, operating
funds from Working Capital Institute for Cooperative Community Development,
other banks, and private foundations.

Hampton City Employment and Training Consortium
Springfield Business Development Fund (SBDF)
1176 Main St.
Springfield, MA 01103   413-781-6900
Eligible applicants are low and moderate income, and minorities located in
Springfield. SBDF provides secondary loans to small business for startup or
expansion within the City of Springfield. It receives funding from the Small
Business Administration and the Economic Development Administration. Loans
are from $10,000 to $50,000 with terms from 5 to 20 years. The interest rate is at
6%.

Hilltown Enterprise Fund
Hilltown Community Development Corporation
P.O. Box 17
Chesterfield, MA 01012   413-296-4536
This loan is available to the 11-town area around Hilltown for businesses that
cannot otherwise get funding. Amounts from $500 to $15,000 are available at
12% interest. The terms of the loan are 6 months to 5 years, depending on the
amount loaned. Funds come from local people.

Working Capital Program
Working Capital
99 Bishop Allen Drive   617-576-8620
Cambridge, MA 02139   Fax: 617-576-8623
E-mail: infor@workingcapital.org
www.workingcapital.org
Borrowers join a business loan group which control the lending process.

Working Capital

Working Capital's loans are set up in
steps with each amount having a
different repayment time. They start
off at $500 and go in steps up to
$10,000, in some cases they will go
as high as $20,000. There is a 16% interest rate for processing loans. Members
also can also take advantage of the business programs and network with other
business owners. This is for the greater Boston area.

Micro Loan
Twin Cities Community Development Corporation
195 Kimball Street
Fitchburg, MA 01420   978-342-9561
The goal of this fund is to increase economic development and income, and to
create assets and jobs. It is available to business owners that have low to
moderate incomes and do not fall within conventional loan guidelines. The

business must be in operation for at least one year and located in the Fitchburg area. The loan amount is up to $50,000 with a term of 3 to 10 years. The interest rate is 12%.

Small Business Loan Fund
Dorchester Bay Economic Development Corporation
594 Columbia Road, Suite 302   617-825-4200
Dorchester, MA 02125   Fax: 617-825-3522
E-mail: DBSBAP@aol.com
This loan is open to residents or small businesses located in Dorchester. It is also available to a client that comes through a Community Development Corporation in another community. They also help with technical assistance, credit repair, financial planning, and more. The maximum loan amount is $25,000. The term is up to 5 years with a compounded interest rate.

Cambodian American League Fund
Cambodian American League of Lowell, Inc.
60 Middlesex Street
Lowell, MA 01852   978-454-3707
After a 7-week training program, small business owners must submit a business plan with their application for a loan. The loan amount is a maximum of $5,000. The loan must be paid back from one to two years, depending on the loan.

Greater Springfield Entrepreneurial Fund
Hampden County Employment and Training Consortium
1176 Main Street
Springfield, MA 01103   413-781-6900 ext. 227
This fund is available to the people in Hampden county except for the Chicopee and Chester areas. Small business owners can apply for a maximum of $25,000. It must be repaid in up to 5 years. The interest rate is 8%.

SEED Micro Loan Program
South Eastern Economic Development Corporation
88 Broadway
Taunton, MA 02780   508-822-1020
The eligible business types for this loan are manufacturing, retail, wholesale, and service. The money can be used for working capital, real estate for the use of the small business, and for machinery and equipment. The loan amount is up to $25,000 with a term up to 5 years. The interest rate is usually the market rate. The business must show potential for creating jobs, especially for low to moderate-income people. The service area of SEED is Barnstable, Bristol, Dukes, Plymouth and Nantucket counties.

Michigan
Wise Program
Ann Arbor Community Development Corp.
2008 Hogback Rd., Suite 12   313-677-1400
Ann Arbor, MI 48105   Fax: 313-677-1465
The WISE Program is to encourage small business development among
women/minorities. This program assists women to become self-sufficient through
self-employment. Loans are from $500 to $7,000. Terms are from 6 months to 7
years. Interest rate is prime rate plus 1%. Closing costs can be included in the
amount of the loan. Receives funding from the City of Ann Arbor, Mott
Foundation, U.S. Department of Health and Human Services, Michigan Women's
Foundation, and the Community Foundation of Southeastern Michigan.

Lansing Community Micro-Enterprise Fund
Lansing Community Micro-Enterprise Fund
520 West Ionia   517-485-4446
Lansing, MI 48933   Fax: 517-485-4761
To become eligible for this loan, the borrower must meet the criteria for low to
moderate income and live in the City of Lansing. Or, the location of their
business or residence must be within the City of Lansing where 70% or more of
households are low to moderate income. They must also show that LCMF is
the best loan option. The loan amount is $500 to $10,000. The term is from 12
months to 4 years at a 7% interest rate. A business training program is
available, but not required.

Project Invest
Northwest Michigan Council of Governments
2194 Dendrinos Drive
P.O. Box 506   231-929-5000
Traverse City, MI 49685-0506   Fax: 231-929-5012
www.cog.mi.us
The goal of this program is to help entrepreneurs develop successful small
businesses to create income and possible employment for others. To achieve
this, a borrower must complete the Enterprise Development Workshops. After
that, a loan of between $250 to $1,500 can be sought. Borrowers must meet
with a loan advisor monthly.

Minnesota
Arrowhead Microenterprise Program
Arrowhead Community Economic Assistance Corporation
702 Third Ave. S.   218-749-2914
Virginia, MN 55792-2775   Fax: 218-749-2913

The aim of this program is to assist with startup or expansion of local businesses
that increase employment opportunities, that
retain existing jobs, identify and develop
local skills and talents, and that provide
economic opportunity for unemployed, low
income and minority citizens. Loans are from
$500 to $10,000. Terms are from 90 days to
10 years. The interest rate is a minimum 8%,
and is adjusted annually. Receives funds from
federal, state and county funds, private loans,
and revenue from operations.

Business Development Services
Women Venture
2324 University Ave., Suite 200   651-646-3808
St. Paul, MN 55114   Fax: 651-641-7223
The aim of this service is to secure a stronger economic future for women through
employment, career development, business development, and financial
responsibility. Eligible applicants are women, with particular interest in reaching
low-income women. Loans are from $50 to $25,000 with terms from three months
to five years. The interest rate is at 10%. Women Venture receives funding from
SBA Microloan Demonstration Grant, state and federal grants, and foundations.

Emerging Entrepreneur Development Program
Northwest Minnesota Initiative Fund
4225 Technology Dr.   218-759-2057
Bemidji, MN 56601   Fax: 218-759-2328
Although this program is available to everyone, it targets women, minorities and
low-income individuals. The mission is to improve the quality of life for the people
who live and work in NW Minnesota. This program provides opportunities for
self-employment and the establishment of new businesses which makes it
economically feasible for people to remain in the region. Loans are from $136 to
$13,500, terms from one month to five years. The interest rate is 8%. Program
receives funding from the SBA and The McKnight Foundation.

Northeast Entrepreneur Fund, Inc.
Northeast Entrepreneur Fund, Inc.
820 Ninth St., N., Suite 140   218-749-4191
Virginia, MN 55792   Fax: 218-741-4249
This is available to unemployed and underemployed individuals. This Fund helped
to revitalize a rural region that has experienced severe economic dislocation in the
last 15 years, and helped start or expand over 120 microbusinesses. The purpose is
to encourage economic self-sufficiency through the growth of small businesses.

Loans are from $100 to $100,000 with terms from 60 days to three years. Funds come from foundations, loans, contracts, fees, and interest.

Revolving Loan Fund (RLF)
North Star Community Development Corporation
604 Board of Trade Building
301 West First St.
Duluth, MN 55802   218-727-6690
North Star CDC is a community based economic development organization providing assistance to small businesses. Focus is placed on assisting low and moderate income individuals to achieve economic self-sufficiency. Loans are from $400 to $20,000 with the terms from 90 days to 5 years. The interest rate is 8%. Funding comes from the Community Development Block Grant. Only for those residing within the city limits of Duluth.

Self-Employment Training Opportunities (SETO)
Women Venture
2324 University Ave., Suite 200   651-646-3808
St. Paul, MN 55114   Fax: 651-641-7223
Eligible applicants are women, with particular interest in low-income women. The aim of SETO is to secure an economic future for women through employment, career development, business development, and financial responsibility. Loans are from $50 to $25,000 with terms from three months to five years. The interest rate is at 10%. Women Venture receives funding from SBA Microloan Demonstration Grant, state and federal grants, and foundations.

Child Care Provider Loan
Arrowhead Community Economic Assistance Corporation
8880 Main Street
P.O. Box 406   218-735-8201
Mountain Iron, MN 55768-0406   Fax: 218-735-8202
E-mail:aceac@rangenet.com
ACEAC's goal is to help start-up and expansion of local businesses in order to create economic opportunities for the area residents. The child care loan is offered between $300 and $7,000. Generally, repayment is from 2 to 3 years. The interest rate is 3 to 8% depending on the borrower's adjusted gross income. Priority is given to people who are open during non-traditional hours, people who care for children with disabilities, and those who operate in areas with a lack of child care. Technical support is available throughout the loan.

Micro Enterprise Loan Program
Neighborhood Development Center
651 1/2 University Avenue   651-291-2480

St. Paul, MN 55104   Fax: 651-291-2597
Small business and start-up loans are available to businesses in the cities of
Minneapolis and St. Paul for up to $10,000. First, a 16-week NDC business
training program must be completed. Repayment is up to 5 years at 10%
interest rate. Business owners that have income below area median for their
area are eligible.

Northeast Entrepreneur Fund
Northeast Entrepreneur Fund
820 Ninth Street North   218-749-4191
Virginia, MN 55792   Fax: 218-749-5213
This fund is offered to small business owners that do not have reasonable
access to other sources of money. The business must be located in, or the
owner must be a resident of, the seven-county Arrowhead Region of northeast
Minnesota. For a start-up or expansion of a business up to $100,000 may be
requested. Repayment period varies from 30 days to 6 years. The interest is at
market rate.

Revolving Loan Fund
North Star Community Development Corporation
301 West First Street, Suite 604
Duluth, MN 55802   218-727-6690
This loan is for low to moderate-income business owners. Currently, it serves
the Duluth area, but it is expected to expand those boundaries soon. Up to
$20,000 can be borrowed at 8% interest. The term of the loan is a maximum of
5 years.

Micro Loan
Phillips Community Development Corporation
1014 East Franklin, Suite #1   612-871-2435
Minneapolis, MN 55404   Fax: 612-871-8131
This loan is for general small businesses in the 8 neighborhood areas. The
business must have been in operation for at least one year. Equity is required
for a loan up to $10,000. The rate is 5 years with an interest of Prime plus 3%.

Dayton Hudson Artists Loan Fund
Resources and Counseling for the Arts   651-292-4381
308 Prince Street, Suite 270   Fax: 651-292-4315
St. Paul, MN 55101   TTY: 651-292-3218
www.rc4arts.org
This program is a community based revolving loan program for artists who
cannot find traditional funding. It is available to those in the Minneapolis-St.
Paul metro area. A loan of $1,000 to $5,000 with a term of 12 to 36 months

can be applied for. The interest rate is 1% over Prime. The money can be used for artistic development and the artist's business development.

Micro Loan Program
Northwest Minnesota Foundation
4225 Technology Drive, NW   218-759-2057
Bemidji, NM 56601   Fax: 218-759-2328
www.nwnf.org
This loan is offered in order to help to develop small businesses and to create self-employment. It is available in the 12 extreme counties of Northwest Minnesota. Up to $20,000 can be applied for with a term of up to 5 years. This is open to either start-up or existing small businesses.

SBA Loan
Women Venture
2324 University Avenue
St. Paul, MN 55114   651-646-3808
This loan is available to help women to gain economic success. It is offered to new or existing small businesses in the 14 county service area. The amount of the loan is from $200 to $25,000 and technical assistance is given with it. The term is 30 days to 6 years with the interest up to 4 percent over prime. Fifty percent collateral is required.

Mississippi
Small Farm Loan
Alcorn State University
Small Farm Development Center
1000 ASU Drive #1080   601-877-6449
Alcorn State, MS 39096-7500   Fax: 601-877-3931
This loan is used to give short-term loans to small farmers. The money can be used for agriculture related expenses. The applicant  must have a minimum farming experience of one year or have an educational background. Additionally, the farmer must have been turned down by 2 or more creditors. Repayment terms are from 1 to 5 years. There is a 1 to 3% service fee for approved loans, but the interest rate is 0%. Preference is given to emerging crop enterprise.

SELF Loan Fund
Economic Alternatives
P.O. Box 5208
Holly Springs, MS 38634
601-252-1575

This micro loan targets low to moderate-income people. The business can be either just starting or an existing one. The loan amount is $500 to $2,500, with a 2-month grace period. The term is for not beyond 3 years with a 5% interest rate. This is available to businesses in Marshall and Benton counties. Funding is from USDA and private foundations.

Missouri
Microloan Program
First Step Fund
1080 Washington, Suite 204   816-474-5111
Kansas City, MO 64105   Fax: 816-472-4207
This loan is only for the graduates of the business training program that are members of the Alumni Group. They must also fall within the federal low to moderate income guidelines. A maximum loan for a first time borrower is $2,500; the next level of loan is up to $5,000. This money can be used for supplies and/or equipment. The average loan is 2 years. The interest rate is the prime rate. The loan is approved by the Borrowers' Group.

SBA Microloan Program
Rural Missouri, Inc.
1014 Northeast Drive   800-234-4971
Jefferson City, MO 65109   Fax: 573-635-5636
This loan is for start-up and expanding businesses to provide funds for working capital, inventory, supplies, furniture, fixtures, machinery and/or equipment. The loan amount is from $500 to $25,000. The term is 1 to 5 years with an interest rate that is NY Prime plus 3% Technical assistance is given on a one to one basis.

Montana
Action for Eastern Montana - Microbusiness Loan
2030 N. Merrill
Glendive, MT 59330-1309   406-377-3564
Receives funds from the Montana Department of Commerce, banks, utilities, Rural Conservation and Development District, and small business donations. The mission is to help create a flourishing microbusiness climate. Eligible applicants are low income, women and minorities. Loans are from $500 to $20,000, interest rate are prime plus 2%. Closing costs/fees can be included in the loan.

Montana Microbusiness Finance Program
Montana Department of Commerce
1424 9th Ave.   406-444-3494
Helena, MT 59620   Fax: 406-444-2808

Eligible applicants are minorities, women and low income individuals. The goal is to provide disadvantage individuals with self-employment opportunities. Loans and terms vary. Receives funds from State legislative appropriation from in-state investment fund, local capital, and operating budget.

Montana Women's Economic Development Group (WEDGO)
Women's Opportunity and Resource Development
127 N. Higgins   406-543-3550
Missoula, MT 59802   Fax: 406-721-4584
Aim is to provide business assistance services including training, consulting and capital access, targeting low and moderate income women. It works with community teams planning and implementing timber diversification strategies, and employ business assistance specialists to assist entrepreneurs. Loans are up to $35,000, terms up to five years. Interest rate is 1-2% above market rate. Receives funds from city, county, and state government, Ms. Foundation, Department of Health and Human Services, and US West Foundation. Only for residents of western Montana.

Opportunities, Inc. - Microbusiness Finance Program
Opportunities, Inc.
P.O. Box 2289
Great Falls, MT 59403   406-761-0310
Eligible applicants are those unable to receive loans from conventional sources. The purpose is to stimulate better coordination among available federal, state, local and private resources to enable low income families and individuals in rural and urban areas, to attain the skills and motivations they need to secure opportunities necessary to become self-sufficient. Loans and terms vary.

Microbusiness Loan
District 7 Human Resources Development Council
P.O. Box 2016   406-247-4710
Billings, MT 59103   Fax: 406-248-2943
E-mail: dist7hrdc@imt.net
www.imt.net/~dist7hrdc
This loan program is available to start-up and existing micro businesses in Big Horn, Carbon, Stillwater, Sweetgrass and Yellowstone Counties. The amount that can be applied for is from $500 to $35,000 with the average term being 36 months. The money can be used for equipment, working capital, and property. There is also technical assistance and training available.

Nebraska

Rural Enterprise Assistance Project
Center for Rural Affairs
P.O. Box 406   402-846-5428
Walthill, NE 68067   Fax: 402-846-5420
The aim of this project is to demonstrate and implement programs to meet the
long-term needs of existing and potential small businesses to succeed in rural areas
of Nebraska. Loans are from $100 to $10,000; terms from 6 months to two years.
Interest rate is prime rate plus 1% and 4%. It receives funding from the Ford
Foundation, Mott Foundation, SBA Grant, The Aspen Institute, and Share Our
Strength.

Rural Business Enterprise Program
Central Nebraska Community Services, Inc.
626 N Street
P.O. Box 509   308-745-0780
Loup City, NE 68853   Fax: 308-745-0824
E-mail; cncsbd@micrord.com
The goal of this loan is to maintain or increase employment in Central
Nebraska.   Small business loans are available from $500 to $15,000 to small
and emerging businesses. The term is a maximum of 5 years at a fixed interest
rate. Free consulting services are also provided.

Northeast Nebraska Microloan Fund
Northeast Nebraska Economic Development District
111 South 1st Street   402-379-1150
Norfolk, NE 68701   Fax: 402-378-9207
www.nenedd.org/mbu.htm
A For Profit Micro business in Northeast Nebraska can apply for this loan. For
each $20,000 borrowed, one job must be created. And of those, at least 51% of
the jobs retained must be for low to moderate-income employees. Security is
required for the loan of $10,000 to $25,000, which must generally be paid back
within 5 years. The interest rate is fixed by NNEDD.

Small Enterprise Economic Development Loan (SEED)
Mid-Nebraska Community Services, Inc.
16 West 11th Street
P.O. 2288
Kearney, NE 68848   308-865-5675
The borrower is asked to attempt conventional financing first. If that fails, they
can apply for a loan up to $5,000. The term is a maximum of 5 years with a
fixed interest rate. This is available to a 27 county area in South Central
Nebraska. With the funding that comes from the USDA, the loan maximum is
$15,000 within a 10 county area.

Lincoln Action Program Loan
Lincoln Action Program
2202 South 11th
Lincoln, NE 68502   402-471-4515
This loan targets small business owners that are in the low-income bracket.
They use a pure lending peer group system. The loans are given in steps; they
start small with a shorter term and when that is repaid, the next loan is larger,
and so on. The maximum loan is $2,000. This is available to Lancaster County.

Micro Loan Program
New Community Development Corporation
3147 Ames Avenue
Omaha, NE 68131   402-451-2939
The goal of this program is to try and make loans available to a population that
has been historically denied access to capital. The loan is available in the
amounts of $100 to $10,000 for up to 36 months. Each loan level comes with a
different origination fee and fixed interest rate. The eligible area is mainly
North Omaha.

Rural Enterprise Assistance Project (REAP)
Center for Rural Affairs
101 Tallman
P.O. Box 406   402-846-5428
Walthill, NE 68067   Fax: 402-846-5420
REAP is designed to enhance the formation of local businesses and to invest in
local people and the future of the community. Local communities form an
association of members between 5 and 20 people. They meet for monthly
training, support, networking and reviewing of loans. The committee can loan
funds between the amounts of $100 and $10,000. This is done by step-up
borrowing, with the first time amount up to $2,000. The next loan amount can
be doubled up to $10,000. The interest for the first 2 loans is Prime +1%, and
after that it is Prime +4%.

Micro Business Training and Development Project
Catholic Charities- Juan Diego Center
5211 South 31st Street
Omaha, NE 68107   402-731-5413
Applicants must go through the training and development program either here
or at their sister agency. Generally, this is for start-up businesses, but an
existing one will be considered if it has been operational for 3 years, with 3
years of tax returns. The funds available are from $250 to $1,000, but they will
go up to $3,000 with sufficient reason. It may be used for inventory, operating
expenses, and equipment. Available in their service area only.

Self Employment Loans Fund of Lincoln
Lincoln Partnership for Economic Development
P.O. Box 83006   402-436-2350
Lincoln, NE 68501-3006   Fax: 402-436-2360
www.lped.com
This Self Employment Loans Fund (SELF) program is available to low or
moderate income business owners. They
must join a Business Loan Group where
the group meets monthly for assistance,
networking, and loan processing. The
loans are given in steps where the first
amount is a maximum of $1,000. The
next loan can be doubled and so on, for a
maximum of $10,000. These loans are not based on credit history, but
character. This program is available in Lincoln Partnership for Economic
Development's (LPED) service area.

Nevada

Nevada Microenteprise Initiative Microloan Funds
Nevada Microenterprise Initiative
116 East 7th Street, Suite 3   702-841-1420
Carson City, NV 89701   Fax: 702-841-2221
It is the goal of the Nevada Microenterprise Initiative to strengthen the
economic and quality of life of low and moderate-income business owners in
the state of Nevada through training, technical assistance, and loans. For those
people that cannot get commercial funding, they must attend NMI's workshop
before applying for a loan. A start-up business can borrow up to $7,500, for
existing or returning borrowers, the maximum loan is $25,000. The term either
is up to 36 or 72 months, depending on the loan. After that, they meet with an
advisor once a month.

New Hampshire

Working Capital-Microenterprise Peer Lending
New Hampshire Community Loan Fund
7 Wall St.   603-224-6669
Concord, NH 03301   Fax: 603-225-7254
This program is available to low and moderate income individuals in the Concord
area. This program assists underserved individuals in meeting their own basic
economic needs by complementing and extending the reach of conventional
lenders and public institutions. Loans are from $500 to $5,000 with the interest rate
at 12%. This fund receives funding from commercial banks.

Working Capital
New Hampshire Community Loan Fund
7 Wall Street   603-224-6669
Concord, NH 03301   Fax: 603-225-7425
This program was created to increase the income and success of small business owners. They use a peer lending system where members apply for loans from their group. All members must be current on their loans for any member to apply for another loan. The available loans are from $500 to $5,000. Call for the service area covered.

Citizens Bank Women Business Owners' Loan Fund
Women's Business Center
150 Greenleaf Avenue, Unit 8
Portsmouth, NH 03801   603-430-2892
The Women's Business Center (WBC) is designed to encourage and support women in all phases of enterprise development in order to create economic development. Technical assistance and workshops must be attended in order to become a member. After that, a loan from $10,000 to $100,000 can be requested if the business is also owned by at least 51% of women. The money can be used for start-up, relocation, and working capital to expand and /or purchase equipment and/or inventory.

Working Capital
Women's Rural Entrepreneurial Network (WREN)
2013 Main Street
P.O. Box 331
Bethlehem, NH 03574   603-869-9736
E-mail: WREN@connriver.net   Fax: 603-869-9738
This program has been created to support self-employed members and to give small business loans. The peer group lending system is used so that the business owner becomes a member of the group where the loan is reviewed. The amount starts at $500 and has a $5,000 maximum. After that, there are meetings where the group gets a report as to how the loan is being used. This is for both start-up and existing businesses in the area.

New Jersey
Micro Loan
Trenton Business Assistance Corporation (TBAC)
36 Broad Street   609-396-8271
Trenton, NJ 08608
Fax: 609-396-8603
E-mail: tbacsba@earthlink.net
www.trentonj.com/tbac.html

About 70% of the funds offered by TBAC are loaned to women and minority business owners. At least 50% of the loans are made to businesses owned by women. The loan amounts are up to $25,000 with a maximum term of 5 years. The interest rate is 10.5%. The for-profit business must be located in Mercer, Burlington, or Hunterdon counties.

New Mexico
Women's Economic Self-Sufficiency Team (WESST Corp.)
Women's Economic Self-Sufficiency Team
414 Silver SW   505-848-4760
Albuquerque, NM 87102-3239   Fax: 505-848-2368
The aim of Women's Economic Self-Sufficiency Team (WESST Corp.) is to help women in New Mexico achieve economic self-sufficiency through sustained self-employment. Eligible applicants are low income women and minorities located in the State of New Mexico. Loans are from $500 to $7,000 with terms from 30 days to 5 years. The interest rate is at prime rate plus 2-4%. WESST Corp. receives funding from Seton Enablement Fund, SBA Microloan Demonstration Program, and in-kind contributions.

Micro Loan Program
ACCION
#20 First Plaza NW, Suite 417
Albuquerque, NM 87102   505-243-8844
The main focus of this loan is to aid those businesses in urban or low-income areas of the Albuquerque area. Traditionally, these owners cannot get funding from banks. The loans are from $100 to $50,000. The repayment depends on the type of loan. The interest rate is from 11% to 14%. Technical assistance is also available.

New York
Adirondack Entrepreneurial Center
Adirondack Economic Development Corporation
P.O. Box 747   518-891-5523
Saranac Lake, NY 12983   Fax: 518-891-9820
The mission is to promote the development of small business. Loans are from $500 to $150,000, with flexible terms and rates. Eligible applicants are low income, women, minorities, and rural entrepreneurs. Receives funds from the Small Business Administration, Farmers Home Administration, Adirondack North County Association, NY State Urban Development Corporation, Rural Economic Development Program, and the Department of Economic Development Entrepreneurial Assistance Program.

Entrepreneurship Training Program
Worker Ownership Resource Center, Inc.
400 E. Church St.   607-737-5212
Elmira, NY 14901   Fax: 607-734-6588
This program assists low income and minority entrepreneurs to start businesses in their communities and to build personal and business assets. Eligible applicants are persons with household income below WIC guidelines and minorities. Loans are from $100 to $5,000 with terms from 6 months to two years. Interest rate is 12%. Receives funding from Diocese of Rochester, and Campaign for Human Development.

Micro-Enterprise Loan and Assistance Program
Church Avenue Merchants Block Association
885 Flatbush Ave., Suite 202   718-287-0010
Brooklyn, NY 11211   Fax: 718-287-2737
The Micro-Enterprise Loan and Assistance Program is devoted to recently arrived refugees. Goal is to enable low income persons attain self-sufficiency through microenterprise development. This program makes loans to persons who have limited or no access to capital for small businesses. Loan amounts are up to $5,000. Terms are 12 or 18 months, with an interest rate at 14%. For residents of New York City.

Minority and Women Business Development Center
Urban League of Rochester, New York, Inc.
215 Tremont St., Door #4
Rochester, NY 14608   212-803-2418
The aim is to provide training, counseling, and technical assistance to minorities and women seeking to start their own businesses. Loans are from $2,000 -$50,000; terms from 1-5 years. Interest rate is prime rate plus 1-2.5%. Receives funds from the Urban Development Corp., and NY State Department of Economic Development Entrepreneurial Assistance Program. Only for residents of greater Rochester - Monroe County.

Neighborhood Micro-Loan Program
Ridgewood Local Development Corporation
59-09 Myrtle Ave.   718-366-3806
Ridgewood, NY 11385   Fax: 718-381-7080
The Neighborhood Micro-Loan Program serves neighborhood retailers, small manufacturers, professionals and health care providers, service businesses. and young businesses and businesses owned by minorities and women. Program is used to contract startup costs, storefront improvements, and purchase new equipment. Loan amounts and terms vary. Only for residents of the greater Ridgewood area in Queens, NY.

N.Y. State Department of Economic Development Entrepreneurial Assistance
Program
Albany-Colonie Regional Chamber of Commerce
1 Computer Dr. S.   518-458-9851
Albany, NY 12205   Fax: 518-458-1055
Purpose of this program is to promote the growth and development
of minority-owned and women-owned businesses by
providing technical assistance and creating access to
capital, networking, and community and business leaders.
Receives funds from NY State Urban Development Corp.,
Albany Local Development Corp., KeyBank USA, and
Town of Colonie I.D.A. Loans are from $1,000 to $5,000,
terms from three to five years. Interest rate is Prime rate plus
2%.

Queens County Overall Economic Development Corporation
- NY State Department of Economic Development
Entrepreneurial Assistance Program
Queens County Overall Economic Development Corp.
120-55 Queens Blvd., Suite 309   718-263-0546
Kew Gardens, NY 11424   Fax: 718-263-0594
Provides a package of services to encourage and train would be entrepreneurs; to
support and assist new startup businesses in surviving the first two years of
business, and assist existing businesses with their relocation and/or expansion
efforts. Eligible applicants are low income and minority residents of Queens.
Loans and terms vary. Funding comes from seven banks and equity investors,
borough presidents, city and state agencies.

Regional Economic Development Assistance Corporation Mini Loan Program
New York City Economic Development Corporation
110 William St.
New York, NY 10038   212-618-8900
This program is for small/startup service, retail, contractor, manufacturing
businesses. Loans are available for machinery and equipment, leasehold
improvements, real estate acquisition and working capital. Loans are from $5,000
to $50,000. Terms are two to five years. Interest rates are prime rate plus 1.5%.

Rural Ventures Fund
Rural Opportunities, Inc.
400 East Ave.   716-340-3387
Rochester, NY 14607   Fax: 716-340-3337
Eligible applicants are low and moderate income individuals denied access to bank
credit. The aim is to promote self-sufficiency and economic independence through

the creation and expansion of small businesses and microenterprises. Loans are from $3,000 to $50,000 with terms from 3 to 60 months. The interest rate is up to 15%. Funding comes from FmHA Industrial Development Grant, SBA Microloan Demonstration Program, CDBG funds, and New York State. For residents of upstate New York, primarily rural and small communities.

WORC Loan Fund
Worker Ownership Resource Center
One Franklin Square
Exchange Street   315-789-5061
Geneva, NY 14456   Fax: 315-789-0261
www.atworc.org
WORC funds are available to people with low to moderate income. In order to be considered for a loan, a training program through the center must be completed. Five thousand dollars is the maximum amount for first time borrowers. After half of that has been paid off on time, additional funds may be applied for. Only the interest is required during the first 3 months of a new loan. After that, repayment is normally 2 years. That may be extended for loan over $5,000. Interest is the prime lending rate at closing. The business or owner must reside in the 10 county service area.

Manhattan Loan Fund
Manhattan Borough Development Corporation
15 Park Row, Suite 510   212-791-3660
New York, NY 10038   Fax: 212-571-0873
This is available to moderate-income business owners located in Manhattan. The amounts of the loan are from $5,000 to $25,000. It can be used for leasehold improvements, machinery and equipment and working capital. The terms are 6 months to 5 years at 10.5% interest.

Micro Loan Program
Project Enterprise
2303 7th Avenue
New York, NY 10030   212-690-2024
This program is for microentrepreneurs in the Brooklyn and Harlem areas that live at or below the poverty level, in order that they can increase their incomes and improve the quality of their lives. A group of peers build up a Group Savings Fund, which is used for loans to members of the group at no interest. Bi-weekly meetings must be attended. The first loan is for a maximum of $750 for 5 months or $1,500 for 12 months. After that the loan amount doubles with a maximum of $10,000. A good credit record or collateral is not needed to enroll in this program.

ACCORD Business Development Program
ACCORD Corporation
50 West Main Street   716-973-2322
Friendship, NY 14739   Fax: 716-973-3014
E-mail: RVC_Fedz@eznet.net
To be able to apply for a loan, a 10-week course or equivalent independent
study must be completed. It is available to business owners that fall within
HUD's low to moderate-income levels. It is for start-up or existing businesses
that need money for working capital, real property, and equipment. Up to
$25,000 can be applied for with the term varying. It is offered in Allegany
County.

Micro Loan Program
ACCION New York
235 Havemeyer Street
Brooklyn, NY 11211   718-599-5170
E-mail: accionnewyork@compuserve.com
www.accion.org
ACCION does not require that a business be formal in their operation. It is
preferred that they have been in business for at least 1 year. The loan is from
$5,000 to $25,000 with a term of 3 months to 24 months. The interest is
ammortized on a monthly basis. This is available to businesses in New York
City that cannot get conventional lending.

Appleseed Trust
MicroCredit Group of Central New York
222 Herald Place, 2nd Floor   315-424-9485
Syracuse, NY 13202   Fax: 315-424-7056
It is the mission of this program to assist low and moderate-income residents in
this community to start, expand, or improve
their business through training, support, and
loan access. Members must join a Peer
Group where they can apply for a first loan of
up to $500. The money can be used for equipment, materials, or advertising and
promotions. Expansions and additional loans can be sought for up to $5,000.

Trickle Up Program
Trickle Up
121 West 27th St., Suite 504
New York, NY 10001   212-362-7958
Over 75% of the recipients of this program either have no credit or bad credit
history. Entrepreneurs are given $700 in conditional start-up capital in two
installments. For the first $500, they must complete a Business Plan, agree to

spend a minimum of 250 hours per person over a 3 month period, and save or reinvest at least 20% of the profits in the business. At the end of three months, and when all of the requirements have been met, they can receive the final $200. Most of the recipients work out of their homes.

North Carolina
Child Care Providers
Self-Help
301 W. Main St.
Durham, NC 27701
www.self-help.org

800-476-7428
919-956-4400
Fax: 919-956-4600

This is a special loan program created by the NC Division of Child Development to help an individual get started or expand, buy indoor or outdoor equipment, upgrade buildings, and improve a particular program's quality. These loans have a below market, fixed interest rate of 5%, and no minimum/maximum loan size. Eligible applicants are anyone who runs or wants to run a registered and licensed child care program that serves or is willing to serve subsidized children.

Good Work
Good Work
115 Market St. #211
Durham, NC 27702

919-682-8473
Fax: 919-687-7033

Aim is to be a resource for those who want to start or expand their small businesses. Eligible applicants are startup and small businesses. Loans are from $100-$10,000 with terms from three months to three years. Interest rate is 13%. Receives funds from Self-Help Credit Union, foundations, and churches.

Microbusiness Development
WAMY Community Action, Inc.
P.O. Box 2688
Boone, NC 28607

828-264-2421
Fax: 828-264-0952

This program allows low-income persons to begin or expand small business efforts in an area where few jobs are available. Eligible applicants are persons below poverty level located in Watauga, Avery, Mitchell and Yancey counties only. Loans are from $500 to $10,000; terms and interest rates vary.

Mountain Microenterprise Fund
Mountain Microenterprise Fund
29 1/2 Page Ave.
Asheville, NC 28801

828-253-2834
Fax: 828-255-7953

Eligible applicants are women and minorities, and low income persons. The aim is to create small businesses and microenterprises through a program of financial and technical assistance. Funding is from NC General Assembly, operating budget, Dogwood Fund, NC Rural Economic Development Center, and the Z. Smith Reynolds/Janirve Foundations. Loans are from $200-$25,000; terms vary.

North Carolina Microenterprise Loan Program (NCMLP)
NC Rural Economic Development Center, Inc.
4021 Carya Dr.   919-250-4314
Raleigh, NC 27610   Fax: 919-250-4325
The NCMLP is one of the largest microenterprise loan funds in the country. It's funded by public and private sources. It offers financing and support for the startup and expansion of small businesses for residents of the 85 counties defined as rural in NC. Borrowers have included mechanics, seamstresses, crafts people, janitorial service operators, building contractors, and retailers. Loans are from $350 to $25,000.

Northeastern Community Development Corporation
154 Highway 158 East   252-338-5466
Camden, NC 27921   Fax: 252-338-5639
The mission of this fund is to make funding available to craft artisans to startup or expand their businesses. The Fund works with low-income people who need loans to buy equipment/supplies in order to begin making crafts, or who need working capital for expanding their business. Loans are from $50 to $750 with terms from one to three months. The interest rate is prime rate plus 2%. This fund receives funding from the Ms. Foundation.

West Greenville CDC Micro Loan Program
West Greenville Community Development Corp.
706 West 5th St.
P.O. Box 1605
Greenville, NC 27835-1605   252-752-9277
Eligible applicants are women, and other high risk borrowers. The aim is to increase economic index in target counties. Loans and terms vary. Also provide business training and planning, individual business counseling, peer support, and mentoring. This program receives funding from the NC Rural Economic Development Center.

Micro Loan
Mountain Microenterprise Fund (MMF)
29 1/2 Page Avenue
Asheville, NC 28801   888-389-3089
www.mtnmicro.org
Either a secured or unsecured loan is available to those small business owners that cannot get a conventional loan through a bank. For an unsecured loan,

$99-$1,500 can be applied for. The first level for a secured loan is $99 to
$2,500. After that has been repaid up to $5,000 can be sought. The last level
of the loan is for up to $8,000. The repayment varies from 12 months to 36
months for the larger loans. Most of the funding comes from the Rural
Economic Development Center.

Micro Loan
Good Work, Inc.
P.O. 25250
Durham, NC 27702   919-682-8473

While the target of this loan is low-income minority
small business owners, anyone in the service area
can apply. In order to be eligible, a technical
training class through the company must be
completed. The loan amounts are $1,000 to
$10,000. The term is from 6 to 12 years. The
interest rate is 13%, but is negotiable depending on
the loan size.

Microenterprise Loan Program
North Carolina Rural Economic Development Center
4021 Carya Drive
Raleigh, NC 27610   919-250-4314
The goal of this program is to help rural people become self-sufficient. It
offers loans to people that could not get conventional funding in order to start-
up or expand their business. Loans up to $25,000 are available. With this
program, five local lending sites have group-based lending programs. The
business owner joins into a group where they are involved in training and get
certification. Each group controls the loan payments. This is for small
businesses in the 85 rural counties of North Carolina. The local lending office
should be contacted for information.

East Carolina Microenterprise Loan Program
East Carolina Microenterprise Loan Program
315 Turner Street   252-504-2424
Beaufort, NC 28516   Fax: 252-504-2248
It is the goal of this program to loan money to microentrepreneurs in order to
create more jobs in rural areas. Participants must attend business sessions and
afterwards they form small groups that administer their own loans. After that
they meet monthly for further training, networking and loan presentations.
From $500 to $8,000 can be applied for in three stages. The terms range from
20 months to 30 months. It is available to either start-up or existing businesses
in the service area.

Ohio
Microenterprise Program
Lima-Allen Council for Community Affairs
405 East Market St.   419-227-2586
Lima, OH 45801   Fax: 419-227-7626
This program is available to low income workers, displaced workers, ADC/JOBS
recipients located in Allen county. The aim is to empower low income individuals
through self-employment, creating self-sufficiency and alleviating poverty. Loans
are up to $1,000, terms from two to five years and interest rate is at prime plus 2%.
Receives funds from various financial institutions and CSBG.

CAC Microenterprise Training Program
Community Action Committee (CAC) of Pike County
941 Market St.
P.O. Box 799   740-289-2371
Piketon, OH 45661   Fax: 740-289-4291
The program is available to low and moderate income persons. The aim is to
improve economic conditions through training, small business development and
support services leading to self-sufficiency. Loans are $500 to $10,000, terms three
months to three years, and interest rate at prime plus 2%. Receives funds from
CDC Grant Program, banks, local housing authority, and organization
contributions.

City of Cleveland Microloan Program
City of Cleveland Department of Economic Development
601 Lakeside Ave., Room 210   216-664-2406
Cleveland, OH 44114   Fax: 216-664-3681
The aim is to provide financial and management support to existing and new
businesses that do not have access to traditional financial sources. Eligible
applicants are businesses in the City of Cleveland. Loan amounts and terms vary.
Receives funds from City of Cleveland and local financial institutions.

Columbus/Franklin County Microloan Program
Columbus Countywide Development Corp.
941 Chatham Lane, Suite 207   614-645-6171
Columbus, OH 43221   Fax: 614-645-8588
This program is available to women and minority-owned businesses, day care
facilities and targeted Columbus neighborhoods. The aim is to encourage the
creation of small micro businesses and provide financing for small projects not
available from conventional lenders. Loans are $1,000 to $25,000, terms 30 days
to 6 years, and interest rate is 10.6% to 11.6%. Receives funds from SBA, Ohio
Department of Development, Columbus Department of Development, and banks.

Food Ventures Project and Product Development Fund
ACEnet
94 N. Columbus Rd.   740-592-3854
Athens, OH 44701   Fax: 740-593-5451
The aim is to transform relationships within communities to allow people with low incomes to successfully enter the economic mainstream by creating opportunities for both business ownership and employment in expanding firms. Eligible applicants are low to moderate-income persons, public assistance recipients, and firms participating in ACEnet business networks in Southeastern Ohio. To promote food manufacturing businesses; funds can be a loan, royalty, or equity. Receives funds from private sources and foundations.

HHWP Community Action Commission
Microenterprise Development Program
HHWP Community Action Commission
122 Jefferson St., P.O. Box 179   419-423-3755
Findlay, OH 45839   Fax: 419-423-4115
Program is available to low income and public assistance recipients. The aim is to create self-employment opportunities that enable low income residents to improve their living conditions and become self-sufficient. Loans are up to $5,000, terms from 3-24 months. Interest rate is prime plus 2%. Receives funds from CSBG and private foundations.

Neighborhood Economic Development Loan Program (NEDL)
Office of Economic Development, City of Toledo
One Government Center, Suite 1850   419-245-1426
Toledo, OH 43604   Fax: 419-245-1462
This program is available to low and moderate income target communities served by CDC housing programs. The aim is to provide commercial credit for neighborhood-based businesses and provide a competitive advantage to neighborhood commercial and industrial areas. Loan amounts and terms vary. Receives funding from City of Toledo and banks.

Women Entrepreneurs, Inc.
Women Entrepreneurs, Inc.
P.O. Box 2662, C-OH45201
36 East 4th St., Suite 92   513-684-0700
Cincinnati, OH 45201   Fax: 513-684-0779
New businesses that are started offer services to the community such as adult day care, home-bound disabled worker assistance and extra support to women in traditional industries. Receives funding from Society National Banks, Liberty National Banks, independent member/corporate contributions, and local foundations. Eligible applicants are AFDC recipients, low and moderate income

individuals located in Hamilton, Clermont, Warren, Butler, Brown, Adams, Highland, Pike and Ross counties, and Northern Kentucky and Southeastern Indiana. Loans and terms vary.

Micro Loan Fund
Neighborhood House, Inc
1000 Atchenson Street   614-252-4544
Columbus, OH 43203   Fax: 614-252-7919
E-mail: lboykin@beol.net
The purpose of this loan is to build up the empowerment zone. It is available to start-up and existing small businesses in that area, or for those business owners that live in the zone. Applications can be made for up to $7,500 for a 3 year term. The interest rate is 12%.

Appalachian Microloan Program
Enterprise Development Corporation   740-797-9646
9080 Hocking Hills Drive   800-822-6096
The Plains, OH 45780   Fax: 740-797-9659
This is for small business located in the 30 counties of Appalachia. It may be used for working capital, equipment and machinery, furniture and fixtures, inventory and supplies, and leasehold improvements. The size of the loan is $100 to $25,000. The term is flexible with a maximum of 6 years. The interest rate is from 11% to 12.75% APR. Funding is from the Small Business Administration.

Child Care Loan
Lima/Allen Council on Community Affairs (LACCA)
540 South Central   419-227-2586
Lima, OH 45804   Fax: 419-227-7626
The Child Care Loan is available to those child care providers that target low income people, infants, workers of 2nd or 3rd shifts, and disabled kids. The maximum amount of the loan is $25,000. It must be repaid in up to 5 years and the interest is Prime + 2. The borrowers must be in the 5 county service area of LACCA.

MicroLoan Program
Hamilton County Development Company, Inc.
1776 Mentor Avenue
Cincinnati, OH 45212   513-631-8292
E-mail: lawalden@hcdc.com
This loan is open to small business owners located in one of the 8 counties of Southwest Ohio. The maximum loan for a start-up business is $7,500. For an

existing business, one year or more, the amount is $15,000. The term is up to 6 years with an interest rate of 16%. Funding is provided by the SBA.

MicroLoan
Columbus Countywide Development Corporation
941 Chatham Lane, Suite 300   614-645-6171
Columbus, OH 43221-2416   Fax: 614-645-85883
E-mail: ccdc@earthlink.net
This program helps healthy growing businesses by offering financial and technical support. The maximum loan for a start-up business is $15,000. For an existing business, the loan starts at $1,000 and has a maximum of $25,000. The term depends on what the loan is being used for, but on an average is 2 years. The interest ranges from 11.6% to 10.6%. Borrowers are required to attend Technical Assistance Group meetings. This available area is in 13 counties of Central Ohio.

Pike County Microloan
CAC of Pike County, Inc.
941 Market Street
Piketon, OH 45661   740-289-2371
While they tend to serve business owners that cannot get loans from the banks, this program is also open to other entrepreneurs in Pike County. After completion of the business class, a loan for up to $10,000 can be applied for. The term is a maximum of 3 years with the interest rate of Prime plus 2.

Oregon
SBA Microloan Program
Cascades West Financial Services, Inc.
1400 Queen Avenue SE
P.O. Box 686   541-924-8480
Albany, OR 97321   Fax: 541-967-4651
E-mail: dsearle@cwcog.cog.or.us
The purpose of this loan is to help women, low income, minority and other business owners get loans that they could not otherwise get. The ultimate goal is to help them become eligible for conventional banking loans. The money available is up to $25,000 for up to 6 years at a fixed rate of up to 14.75%. Technical support is offered throughout the life of the loan. The business must be located in the 14 county service area of Cascades West.

Microenterprise Loan
O.U.R. Federal Credit Union
P.O. Box 11922
Eugene, OR 97440   541-485-1190

This loan is for businesses that have been operational at least 12 months and have proof of business activity. They must be members of the credit union and have participated with or in a health or human services agency in Lane County. The loan amount is a maximum of $5,000 at 13.9% interest. The term is up to 36 months.

Micro Loan
Southern Oregon Women's Access to Credit
33 North Central, Suite 209
Medford, OR 97501   541-779-3992
Start-up or expansion businesses in the Jackson County area can apply for a loan of up to $25,000. The term is 5 years with an interest rate of 3 1/2 points over prime. A written business plan must be submitted before applying for the loan. The funds can be used for working capital.

Child Care Neighborhood Network Loan Fund
Rose Community Development Corporation
7211 NE 62nd Avenue
Portland, OR 97206   503-788-0826
Through community based microenterprise development, Rose CDC helps to increase the character of child care and secure the providers' businesses. These loans are established in order to help child care providers who have difficulty getting conventional loans. The loan amounts are $500 to $5,000 with a term between 24 and 48 months. The money may be used for business improvements, equipment or toys, and related business expenses.

Pennsylvania
Ben Franklin Enterprise Growth Fund
Ben Franklin Technology Center of Southeastern Pennsylvania
1110 Penn Center
1835 Market St., Suite 1100   215-972-0877
Philadelphia, PA 19103   Fax: 215-972-5588
Fund was established to make capital available to low income, minority, and women business owners, startups, and to help client businesses obtain credit from conventional sources in Bucks, Chester, Delaware, Montgomery, and Philadelphia counties. Loans are from $5,000 to $15,000. Interest rate is fixed at prime rate plus 3%. Closing fees are up to $350 (can be financed in the loan).

Local Enterprise Assistance Program (LEAP)
Bloomsburg University College of Business
243 Sutliff Hall   570-389-4591
Bloomsburg, PA 17815   Fax: 570-389-3892

The aim is to create opportunities for startup and self-employed business persons to earn equitable incomes and control productive resources. Dedicated to building the economic capacity of rural communities through small enterprises by providing access to credit, business training and self-management skills. Eligible applicants are the unemployed, rural microentrepreneurs, and AFDC recipients. Loans and terms vary.

Micro-Enterprise Development
Lutheran Children and Family Service
45 Garrett Rd.   610-734-3363
Upper Darby, PA 19082   Fax: 610-734-3389

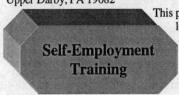

This program is available to refugees in the U.S. less than five years, who are AFDC recipients, low/moderate income located in Philadelphia. Receives funding from the Office of Refugee Resettlement. Loans and terms vary.

Service for Self-Employment Training and Support (ASSETS)
Mennonite Economic Development Associates
447 S. Prince St.
Lancaster, PA 17603   717-393-6089
This program is available to low income individuals as defined by HUD guidelines. The Associates have assisted new businesses to start or expand in the most disadvantaged areas of Lancaster. The purpose is to increase personal income, create jobs, foster economic linkages, develop human potential and encourage community development through small business. Loans are from $500 to $5,000 with terms from 6 months to three years. The interest rate is prime rate.

Micro Loan
ASSETS
447 South Prince Street   717-393-6089
Lancaster, PA 17603   Fax: 717-290-7936
In order to apply for this loan, applicants must complete a 13-week training program. It is available to people with low to moderate income that live in Lancaster. Up to $5,000 can be loaned with a term of up to 3 years. The interest rate is the Prime lending rate.

Micro Loan
Community Action Development Corporation of the Lehigh Valley
605 Turner Street
Allentown, PA 18102   610-433-5703
This program was designed to help to build up the community and to establish business owners. Before applying for the loan, the Start Your Business

Program must be completed. Graduates can apply for a loan up to $5,000. The terms and interest rate of the loan vary case by case. It is available for the areas of Center City, Allenton, and South Side.

Community Capital Works
Philadelphia Development Partnership
1334 Walnut Street
Philadelphia, PA 19107   215-545-3100
Applicants must go through the customized business training to qualify for this small business loan. After that, they join a peer lending group which governs the loan. The funds are loaned in steps starting with $500. After that amount is repaid the business owner can apply for $1,000. This goes up to a maximum amount of $5,000. The amount of time to repay the loan depends on the amount. The interest rate is a 12% annual rate. Borrowers must be in the service are of PDP.

Women's Opportunities Resource Program
Women's Opportunities Resource
1930 Chestnut Street, Suite 1600
Philadelphia, PA 19103   215-564-5500
After applicants have attended the free business classes, they can apply for a loan. The maximum amount available is $2,500 for a term of 24 months. It is intended for minority, woman, refugee and immigrant business owners. They say they are a "fund of last resort" in the 5 county area that is served.

Enterprise Growth Fund
Ben Franklin Technology Center of Southeastern Pennsylvania
11 Penn Center
1835 Market St., Suite 1100   215-972-6700
Philadelphia, PA 19103   Fax: 215-972-5588
This Fund was created to make capital available to small businesses in Bucks, Chester, Delaware, Montgomery, and Philadelphia counties, so that they may be able to get conventional funding in the future. Eligible businesses are owned by credit-challenged women, minorities, low to moderate income people, and those that are located in economically distresses areas. The maximum loan is $25,000 for existing businesses and $5,000 for start-ups to be used for development and expansion.

South Dakota
Revolving Loan Fund Program
Northeast South Dakota Economic Corporation
414 Third Ave. East   605-698-7654
Sisseton, SD 57262   Fax: 605-698-3038

This program receives funding from Northwest Area Foundation, CDBG, SBA Microloan Demonstration Program, East River Electric Power Corp., and the First State Bank of Roscoe. The program addresses the economic needs of small rural communities as they relate to business development and job creation. Eligible applicants are low income, disadvantaged persons, minorities, and women. Loans are from $100 to $150,000 with terms from 6 months to 25 years. For residents of northeastern South Dakota.

Tennessee
Community Microloan Program
Knoxville's Community Development Corporation
Economic Ventures, Inc.
P.O. Box 3550   423-594-8762
Knoxville, TN 37927-3550   Fax: 423-594-8659
This program helps individuals in getting their businesses established through financial and technical assistance. Borrowers join a peer group where they get training, support, and apply for the loans. All members must be current for one to get a loan. The loans are given in 5 stages, the first is $500 and the maximum is $10,000. Terms are from 6 months to 48 month. This is available to low to moderate-income people, women, and minorities in East Tennessee.

Micro Loan Program
Firestone Retirees CDC
659 North Manassas Street, Room 106-107
Memphis, TN 38107
P.O. Box 80073
Memphis, TN 38108   901-454-9524

Firestone Retirees is trying to help people in poverty to become income achievers. While they offer business training courses, it is not a requirement for a loan. The Peer Lending Group method is used with a 10-person group administering the loans. The loan amounts range from $250 to $5,000 with the term varying from 5 months to 25 months, depending on the loan. The interest rate is currently 10% and subject to change. It is available to their service area.

Texas
Micro Loan
ACCION El Paso
7744 North Loop Road, Suite A
El Paso, TX 79915   915-779-3727

This loan requires that a business has one year of experience or is a start-up in El Paso. It is for those that have limited access to bank credit. The amount loaned to a small business is $250 to $1,000, the medium business loan is for $1,000 to $3,000, and the large fund is for the maximum of $10,000. The term depends on the type of loan issued. The rate is an 18% simple interest.

Tyler Development Fund
Tyler Economic Development Council, Inc.
P.O. Box 2004   903-593-2004
Tyler, TX 75710   Fax: 903-597-0699
The goal of the Council is to create a
solid economy for small and minority
business owners with low to moderate
income. This fund is for those that have
results within 18 months of operation and
located in Smith County. The maximum
amount of a loan is $50,000 with bank
participation for loans over $25,000. The
terms depend on the loan and the interest rate is fixed.

MicroLoan Program
Corporation for Economic Development of Harris County, Inc.
2223 West Loop South, Suite 400   713-840-8804
Houston, TX 77027   Fax: 713-840-8806
Their mission is to enhance the economic and community development in Harris County and the Gulf Coast Region. The target is low to moderate income people who are having trouble finding conventional funding. The amounts available for a loan are $500 to $25,000.

MicroLoan Program
Corporation for Economic Development of Harris County, Inc.
2223 West Loop South, Suite 400   713-840-8804
Houston, TX 77027   Fax: 713-840-8806
The goal with CEDHC is to provide gap financing in order to create permanent jobs that will improve the community economically. This is available for low to moderate business owners in Harris County and the Gulf Coast Region. The loan amount is from $500 to $25,000. Technical seminars and one-on-one counseling are also offered.

Utah
Utah Microenterprise Loan Fund
Utah Microenterprise Loan Fund
3595 South Main Street
Salt Lake City, UT 84115   801-269-8408

This Fund was developed to help socially and economically disadvantaged people. It is available for small businesses in Salt Lake, Davis, Summit, Toouele and Morgan Counties. Up to $10,000 can be borrowed with a term of 5 years. The interest rate varies.

Vermont
Burlington Revolving Loan Fund
Community and Economic Development Office
Room 32, City Hall   802-865-7144
Burlington, VT 05461   Fax: 802-865-7024
The aim is to create a sustainable local economy that equitably distributes costs and provides meaningful opportunities for participation by residents in essential resource allocation decisions. The fund is aimed at low and moderate-income individuals located in the Champlain Valley. Loans are from $4,000 to $100,000, terms from 3-10 years, and the interest rate is variable.

Micro-Business Development Program
Central Vermont Community Action Council, Inc.
195 US Route 302/Berlin   802-479-1053
Barre, VT 05641   Fax: 802-479-5353
The aim of this program is to eliminate poverty by opening to everyone the opportunity to live in decency and with dignity. It is aimed at low-income persons. Loans and terms vary. Closing costs can be included in the loan amount. Receives funding from the Family Foundation, HeadStart, Vermont Community Development Program, Vermont State, USDA Food Stamps, Veterans grant, and CDBG discretionary grant.

Virginia
Eagle Staff Fund - Seed Grants
First Nations Development Institute
The Stores Building
11917 Main St.
Fredericksburg, VA 22408   540-371-5615

Seed Grants This Fund is dedicated to promoting economic understanding among Native people. Seed grants are to identify and develop ideas and concepts about economic development, and provide funds for training, convening meetings, and community organizing.
Amounts are from $1,500 to $5,000. The applicant's proposed budget must accurately reflect the project scope.

Northern Virginia Microenterprise Loan - SBA
Ethiopian Community Development Council, Inc.
1038 S. Highland St.
Arlington, VA 22206   703-685-0510
Applicants must be opening or expanding a small business, unable to find
alternative sources of financing. Loans are up to $25,000 with the interest rate at
prime rate plus 4%.

Refugee Microenterprise Loan - ORR
Ethiopian Community Development Council, Inc.
1038 S. Highland St.
Arlington, VA 22204   703-685-0510
Applicants must be refugees and political asylees in the U.S. for less than five
years, and have proper documents; want to open or expand a business, and are
willing to write a business plan. Loans are up to $10,000 at prime rate plus 2%.

Microloan Fund
Small Business Development Center, Inc.
147 Mill Ridge Rd.
Lynchburg, VA 24502   804-582-6170
This program is available to low to moderate-income individuals who lack access
to bank or other financing. All new business owners must complete the Self-
Employment Training Program prior to making application for the loan fund.
(Training Program covers the basics of owning your own business). Loan amounts
range from $50.00 to $10,000 with terms from 1-3 years for long term loans, and
0-12 months for short-term loans. Interest rate is prime plus 3, which is fixed at
time of closing. This program is sponsored by the SBA, Virginia Department of
Economic Development, Greater Lynchburg Chamber of Commerce, Virginia's
Region 2000, and the City of Lynchburg. For residents of Lynchburg and these
counties: Amherst, Appomattox, Bedford, and Campbell.

Business Loan Program
South Fairfax Regional Business Partnership, Inc.
6911 Richmond Highway   703-768-1440
Alexandria, VA 22306   Fax: 707-768-0547
Loans are provided for entrepreneurs that can not get conventional loans. They
are for start-up or small businesses in the southeast Fairfax County. Direct
loans of $3,500 to $25,000 are available with interest rates in the range of
Prime + 3% to Prime + 7%. The repayment period is 3 years on an average.
The funds can be used for business machinery and equipment, working capital
and paying marketing expenses. The owner must be in the low or moderate-
income bracket.

Micro Loan
VA Eastern Shore Economic Empowerment and Housing Corp.
P.O. Box 814   757-442-4509
Nassawadox, VA 23413   Fax: 757-442-7530
This loan assists low to moderate-income people to start-up or improve an
existing business. The funds that may be applied for are from $500 to $50,000.
The interest is 6.5% plus costs. This is only for residents of Virginia Eastern
Shore.

New Enterprises Loan Fund
New Enterprises Fund
930 Cambria Street
Christiansburg, VA 24073   540-382-2002

This fund is available in the New River Valley of
southwest Virginia. Its goal is to promote the
development of micro-enterprises through
training, technical assistance, loaning of
funds, and follow-up support. After
completing the training program, a loan from
$1,000 to $25,00 can be applied for. The terms
are from 1 to 4 years at an 8% interest rate. This is
for both start-up and existing businesses.

Northern Neck Enterprise Program
Northern Neck Planning District Commission
153 Yankee Point Road
Lancaster, VA 22503   804-333-1900
www.nnpdc17.state.va.us
This loan is available to micro start-up or expansion businesses in the Northern
Neck Area. They must have been turned down by a bank and pass the loan
committee review. Up to $25,000 can be applied for and the term is up to 3
years.

MicroLoan Program
Virginia Economic Development Corporation
P.O. Box 1505   804-979-0114
Charlottesville, VA 22902-1505   Fax: 804-979-1597
E-mail: microloan.tjpd@state.va.us
www.avenue.org/Gov/TJPDC
This program is accessible to small business owners that live and operate their
businesses in the Thomas Jefferson Planning District. There is an emphasis on
women and minority owners. An Entrepreneur Training Course or equal
training and/or experience is a requirement before applying for a loan. The

maximum loan is $25,000 with a variable interest rate at Prime plus 1.5% to 5%. Collateral and a credit check are needed.

Washington
African American Community Endowment Fund
Black Dollar Days Task Force
116-21st Ave.
Seattle, WA 98122   206-323-0534
This is a new program that hopes to make its first micro-enterprise loan this year (1996). This proposed microenterprise loan fund hopes to foster an entrepreneurial spirit and encourage self-sufficiency through the growth of small business opportunities primarily in the economically depressed areas of Seattle. This micro-enterprise loan is a source of business financing for people who are unable to access capital from other sources. As this is a new program, the amount of loans, interest, etc. are not know as yet. For further information, contact the above number.

Cascadia Revolving Fund
Cascadia Revolving Fund
119 1st Ave. S., Suite 100   206-447-9226
Seattle, WA 98104   Fax: 206-682-4804
This is a tax-exempt nonprofit corporation that provides loans and technical assistance to socially/environmentally based enterprises and nonprofit organizations. Loans can be up to $150,000 with variable interest rates and terms. Eligible applicants are low income women, minorities, and refugees. Receives funds from individual investors, religious orders, nonprofit corporations, earnings and individual gifts.

DownHome Washington Microloan Program
Snohomish County Private Industry Council   425-743-9669
728 134th Street SW, Bldg. A, Suite 211   425-353-2025
Everett, WA 98204   Fax: 425-742-1177
E-mail: snopic@gte.net
This program is designed for those borrowers who do not fit into the general banking guidelines. It is offered with technical assistance and available to those who have their business within the 16 county service area of the program. The loan amounts are from $500 to $25,000. Funding is from the SBA.

CASH Loan Program
Washington CASH- Community Alliance for Self-Help
410 Boston Street   206-352-1945
Seattle, WA 98109   Fax: 206-352-1899

E-mail: washcash@nwlink.com
www.washingtoncash.org
This program was established to create self-sufficiency and self-employment
for low-income women, people with disabilities, and new immigrants and
refugees. It uses a peer support group lending model. Each group regulates its
own loans and repayment. The first loan amount is $500. After that has been
successfully repaid, up to $5,000 can be applied for. A required 12-week
business training course, post loan technical assistance and peer support are
part of this program. It is available within CASH's service area.

Micro Loan Program
Tri-Cities Enterprise Association
2000 Logston Boulevard
Richland, WA 99052   509-375-3268
www.owt.com/tea
TEA wants to promote the growth and development of new businesses in order
to economically benefit the community. The small business loans are available
to for-profit start up businesses in Benton or Franklin counties. The money can
be used for working capital or acquisition of materials, supplies, furniture,
fixtures or equipment. From $500 to $7,500 is available for a loan, but up to
$25,000 may be considered. The average term is 18 to 36 months with up to 6
years as the maximum.

SNAP Program
Spokane Neighborhood Action Programs
212 South Wall
Spokane, WA 99201   509-456-7174
E-mail: lancaster@snapwa.org

Northwest Business Development Association
9 South Washington, Suite 215
Spokane, WA 99201   509-458-8555
This loan requires that the Technical Assistance Program be attended. Funds
are available to start-up or existing businesses where the owners are in the low
to medium income bracket in their area. The loan amount is up to $10,000 with
repayment in a maximum of 5 years. The interest rate is Prime plus 2%. This
is only for the Spokane County area. The training program is offered by
SNAP and the loan comes from Northwest Business Development.

West Virginia
Monroe Neighborhood Enterprise Center
Monroe County Community Services Council
P.O. Box 403   304-772-3381

Union, WV 24883   Fax: 304-772-4014
The aim is to improve the income and self-sufficiency of low to moderate-income
persons by providing loans, business training, and opportunities for
microenterprises. This center receives funding from banks of Monroe, Union,
West Virginia by providing lines of credit, operating funds from Neighborhood
Reinvestment Corp., and Benedum Foundation. Loans are from $500 to $10,000
with terms from one to five years. Loan review committees will determine loan
conditions.

Lighthouse MicroLoan
Lightstone CDC
H 363 Box 73   304-249-5200
Moyers, WV 26815   Fax: 304-249-5310
www.lightstone.org
Lightstone has developed this loan in order to help create and sustain new
business development in rural areas. It is available
in 10 counties in the Eastern Panhandle of West
Virginia, and 2 counties in Virginia. After working
with the Small Business Development Center, a
loan with a maximum amount of $10,000 can be
applied for. The maximum term is 5 years. This is often used by low and
moderate-income entrepreneurs. They are CDFI.

Wisconsin
ADVOCAP Business Development Loan Fund
ADVOCAP, Inc.
19 W. 1st St.   920-922-7760
Fond du Lac, WI 54935   Fax: 920-922-7214
This Loan Fund is to help low income persons become self-sufficient by
developing businesses that will create jobs. Loans are from $100 to $15,000.
Terms are from 30 days to 6 years. Interest rate can be from 7 to 10%. Closing
costs/fees can be included in the amount of the loan. Receives funding from
ADVOCAP business development fund, SBA Microloan Demonstration, C.O.E.
fund from agency funds. Only for residents of Fond du Lac, and Winnebago and
Green Lake counties.

Business Ownership and Operations
Juneau Business High School
6415 West Mount Vernon
Milwaukee, WI 53213   414-476-5480
Program is available to 15-19 year old multi-cultural students, of which a large
percentage are low income. It provides high school students with practical, hands-

on experience in business ownership and operations. Provides youth with alternative career options and education in the areas of economics, citizenship and ethics. Loans are from $50 to $500 with terms at 9 months. Interest rate is 12%.

Economic Development Project
West Cap
525 2nd St.   715-265-4271
Glenwood City, WI 54013   Fax: 715-265-7031
The aim is to create opportunities that allow people to achieve self-sufficiency for themselves, their families, and their communities. Eligible applicants are low income individuals with special emphasis on women. Loans are up to $15,000. Receives funding from Farmers Home Administration and the Bremer Foundation.

Self-Employment Project
CAP Services, Inc.
1725 W. River Dr.   715-345-5200
Stevens Point, WI 54481   Fax: 715-345-6508
The aim is to mobilize public and private resources to help low income individuals to attain self-sufficiency. Loans are up to $10,000; terms up to five years. Interest rate is at 8%. Receives funds from the U.S. Office of Community Services, corporate contributions, State of Wisconsin, and CDBG funds. For residents of these counties only: Portage, Waupaca, Outagamie, Waushara, Marquette.

Small Business Loan
Wisconsin Women's Business Initiative
2745 N. Dr. Martin Luther King Jr. Drive
Milwaukee, WI 53212   414-263-5450
www.wwbic.com
E-mail: info@wwbic.com
Although this loan is open to any small start-up business in Wisconsin, women, minority and low-income entrepreneurs are targeted. Those businesses that cannot get conventional loan funding may apply for up to $25,000. The money is to be used for tangible items, but working capital will be allowed. Terms are generally from 3 to 5 years. The interest rate is a flexible one.

Job and Business Development Loan
Wisconsin Coulee Region Community Action Program
201 Melby Street
Westby, WI 54667   608-634-3104
This new fund is available to help low to moderate-income people who want to start a new business. To be able to apply for the loan, borrowers must complete the Business Program. It is offered in the 4 county area of LaCross, Monroe, Crawford and Vernon. The loan can be obtained from $100 to $500. This

funding amount is expected to increase. There are 12 months to repay the loan and at this point in time, there is no interest.

Revolving Loan Fund
CAP Services
1725 West River Drive
Stevens Point, WI 54481   715-345-5200
This loan is specific to a 5 county area of Wisconsin; Marquette, Waushara, Portage, Waupaca, and Outagamie. It is available for low to moderate-income entrepreneurs or those that create jobs for low to moderate-income people. There is a maximum of $10,000 available at 8% for a maximum term of 5 years. It requires a matching conventional loan.

West CAP Child Care Loan
West Central Wisconsin Community Action Agency, Inc. (West CAP)
119 West 6th Avenue
Menomonie, WI 54751   715-235-8525
This small business loan is available to child care providers. If the business is run out of a center, the owner must be low income to be eligible for a maximum loan of $15,000. If they are licensed or certified to work out of the home, they must target low income clients for a loan of up to $5,000. The term is up to 5 or 6 years, depending on the loan. This is available to those businesses in a seven county area.

Free Business Assistance Programs

A helping hand is just a phone call away for individuals who want to enter into a small business or microenterprise. If you fall into any of the following categories: low to moderate income, Native American, minorities, women, welfare recipients, or have little or no money, you may be eligible for a wide range of assistance. These programs are aimed to assist individuals toward self-sufficiency.

Imagine getting training, counseling, peer support and exchange, and mentoring for free to help you get the knowledge you need to start your own business. Learn how to prepare a business plan and get guidance from the best instructors in the country. One such program is NOVA, located in Arkansas. Their program has four major components: Group Training; Individual Sessions; Business Start-Up; and Networking and Mentoring.

Kidpreneur Enterprises

Imagine youths able to receive effective business course training. One such program is Kidpreneur Enterprises, located in Michigan. This program is available to all youths who express an interest in owning and operating their own small business. Kidpreneur is designed to provide and instill concepts and experiences in the minds of youths.

Doors can open for entrepreneurs, like Adina Rosenthal, owner of Threadbearer, a fabric and accessory shop located on Capitol Hill. At a very young age, Adina knew she wanted to work with fabrics. At age 17, she lost the use of her right arm when she was hit by a logging truck. After receiving her degree from the Fashion Institute of Design and Merchandising she attempted to get work at various design companies only to be passed over time and time again. A friend suggested she join the Black Dollar Days' program for entrepreneurs. After completing their entrepreneurial program, Adina opened Threadbearer. She accredits her success to the assistance she received, and is still receiving, from the Black Dollar Days Task Force.

Daryl Anderson an experienced roofer, lacked the necessary skills to run a business of his own. In 1994, Daryl began his involvement with the Cottage Industry Programs offered by the Portsmouth Community Development Group (PCDG) in Montana. After a year of technical assistance, the use of an office, and hours of encouragement, Daryl and his wife Karen were able to open Quality Roofing and Siding. Daryl admits he never would have made it without PCDG's commitment to business counseling and training.

The aim of these programs is to develop a participant's confidence and skills in understanding business enterprise and to further the development of viable business ideas.

Technical Assistance Programs

Arizona
Micro Industry Credit Rural Organization
P.P.E.P. Microbusiness and Housing Development Corporation, Inc.
1100 E. Ajo Way, Suite 209   520-806-9513
Tucson, AZ 85713   Fax: 520-806-9515
Provides business training and planning, cash flow analysis, individual business
planning, and peer support. The aim is to enhance family self-sufficiency and
quality of life by facilitating the development, growth, and participation of family
based, micro, and small business enterprises in their local economies. Receives
funding from Ford Foundation, City of Douglas, Mott Foundation, Tides
Foundation, and Calvert Social Investment Fund.

Arkansas
New Opportunities for Venture Alternatives (NOVA)
Good Faith Fund (GFF)
2304 W. 29th Ave.
Pine Bluff, AR 71603   870-535-6233
NOVA is a program funded by the Office of Community Services/Health and
Human Services. It is designed to help AFDC recipients and others on public
assistance work toward self-sufficiency. The program has four major components:
Group training: A 12-week training program designed to enhance personal
effectiveness and build basic business skills; Individual Sessions: Participants meet
with business counselors and instructors, and NOVA personnel for case
management and individual business counseling; Business Start-Up: Participants
create a working business plan and take the steps necessary for starting their own
enterprise; and Networking and Referrals: Participants are directed to other area
resources that can be called upon for assistance, including governmental,
educational, and social programs. Anyone who is receiving or is eligible to receive
Aid to Families with Dependent Children (AFDC), Food Stamps, no or low
income may participate in NOVA.

California
Arcata Economic Development Corporation
Arcata Economic Development Corporation
100 Ericson Court, Suite 100   707-822-4616
Arcata, CA 95521 ·   Fax: 707-822-8982
This corporation provides services that enhance the growth and development in
Arcata. Business training, business planning, individual business counseling, peer
support, and exchange are available to low income women, minorities, and
displaced workers.

California Indian Manpower Consortium
4153 Northgate Blvd.   916-920-0285
Sacramento, CA 95834   Fax: 916-641-6338
The aim is to promote the social, educational, and economic advancement of
member tribes and Indian organizations, Indians, and other Native Americans who
are unemployed and underemployed or economically disadvantaged. All programs
are designed to increase self-sufficiency in rural, reservation, and urban areas.
Provides business training and planning, information, and referrals.

Center for Community Futures
P.O. Box 5309
Elmwood Station   510-339-3801
Berkeley, CA 94705   Fax: 510-339-3803
Provides business training, individual business counseling, peer support, and
program development services to nonprofits seeking to begin/expand
microbusiness programs. The aim is to promote quality development through a
training program and consulting services.

Micro Enterprise Assistance Program of Orange County
18011 Skypark Circle, Suite E
Irvine, CA 92614   949-252-1380
Provides business training, peer support, and mentoring to women and minorities
located in Orange County. The aim is to provide access to credit, training, and
support so that they may become self-sufficient. Receives funds from bank and
private contributions.

Private Industry Council
2425 Bisso Lane, Suite 200   925-646-5377
Concord, CA 94520   Fax: 925-646-5299
Provides business training, individual business
counseling, peer support, and mentoring to existing
businesses or start-ups planning to hire low to moderate
income individuals within the next 12-18 months. The
aim is to provide technical assistance and resources to
small business owners, or potential owners, that will
enhance their chance of business growth.

> *Private*
> *Industry*
> *Council*

Self-Employment Microenterprise Development (SEMED)
Economic and Employment Development Center (EEDC)
241 S. Figueroa St.
Los Angeles, CA 90012   213-617-3953
Provides business training and planning, individual business counseling, peer
support, and mentoring to refugees admitted to the U.S. within the last 5 years and

who are under the national poverty level. The aim is to assist the Southeast Asian Community to attain economic self-sufficiency and achieve a positive acculturation. Receives funding from the Office of Refugee Resettlement.

The West Company
The West Enterprise Center
367 North State St., Suite 206   707-468-3553
Ukiah, CA 95482   Fax: 707-462-8945
Provides business training, individual business counseling, peer support, advanced marketing, and financial training to low income women and minorities located in Mendocino county. The aim is to stimulate the growth of economic opportunity. Emphasis is on small business. Receives funds from foundation, banks, utilities, CAP agency, local, state and federal government, donations, and fees.

Training, Network and Business Incubator
San Francisco Renaissance
275 5th St.   415-541-8580
San Francisco, CA 94103   Fax: 415-541-8589
Provides business planning, individual business counseling, peer support, and exchange and loan packaging for SEED loan to low income people, women, and minorities in San Francisco and Greater Bay Area. The aim is to increase the entrepreneurial capabilities of low and moderate income people. Works with other microenterprise development programs such as Mayor's Office, SCORE, SBA, Chamber of Commerce, Hispanic and Black Chambers of Commerce, and local banks.

Women's Economic Ventures of Santa Barbara
1216 State St., Suite 610   805-965-6073
Santa Barbara, CA 93101   Fax: 805-962-9622
Provides business training and planning, peer support, and mentoring to low to moderate income women. The aim is to help women become self-sufficient through entrepreneurship. Receives funding from sale of real estate, foundation grants, corporate and individual gifts, and interest payments.

Colorado
Mi Casa Resource Center for Women
Mi Casa Resource Center for Women
571 Galapago St.   303-573-1302
Denver, CO 80204   Fax: 303-595-0422
Provides business training and planning, individual business counseling, peer support and exchange, free continuing education seminars, and a listing in business directory to low income Hispanic women, and women receiving welfare benefits

in Denver. The aim is to assist women and youth in achieving economic self-sufficiency. This Women's Center was recognized as a top site in the nation by the National Academy of Public Administration, and was given the "Outstanding Non-Profit" award by a local foundation.

Connecticut
Aid to Artisans, Inc.
14 Brick Walk Lane
Farmington, CT 06032
The mission of Aid to Artisans, Inc. is to create
employment opportunities for disadvantaged
artisans worldwide. The services they provide are
business training, product development, and
marketing. Their plans are to develop more working
relationships between American artisan groups and
foreign artisan groups and expand our worldwide
Artisans and Ecology Program.

860-677-1649
Fax: 860-676-2170

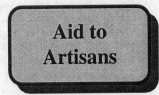

Entrepreneurial Center for Women
Hartford College for Women
50 Elizabeth St.
Hartford, CT 06105
860-768-5681
Fax: 860-768-5622
Provides business training, individual business counseling, and peer support to low income women (not exclusively) located in Connecticut. The aim is to promote self-employment as a alternative through training, technical assistance, networking, personal development, and assistance with access to financing. Receives funds from fees, CDBG, SOS, Department of Social Services, and Department of Labor.

Hartford Economic Development Corporation
Hartford Economic Development Corporation
15 Lewis St.
Hartford, CT 06103
860-527-1301
Fax: 860-727-9224
Provides business training and planning, and individual business counseling to low/moderate income individuals located in the City of Hartford. The aim is the creation and retention of jobs. Receives funds from CDBG funds, membership fees, and dues.

District of Columbia
Accion International
Department of U.S. Operations
733 15th St. NW, Suite 700
202-393-5113

Washington, DC 20005   Fax: 202-393-5115
Eligible applicants are low-income microentrepreneurs, with emphasis on the
Hispanic population. They provide program development support to start new
affiliates; feasibility study, business plan, staff training, and board development for
implementing organizations.

LEDC Microenterprise Loan Fund
Latino Economic Development Corp., Inc.
2316 18th St., NW   202-588-5102
Washington, DC 20009   Fax: 202-588-5204
Provides business training and individual business counseling to low income
entrepreneurs of Latino, African, Asian and African-American origins. The aim is
to provide credit, training, and technical assistance to new small businesses,
particularly those who cannot access formal lending institutions. Receives funds
from First National Bank of Maryland, DC CDBG funds, National Council of
LaRaza, and NationsBank.

New Enterprise Training for Profits (NET/PRO)
Venture Concepts
325 Pennsylvania Ave., SE   202-543-1200
Washington, DC 20003   Fax: 202-543-0254
Provides business training, planning, and screening of potential entrepreneurs to all
would-be entrepreneurs located in the U.S. and Canada. The aim is provide quality
training to would-be and existing entrepreneurs by installing training and technical
assistance capabilities.

SCORE
National SCORE Office
409 3rd St., SW
Washington, DC 20024   800-634-0245
SCORE is a nonprofit association providing free business counseling by persons
who have had successful business careers as company executives or owners of
businesses. They are willing to share their knowledge and experience at absolutely
no charge. They are as close as your phone. SCORE has counselors in all 50 states,
Puerto Rico, Guam, the Virgin Islands, and the District of Columbia.

Youth Microloan Fund
The Entrepreneurial Development Institute
P.O. Box 65882
Washington, DC 20035-5882   202-822-8334
Provides business training, peer support and exchange, individual business
counseling, and mentoring to minority youths ages 7-21 years old located in the
Washington, DC metropolitan area. The aim is to assist disadvantaged youth to

develop their own businesses, avoid drugs and crime, sharpen academic skills, and form positive attitudes about themselves and their communities. Receives funds from banks, foundations, and corporations.

Georgia
Entrepreneurial Training
Grasp Enterprises
55 Marietta, Suite 2000   404-659-5955
Atlanta, GA 30303   Fax: 404-880-9561
Provides business training and planning, individual
business counseling, peer support/exchange,
mentoring, and entrepreneurial lifestyle skills
training to low income dislocated workers and
entrepreneurs located in Greater Atlanta. The
aim is to provide comprehensive services for
the growth and development of small businesses.
Receives funds from SBA Microloan fund,
Department of Health and Human Services, local banks, City of Atlanta, and client fees.

Hawaii
Pacific Business Center Program
University of Hawaii
BUS-AD 413
2404 Maile Way
Honolulu, HI 96822   808-956-6286
Offers management and technical assistance to large and small businesses, entrepreneurs, government agencies, and community organizations. Through the program, the faculty, students, and some physical resources of the University of Hawaii may be accessed quickly. The program works with the faculty and students to develop proposals for more extensive projects.

Refugee Enterprise Development Project
Immigrant Center
720 North King St.   808-845-3918
Honolulu, HI 96817   Fax: 808-842-1962
Provides business training and planning, individual business counseling, peer support, and exchange to refugees located in Oahu. The aim is to advance economic self-sufficiency among recently arrived refugees by providing culturally sensitive lending and support programs for the startup or expansion of microenterprise in Hawaii.

Illinois

Chicago Association of Neighborhood Development Organizations
Chicago Association of Neighborhood Development Organizations
123 W. Madison St., Suite 1100   312-372-2636
Chicago, IL 60602   Fax: 312-372-2637
Provides business training and mentoring to low to moderate-income individuals
throughout Chicago. This organization is committed to the revitalization of all
Chicago neighborhoods, retail, and industrial areas. Receives funding from PRC
Foundation and Neighborhood Capital Corporation.

Community Enterprising Project
Uptown Center Hull House Association
4520 North Beacon St.   312-561-3500
Chicago, IL 60640   Fax: 312-561-3507
Provides business training, individual business counseling, and peer support to low
to moderate-income people located in the Uptown, Edgewater, and Ravenswood
neighborhoods. The aim is to help people help themselves by assisting low and
moderate-income residents to increase their income and overall economic capacity.
Receives funds from foundations, corporations, government agencies, and
individuals.

Peoria Area Micro Business Development Program
The Economic Development Council for The Peoria Area, Inc.
124 South West Adams St., Suite 300   309-676-7500
Peoria, IL 61602   Fax: 309-676-7534

Provides business training and individual
counseling to low income existing or startup
businesses, minorities, and females. Aim is to
assist in the development of small and
microbusinesses and helping them overcome
obstacles to growth. Receives funds from SBA
Microloan Demonstration Program, and City and County of Peoria.

Prison Small Business Project
Self-Employment Research Project
Roosevelt University
430 South Michigan Ave.
Chicago, IL 60605   312-341-3696
Provides business training, training materials, and mentoring to prison inmates.
The aim is to develop programs and teaching materials for self-employment
assistance to prison inmates and ex-offenders. The Project engages in research on
the topic of self employment targeted to poor people, and advocates for the low
income self employed. Receives funds from grants and out-of-pocket resources.

Women's Business Development Center
8 South Michigan Ave., Suite 400
Chicago, IL 60603

312-853-3477
Fax: 312-853-0145

Provides business training and planning, individual business counseling, peer support, and exchange and mentoring to underemployed women located in the Chicago area. The aim is to support women in their quest for economic self-sufficiency through entrepreneurship. Receives funds from loans from various foundations and banks.

Women's Self-Employment Project
20 N. Clark St.
Chicago, IL 60602

312-606-8255
Fax: 312-606-9215

Provides business training and planning, individual business counseling, peer support, and exchange to low to moderate income women located in Chicago. The aim is to raise the self-sufficiency of women through a strategy of self employment. Receives funds from SBA Microloan Demonstration, foundations, corporations, government contracts, individual donors, and consulting contracts.

Women's Economic Venture Enterprise (WEVE)
YWCA
229 16th St.
Rock Island, IL 61201

309-788-9793
Fax: 309-788-9825

Provides business training and planning, individual counseling, peer support, and mentoring to women between the ages of 18-70 located in Scott County, Iowa; Rock Island County, Illinois, and Metropolitan Quad Cities. The aim is to assist women in achieving self-sufficiency through business ownership. Receives funds from banks, SBA, foundations, program fees, individuals, and corporations.

Indiana
Eastside Community Fund
Eastside Community Investments (ECI)
26 North Arsenal Ave.
Indianapolis, IN 46220

317-637-7300
Fax: 317-637-7581

Provides business training and planning, individual business counseling, and peer support to low income persons located near the east side of Indianapolis. The aim is to loan money and provide technical assistance to both startup businesses and existing small businesses. Receives funding from SBA, OCS, NDDP, Mott Foundation, state loan money, and the Partnership for Common Good Loan Fund.

Indiana Small Business Development Center Network
One North Capitol
Suite 1275   317-264-6871
Indianapolis, IN 46204   Fax: 317-264-2806
Provides business training and planning, individual business counseling, peer
support, and exchange and mentoring to potential new and existing small business
located in Indiana. The aim is to increase the rate of successful new business
formation and to enhance and encourage existing businesses. Receives funds from
SBA, Indiana Chamber of Commerce, 14 local regional economic development
foundations, local churches, universities, and private corporations.

Iowa

Siouxland Economic Development Corporation (SEDC)
428 Insurance Centre   712-279-6286
Sioux City, IA 51102   Fax: 712-279-6920
Provides individual counseling, peer support, and exchange and mentoring to low
to moderate income individuals located in Woodbury, Plymouth, Cherokee, Ida,
and Monona counties. The aim is to further the economic development of
Siouxland regions. Within the microlending program, the aim is to provide access
to capital to those excluded from traditional sources and also to provide technical
assistance designed to increase business success. Receives funds from SBA grant,
SEDC cash match, and other SEDC operating surplus and revenue.

Small Enterprise Development
Institute for Social and Economic Development
1901 Broadway, Suite 313   319-338-2331
Iowa City, IA 52240   Fax: 319-338-5824
Provides business training, individual business counseling, peer support, and
exchange and mentoring to low income, ethnic minorities, and women. The aim is
to facilitate the empowerment of disadvantaged populations through the integration
of social and economic development strategies. Receives funds from foundations,
corporations, civic and religious organizations, federal/state grants and contracts,
and private contributions.

Kentucky
Community Loan Fund
Human/Economic Appalachian Development Corporation
P.O. Box 504   606-986-8423
Berea, KY 40403   Fax: 606-986-1299
Provides business planning, individual business counseling, peer support and
exchange to low income persons and women located in central Appalachia. The
aim is to strengthen low income communities and foster the development of an

economy that supports its people and encourages cooperative economic structures in the workplace. Receives funds from permanent capital, grants, and donations.

Community Ventures Corporation Bluegrass Microenterprise Program
1450 North Broadway
Lexington, KY 40506   606-231-0054
Upon joining the small business training program, you will have access to classes designed to help with specific areas of self employment and business ownership. Classroom instruction is offered in the following areas:

* **Business Feasibility and Planning:** Do you have a sound business idea? Do you have a product/service that customers want or need? How should you describe it? Do you have what it takes to be self-employed? An indepth look at these issues will help you decide whether or not your business idea is feasible and worth pursuing.

* **Marketing:** A basic introduction to market research and the development of a marketing plan. A comprehensive market research analysis and customer survey will help you determine information crucial to the success of your business.

* **Financial Management:** Learn the basics of filing/accounting systems, record keeping, cash flow, income statements, break-even analysis, personal budgeting. Technical assistance is also available to help you develop systems appropriate for your business.

* **Child Care Management:** This training gives you the basics needed to develop a home child care business. Learn about the certification application, policies/procedures, parent handbook, activity development, communication, health, safety, sanitation/nutrition, and how to recognize child abuse.

These classes will help you determine what it takes to make a business successful, how to market your product or service, how much capital is needed to open a particular business, and most important, how to develop a comprehensive business plan.

Maine
Androscoggin Valley Council of Governments (AVCOG's)
125 Manley Rd.   207-783-9186
Auburn, ME 04210   Fax: 207-783-5211
The primary goal of the economic development programs and services of the Androscoggin Valley Council of Governments (AVCOG's) is to stimulate business that results in job creation and retention. They offer information referral,

seminars, workshops, individual counseling, mentoring, library resources, and computer training.

Aroostook County Action Programs, Inc.
771 Main St.   207-764-3721
Presque Isle, ME 04769   Fax: 207-768-3040
The mission of this program is to become a reliable, consistent source of technical assistance while providing loan resources. They offer information referral, seminars, workshops, business courses, individual counseling, mentoring, library resources, and computer training to low income individuals residing in Northern Maine.

Community Concepts Inc. (CCI)
P.O. Box 278, Market Square   207-743-7716
South Paris, ME 04281   Fax: 207-743-6513

Community Concepts

CCI's mission is to help people in need build opportunities for a better tomorrow. Provides information referral, seminars, peer support and exchange, training, workshops, and individual counseling to low income minorities denied conventional funding located in Androscoggin and Oxford counties. Receives funding from Maine Job Start Program, SBA Microloan Demonstration Program, and CDBG funds.

Enterprise Development Fund
Coastal Enterprises, Inc.
P.O. Box 268, Water St.   207-882-7552
Wiscasset, ME 04578   Fax: 207-882-7308
Provides business training, individual business counseling, peer support and exchange, mentoring, trade association organizing assistance, and policy development for state delivery system to women, low income, unemployed and refugees. Receives funding from the Ford Foundation, SBA, Mott Foundation, Betterment Fund, U.S. Department of Health and Human Services, national churches, and Maine Department of Economic and Community Development.

Greater Portland Economic Development Council
145 Middle St.   207-772-1109
Portland, ME 04101   Fax: 207-772-1179
Eligible applicants are startup businesses, businesses that create jobs, and manufacturing businesses. The Council provides seminars, information referral, workshops, individual counseling, mentoring, peer support and exchange, and library resources.

Growth Council of Oxford Hills
150 Main St.   207-743-8830
South Paris, ME 04281   Fax: 207-743-5917
The Council provides technical assistance, training and education, business
resources, small business incubators, and regulatory approval assistance. All
businesses are eligible who focus primarily on manufacturing, information
management, and export.

Maine Centers for Women, Work and Community
46 University Dr.   207-621-3440
Augusta, ME 04330   Fax: 207-621-3429
The Center provides community development and entrepreneurship training and
services for displaced homemakers, single parents, and other workers in transition.
Provides information referral, seminars, business training, peer support and
exchange, and staff support.

New Ventures
Maine Centers for Women, Work, and Community
Stoddard House, University of Maine   207-621-3433
Augusta, ME 04330   Fax: 207-621-3429
Provides business training, peer support, and follow-up support training to
displaced homemakers, single parents,
refugees, and the unemployed. The aim is
to empower women to move to self-
sufficiency and to support/ advocate for
their participation in our economy. Receives funds from Carl Perkins Vocational
Education, Department of Health and Human Services, and Office of Refugee
Resettlement.

Service Corps of Retired Executives (SCORE)
SCORE
66 Pearl St.
Portland, ME 04101   207-772-1147
SCORE matches volunteers with small businesses that need sound business
advice. They provide information referral, seminars, workshops, individual
counseling, and library resources to potential SBA borrowers only.

University of Maine Cooperative Extension
5741 Libby Hall, Room 106   207-581-3167
Orono, ME 04469-5741   Fax: 207-581-1387
The University of Maine Cooperative Extension provides Maine people with
research based education programs in a variety of areas. It provides business
management educational programs targeting home based and natural resource

based businesses, educational programs in Nutrition and Health; Food Safety; Forestry and Wildlife; 4-H and Youth Development; Marine Resources; Pest Management; Sustainable Agriculture; Waste Management; and Water Quality. Provides workshops, seminars, educational publications, consultation, and technical assistance.

USM School of Applied Science/
Department of External Programs
University of Southern Maine
37 College Ave.   207-780-5439
Graham, ME 04038   Fax: 207-780-5129
The University of Southern Maine (USM) provides information referral, seminars, workshops, business courses, individual counseling, peer support, mentoring, computer training, and laboratory access. The aim is to develop and maintain linkages between business and industry and higher and secondary education. Eligibility would apply to a startup business, an existing business, or a business in manufacturing, service, or education.

Maryland

Business Owners Start-Up Services (BOSS)
Council of Economic and Business Opportunities
800 North Charles St., Suite 300   410-576-2326
Baltimore, MD 21201   Fax: 410-576-2498
Provides business training and planning, individual business counseling, peer support, and mentoring to AFDC recipients, Title III dislocated workers, and residents of Housing Authority of Baltimore County. The aim is to develop microenterprises via training and funding and to maintain microenterprises through technical assistance, support, and funding. Receives funding from SBA loans via council on Economic Business Opportunities, CDBG funds, SEID Grant, state, city, county PI and Title III contracts, and grants from HUD.

Women Entrepreneurs of Baltimore, Inc.
1118 Light St., Suite 202   410-727-4921
Baltimore, MD 21230   Fax: 410-727-4989
Provides business training and planning, individual business counseling, peer support, mentoring, community organizing, and outreach resource sharing to economically disadvantaged women located in Baltimore City and County. The aim is to provide entrepreneurial support and training to women who have a viable business idea and the spirit to make their business a success. Receives funds from foundations and bank contributions.

Training
And
Planning

Massachusetts
Berkshire Enterprises
University of Massachusetts Donahue Institute
24 Depot St.
P.O. Box 2297   413-448-2755
Pittsfield, MA 01201   Fax: 413-448-2749
Provides business training, individual business counseling, and peer support and
exchange to dislocated workers, low income and minorities. The aim is to assist in
the creation of a positive business environment through services that aid,
encourage, and advise present and future business owners and to collaborate with
others having similar missions. Receives funds from ICCD-Working Capital
Program, Massachusetts Industrial Services Program, and HUD-Pittsfield
Enterprise Collaboration.

Brightwood Development Corporation
2345 Main St.   413-734-2144
Springfield, MA 01107   Fax: 413-746-3934
The aim of this Corporation is to provide affordable housing and economic
development. Provides business training courses, business planning, individual
business counseling and mentoring to low and moderate income Hispanics and
Puerto Ricans. Receives funds from City CDBG funds, Springfield Chamber of
Commerce, SBA, and HUD.

Hilltown Enterprise Fund
Hilltown Community Development Corporation
432 Main Rd. #A   413-296-4536
Chesterfield, MA 01012   Fax: 413-296-4020
Provides business training, counseling, and peer support to individuals with limited
resources who wish to start or expand a business. The aim is to promote
cooperation as a way to ensure the best quality of life for all residents; to enable
them to help themselves in addressing economic and housing needs, and to create
and expand opportunities for those with limited resources. Receives funds from
state and federal grants, loans from individuals, Western Massachusetts Enterprise
Fund, and contributions. Program is for Hilltown residents only.

Microenterprise Training and Loan Program for Refugees
Jewish Vocational Service
105 Chauncy St., 4th Floor   617-451-8147
Boston, MA 02111   Fax: 617-451-9973
Provides business training, individual business counseling, and peer support and
mentoring to refugees who have been in the U.S. for less than five years. The aim
is to provide employment, training, and career services to disadvantaged and
disabled individuals. Receives funds from the Office of Refugee Resettlement and
the Jewish Vocational Service.

Community Economic Development Center
166 William St.   508-979-4684
New Bedford, MA 02740   Fax: 508-990-0199
Provides peer support and exchange, mentoring, and self-taught tutorials to
low/moderate income, racially, and culturally diverse people located in SE
Massachusetts. The aim is to increase the income of the self-employed by
providing loans, business assistance, and a forum for peer support of self-
employed, low/moderate income people in New Bedford. Receives funds from
credit through Fleet Banks, funds from Working Capital-Institute for Cooperative
Community Development, banks, and private foundations.

Small Business Development System (SBDS)
The Howells Group
SIS Management
930 Commonwealth Ave., South   717-264-6205
Boston, MA 02215   Fax: 717-731-6531
Provides business training and planning, mentoring, and market identification for
targeted urban areas and regions to minorities, the physically disabled, and those
living in low income or disadvantaged areas. The aim is to encourage the creation
or expansion of microenterprises among disadvantaged populations.

The Trusteeship Institute
15 Edwards Square
Northampton, MA 01060   413-259-1600
The Trusteeship Institute is a consulting firm that assists companies and
organizations which seek to become employee owned and controlled. They are
usually asked to provide assistance when such a firm is being created; when an Employee Stock Ownership Plan (ESOP) is being established with the ultimate goal of the employees having majority ownership and control; or when the voting rights of the ESOP stock have passed through to the employees, giving them majority control of the firm. The Institute's expertise is in the area of the conversion of firms to democratic ownership and control by their employees. They have been providing legal, financial, and training services to such firms since 1973.

Michigan
Ann Arbor Community Development Corporation
2008 Hogback Rd., Suite 12   313-677-1400
Ann Arbor, MI 48105   Fax: 313-677-1465

The program assists women to become self-sufficient through self employment. The aim of this program is to encourage small business development among women and minorities, and to provide business training and planning, counseling, peer support, and exchange.

Grand Rapids Opportunities for Women (GROW)
Center for Women
25 Sheldon Blvd. SE, Suite 210
Grand Rapids, MI 49503   616-458-3404
GROW is a nonprofit organization which provides economic opportunities through self employment to women in Kent and Ottawa Counties. Women from diverse backgrounds receive self-employment training, personal consultation, peer support, and assistance in gaining access to seed money. Provides individualized orientation, training and technical assistance, financial overview and linkages, and continuing support. Receives funds from Kent County Department of Social Services, The Michigan Women's Foundation, The Grand Rapids Foundation, Steelcase Foundation, and the Frey Foundation.

Kidpreneur Enterprises
Metropolitan Chamber of Commerce
400 N. Saginaw St., Suite 101A   810-235-5514
Flint, MI 48502   Fax: 810-235-4407
Kidpreneur is a program designed specifically for youth to provide and instill concepts and experiences in the minds of youth enabling them to become successful entrepreneurial adults. The object of the program is to work with businesses and organizations to inform the community at large of the Kidpreneur concept. Program is available to all youth that express an interest in Genesee County.

Northern Economic Initiatives Corporation
Northern Economic Initiatives Corporation
1009 West Ridge   906-228-5571
Marquette, MI 49855   Fax: 906-228-5572
Provides business training and planning, business counseling, and mentoring to startup and expanding small business owners. The aim is to improve the competitive position of the economy by inspiring action among value-added firms, and working to gain access to capital and markets for these Upper Peninsula firms, and developing customers, management, and emerging workforce through public and private collaboration. Receives funds from SBA Microloan Demonstration Program, Joyce Foundation, and State of Michigan.

Supportive Entrepreneurial Program
Community Action Agency of South Central Michigan
175 Main St.   616-965-7766
Battle Creek, MI 49014   Fax: 616-965-1152

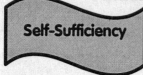

Provides business training and planning, individual business counseling, and marketing assistance to low income women located in Calhoun, Barry, Branch, and St. Joseph counties. The aim is to assist women who wish to create a successful business enterprise that will lead to self-sufficiency. Receives funding from Michigan Women's Foundation (Mott) and Battle Creek Community Foundation.

Minnesota
American Institute of Small Business
7515 Wayzata Blvd., Suite 129   612-545-7001
Minneapolis, MN 55426   Fax: 612-545-7020
The Institute provides business training, planning, business counseling, and publishing of books, videos, and software to native American Indians, Hispanics, and African-Americans. The goal is to generate jobs for Native American youth by obtaining loans to start up new businesses. Provides on-site visits with similar type businesses such as accountants, advertising agencies, and market researchers.

Arrowhead Community Economic Assistance Corporation
702 Third Ave. South   218-749-2914
Virginia, MN 55792-2775   Fax: 218-749-2913
Business planning, individual counseling, and peer support and exchange are available to unemployed and low income and minority residents located in the Taconic Tax Relief Area. The goal is to assist with the startup and expansion of local businesses that increase employment opportunities and that retain existing jobs, by developing local skills and providing economic opportunity.

Emerging Entrepreneur Development Program
Northwest Minnesota Initiative Fund
4225 Technology Dr.   208-759-2057
Bemidji, MN 56601   Fax: 208-759-2328
Provides business planning, business counseling, peer support and mentoring to women, minorities and low income persons located in Beltrami, Clearwater, Hubbard, Kittson, Lake of the Woods, Mahnomen, Marshall, Norman, Pennington, Polk, Redlake, and Roseau. The aim is to improve the quality of life for the people who live and work in NW Minnesota by encouraging them to devise greater responses to change that will build a future with greater economic opportunity. Receives funds from SBA and the McKnight Foundation.

Northeast Entrepreneur Fund, Inc.
820 Ninth St., North, Suite 140   218-749-4191
Virginia, MN 55792   Fax: 218-741-4249
Provides business training and planning, individual business counseling, and peer
support to unemployed and underemployed persons. The aim is to foster and
encourage self-sufficiency through the growth of small business opportunities.
Receives funds from foundations, loans, contracts, fees, and interest.

Self-Employment Investment Demonstration (SEID)
Minnesota Department of Human Services
444 Lafayette Rd.   651-297-1316
St. Paul, MN 55155-3814   Fax: 651-215-6388
www.dhs.state.mn.us/ecs/program/seid.htm
Minnesota operated the Self-Employment Investment Demonstration (SEID) as
part of a five-state demonstration project from March 1988 to September 1991.
Minnesota received federal approval to continue the program for each federal
fiscal year thereafter. Service providers operate the program in counties that
choose to offer SEID. The aim is to serve as administrative coordinator of the
program, coordinating programs run by individual service providers, provide
technical services, and coordination with federal and state agencies, and private
nonprofit organizations. Each service provider delivers a program that combines
business training, personal effectiveness training, access to seed capital, and
ongoing support for interested AFDC clients.

North Star Community Development Corporation
615 Board of Trade Building
301 West First St., Suite 604
Duluth, MN 55802   218-727-6690
Provides business training and planning, individual business counseling, peer
support, and exchange to low and moderate income persons and public housing
residents. This is a community based economic development organization
providing assistance to small businesses. Focus is placed on assisting low and
moderate income persons to achieve self-sufficiency. Receives funds from
Community Development Block Grant, Duluth Housing and Redevelopment
Authority.

Missouri
Create Your Own Job
Missouri Western State College
4525 Downs Dr.
St. Joseph, MO 64507   816-271-5830
Provides business training, planning, and individual business counseling to anyone
interested in opening a business in Northwest Missouri. The aim is to develop a

participant's confidence and skills in understanding business enterprise and to further develop viable business ideas.

Montana
Action for Eastern Montana
2030 N. Merrill
Glendive, MT 59330-1309   406-377-3564
Action's mission is to help create a flourishing microbusiness climate in eastern Montana. Eligible applicants are low income, women, and minorities. They provide business training courses, business planning, individual business counseling, peer support, and mentor program. Also provides individual counseling, child care, transportation, leadership, and self-esteem courses.

Montana Women's Economic Development Group (WEDGO)
Women's Opportunity and Resource Development
127 North Higgins   406-543-3550
Missoula, MT 59802   Fax: 406-721-4584
Provides business training, planning, and individual business counseling to low and moderate income women. Receives funds from city, county, and state government, the Ms. Foundation, Department of Health and Human Services, U.S. West Foundation, and service contracts. Only for residents of western Montana.

Opportunities, Inc.
Opportunities, Inc.
905 1st Ave. North
Great Falls, MT 59403   406-761-0310
Provides business training and planning, individual business counseling, peer

 support, and exchange and mentoring to persons unable to receive loans from conventional sources located in Cascade, Chauteau, Teton, Foale, Pondera, and Glacier. The aim is to stimulate

coordination among available federal, state, local, and private resources to enable low-income individuals, in rural and urban areas, to attain the skills, knowledge, and motivations they need to secure opportunities necessary to become self-sufficient. Receives funds from grants to loans from Montana Department of Commerce.

Nebraska
Rural Enterprise Assistance Project
Center for Rural Affairs
P.O. Box 406   402-846-5428
Walthill, NE 68067   Fax: 402-846-5420

Provides business training, business planning, individual business counseling, and peer support and exchange to low and moderate income individuals in rural Nebraska. The mission is to demonstrate and implement programs to meet the long term needs of existing and potential small businesses to succeed in rural areas. Receives funding from the Ford Foundation, the Mott Foundation, SBA Grant, the Aspen Institute, and Share Our Strength (SOS).

New Mexico
Women's Economic Self-Sufficiency Team (WESST Corp.)
414 Silver SW   505-848-4760
Albuquerque, NM 87102-3239   Fax: 505-848-2368
Provides business training and planning, individual business counseling, and mentoring to low income women and minorities located in the State of New Mexico. The aim is to help women achieve self-sufficiency through sustained self-employment. Receives funding from Seton Enablement Fund, SBA Microloan Demonstration Program, and in-kind contributions.

New York
ACCION New York
235 Havemeyer St., 3rd Floor   718-599-5170
Brooklyn, NY 11211   Fax: 718-387-9686
ACCION was founded for the purpose of combating poverty and hunger in the poorest communities of America. It supports the economic initiatives of the poor by providing market rate loans and basic business training to family-run businesses.

Microenterprise Loan and Assistance Program
Church Avenue Merchants Block Association, Inc.
885 Flatbush Ave.   718-287-0100
Brooklyn, NY 11226   Fax: 718-287-2737
Provides business training, individual business counseling, and peer support and exchange to refugees located in Brooklyn and New York City. The aim is to provide refugees who want to start businesses with training and loans to do so. Receives funds from the Office of Refugee Resettlement, and the U.S. Department of Health and Human Services.

Ms. Foundation for Women
Ms. Foundation
120 Wall St., Floor 33   212-742-2300

New York, NY 10005   Fax: 212-742-1653
This Foundation supports the efforts of women to govern their own lives and influence the world around them. They fund and assist women's self-help organizing efforts and pursue changes in public consciousness, law, philanthropy, and social policy. Provides program planning and organizational growth to women and nonprofit organizations assisting women to become self-sufficient through self employment. Receives funds from private and corporate foundations, individuals, and limited endowment income.

New York Department of Economic Development
Local Development Corporation of East New York
80 Jamaica Ave.   718-385-6700
Brooklyn, NY 11207   Fax: 718-385-7505
Provides business training and planning, individual business counseling, peer support, and mentoring to women and minority entrepreneurs located in Brooklyn. The aim is to provide microenterprise development assistance as a way to promote economic development and job creation. Receives funds from New York Urban Development Corporation and European American Bank.

New York State Department of Economic Development
Entrepreneurial Assistance Program
Queens County Overall Economic Development Corp.
120-55 Queens Blvd. #309   718-263-0546
Jamaica, NY 11424   Fax: 718-263-0594
Provides business training and planning, individual business counseling, peer support, mentoring, seminars, and workshops to low income and minority residents of Queens. Provides a comprehensive package of services to: encourage and train would-be entrepreneurs; to support and assist startup businesses to survive the first 24 months of business; and to assist existing businesses with their relocation and/or expansion efforts. Receives funds from seven banks and equity investors, borough presidents, and city and state agencies.

Rural Venture Fund
Rural Opportunities, Inc.
400 East Ave.   716-340-3387
Rochester, NY 15607   Fax: 716-340-3337

Provides business planning, individual business counseling, marketing analysis, and cash flow analysis to low and moderate income persons located in Western NY State who have been denied access to bank credit. The aim is to promote self-sufficiency and economic independence through the creation and expansion of microenterprises and small businesses. Receives funds from FmHA Industrial Development Grant, SBA Microloan Demonstration Program, CDBG funds, and NY State.

North Carolina
Rural Economic Development Centers, Inc.
Rural Economic Development Center
4021 Carya Dr.   919-250-4314
Raleigh, NC 27610   Fax: 919-250-4325
It's hard to succeed in business. Being able to make a good product or offer a good service is only a start. That's why this program combines its financing with training and advice from local business counselors. The following is what you can expect: Help developing a business plan: experts will help you think through all of the decisions you need to make, such as who your customers will be and where to buy supplies; Classes and Workshops: these will cover issues you have to deal with in running your business; Support From Other Business People: many local business owners are happy to share

their experiences with people in the microenterprise program. If you're in the group lending program, you will get advice and support from other group members. Expert Advice: regularly, you will go over the progress of your business with someone who can let you know what you are doing right and what you can do more effectively.

WAMY Community Action, Inc.
P.O. Box 2688   828-264-2421
Boone, NC 28607   Fax: 828-264-0952
WAMY provides business training, planning, and individual business counseling to persons below poverty level located in Watauga, Avery, Mitchell, and Yancey counties only. The aim is to improve economic, social, and physical conditions of low-income persons. Receives funds from CDBG and repaid funds.

Northeastern Community Development Corporation
154 US Highway 158 East   252-338-5466
Camden, NC 27921   Fax: 252-338-5639
This corporation provides business training and planning, individual business counseling, peer support, and exchange and mentoring to Watermark members located in Northeastern North Carolina. Works with low and moderate-income persons who need loans to buy equipment and supplies to begin making crafts, and those who need working capital for expanding their business. The aim is to make

funding available to those with low and moderate income to startup, expand, or help their businesses in emergency situations. Receives funds from the Ms. Foundation.

North Dakota
Center for Innovation and Business Development
Box 8372, UND   701-777-3132
Grand Forks, ND 58202   Fax: 701-777-2339
The Center for Innovation and Business Development provides business training courses, business planning, individual business counseling, peer support and exchange, mentoring, market plans, technical evaluation, patent searches, and new product development to low and moderate income, rural small manufacturers, entrepreneurs, researchers, colleges, and universities. The aim to help manufacturers and entrepreneurs start up new ventures and bring new products and technologies to market.

Ohio
The Appalachian Center for Economic Networks (ACEnet)
94 North Columbus Rd.   740-592-3854
Athens, OH 45701   Fax: 740-593-5451
The Appalachian Center for Economic Networks (ACEnet) has generated broad involvement of educational institutions, banks, social service agencies, and community groups in the development of support projects in five areas: (1) Training and Workforce Development: enables people receiving public assistance to obtain jobs in flexible manufacturing networks (FMN) firms or to start their own small businesses; (2) Access to Capital: a loan fund for very small loans; (3) Modernization and Business Assistance: introduces more current production and organizational technologies to FMN firms; (4) Telecommunications: firms are introduced to various information technologies; and (5) Market Niche Development: assists entrepreneurs in identifying niche markets and potential purchasing partners, and explores export opportunities.

The Chamber of Women's Business Initiative Program
37 North High St.
Columbus, OH 43215   614-225-6910
The Chamber of Women's Business Initiative Program provides business training and planning, business counseling, peer support, mentoring, and procurement assistance to women who are unemployed, underemployed, or receiving public assistance; women who have started their own business, or women who are interested in self employment. The aim of this program is to provide assistance in order to increase participation of women in the economy. Receives funds from federal and city funds, banks, and private foundations.

Ventures in Business Ownership
Columbiana Career Center
9364 St. Rt. 45   330-424-9561, ext. 34
Lisbon, OH 44432   Fax: 330-424-9719
(Serving Columbiana, Mahoning, Carroll counties and parts of Pennsylvania and
West Virginia)

Ehove Career Center
316 West Mason Rd.   419-499-4663
Milan, OH 44846   Fax: 419-499-4076
www.ehove-jvs.k12.oh.us
(Serving Huron, Erie and Ottawa counties)

Guernsey-Noble Career Center
57090 Vocational Rd.   740-685-2516
Senecaville, OH 43780   Fax: 740-685-2518
(Serving Guernsey, Noble, Muskingum and Perry counties)

Greene County Career Center
2960 West Enon Rd.   937-426-6636
Xenia, OH 45385   Fax: 937-372-8283
(Serving Montgomery, Greene, Clark and Miami counties)

Medina County Career Center
1101 West Liberty St.   330-725-8461
Medina, OH 44256   Fax: 330-725-3842
(Serving Medina county and surrounding area)

Penta County Vocational School
30095 Oregon Rd.   419-666-1120
Perrysburg, OH 43551   Fax: 419-666-6049
(Serving Northwest Ohio)

Polaris Career Center
7285 Old Oak Blvd.   440-891-7703
Middleburg, OH 44130   Fax: 440-826-4330
www.polaris.edu
(Serving Cuyahoga county)

Upper Valley Applied Technology Center
8811 Career Dr.
Piqua, OH 45356   937-778-8419
(Serving Miami, Shelby, Darke and portions of surrounding counties)

Provides a 100-hour business planning and management program, and a 60 hour class-run business operation module. This is available to single parents, displaced homemakers,, and single pregnant women. The aim is to provide small business training and technical assistance enabling these individuals to become independent.

Women's Business Resource Program of Southeast Ohio
20 East Circle Dr., Suite 155   740-593-0474
Athens, OH 45701   Fax: 740-593-1795
This program provides business training and planning, individual business counseling, peer support, networking, and mentoring to underemployed and unemployed women. The aim is to develop successful women's entrepreneurship. Receives funds from SBA, individual and corporate donations, Ohio Department of Development, and Ohio University.

Women Entrepreneurs, Inc.
36 East 4th St. #92   513-684-0700
Cincinnati, OH 45202   Fax: 513-684-0779
Provides business training and planning, business counseling mentoring, and certification assistance to low and moderate income people located in Cincinnati. The aim is that through community leadership, professional development, business support, and networking, Women Entrepreneurs, Inc. promotes successful entrepreneurship. Receives funds from banks, independent member contributions, local foundations, and corporate contributions.

Women's Network Mentoring Program
Women's Network
526 S. Main St., Suite 221   330-379-9280
Akron, OH 44311   330-379-3454
This mentoring program is available to women business owners in business for at

least one year in Summit, Portage, Stark, Wayne, or Medina Counties. The aim is to stimulate the economy by encouraging the growth of small women owned businesses in the community through the provision of mentoring services. Receives funds from SBA and banks.

Pennsylvania
A Service for Self-Employment Training and Support (ASSETS)
Mennonite Economic Development Associates
447 S. Prince St.
Lancaster, PA 17603   717-393-6089

Provides business training and planning, individual business counseling, peer support, and mentoring to low income individuals as defined by HUD guidelines. The aim is to increase personal income, create jobs, foster economic linkages, develop human potential through small businesses, and provide credit and training to make small businesses profitable. Receives funds from PA Mennonite Credit Union corporate contributions, CDBG funds, and foundations.

Micro-Enterprise Development
Lutheran Children and Family Service
45 Garrett Rd.   610-734-3363
Upper Darby, PA 19082   Fax: 610-734-3389
Provides business training, planning, and individual business counseling to refugees, mostly Vietnamese and Russian, who have been in the U.S. less than five years, and who are located in the Philadelphia area. This Service has a loan agreement with PNC Bank and receives assistance from lawyers and other area professionals.

Philadelphia Small Business Loan Fund
LaSalle University Small Business Development Center
1900 West Olney Ave., Box 828   215-951-1416
Philadelphia, PA 19141   Fax: 215-951-1597
This fund provides business training, planning, and individual business counseling to applicants who have been declined by other funding sources. The aim is to provide small business financing of less than $25,000 to entrepreneurs who have been declined by a financial institution or public program. Receives funds from major corporations and six major banks within the Delaware Valley.

Rhode Island
Elmwood Neighborhood Housing Services, Inc. (N.H.S.)
9 Atlantic Ave.
Providence, RI 02907   401-461-4111
There is plenty of help and information available to get your new business started and to help you make your business successful. At Elmwood Neighborhood Housing Services, Inc. (N.H.S.), there is a full-fledged MicroBusiness Program that offers business workshops, peer lending groups, and small business loans. Programs are available to minority and disadvantaged residents of Elmwood, Upper and Lower S. Providence, West End, Reservoir Triangle, and Washington Park. Receives funds from Citizens Bank, RI Hospital Trust Bank, RI Department of Economic Development, Neighborhood Reinvestment, Hazard Trust, and the Campaign for Human Development.

South Dakota
Northeast South Dakota Energy Conservation Corporation
NE South Dakota Energy Conservation Corp.
414 Third Ave. East
Sisseton, SD 57262   605-698-7654
The Northeast South Dakota Energy Conservation Corporation provides business
planning, individual business counseling, and financial record keeping to low
income, disadvantaged persons, minorities, and women. The aim is to address the
economic needs of small rural communities as they relate to business development.
Also, the agency seeks to become directly involved in community based economic
development and serve as an institution for developing an economic power base
controlled by low income persons. Receives funds from Northwest Area
Foundation, CDBG, SBA Microloan Demonstration Program, East River Electric
Power Coop, and First State Bank of Roscoe.

Vermont
Burlington Revolving Loan Fund
Community and Economic Development Office
Room 32, City Hall
Burlington, VT 05461   802-865-7144
Provides business training and planning, individual business counseling, peer
support, and mentoring to low and moderate income individuals located in
Champlain Valley. Receives funding from CDBG, loan money from banks, and
affiliation with Working Capital.

Micro-Business Development Program
Central Vermont Community Action Council, Inc.
195 US Route 302/Berlin   802-479-1053
Barre, VT 05641   Fax: 802-479-5353
Provides business training and planning, individual business counseling, and peer
support to low income persons located in 56 towns in central Vermont. The
mission is to eliminate poverty by opening to everyone the opportunity to
education, training, and the ability to work. Receives funding from family
foundations, HeadStart, Vermont Community Development Program, Vermont
State, USDA food stamps, Veterans grant, and CDBG discretionary grant.

Virginia
Association of Farmworker Opportunity Programs
1611 N. Kent St., Suite 910   703-528-4141
Arlington, VA 22209   Fax: 703-528-4145
Business training courses, business planning, individual business counseling, and
peer support are available to low income, migrant and seasonal farmworkers,

672   *Information USA, Inc.*

minorities, and men and women. The goal is to provide a clearinghouse for the provision of information, training, support, and education, so that the lives of low income farmworkers and other rural poor can be improved.

Oweesta Program
First Nations Development Institute
The Stores Bldg.
11917 Main St.   540-371-5615
Falmouth, VA 22408   Fax: 540-371-3505
Provides business planning and loan fund start up to
American Indians living on reservations. The aim is to
help tribes achieve financial self-sufficiency through
culturally sensitive economic development; to
decrease reliance on federal funding and other
dependencies; and to combine direct support with
national programs and policy development. Receives funds
from Program Related Investments (PRIs) and individual investors.

United Community Ministries (UCM)
7511 Fordson Rd.   703-768-7106
Alexandria, VA 22306   Fax: 703-768-4788
Provides business training and planning, individual business counseling, peer support, and mentoring to low and moderate income people who are clients of UCM, located in SE Fairfax County. The aim is to enable selected UCM clients to supplement, stabilize, and increase their incomes through microenterprises.

Washington
Cascadia Revolving Fund
119 1st Ave. S., Suite 100   206-447-9226
Seattle, WA 98104   Fax: 206-682-4804
Provides business planning, business counseling, peer support, and mentoring to low income women and minorities, refugees, and displaced timber workers. Provides technical assistance and loans to both for-profit and nonprofit entrepreneurs who cannot find these services from traditional sources. They focus on low income women, minorities, rural communities, and businesses that preserve the environment. Receives funds from individual investors, religious orders, nonprofit corporations, earnings, and individual gifts.

The Inner-City Entrepreneurial Training Program (ICETP)
Black Dollar Task Force
116-21st Ave.   206-323-0534
Seattle, WA 98122   Fax: 206-323-4701

The Inner-City Entrepreneurial Training Program (ICETP) provides ten weeks of training to low income individuals who aspire to be entrepreneurs. Selection is based upon their income, education, and experience in the industry and their desire to start up and maintain a business. Each student is required to complete an internship with a similar business, and must write a business plan. The ICETP works with the following agencies and organizations: Seattle University Small Business Entrepreneurship Center, SBA, Department of Social and Health Services, Employment Security, Department of Vocational Rehabilitation, Representatives from the Banking and Lending Community, and the Department of Community Trade and Economic Development.

West Virginia
Center for Economic Options
601 Delaware Ave.   304-345-1298
Charleston, WV 25302   Fax: 304-342-0641
The Center for Economic Options provides assistance to rural entrepreneurs in developing market driven businesses, and provides technical assistance and leadership skill training to community groups. Program is available to rural residents, with emphasis on women. The aim is to promote home and community based enterprises and equal access to better paying jobs. Receives funding from foundations, corporations, and the government.

Monroe Neighborhood Enterprise Center
Monroe County Community Services Council
P.O. Box 403   304-772-3381
Union, WV 24883   Fax: 304-772-4014
Provides business training, peer support, and exchange to low to moderate income persons. The aim is to improve the income and self-sufficiency of persons by providing loans, business training, and opportunities for peer support to microenterprises. Receives funds from banks of Monroe and Union, West Virginia providing lines of credit, operating funds from Neighborhood Reinvestment Corporation, and the Benedum Foundation.

Wisconsin
Advocap, Inc.
19 W. 1st St.   920-922-7760
Fond du Lac, WI 54935   Fax: 920-922-7214
The aim of Advocap, Inc. is to help low income persons become self-sufficient by developing businesses. Provides business training and planning, individual

business counseling, peer support and exchange, mentoring, and loan packaging to poor and low income persons.

Business Ownership and Operations
Juneau Business High School
6415 West Mount Vernon
Milwaukee, WI 53213   414-476-5480
Provides business training and planning, individual business counseling, peer support and exchange, and mentoring to 15-19 year old multi-cultural students. Provides high school students with practical experience in business ownership and operations.

Cap Services, Inc.
5499 Highway 10 East   715-345-5200
Stevens Point, WI 54481   Fax: 715-345-5206
Provides business planning, counseling, peer support, and mentoring to low income individuals. Aim is to mobilize public and private resources to enhance the ability of persons to attain self-sufficiency. Receives funds from U.S. Office of Community Services, corporate contributions, state of Wisconsin, and CDBG funds.

Economic Development Project
West Cap
525 2nd St.   715-265-4271
Glenwood City, WI 54013   Fax: 715-265-7031
Provides business training, planning, and individual business counseling to low income persons, with emphasis on women located in West Central Wisconsin. Aim is to create opportunities that empower people to achieve self-sufficiency for themselves. Receives funds from Farmers Home Administration and the Bremer Foundation.

Women's Business Initiative Corporation
2745 Dr. M.L. King Dr.   414-372-2070
Milwaukee, WI 53212   Fax: 414-263-5456
Provides business training, individual counseling, and mentoring to minority and low income persons. The aim is to provide business seminars, consulting services, and microloans to individuals who are owners of startup or expanding small businesses. Focus is on women who are underemployed or unemployed striving for self-sufficiency. Receives funds from SBA Microloan Demonstration Project, Wisconsin Department of Economic Development, Milwaukee County, and foundations.

Venture Capital: Finding A Rich Angel

With federal and state money getting harder to come by, and banks experiencing serious problems of their own that restrict their willingness to loan money, anyone interested in starting his own business or expanding an existing one may do well to look into venture capital. Venture capitalists are willing to invest in a new or growing business venture for a percentage of the equity. Below is a listing of some of the associations, government agencies, and businesses that have information available on venture capital.

In addition, there are Venture Capital Clubs throughout the country where entrepreneurs have a chance to present their ideas to potential investors and learn about the process of finding funds for ventures that might be long on innovative ideas for a business, but short on proven track records.

Associations

The National Venture Capital Association (NVCA)
1655 N. Fort Meyer Dr., Suite 850   703-524-2549
Arlington, VA 22209   Fax: 703-524-3940
www.nvca.org

The association works to improve the government's knowledge and understanding of the venture capital process. Staff members can answer questions about federal legislation and regulations, and provide statistical information on venture capital. NVCA members include venture capital organizations, financiers, and individuals interested in investing in new companies. The association publishes a membership directory that includes a listing of their members with addresses, phone numbers, fax numbers and contacts. There are currently about 289 members. The directory is available for $99.

The Western Association of Venture Capitalists
3000 San Hill Rd.
Bldg. 1, Suite 190
Menlo Park, CA 94025   650-854-1322
Publishes a directory of its 130 members. The cost is $100.

National Association of Investment Companies
733 15th St. NW, Suite 700   202-289-4336
Washington, DC 20005   Fax: 202-289-4329
It is composed of specialized Small Business Investment Companies (SSBICs). The SSBIC Directory lists about 120 companies across the country including names, addresses, and telephone numbers. It also describes each company's investment preferences and policies. The 23-page publication costs $25.98. It also publishes *Perspective*, a monthly newsletter geared toward specialized small business investment companies. This newsletter includes articles about legislation and regulations affecting SSBICs. (Note: This association was formerly called the American Association of Minority Enterprise Small Business Investment Companies (AAMESBIC)).

Technology Capital Network at MIT
201 Vassar St.   617-253-7163
Cambridge, MA 02139   Fax: 617-258-7395
www.tcnmit.org
This nonprofit corporation tries to match entrepreneurs in need of capital with venture capital sources. Investors and entrepreneurs register with the network for up to 12 months for $300.

Venture Capital Clubs

There are more than 150 Venture Capital Clubs worldwide where inventors can present their ideas to potential investors. At a typical monthly meeting, several entrepreneurs may give short presentations of their ideas. It is a great way for entrepreneurs and potential investors to talk informally.

The International Venture Capital Institute (IVCI)
P.O. Box 1333
Stamford, CT 06904   203-323-3143
The IVCI publishes an annual directory of domestic and international venture groups (venture capital clubs). The cost of the *1995 IVCI Directory of Domestic and International Venture Groups*, which includes contact information for all of the clubs, is $19.95.

Below is a partial listing of clubs in the United States.

Alabama
Birmingham Venture Club
Chamber of Commerce
P.O. Box 10127
Birmingham, AL 35202
205-323-5461
Fax: 205-250-7669
www.birminghamchamber.com

Mobile Venture Club
c/o Mobile Area Chamber of
Commerce
451 Government St.
Mobile, AL 36652
334-433-6951
Fax: 334-431-8646
www.mobcham.org
Attn: Walter Underwood

Arkansas
Venture Capital Investors

400 W. Capital, Suite 1845
Little Rock, AR 72201
501-372-5900
Fax: 501-372-8181

California
Tech Coast Venture Network
195 S. C St., Suite 250
Tustin, CA 92780
714-505-6493
Fax: 714-669-9341
www.tcvn.org
Attn: Alonzo

Orange Coast Venture Group
P.O. Box 2011
Laguna Hills, CA 92654
949-859-3646
Fax: 949-859-1707
www.ocvg.org
Attn: Gregory Beck

Community Entrepreneurs
Organization
P.O. Box 9838
San Rafael, CA 94912
415-435-4461
Attn: Dr. Rick Crandall

San Diego Venture Group
750 B St., Suite 2400
San Diego, CA 92101
619-272-1985
Fax: 619-272-1986
www.sdvgroup.org

Colorado
Rockies Venture Club, Inc.
190 E. 9th Ave., Suite 440
Denver, CO 80203
303-831-4174
Fax: 303-832-4920
www.rockiesventureclub.org
Attn: Josh

Connecticut
Connecticut Venture Group
1891 Post Rd., Suite F
Fairfield, CT 06430
203-256-5955
Fax: 203-256-9949
www.ct-venture.org

District of Columbia
Baltimore-Washington Venture
Group
Michael Dingman Center for
Entrepreneurship
College Park, MD 20742-7215
301-405-2144
Fax: 301-314-9152
www.rhsmith.umd.edu/dingman

Florida
Gold Coast Venture Capital Club
22783 S. State Rd. 7, #56
Boca Raton, FL 33428
561-488-4505
Fax: 561-451-4746
www.beaconmgmt.com/gcvcc

Hawaii
Hawaii Venture Group
University of Hawaii, OTTED
2800 Woodlawn Dr., Suite 280
Honolulu, HI 96822
805-533-1400
Fax: 808-524-2775
www.hawaiiventuregroup.com

Investment Capital

Idaho
Rocky Mountain Venture Group
2300 N. Yellowstone, Suite E
Idaho Falls, ID 83402
208-526-9557
Fax: 208-526-0953
Attn: Dennis Cheney

Treasure Valley Venture Capital
Forum
Idaho Small Business Development
Center
Boise State University College of
Business
1910 University Dr.
Boise, ID 83725
208-426-1640
Fax: 208-426-3877
www.boisestate.edu/isbdc

Iowa
Iowa City Development
ICAD Group
P.O. Box 2567
Iowa City, IA 52244
319-354-3939
Fax: 319-338-9958
Attn: Marty Kelley

Illinois
Madison Dearborn Partners
70 W. Madison, 8th Floor
Chicago, IL 60602
312-895-1000
Fax: 312-895-1001

Kentucky
Kentucky Investment Capital
Network
67 Wilkinson Blvd.
Frankfort, KY 40601
502-564-4300, ext. 4315
Fax: 502-564-9758
www.state.kentucky.us
Attn: Norris Christian

Mountain Ventures Inc.
P.O. Box 1738
London, KY 40743
606-864-5175
Fax: 606-864-5194
www.ezec.gov

Louisiana
Chamber Small Business Hotline
1-800-949-7890

Maryland
Mid Atlantic Venture Association
(MAVA)
2345 York Rd.

Timonium, MD 21093
410-560-5855
Fax: 410-560-1910
www.mava.org
Attn: Maryanne Gray

Massachusetts
Venture Capital Fund of New
England
160 Federal St., 23rd Floor
Boston, MA 02110
617-439-4646
Fax: 617-439-4652

Michigan
Southeastern Venture Capital
The Meyering Corporation
206 30 Harper Ave., Suite 103
Harper Woods, MI 48225
313-886-2331
Attn: Carl Meyering

Ann Arbor Chamber of Commerce
425 S. Main St.
Ann Arbor, MI 48104
734-665-4433
www.annarborchamber.org
Attn: Barb Sprague

Minnesota
The Entrepreneurs Network
4555 Erin Dr., Suite 200
Eagan, MN 55122
651-683-9141
Fax: 651-683-0584
www.ens.net

St. Paul Venture Capital
10400 Viking Drive, Suite 550
Bloomington, MN 55444
612-995-7474

Fax: 612-995-7475
www.st.paulvc.com

Missouri
Kansas City Venture Group
10551 Barkley, Suite 400
Overland Park, KS 66212
913-341-8992
Fax: 913-341-8981

Missouri Innovation Center
5650 A S. Sinclair Rd.
Columbia, MO 65203
573-446-3100
Fax: 573-446-3106

Montana
Montana Private Capital Network
7783 Valley View Rd.
Poulson, MT 59860
406-883-5677
Fax: 406-883-5677
Attn: Jon Marchi, President

Nebraska
Grand Island Industrial Foundation
309 W. 2nd St.
P.O. Box 1486
Grand Island, NE 68802-1486
308-382-9210
Fax: 308-382-1154
www.gichamber.com
Attn: Andrew G. Baird, II CED

New Jersey
Venture Association of New Jersey, Inc.
177 Madison Ave., CN 1982
Morristown, NJ 07960
973-631-5680
Fax: 973-984-9634

www.zanj.com
Attn: Amy or Jay Trien

CHAMBER OF COMMERCE

New York
Long Island Venture Group
CW Post Campus
Long Island University
College of Management
Deans Office, Worth Hall
Room 309, North Blvd.
Brookville, NY 11548
516-299-3017
Fax: 516-299-2786
www.liv.edu
Attn: Carol Caracappa

New York Venture Group
605 Madison Ave., Suite 300
New York, NY 10022-1901
212-832-7300
Fax: 212-832-7338
www.nybusiness.com
Attn: Burt Alimansky

Westchester Venture Capital
Network
c/o Chamber of Commerce
235 Mamaroneck Ave.
White Plains, NY 10605
914-948-2110
Fax: 914-948-0122
www.westchesterny.org

Rochester Venture Capital Group
100 Corporate Woods, Suite 300
Rochester, NY 14623

Ohio
Greater Columbus Chamber of
Commerce
Columbus Investment Interest
Group
37 N. High St.
Columbus, OH 43215
614-225-6087
Fax: 614-469-8250
www.columbus.org
Attn: Diane Essex

Ohio Venture Association, Inc.
1120 Chester Ave.
Cleveland, OH 44114
216-566-8884
Fax: 216-696-2582
Attn: Joan McCarthy

Oklahoma
Oklahoma Venture Forum
211 Robinson, Suite 210
P.O. Box 26788
Oklahoma City, OK 73126-0788
405-636-9736
405-270-1050
Fax: 405-416-1035
Attn: Steve Thomas

Oregon
Oregon Entrepreneur Forum
2611 SW Third Ave., Suite 200
Portland, OR 97201
503-222-2270
Fax: 503-241-0827
www.oes.org

Portland Venture Group
P.O. Box 2341
Lake Oswego, OR 97035
503-697-5907

Fax: 503-697-5907
Attn: Glen Smith

Pennsylvania
Enterprise Venture Capital
Corporation of Pennsylvania
111 Market St.
Johnstown, PA 15901
814-535-7597
Fax: 814-535-8677

South Dakota
Dakota Ventures Inc.
P.O. Box 8194
Rapid City, SD 57709
605-348-8441
Fax: 605-348-8452
Attn. Don Frankenfeld

Texas
Capital Southwest Venture
Corporation
12900 Preston Rd., Suite 700
Dallas, TX 75230
972-233-8242
Fax: 972-233-7362
www.capitalsouthwest.com

Utah
Utah Ventures
423 Wakara Way, Suite 306
Salt Lake City, UT 84108
801-583-5922
Fax: 801-583-4105

Vermont
Vermont Venture Network
P.O. Box 5839
Burlington, VT 05402
802-658-7830
Fax: 802-658-0978

Virginia
Richmond Venture Capital Club
c/o 4900 Augusta Ave., Suite 103
Richmond, VA 23230
804-359-1139
www.ventureclub.com
Attn: Smoky Sizemore

Washington
Northwest Venture Group
P.O. Box 21693
Seattle, WA 98111-3693
425-746-1973

West Virginia
Enterprise Venture Capital
Company
P.O. Box 460
Summerville, WV 26651
304-872-3000
Fax: 304-872-3040
Attn: William Bright

Wisconsin
Wisconsin Venture Network
P.O. Box 510103
Milwaukee, WI 53203
414-224-7070
www.maxnetwork.com/wvn
Attn: Paul Sweeny

International Clubs
Puerto Rico Venture Capital Club
P.O. Box 2284

Hato Rey, PR, 00919
1-809-787-9040
Attn: Danol Morales

Johannesburg Venture Capital Club
162 Anderson St.
P.O. Box 261425
EXCOM 2023 RSA
Johannesburg, South Africa, 2001
Attn: Graham Rosenthal

Cape Town Venture Capital
Association
c/o Arthur Anderson and Company
12th Floor, Shell House
Capetown, South Africa, 8001
Attn: Colin Hultzer

Canada Clubs
Edmonton Chamber of Commerce
600 10123 99th St.
Edmonton, Alberta Canada, T5J
3G9
780-426-4620
Attn: Ace Cetinski

Venture Capital/Entrepreneurship
Club of Montreal, Inc.
1670 Sherbrooke St.
East Montreal (Quebec) Canada,
H2L 1M5
514-526-9490
Attn: Claude Belanger

Other groups with information on venture capital include:

The CPA Firm Coopers and Lybrand
1177 Avenue of the Americas   212-596-8000
New York, NY 10020   Fax: 212-596-8910

www.pwc.com

The firm publishes several publications on venture capital including *Venture Capital: The Price of Growth*, 1998, and *Venture Capital Advisory and Survey*, 1996 update. There is no charge for these publications.

Venture Economics, Inc.
22 Thompson Place
Boston, MA 02210   617-345-2504
Attn: Kelly McGow

Publications are available from:
Securities Data Publishing
40 W. 57th St., 11th Floor   212-765-5311
New York, NY 10019   Fax: 212-956-0112
Attn: Esther Miller

Venture Capital Journal, a monthly periodical that cites new issues and trends in venture capital investments. Subscription rate is $1095.

Pratt's Guide to Venture Capital Sources, an annual directory that lists 800 venture capital firms in the U.S. and Canada. It also includes articles recommending ways to raise venture capital. The cost is $385 plus shipping and taxes.

Additional Reading Material

A Venture Capital Primer for Small Business, a U.S. Small Business Administration publication that identifies what venture capital resources are available and explains how to develop a proposal for obtaining these funds ($2). SBA Publications, P.O. Box 30, Denver, CO 80201-0030. Item number FM5.

The Ernst & Young Guide to Financing for Growth. This is part of their entrepreneur series and includes bibliographical references and index. ($14.95) John Wiley & Son, 1 Wiley Dr., Somerset, NJ 08875; 800-225-5945. 1994.

Uncle Sam's Venture Capital

What Do Federal Express, Apple Computer, Staples and A Porno Shop on 42nd Street All Have In Common? They All Used Government Venture Money To Get Started

A few years ago I read that the government provided money to a porno shop in New York City through a program call Small Business Investment Companies (SBIC). Since 1960 these organizations have provided venture capital to over 75,000 businesses, so it's easy to see that one of those businesses might be a porno shop. Porno is a legitimate businesses in many areas of the country.

SBICs are licensed by the U.S. Small Business Administration but are privately owned and operate on a for profit basis. Their license allows companies to pool their money with borrowed money from the government in order to provide financing to small businesses in the form of equity securities or long-term debt. These government subsidized investment companies have helped Compaq, Apple, Federal Express and Staples make it to the big time. They have also helped smaller companies achieve success. They've financed Spencer and Vickie Jacobs' hot tub business in Columbus, Ohio, as well as taxi drivers in New York City who needed money to pay for the medallions which allows them to operate their own cabs.

Uncle Sam's Venture Capital Boom

In 1994, new government regulations were imposed that make it easier to become an SBIC. The budget for this program was also greatly expanded. As a result of this change, there will now be over $6 billion worth of financing available to entrepreneurs over the next several years. Now, that's not small change, even to a hotshot entrepreneur. With these new regulations and budget in place, the government expects that there will soon be 200 additional SBICs waiting to serve American entrepreneurs.

Who Gets The Money?

 Basically you have to be a small business to apply for this money, and the government's definition includes companies that have less than $18 million in net worth and less than $6 million in profits. Wow, that's some small business! They seem particularly interested in businesses that offer a new product or service that has a strong growth potential. There is special consideration given to minorities and Vietnam Veterans applying for this money.

You do have to be armed with a business plan, which should include the following:

1) Identify Your Company
2) Identify Your Product Or Service

Information USA, Inc.

3) Describe Your Product Facilities And Property
4) Detail Your Marketing Plan
5) Describe Your Competition
6) Describe Your Management Team
7) Provide A Financial Statement

Where to Apply

You can apply to more than one SBIC at the same time. Each

acts as an independent company and they can provide money to both local or out-of-state businesses. At the end of this section is a listing of SBA licensed Small Business Investment Companies. However, this list is growing every day so it would be wise to contact the following office to obtain a current list: Associate Administrator for Investment, U.S. Small Business Administration, Washington, DC 20416; 202-205-6510; {www.sba.gov/inv}.

States Have Venture Money, Too

It's not enough to only look at federal venture capital programs, because some state governments also have venture capital programs. More and more states continue to start new programs every month. Some states, like Maryland, see the value in the new rule changes for becoming an SBIC, and are beginning to apply to become a licensed participant of the Small Business Administration's program. Here is what is available from state governments at the time this book went to press. Be sure to check with your state to see what's new:

1) **Arkansas** - Seed Capital Investment Program
2) **Connecticut** - Risk Capital
   - Product Design Financing
   - Seed Venture Fund
3) **Illinois** - Technology Investment Program
   - Illinois Venture Capital Fund
4) **Iowa** - Venture Capital Resources Fund
5) **Kansas** - Venture Capital and Seed Capital
   - Seed Capital Fund
   - Ad Astra Fund
   - Ad Astra Fund II
6) **Louisiana** - Venture Capital Incentive Program
7) **Massachusetts** - Venture Capital Program
8) **Michigan** - Enterprise Development Fund
   - Onset Seed Fund
   - Diamond Venture Associates
   - Semery Seed Capital Fund
   - Michigan Venture Capital Fund
9) **Montana** - Venture, Equity & Risk Capital
10) **New Mexico** - Venture Capital Investment Program
11) **New York** - Corporation for Innovation Development
12) **North Carolina** - North Carolina First Flight Inc.
13) **North Carolina** - Seed and Incubator Capital
14) **Pennsylvania** - Seed Venture Capital
15) **South Carolina** - Venture Capital Funding Program
16) **Tennessee** - Venture Capital

Contact your state office of economic development in your state capital for further information on venture capital available in your state (also see the chapter entitled "State Money and Help For Your Business").

Small Business Investment Companies

Alabama

Alabama Capital Corporation
David C. DeLaney, President
16 Midtown Park East
Mobile, AL 36606
334-476-0700
Fax: 334-476-0026

FJC Growth Capital Corporation
William B. Noojin, Manager
200 Westside Court Square
Suite 340
Huntsville, AL 35801
256-922-2918
Fax: 256-922-2909

First SBIC of Alabama
David C. DeLaney, President
16 Midtown Park East
Mobile, AL 36606
334-476-0700
Fax: 334-476-0026

Hickory Venture Capital
Corporation
J. Thomas Noojin, President
301 Washington St., Suite 301
Huntsville, AL 35801
256-539-1931
Fax: 256-539-5130
www.hvcc.com

Javelin Capital Fund, L.P.
Lyle Hohnke and Joan Neuschaler,
Partners
2850 Cahaba Rd., Suite 240
Birmingham, AL 35223
205-870-4811
Fax: 205-870-4822

Arizona

Sundance Venture Partners, L.P.
Brian Burns, General Manager
5030 E. Sunrise Dr., Suite 200
Phoenix, AZ 85044
602-785-0725
Fax: 602-785-0753

Sundance Venture Partners, L.P.
(Main Office: Cupertino, CA)
Gregory S. Anderson, VP
5030 E. Sunrise Dr., Suite 200
Phoenix, AZ 85004
480-785-0725
Fax: 480-257-8111

Arkansas

Small Business Inv. Capital, Inc.
Jerry W. Davis, President
12103 Interstate 30
P.O. Box 3627
Little Rock, AR 72203
501-455-6599
Fax: 501-455-6556

California

Allied Business Investors, Inc.
(SSBIC)
Jack Hong, President
301 W. Valley Blvd., Suite 208
San Gabriel, CA 91776
626-289-0186
Fax: 626-289-2369

Ally Finance Corp.
Eric Steinmann, CEO
14011 Park Ave., Suite 310
Victorville, CA 92392
760-241-7025
Fax: 760-241-8232

Asian American Capital
Corporation
Jennie Chien, Manager
1251 W. Tennyson Rd., Suite #4
Hayward, CA 94544
510-887-6888
Fax: 510-887-6897

Aspen Ventures West II, L.P.
Alexander Cilento and David
Crocket, Managers
1000 Fremont Ave., Suite V
Los Altos, CA 94024
650-917-5670
Fax: 650-917-5677
www.aspenventures.com

Astar Capital Corp.
George Hsu, President
9537 E. Gidley St.
Temple City, CA 91780
626-350-1211
Fax: 626-443-5874

AVI Capital, L.P.
P. Wolken, B. Weinman and B.
Grossi, Managers
One First St., Suite 12
Los Altos, CA 94022
650-949-9862
Fax: 650-949-8510
www.avicapital.com

BT Capital Partners, Inc.
(Main Office: New York, NY)

300 S. Grand Ave.
Los Angeles, CA 90071
www.bankerstrust.com/btcapital

BankAmerica Ventures, Inc.
Carla Perumean, Senior VP
950 Tower Lane, Suite 700
Foster City, CA 94404
650-378-6000
Fax: 650-378-6040

Bay Partners SBIC, L.P.
John Freidenrich and Neal
Dempsey, Managers
10600 N. De Anza Blvd., Suite 100
Cupertino, CA 95014
408-725-2444
Fax: 408-446-4502
www.baypartners.com

Bentley Capital
John Hung, President
592 Vallejo St., Suite #2
San Francisco, CA 94133
415-362-2868
Fax: 415-398-8209

Best Finance Corporation
Yong Ho Park, General Manager
3540 W. Wilshire Blvd., Suite 804
Los Angeles, CA 90010
213-385-7030
Fax: 213-385-7130

Calsafe Capital Corp.
Ming-Min Su, President,
Director and Manager
245 E. Main St., Suite 107
Alhambra, CA 91801
626-289-3400
Fax: 626-300-8025

Canaan Venture Partners
Main Office: Rowayton, CT-
Eric Young, Manager
2884 Sand Hill Rd.
Menlo Park, CA 94025
650-854-8092
Fax: 650-854-8127
www.canaan.com

Capstone Ventures SBIC, L.P.
Barbara Santry and Gene Fischer,
Managers
3000 Sand Hill Rd.
Building 1, Suite 290
Menlo Park, CA94025
650-854-2523
Fax: 650-854-9010
www.capstonevc.qpg.com

Charterway Investment Corporation
Edmund C. Lau, Chairman
9660 Flair Dr., Suite 328
El Monte, CA 91731
626-279-1189
Fax: 626-279-9062

Critical Capital Growth Fund, L.P.
Steven Sands & Allen Gold, Mgrs.
17 E. Sir Francis Drake Blvd.
Suite 230
Larkspur, CA 94939
415-464-5720
Fax: 415-464-5701

Draper Associates (a California LP)
Timothy C. Draper, President
400 Seaport Court, Suite 250
Redwood City, CA 94063
650-599-9000
Fax: 650-599-9726
www.drapervc.com

Draper-Richards L.P.
William Draper III, President
50 California St., Suite 2925
San Francisco, CA 94111
415-616-4050
Fax: 415-616-4060
www.draperintl.com

Far East Capital Corp.
Tom Wang, Manager
977 N. Broadway, Suite 401
Los Angeles, CA 90012
213-687-1361
Fax: 213-626-7497

First American Capital Funding,
Inc.
Chuoc Vota, President
10840 Warner Ave., Suite 202
Fountain Valley, CA 92708
714-965-7190
Fax: 714-965-7193

Fourteen Hill Capitol
Bradley Rotter and Alan Perper,
Managers
1700 Montgomery St., Suite 250
San Francisco, CA 94111
415-394-9469
Fax: 415-394-9471
www.fourteenhill.com

Fulcrum Venture Capital Corp.
Brian Argrett, President
3683 Corporate Pointe, Suite 380
Culver City, CA 90230
310-645-1271
Fax: 310-645-1272

Hall Capital Management
Ronald J. Hall, Managing Director

26161 La Paz Rd., Suite E
Mission Viejo, CA 92691
949-707-5096
Fax: 949-707-5121

Imperial Ventures, Inc.
Christian Hobbs, VP
9920 S. La Cienega Blvd.
Suite 1030
(P.O. Box 92991
L.A. 90301)
Inglewood, CA 90301
310-417-5960
Fax: 310-417-5781

Kline Hawkes California SBIC, LP
Frank R. Kline, Manager
11726 San Vicente Blvd.
Suite 300
Los Angeles, CA 90049
310-442-4700
Fax: 310-442-4707
www.klinehawkes.com

LaiLai Capital Corp.
Danny Ku, Pres. & General Mgr.
223 E. Garvey Ave., Suite 228
Monterey Park, CA 91754
626-288-0704
Fax: 626-288-4101
www.lailai.com

Magna Pacific Investments
David Wong, President
330 N. Brand Blvd., Suite 670
Glendale, CA 91203
818-547-0809
Fax: 818-547-9303

Marwit Capital Corp.
Matthew Witte, President
180 Newport Center Dr., Suite 200

Newport Beach, CA 92660
949-640-6234
Fax: 949-720-8077
www.marwit.com

New Vista Capital Fund
Roger Barry, Manager
540 Cooper St., Suite 200
Palo Alto, CA 94301
650-329-9333
Fax: 650-328-9434
www.nvcap.com

Novus Ventures, L.P.
Daniel Tompkins, Manager
20111 Stevens Creek Blvd.
Suite 130
Cupertino, CA 95014
408-252-3900
Fax: 408-252-1713

Opportunity Capital Corporation
J. Peter Thompson, President
2201 Walnut Ave., Suite 210
Fremont, CA 94538
510-795-7000
Fax: 510-494-5439

Opportunity Capital Partners II,
L.P.
J. Peter Thompson, Gen. Partner
2201 Walnut Ave., Suite 210
Fremont, CA 94538
510-795-7000
Fax: 510-494-5439

Pacific Mezzanine Fund, L.P.
Nathan W. Bell, General Partner
2200 Powell St., Suite 1250
Emeryville, CA 94608
510-595-9800
Fax: 510-595-9801

Pinecreek Capital Partners, L.P.
Randall F. Zurbach, President
24 Corporate Plaza, Suite 160
Newport Beach, CA 92660
949-720-4620
Fax: 949-720-4629

Positive Enterprises, Inc.
Kwok Szeto, President
1489 Webster St., Suite 228
San Francisco, CA 94115
415-885-6600
Fax: 415-928-6363

San Joaquin Business Investment
Group Inc.
Eugene Waller, President
1900 Mariposa Mall, Suite 100
Fresno, CA 93721
559-233-3580
Fax: 559-233-3709

Sorrento Growth Partners
Robert Jaffe, Manager
4370 La Jolla Village Dr.
Suite 1040
San Diego, CA 92122
619-452-3100
Fax: 619-452-7607
www.sorrentoventures.com

Tangent Growth Fund
Alexander Schilling, Manager
180 Geary St., Suite 500
San Francisco, CA 94108
415-392-9228
Fax: 415-392-1928

TeleSoft Partners IA L.P.
Arjun Gupta, Manager
1450 Fashion Island Blvd.

Suite 610
San Mateo, CA 94404
650-358-2500
Fax: 650-358-2501

UnionBanCal Venture Corporation
Robert S. Clarke, President
445 S. Figueroa St., 9th Floor
P.O. Box 3100
Los Angeles, CA 90071
213-236-4092
Fax: 213-629-5328

VK Capital Company
Franklin Van Kasper, General
Partner
600 California St., Suite 1700
San Francisco, CA 94108
415-391-5600
Fax: 415-397-2744
www.vkco.com

Sorrento Growth Partners

Viridian Capital, L.P.
Christine Cordaro, Contact
220 Montgomery St., Suite 946
San Francisco, CA 94104
415-391-8950
Fax: 415-391-8937

Walden-SBIC, L.P.
Arthur S. Berliner, Manager
750 Battery St., 7th Floor
San Francisco, CA 94111
415-391-7225
Fax: 415-391-7262
www.waldenvc.com

Wells Fargo SBIC, Inc.
Richard Green, Steven Burge,
Managers
One Montgomery St.
West Tower, Suite 2530
San Francisco, CA 94104
800-411-4932
Fax: 415-765-1569
www.wallsfargo.com

Western General Capital Corp.
Alan Thian, President
13701 Riverside Dr., Suite 610
Sherman Oaks, CA 91423
818-907-8272
Fax: 818-905-9220

Woodside Fund III SBIC, L.P.
Vincent Occhipinti and Frank
Mendicino
850 Woodside Dr.
Woodside, CA 94062
650-368-5545
Fax: 650-368-2416
www.woodsidefund.com

Colorado
CapEx, L.P.
Jeffrey Ross, Manager
1670 Broadway, Suite 3350
Denver, CO 80202
303-869-4700
Fax: 303-869-4602

Hanifen Imhoff Mezzanine Fund,
L.P.
Edward C. Brown, Manager
1125 17th St., Suite 1820
Denver, CO 80202
303-291-5209
Fax: 303-291-5327
www.rockycapital.com

Rocky Mountain Mezzanine Fund
II
Edward Brown, Paul Lyons, Mgrs.
1125 17th St., Suite 1500
Denver, CO 80202
303-291-5209
Fax: 303-291-5327
www.rockycapital.com

Connecticut
AB SBIC, Inc.
Adam J. Bozzuto, President
275 School House Rd.
Cheshire, CT 06410
203-272-0203
Fax: 203-250-2954

Canaan SBIC, L.P.
Gregory Kopchinsky, Manager
105 Rowayton Ave.
Rowayton, CT 06853
203-855-0400
Fax: 203-854-9117
www.canaan.com

Capital Resource Co. of
Connecticut
Morris Morgenstein, General
Partner
Two Bridgewater Rd.
Framington, CT 06032
860-677-1113
Fax: 860-677-5414

Imprimis SB, L.P.
Charles Davidson, Joseph Jacobs,
Managers
411 W. Putnam Ave.
Greenwich, CT 06830
203-862-7074
Fax: 203-862-7374

First New England Capital, LP
Richard C. Klaffky, President
100 Pearl St.
Hartford, CT 06103
860-293-3333
Fax: 860-293-3338
www.firstnewenglandcapital.com

Marcon Capital Corp.
Robert Mahoney and Todd Enright,
Managers
1470 Barnum Ave., Suite 301
Bridgeport, CT 06610
203-337-4444
Fax: 203-337-4449
www.marconcapital.com

RFE Capital Partners, L.P.
Robert M. Williams, Managing
Partner
36 Grove St.
New Canaan, CT 06840
203-966-2800
Fax: 203-966-3109

SBIC of Connecticut Inc. (The)
Kenneth F. Zarrilli, President
965 White Plains Rd.
Trumbull, CT 06611
203-261-0011
Fax: 203-452-9699

Delaware
Blue Rock Capital, L.P.
Virginia Bonker and Paul Collison,
Managers
5803 Kennett Pike, Suite A
Wilmington, DE 19807-1135
302-426-0981
Fax: 302-426-0982

District of Columbia
Allied Investment Corporation
Kelly Anderson, Controller
1919 Pennsylvania Ave., NW
Washington, DC 20006-3434
202-973-6328
Fax: 202-659-2053
www.alliedcapital.com

Broadcast Capital, Inc. SSBIC
John E. Oxendine, President
1700 K St., NW, Suite 405
Washington, DC 20006
202-496-9250
Fax: 202-496-9259

Capitol Health Partners, L.P.
Debora Guthrie, Manager
2620 P St., NW
Washington, DC 20007
202-342-6300
Fax: 202-342-6399

Multimedia Broadcast Investment
Corp. SSBIC
Walter L. Threadgill, President
3101 South St., NW
Washington, DC 20007
202-293-1166
Fax: 202-293-1181

Women's Growth Capital Fund,
LLLP
Patty Abramson and Rob Stein,
Managers
1029 31st St., NW
Washington, DC 20007-1203
202-342-1431
Fax: 202-342-1203
www.womensgrowthcapital.com

Florida

Capital International
Marvel Iglesias, Contact
One SE Third Ave., Suite 2255
Miami, FL 33131
305-373-6500
Fax: 305-373-6700
www.net-invest.com

Market Capital Corp.
Eugene C. Langford
1715 W. Cleveland St.
Tampa, FL 33606
813-251-6055
Fax: 813-251-1900
www.langfordhill.com

PMC Investment Corporation
(Main Office: Dallas, TX)
AmeriFirst Bank Building
2nd Floor S
18301 Biscayne Blvd.
N. Miami Beach, FL 33160
305-933-5858
Fax: 305-931-3054

Western Financial Capital Corp.
(Main Office: Dallas, TX)
AmeriFirst Bank Building
2nd Floor S
18301 Biscayne Blvd.
N. Miami Beach, FL 33160
305-933-5858
Fax: 305-932-3730
www.pmcapital.com

Georgia

Cordova Enhanced Fund, L.P.
Paul DiBella and Ralph Wright,
Managers
2500 North Winds Pkwy, Suite 475
Alpharetta, GA 30004
678-942-0300
Fax: 678-942-0301
www.cordovaventures.com

EGL/NatWest Ventures USA, L.P.
Salvatore Massaro, Manager
6600 Peachtree-Dunwoody Rd.
300 Embassy Row, Suite 630
Atlanta, GA 30328
404-949-8300
Fax: 404-949-8311
www.eglholdings.com

First Growth Capital, Inc.
Vijay K. Patel, President
P.O. Box 815
I-75 and GA 42
Best Western Plaza
Forsyth, GA 31029
912-994-4620
Fax: 912-994-1280

Waschovia Capital Associates, Inc.
Matthew J. Sullivan, Managing Dir.
191 Peachtree St., NE, 26th Floor
Atlanta, GA 30303
404-332-1437
Fax: 404-332-1455
www.waschovia.com

Hawaii

Pacific Century SBIC, Inc.
Robert Paris, President
130 Merchant St., 12th Floor

(P.O. Box 2900,
Honolulu, 96846-6000)
Honolulu, HI 96813
808-537-8613
Fax: 808-521-7602
www.boh.com

Pacific Venture Capital, Ltd.
Dexter J. Taniguchi, President
222 S. Vineyard St., PH.1
Honolulu, HI 96813
808-521-6502
Fax: 808-521-6541
E-mail: hedco@gle.com

Illinois

ABN AMRO Capital
Paul Widuch, Chairman
135 S. Lasalle St.
Chicago, IL 60674
312-904-6445
Fax: 312-904-6376
www.abnamro.com

BMO Nesbitt Burns Equity
Investments
William Morro, President
111 W. Monroe St., 20th Floor
Chicago, IL 60603
312-461-2021
Fax: 312-765-8000

Continental Illinois Venture Corp.
Christopher J. Perry, President
209 S. LaSalle St.
(Mail: 231 S. LaSalle St.)
Chicago, IL 60697
312-828-8021
Fax: 312-987-0763
www.civc.com

First Chicago Equity Corp.
David J. Vitale, President
Three First National Plaza
Suite 1330
Chicago, IL 60670
312-895-1000
Fax: 312-895-1001

Heller Equity Capital Corporation
Charles Brisman, Steven Miriani
500 W. Monroe St.
Chicago, IL 60661
312-441-7000
Fax: 312-441-7208
www.hellersin.com

Midwest Mezzanine Fund
David Gezon and Allan Kayler,
Managers
208 S. Lasalle St., 10th Floor
Chicago, IL 60604
312-855-7140
Fax: 312-553-6647
www.abnequity.com

Peterson Finance and Investment
Company
James S. Rhee, President
3300 W. Peterson Ave., Suite A
Chicago, IL 60659
773-539-0502
Fax: 773-583-6714

Polestar Capital, Inc.
Wallace Lennox, President
180 N. Michigan Ave., Suite 1905
Chicago, IL 60601
312-984-9875
Fax: 312-984-9877
www.polestarvc.com

Prairie Capital Mezzanine Fund, L.P.
Bryan Daniels and Stephen King, Partners
300 S. Wacker Dr., Suite 1050
Chicago, IL 60606
312-360-1133
Fax: 312-360-1193

Capital Corporations

Shorebank Capital Corp.
David Shryock, CEO
7936 S. Cottage Grove Ave.
Chicago, IL 60619
773-371-7030
Fax: 773-371-7035
www.sbk.com

Walnut Capital Corp.
Burton W. Kanter, Chairman of the Board
Two N. LaSalle St., Suite 2200
Chicago, IL 60602
312-269-1700
Fax: 312-269-1747

Indiana
1st Source Capital Corporation
Eugene L. Cavanaugh, Jr., VP
100 N. Michigan St.
(Mailing address: P.O. Box 1602
South Bend 46634)
South Bend, IN 46601
219-235-2180
Fax: 219-235-2227

Cambridge Ventures, LP
Ms. Jean Wojtowicz, President

8440 Woodfield Crossing, #315
Indianapolis, IN 46240
317-469-9704
Fax: 317-469-3926

White River Venture
Sam Surphin and Mark Delong, Managers
3603 E. Raymond St.
Indianapolis, IN 46203
317-780-7789
Fax: 317-791-2935

Iowa
Berthel SBIC, LLC
Jim Thorp & Henry Madden, Mgrs.
100 2nd St., SE
Cedar Rapids, IA 52407
319-365-2506
Fax: 319-365-9141
www.berthel.com

MorAmerica Capital Corporation
David R. Schroder, President
101 2nd St., SE, Suite 800
Cedar Rapids, IA 52401
319-363-8249
Fax: 319-363-9683

North Dakota SBIC, L.P.
David R. Schroder, Manager
101 Second St. SE, Suite 800
Cedar Rapids, IA 52401
701-298-0003
Fax: 701-293-7819

Kansas
Kansas Venture Capital, Inc.
Carol Laddish, Manager
6700 Antioch Plaza, Suite 460
Overland Park, KS 66204

913-262-7117
Fax: 913-262-3509

Enterprise Fund
Randall Humphreys, Manager
7400 W. 110th St., Suite 560
Overland Park, KS 66210
913-327-8500
Fax: 913-327-8505

Kentucky
Equal Opportunity Finance, Inc.
David A. Sattich, President
420 S. Hurstbourne Pkwy.
Suite 201
Louisville, KY 40222
502-423-1943
Fax: 502-423-1945

Mountain Ventures, Inc.
L. Ray Moncrief, Executive VP
P.O. Box 1738
362 Old Whitely Rd.
London, KY 40743
606-864-5175
Fax: 606-864-5194

Louisiana
Banc One Equity Investors, Inc.
Thomas J. Adamek, President
451 Florida St.
P.O. Box 1511
Baton Rouge, LA 70821
225-332-4421
Fax: 225-332-7377

Hibernia Capital Corp.
Thomas Hoyt, President
313 Carondelet St.
New Orleans, LA 70130
504-533-5988

Fax: 504-533-3873
www.hibernia.com

Maine
North Atlantic Venture Fund
David M. Coit, Manager
Seventy Center St.
Portland, ME 04101
207-772-1001
Fax: 207-772-3257
www.northatlanticcapital.com

Maryland
Anthem Capital
William Gust, Manager
16 S. Calvert St., Suite 800
Baltimore, MD 21202
410-625-1510
Fax: 410-625-1735
www.anthemcapital.com

MMG Ventures
Stanley W. Tucker, Manager
826 E. Baltimore St.
Baltimore, MD 21202
410-333-2548
Fax: 410-333-2552
www.mmggroup.com

Security Financial and Investment
Corporation
7720 Wisconsin Ave., Suite 207
Bethesda, MD 20814
301-951-4288
Fax: 301-951-9282

Syncom Capital Corp.
Terry L. Jones, President
8401 Colesville Rd., #300
Silver Spring, MD 20910
301-608-3207
Fax: 301-608-3307

Massachusetts

Argonauts MESBIC Corporation
Kevin Chen, General Manager
929 Worcester Rd.
Framingham, MA 01701
508-875-6939
Fax: 508-872-3741

BancBoston Ventures, Inc.
Frederick M. Fritz, President
100 Federal St.
P.O. Box 2016
Stop 01-32-01
Boston, MA 02106
617-434-2442
Fax: 617-434-1153
www.bancboscap.com

Cadeuceus Capital Health Ventures
Bill Golden, Manager
101 Arch St., Suite 1950
Boston, MA 02110
617-330-9345
Fax: 617-330-9349

Chestnut Street Partners, Inc.
David D. Croll, President
75 State St., Suite 2500
Boston, MA 02109
617-345-7220
Fax: 617-345-7201
www.mcventurepartners.com

Citizens Ventures, Inc.
Robert Garrow and Gregory
Mulligan, Managers
28 State St., 15th Floor
Boston, MA 02109
617-725-5635
Fax: 617-725-5630

Commonwealth Enterprise Fund
Inc
Charles G. Broming, Fund
Manager
10 Post Office Square
Suite 1090
Boston, MA 02109
617-482-1881
Fax: 617-482-7129

GMN Investors II, L.P.
James M. Goodman, Manager
20 William St.
Wellesley, MA 02481
781-237-7001
Fax: 781-237-7233
www.gemini-investors.com

Geneva Middle Market Investors
James Goodman, Manager
20 William St.
Wellesley, MA 02481
781-237-7001
Fax: 781-237-7233
www.gemini-investors.com

Marathon Investment Partners
10 Post Office Square, Suite 1225
Boston, MA 02109
617-423-2494
Fax: 617-423-2719
www.marathoninvestment.com

New England Partners Capital, L.P.
Robert Hanks, Prin. and Todd
Fitzpatrick
One Boston Place, Suite 2100
Boston, MA 02108
617-624-8400
Fax: 617-624-8416

Northeast SBI Corp.
Joseph Mindick, Treasurer
212 Tosca Dr.
Stoughton, MA 02072
781-297-9235
Fax: 781-297-9236

Norwest Equity Partners IV
Main Office: Minneapolis, MN
40 William St., Suite 305
Wellesley, MA 02181
617-237-5870
Fax: 617-237-6270
www.norwestvc.com

Pioneer Ventures Limited
Partnership
Leigh Michl, General Partner
60 State St., 19th Floor
Boston, MA 02109
617-742-7825
Fax: 617-742-7315
www.pioneerfunds.com

Seacost Capital Partners
Walt Leonard, Manager
55 Ferncroft, Rd.
Danvers, MA 01923
978-750-1310
Fax: 978-750-1301

UST Capital Corp.
Arthur F. Snyder, President
40 Court St.
Boston, MA 02108
617-726-7000
Fax: 617-695-4185
www.ustrustboston.com

Zero Stage Capital V, L.P.
Paul Kelley, Manager

Kendall Square
101 Main St., 17th Floor
Cambridge, MA 02142
617-876-5355
Fax: 617-876-1248
www.zerostage.com

Michigan
Capital Fund, Inc.
Barry Wilson, President
6412 Centurion Dr., Suite 150
Lansing, MI 48917
517-323-7772
Fax: 517-323-1999

Dearborn Capital Corp.
Michael J. Kahres, President
c/o Ford Motor Credit Corp.
P.O. Box 1729
Dearborn, MI 48121
313-337-8577
Fax: 313-248-1252

Investcare Partners
Malcolm Moss, Manager
31500 Northwest Hwy., Suite 120
Farmington Hill, MI 48334
248-851-9200
Fax: 248-851-9208

Merchants Capital Partners, L.P.
Pat Beach, Dick Goff, Ross Martin,
Managers
24 Frank Lloyd Wright Dr.
Lobby L, 4th Floor

Ann Arbor, MI 48106
734-994-5505
Fax: 734-994-1376
www.captec.com

Motor Enterprises, Inc.
Mark Fischer, VP and Treasurer
NAO Headquarters Bldg., 1-8
30400 Mound Rd., Box 9015
Warren, MI 48090
810-986-8420
Fax: 810-986-6703

Pacific Capital
Lois F. Marler, VP
2401 Plymouth Rd., Suite B
Ann Arbor, MI 48105
734-747-9401
Fax: 734-747-9704
www.whitepines.com

White Pines Capital Corp.
Mr. Ian Bund, President
2401 Plymouth Rd.
Ann Arbor, MI 48105
734-747-9401
Fax: 734-747-9704
www.whitepines.com

Minnesota
Agio Capital Partners
Kenneth F. Gudolf, Pres. and CEO
First Bank Place
601 Second Ave. S., Suite 4600
Minneapolis, MN 55402
612-339-8408
Fax: 612-349-4232
www.agio-capital.com

Baynew Capital Partners
Cary Musech, Manager

61 E. Lake St., Suite 230
Waycata, MN 55391
612-475-4935
Fax: 612-476-7820
www.bayviewcap.com

Milestone Growth Fund, Inc.
Esperanza Guerrero, President
401 Second Ave. S., Suite 1032
Minneapolis, MN 55401
612-338-0090
Fax: 612-338-1172

Mezzain Capital Partners
Gerald Slater and Lar Sovenson
150 S. 5th St., Suite 1720
Minneapolis, MN 55402
612-343-5540
Fax: 612-333-6118

Medallion Capital, Inc.
Tom Hunt, President
7831 Glenroy Rd., Suite 480
Minneapolis, MN 55439-3132
612-831-2025
Fax: 612-831-2945
www.medallionfinancial.com

Norwest Venture Partners
Robert F. Zicarelli, Manager
2800 Piper Jaffray Tower
222 S. Ninth St.
Minneapolis, MN 55402
612-667-1650
Fax: 612-667-1660
www.norwestvc.com

Piper Jaffray Healthcare Capital
Lloyd Benson, Manager
222 S. Ninth St.
Minneapolis, MN 55402

612-342-6335
Fax: 612-342-8514
www.pjc.com

Piper Jaffray Technology Capital
Gary Blauer, Buzz Benson, Mgrs.
222 South 9th St.
Minneapolis, MN 55402
612-342-6368
Fax: 612-342-8514
www.pjc.com

Norwest Venture Partners
Daniel J. Haggerty, Manager
2800 Piper Jaffray Tower
Minneapolis, MN 55402
612-667-1650
Fax: 612-667-1660
www.norwestvc.com

Wells Fargo SBIC, Inc.
John Whaley
2800 Piper Jaffray Tower
222 S Ninth St.
c/o Norwest Venture Capital
Minneapolis, MN 55402
612-667-1667
Fax: 612-667-1660
www.norwestvc.com

Mississippi
CapSource Fund, L.P.
Bobby Weatherly and James
Herndon, Managers
800 Woodlands Parkway, Suite 102
Ridgeland, MS 39157
601-899-8980
Fax: 601-952-1334

Sun-Delta Capital Access Center,
Inc.
Howard Boutte, Jr., VP

819 Main St.
Greenville, MS 38701
601-335-5291
Fax: 601-335-5295

Missouri
Bankers Capital Corp.
Raymond E. Glasnapp, President
3100 Gillham Rd.
Kansas City, MO 64109
816-531-1600
Fax: 816-531-1334

BOME Investors, Inc.
Gregory R. Johnson and John
McCarthy, Managers
8000 Maryland Ave., Suite 1190
St. Louis, MO 63105
314-721-5707
Fax: 314-721-5135
www.gatewayventures.com

CFB Venture Fund I, Inc.
James F. O'Donnell, Chairman
11 S. Meramec, Suite 1430
St. Louis, MO 63105
314-746-7427
Fax: 314-746-8739

CFB Venture Fund II, Inc.
James F. O'Donnell, President
11 S. Meramec, Suite 1430
St. Louis, MO 63105
314-746-7427
Fax: 314-746-8739

Civic Ventures Investment Fund,
L.P.
Bryon E. Winton, Manager
One Metropolitan Square
211 North Broadway, Suite 2380

St. Louis, MO 63102
314-436-8222
Fax: 314-436-2070

Enterprise Fund, L.P.
Joseph D. Garea, Managing Dir.
150 North Meramec
Clayton, MO 63105
314-725-5500
Fax: 314-725-1732

Gateway Partners

Gateway Partners
John S. McCarthy
8000 Maryland Ave., Suite 1190
St. Louis, MO 63105
314-721-5707
Fax: 314-721-5135
www.gatewayventures.com

KCEP I, L.P.
William Reisler, Manager
233 W. 47th St.
Kansas City, MO 64112
816-960-1771
Fax: 816-960-1777
www.kcep.com

MorAmerica Capital Corporation
(Main Office: Cedar Rapids, IA)
911 Main St., Suite 2424
Commerce Tower Bldg.
Kansas City, MO 64105
816-842-0114
Fax: 816-471-7339

United Missouri Capital Corp.
Noel Shull, Manager
1010 Grand Blvd.
P.O. Box 419226
Kansas City, MO 64141
816-860-7914
Fax: 816-860-7143
www.umb.com

Nevada
Atalanta Investment Company, Inc.
L. Mark Newman, Chairman of the
Board
601 Fairview Blvd.
Call Box 10,001
Incline Village, NV 89450
775-833-1836
Fax: 775-833-1890

New Jersey
DFW Capital Partners
Donald Demuth, Manager
Glenpointe Center East, 5th Floor
300 Frank W. Burr Blvd.
Teaneck, NJ 07666
201-836-2233
Fax: 201-836-5666

CIT Group/Venture Capital, Inc.
Colby W. Collier, Manager
650 CIT Dr.
Livingston, NJ 07039
973-740-5429
Fax: 973-740-5555
www.citgroup.com

Capital Circulation Corporation
Judy Kao, Manager
2035 Lemoine Ave., Second Floor
Fort Lee, NJ 07024

201-947-8637
Fax: 201-585-1965

Early Stage Enterprises
Ronald Hahn, James Miller, Mgrs.
995 Route 518
Skillman, NJ 08558
609-921-8896
Fax: 609-921-8703

First Fidelity
Stephen Lane, President
190 River Rd.
Summit, NJ 07901
908-598-3363
Fax: 908-598-3375

Midmark Capital
Dennis Newman, Manager
466 Southern Blvd.
Chatham, NJ 07928
973-822-2999
Fax: 973-822-8911
www.midmarkcapital.com

Rutgers Minority Investment Co.
Oscar Figueroa, President
180 University Ave., 3rd Floor
Newark, NJ 07102
973-353-5627

Tappan Zee Capital Corporation
Jeffrey Birnberg, President
201 Lower Notch Rd.
P.O. Box 416
Little Falls, NJ 07424
973-256-8280
Fax: 973-256-2841

Transpac Capital Corporation
Tsuey Tang Wang, President

1037 Route 46 East
Clifton, NJ 07013
973-470-8855
Fax: 973-470-8827

Penny Lane Partners
Stephen Shaffer, Resident Manager
One Palmer Square, Suite 309
Princeton, NJ 08542
609-497-4646
Fax: 609-497-0611

New Mexico
TD Origen Capital Fund
J. Michael Schafer, Manager
150 Washington Ave., Suite 201
Santa Fe, NM 87501
505-982-7007
Fax: 505-982-7005

New York
399 Venture Partners
William Comfort, Chairman
399 Park Ave., 14th Floor, Zone 4
New York, NY 10043
212-559-1127
Fax: 212-888-2940

BOCNY, LLC
Shelley G. Whittington, Manager
10 E. 53rd St., 32nd Floor
New York, NY 10022
225-332-7721
Fax: 225-332-7377

American Asian Capital Corp.
Howard H. Lin, President
130 Water St., Suite 6-L
New York, NY 10005
212-422-6880
Fax: 212-422-6880

Argentum Capital Partners, LP
Daniel Raynor, Chairman
405 Lexington Ave., 54th Floor
New York, NY 10174
212-949-6262
Fax: 212-949-8294

Bank Austria Creditanstalt SBIC,
Inc.
Dennis O'Dowd, President
245 Park Ave., 32nd Floor
New York, NY 10167
203-861-1410
Fax: 203-861-1477
www.bacai.com/

BT Capital Partners, Inc.
Doug Brent, Managing Director
130 Liberty St., 25th Floor
New York, NY 10006
212-250-7577
Fax: 212-250-7651
www.bankerstrust.com/btcapital

Barclays Capital Investors
Corporation
Lorne Stapleton, President
222 Broadway, 11th Floor
New York, NY 10038
212-412-5832
Fax: 212-412-7600
www.barcat.com

CB Investors, Inc.
George E. Kells, Managing
Director
380 Madison Ave., 12th Floor
New York, NY 10017
212-622-3100
Fax: 212-622-3799
www.chasecapitalpartners.com

CIBC Wood Gundy Ventures, Inc.
Robi Blumenstein, Managing Dir.
425 Lexington Ave., 9th Floor
New York, NY 10017
212-856-3713
Fax: 212-697-1554
www.cibcwm.com

CMNY Capital II, L.P.
Robert G. Davidoff, G.P.
135 E. 57th St., 26th Floor
New York, NY 10022
212-909-8432
Fax: 212-980-2630

Cephas Capital Partners
Clint Campbell, Jeff Holmes, Mgrs.
16 W. Main St.
Rochester, NY 14614
716-231-1528
Fax: 716-231-1530

Capital Investors & Management
Corp.
Rose Chao, Manager
210 Canal St., Suite 611
New York, NY 10013
212-964-2480
Fax: 212-349-9160

Chase Manhattan Capital Corp.
George E. Kells, Managing Dir
380 Madison Ave., 12th Floor
New York, NY 10017
212-552-6275
Fax: 212-622-3799
www.chase.com

Chase Venture Capital Assoc.
Jeffrey C. Walker, Managing
General Partner

380 Madison Ave., 12th Floor
New York, NY 10017
212-270-3220
Fax: 212-622-3101
www.chase.com

Credit Suisse First Boston SB Fund
David DeNunzio, John Hennessy,
Managers
11 Madison Ave., 26th Floor
New York, NY 10010
212-325-2000
Fax: 212-325-2699
www.csfb.com

Citicorp Venture Capital, Ltd.
William Comfort
Chairman of the Board
399 Park Ave., 14th Floor, Zone 4
New York, NY 10043
212-559-1127
Fax: 212-793-6164

Dresdner Kleinwort Benson Private
Equity
Christopher Wright, President
75 Wall St., 24th Floor
New York, NY 10005
212-429-2100
Fax: 212-429-2929
www.dresdner-bank.com

Edwards Capital Corporation
Michael Kowalsky, President
437 Madison Ave.
New York, NY 10022
212-328-2110
Fax: 212-328-2125
www.medallionfinancial.com

Eos Partners SBIC II, L.P.
Steven Friedman and Brian Young,
Managers

320 Park Ave., 22nd Floor
New York, NY 10022
212-832-5800
Fax: 212-832-5805
www.eospartners.com

East Coast Venture Capital, Inc.
Zindel Zelmanovitch, President
570 Seventh Ave., Suite 1802
New York, NY 10018
212-869-7778
Fax: 212-819-9764

East River Ventures
Alexander Paluch and Walter
Carozza
150 E. 58th St., 16th Floor
New York, NY 10155
212-644-6211
Fax: 212-980-6603

Elk Associates Funding Corp.
Gary C. Granoff, President
747 Third Ave.
New York, NY 10017
212-421-2111
Fax: 212-759-3338

Empire State Capital Corporation
Dr. Joseph Wu, President
170 Broadway, Suite 1200
New York, NY 10038
212-513-1799
Fax: 212-513-1892

Esquire Capital Corp.
Wen-Chan Chin, President
69 Veterans Memorial Highway
Commack, NY 11725
516-462-6944
Fax: 516-864-8152

Exim Capital Corp.
Victor K. Chun, President
241 5th Ave., 3rd Floor
New York, NY 10016
212-683-3375
Fax: 212-689-4118

Fair Capital Corp.
Rose Chao, Manager
210 Canal St., Suite 611
New York, NY 10013
212-964-2480
Fax: 212-349-9160

EOS Partners, SBIC
Steven Friedman, Partner
520 Madison Ave., 42nd Floor
New York, NY 10022
212-832-5814
Fax: 212-832-5815
www.eospartners.com

Exeter Capital Lenders
Keith Fox, Manager
10 E. 53rd St.
New York, NY 10022
212-872-1170
Fax: 212-872-1198
www.exeterfunds.com

First County Capital, Inc.
Orest Glut, Financial Manager
135-14 Northern Blvd., 2nd Floor
Flushing, NY 11354

718-461-1778
Fax: 718-461-1835

Flushing Capital Corporation
Frank J. Mitchell, President
39-06 Union St., Room 202
Flushing, NY 11354
718-886-5866
Fax: 718-939-7761

Freshstart Venture Capital
Corporation
Zindel Zelmanovich, President
24-29 Jackson Ave.
Long Island City, NY 11101
718-361-9595
Fax: 718-361-8295
www.defertax.com

Fundex Capital Corp.
Larry Linksman, President
780 Third Ave., 48th Floor
New York, NY 10017
212-527-7135
Fax: 212-527-7134

Genesee Funding, Inc.
Stuart Marsh, President & CEO
70 Linden Oaks, 3rd Floor
Rochester, NY 14625
716-383-5550
Fax: 716-383-5305

Hanam Capital Corp.
Robert Schairer, President
38 W. 32nd St., Suite 1512
New York, NY 10001
212-564-5225
Fax: 212-564-5307

Hudson Venture Partners, L.P.
Lawrence Howard, Marilyn Adler

660 Madison Ave., 14th Floor
New York, NY 10022
212-644-9797
Fax: 212-583-1849

ING Furman Selz Invest
Brian Friedman, Manager
230 Park Ave.
New York, NY 10169
212-309-8348
Fax: 212-692-9147

IBJ Whitehall Capital Corp.
Pete Hardy, President
One State St., 8th Floor
New York, NY 10004
212-858-2000
Fax: 212-952-1629

Ibero American Investors Corp.
Emilio Serrano, President
104 Scio St.
Rochester, NY 14604
716-262-3440
Fax: 716-262-3441
www.iberoinvestors.com

InterEquity Capital Corporation
Irwin Schlass, President
220 Fifth Ave., 12th Floor
New York, NY 10001
212-779-2022
Fax: 212-779-2103
www.interequity-capital.com

International Paper Cap.
Formation, Inc.
(Main Office: Memphis, TN)
John Jepsen, President
Two Manhattanville Rd.
Purchase, NY 10577

914-397-1578
Fax: 914-397-1909
www.internationalpaper.com

J.P. Morgan Investment Corp.
Brian F. Watson, Managing Dir.
60 Wall St.
New York, NY 10260
212-483-2323
Fax: 212-648-5032
www.jpmorgan.com

KOCO Capital Company
Paul Echausse, President
111 Radio Circle
Mount Kisco, NY 10549
914-242-2324
Fax: 914-244-3985

M & T Capital Corp.
Tom Scanlon, President
One Fountain Plaza, 9th Floor
Buffalo, NY 14203
716-848-3800
Fax: 716-848-3150
www.mandtbank.com

LEG Partners Debenture
Lawrence Golub, Manager
230 Park Ave., 19th Floor
New York, NY 10169
212-207-1423
Fax: 212-207-1579

Medallion Funding Corporation
Alvin Murstein, President
437 Madison Ave.
New York, NY 10022
212-328-2110
Fax: 212-328-2125
www.medallionfinancial.com

Mercury Capital, L.P.
David Elenowitz, Manager
153 E. 53rd St.
New York, NY 10022
212-838-0888
Fax: 212-759-3897

NBT Capital Corporation
Daryl Forsythe and Joe Minor,
Managers
19 Eaton Ave.
Norwich, NY 13815
607-337-6810
Fax: 607-336-8730
www.nbtbank.com

NYBDC Capital Corp.
Robert W. Lazar, President
41 State St.
P.O. Box 738
Albany, NY 12207
518-463-2268
Fax: 518-463-0240
www.nybdc.com

NatWest USA Capital Corporation
Elliot Jones, President
660 Madison Ave., 14th Floor
New York, NY 10021
212-401-1330
Fax: 212-401-1390
www.natwest.com

Norwood Venture Corp.
Mark R. Littell, President
1430 Broadway, Suite 1607
New York, NY 10018
212-869-5075
Fax: 212-869-5331
www.norven.com

Needham Capital
John Michaelson, Manager
445 Park Ave.
New York, NY 10022
212-705-0297
Fax: 212-751-1450
www.needhamco.com

Paribas Principal Incorporated
Steven Alexander, President
787 Seventh Ave., 32nd Floor
New York, NY 10019-8018
212-841-2000
Fax: 212-841-3558
www.parbas.com

Pierre Funding Corp.
Elias Debbas, President
805 Third Ave., 6th Floor
New York, NY 10022
212-888-1515
Fax: 212-688-4252

Prospect Street NYC Discovery
Fund, L.P.
Richard E. Omohundro, CEO
250 Park Ave., 17th Floor
New York, NY 10177
212-448-0702
Fax: 212-448-0702
www.prospectstreet.com

Pyramid Ventures, Inc.
Brian Talbot, VP

130 Liberty St., 31st Floor
New York, NY 10006
212-250-9571
Fax: 212-250-7651
www.bankerstrust/btcapitalpartners

RBC Equity Investments
Stephen Stewart, Manager
One Liberty Plaza
New York, NY 10002
212-428-3035
Fax: 212-858-7468

Regent Capital Partners
J. Oliver Maggard, Managing Ptnr.
505 Park Ave., Suite 1700
New York, NY 10022
212-735-9900
Fax: 212-735-9908

Situation Ventures Corp.
Sam Hollander, President
56-20 59th St.
Maspeth, NY 11378
718-894-2000
Fax: 718-326-4642

Sixty Wall Street
Brian Watson, Managing Director
60 Wall St.
New York, NY 10260
212-344-7538
Fax: 212-648-5032

Societe Generale Capital Corp.
Steven Baronoff, President
1221 Ave. of the Americas, 8th Flr.
New York, NY 10020
212-278-5400
Fax: 212-278-5387
www.socgen.com

Sterling/Carl Marks Capital, Inc.
Harvey L. Granat, President
175 Great Neck Rd., Suite 408
Great Neck, NY 11021
516-482-7374
Fax: 516-487-0781

TLC Funding Corp.
Philip G. Kass, President
660 White Plains Rd.
Tarrytown, NY 10591
914-939-0518
Fax: 914-332-5660

Transportation Capital Corp.
Michael Fanger, President
437 Madison Ave.
New York, NY 10022
212-328-2110
Fax: 212-328-2125
www.medallionfinancial.com

Triad Capital Corp. of New York
Oscar Figueroa, Manager
305 Seventh Ave., 20th Floor
New York, NY 10001
212-243-7360
Fax: 212-243-7647
www.bcf-triad.org

Trusty Capital Inc.
Yungduk Hahn, President
350 Fifth Ave., Suite 2026
New York, NY 10118
212-736-7653
Fax: 212-629-3019

United Capital Investment Corp.
Paul Lee, President
60 E. 42nd St., Suite 1515
New York, NY 10165

212-682-7210
Fax: 212-573-6352

UBS Capital, II LLC
Justin S. Maccarone, President
299 Park Ave.
New York, NY 10171
212-821-6490
Fax: 212-821-6333

Venture Opportunities Corp.
A. Fred March, President
150 E. 58th St., 16th Floor
New York, NY 10155
212-832-3737
Fax: 212-980-6603

Wasserstein Adelson Ventures,
L.P.
Townsend Ziebold, Jr., Manager
31 West 52nd St., 27th Floor
New York, NY 10019
212-969-2690
Fax: 212-969-7879
www.wassersteinparilla.com

Winfield Capital Corp.
Stanley M. Pechman, President
237 Mamaroneck Ave.
White Plains, NY 10605
914-949-2600
Fax: 914-949-7195

Walden Capital Partners
John Costantino, Allen Greenberg,
Managers
150 E. 58th St., 34th Floor
New York, NY 10155
212-355-0090
Fax: 212-755-8894
www.waldencapital.com

North Carolina
BB&T Capital Partners, LLC
David Townsend and Martin
Gilmore, Managers
200 West Second St., 4th Floor
Winston-Salem, NC 27101
336-733-2420
Fax: 336-733-2419
www.bbtcapital.com

First Union Capital Partners Inc
Tracey M. Chaffin, CFO
One First Union Center, 5th Floor
301 S. College St.
Charlotte, NC 28288
704-374-4768
Fax: 704-374-6711
www.firstunion.com

Blue Ridge Investors
Edward McCarthy, Executive VP
300 N. Greene St., Suite 2100
Greensboro, NC 27401
336-370-0576
Fax: 336-274-4984

Centura SBIC, Inc.
Robert R. Anders, Jr., President
200 Providence Rd., 3rd Floor
P.O. Box 6261
Charlotte, NC 28207
704-331-1451
Fax: 704-331-1761
www.centura.com

NationsBanc SBIC Corporation
George Carter, President
Elyn Dortch, VP
101 S. Tryon St., 18th Floor
NC-1-002-18-02
Charlotte, NC 28255

704-386-7549
Fax: 704-386-1930

NationsBanc Capital Corporation
Walter W. Walker, Jr., President
100 North Tryon St., 25th Floor
NCI-007-25-02
Charlotte, NC 28255
704-386-8063
Fax: 704-388-9049
www.bankofamerica.com

Oberlin Capital
Robert Shepley, Manager
702 Oberlin Rd., Suite 150
Raleigh, NC 27605
919-743-2544
Fax: 919-743-2501

North Dakota
North Dakota SBIC, L.P.
Main Office: Cedar Rapids, IA
406 Main Ave., Suite 404
Fargo, ND 58103
701-298-0003
Fax: 701-293-7819

Ohio
Enterprise Ohio
Steven Budd, President
8 N. Main St.
Dayton, OH 45402
937-226-0457
Fax: 937-222-7035

Banc One Capital Partners Corp.
William Leahy, Managing Director
150 E. Gay St., 24th Floor
Columbus, OH 43215
614-217-1100
Fax: 614-217-1217

Financial Opportunities, Inc.
Gregg R. Budoi, Manager
300 Executive Parkway West
Hudson, OH 44236
330-342-6664
Fax: 330-342-6675

Key Equity Capital Corp.
David Given, President
127 Public Square, 28th Floor
Cleveland, OH 44114
216-689-5776
Fax: 216-689-3204

Clarion Capital Corp.
Morris H. Wheeler, President
Ohio Savings Plaza, Suite 510
1801 E. 9th St.
Cleveland, OH 44114
216-687-8941
Fax: 216-694-3545

National City Capital Corp
William H. Schecter, President &
GM
1965 E. Sixth St, Suite 1010
Cleveland, OH 44114
216-575-2491
Fax: 216-575-9965

River Cities Capital

River Cities Capital
R. Glen Mayfield, Manager
221 E. Fourth St., Suite 2250
Cincinnati, OH 45202
513-621-9700
Fax: 513-579-8939
www.rccf.com

Key Mezzanine Capital
Stephen Stewart, Manager
10th Floor, Banc One Bldg.
600 Superior Ave.
Cleveland, OH 44114
216-858-6090
Fax: 216-263-3577

Oklahoma
BancFirst Investment Corporation
T. Kent Faison, Manager
101 North Broadway
Mail: P.O. Box 26788
Oklahoma City, OK 73126
405-270-1000
Fax: 405-270-1089
www.bancfirst.com

First United Venture Capital Corp.
John Massey and Greg Massey,
Managers
1400 West Main St.
Durant, OK 74701
580-924-2256
Fax: 580-924-2228

Oregon
Northern Pacific Capital Corp.
Joseph P. Tennant, President
937 S.W. 14th St., Suite 200
P.O. Box 1658
Portland, OR 97207
503-241-1255

Shaw Venture Partners
Ralph R. Shaw, Manager
400 SW Sixth Ave., Suite 1100
Portland, OR 97204
503-228-4884
Fax: 503-227-2471
www.shawventures.com

Pennsylvania
CIP Capital, Inc.
Winston Churchill, Jr., Manager
435 Devon Park Dr., Bldg. 300
Wayne, PA 19087
610-964-7860
Fax: 610-964-8136

CEO Venture Fund
James Colker, Manager
2000 Technology Dr., Suite 160
Pittsburgh, PA 15219
412-687-0200, ext. 236
Fax: 412-687-8139
www.ceoventurefund.com

GS Capital, L.P.
Kenneth S. Choate, Managing
Director
433 Devon Park Dr., Suite 612
Wayne, PA 19087
610-293-9151
Fax: 610-293-1979

Greater Phila. Venture Capital
Corp., Inc.
Fred S. Choate, Mgr.
351 E Conestoga Rd.
Wayne, PA 19087
610-688-6829
Fax: 610-254-8958

Mellon Ventures
Lawrence Mock, Ronald Coombs,
Managers
One Mellon Bank Center
Room 3200
Pittsburgh, PA 15258
412-236-3594
Fax: 412-236-3593
www.mellon.com

Meridian Venture Partners
Raymond R. Rafferty, Gen Part
The Fidelity Court Building
259 Radnor-Chester Rd., Suite 140
Radnor, PA 19087
610-254-2999
Fax: 610-254-2996

Argosy Investment Partners
Kunte Albrecht, Manager
950 W. Valley Rd., Suite 2902
Wayne, PA 19087
610-971-0558
Fax: 610-964-9524
www.argosycapital.com

Liberty Ventures
Thomas R. Morse, Manager
The Bellevue
200 Broad St.
Philadelphia, PA 19102
215-732-4445
Fax: 215-732-4644

Puerto Rico
North American Inv. Corporation
Marcelino Pastrana Torres,
President
Mercantil Plaza Bldg.
Suite 813
P.O. Box 1831
Hato Rey, PR 00919
787-754-6178
Fax: 787-754-6181

Rhode Island
Domestic Capital Corp.
Nathaniel B. Baker, President
815 Reservoir Ave.
Cranston, RI 02910
401-946-3310

Fax: 401-943-6708
www.domesticbank.com

Fleet Equity Partners
Robert Van Degna, Habib Gorgi,
Managers
50 Kennedy Plaza, 12th Floor
Providence, RI 02903
401-278-6770
Fax: 401-278-6387
www.fleetequity.com

Liberty Ventures

Fleet Venture Resources, Inc.
Robert M. Van Degna, President
50 Kennedy Plaza, 12th Floor
Mail Stop: RI MO F12C
Providence, RI 02903
401-278-6770
Fax: 401-278-6387
www.fleetequity.com

South Carolina
Charleston Capital Corporation
Henry Yaschik, President
111 Church St.
P.O. Box 328
Charleston, SC 29402
843-723-6464
Fax: 843-723-1228

CF Investment Co.
William S. Hummers, III, Manager
102 S. Main St.
Greenville, SC 29601

864-255-4919
Fax: 864-239-6423

TransAmerica Mezzanine
John J. Sterling, President
7 N. Laurens St., Suite 603
P.O. Box 10447
Greenville, SC 29601
864-232-6198
Fax: 864-241-4444

South Dakota
Bluestem Capital Partners II, L.P.
Steve Kirby and Paul Schock,
Managers
122 South Phillips Ave., Suite 300
Sioux Falls, SD 57104
605-331-0091
Fax: 605-334-1218

Tennessee
Capital Across America
Whitney Johns and Chris Brown,
Managers
414 Union St., Suite 2025
Nashville, TN 37219
615-254-1414
Fax: 615-254-1856

Commerce Capital, L.P.
Andrew Higgins, Pres and Rudy
Ruark, V.P.
611 Commerce St., Suite 2602
Nashville, TN 37203
615-726-0202
Fax: 615-242-1407

Equitas, L.P.
D. Shannon LeRoy,
President of CGP
2000 Glen Echo Rd., Suite 100

Mail: P.O. Box 158838
Nashville, TN 37215
615-383-8673
Fax: 615-383-8693
E-mail: sleroy@equitaslp.com

International Paper Cap.
Formation, Inc.
Bob J. Higgins, VP and Controller
International Place II
6400 Poplar Ave.
Memphis, TN 38197
901-763-6282
Fax: 901-763-6076
www.internationalpaper.com

Pacific Capital, L.P.
Clay R. Caroland, III, President
3100 West End Ave.
Suite 1070
Nashville, TN 37203
615-292-3166
Fax: 615-292-8803
www.whitepine.com

Sirrom Investments, Inc.
George M. Miller, II, President
500 Church St., Suite 200
Nashville, TN 37219
615-256-0701
Fax: 615-726-1208
www.finova.org

Southern Venture Fund
Don Johnston, President
310 25th Ave., N.
Suite 103
Nashville, TN 37203
615-329-9448
Fax: 615-329-9237
www.masseyburch.com

Valley Capital Corp.
Lamar J. Partridge, President
Suite 212, Krystal Building
100 W. Martin Luther King Blvd.
Chattanooga, TN 37402
423-265-1557
Fax: 423-265-1588

West Tennessee Venture Capital
Corporation
Frank Banks, President
5 N. Third St.
Memphis, TN 38103
901-522-9237
Fax: 901-527-6091

Texas
AMT Capital, Ltd.
Tom H. Delimitros, CGP
8204 Elmbrook Dr., Suite 101
Dallas, TX 75247
214-905-9760
Fax: 214-905-9761
www.amtcapital.com

Alliance Business Investment Co.
(Main Office: Tulsa, OK)
1221 McKinney St.
Suite 3100
Houston, TX 77010
713-659-3131
Fax: 713-659-8070

Legacy Private Capital
Management
Suzanne B. Kriscunas, Managing
Director
3811 Turtle Creek Blvd.
Suite 1600
Dallas, TX 75219
214-219-0363

Fax: 214-219-0769
www.legacyfund.com

Capital Southwest Venture Corp.
William R. Thomas, President
12900 Preston Rd., Suite 700
Dallas, TX 75230
972-233-8242
Fax: 972-233-7362
www.capitalsouthwest.com

Catalyst Fund, Ltd., (The)
Richard L. Herrman, Manager
Three Riverway, Suite 770
Houston, TX 77056
713-623-8133
Fax: 713-623-0473
www.the-catalyst-group.com

Chen's Financial Group, Inc.
Samuel S. C. Chen, President
10101 Southwest Freeway
Suite 370
Houston, TX 77074
713-772-8868
Fax: 713-772-2168

First Capital Group of Texas
Messrs. Blanchard, Greenwood &
Lacy
750 E. Mulberry, Suite 305
San Antonio, TX 78212
210-736-4233
Fax: 210-736-5449
www.firstcapitalgroup.com

HCT Capital Corp.
Vichy Woodward Young, Jr., Pres.
4916 Camp Bowie Blvd.
Suite 200
Ft. Worth, TX 76107

817-763-8706
Fax: 817-377-8049

Houston Partners, SBIP
Glenda Overbeck, President, CGP
401 Louisiana, 8th Floor
Houston, TX 77002
713-222-8600
Fax: 713-222-8932
www.houstonpartners.com

Jardine Capital Corporation
Lawrence Wong, President
7322 Southwest Parkway
Suite 787
Houston, TX 77074
713-271-7077
Fax: 713-271-7577

MESBIC Ventures, Inc.
Donald R. Lawhorne, President
12655 N. Central Plaza
Suite 710
Dallas, TX 75243
972-991-1598
Fax: 972-991-1647

Mapleleaf Capital Ltd.
Patrick A. Rivelli, Manager
Three Forest Plaza, Suite 935
12221 Merit Dr.
Dallas, TX 75251

972-239-5650
Fax: 972-701-0024

NationsBanc Capital Corporation
(Main Office: Charlotte, NC)
901 Main St., 66th Floor
Dallas, TX 75202
214-508-0932
Fax: 214-508-0985

North Texas MESBIC, Inc.
Allan Lee, President
9500 Forest Lane, Suite 430
Dallas, TX 75243
214-221-3565
Fax: 214-221-3566

PMC Investment Corporation
Andrew S. Rosemore, President
18111 Preston Rd., Suite 600
Dallas, TX 75252
972-349-3200
Fax: 972-349-3265
www.pmccapital.com

Retail and Restaurant Growth
Capital, L.P.
Raymond Hemmig, Joseph
Harberg, Managers
10000 N. Central Expressway,
Suite 1060
Dallas, TX 75231
214-750-0065
Fax: 214-750-0060
www.rrgcsbic.com

SBIC Partners
Gregory Forsot and Jeffrey Brown,
Managers
201 Main St., Suite 2302
Fort Worth, TX 76102

949-729-3222
Fax: 949-729-3226

SBIC Partners II, L.P.
Nicholas Binkley and Gregory
Forrest, Managers
201 Main St., Suite 2302
Fort Worth, TX 76102
817-339-7020
Fax: 817-338-2047

Southwest/Catalyst Capital, Ltd.
Ronald Nixon and Rick Herrman,
Managers
Three Riverway
Suite 770
Houston, TX 77056
713-623-8133
Fax: 713-623-0473
www.the-catalyst-group.com

Stratford Capital
Michael Brown, John Fannin,
Darin Winn
200 Crescent Court
Suite 1650
Dallas, TX 75201
214-740-7377
Fax: 214-740-7340

United Oriental Capital Corp.
Jai Min Tai, President
908 Town and Country Blvd.
Suite 310
Houston, TX 77024
713-461-3909
Fax: 713-465-7559

Victoria Capital Corp.
Steve Selinske, Acting President
16416 San Pedro

San Antonio, TX 78232
210-856-4468
Fax: 210-856-8848

Western Financial Capital Corp.
Andrew S. Rosemore, President
17290 Preston Rd., Suite 600
Dallas, TX 75252
972-349-3200
Fax: 972-349-3265
www.pmccapital.com

Utah
First Security Business Investment
Corporation
Louis D. Alder, Manager
15 East 100 South, Suite 100
Salt Lake City, UT 84111
801-246-5737
Fax: 801-246-5740
www.firstsecurity.com

STRATfORd CApiTAl

Utah Ventures II L.P.
Alan Dishlip and James Dreyfous,
Managers
423 Wakara Way
Suite 206
Salt Lake City, UT 84108
801-583-5922
Fax: 801-583-4105

Wasatch Venture Corporation
Todd J. Stevens, Secretary
1 South Main St.
Suite 1400

Salt Lake City, UT 84133
801-524-8939
Fax: 801-524-8941
www.wasatchvc.com

Vermont
Green Mountain Capital, L.P.
Michael Sweatman, General
Manager
RR1 Box 1503
Waterbury, VT 05676
802-244-8981
Fax: 802-244-8990
E-mail: ims@gmtcap.com

Virginia
Continental SBIC
Arthur Walters, President
4141 N. Henderson Rd., Suite 8
Arlington, VA 22203
703-527-5200
Fax: 703-527-3700

East West United Investment
Company
Dung Bui, President
1568 Spring Hill Rd.
Suite 100
McLean, VA 22102
703-442-0150
Fax: 703-442-0156
www.ewmortgage.com

Virginia Capital SBIC
Frederick Russell, Tom Deardorff,
Managers
9 S. 12th St., Suite 400
Richmond, VA 23219

Waterside Capital Corp.
Alan Lindower, President

300 E. Main St.
Suite 1380
Norfolk, VA 23510
757-626-1111
Fax: 757-626-0114
www.watersidecapital.com

Walnut Capital Corp.
(Main Office: Chicago, IL)
8000 Tower Crescent Dr.
Suite 1070
Vienna, VA 22182
703-448-3771
Fax: 703-448-7751

Washington
Northwest Venture Partners II, L.P.
Thomas Simpson and Jean Balek-
Miner, Managers
221 North Wall St., Suite 628
Spokane, WA 99201
509-747-0728
Fax: 509-747-0758
www.nwva.com

Pacific Northwest Partners SBIC,
L.P.
Theodore M. Wight, Manager
305 - 108th Ave. NE, 2nd Floor
Bellevue, WA 98004
425-455-9967
Fax: 425-455-9404
www.pnwp.com

West Virginia
Shenandoah Venture Capital L.P.
Thomas E. Loehr, President
208 Capital St., Suite 300
Charleston, WV 25301
304-344-1796
Fax: 304-344-1798

WestVen Limited Partnership
Thomas E. Loehr, President
208 Capitol St., Suite 300
Charleston, WV 25301
304-344-1794
Fax: 304-344-1798

Whitney Capital Corporation
Thomas Loehr, Manager
707 Virginia St., East, Suite 1700
Charleston, WV 25301
304-345-2480
Fax: 304-345-7258

Wisconsin
Capital Investments, Inc.
Steve Ripple, Executive VP
1009 W. Glen Oaks Ln., Suite 103
Mequon, WI 53092
414-241-0303
Fax: 414-241-8451
www.capitalinvestmentsinc.com

Future Value Ventures, Inc.
William P. Beckett, President
2821 N. 4th St., Suite 526
Milwaukee, WI 53212
414-264-2252
Fax: 414-264-2253

M & I Ventures L.L.C.
John T. Byrnes, President
770 North Water St.
Milwaukee, WI 53202
414-765-7910
Fax: 414-765-7850
www.masonwells.com

MorAmerica Capital Corporation
(Main Office: Cedar Rapids, IA)
600 East Mason St.
Suite 304
Milwaukee, WI 53202
414-276-3839
Fax: 414-276-1885

Government Contracts: How to Sell Your Goods and Services To The World's Largest Buyer

If you produce a product or service, you've probably always wondered how you could offer what you produce to the biggest client in the world — the Federal government. Have you thought of the government as being a "closed shop" and too difficult to penetrate? Well, I'm happy to say that you're entirely wrong on that score. The Federal government spends over $180 billion each year on products ranging from toilet paper to paper clips and writes millions of dollars in contracts for services like advertising, consulting, and printing. Most Americans believe that a majority of those federal purchasing contracts have been eliminated over the last few years, but that's simply not true — they've just been replaced with new contracts that are looking for the same kinds of goods and services. Last year the government took action (either initiating or modifying) on over 350,000 different contracts. They buy these goods and services from someone, so why shouldn't that someone be you? To be successful doing business with the government, you need to learn to speak "governmenteze" to get your company into the purchasing loop, and I can show you how to accomplish that in just a few easy steps.

Step 1

Each department within the Federal government has a procurement office that buys whatever the department requires.

Most of these offices have put together their own *Doing Business With the Department of* _____ publication, which usually explains procurement policies, procedures, and programs. This booklet also contains a list of procurement offices, contact people,

> *Doing Business With the Department of* _____

subcontracting opportunities, and a solicitation mailing list. Within each department there is also an Office of Small and Disadvantaged Business Utilization, whose sole purpose is to push the interests of the small business, and to make sure these companies get their fair share of government contracts. Another good resource is your local Small Business Administration Office that should have a listing of U.S. Government Procurement Offices in your state.

Step 2

Once you have familiarized yourself with the process, you need to find out who is buying what from whom and for how much. There are three ways to get this important information.

A. Daily Procurement News

Each weekday, the *Commerce Business Daily* (CBD) gives a complete listing of products and services (that cost over $25,000) wanted by the U.S. government — products and services that your business may be selling. Each listing includes the following: the product or service, along with a short description; name and address of the agency; deadline for proposals or bids; phone number to request specifications; and the solicitation number of the product or service needed. Many business concerns, including small businesses, incorporate CBD review into their government marketing activities. To obtain a subscription for $275 a year, contact: Superintendent of Documents, U.S. Government Printing Office, Washington, DC 20402; 202-512-1800; {www.gpo.gov}.

B. Federal Data Systems Division (FDSD)

This Center distributes consolidated information about federal purchases, including research and development. FDSD can tell you how much the Federal government spent last quarter on products and services, which agencies made those purchases, and what contractors did business with the government. FDSD summarizes this information through two types of reports: The FDSD standard report and the FDSD special report. The standard report is a free, quarterly compilation containing statistical procurement information in "snapshot" form for over 60 federal agencies, as well as several charts, graphs, and tables which compare procurement activities by state, major product and service codes, method of

procurement, and contractors. The report also includes quarterly and year-to-year breakdowns of amounts and percentages spent on small, women owned, and minority businesses. Special reports are prepared upon request for a fee, based on computer and labor costs. They are tailored to the specific categories, which can be cross-tabulated in numerous ways. A special report can help you analyze government procurement and data trends, identify competitors, and locate federal markets for individual products or services. Your Congressman may have access to the Federal Procurement Database from his/her office in Washington, which you may be able to use for free. For more information, contact: Federal Data Systems Division, General Services Administration, 7th and D St., SW, Room 5652, Washington, DC 20407; 202-401-1529.

C. Other Contracts

For contracts under $25,000, you must be placed on a department's list for solicitation bids on those contracts. The mailing list forms are available through the Procurement Office, the Office of Small and Disadvantaged Business Utilization, or your local Small Business Association office. Last year 18.7 billion dollars was spent on these "small" purchases, so these contracts should not be overlooked. Smaller contracts, completed over the course of a fiscal year, can mean lots of revenue for your business bottom line.

Step 3: Subcontracting Opportunities

All of the federal procurement offices or Offices of Small and Disadvantaged Business Utilization (SDBU) can provide you with information regarding subcontracting. Many of the departments' prime contracts require that the prime contractor maximize small business subcontracting opportunities. Many prime contractors produce special publications, which can be helpful to those, interested in subcontracting.

Small Business Administration 1-800-827-5722

The SDBU Office can provide you with more information on the subcontracting process, along with a directory of prime contractors. Another good source for subcontract assistance is your local Small Business Administration (SBA) office, 1-800-827-5722. SBA develops subcontracting opportunities for small business by maintaining close contact with large business prime contractors and by referring qualified small firms to them. The SBA has developed agreements and close working relationships with hundreds of prime contractors who cooperate by offering small firms the opportunity to compete for their subcontracts. In addition, to complete SBA's compliance responsibilities, commercial market representatives monitor prime contractors in order to assess their compliance with laws governing subcontracting opportunities for small businesses.

Step 4: Small Business Administration's 8(a) Program

Are you a socially or economically disadvantaged person who has a business? This group includes, but is not limited to, Black Americans, Hispanic Americans, Native Americans, Asian Pacific Americans, and Subcontinent Asian Americans. Socially and economically disadvantaged individuals represent a significant percentage of U.S. citizens, yet account for a disproportionately small percentage of total U.S. business revenues. The 8(a) program assists firms in participating in the business sector and to become independently competitive in the marketplace. SBA may provide participating firms with procurement, marketing, financial, management, or other technical assistance. A Business Opportunity Specialist will be assigned to each firm that participates, and is responsible for providing the firm with access to assistance that can help the firm fulfill its business goals. SBA undertakes an extensive effort to provide government contracting opportunities to participating businesses.

The SBA has the Procurement Automated Source System (PASS) which places your company's capabilities online so that they may be available to government agencies and major corporations when they request potential bidders for contracts and subcontracts. To apply for the 8(a) program, you must attend an interview session with an official in the SBA field office in your area. For more information, contact your local Small Business Administration Office, or call 1-800-827-5722, or [www.sba.gov] for the SBA office nearest you.

Step 5: Bond

A Surety bond is often a prerequisite for government and private sector contracts. This is particularly true when the contract involves construction. In order for the company to qualify for an SBA Guarantee Bond, they must make the bonding company aware of their capabilities based on past contract performance and meeting of financial obligations. SBA can assist firms in obtaining surety bonding for contracts that do not exceed $1,250,000. SBA is authorized, when appropriate circumstances occur, to guarantee as much as 90 percent of losses suffered by a surety resulting from a breach of terms of a bond.

Step 6: Publications

The Government Printing Office has several publications for sale which explain the world of government contracts. For ordering information, contact Superintendent of Documents, Government Printing Office, Washington, DC 20402; 202-512-1800; {www.gpo.gov}.

◆ *U.S. Government Purchasing and Sales Directory* ($25): The Directory is an alphabetical listing of the products and services bought by the military departments, and a separate listing of the civilian agencies. The Directory also includes an explanation of the ways in which the SBA can help a business obtain government prime contracts and subcontracts, data on government sales of surplus property, and comprehensive descriptions of the scope of the government market for research and development.

♦ *Selling to the Military* ($14.00)

♦ *Women Business Owners; Selling to the Federal Government* ($3.75)

♦ *Subcontracting Opportunities with DOD Major Prime Contractors* ($23.00)

Step 7: What is GSA?

General Services Administration (GSA) is the Government's business agent. On an annual budget of less than half a billion dollars, it directs and coordinates nearly $8 billion a year worth of purchases, sales, and services. Its source of supply is private enterprise, and its clients include all branches of the Federal government. GSA plans and manages leasing, purchase, or construction of office buildings, laboratories, and warehouses; buys and delivers nearly $4 billion worth of goods and services; negotiates the prices and terms for an additional $2.3 billion worth of direct business between federal groups and private industry; sets and interprets the rules for federal travel and negotiates reduced fares and lodging rates for federal travelers; and manages a 92,000 vehicle fleet with a cumulative yearly mileage of over 1 billion.

For a copy of *Doing Business With GSA, GSA's Annual Report*, or other information regarding GSA, contact: Office of Publication, General Services Administration, 18th and F Streets, NW, Washington, DC 20405; 202-501-1235. For information on GSA's architect and engineer services, such as who is eligible for GSA professional services contracts, how to find out about potential GSA projects, what types of contracts are available, and where and how to apply, contact: Office of Design and Construct)on, GSA, 18th and F Streets, NW, Washington, DC 20405; 202-501-1888. Information on specifications and standards of the Federal government is contained in a booklet, *Guide to Specifications and Standards*, which is available free from Specifications Sections, General

Services Administration, 470 E L'Enfant Plaza, SW, Suite 8100, Washington, DC 20407; 202-619-8925.

Step 8: Bid and Contract Protests

The General Accounting Office (GAO) resolves disputes between agencies and bidders of government contracts, including grantee award actions. The free publication, *Bid Protests at GAO; A Descriptive Guide*, contains information on GAO's procedures for determining legal questions arising from the awarding of government contracts. Contact Information Handling and Support Facilities, General Accounting Office, Gaithersburg, MD 20877; 202-512-6000.

For Contract Appeals, the GSA Board of Contract Appeals works to resolve disputes arising out of contracts with GSA, the Departments of Treasury, Education, Commerce, and other independent government agencies. The Board also hears and decides bid protests arising out of government-wide automated data processing (ADP) procurements. A contractor may elect to use either the GSA Board or the General Accounting Office for resolution of an ADP bid protest. Contractors may elect to have their appeals processed under the Board's accelerated procedures if the claim is $50,000 or less, or under the small claims procedure if the claim is $10,000 or less. Contractors may also request that a hearing be held at a location convenient to them. With the exception of small claims decisions, contractors can appeal adverse Board decisions to the U.S. Court of Appeals for the Federal Circuit.

For more information, contact: Board of Contract Appeals, General Services Administration, 18th and F Streets, NW, Washington, DC 20405; 202-501-0720. There are other Contract Appeals Boards for other departments. One of the last paragraphs in your government contract should specify which Board you are to go to if a problem with your particular contract should arise.

Free Local Help: The Best Place To Start To Sell To The Government

Within each state there are offices that can help you get started in the federal procurement process. As stated previously, your local Small Business Administration (SBA) office is a good resource. In addition to their other services, the SBA can provide you with a list of Federal Procurement Offices based in your state, so  you can visit them in person to gather valuable information. Another place to turn is your local Small Business Development Center (look under Economic Development in your phone book). These offices are funded jointly by federal and state governments, and are usually associated with the state university system in your area. They are aware of the federal procurement process, and can help you draw up a sensible business plan that will be successful.

Some states have established programs to assist businesses in the federal procurement process for all departments in the government. These programs are designed to help businesses learn about the bidding process, the resources available, and provide information on how the procurement system operates. They can match the product or service you are selling with the appropriate agency, and then help you market your product. Several programs have online bid matching services, whereby if a solicitation appears in the *Commerce Business Daily* that matches what your company markets, then the program will automatically contact you to start the bid process. The program office can then request the appropriate documents, and assist you in achieving your goal. These Procurement Assistance Offices (PAOs) are partially funded by the Department of Defense to assist businesses with Defense Procurement. For a current listing of PAOs contact:

Defense Logistics Agency
Office of Small and Disadvantaged Utilization
Bldg. 4, Cameron Station, Room 4B110
Alexandria, VA 22304-6100
703-767-1661
{www.dla.mil}, then go to the small business site

Let Your Congressman Help You

Are you trying to market a new product to a department of the Federal government? Need to know where to try to sell your wares? Is there some problem with your bid? Your Congressman can be of assistance. Because they want business in their state to boom, most Congressmen will make an effort to assist companies in obtaining federal contracts. Frequently they will write a letter to accompany your bid, or if you are trying to market a new product, they will write a letter to the procurement office requesting that they review your product. Your Congressman can also be your personal troubleshooter. If there is some problem with your bid, your

Congressman can assist you in determining and resolving the problem, and can provide you with information on the status of your bid. Look in the blue pages of your phone book for your Senators' or Representatives' phone numbers, or call them in Washington at 202-224-3121.

Small Business Set-Asides

The Small Business Administration (SBA) encourages government purchasing agencies to set aside suitable government purchases for exclusive small business competition. A purchase which is restricted to small business bidders is identified by a set aside clause in the invitation  for bids or request for proposals. There is no overall listing of procurements that are, or have been, set aside for small business. A small business learns which purchases are reserved for small business by getting listed on bidders' lists. It also can help keep itself informed of set aside opportunities by referring to the *Commerce Business Daily*. Your local SBA office can provide you with more information on set asides, and so can the Procurement Assistance Offices listed at the end of this section. To locate your nearest SBA office, call 1-800-827-5722 or {www.sba.gov}.

Veterans Assistance

Each Small Business Administration District Office has a Veterans Affairs Officer that can assist veteran-owned businesses in obtaining government contracts. Although there is no such thing as veterans set aside contracts, the

Veterans Administration does make an effort to fill its
contracts using veteran-owned businesses whenever possible.
Contact your local SBA office for more information.

Woman-Owned Business Assistance

There are over 3.7 million women-owned businesses in the
United States, and the number is growing each year. Current
government policy requires federal contracting officers to increase their purchases from women-owned businesses.
Although the women-owned firms will receive more opportunities to bid, they still must be the lowest responsive and
responsible bidder to win the contract. To assist these
businesses, each SBA district office has a Women's Business
Representative, who can provide you with information
regarding government programs. Most of the offices hold a
Selling to the Federal Government seminar, which is
designed to educate the business owner on the ins and outs of
government procurement. There is also a helpful publication,
*Women Business Owners: Selling to the Federal
Government*, which provides information on procurement
opportunities available. Contact your local SBA office or
your Procurement Assistance Office (listed below) for more
information.

Minority and Labor Surplus Area Assistance

Are you a socially or economically disadvantaged person
who has a business? This group includes, but is not limited
to, Black Americans, Hispanic Americans, Native
Americans, Asian Pacific Americans, and Subcontinent

Asian Americans. Socially and economically disadvantaged individuals represent a significant percentage of U.S. citizens yet account for a disproportionately small percentage of total U.S. business revenues. The 8(a) program assists firms to participate in the business sector and to become independently competitive in the marketplace. SBA may provide participating firms with procurement, marketing, financial, management, or other technical assistance. A Business Opportunity Specialist will be assigned to each firm that participates, and is responsible for providing that company with access to assistance that can help it fulfill its business goals.

Some areas of the country have been determined to be labor surplus areas, which means there is a high rate of unemployment. Your local SBA office can tell you if you live in such an area, as some contracts are set-asides for labor surplus areas. For more information, contact your local Small Business Administration office (call 1-800-827-5722 for the SBA office nearest you; or online at {www.sba.gov}), or call the Procurement Assistance Office in your state (listed below).

Federal Procurement Assistance Offices

Alabama
Charles A. Hopson
University of Alabama at
Birmingham

1717 11th Ave., S, Suite 419
Birmingham, AL 35294-4410
205-934-7260
Fax: 205-934-7645

Alaska
Mike Taylor
University of Alaska Anchorage
Small Business Development
Center
430 W. 7th Ave., Suite 100
Anchorage, AK 99501-3550
907-274-7232
Fax: 907-274-9524

Arizona
Linda Alexius Hagerty
The National Center for AIED
National Center Headquarters
953 E. Juanita Ave.
Mesa, AZ 85204
602-545-1298
Fax: 602-545-4208

Paul R. Roddy
Aptan, Inc.
1435 N. Hayden Rd.
Scottsdale, AZ 85257-3773
602-945-5452
Fax: 602-945-4153
E-mail: aptan@pnmenet.com
www.aptan.com

Arkansas
Toni Tosch
Board of Trustees
University of Arkansas
Cooperative Extension Service
103 Page
Malvern, AR 72104
501-337-5355
Fax: 501-337-5045
E-mail: info@apacua.org
www.apacua.org

California
Lane Stafford
Riverside Community College
District
3985 University Ave.
Riverside, CA 92501-3256
909-684-8469
Fax: 909-684-8369
E-mail: stafford@rccd.cc.ca.us
www.rccd.resources4u.com/pac/

Jane E. McGinnis
Action Business Center
California Central Valley PTAC
3180 Collins Dr., Suite A
Merced, CA 95348
209-385-7686
Fax: 209-383-4959
E-mail: cpc@cell2000.net
www.cell2000.net/cpc

J. Gunnar Schalin
Southwestern Community College
Contracting Opportunities Center
3443 Camino Del Rio South
Suite 116
San Diego, CA 92108-3913
619-285-7020
Fax: 619-285-7030
E-mail: sdcoc@pacbell.net
http://home.pacbell.net/sdcoc

Colorado
No PTA awarded

Connecticut
Arlene M. Vogel
Southeastern Connecticut
Enterprise Region (seCTer)
190 Governor Winthrop Blvd

Suite 300
New London, CT 06320
860-701-6056
1-888-6-SECTER
Fax: 860-437-4662
E-mail: avogel@secter.org
www.secter.org/cptap/main.htm

Delaware
No PTA awarded

District of Columbia
No PTA awarded

Florida
Laura Subel
University of West Florida
Florida PTA Program
19 W. Garden St., Suite 300
Pensacola, FL 32501
850-595-6066
Fax: 850-595-6070

Georgia
Zack Osborne
Georgia Technical Research Corp.
GA Institute of Technology
400 Tenth St.
CRB Room 246
Atlanta, GA 30332-0420
912-953-1460
Fax: 912-953-3169

Hawaii
No PTA awarded

Idaho
Larry Demirelli
Idaho Department of Commerce
State of Idaho
700 West State St.

Boise, ID 83720-0093
208-334-2470
Fax: 208-334-2631

PROCUREMENT CENTERS

Illinois
D. Lorenzo Padron
Latin American Chamber of
Commerce
The Chicago Pac
2539 N. Kedzie Ave.
Chicago, IL 60647
773-252-5211
Fax: 773-252-7065
www.lacc1.com

Lois Van Meter
State of Illinois
Department of Commerce and
Community Affairs
620 E. Adams St., Third Floor
Springfield, IL 62701
217-557-1823
Fax: 217-785-6328
E-mail: ivanmete@commerce.
state.il.us
www.commerce.state.il.us

Indiana
Kathy DeGuilio-Fox
Partners in Contracting Corporation
PTA Center
6100 Southport Rd.
Portage, IN 46368
219-762-8644
Fax: 219-763-1513

A. David Schaaf
Indiana Small Business
Development Corporation
Government Marketing Assistance
Group
One N. Capitol Ave., Suite 1275
Indianapolis, IN 46204-2026
317-264-5600
Fax: 317-264-2806
www.isbdcorp.org

Iowa
Bruce Coney
State of Iowa
Iowa Department of Economic
Development
200 E. Grand Ave.
Des Moines, IA 50309
515-242-4888
Fax: 515-242-4893
E-mail: bruce.coney@ided.
state.ia.us
www.state.ia.us/sbro/ptac.htm

Kentucky
James A. Kurz
Kentucky Cabinet For Economic
Development
Department of Community
Development

500 Mero St.
22nd Floor Cap Plaza Tower
Frankfort, KY 40601
800-838-3266
Fax: 502-564-5932
E-mail: jkurz@mail.state.ky.us
www.state.ky.us/edc/kpp.htm

Louisiana
Sherrie Mullins
Louisiana Productivity Center
University of Southwest Louisiana
P.O. Box 44172
241 E. Lewis St.
Lafayette, LA 70504-4172
318-482-6767
Fax: 318-262-5472
E-mail: sbm3321@usl.edu

Kelly Ford
Northwest Louisiana Government
Procurement Center
Shreveport COC
400 Edwards St.
P.O. Box 20074
Shreveport, LA 71120-0074
318-677-2529
Fax: 318-677-2534
E-mail: kmford@iamenca.net

Maine
Michael Robinson
Eastern Maine Development Corp.
Market Development Center
One Cumberland Pl., Suite 300
P.O. Box 2579
Bangor, ME 04402-2579
207-942-6389
Fax: 207-942-3548
E-mail: mrobinson@emdc.org
www.mdcme.org

Information USA, Inc.

Maryland
Michael J. Wagoner, Inc.
Tri County Council For Western
Maryland
111 S. George St.
Cumberland, MD 21502
301-777-2158
Fax: 301-777-2495

Massachusetts
No PTA awarded

Michigan
Sheila A. Auten
Genesee County Metropolitan
Planning Commission
PTA Center
1101 Beach St., Room 223
Flint, MI 48502-1470
810-257-3010
Fax: 810-257-3185

Amy Reid
Schoolcraft College
18600 Haggerty Rd.
Livonia, MI 48152-2696
734-462-4400, ext. 5309
Fax: 734-462-4439
E-mail: 2382@softshare.com
www.schoolcraft.cc.mi.us

Michael Black
Kalamazoo Chamber of Commerce
SW & NE Michigan Technical
Assistance Center
346 W. Michigan Ave.
Kalamazoo, MI 49007-3737
616-381-2977, ext. 3242
Fax: 616-343-1151
E-mail: swmitac@iserv.net

Paula Boase
Downriver Community Conference
Economic Development
15100 Northline
Southgate, MI 48195
734-281-0700, ext. 129
Fax: 734-281-3418

Janet E. Masi
Warren, Center Line
Sterling Heights Chamber of
Commerce
30500 Van Dyke Ave., Suite 118
Warren, MI 48093
810-751-3939
Fax: 810-751-3995
E-mail: jmasi@wcschamber.com
www.michigantac.org

Pamela Vanderlaan
West Central Michigan
Employment and Training
Consortium
PTA Center
110 Elm St.
Big Rapids, MI 49307
616-796-4891
Fax: 616-796-8316

James F. Haslinger
Northwestern Michigan Council of
Governments
PTA Center
P.O. Box 506
2194 Dendrinos Dr.

Traverse City, MI 49685-0506
616-929-5036
Fax: 616-929-5012

Minnesota
George Johnson
Minnesota Project Innovation, Inc.
Procurement Technical Assistance
Center
100 Mill Place
Suite 100, 111 Third Ave. South
Minneapolis, MN 55401-2551
612-347-6745
Fax: 612-349-2603
E-mail: gjohnson@mpi.org
www.mpi.org

Project Innovation

Mississippi
Richard L. Speights
Mississippi Contract Procurement
Center, Inc.
1636 Poppsferry Rd., Suite 229
Biloxi, MS 39532
228-396-1288
Fax: 228-396-2520
E-mail: mprogoff@aol.com
www.mscpc.com

Missouri
Morris Hudson
The Curators of University of
Missouri
Outreach & University Extension
310 Jesse Hall
Columbia, MO 65211

573-882-3597
Fax: 573-884-4297

Guy M. Thomas
Missouri Southern State College
3950 E. Newman Rd.
Joplin, MO 64801-1595
417-625-3001
Fax: 417-625-9782

Montana
James Ouldhouse
Big Sky Economic Development
Authority
2722 Third Ave., North
Suite 300 West
Billings, MT 59101-1931
406-256-6871
Fax: 406-256-6877
E-mail: jewell@bigskyeda.org
E-mail: ouldhouse@bigskyeda.org

Nebraska
Jerry Dalton
Board of Regents of the University
of Nebraska
Nebraska Business Development
Center
1313 Farnam St., Suite 132
Omaha, NE 68182-0210
402-595-3511
Fax: 402-595-3832

Nevada
Roger Tokarz
State of Nevada
Commission on Economic
Development
5151 S. Carson St.
Carson City, NV 89701
702-687-1813
Fax: 702-687-4450

New Hampshire
Joseph Flynn
State of New Hampshire
Office of Business and Industrial
Development
P.O. Box 1856
172 Pembroke Rd.
Concord, NH 03302-1856
603-271-2591
Fax: 603-271-6784
E-mail: j-flynn@drred.state.nh.us
www.ded.state.nh.us/obid/ptac

New Jersey
John Fedkenheuer
County Economic Development
Corp.
PTA Program
1085 Morris Ave., Suite 531
Lib Hall Center
Union, NJ 07083
908-527-1166
Fax: 908-527-1207

Dolcey Chaplin
Foundation At New Jersey Institute
of Technology (NJIT)
PTA Center
University Heights
Newark, NJ 07102
973-596-3105
Fax: 973-596-5806
E-mail: chaplin@admin.njit.edu
www.nyit.edu/DPTAC

New Mexico
Charles Marquez
State of New Mexico General
Services Department
Procurement Assistance Program
1100 St. Francis Dr., Room 2006

Santa Fe, NM 87503
505-827-0425
Fax: 505-827-0499
E-mail: cmarquez@state.nm.us

New York
Keith Cook
South Bronx Overall Economic
Development Corporation
370 E. 149th St.
Bronx, NY 10455
718-292-3113
Fax: 718-292-3115

Thomas M. Livak
Cattaraugus County
Department of Economic
Development
Plan and Tour
303 Court St.
Little Valley, NY 14755
716-938-9111
Fax: 716-938-9431

Solomon Soskin
Long Island Development
Corporation
PTA Program
255 Executive Dr.
Plainview, NY 11803
516-349-7800
Fax: 516-349-7881
E-mail: gov_contracts@lidc.org
www.lidc.org

Gordon Richards
New York City Dept. of Business
Services
Procurement Outreach Program
110 William St., 2nd Floor
New York, NY 10038

212-513-6472
Fax: 212-618-8899

Roberta J. Rodriquez
Rockland Economic Development
Corporation
Procurement
One Blue Hill Plaza, Suite 1110
Pearl River, NY 10965-1575
914-735-7040
Fax: 914-735-5736

North Carolina
Robert Truex
University of North Carolina at
Chapel Hill
Small Business and Tech
Development Center
Room 300, Bynum Hall
Chapel Hill, NC 27599-4100
919-715-7272
Fax: 919-715-7777
E-mail: rtruex@sbtdc.org

North Dakota
No PTA awarded

Ohio
Caretha Brown-Griffin
Community Improvement
Corporation of Lake County Ohio
NE Ohio Government Contract
Assistance Center Lake Erie
391-W. Washington College

Painesville, OH 44077
440-357-2294
Fax: 440-357-2296
E-mail: neogcac@lcedc.org

Connie S. Freeman
Lawrence Economic Development
Corporation
Procure Outreach Center
216 Collins Ave.
P.O. Box 488
South Point, OH 45680-0488
740-377-4550
Fax: 740-377-2091
E-mail: procure@zoomnet.net
www.zoomnet.net/~procure/

Oklahoma
C.L. Vache
Oklahoma Dept. of Vocational and
Technical Education
Oklahoma Bid Assistance Network
1500 W. Seventh Ave.
Stillwater, OK 74074-4364
405-743-5571
Fax: 405-743-6821

Roy Robert Gann, Jr.
Tribal Government Institute
421 E. Comanche, Suite B
Norman, OK 73071
405-329-5542
Fax: 405-329-5543

Oregon
Jan Hurt
The Organization for Economic
Initiatives
Government Contract Acquisition
Program
99 W. 10th Ave., Suite 330

Eugene, OR 97401
541-344-3537
Fax: 541-687-4899

Pennsylvania
Joseph E. Hopkins
Mon-Valley Renaissance
CA University of Pennsylvania
250 University Ave.
California, PA 15419
724-938-5881
Fax: 724-938-4575
E-mail: wojak@cup.edu

Richard A. Mihalic
NW Pennsylvania Regional
Planning and Development
Commission
614 Eleventh St.
Franklin, PA 16323
814-677-4800
Fax: 814-677-7663
E-mail: nwpaptac@nwpian.org

Chuck Burtyk
PIC of Westmoreland/Fayette, Inc.
Procurement Assistance Center
531 S. Main St.
Greensburg, PA 15601
724-836-2600
Fax: 724-836-8058
E-mail: cburtyk@sgi.net

Robert J. Murphy
Johnstown Area Regional
Industries
Defense PAC
111 Market St.
Johnstown, PA 15901
814-539-4951
Fax: 814-535-8677

A. Lawrence Barletta
Seda Council of Governments
RR 1, Box 372
Lewisburg, PA 17837
570-524-4491
Fax: 570-524-9190
E-mail: sedapta@seda.cog.org
www.seda.cog.org

Thomas E. Wren
University of Pennsylvania-
Wharton
SE-PA PTAP, 3733 Spruce St.
Vance Hall, 4th Floor
Philadelphia, PA 19104-6374
215-898-1282
Fax: 215-573-2135

David Kern
Economic Development Council of
Northeast Pennsylvania
Local Development District
1151 Oak St.
Pittston, PA 18640
570-655-5581
Fax: 570-654-5137

Kerry A. Meehan
Northern Tier Regional Planning
and Development Commission
Economic/Community
Development
507 Main St.
Towanda, PA 18848-1697
570-265-9103
Fax: 570-265-7585
E-mail: meehan@northerntier.org
www.northerntier.org

Millicent Brown
West Chester University

Procurement Assistance Center
211 Carter Dr., Suite E
West Chester, PA 19383
610-436-3337
Fax: 610-436-2593
pac.btcwcu.org

Puerto Rico
Wilson Baez
Commonwealth of Puerto Rico
Economic Development
Administration
355 Roosevelt Ave.
Hato Rey, PR 00918
787-753-6861
Fax: 787-751-6239

Rhode Island
Michael H. Cunningham
Rhode Island Development
Corporation
Business Expansion Division
One W. Exchange St.
Providence, RI 02903
401-277-2601
Fax: 401-277-2102
E-mail: mcunning@riedc.com

Bid Assistance

South Carolina
John M. Lenti
University of South Carolina
Frank L. Roddey SBDC of South
Carolina
College of Business Administration
Columbia, SC 29208
803-777-4907
Fax: 803-777-4403

South Dakota
No PTA awarded

Tennessee
Becky Peterson
Center for Industrial Services
University of Tennessee
226 Capitol Blvd., Suite 606
Nashville, TN 37219-1804
615-532-4906
Fax: 615-532-4937

Texas
Doug Nelson
Panhandle Regional Planning
Commission
Economic Development Unit
P.O. Box 9257
Amarillo, TX 79105-9257
806-372-3381
Fax: 806-373-3268

Rogerio Flores
University of Texas at Arlington
Automation and Robotics Research
Institute
Office of President
Box 19125
Arlington, TX 76019
817-272-5978
Fax: 817-272-5952

Rosalie Manzano
University of Texas at Brownsville
ITSC
Center for Business and Economic
Development
1600 E. Elizabeth St.
Brownsville, TX 78520
956-548-8713
Fax: 956-548-8717

Carey Joan White
University of Houston, TIPS
1100 Louisiana, Suite 500
Houston, TX 77204
713-752-8466
Fax: 713-756-1515

Otilo Castellano
Texas Technical University
College of Business Administration
203 Holder
Lubbock, TX 79409-1035
806-745-1637
Fax: 806-745-6207

Thomas E. Breuer, Jr.
Angelina College
Procurement Assistance Center
P.O. Box 1768
Lufkin, TX 75902-1768
409-639-3678
Fax: 409-639-3863
E-mail: acpac@lcc.net
www.oecrc.org/acpac/

Terri L. Williams
San Antonio Procurement Outreach
Program
Economic Development
Department
P.O. Box 839966
San Antonio, TX 78283
210-207-3910
Fax: 210-207-3909

Frank Delgado
El Paso Community College
Resource Development
P.O. Box 20500
El Paso, TX 79998

915-831-4405
Fax: 915-831-4420

Utah
Johnny C. Bryan
Utah Department of Community
and Economic Development
Utah Procurement Technical
Assistance Center (UPTAC)
324 South State St., Suite 504
Salt Lake City, UT 84111
801-538-8791
Fax: 801-538-8825

Vermont
Greg Lawson
State of Vermont
Department of Economic
Development
109 State St.
Montpelier, VT 05609
802-828-5237
Fax: 802-828-3258

Virginia
James Regan
George Mason University
Entrepreneurship Center
4400 University Dr.
Fairfax, VA 22030
703-277-7750
Fax: 703-352-8195
E-mail: ptap@gmu.edu
www.gmu.edu/gmu/PTAP

Dennis K. Morris
Crater Planning District
Commission
The Procurement Assistance Center
1964 Wakefield St.
P.O. Box 1808

Petersburg, VA 23805
804-861-1667
Fax: 804-732-8972
E-mail: ptac111@aol.com

Glenda D. Calver
Southwestern Virginia Community
College
Economic Development Division
P.O. Box SVCC
Richlands, VA 24641
540-964-7334
Fax: 540-964-7575
www.sw.cc.va.us/pac.html

Washington
Brent C. Helm
Economic Development Council of
Snohomish County
728 134th St., SW
Bldg. A, Suite 219
Everett, WA 98204
425-743-4567
Fax: 425-745-5563
E-mail: ptac@snoedc.org
www.snoedc.org/patc/html

West Virginia
R. Conley Salyer
Regional Contracting Assistance
Center, Inc.
1116 Smith St., Suite 202

Charleston, WV 25301
304-344-2546
Fax: 304-344-2574
www.rcacwv.com

Belinda Sheridan
Mid-Ohio Valley Regional Council
PTA Center
P.O. Box 5528
Parkersburg, WV 26105
304-428-6889
Fax: 304-428-6891
E-mail: ptac@access.mountain.net

Wisconsin
Denise Kornetzke
Madison Area Technical College
Small Business PAC
211 North Carroll St.
Madison, WI 53703
608-258-2350
Fax: 608-258-2329
http://bpac.madison.tec.wi.us

Joseph W. Hurst
Wisconsin Procurement Institute,
Inc.
756 N. Milwaukee St.
Milwaukee, WI 53202
414-443-9744
Fax: 414-443-1122
E-mail: wispro@execpc.com

How To Become a Consultant With The Government

If you are between jobs or just thinking about quitting the one you have and want something to tide you over until you get your next one, you should seriously think about freelancing for the Federal government.

The Interior Department hires ecologists and geologists. The Justice Department hires business consultants. The Department of Energy hires conservation consultants. Here's a sample listing of the kinds of projects freelance consultants do for the Federal government:

Types of Government Freelancing

Landscaping
Carpentry Work
Painting and Paper Hanging
Security Guards
Computer Services
Data Processing
Detective Services
Electrical Work
Plumbing
Accounting Services
Chaplain Services (Priest)
Management Consulting
Engineering Services

Information Retrieval Services
Real Estate Agents
Secretarial Services
Court Reporting
Legal Services
Business Consulting
Photography
Insurance Agents
Computer Programming
Research
Drafting
Interior Decorating
Library Services

Word Processing
Translation Services
Courier and Messenger Services
Cleaning Services
Food Service
Auditing Services
Advertising Services
Nursing Services
Housekeeping Services
Administrative Support
Services
Education and Training
Medical Services
Social Services

Special Study and Analysis
Wildlife Management
Salvage Services
Travel Agent
Personnel Testing Services
Photography
Animal Care
Mathematics and Computer
Science
Environmental Research
Historians
Recreation Research
Economic Studies
More, More, More...

Practically every major government agency hires freelance consultants to work on both small and large projects — which might be exactly what you need until you land a full time job down the road.

The feds hire all kinds of professionals to perform consulting work, from accountants and business specialists, to computer experts, social scientists, and security and surveillance consultants. The offices listed below, called **Offices of Small and Disadvantaged Business Utilization**, specialize in helping individuals and small businesses get involved in contracting with their agency.

Subcontracting

Not only do the feds themselves hire consultants, so do the large prime contractors who sell their products and services to the government. By law, any large company that receives contracts worth $500,000 or more from the Federal government must make an effort to subcontract some of that work to small businesses. So, for example, if a company gets a large computer consulting contract with the Defense Department, they have to make an effort to hire some freelance computer consultants to work on that contract. And that could be you.

How to Find Subcontracting Work

All of the federal procurement offices or Offices of Small and Disadvantaged Business Utilization (SADBU) (see list below) can provide you with information regarding subcontracting. Many of the departments' prime contracts require that the prime contractor maximize small business subcontracting opportunities. The SADBU offices can show you the way to get this work.

> **A great lead on new job openings that probably won't be listed in the Sunday newspaper!**

Each of the large federal agencies listed below, except the Department of Education, maintain directories of large contractors who are looking to do work with the feds in your area of expertise. And since the companies listed in these directories, for the most part, have just landed big government contracts, they might very well be looking to take on more full-time employees to help fulfill those contracts. A great lead on new job openings that probably won't be listed in the Sunday newspaper!

Offices of Small and Disadvantaged Business Utilization

Note: Offices designated as Offices of Small and Disadvantaged Business Utilization (OSDBUs) provide procurement assistance to small, minority, 8(a) and women-owned businesses. Their primary function is to ensure that small and disadvantaged businesses receive their fair share of U.S. Government contracts. "OSDBUs" are the contacts for their respective agencies and are excellent sources of information.

Agency for International Development
Ronald Reagan Building
1300 Pennsylvania Ave., NW
Washington, DC 20523-1414
202-712-1500
Fax: 202-216-3056
www.info.usaid.gov

Corporation for National and Community Service
1100 Vermont Ave., NW
Room 2101
Washington, DC 20525
202-606-5020
Fax: 202-606-5126

Department of Agriculture
14th and Independence Ave., SW
Room 1323, South Bldg.
Washington, DC 20250-9400
202-720-7117
Fax: 202-720-3001
www.usda.gov/da/smallbus.html

Department of Commerce
14th and Constitution Ave, NW
Room 6411
Washington, DC 20230
202-482-1472
Fax: 202-482-0501
www.osec.doc.gov/osdbu

Department of Education
600 Independence Ave., SW
Room 3120-ROB-3
Washington, DC 20202-0521
202-708-9820
Fax: 202-401-6477
www.ed.gov/offices/ODS

Department of Energy
1000 Independence Ave., SW,
Room 5B110
Washington, DC 20585
202-586-8383
Fax: 202-586-3075
www.hr.doe.gov/ed/osdbu.htm

Department of Health and Human Services
200 Independence Ave., SW
Room 517D
Washington, DC 20201
202-690-7300
Fax: 202-690-8772

Department of Housing and Urban Development
451 7th St., SW
Room 3130
Washington, DC 20410
202-708-1428
Fax: 202-708-7642
www.hud.gov/osdbu/osdbu.html

Department of the Interior
18th & C St., NW, Room 2727
Washington, DC 20240
202-208-3493
Fax: 202-208-5048
www.doi.gov/osdbu/osdbu.html

Department of Justice
1331 Pennsylvania Ave., NW
Room 1010, National Place Bldg.
Washington, DC 20530
202-616-0521
Fax: 202-616-1717
www.usdoj.gov/jmd/pss/
home.osd.htm

Department of Labor
200 Constitution Ave., NW
Room C-2318
Washington, DC 20210
202-219-9148
Fax: 202-219-0167
www.dol.gov/dol/ospl

Department of State
Room 633 (SA 6)
Washington, DC 20522-0602
703-875-6824
Fax: 703-875-6825
http://statebuy.inter.net/osdbul.htm

Department of Transportation
400 7th St., SW, Room 9414
Washington, DC 20590
202-366-1930
Fax: 202-366-7228
http://osdbuweb.dot.gov

Department of the Treasury
1500 Pennsylvania Ave., NW
Room 6100 - Annex

Washington, DC 20220
202-622-0530
Fax: 202-622-2273
www.ustreas.gov/sba

Department of Veterans Affairs
810 Vermont Ave., NW
Washington, DC 20420
202-565-8124
Fax: 202-565-8156
www.va.gov/osdbu

Environmental Protection Agency
401 M St., SW
Mail Code A-123O-C
Washington, DC 20460
202-260-4100
Fax: 202-401-1080

Export-Import Bank of the U.S.
811 Vermont Ave., NW
Room 1017
Washington, DC 20571
202-565-3338
Fax: 202-565-3528

Federal Emergency Management Agency
500 C St., SW, Room 726
Washington, DC 20472
202-646-3743
Fax: 202-646-3846
www.fema.gov/ofm

Federal Trade Commission
6th and Pennsylvania Ave., NW,
Room H-700
Washington, DC 20580

202-326-2258
Fax: 202-326-3529
www.ftc.gov

Federal Procurement

General Services Administration
18th and F Sts., NW, Room 6029
Washington, DC 20405
202-501-1021
Fax: 202-208-5938
www.gsa.gov/oed

National Aeronautics and Space Administration
Headquarters, Code K
Room 9K70, 300 E St., SW
Washington, DC 20546
202-358-2088
Fax: 202-358-3261
www.hq.nasa.gov/office/codek

National Science Foundation
4201 Wilson Blvd.
Arlington, VA 22230
703-306-1390
Fax: 703-306-0337
www.eng.nsf.gov/sbir/index.html

Nuclear Regulatory Commission
Mailstop T2 F-18
Washington, DC 20555
301-415-7380
301-415-5953

Executive Office of the President
725 17th St., NW, Room 5001
Washington, DC 20503
202-395-7669
Fax: 202-395-1155

Office of Personnel Management
1900 E St., NW, Room 5542
Washington, DC 20415
202-606-2180
Fax: 202-606-1464

Small Business Administration
Director, Office of Procurement
and Grants Management
409 Third St., SW, 8th Floor
Washington, DC 20416
202-205-7701
Fax: 202-693-7004

Smithsonian Institution
Small and Disadvantaged Business
Utilization Program
995 L'Enfant Plaza, SW
Washington, DC 20506
202-287-3343
Fax: 202-287-3492

Tennessee Valley Authority
1101 Market St., EB2B
Chattanooga, TN 37402-2801
423-751-7203
Fax: 423-751-7613
www.tva.gov

U.S. Postal Service
475 L'Enfant Plaza, SW
Room 3821

Washington, DC 20260-5616
202-268-6578
Fax: 202-268-6573
www.usps.gov

**United States Information
Agency**
400 6th St., SW
Room 1725
Donahue Building
Washington, DC 20547
202-205-9662
Fax: 202-401-2410

**Office of Federal Procurement
Policy**
725 17th St., NW
Room 9013
Washington, DC 20503
202-395-3302
Fax: 202-395-5705
www.arnet.gov

Civic Transportation Board
12th & Constitution Ave., NW
Room 3148
Washington, DC 20423
202-565-1674
202-565-1596

Railroad Retirement Board
844 N. Rush St.
Chicago, IL 60611
312-751-4565
Fax: 312-751-4923
www.rrb.gov

**Minority Business
Development Agency**
Department of Commerce
14th & Constitution Ave., NW
Room 5093
Washington, DC 20230
202-482-1712
Fax: 202-482-5117

State Procurement Assistance

Have you ever wondered where the government buys all of the products that it works with each day? You might be surprised to learn that they buy from small businesses just like yours that produce products such as:

★ work clothing
★ office supplies
★ cleaning equipment
★ miscellaneous vehicles
★ medical supplies and equipment

Imagine what your bottom line could look like each year if  you won just ONE lucrative government contract that would provide your business with a secure income! It might even buy you the freedom to pursue other clients that you wouldn't have the time or money to go after otherwise. If your business performs well and completes a government contract satisfactorily, chances are you'll have a shot at more and maybe even bigger contracts.

The offices listed below are starting places for finding out who in the state government will purchase your products or services.

State Procurement Offices

Alabama
Finance Department
Purchasing Division
11 S. Union, Room 200
Montgomery, AL 36130
205-242-7250

Alaska
State of Alaska
Department of Administration
Division of General Services and
Supply
P.O. Box 110210
Juneau, AK 99811-0210
907-465-2253

Arizona
State Purchasing
Executive Tower, Suite 101
1700 W. Washington
Phoenix, AZ 85007
602-542-5511

Arkansas
Office of State Purchasing
P.O. Box 2940
Little Rock, AR 72203
501-324-9312

California
Office of Procurement
Department of General Services
1823 14th St.
Sacramento, CA 95814
916-445-6942

Colorado
Division of Purchasing
225 E. 16th Ave., Suite 900

Denver, CO 80203
303 866-6100

Connecticut
State of Connecticut
Department of Administrative
Services
Bureau of Purchases
460 Silver St.
Middletown, CT 06457
203-638-3280

Delaware
Purchasing Division
Purchasing Bldg.
P.O. Box 299
Delaware City, DE 19706
302-834-4550

District of Columbia
Department of Administrative
Services
441 4th St. NW, Room 710
Washington, DC 20001
202-727-0171

Florida
General Service Department
Division of Purchasing
Knight Bldg.
2737 Centerview Dr., 2nd Floor
Tallahassee, FL 32399-0950
904-488-8440

Georgia
Administrative Services
Department
200 Piedmont Ave.
Room 1308 SE

Atlanta, GA 30334
404-656-3240

Hawaii
Purchasing Branch
Purchasing and Supply Division
Department of Accounting and
General Services
Room 416, 1151 Punch Bowl
Honolulu, HI 96813
808-586-0575

Idaho
Division of Purchasing
Administration Department
5569 Kendall
State House Mall
Boise, ID 83720
208-327-7465

Illinois
Department of Central
Management Services
Procurement Services
801 Stratton Bldg.
Springfield, IL 62706
217-782-2301

**Purchasing
Offices**

Indiana
Department of Administration
Procurement Division
402 W. Washington St.
Room W-468
Indianapolis, IN 46204
317-232-3032

Iowa
State of Iowa
Department of General Services
Purchasing Division
Hoover State Office Building
Des Moines, IA 50319
515-281-3089

Kansas
Division of Purchasing
Room 102 North
Landon State Office Bldg.
900 SW Jackson St.
Topeka, KS 66612
913-296-2376

Kentucky
Purchases, Department of Finance
Room 367, Capital Annex
Frankfort, KY 40601
502-564-4510

Louisiana
State Purchasing Office
Division of Administration
P.O. Box 94095
Baton Rouge, LA 70804-9095
504-342-8010

Maine
Bureau of Purchases
State House Station #9
Augusta, ME 04333
207-287-3521

Maryland
Purchasing Bureau
301 W. Preston St.
Mezzanine, Room M8
Baltimore, MD 21201
410-225-4620

Massachusetts
Purchasing Agent Division
One Ashburton Place, Room 1017
Boston, MA 02108
617-727-7500

Michigan
Office of Purchasing
Mason Bldg.
P.O. Box 30026
Lansing, MI 48909
or 530 W. Ellegan, 48933
517-373-0330

Minnesota
State of Minnesota
112 Administration Bldg.
50 Sherburne Ave.
St. Paul, MN 55155
651-296-6152

Mississippi
Office of Purchasing and Travel
1504 Sillers Bldg.
550 High St., Suite 1504
Jackson, MS 39201
601-359-3409

Missouri
State of Missouri
Division of Purchasing
P.O. Box 809
Jefferson City, MO 65102
314-751-3273

Montana
Department of Administration
Procurement Printing Division
165 Mitchell Bldg.
Helena, MT 59620-0135
406-444-2575

Nebraska
State Purchasing
Material Division
301 Centennial Mall S.
P.O. Box 94847
Lincoln, NE 68509
402-471-2401

Nevada
Nevada State Purchasing Division
209 E. Musser St.
Room 304
Blasdel Bldg.
Carson City, NV 89710
702-687-4070

New Hampshire
Plant and Property Management
25 Capitol St.
State House Annex, Room 102
Concord, NH 03301
603-271-2201

New Jersey
Division of Purchase and Property
CN-039
Trenton, NJ 08625
609-292-4886

New Mexico
State Purchasing Division
1100 St. Frances Dr.
Joseph Montoya Bldg.
Room 2016
Santa Fe, NM 87503
505-827-0472

New York
Division of Purchasing
Corning Tower
Empire State Plaza, 38th Floor

Albany, NY 12242
518-474-3695

North Carolina
Department of Administration
Division of Purchase and Contract
116 W. Jones St.
Raleigh, NC 27603-8002
919-733-3581

State Procurement

North Dakota
Central Services Division of State
Purchasing
Purchasing
600 E Blvd., I Wing
Bismarck, ND 58505-0420
701-224-2683

Ohio
State Purchasing
4200 Surface Rd.
Columbus, OH 43228-1395
614-466-5090

Oklahoma
Office of Public Affairs
Central Purchasing Division
Room B4, State Capital Bldg.
Oklahoma City, OK 73105
405-521-2110

Oregon
General Services
Purchasing
1225 Ferry St.

Salem, OR 97310
503-378-4643

Pennsylvania
Procurement Department Secretary
N. Office Bldg., Room 414
Commonwealth and North St.
Harrisburg, PA 17125
717-787-5295

Rhode Island
Department of Administration
Purchases Office
One Capital Hill
Providence, RI 02908-5855
401-277-2317

South Carolina
Materials Management Office
General Service Budget and
Control Board
1201 Main St., Suite 600
Columbia, SC 29201
803-737-0600

South Dakota
Division of Purchasing
118 W. Capitol Ave.
Pierre, SD 57501
605-773-3405

Tennessee
Purchasing Division
C2-211, Central Services Bldg.
Nashville, TN 37219
615-741-1035

Texas
State Purchasing and General
Services Commission
P.O. Box 13047

Austin, TX 78711
512-463-3445

Utah
Purchasing Division
Department of Administrative
Services
State Office Bldg., Room 3150
Salt Lake City, UT 84114
801-538-3026

Vermont
Purchasing Division
128 State St., Drawer 33
Montpelier, VT 05633-7501
802-828-2211

Virginia
Department of General Services
Purchasing Division
P.O. Box 1199
Richmond, VA 23209
804-786-3172

Washington
Office of State Procurement
216 GA Building

P.O. Box 41017
Olympia, WA 98504-1017
206-753-6461

West Virginia
Department of Administration
Purchasing Section
Room E102, Building One
1900 Kanawha Blvd. E
Charleston, WV 25305-0110
304-558-2306

Wisconsin
Division of State Agency Services
Bureau of Procurement
101 E. Wilson, 6th Floor
P.O. Box 7867
Madison, WI 53707-7867
608-266-2605

Wyoming
Department of Administration
Procurement Services
2001 Capitol Ave.
Cheyenne, WY 82002
307-777-7253

How Freelance Writers and Editors Can Get Government Contracts

Writers don't have to be starving artists these days — the Federal government hires freelancers to do all kinds of work, such as script writing, technical writing, editing, translations, and much more. Believe it or not, your creative talent can find an outlet (and a paycheck!) within the halls of several Federal agencies. Consider this:

🖊 If you're a consumer writer, the Food and Drug Administration might be interested in using your skills to write an article on food safety for $1,200.

🖊 If you're an editor, the U.S. Department of Agriculture might want to use you at a rate of $1,225 per week.

🖊 Technical writers can land $25,000 contracts that NASA awards each year.

While many agencies have writers on staff, sometimes the work load is just too much and they'll look outside for freelancers to handle the overflow. Not all hire freelance writers, so we've done the leg work for you and found out which agencies do.

Information USA, Inc.

To be considered for any kind of contract work with the government, you'll need to submit a standard capabilities statement with each agency with which you would like to work. This statement should be submitted on a standard form 129 (*SF-129*), which is available free from any of the contracting offices listed below.

> An agency will put you on the bidders mailing list so that when writing opportunities come up, you'll be notified.

Once they've received your *SF-129*, an agency will put you on the bidders mailing list so that when writing opportunities come up, you'll be notified. You'll then be asked to submit a closed bid for the project, with the lowest bid getting the work. Keep in mind, though, that on larger contracts of $25,000 and up, the government usually pays only on completion of the project, which could be six months or a year, depending on the size. So if you're going to bid for a project, be sure you can survive that long before you get paid.

Here are some success stories of individuals and small businesses that have received writing contracts worth more than $25,000:

✔ **International Computer and Telecommunications** of Lanham, MD, received *$1.99 million* to provide NASA headquarters with technical writing support services.

✔ **Gottlieb Associates** of Washington, DC, received *$55,310* to edit a science magazine for the National Science Foundation.

✔ **Stone and Webster Engineering Corp.** of Engelwood, CO, received *$192,839* to revise and update a book for the Department of Energy.

✔ **Graph Tech, Inc.**, of Arlington, VA, received *$57,418* to provide editorial services to the Federal Emergency Management Administration.

✔ **Bruce Valley** of Alexandria, VA, received *$38,289* to write speeches for the Chairman of the Federal Deposit Insurance Corp.

✔ **The Blue Pencil Group, Inc.**, of Reston, VA, received *$27,900* to edit a scientific journal for the National Science Foundation.

Not all freelance writers get work through this kind of formal, bidded contract. Most writing and editing jobs are smaller, valued under $25,000, and are given out on a less formal basis — the procurement office might contact only three writers they know of and ask for bids, with the lowest getting the job.

Even smaller jobs in the range of, say, $2,500 or under are often awarded to writers that the **Small Purchases Agent** for an agency might have in his/her Rolodex, especially those writers who can do work on an as needed, last minute basis. So make sure that the Small Purchases Agent in each agency knows your name and has your resume on file — it's usually the people who are freshest in the agent's mind that gets these small, though often lucrative assignments.

Here are some examples of these smaller contracts:

✔ **Briere Associates** of Arlington VA received *$2,000* to edit an investigation report for the International Trade Commission.

✔ **Richard Bellman** received *$511* to write a paper on fair housing for the Department of Housing and Urban Development.

 Information USA, Inc.

✔ **Peter Petrakis** of Annapolis, MD, received *$2,500* to write a scientific report for the Public Health Service.

✔ **Paragon Solutions** received *$23,011* to develop a users manual for the Department of Housing and Urban Development.

✔ **Rowena Itchon** of Washington, DC, received *$2,000* for editing services from the Securities and Exchange Commission.

✔ **Barbara Snyder** of Falls Church, VA, received *$625* to write a paper on drug abuse for the Department of Health and Human Services.

✔ **Don Hill** of Virginia received *$2,500* to produce a series of training conference reports for the Office of Personnel Management.

In fact, when first starting out in government contracting, it's a good idea to complete a few of these smaller contracts before you try to land any of the larger ones valued over $25,000. Showing a government agency that you have successfully completed smaller contracting work for them will make them more likely to award you larger jobs when you submit bids on them. Just as it is in the private sector, if all other things are equal, contracts often go to those companies with whose work the agency is most familiar.

Writers Contacts

Drug Enforcement Administration
Mr. Burdette Burton
Office of Procurement
700 Army Navy Dr., Room W5140
Arlington, VA 22202   202-307-7182
www.usdoj.gov/dea
The Drug Enforcement Administration (DEA) occasionally hires freelance writers and editors. Send a resume outlining your capabilities to this office.

Energy Department
David Hoexter
Office of Procurement and Assistance Management
U.S. Department of Energy
1000 Independence Ave., SW
Washington, DC 20585-0705   202-586-9062
E-mail: david.hoexter@hq.doe.gov
www.doe.gov

The Office of Procurement and Assistance Management sponsors a special
website designed to assist individuals and companies in doing business with the
Department of Energy. It can be accessed online at {www.pr.doe.gov/prbus.
html}. When freelance writing opportunities are posted, resumes should be sent to
the program office announcing the requirement.

Federal Emergency Management Administration
Office of Acquisition Management
Federal Emergency Management Administration
500 C St., SW
Washington, DC 20472   202-646-4006
www.fema.gov

The Federal Emergency Management Administration (FEMA) publishes

educational and training materials relating to disaster
management and, at times, hires freelance writers
and editors to work on these projects. By calling or
writing FEMA, you can obtain a list of the latest
disaster contracting locations and phone numbers,
small business opportunities (including how to
register as a bidder) and solicitation information.

Fish and Wildlife Service
Meghan Durham
Public Affairs
U.S. Fish and Wildlife Service
1849 C St., NW, Room 3361
Mail Stop 3024 MIB
Washington, DC 20240   202-208-4131
E-mail: Megan_Durham@FWS.GOV
www.fws.gov

The Fish and Wildlife Service's Public Affairs Office occasionally hires freelance
writers to work on wildlife projects. To be considered for writing opportunities,
submit a resume and work samples to this office. The Fish and Wildlife Service's
website also features a section entitled "Doing Business with the U.S. FWA,"

which includes a list of products and services contracted, an acquisition forecast for the year and other business opportunities available within the Department of the Interior.

Food and Drug Administration
Isadora Stehlin, Editor
FDA Consumer
Food and Drug Administration (HFI-40)
5600 Fishers Lane, Room 15A19
Rockville, MD 20857   301-827-7130
www.fda.gov

The Food and Drug Administration (FDA) publishes a magazine called the *FDA Consumer*, which specializes in food and drug issues. This magazine sometimes uses freelance writers to research and write articles which the FDA is interested in having completed. To be considered for freelance work with the *FDA Consumer*, send a resume and samples of your writing to the editor at the address listed above.

Forest Service
U.S. Forest Service
U.S. Department of Agriculture
P.O. Box 96090
Room 707 RP-E
Washington, DC 20090-6090   703-235-8165
www.fs.fed.us

On occasion, the Forest Service hires freelance editors, proofreaders, and technical writers to do contract work. This work often specializes in the earth sciences and may involve technical engineering reports. If you'd like to be notified when these contract opportunities arise, you'll need to submit an *SF-129* that outlines your capabilities and experience.

General Services Administration
Mary Rudbeck
U.S. General Services Administration (XM)
1800 F St., NW, Room 6002
Washington, DC 20405   202-501-0937
E-mail: mary.rudbeck@gsa.gov
www.gsa.gov

The General Services Administration (GSA) has a limited need for freelance writers and editors. To be considered for projects, submit a resume and work samples. Your resume will be kept on file until a contract opportunity arises.

Health and Human Services
    Linda Danley
    General Acquisitions
    Public Health Service
    U.S. Department of Health and Human Services
    5600 Parklawn Ave., Room 5C26
    Rockville, MD 20857   301-443-1715
The U.S. Department of Health and Human Services (HHS) hires freelance
editors and writers to work on health related reports and publications. To be
considered for this work, you'll need to submit an *SF-129* that outlines your
capabilities and experience to this office. Once on file, the office will notify you
when any projects come up that they think match your talents.

Housing and Urban Development
    Office of Procurement and Contracts
    U.S. Department of Housing and Urban Development
    451 7th St., SW, Room 5272
    Washington, DC 20410   202-708-1290
    www.hud.gov

 The U.S. Department of Housing and Urban
Development (HUD) does not routinely hire freelance
writers and editors. But on those occasions when a
freelance need arises, the procurement is
announced 15 days prior to its release in the
Commerce Business Daily (CBD). The CBD is
available for free online at {//cbdnet.access.
gpo.gov}. When the solicitation for bids is officially
issued, it is posted on the "Current Contracting Opportunities" page of HUD's
website, located at {www.hud.gov/cts/ctsoprty.html}.

Interior Department
    Kris Damsgaard
    Office of Aircraft Services
    Branch of Training
    2741 Airport Way
    Boise, ID 83705   208-387-5812
    E-mail: kris_damsgaard@oas.gov
    www.oas.gov
The Office of Aircraft Services (OAS) within the Department of Interior does not
typically hire freelance writers and editors, but may have a need on an intermittent
basis. Contact this office for more information.

Justice Department
Office of Justice Programs
Office of Personnel
810 7th St., NW, 3rd Floor
Washington, DC 20531   202-307-0730
www.ojp.usdoj.gov

At times, the Office of Justice Programs (OJP) requires
freelance editors and writers for project support. If
you're interested in being considered for this work,
you'll first need to submit a capabilities statement
to this office. If they're interested in possibly
using you, they may set up an interview to further
discuss your capabilities. After that, you'll be
notified when any relevant work comes up that they think
best matches your abilities.

Labor Department
Brenda Butler
Office of Procurement Services
U.S. Department of Labor
200 Constitution Ave., NW, Room N5416
Washington, DC 20120   202-219-9355
E-mail: butler-brenda@dol.gov

The U.S. Department of Labor hires freelancers to work on different projects,
such as script writers for video projects. If you're interested in being considered
for this work, you'll first need to submit an *SF-129* capabilities statement to this
office. If they're interested in possibly using you, they may set up an interview to
further discuss your capabilities. After that, you'll be notified when any relevant
work comes up that they think best matches your abilities.

National Aeronautics and Space Administration
NASA Headquarters
Washington, DC 20546-0001   202-358-0000
www.nasa.gov

There are several ways to access freelance writing and editing opportunities with
NASA. If you are interested in working for NASA Headquarters, call the Goddard
Space Flight Center listed below and ask for Headquarters Operations. If you are
interested in working for any of the other 11 NASA centers, you can contact the
procurement officers listed below. Another approach is to submit your resume and
work samples to those companies that supply services to NASA. Several of the
space centers list their contractors on their websites. The final option is to

subscribe to NASA's online service, NASA Acquisition Internet Service (NAIS), which allows you to search for freelance contract opportunities in its database and also notified you by e-mail when procurement announcements are made. NAIS, however, doese not always post smaller contracts (under $25,000), so it is best to contact the individual NASA centers to find out about those opportunities.

Ames Research Center
Charles W. Duff
Mail Stop 241-1
Moffett Field, CA 94035-1000   650-604-5000
E-mail: cduff@mail.arc.nasa.gov
www.arc.nasa.gov

Dryden Flight Research Center
Russ Davis
P.O. Box 273
Edwards, CA 93523-0273   661-258-3311
E-mail: russ.davis@dfrc.nasa.gov

Glenn Research Center
Bradley J. Baker
Mail Stop 500-313
21000 Brookpark Rd.
Cleveland, OH 44135-3191   216-433-4000
E-mail: bradley.j.baker@grc.nasa.gov
www.grc.nasa.gov

Goddard Space Flight Center
Michael J. Ladomirak
Code 200
Greenbelt, MD 20771-0001   301-286-2000
E-mail: mladomir@pop200.gsfc.nasa.gov
www.gsfc.nasa.gov
The Goddard Space Flight Center handles all acquisitions for NASA Headquarters. When calling, ask for Headquarters Operations.

Jet Propulsion Laboratory
4800 Oak Grove Dr.
Pasadena, CA 91109-8099   818-354-4321
www.jpl.nasa.gov
The Jet Propulsion Laboratory has a staff made up primarily of contractors.

Kennedy Space Center
James E. Hattaway
Code OP
Kennedy Space Center, FL 32899-0001   407-867-7110
E-mail: james.hattaway@ksc.nasa.gov
www.ksc.nasa.gov

Langley Research Center
Sandra Ray
Mail Stop 134
Hampton, VA 23681-0001   757-864-1000
E-mail: s.s.ray@larc.nasa.gov
www.larc.nasa.gov

Marshall Space Flight Center
Stephen Beale
Code PS01
Marshal Space Flight Center, AL 35812-0001   256-544-2121
E-mail: steve.beale@msfc.nasa.gov
www1.msfc.nasa.gov

Michoud Assembly Facility
P.O. Box 29300
New Orleans, LA 70189   504-257-3311
www.lmco.com/michoud
The Michoud Assembly Facility has a staff made up primarily of contractors.

Stennis Space Center
Kimberly Stone
Code DA00
Stennis Space Center, MS 39529-6000   228-688-2211
E-mail: kim.stone@scc.nasa.gov
www.ssc.nasa.gov

National Park Service
Dyra Monroe
National Park Service
Contract Operations Branch
P.O. Box 37127
Washington, DC 20013-7127   202-523-0092
www.nps.gov

Government Contracts

The National Park Service hires freelance writers and editors for contract work

when projects arise. If you're interested in being placed on their bidders list so that you can receive notice when new contracts need filling, you'll need to submit an *SF-129* capabilities statement with this office.

National Science Foundation
Veronica Bankins
Chief, Systems and Services Branch
Division of Administrative Services
National Science Foundation
4201 Wilson Blvd., Room 295 N
Arlington, VA 22230   703-306-1125, ext. 2065
E-mail: vbankins@nsf.gob
www.nsf.gov

Freelance writers and editors interested in working for the National Science Foundation should contact the office listed above.

National Technical Information Service
Anita Tolliver
National Technical Information Service
U.S. Department of Commerce
5285 Port Royal Rd., Room 203
Springfield, VA 22161   703-487-4720
www.ntis.gov

National Technical Information Service (NTIS), the largest publisher and distributor of government technical information, occasionally hires freelance editors and writers to work on their publications. To be considered for this contract work, you'll need to submit an *SF-129* summarizing your capabilities and experience. When relevant contracts arise, you'll be notified to submit bids on the projects.

Office of Personnel Management
U.S. Office of Personnel Management
Contracting Division
1900 E St., NW
Washington, DC 20415-0001   202-606-2240 (press option 9)
www.opm.gov

Write or call the OPM's Contracting Division to obtain procurement information (including a forecast of opportunities) and copies of OPM solicitations. A packet will be mailed to you within five working days.

Postal Service
 Headquarters Purchasing
 Barbara Sauls
 Services Purchasing
 U.S. Postal Service
 475 L'Enfant Plaza West, SW
 Washington, DC 20260-6237   202-268-4100
 www.usps.gov

For writing contracts worth $25,000 and over, you'll need to be placed on the
Postal Service's list of suppliers. This office can send
you the appropriate applications. When writing
contracts arise, you'll be notified to submit
competitive bids. The Postal Service awards
contracts for both technical writing and technical
manual production services, which includes editorial
services such as proofreading, copy markup, and text
writing. The Commodity Codes for these services are T013A and T013B. The
code for Speech Writing is R416A, and for Language Translation it's R416.

Securities and Exchange Commission
 Office of Administrative and Personnel Management
 U.S. Securities and Exchange Commission
 450 5th St., NW
 Washington, DC 20549   202-942-4000
 www.sec.gov

The Securities and Exchange Commission (SEC) occasionally hires freelance
writers and editors. Contact this office for more information.

Smithsonian Institution
 Office of Contracting and Property Management
 Smithsonian Institution
 955 L'Enfant Plaza, SW, Suite P114
 Washington, DC 20024   202-287-3343
 www.si.edu

The Smithsonian often hires freelancers to work on their publications. Keep in
mind, though, that this work does not include work on the *Smithsonian Magazine*,
which is a completely separate entity. This part of the Smithsonian provides
administrative publication support, along with the many different books that they
publish. To be considered for this work, you'll need to submit an *SF-129* outlining
your capabilities and experience, and if they're interested in using you, you'll be
notified when opportunities arise.

Transportation Department
Cindy Blackmon
U.S. Department of Transportation
400 7th St., SW
Washington, DC 20590   202-366-4968
www.dot.gov

The Department of Transportation occasionally hires freelance writers. To be considered for projects, submit a resume to this office.

Treasury Department
Wesley Hawley
Procurement Services Division
Treasury Department
1500 Pennsylvania Ave., NW, Room 1438
Washington, DC 20220   202-622-1300
www.ustreas.gov

To be considered for any writing and editing contracts that might arise, you'll need to submit a capabilities statement to this office or an *SF-129*.

Office of Procurement
SBA-PCR
Ollie Snyder
1301 Constitution Ave., NW
ICC Building, Room 3379
Washington, DC 20229   202-927-7131

On occasion, FMS requires the services of freelance editors and writers, and to get
 on the bidders' list, you need to submit an *SF-129* that outlines your capabilities.

Michelle James
Internal Revenue Service
Room 700 Constellation Centre
6009 Oxon Hill Rd.
Oxon Hill, MD 20749   202-283-1350

Doug Mason
Senior Contract Specialist/Procurement Office
Office of Thrift Supervision
1700 G St., NW
Washington, DC 20552   202-906-7624
www.ots.treas.gov

While the Office of Thrift Supervision does not hire freelance writers on a regular basis, inquiries and resumes can be sent to this office. Notice of job vacancies can be obtained by calling 202-906-6071 or visiting the OTS website.

The above departments within the U.S. Department of the Treasury contract for the service of writers and editors. To bid on writing contracts valued over $25,000, you'll need to complete and submit an *SF-129* application to be put on their solicitation mailing lists. These agencies also make smaller purchases of these services, and with your *SF-129* on file, they will contact you when any appropriate work comes up. Once on the mailing lists, you'll receive notice whenever these agencies are looking for bids on writing contracts.

U.S. Geological Survey
   Kathleen Craig
   U.S. Geological Survey
   12201 Sunrise Valley Dr.
   MS 205 B
   Reston, VA 20192   703-648-7357
   E-mail: kcraig@usgs.gov
   www.usgs.gov

The U.S. Geological Survey (USGS) does not routinely hire freelance writers, but does occasionally offer miscellaneous editing jobs, for which vendors compete. Contact this office to have bidding information faxed or mailed to you.

Help For Inventors

Patents, Trademarks, and Copyrights

Most inventors realize that it's vitally important to protect their idea by copyrighting it and obtaining the necessary patents and copyrights, but did you know that it's also important to look around for loans and other grants to support your business while working on your invention? If you want an idea to become an actual product, you have to invest an awful lot of your time into its research, and not just on a part time basis. Loans and grants programs for inventors help you do just that — for example, Hawaii offers low cost loans to inventors, as do other states around the country. First, let's talk about getting the necessary information concerning trademark and patent procedures.

Patent and Trademark Office

United States patent and trademark laws are administered by the Patent and Trademark Office (PTO). States also have trade secret statutes, which generally state that if you guard your trade secret with a reasonable amount of care, you will protect your rights associated with that secret. The PTO examines patent and trademark applications, grants protection for qualified inventions, and registers trademarks. It also collects, assembles, and disseminates the technological information patent grants. The PTO maintains a collection of almost 6 million United States patents issued to date, several million foreign patents, and more than 2.2 million

Information USA, Inc.

trademarks, together with supporting documentation. Here's how to find out what you need to do to patent your idea.

What a Great Idea

To help you get started with patenting your invention, the Patent and Trademark Offices will send you a free booklet upon request called *Basic Facts About Patents*. There are three legal elements involved in the process of invention: the conception of the idea, diligence in working it out, and reducing it to

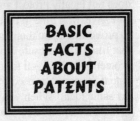

practice — i.e., getting a finished product that actually works. If you have a great idea you think might work, but you need time to develop it further before it is ready to be patented, what should you do?

Protect Your Idea for $10

You can file a Disclosure Statement with the Patent and Trademark Office, and they will keep it in confidence as evidence of the date of conception of the invention or idea.

> ***Disclosure Statement***
> Assistant Commissioner of Patents
> Box DD
> Washington, DC 20231
> Disclosure Office
> 800-786-9199
> 703-308-HELP

Send an 8 1/2 x 11" drawing, a copy, signed disclosure, SASE, and a check or money order for $10 to file. Upon request, the above office will also send you a free brochure on Disclosure Statements.

This is the best way to keep the idea you are working on completely secret and yet document the date you conceived the idea. You can file the Disclosure Statement at any time after the idea is conceived, but the value of it will depend on how much information you put into it — so put as much detail into this statement as you can.

The Purpose of Documenting The Date of Conception

If someone else should try to patent your idea, filing a Disclosure Statement shows that you thought of it first, although filing this statement does not legally protect your invention. Documentation of the conception date gives you time to patent your invention, and is invaluable if you need to prove when you thought of your idea if a dispute should arise. (Note that filing a Disclosure Statement gives you limited defensive legal protection only if you follow it up with a patent in two years. Unlike a patent, it cannot be used offensively, to stop someone else from patenting the same idea.) When you go to file for a patent, if you and a competitor get into a dispute as to who was the first to invent it, the Patent and Trademark Office (PTO) will hold an Interference Proceeding. If you thought of the idea first, your Disclosure Statement will go a long way towards establishing that you were the first inventor and should therefore receive the patent for it.

Research Resources That Can Help You Turn Your Idea Into Reality

While diligently working out the details of your invention you can use the extensive resources of over 190,000 scientific and technical journals, articles, and books at the Scientific Document Library at the PTO in Crystal City, VA.

Facilitating public access to the more than 25 million cross-referenced United States patents is the job of PTO's Office of Technology Assessment and Forecast (OTAF), 703-306-2600. It has a master database which covers all United States patents, and searches are available free. An OTAF search will not result in an in-depth patent search. (More on that, and how to find classifications in the *Conducting Your Own Patent Search* section below.) OTAF extracts information from its database and makes it available in a variety of formats, including publications, custom patent reports, and statistical reports. The purpose of most of the reports generated by an OTAF search is to reveal statistical information.

Copies of the specifications and drawings of all patents are available from PTO. Design patents and trademark copies are $3 each. Plant patents not in color are $10 each, while plant patents in color are $20 each. To make a request, you must have the patent number. For copies, contact:

Assistant Secretary and Commissioner
P.O. Box 9
ATTN: PTCS
Washington, DC 20231
Public Information Line
703-305-8716

Patenting Your Invention

To patent your invention, start by ordering the Patent Booklet called *General Information Concerning Patents*, and Application Form.

Superintendent of Documents
U.S. Government Printing Office
P.O. Box 371954
Pittsburgh, PA 15250-7954
202-512-1800

The cost is $4 and may be charged to Mastercard, VISA or Discover Card.

The application will ask you for a written description, oath, and drawing where possible. The cost to file for a patent to individuals or small businesses of under 500 employees (defined by SBA standards) is $380. It generally takes 18 months to two years for the PTO to grant a patent, and rights start the date the patent is granted. If you use your invention prior to being granted a patent, you can put "patent pending" on your product. This warns competitors that you have taken the necessary steps, but otherwise affords you no legal protection. Before embarking on the patenting process, you should conduct a patent search to make sure no one else has preceded you.

Conducting Your Own Patent Search

Before investing too much time and money on patenting your idea, you will want to see if anyone has already patented it. You may conduct the search yourself on the PTO website at {http://www.uspto.gov} or hire someone to do it for you. If you wish to hire a professional to do your patent search, consult the local yellow pages or again, search the PTO website for a roster of patent attorneys. Even if your search is not as in-depth as that of a patent attorney or a patent agent, you may still find the information that you need. You may also conduct your patent search at the Patent and Trademark Office Search Room.

Patent and Trademark Office (PTO)
Patent and Trademark Search Room
2021 South Clark Place
Crystal Plaza 3
Arlington, VA 22202
703-305-4463

For information about the Patent Depository Library Program, contact the office listed below.

Patent and Trademark Depository Library Program
U.S. Patent and Trademark Office
Crystal Park 3, Suite 461
Washington, DC 20231
Fax: 703-306-2654

Patent Search

You may also conduct your patent search at any of the 83 Patent Depository Libraries (PDLs) throughout the country as listed below.

Alabama
Auburn University: Ralph Brown Draughon Library, Auburn University; 334-844-1747
Birmingham: Birmingham Public Library; 205-226-3620

Alaska
Anchorage: Z.J. Lottssac Public Library, Anchorage Municipal Libraries; 907-562-7323

Arizona
Tempe: Daniel F. Noble Science and Engineering Library/Science/Reference, Arizona State University; 602-965-7010

Arkansas
Little Rock: Little Rock, Arkansas State Library; 501-682-2053

California
Los Angeles: Los Angeles
Public Library; 213-228-
7220
Sacramento: California
State Library, Library
Courts Building; 916-654-0069

San Diego: San Diego Public Library; 619-236-5813
San Francisco: San Francisco Public Library; 415-557-4500
Sunnyvale: Sunnyvale Center for Innovation, Invention & Ideas; 408-730-
7290

Colorado
Denver: Denver Public Library; 303-640-6220

Connecticut
Hartford: Hartford Public Library; not yet operational
New Haven: New Haven Free Public Library; 203-946-8130

Delaware
Newark: University of Delaware Library; 302-831-2965

District of Columbia
Washington: Founders Library, Howard University; 202-806-7252

Florida
Fort Lauderdale: Broward County Main Library; 954-357-7444
Miami: Miami-Dade Public Library; 305-375-2665
Orlando: University of Central Florida Libraries; 407-823-2562
Tampa: Tampa Campus Library, University of South Florida; 813-974-
2726

Georgia
Atlanta: Library and Information Center, Georgia Institute of Technology;
404-894-4508

Hawaii
Honolulu: Hawaii State Library; 808-586-3477

Idaho
Moscow: University of Idaho Library; 208-885-6235

Illinois
Chicago: Chicago Public Library; 312-747-4450
Springfield: Illinois State Library; 217-782-5659

Indiana
Indianapolis: Indianapolis-Marion County Public Library; 317-269-1741
West Lafayette: Siegesmund Engineering Library, Purdue University;
317-494-2872

Iowa
Des Moines: State Library of Iowa; 515-281-4118

Kansas
Wichita: Ablah Library, Wichita State University; 316-978-3155

Kentucky
Louisville: Louisville Free Public Library; 502-574-1611

Louisiana
Baton Rouge: Troy H. Middleton Library, Louisiana State University;
504-388-8875

Maine
Orono: Raymond H. Fogler Library, University of Maine; 207-581-1678

Maryland
College Park: Engineering and Physical Sciences Library, University of
Maryland; 301-405-9157

Massachusetts
Amherst: Physical Sciences and Engineering Library, University of
Massachusetts; 413-545-1370
Boston: Boston Public Library; 617-536-5400, ext. 265

Information USA, Inc.

Michigan
Ann Arbor: Media Union Library, The University of Michigan; 313-647-5735
Big Rapids: Abigail S. Tunme Library, Ferris State University; 616-592-3602
Detroit: Great Lakes Patent and Trademark Center, Detroit Public Library; 313-833-3379

Minnesota
Minneapolis: Minneapolis Public Library & Information Center; 612-630-6120

Mississippi
Jackson: Mississippi Library Commission; 601-359-1036

Missouri
Kansas City: Linda Hall Library; 816-363-4600
St. Louis: St. Louis Public Library; 314-241-2288, ext. 390

Montana
Butte: Montana Tech of the University of Montana Library; 406-496-4281

Nebraska
Lincoln: Engineering Library, Nebraska Hall, 2nd Floor West; 402-472-3411

Nevada
Reno: University Library, University of Nevada-Reno; 702-784-6500, ext. 257

New Hampshire
Concord: New Hampshire State Library; 603-271-2239

New Jersey
Newark: Newark Public Library; 973-733-7779
Piscataway: Library of Science and Medicine, Rutgers University; 732-445-2895

New Mexico

Albuquerque: Centennial Science and Engineering Library, The University of New Mexico; 505-277-4412

New York

Albany: New York State Library, Science, Industry and Business Library; 518-474-5355
Buffalo: Buffalo and Erie County Public Library; 716-858-7101
New York: Science, Industry and Business Library; 212-592-7000
Stony Brook: Engineering Library, State University of New York; 516-632-7148

North Carolina

Raleigh: D.H. Hill Library, North Carolina State University; 919-515-2935

North Dakota

Grand Forks: Chester Fritz Library, University of North Dakota; 701-777-4888

Ohio

Akron: Akron-Summit County Public Library; 330-643-9075
Cincinnati: The Public Library of Cincinnati and Hamilton County; 513-369-6971
Cleveland: Cleveland Public Library; 216-623-2870
Columbus: Ohio State University Libraries; 614-292-6175
Toledo: Toledo/Lucas County Public Library; 419-259-5212

Oklahoma

Stillwater: Oklahoma State University; 405-744-7086

Oregon

Portland: Paul L. Boley Law Library, Lewis & Clark College; 503-768-6786

Pennsylvania

Philadelphia: The Free Library of Philadelphia; 215-686-5331
Pittsburgh: The Carnegie Library of Pittsburgh; 412-622-3138

University Park: Pattee Library - C207, Pennsylvania State University; 814-865-4861

Puerto Rico
Mayaguez: General Library, University of Puerto Rico; 787-832-4040, ext. 3459

Rhode Island
Providence: Providence Public Library; 401-455-8027

South Carolina
Clemson: R.M. Cooper Library, Clemson University; 864-656-3024

South Dakota
Rapid City: Devereaux Library, South Dakota School of Mines and Technology; 605-394-1275

Tennessee
Memphis: Memphis & Shelby County Public Library and Information Center; 901-725-8877
Nashville: Stevenson Science and Engineering Library, Vanderbilt University; 615-322-2717

Texas
Austin: McKinney Engineering Library, The University of Texas at Austin; 512-495-4500
College Station: Sterling C. Evans Library, Texas A&M University; 409-845-3826
Dallas: Dallas Public Library; 214-670-1468
Houston: Fondren Library, Rice University; 713-527-8101, ext. 2587
Houston: South Central Intellectual Property Partnership at Rice University (SCIPPR); 713-285-5196
Lubbock: Texas Tech University; 806-742-2282

Utah
Salt Lake City: Marriott Library, University of Utah; 801-581-8394

Vermont
Burlington: Bailey/Howe Library, University of Vermont; 802-656-2542

Virginia
Richmond: James Branch Cabell Library, Virginia Commonwealth University; 804-828-1104

Washington
Seattle: Engineering Library, University of Washington; 206-543-0740

West Virginia
Morgantown: Evansdale Library, West Virginia University; 304-293-2510, ext. 5113

Wisconsin
Madison: Kurt F. Wendt Library, University of Wisconsin-Madison; 608-262-6845
Milwaukee: Milwaukee Public Library; 414-286-3051

Wyoming
Casper: Natrona County Public Library; 307-237-4935

The Patent and Trademark Library Program distributes the information to the 83 PDLs. The information is kept on CD-Rom discs, which are constantly updated, and you can use them to do a patent search. CD-Rom discs have been combined to incorporate CASSIS (Classification and Search Support Information System). CD-Rom discs do not give you online access to the PTO database. Online access is available through APS (Automated Patent Systems), and is presently available to public users of the PTO Search Room and to the 83 Patent Libraries. Each PDL with the online APS has its own rules regarding its use. To use the online APS at the PTO Search Room, you must first sign up and take a class at the Search Room. This class is held for 3 consecutive 1/2 days and is given once per month for a cost of $25. Online access costs $40 per connect hour, and the charge for paper used for printouts is an additional $.25 per sheet.

If you do not live near a PDL, several CD-Rom discs are available through subscription. You may purchase the Classification disc, which dates back to 1790, for $300; the Bibliography disc, which dates back to 1969, for $300; and the ASIST disc, which contains a roster of patent attorneys, assignees, and other information for $200. You can also conduct your patent search and get a copy of it through commercial database services such as:

MeadData Central, Nexis, Lexis: 1-800-843-6476. Patent searches are done for $25. If found, there is a charge of $5 per page of printout and $5 more if there is a drawing. Abstracts are $3. For Trademarks, the charge is $50 and $5 for the drawing. If you intend on doing many searches over time, Nexis Lexis will customize a package for you as a subscriber for approximately $250 per month.

Derwent, 1725 Duke St., Suite 250, Alexandria, VA 22314; 1-800-336-5010, 1-800-523-7668, Fax: 1-800-457-0850. Patent searches are free, but the printouts range from $3.95 to $29.50 per page plus shipping.

If you are going to do your own patent search at your local Patent Depository Library, begin with the *Manual and Index to U.S. Patent Classifications* to identify the subject area where the patent is placed. Then use the CD-Rom discs to locate the patent. CD-Rom discs enable you to do a complete search of all registered patents but do not enable you to view the full patent, with all its specific details. Lastly, view the patent, which will be kept on microfilm, cartridge, or paper. What information there is to view varies by library, depending on what they have been able to purchase. If the library you are using does not have the patent you want, you may be able to obtain it through inter-library loan.

Copies of patents can be ordered from the PTO at 703-308-9726, for $3 per copy.

To obtain a certified copy of a patent, call 703-308-9726 (Patent Search Library at the PTO). The fee is $25 and you must have the patent number. For a certified copy of an abstract of titles, the fee is $25. For a certified copy of patent assignments, with a record of ownership from the beginning until present, call 703-308-9726. The cost is $25, and to request specific assignments you must have the reel and frame number.

Trademarks

Registering a trademark for your product or service is the way to protect the recognition quality of the name you are building. The PTO keeps records on more than 2.2 million trademarks and records. Over 500,000 active trademarks are kept on the floor of the library, while "dead" trademarks are kept on microfilm. Books contain every registered trademark ever issued, starting in 1870. You can visit the Patent and Trademark Office to research a trademark. You can then conduct your search manually for no charge or use their Trademark Search System (T-Search) for $40 per hour, plus $.25 cents per page.

Assistant Commissioner of Trademarks
Trademark Search Library
2900 Crystal Dr.
Second Floor, Room 2B30
Arlington, VA 22202
703-308-9800/9805

If you can't do it yourself, you can hire someone to do the search for you. For an agent to do this, consult the local yellow pages under "Trademark Agents/Consultants" or "Trademark Attorneys". You can also locate an agent by calling your local bar association for a referral.

To conduct your own search at a Patent Depository Library, use the CD-Rom disc on trademarks. It is available for purchase. The CD-Rom discs deliver patent and trademark information including full-text facsimile images and searchable text records. Images can be found in the *Official Gazette*, which contains most current and pending trademarks. Subscriptions to the *Gazette* for trademarks cost $640 per year. The *Gazette* for patents costs $711 per year. Both are issued every Tuesday and can be ordered from the U.S. Government Printing Office. You can also purchase an image file which contains pending and registered trademarks and corresponding serial or registration numbers through Thomson and Thomson by calling 1-800-692-8833. The information contained in it dates back to April 1, 1987 and is updated by approximately 500 images weekly. However, the PDL you use is likely to have an image of the trademark on microfilm or cartridge, and also have copies of the *Official Gazette*. If not, and you have the registration number, you may obtain a copy of the trademark you want for $3 from the PTO. Contact:

Assistant Commissioner of Trademarks
2900 Crystal Dr.
Second Floor, Room 2B30
Arlington, VA 22202
703-308-9800

There are also several commercial services you can use to conduct trademark searches.

Trademark Scan produced by Thomson and Thomson. It can be purchased by calling 1-800-692-8833 (ask for online services), or accessed directly via Saegis. Trademark Scan is updated three times per week, and includes state and federal trademarks, foreign and domestic. To access Trademark Scan you must already have Dialog or Saegis. Many online options are free. The Internet address is {www.thomson-thomson.com}.

Derwent, 1-800-336-5010, is a commercial service that will conduct patent searches only. The cost ranges from $100 and up with a turnaround time of 2-5 days. The Internet address is {www.derwent.com}.

Online services and database discs for both patents and trademarks are constantly being expanded. For information on an extensive range of existing and projected products, call the PTO Office of Electronic Information at 703-306-2600 and ask for the U.S. Department of Commerce, PTO Office of Information Systems' *Electronic Products Brochure*. For example, there is a Weekly Text File, containing text data of pending and registered trademarks. Information can be called up by using almost any term. It can be purchased from AvantIQ and Thomson & Thomson. You can reach AvantIQ at 1-800-320-6366, 610-584-4380, or online at {http://www.avantiq.lu/}. You can reach Thomson & Thomson at 1-800-692-8833 or online at {www.thomson-thomson.com}.

How to Register a Trademark

Get a copy of the booklet, *Basic Facts about Trademarks* from the U.S. Government Printing Office. It is free upon request from the Trademark Search Library by calling 703-308-9000. The mark you intend to use needs to be in use before you apply. The fee to register your trademark is $245. The time to process your registration can take from 12-15 months.

The Right Way to Get a Copyright

Copyrights are filed on intellectual property. A copyright protects your right to control the sale, use of distribution, and royalties from a creation in thought, music, films, art, or books. For more information, contact:

Library of Congress
Copyright Office
Washington, DC 20559
Public Information Office
202-707-3000
www.loc.gov
http://lcweb.loc.gov/copyright

If you know which copyright application you require, you can call the Forms Hotline, open 7 days per week, 24 hours per day at 202-707-9100. The fee is $20 for each registration.

The Library of Congress provides information on copyright registration procedures and copyright card catalogs that cover several million works that have been registered since 1870. The Copyright Office will research federal copyrights only for varying fees. Requests must be made in writing and you must specify exactly what information you require. Contact the Copyright Office, Reference and Bibliography, Library of Congress, 101 Independence Ave., SE, Washington, DC 20559; 202-707-6850, Public Information 707-3000.

Invention Scams: How They Work

Fake product development companies prey on amateur inventors who may not be as savvy about protecting their idea or invention as experienced inventors might be. Most of the bogus/ fake companies use escalating fees.

The following is a description of how most of them operate:

♦ The inventor is invited to call or write for free information.

♦ The inventor is then offered a free evaluation of his idea.

♦ Next comes the sales call. The inventor is told he has a very good potential idea and that the company is willing to share the cost of marketing, etc. Actual fact, there is no sharing with these companies. Most times the inventor has to come up with the money (usually several hundred dollars or more) for a patent search and a market analysis. Neither of these are worth anything.

♦ Then the inventor receives a professional/ impressive looking portfolio which contains no real information at all. All the paper crammed into this portfolio looks topnotch, but it's all computer generated garbage.

♦ Upon receiving this portfolio, the inventor is lured into signing a contract that commits him to giving the company thousands of dollars to promote/license the product. The company sends some promotional letters to fulfill their obligation, but large manufacturers simply toss them into the trash.

After all this, the inventor has spent thousands of dollars, wasted a lot of time, and gotten nowhere with his product.

How To Avoid Losing a Fortune

According to the experts, the inventor should:

♦ Beware of the come-ons offered by these unethical companies. Avoid using the invention brokers who advertise on TV late in the evening; in public magazines; those who offer 800 numbers; and those on public transit display signs.

♦ When upfront money is required, look out. There are very few legitimate consultants who insist on a retainer or hourly fee.

♦ Don't allow the enthusiasm of your idea to take over your inherent common sense. Talk to your patent attorney and see if he knows anything about this company. Plus, check with inventors associations in the state, and see what they have to say about this particular company.

♦ Demand to know what percentage of ideas the company accepts. Legitimate brokers might accept 2 ideas out of every 100. The fake companies tend to accept about 99 out of 100.

♦ Find out their actual success rate. Any corporation/ company that will not give you their success rate (not licensing agreements) is a company to stay away from.

♦ Get an objective evaluation of your invention from reputable professionals. This will save you plenty of money on a bad idea.

A number of highly recommended programs are listed in the next section.

Free Help For Inventors

If you have a great idea and want to turn it into reality, don't rush out and spend what could be thousands of dollars for a private invention company and a patent attorney. You can get

a lot of this help for free or at a fraction of the cost. There is a lot of help out there; university-sponsored programs, not-for-profit groups, state affiliated programs, profit-making companies, etc.

Depending on the assistance and the organization, some services are free, others have reasonable fees.

Many of the inventors' organizations hold regular meetings where speakers share their expertise on topics such as licensing, financing and marketing. These groups are a good place for inventors to meet other inventors, patent attorneys, manufacturers, and others with whom they can talk and from whom they can get help.

If the listings in the state-by-state section of this chapter do not prove to be useful, you can contact one of the following organizations for help.

1. **Small Business Development Center**
   Washington State University
   Parkplace Building
   1200 6th Ave., Suite 1700

Seattle, WA 98101
206-553-7328
Fax: 206-553-7044
www.sbdc.wsu.edu/franz.htm

This service will evaluate your idea for a fee. They also provide counseling services and can assist you with your patent search.

2. **Wisconsin Innovation Service Center/Technology**
   Small Business Development Center
   Ms. Debra Malewicki, Director
   University of Wisconsin - Whitewater
   402 McCutchan Hall
   Whitewater, WI 53190
   414-472-3217
   Fax: 414-472-1600

The only service that is guaranteed is the evaluation. However, efforts are made to match inventors with exceptional high evaluation scores with manufacturers seeking new product ideas. (Do not offer direct invention development or marketing services). WISC charges a $495 flat fee for an evaluation. The goal is to keep research as affordable as possible to the average independent inventor. Most evaluations are completed within 30 - 45 days. Those inventions from specialized fields may require more time. WISC also provides preliminary patent searches via on-line databases to client.

3. **Drake University**
   Small Business Development Center
   Mr. Benjamin C. Swartz, Director
   Drake Business Center
   2507 University
   Des Moines, IA 50311-4505
   515-271-2655
   1-800-532-1216
   Fax: 515-271-1899
   www.iabusnet.org

INVENTURE is a program of the Drake University Business Development and Research Institute designed to encourage the development of valid ideas through the various steps to becoming marketable items. INVENTURE has no paid staff. The entire panel is made up of volunteers. The administration of the program is handled by existing staff from the Small Business Development Center and the College of Business and Public Administration. They will review items from **any person** regardless of their place of residence. They will review a product idea and check it for market feasibility. INVENTURE may link individuals with business and/or financial partners.

INVENTURE screens every product submitted, but will not consider toy/game or food items. Products are evaluated on 33 different criteria, (factors related to legality, safety, business risk, and demand analysis, to market acceptance/ competition). It normally takes up to 6 weeks to receive results of the evaluation. Evaluators are experienced in manufacturing, marketing, accounting, production, finance and investments.

INVENTURE acts in a responsible manner to maintain confidence of an idea, but cannot guarantee confidentiality.

For assistance with business plans, financial projections, and marketing help, you're encouraged to contact your Small Business Development Center (SBDC).

4. **The Wal-Mart Innovation Network (WIN)**
    Center for Business and Economic Development
    Southwest Missouri State University
    901 S. National
    Springfield, MO 65804
    415-836-5671
    www.innovation-institute.com

The WIN program is essentially an innovation evaluation service designed to provide inventors with an honest and objective third-party analysis of the risks and potential of their ideas and inventions. If the invention or new product idea passes the tough screening process, the Center will automatically send your idea to Wal-Mart for an Assessment of Marketability. Their expertise allows them to provide qualified inventors with a second analysis of the marketability of their invention/new product idea. A WIN endorsement will increase the chances that others will be willing to listen. If the invention/ product idea receives a "Fully recommended" market assessment, WIN will not take the development or commercialization of your invention or idea. But, if the invention has a reasonable chance of success, WIN will supply information about the Innovation Network (IN) resources in a particular state, (Do not assume their services are free). The only advance payment charged by WIN is the $175 evaluation fee. A "fully recommended" WIN Assessment of Marketability does not obligate Wal-Mart in any way. The WIN program is limited to consumer related ideas and inventions. The only promise is an honest and objective preliminary evaluation.

5. **U.S. Department of Energy**
   Mail Stop EE-24
   1000 Independence Ave., SW
   Washington, DC 20585
   202-586-1478
   Fax: 202-586-7114
   www.oit.doe.gov/inventions/
Financial assistance is available at 2 levels: up to $40,000 and up to $200,000 by the Inventions and Innovations program as stated by the Office of Industrial Technologies (OIT) Department of Energy (DOE) for ideas that significantly impact energy savings and future commercial market potential. Successful applicants will find technical guidance and commercialization support in addition to financial assistance.

DOE has given financial support to more than 500 inventions with nearly 25% of these reaching the marketplace bringing in nearly $710 million in cumulative sales.

6. **U.S. Environmental Protection Agency**
   Center for Environmental Research Information
   Cincinnati, OH 45260
   513-569-7562
   www.epa.gov
Directory Description: Environmental Protection Agency, Office of

Research and Development, 401 M Street, SW, Washington, DC 20460;
202-260-7676, Fax: 202-260-9761
The Office of Research and Development conducts an Agency wide
integrated program of research and development relevant to pollution
sources and control, transport and fate processes, health/ecological
effects, measurement/monitoring, and risk assessment. The office
provides technical reviews, expert consultations, technical
assistance, and advice to environmental decision-makers
in federal, state, local, and foreign governments.

**Center for Environmental Research
Information**
26 W. ML King Drive, Cincinnati, OH 45268,
Calvin O. Lawrence, Director; 513-569-7562;
Fax: 513-569-7566.
A focal point for the exchange of scientific/
technical information both within the federal
government and to the public.

Office of Research and Development
Is responsible for working with laboratories, program offices, regions to
produce information products that summarize research, technical,
regulatory enforcement information that will assist non-technical
audiences in under-standing environmental issues. Contact Office of
Research and Development, U.S. Environmental Protection Agency, 401
M St., SW, Washington, DC 20460; 202-260-5767.

Office of Exploratory Research
Robert Menzer, Acting Director, 401 M Street, SW, Washington, DC
20460; 202-564-6849, Fax: 202-260-0450.
The Office of Exploratory Research (OER) plans, administers, manages,
and evaluates the Environmental Protection Agency's (EPA) extramural
grant research. It supports research in developing a better understanding
of the environment and its problems. Main goals are: to support the
academic community in environmental research; maintain
scientific/technical personnel in environmental science/ technology; to
support research for the identification/solution of emerging environmental
problems.

Goals are accomplished through four core programs:

1. The Research Grants Program:
Supports research initiated by individual investigators in areas of interest to the agency.

2. The Environmental Research Centers Program:
Has two components: The Academic Research Center Program (ARC) and the Hazardous Substance Research Centers Program (HSRC).
3. The Small Business Innovation Research (SBIR) Program:
Program supports small businesses for the development of ideas relevant to EPA's mission. Focuses on projects in pollution control development. Also receives 1.5% of the Agency's resources devoted to extramural Superfund research.

4. The Visiting Scientists Program:
Components are an Environmental Science and Engineering Fellows Program and a Resident Research Associateship Program. The Fellows Program supports ten mid-career post-doctoral scientists and engineers at EPA headquarters & regional offices. The Research Associateship Program attracts national and international scientists and engineers at EPA research laboratories for up to 3 years to collaborate with Agency researchers on important environmental issues.

Other programs available are:
A Minority Fellowship Program
A Minority Summer Intern Program
The Agency's Senior Environmental Employment Program (SEE)
The Federal Workforce Training Program
An Experimental Program to Stimulate Competitive Research
(EPSCoR).

To learn more, contact Grants Administration, U.S. Environmental Protection Agency, 401 M St., SW, 3903E, Washington, DC 20460; 202-564-5315. The best way, though, is to search for the word "grant" at the EPA's website, {www.epa.gov}.

State Sources for Inventors

Below is a listing of a variety of inventors groups, listed state by state. Some organizations listed under the state where they are located are regional or national in scope. In states where there is no specific program for inventors, the Small Business Development Centers (under the U.S. Small Business Administration) can often be of help. They are usually found at the colleges and universities. The Small Business Development Center office is located at 409 Third St., SW, Suite 4600, Washington, DC 20416; 202-205-6766; {www.sba.gov}.

Alabama

Office for the Advancement of Developing Industries
University of Alabama - Birmingham
2800 Milan Ct.
Birmingham, AL 35211   205-934-6560
www.uab.edu/oad
Inventors can receive help on the commercialization and patent processes and critical reviews of inventions in this office. Assessments can be made on an invention's potential marketability and assistance is available for patent searches. There is a charge for services.

Small Business Development Center
University of Alabama at Birmingham
9015 15th St.   205-934-6760
Birmingham, AL 35294   Fax: 205-934-0538
www.business.uab.edu/school.sbdc/seminar.html

The center offers counseling for a wide range of business issues and problems.

U.S. Small Business Administration
Business Development
2121 8th Avenue, N, Suite 200   205-731-1338
Birmingham, AL 35203-2398   Fax: 205-731-1404
www.sba.gov
This office offers counseling for a wide range of business issues and problems.

Alabama Technology Assistance Program
University of Alabama at Birmingham
1717 11th Avenue S, Suite 419   205-934-7260
Birmingham, AL 35294   Fax: 205-934-7645
This program provides general assistance/funding information. Inventors meet other inventors and investors.

Alaska
UAA Small Business Development Center of Alaska
430 W. 7th Ave., Suite 110   907-274-7232
Anchorage, AK 99501   Fax: 907-274-9524
www.sba.gov/regions/states/ak/
The SBDC provides general assistance, including free counseling to inventors on commercialization and patent processes, and arranging meetings between inventors, investors, manufacturers, and others who can be of help.

Arizona
Arizona SBDC Network
108 N. 40th Street, Suite 148   602-392-5224
Phoenix, AZ 85034   Fax: 602-392-5300
The center offers counseling for a wide range of business issues and problems.

Maricopa Community Colleges
Small Business Development Center

702 E. Osborn Rd., Suite 150   602-230-7308
Phoenix, AZ 85014   Fax: 602-230-7989
www.dist.maricopa.edu/sbdc
The center provides inventor assistance and funding information to
inventors.

Arkansas
Small Business Development Center
University of Arkansas at Little Rock
100 S. Main, Suite 401   501-324-9043
Little Rock, AR 72201   Fax: 501-324-9049
www.asbdc.ualr.edu
The center offers counseling for a wide range of business issues and
problems.

California
Inventors Workshop International
Inventor Center, Suite 304
3201 Corte Malpaso
Camarillo, CA 93012   805-962-5722
This foundation has chapters nationwide. They hold meetings, conduct
seminars, and counsel inventors on important issues, including product
development and market research. The foundation
publishes journals and a guidebook. There are
dues and subscription fees.

COUNSELING

Small Business Development Center
1410 Ethan Way   916-563-3210
Sacramento, CA 95825   Fax: 916-563-2366
www.sbdc.net
The center offers counseling for a wide range of business issues and
problems.

Colorado
Affiliated Inventors Foundation, Inc.
1405 Porter St., #107   719-380-1234

Colorado Springs, CO 80909   Fax: 719-380-1144
This foundation counsels inventors on commercialization and patent
processes, and provides detailed information on the steps needed to reach
commercialization. Preliminary appraisals, evaluations and other services
are available for a fee.

Small Business Development Center
Office of Economic Development
1625 Broadway, Suite 1710   303-892-3840
Denver, CO 80202   Fax: 303-892-3848
www.state.co.us/gov_dir/oed/sbdc.html
The center offers counseling for a wide range of business issues and
problems.

Connecticut
Small Business Development Center
2 Bourn Place   860-486-4135
Storrs, CT 06269-1594   Fax: 860-486-1576
www.sbdc.uconn.edu
The center offers counseling for a wide range of business issues and
problems.

Delaware
Small Business Development Center
University of Delaware
102 MBNA America Hall   302-831-1555
Newark, DE 19716   Fax: 302-831-1423
www.delawaresbdc.org
The office offers management counseling and seminars on various topics,
and can counsel inventors on areas such as the commercialization and
patenting processes. Services are by appointment only.

Delaware Economic Development
99 Kings Highway   302-739-4271
Dover, DE 19901   Fax: 302-739-5749
www.state.de.us

Assistance is available to any applicant located in Delaware or relocating to Delaware, who has been granted a phase I SBIR award and has submitted a Phase II SBIR application.

District of Columbia
U.S. Department of Commerce
U.S. Patent and Trademark Office
Washington, DC 20231

800-PTO-9199
703-308-4357

District of Columbia Small Business Development Center
Howard University
2600 6th St., NW, Suite 128
Washington, DC 20059

202-806-1550
Fax: 202-806-1777

The center offers counseling for a wide range of business issues and problems.

U.S. Small Business Administration
2328 19th St., NW
Washington, DC 20009
www.sba.gov

202-606-4060
Fax: 202-205-7064

This office provides general assistance and information on funding.

Florida
Small Business Development Center
1531 NW 6th St.
Gainesville, FL 32606

352-377-5621

The center offers counseling for a wide range of business issues and problems.

Small Business Development Center
University of West Florida
1170 Martin L. King, Jr. Blvd.
Fort Walton Beach, FL 32547
www.sbdc.uwf.edu

850-595-5480
Fax: 850-595-5487

The center offers counseling for a wide range of business issues and problems.

Florida SBDC Network
19 W. Garden St., Suite 300   850-595-6060
Pensacola, FL 32501   Fax: 850-595-6070
www.floridasbdc.com
The network provides general assistance; conducts
market/ technical assessments; offers legal advice on
patents and licensing; provides funding information;
and assists in building a prototype. Inventor get to
showcase their inventions and meet with other
inventors and investors.

University of Central Florida
Small Business Development Center
P.O. Box 161530   407-823-3073
Orlando, FL 32816-1530   Fax: 407-823-3073
www.bus.ucs.edu.sbdc
The center provides general assistance, funding information and conducts
market assessments. Inventors meet other inventors.

Georgia
Small Business Development Center
University of Georgia
Chicopee Complex
1180 East Broad Street   706-542-7436
Athens, GA 30602   Fax: 706-542-6803
The center offers counseling for a wide range of business issues and
problems.

Hawaii
Small Business Development Center
University of Hawaii at Hilo
1111 Bishop St., Suite 204   808-933-3515
Honolulu, HI 96813   Fax: 808-933-3683
http://hawaii-sbdc.org
The center offers counseling for a wide range of business issues and
problems.

Help For Inventors

Idaho

Idaho Research Foundation, Inc.
University of Idaho
121 Sweet Ave.
Moscow, ID 83843-2309   208-885-3548
This foundation counsels inventors on commercialization and patent
processes, and provides critical reviews on inventions. Computerized data
searching and marketing service is available. It takes a percentage of
intellectual property royalties.

Small Business Development Center
Boise State University
1910 University Drive
Boise, ID 83725   208-426-1640
The center offers counseling for a wide range of business issues and
problems.

Idaho Small Business Development Center
P.O. Box 1238
315 Falls Ave.   208-733-9554
Twin Falls, ID 83303-1238   Fax: 208-733-9316
www.csi.cc.id.us - click on community services
The center conducts market assessments and provides funding
information.

Idaho Small Business Development Center
Lewis-Clark State College
500 8th Ave.
Lewiston, ID 83501   Fax: 208-799-2831
www.idbsu.edu/isbdc
The center provides general assistance and funding information. They
also conduct market assessments.

Idaho State University
Small Business Development Center
2300 N. Yellowstone   208-523-1087
Idaho Falls, ID 83401   Fax: 208-528-7127
The center provides general assistance and funding information, and
conducts technical assessments. Inventors meet with other inventors and
investors.

Illinois

Inventor's Council
431 S. Dearborn, Suite 705
Chicago, IL 60605   312-939-3329
www.donmeyer.com
This group provides a liaison between inventors and industries. It holds
meetings and workshops on commercialization, evaluation, marketing,
financing, etc., for U.S. and Canadian inventors. Dues are required.

Small Business Development Center
Department of Commerce and Community Affairs
620 East Adams St., 3rd Floor   217-524-5856
Springfield, IL 62701   Fax: 217-785-6328
www.commerce.state.il.us
The center offers counseling for a wide range of business issues and
problems, including commercialization and patent processes.

Small Business Development Center
Evanston Business Investment Corp.
1840 Oak Avenue   847-866-1817
Evanston, IL 60201   Fax: 847-866-1808
The center provides general assistance and funding information.

Western Illinois University
Technical Center and Small Business Development Center
Seal Hall 214
Macomb, IL 61455   Fax: 309-298-2520
www.wiu.edu/sbdc
The center provides general assistance; conducts market/technical
assessments; provides investment and funding information; and aids in
building a prototype. Inventors meet with other inventors and investors,
and get the chance to showcase their inventions.

Indiana

Small Business Development Center
One North Capitol, Suite 1275   317-246-6871
Indianapolis, IN 46204   Fax: 317-264-6855

www.isbdcorp.org
The center offers counseling for a wide range of business issues and
problems.

Iowa
Drake Small Business Development Center
2429 University Ave.   515-271-2655
Des Moines, IA 46204   Fax: 515-271-1899
This center evaluates innovations for marketability, counsels inventors on
commercialization, and helps match inventors with businesspersons. The
fee for invention assessment is $125.

Small Business Development Center
Administrative Office
Iowa State University
137 Lynn Avenue   515-292-6351
Ames, IA 50014   Fax: 515-292-0020
www.iowasbdc.org
The center offers counseling for a wide range of business
issues and problems.

Kansas
Small Business Development Center
Wichita State University
Campus Box 148
1845 Fairmont   316-978-3193
Wichita, KS 67260-0148   Fax: 316-978-3647
www.twsu.edu/~ksbdc
The center offers counseling for a wide range of business issues and
problems.

Kentucky
Small Business Development Center
University of Louisville
Burhans Hall, Room 137, Shelby Campus   502-852-7854

Louisville, KY 40292   Fax: 502-852-8573
This center counsels inventors on commercialization and patent processes
and provides critical reviews of inventions. It provides assistance in
technically refining inventions. There are no fees.

Small Business Development Center
Kentucky Small Business Development Center
Center for Business Development
College of Business and Economics Building
225 Business and Economics Building
University of Kentucky   606-257-7668
Lexington, KY 40506   Fax: 606-323-1907
The center offers counseling for a wide range of business issues and
problems.

Kentucky Transportation Center
176 Oliver H. Raymond Bldg.   606-257-4513
Lexington, KY 40506   Fax: 606-257-1815
www.engrouky.edu/ktc/
The center works closely with various federal, state and local agencies, as
well as the private sector to conduct research supported by a wide variety
of sources.

Louisiana
Small Business Development Center
Northeast Louisiana University
College of Business Administration
700 University Avenue   318-342-5506
Monroe, LA 71209   Fax: 318-342-5510
The center offers counseling for a wide range of business issues and
problems.

Louisiana Department of Economic Development
P.O. Box 94185
Baton Rouge, LA 70804-9185   225-342-3000
www.lded.state.la.us
The department provides general assistance.

Maine

Industrial Cooperation
University of Maine
5717 Corbett Hall, Room 435
Orono, ME 04469-5717   207-581-2200
www.umaine.edu/dic
This center counsels inventors on the commercialization process, provides
referrals for critical reviews of inventions and for financial and patent
assistance, and conducts inventors' forums. It publishes a newsletter and
bulletins. The communicative services are usually free; there are fees for
educational services and materials.

Sunrise County Economic Council
P.O. Box 679
Machias, ME 04654   389-255-3313
The center offers counseling for a wide range of business issues and
problems.

Department of Industrial Cooperation
5711 Boardman Hall, Room 117   207-581-1488
Orono, ME 04469-5711   Fax: 207-581-2202
www.umaine.edu/dic
On March 15, 1984, the Inventors Forum of Maine, Inc. (IFM), was
formed and became a nonprofit corporation in the state of Maine. It was
organized to stimulate inventiveness and entrepreneurship, and to help
innovators and entrepreneurs develop and promote their ideas. It allows
inventors and entrepreneurs to join together, share ideas and hopefully
improve the chance for success. It gives encouragement, professional
expertise, evaluation assistance, confidentiality and moral support of the
University of Maine's Network and the University of Southern Maine's
Small Business Development Center.

The Inventors Forum of Maine generally meets on the first Tuesday
evening of each month at the University of Southern Maine, Campus
Center, Room A, B & C on Bedford Street in Portland. Membership is
open to all. For information regarding the Inventors Forum of Maine,
contact Jake Ward, 207-581-1488.

Maryland
Inventions and Innovations
Department of Energy
Forrestal Building
1000 Independence Ave., SW
Washington, DC 20585   202-586-2079
www.oit.doe.gov/inventions
The office evaluates all promising non-nuclear energy-related inventions,
particularly those submitted by independent inventors and small
companies for the purpose of obtaining direct grants for their
development from the U.S. Department of Energy.

Small Business Development Center
MMG, Inc.   410-333-4270
Baltimore, MD 21202   Fax: 410-333-2552
www.mmggroup.com
The center offers counseling for a wide
range of business issues and problems.

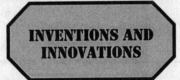

INVENTIONS AND
INNOVATIONS

Massachusetts
Massachusetts Small Business Development Center
Salem State College
352 Lafayette St.
Salem, MA 01970   978-542-6345
The center offers counseling for a wide range of business issues and
problems.

Small Business Development Center
205 School of Management
University of Massachusetts   413-545-6301
Amherst, MA 01003   Fax: 413-545-1273
The center provides general assistance and funding information.

Smaller Business Association of New England
252 2nd Ave.   781-890-9070
Waltham, MA 02451   Fax: 781-890-4567
www.sbane.org
The association provides general assistance and funding information.

Michigan
Small Business Development Center
2727 Second Avenue
Detroit, MI 48201
313-226-7947
Fax: 313-577-4222
The center offers counseling for a wide range of business issues and problems.

Minnesota
Minnesota Project Innovation, Inc.
111 3rd Ave. S., Suite 100
Minneapolis, MN 55401-2551
www.mpi.org
612-338-3280
Fax: 612-349-2603
This project is affiliated with the Minnesota Dept. of Energy and Economic Development, U.S. Small Business Administration, and private companies. It provides referrals to inventors for sources of technical assistance in refining inventions.

Minnesota Inventors Congress (MIC)
805 East Bridge Street
P.O. Box 71
Redwood Falls, MN 56283
www.invent1.org
507-637-2344
Fax: 507-637-8399
The Minnesota Inventors Congress (MIC) is a nonprofit organization established in 1958 to promote creativity, innovation, entrepreneurship by assisting the inventor and entrepreneur with education, promotion and referral. It's a professional organization composed of private individuals and corporations, who are creating and developing useful technologies. MIC is for inventors at every development stage — the novice and experienced; male or female; young and old; and supporters of invention and innovation. Workshops are also available. These are for individuals with ideas or inventions not yet successfully on the market; for companies, entrepreneurs looking for such inventions or new products.

"World's Oldest Annual Invention Convention," promotes the spirit of invention and innovation. Each year a 3 day convention presents more than 200 inventions and attracts some 10,000 visitors from around the world. The MIC provides a meeting place for:

1) Inventors to showcase their new products, connecting with manufacturers/investors, product test market, educational seminars, publicity, inventors network, and $1,500 in cash awards.
2) Manufacturers, marketers, investors and licenses seeking new products.
3) Inventors, viewers and exhibitors, seeking free counsel and literature on the invention development process.
4) Public to view the latest inventions, by adults and students, purchase MarketPlace products and meet global inventors.

Small Business Development Center
1125 Harmon Pl.   651-962-4500
St. Paul, MN 55403   Fax: 651-962-4508
The center offers counseling for a wide range of business issues and problems.

Mississippi
Small Business Development Center
Old Chemistry Building, Suite 216   601-232-5001
University, MS 38677   Fax: 601-232-5650
www.olemiss.edu/depts/mssbdc
The center offers counseling for a wide range of business
issues and problems.

Legal Advice

Mississippi State University
Small Business Development Center
P.O. Box 5288   601-325-8684
Mississippi State, MS 39762   Fax: 601-325-4016
The center provides general assistance; conducts market assessments; and provides funding information.

Small Business Development Center
Meridian Community College
910 Highway 19 North   601-482-7445
Meridian, MS 39307   Fax: 601-482-5803
The center provides general assistance and funding information; conducts market/technical assessments; and offers legal advice on patents and licensing. Inventors meet with other inventors and investors.

Missouri
Missouri Innovation Center
5658 Sinclare Rd.   573-446-3100
Columbia, MO 65203   Fax: 573-443-3748
This group provides communications among inventors, manufacturers,
patent attorneys and venture capitalists, and provides general
consultations. It is sponsored by the state, city of Columbia, and the
University of Missouri. There are fees for some services.

Inventors Association of St. Louis
P.O. Box 16544
St. Louis, MO 63105   314-432-1291
The group holds monthly meetings, provides communications among
inventors, manufacturers, patent attorneys, and venture capitalists. It
publishes a newsletter. There are annual dues.

Small Business Development Center
University of Missouri - Columbia
1205 University Ave.
Suite 1800 University Pl.   573-882-7096
Columbia, MO 65211   Fax: 573-882-9931
www.tiger.bpa.missouri.edu/Research/Training/sbdc.homepage.htm
The center offers counseling for a wide range of business issues and
problems.

Montana
Small Business Development Center
Montana Department of Commerce
1424 Ninth Avenue   406-444-4780
Helena, MT 59620   Fax: 406-444-1872
www.state.mt.us
The center offers counseling for a wide range of business issues and
problems.

Nebraska
University of Nebraska - Lincoln
W 191 Nebraska Hall

Lincoln, NE 68588-0525   402-472-5600
www.engext.unl.edu/engext.html
Upon request, the University will send a packet of information so that the
individual may go to the location and conduct their own Patent and
Trademark search.

Small Business Development Center
University of Nebraska at Omaha
60th and Dodge Street
CBA, Room 407   402-554-2521
Omaha, NE 68182   Fax: 402-554-3473
The center offers counseling for a wide range of business issues and
problems.

Association of SBDCs
3108 Columbia Pike, Suite 300
Arlington, VA 22204   703-271-8700
www.asbdc-us.org
Organization's name and address may be
given to individual inventors for referrals.   **REFERRALS**

Nevada
Nevada Small Business Center
University of Nevada - Reno
College of Business Administration/032   775-784-1717
Reno, NV 89557-0100   Fax: 775-784-4337
www.nsbdc.org
The center provides general assistance and funding information. Inventors
meet with other inventors and get to showcase their inventions.

Nevada Small Business Center
3720 Howard Hughes Parkway, Suite 130   702-734-7575
Las Vegas, NV 89109   Fax: 702-734-7633
www.Nevadasbdc.com
The center provides general assistance and funding information. Inventors
meet with other inventors.

New Hampshire
Small Business Development Center
University of New Hampshire
108 McConnell Hall   603-862-2200
Durham, NH 03824   Fax: 603-862-4876
www.nhsbdc.org
The center offers counseling for a wide range of business issues and
problems.

Small Business Development Center
OEI-MMC
1001 Elm Street   603-624-2000
Manchester, NH 03101   Fax: 603-647-4410
www.nhsbdc.org
The Small Business Development Center provides general assistance and
funding information, and offers legal advice on patents and licensing.
Inventors meet with other inventors.

New Jersey
Small Business Development Center
Rutgers University
43 Bleeker St.   973-353-5621
Newark, NJ 07102-1913   Fax: 973-353-1030
www/nj.com/smallbusiness
The Small Business Development Center offers counseling for a wide
range of business issues and problems.

New Mexico
Albuquerque Invention Club
P.O. Box 30062
Albuquerque, NM 87190   505-266-3541
The contact is Dr. Albert Goodman, president of the club. The club meets
on a monthly basis for speakers and presentations by different inventors.
Members include patent attorneys, investors, and manufacturers.

Small Business Development Center
Santa Fe Community College

6401 Richards Ave.
Santa Fe, NM 87505
www.nmsbdc.org
The center offers counseling for a wide range of business issues and
problems.

505-428-1343
Fax: 505-428-1469

New York
Small Business Development Center
State University Plaza
41 State St.
Albany, NY 12246
www.nys-sbdc.suny.edu
The center offers counseling for a wide range of business issues and
problems.

518-443-5398
Fax: 518-443-5275

New York State Energy Research and Development Authority
Corporate Plaza West
286 Washington Ave. Ext.
Albany, NY 12203-6319
www.nyserda.org
The office provides general assistance and investment and funding
information. It assists in building a prototype.

518-862-1090
Fax: 518-862-1091

SUNY Institute of Technology
Small Business Development Center
P.O. Box 3050
Utica, NY 13504
www.sunyit.edu.sbdc/
The center provides general assistance and funding information; conducts
market/technical assessments; offers legal advice on patents and licensing,
and assists in building a prototype. Inventors meet with other inventors.

315-792-7546
Fax: 315-792-7554

Small Business Technical Inv. Fund
New York State Science and Technology Foundation
99 Washington Avenue, Suite 1731
Albany, NY 12210
www.empire.state.ny.us/stf/stf.htm
The program provides financing assistance for technology-based start-up
companies with initial investment as much as $300,000.

518-473-9741

North Carolina
Small Business Development Center
University of North Carolina
333 Fayetteville Street Mall, #1150   919-715-7272
Raleigh, NC 27601   Fax: 919-715-7777
The center offers counseling for a wide range of business issues and
problems.

North Dakota
Center for Innovation and Business Development
University of North Dakota
University Station, Box 8372   701-777-3132
Grand Forks, ND 58202   Fax: 701-777-2339

www.innovators.net
This center conducts occasional seminars and workshops
with speakers; counsels on the commercialization and
patenting process; provides communications among
inventors, manufacturers, and patent attorneys. There are
fees for services, but the first consultation is free.

Small Business Development Center
118 Gamble Hall
University of North Dakota, Box 7308   701-777-3700
Grand Forks, ND 58202-7308   Fax: 701-777-3225
www.und.nodak.edu/dept/nsbdc/
The center offers counseling for a wide range of business issues and
problems.

Ohio
Inventors Connection of Greater Cleveland
17145 Misty Lake Dr.
Strongsville, OH 44106   440-238-3083
This association meets on a regular basis and provides communication
among inventors. There are no dues.

Inventors Council of Dayton
Mr. George Pierce, President

P.O. Box 611
Dayton, OH 45409   937-224-8513
This association meets on a regular basis and provides communication
among inventors, manufacturers, patent attorneys, etc., and often
publishes newsletters.

Docie Marketing
9855 Sand Ridge Rd.
Millfield, OH 45761   740-594-2200
This profit-making company counsels inventors on the commercialization
process, provides critical review of inventions and arranges meetings
between inventors and manufacturers.

Small Business Development Center
Department of Development
30 East Broad Street, 23rd Floor
P.O. Box 1001   614-466-2711
Columbus, OH 43226   Fax: 614-466-0829
www.odod.ohio.gov
The center offers counseling for a wide range of business issues and
problems.

Oklahoma
Invention Development Center
8230 SW 8th Street
Oklahoma City, OK 73128   405-632-0999
The center holds regular meetings, often with speakers, publishes a
newsletter, and offers counseling and technical assistance to inventors.
Annual dues are $25.

Small Business Development Center
Southeastern Oklahoma State University
517 University   580-924-0277
Durant, OK 74701   Fax: 580-924-7071
The center offers counseling for a wide range of business issues and
problems.

Inventors Assistance Program
395 Cordell South
Stillwater, OK 74078
http://techweb.ceat.okstate.edu/ias

405-744-8727
Fax: 405-744-7399

This is a service to help inventors navigate the process from idea to marketplace using information, education and referrals. The service itself is free.

Oregon

Eastern Oregon University
Small Business Development Center
1410 L Ave.
La Grande, OR 97850

541-962-3391
Fax: 541-962-3668

Oregon Institute of Technology
Small Business Development Center
3201 Campus Dr., South 314
Klamath Falls, OR 97601

541-885-1760
Fax: 541-885-1855

Southern Oregon University
Small Business Development Center
332 W. 6th St.
Medford, OR 97501

541-772-3478
Fax: 541-734-4813

Small Business Development Centers (SBDCs) at three state colleges and the community colleges can counsel inventors and direct them where to go for patent process, etc.

Oregon Small Business Development Center
44 W. Broadway, Suite 501
Eugene, OR 97401

541-726-2250
Fax: 541-345-6006

The center provides general assistance and funding information.

Small Business Development Center
2701 NW Vaughn St.
Portland, OR 97210
www.sbdc.citysearch.com

503-978-5080
Fax: 503-222-2570

The center provides general assistance and funding information.

Oregon State Library
State Library Building
250 Winter St., NE   503-378-4277
Salem, OR 97310   Fax: 503-588-7119
www.osl.state.or.us
Organization's name and address may be given to individual inventors for
referrals.

Pennsylvania
American Society of Inventors
P.O. Box 58426
Philadelphia, PA 19102-8426   215-546-6601
Members are counseled on the commerciali-
zation and patent processes; critical reviews
of inventions, and assessments of market
potential are provided. The Society also
offers technical assistance and referrals.
There are dues.

Small Business Development Center
Bucknell University
Dana Engineering Building, 1st Floor   570-524-1249
Lewisburg, PA 17837   Fax: 570-524-1768
www.bucknell.edw/~sbdc
The center offers counseling for a wide range of business issues and
problems.

Pennsylvania Small Business Development Center
Vance Hall, 4th Floor
3733 Spruce Street   215-898-4861
Philadelphia, PA 19104   Fax: 215-898-1063
www.pasbdc.org
The center provides general assistance and funding information. It also
conducts market and technical assessments. It also oversees all centers in
Pennsylvania.

Rhode Island
Service Corps of Retired Executives (SCORE)
c/o U.S. Small Business Administration
380 Westinghouse, Room #511
Providence, RI 02903   401-528-4571

 Volunteers in the SCORE office are experts in many
areas of business management and can offer advice to
inventors in areas including marketing and the
commercialization process.

Small Business Development Center
7 Jackson Walkway
Providence, RI 02903   401-831-1330
The center offers counseling for a wide range of business issues and
problems.

Small Business Development Center
Bryant College
1150 Douglas Pike   401-232-6111
Smithfield, RI 02917   Fax: 401-232-6933
www.risbdc.org
The center provides general assistance and conducts market and technical
assessments.

South Carolina
Small Business Development Center
South Carolina State University
School of Business
300 College St.
Campus Box 7176   803-536-8445
Orangeburg, SC 29117   Fax: 803-536-8066
The center offers counseling for a wide range of business issues and
problems.

South Carolina Small Business Development Center
University of South Carolina
College of Business Administration   803-777-4907

Columbia, SC 29208   Fax: 803-777-4403
The center provides general assistance and funding information.

South Dakota
Business and Education Institute
Dakota State University
Madison, SD 57042   605-256-5555
www.bei.dsu.ed.com
This office can provide guidance to inventors on a wide range of issues:
commercialization, patent process, marketability, etc. It has grant money
available.

Small Business Development Center
University of South Dakota
School of Business
414 East Clark St.   605-677-5287
Vermillion, SD 57069-2390   Fax: 605-677-5427
www.uso.edu/brbinfo
The center offers counseling for a wide range of business issues and
problems.

Tennessee
Tennessee Inventors Association
P.O. Box 11225
Knoxville, TN 37939-1225   423-539-4466
www.state.tn.us
Monthly meetings are held where a wide range of topical subjects are
discussed: patenting, venture capital, marketing, etc. Workshops and
invention exhibitions are held periodically.

Jackson State Community College
Small Business Development Center
2046 North Parkway Street   901-424-5389
Jackson, TN 38301   Fax: 901-425-2641
The center offers counseling for a wide range of business issues and
problems.

Texas

Technology and Economic Development
DivTEEX
301 Terrow Bldg.
College Station, TX 77840-7896   409-845-3559
www.tedd.org
The organization conducts workshops, provides
counseling on commercialization and patent
processes, offers critical reviews of inventions
on a selected basis, assesses invention's
marketability, and assists with patent searches.
State appropriations, federal grants and
subscriptions to newsletter are available on a limited basis.

Critical Review of Inventions

North Texas-Dallas Small Business Development Center
Dallas Community College District
1402 Corinth Street   214-860-5850
Dallas, TX 75215   Fax: 214-565-5815
The center offers counseling for a wide range of business issues and
problems.

Texas Tech University
Small Business Development Center
2579 S. Loop 289, St. 114   806-745-3973
Lubbock, TX 79423   Fax: 806-745-6207
www.nwtsbdc.com
The center provides general assistance and funding information.

University of Houston
Small Business Development Center
Manufacturers Assistance Center
1100 Louisiana, Suite 500   713-752-8440
Houston, TX 77002   Fax: 713-756-1515
http://smbizsolutions.uh.edu
The center provides general assistance and funding information; conducts
market and technical assessments; and assists in building a prototype.
Inventors meet with investors.

Utah
Utah Small Business Development Center
1627 S. State St.   801-957-3480
Salt Lake City, UT 84115   Fax: 801-957-3489
www.slcc.edu
The center provides general assistance and funding information, and
conducts market and technical assessments. Inventors meet with inventors
and investors.

Vermont
Economic and Development Office
State of Vermont
National Library Bldg.   802-828-3211
Montpelier, VT 05620-0501   Fax: 802-828-3258
www.state.vt.us/dca
Inventors will be counseled on the commercialization and marketing
processes as well as other areas, and will be referred to other places as
needed.

Small Business Development Center
60 Main St., Suite 103   802-658-9228
Burlington, VT 05401   Fax: 802-860-1899
www.vermont.org
The center offers counseling for a wide range of business issues and
problems.

Virginia
Virginia Small Business Development Center
707 E. Main St.
P.O. Box 446
Richmond, VA 23288-0446   804-371-8258
www.dba.state.va.us
The center offers counseling for a wide range of business issues and
problems.

Small Business Development Center
1001 E. Market St.   804-295-8198
Charlottesville, VA 22903   Fax: 804-295-7066
http://avenue.gen.va.us/Market/SBDC
The center provides general assistance, and conducts market and technical assessments.

U.S. Department of Commerce
Patent and Trademark Office   1-800-PTO-9199
Washington, DC 20231   703-308-4357
www.uspto.gov
The office provides general assistance on patents and licensing.

Washington
Innovation Assessment Center
108 Nickerson St., Suite 207   206-464-5450
Seattle, WA 98109   Fax: 206-464-6357
www.sbdc.wsu.edu
Part of the Small Business Development Center, this center performs commercial evaluations of inventions, counseling and provides assistance with patentability searches. There are fees for services.

Small Business Development Center
Johnson Tower, Room 501
P.O. Box 644851   509-335-6415
Pullman, WA 99164-4851   Fax: 509-335-0949
www.sbdc.wsu.edu
The center offers counseling for a wide range of business issues and problems.

Small Business Development Center
Western Washington University
308 Parks Hall   360-650-3899
Bellingham, WA 98225   Fax: 360-650-4831
The center provides general assistance, and investment and funding information.

West Virginia
Small Business Development Center
West Virginia University
912 Main St.   304-465-1434
Oak Hill, WV 25901   Fax: 304-465-8680
The center offers counseling for a wide range of business issues and
problems.

West Virginia Small Business Development Office
2000 7th Ave.   304-696-6798
Huntington, WV 25703-1527   Fax: 304-696-4835
www.marshall.edu
The center provides
information on investment
and funding.

**Information on
Investment and Funding**

Wisconsin
Center for Innovation and Development
University of Wisconsin - Stout
278 Jarvis Hall
Menomonie, WI 54751   715-232-5026
http://nwmoc.uwstout.edu
The center counsels inventors on the commercialization and patent
processes; provides critical reviews of inventions; assists inventors on
technically refining inventions; and provides prototype development.
There are fees for services.

Wisconsin Innovation Service Center
402 McCutchan Hall
UW-Whitewater   414-472-1365
Whitewater, WI 53190   Fax: 414-472-1600
www.uww.edu/business/innovate/innovate.htm
Provides early stage market research for inventors. There is a flat fee of
$495 for services.

Small Business Development Center
University of Wisconsin

432 North Lake Street, Room 423   608-263-7794
Madison, WI 53706   Fax: 608-263-7830
www.uwex.edu/sbdc
The center offers counseling for a wide range of business issues and
problems.

Wisconsin Department of Commerce
P.O. Box 7970   608-266-9467
Madison, WI 53707   Fax: 608-267-2829
www.commerce.state.wi.us
The office provides information on investment and funding.

Wyoming
Small Business Development Center
111 W. 2nd St., Suite 502
Casper, WY 82601   307-234-6683
www.uwyo.edu/sbdc
Dr. Leonard Holler, who works in the office, is able to help inventors on a
wide range of issues including patenting, commercialization and
intellectual property rights. There are fees for services.

Canada
Innovative Center
156 Columbia Street W.
Waterloo, Ontario NN 26363   519-885-5870
www.innovationcentre.ca
Provides inventors with market research, idea testing, and helps guide
inventors up to the patent stage.

Money and Help To Sell Your Goods And Services Overseas

If you've found that the domestic market for your product or service is dwindling, it's time to consider broadening your sales base by selling overseas. Hey, it's not as complicated as you might think. There is a lot of information available to us in this country about other countries that isn't even available in that particular country. In other words, we have access to things like marketing trend reports on countries like Turkey that business people in Turkey can't even get! Important expertise and assistance for new and more experienced exporters continue to increase at both the federal and state level.

That widget that you invented in your garage so many years ago is now found in every hardware store in this country — why shouldn't it be in every French hardware store? Or the line of stationery that sold so well for you in this country could definitely be a hit in British stores that specialize in selling fine writing papers. So how do you go about finding what countries are open to certain imports and what their specific requirements are? If you're smart, you go to the best source around — the government — and make it work for you.

Polypropylene In Countries That Don't Even Count People

A few years ago a Fortune 500 company asked us to identify the consumption of polypropylene resin for 15 lesser-developed countries. It was a project they had been working on without success for close to a year. After telexing all over the world and contacting every domestic expert imaginable, we too came up empty handed. The basic problem was that we were dealing with countries that didn't even count people, let alone polypropylene resin.

Our savior was a woman at the U.S. Commerce Department

WORLD TRADE REFERENCE ROOM

named Maureen Ruffin, who was in charge of the World Trade Reference Room. Ms. Ruffin and her colleagues collect the official import/export statistical documents for every country in the world as soon as they are released by the originating countries. Although the data are much more current and more detailed than those published by such international organizations as the United Nations, the publications available at this federal reference room are printed in the language of origin. Because none of

the 15 subject countries manufacture polypropylene resin,
Ms. Ruffin showed us how to get the figures by identifying
those countries which produce polypropylene and counting
up how much each of them exported to the countries in ques-
tion. To help us even further, she also provided us with free
in-house translators to help us understand the foreign
documents.

Exporter's Hotline

The Trade Promotion Coordinating Committee has
established this comprehensive "one-
stop shop" for information on U.S.
Government programs and
activities that support exporting
efforts. This hotline is staffed by
trade specialists who can provide
information on seminars and
conferences, overseas buyers and
representatives, overseas events, export financing, technical
assistance, and export counseling. They also have access to
the National Trade Data Bank.

Trade
Promotion
Coordinating
Committee

Trade Information Center
800-USA-TRADE
infoserv2.ita.doc.gov/tic.nsf

U.S. Department of Commerce
Washington, DC 20230
202-482-0543
Fax: 202-482-4473
TDD: 800-833-8723
www.doc.gov

Country Experts

If you are looking for information on a market, company or most any other aspect of commercial life in a particular country, your best point of departure is to contact the appropriate country desk officer at the U.S. Department of Commerce. These experts often have the information you need right at their fingertips or they can refer you to other country specialists that can help you.

U.S. and Foreign Commercial Services (FCS)
International Trade Administration
U.S. Department of Commerce, Room 2810
Washington, DC 20230
202-482-5777
Fax: 202-482-5013
www.ita.doc.gov/uscs

All the Department of Commerce/US & FCS field offices around the country are listed later in this chapter. (You will also find a separate roster of international trade offices maintained by the states.)

ITA Country Desk Officers

A

Afghanistan	202-482-2954	2029B
Albania	202-482-4915	3413
Algeria	202-482-1870	2039

Angola	202-482-4228	3021
Anguilla	202-482-2527	3021
Antigua/Barbuda	202-482-2527	3021
Argentina	202-482-1548	3021
Aruba	202-482-2527	3020
Australia	202-482-3696	2036
Austria	202-482-2920	3039
Armenia	202-482-2354	3318
Azerbaijan	202-482-2354	3318

B

Bahamas	202-482-2527	3021
Bahrain	202-482-5545	2039
Baltic States	202-482-3952	3318
Bangladesh	202-482-2954	2029B
Barbados	202-482-2527	3021
Belarus	202-482-2354	3318
Belgium	202-482-5401	3042
Belize	202-482-2527	3021
Benin	202-482-4228	3317
Bermuda	202-482-2527	3021
Bhutan	202-482-2954	2029B
Bolivia	202-482-1659	3029
Botswana	202-482-4228	3317
Brazil	202-482-3871	3017
Brunei	202-482-3875	2308
Bulgaria	202-482-4915	3413
Burkina Faso	202-482-4388	3317
Burma	202-482-3875	2308
Burundi	202-482-4388	3317

C

Cambodia	202-482-3875	2308
Cameroon	202-482-5149	3317
Canada	202-482-3103	3033
Cape Verde	202-482-4388	3317
Caymans	202-482-2527	3021
Central Africa Republic	202-482-4388	3020
Chad	202-482-4388	3317
Chile	202-482-1495	3017
China	202-482-2462	2317
Colombia	202-482-1659	3025

Comoro Islands	202-482-4564	3317
Congo	202-482-5149	3317
Costa Rica	202-482-2527	3021
Cuba	202-482-2527	3021
Cyprus	202-482-3945	3044
Czechoslovakia	202-482-2645	3143

D

D'Jibouti	202-482-4564	3317
Denmark	202-482-3254	3413
Dominica	202-482-2527	3021
Dominican Republic	202-482-2527	3021

E

Ecuador	202-482-1659	3025
Egypt	202-482-4441	2039
El Salvador	202-482-2527	3020
Equatorial Guinea	202-482-4228	3317
Ethiopia	202-482-4564	3317
European Community	202-482-5278	3036

F

Finland	202-482-3254	3413
France	202-482-8008	3042

G

Gabon	202-482-5149	3317
Gambia	202-482-4388	3317
Germany	202-482-2434	3409
Ghana	202-482-5149	3317
Greece	202-482-3945	3042
Grenada	202-482-2527	2039
Guadaloupe	202-482-2527	3021
Guatemala	202-482-2528	3021
Guinea	202-482-4388	3317
Guinea-Bissau	202-482-4388	3317
Guyana	202-482-2527	3021

H

Haiti	202-482-2521	3021
Hong Kong	202-482-3832	2317
Hungary	202-482-2645	3413

Information USA, Inc.

I

Iceland	202-482-3254	3037
India	202-482-2954	2029
Indonesia	202-482-3875	2308
Iran	202-482-1870	2039
Iraq	202-482-4441	2039
Ireland	202-482-2177	3039
Israel	202-482-1870	2039
Italy	202-482-2177	3045
Ivory Coast	202-482-4388	3317

J

Jamaica	202-482-2527	3021
Japan	202-482-2425	2318
Jordan	202-482-1857	2039

K

Kenya	202-482-4564	3317
Korea	202-482-4957	2308
Kuwait	202-482-1860	2039
Kazakhstan	202-482-2354	3318
Kyrgyzstan	202-482-2354	3318

L

Laos	202-482-3875	2308
Lebanon	202-482-1860	2039
Lesotho	202-482-4220	3317
Liberia	202-482-4388	3317
Libya	202-482-5545	2039
Luxembourg	202-482-5401	3046

M

Macau	202-482-2462	2317
Madagascar	202-482-4504	3317
Malawi	202-482-4228	3317
Malaysia	202-482-3815	2308
Maldives	202-482-2954	2029B
Mali	202-482-4388	3317
Malta	202-482-3748	3049
Martinique	202-482-2527	3021
Mauritana	202-482-4388	3317

Mauritius	202-482-4564	3317
Mexico	202-482-0300	3028
Mongolia	202-482-2462	2317
Montserrat	202-482-2527	3314
Morocco	202-482-5545	2039
Mozambique	202-482-5148	3317
Moldova	202-482-2354	3318

N

Namibia	202-482-4228	3317
Nepal	202-482-2954	2029B
Netherlands	202-482-5401	3039
Netherlands Antilles	202-482-2527	3021
New Zealand	202-482-3647	2308
Nicaragua	202-482-2521	3021
Niger	202-482-4388	3317
Nigeria	202-482-4288	3317
Norway	202-482-5149	3037

O

Oman	202-482-1870	2039

P

Pacific Islands	202-482-3647	2308
Pakistan	202-482-2954	2029B
Panama	202-482-2527	3020
Paraguay	202-482-1548	3021
People/China	202-482-3583	2317
Peru	202-482-2521	2038
Philippines	202-482-3875	2038
Poland	202-482-2645	3413
Portugal	202-482-4508	3044
Puerto Rico	202-482-2527	3021

Q

Qatar	202-482-1070	2039

R

Romania	202-482-2645	6043
Russia	202-482-2354	3318
Rwanda	202-482-4388	3317

S

Sao Tome & Principe	202-482-4338	3317
Saudi Arabia	202-482-4652	2039
Senegal	202-482-4388	3317
Seychelles	202-482-4564	3317
Sierra Leone	202-482-4388	3317
Singapore	202-482-3875	2038
Somalia	202-482-4564	3317
South Africa	202-482-5498	3317
Spain	202-482-4508	3045
Sri Lanka	202-482-2954	2029B
St. Bartholomy	202-482-2527	3021
St. Kitts-Nevis	202-482-2527	3021
St. Lucia	202-482-2527	3021
St. Martin	202-482-2527	3021
St. Vincent Grenadines	202-482-2527	3021
Sudan	202-482-4564	3317
Suriname	202-482-2527	3021
Swaziland	202-482-5148	3317
Sweden	202-482-4414	3037
Switzerland	202-482-2920	3039
Syria	202-482-4441	2039

T

Taiwan	202-482-4957	2308
Tajikistan	202-482-2354	3318
Tanzania	202-482-4228	3317
Thailand	202-482-3875	2038
Togo	202-482-5149	3317
Trinidad/Tobago	202-482-2527	3021
Tunisia	202-482-1860	2039
Turkey	202-482-5373	3045
Turkmenistan	202-482-2354	3318
Turks & Caicos Islands	202-482-2527	3021

U

Uganda	202-482-4564	3317
Ukraine	202-482-2354	3318
United Arab Emirates	202-482-5545	2039
United Kingdom	202-482-3748	3045
Uruguay	202-482-1495	3021

V

Venezuela	202-482-4303	3029
Vietnam	202-482-3875	2038
Virgin Islands (UK)	202-482-2527	3021

Y

Yemen, Rep of	202-482-1870	2039
Yugoslavia	202-482-2615	3413

Z

Zaire	202-482-5149	3317
Zambia	202-482-4228	3317
Zimbabwe	202-482-4228	3317

State Department Country Experts

If you need information that is primarily political, economic or cultural in nature, direct your questions first to the **State Department Country Desk Officers**. An operator at the number listed below can direct you to the appropriate desk officer.

U.S. Department of State
2201 C Street, NW
Washington, DC 20520
202-647-4000
www.state.gov

Foreign Specialists At Other Government Agencies

The following is a listing by subject area of other departments within the federal government which maintain country experts who are available to help the public:

1) **Foreign Agriculture:**
   Foreign Agriculture Service, Agriculture and Trade Analysis Division, U.S. Department of Agriculture, Room 732, 1301 New York Ave., NW, Washington, DC 20005, 202-219-0700; {www.fas.usda.gov}.

   Food Safety and Inspection Service, International Programs, U.S. Dept. of Agriculture, Room 341-E, 14th and Independence Ave., SW, Washington, DC 20250-3700, 202-720-3473; {www.fsis.usda.gov}.

   Animal and Plant Health Inspection Service, Import-Export, U.S. Department of Agriculture, 6505 Bellcrest Rd., Hyattsville, MD 20782, 301-436-8590; {www.aphis.usda.gov}.

2) **Energy Resources:**
   Office of Export Assistance, U.S. Department of Energy, 1000 Independence Ave., SW, Washington, DC 20585, 202-586-7997; {www.doe.gov}.

   Office of Fossil Energy, U.S. Dept. of Energy, 1000 Independence Ave., SW, Washington, DC 20585, 202-586-6503; Fax: 202-586-5146; {www.fe.doe.gov}.

3) **Economic Assistance to Foreign Countries:**
   Business Office, U.S. Agency for International Development, 320 21st St. NW, Washington, DC 20523, 703-875-1551; {gaia.usaid.gov}.

4) **Information Programs and Cultural Exchange:**
   U.S. Information Agency, 301 4th St. SW, Washington, DC 20547, 202-619-4700; Fax: 202-619-6988; E-mail: {inquiry@usia.gov}; {www.usia.gov}.

5) **Metric:**
   Office of Metric Programs, National Institute of Standards and Technology, 100 Bureau Drive, Building 411, Room A146, Gaithersburg, MD 20899, 301-975-6259; {ts.nist.gov/ts}.

6) **Telecommunications Information:**
Bureau of International Communications and Information Policy,
U.S. Department of State, Washington, DC 20520, 202-647-5212.

7) **Fisheries:**
Office of Trade and Industry Services, Fisheries Promotion and
Trade Matters, National Marine Fisheries Service, 1315 East-West
Highway, Silver Spring, MD 20910, 301-713-2379;
{www.nmfs.gov}.

Money for Selling Overseas

1) **State Government Money Programs:**
Some state government economic development programs offer
special help for those who need financial assistance in selling
overseas. See the section presented later in this chapter entitled *State
Government Assistance To Exporters.*

2) **Export-Import Bank Financing (Eximbank):**
The Export-Import Bank facilitates and aids in the financing of
exports of United States goods and services. Its programs include
short-term, medium-term, and long-term credits, small business support, financial guarantees, and insurance. In addition, it sponsors
conferences on small business exporting, maintains credit information on thousands of foreign firms, supports feasibility studies of
overseas programs, and offers export and small business finance
counseling. To receive *Marketing News* Fact Sheets, or the *Eximbank
Export Credit Insurance* booklet, or the Eximbank's *Program
Selection Guide,* contact: Export-Import Bank, 811 Vermont Ave.
NW, Washington, DC 20571, 202-566-4490, 1-800-424-5201; Fax:
202-566-7524; {www.exim.gov}.

3) **Small Business Administration (SBA) Export Loans:**
This agency makes loans and loan guarantees to small business concerns as well as to small business investment companies, including
those that sell overseas. It also offers technical assistance, counseling,
training, management assistance, and information resources,

including some excellent publications to small and minority businesses in export operations. Contact your local or regional SBA office listed in the blue pages of your telephone book under Small Business Administration, or Small Business Administration, Office of International Trade, 409 3rd St., SW, Washington, DC 20416, 202-205-6720; {www.sbaonline.sba.gov/oit/ finance}.

4) **Overseas Private Investment Corporation (OPIC):**
This agency provides marketing, insurance, and financial assistance to American companies investing in 140 countries and 16 geographic regions. Its programs include direct loans, loan guarantees, and political risk insurance. OPIC also sponsors U.S. and international seminars for investment executives as well as conducts investment missions to developing countries. The Investor Services Division offers a  computer service to assist investors in identifying investment opportunities worldwide. A modest fee is charged for this service and it is also available through the Lexis/Nexis computer network. OPIC has supported investments worth nearly $112 billion, generated $56 billion in U.S. exports, and helped to create 230,000 American jobs. Specific Info-Kits are available identifying basic economic, business, and political information for each of the countries covered. In addition, it operates:

Program Information Hotline
Overseas Private Investment Corporation
1100 New York Ave., NW
Washington, DC 20527
202-336-8799 (Hotline)
202-336-8400 (General Information)
202-336-8636 (Public Affairs)
202-336-8680 (Press Information)
202-408-9859 (Fax)
E-mail: {info@opic.gov}
www.opic.gov

5) **Agency for International Development (AID):**
The Agency for International Development was created in 1961 by John F. Kennedy. AID offers a variety of loan and financing guarantee programs for projects in developing countries that have a substantial developmental impact or for the exportation of manufactured goods to AID-assisted developing countries. Some investment opportunities are region specific, which include the Association of Southeast Asian National, the Philippines, and Africa. For more information, contact the Office of Investment, Agency for International Development, 515 22nd St. NW, Room 301, Washington, DC 20523-0231; 703-875-1551; {www.info.usaid.gov}.

6) **Grants to Train Local Personnel**
The Trade and Development Agency has the authority to offer grants in support of short-listed companies on a transaction specific basis. These are usually in the form of grants to cover the cost of training local personnel by the company on the installation, operation, and maintenance of equipment specific to bid the proposal. The average grant awarded is $320,000. Contact: Trade and Development Agency, 1621 N. Kent St., Suite 200, Arlington, VA 22209; 703-875-4357; Fax: 703-875-4009.

7) **Consortia of American Businesses in Eastern Europe (CABEE):**
CABEE provides grant funds to trade organizations to defray the costs of opening, staffing, and operating U.S. consortia offices in Eastern Europe. The CABEE grant program initially began operations in Poland, the Czech Republic, Slovikia, and Hungary, targeting five industry sectors: agribusiness/agriculture, construction/housing, energy, environment, and telecommunications. Contact: CABEE, Department of Commerce, 14th and Constitution Avenue, Room 1104, Washington, DC 20230, 202-482-5004; Fax: 202-482-1790; {www.ita.doc.gov/oetca}.

8) **Consortia of American Businesses in the Newly Independent States (CABNIS):**
This program was modeled after CABEE and stimulates U.S. business in the Newly Independent States (NIS) and assists the region in its move toward privatization. CABNIS is providing grant funds to

nonprofit organizations to defray the costs of opening, staffing, and operating U.S. consortia offices in the NIS. Contact: CABNIS, Department of Commerce, 14th and Constitution Ave., Washington, DC 20230, 202-482-5004; {www.ita.doc.gov/export_admin/ brochure.html - info}. For financing and a listing of grantees, contact {www.itaiep.doc.gov/bisnis/finance/cabnis.htm}.

Marketing Data, Custom Studies, and Company Information

Further information on any of the following services and products can be obtained by contacting a U.S. Department of Commerce/ US & FCS field office listed later in this chapter, or by contacting the US & FCS at: United States and Foreign Commercial Services, U.S. Department of Commerce, Room 3810, HCH Building, 14th and Constitution Ave., NW, Washington, DC 20230, 202-482-4767 or call 1-800-USA-TRADE.

1) **International Industry Experts:**
   A separate Office of Trade Development at the Commerce Department handles special marketing and company problems for specific industries. Experts are available in the following international market sectors:

   Technology and Aerospace Industries: 202-482-1872

   Office of Automotive Affairs: 202-482-0554
   www.ita.doc.gov/auto

   Basic Industries: 202-482-0614
   Capital Goods and International Construction: 202-482-5023
   Environmental Technologies Exports 201-482-5225
   Office of Computers and Business Equipment 202-482-0952
   infoserv2.ita.doc.gov/ocbe/ocbehome.nsf

Telecommunications:	202-482-4466
	infoserv2.ita.doc.gov/ot/home.nsf
Service, Industries and Finance:	202-482-5261
Textiles, Apparel and Consumer Goods:	202-482-3737
	otexa.ita.doc.gov

You can also talk to industry desk officers at the Department of Commerce. They can provide information on the competitive strengths of U.S. industries in foreign markets from abrasives to yogurt. You can call the Department of Commerce at 202-482-2000 (main office) or 1-800-872-8723 (trade information) to locate specific industry analysts. You can also contact them online at {www.ita.doc.gov/ita_home/itatdhom.html}.

2) **Trade Lists:**
Directories of overseas customers for U.S. exports in selected industries and countries: They contain the names and product lines of foreign distributors, agents, manufacturers, wholesalers, retailers, and other purchasers. They also provide the name and title of key officials as well as telex and cable numbers, and company size data. Prices range up to $40 for a list of a category.

3) **Country Statistics:**
There are multiple ways to get up to date statistics for most countries worldwide. The Census Bureau maintains a listing of country statistics on its website: {www.census.gov/main/www/state_int.html}.

InfoNation is another easy to use database for quick statistical information for every country that is a member of the United Nations. Maintained by the U.N., InfoNation is a very helpful site for being able to easily compare statistics using its two-step database. Contact InfoNation at {www.un.org/Pubs/ CyberSchoolBus/ infonation/e_infonation.htm}.

4) **Demographic and Social Information:**
The Center for International Research compiles and maintains up to date global demographic and social information for all countries in its

International Data Base (IDB). Last year, the IDB represented 227 countries and areas worldwide. The IDB has all vital information available for easy download from its website. The only requirements are that your machine must be a PC compatible, 386 computer (or higher). Contact: Systems Analysis and Programming Staff, 301-457-1403; Fax: 301-457-1539; E-mail: {idb@census.gov}; {census.gov/pub/ipc/www/idbnew.html}.

5) **Customized Export Mailing Lists:**
Selected lists of foreign companies in particular industries, countries, and types of business can be requested by a client. Gummed labels are also available. Prices start at $35.

6) **World Traders Data Reports:**
Background reports are available on individual firms containing information about each firm's business activities, its standing in the local business community, its creditworthiness, and overall reliability and suitability as a trade contact for exporters. The price is $100 per report.

7) **Agent Distributor Service (ADS):**
This is a customized search for interested and qualified foreign representatives on behalf of an American client. U.S. commercial officers overseas conduct the search and prepare a report identifying up to six foreign prospects which have personally examined the U.S. firm's product literature and have expressed interest in representing the firm. A fee of $250 per country is charged. Contact them online at {www.ita.doc.gov/uscs/ uscsads.html}.

8) **New Product Information Service:**
This service is designed to help American companies publicize the availability of new U.S. products in foreign markets and simultaneously test market interest in these products. Product information which meets the criteria is distributed worldwide through *Commercial News USA* and Voice of America broadcasts. A fee is charged for participation.

9) **Customized Market Analysis (CMA):**
   At a cost of $800 to $13,500 per country per product, these studies are called "Comparison Shopping Service". They are conducted by the U.S. Embassy foreign commercial attaches and can target information on quite specific marketing questions such as:

   ➡ Does the product have sales potential in the country?
   ➡ Who is the supplier for a comparable product locally?
   ➡ What is the going price for a comparable product in this country?
   ➡ What is the usual sales channel for getting this type of product into the market?
   ➡ What are the competitive factors that most influence purchases of these products in the market (i.e., price, credit, quality, delivery, service, promotion, brand)?
   ➡ What is the best way to get sales exposure in the market for this type of product?
   ➡ Are there any significant impediments to selling this type of product?
   ➡ Who might be interested and qualified to represent or purchase this company's products?
   ➡ If a licensing or joint venture strategy seems desirable for this market, who might be an interested and qualified partner for the U.S. company?

10) **Special Opportunities in the Caribbean Basin and Latin America:**
    Under the Caribbean Economic Recovery Act of 1983, the government has established special incentives for American firms wishing to do business with Latin American and Caribbean Basin companies. Seminars, workshops, business development missions, business counseling, as well as marketing and competitive information are available.

    Latin America/Caribbean Business Development Center
    U.S. Department of Commerce
    Room 1235

Washington, DC 20230
202-482-0841
Fax: 202-482-5364

11) **New Markets in Eastern European Countries (EEBIC):**
The Eastern Europe Business Information Center is stocked with a
wide range of publications on doing business in Eastern Europe.
These include lists of potential partners, investment regulations,
priority industry sectors, and notices of upcoming seminars,
conferences, and trade promotion events. The center also serves as a
referral point for programs of voluntary assistance to the region.

Eastern Europe Business Information Center
U.S. Department of Commerce
Room 7412
Washington, DC 20230
202-482-2645
Fax: 202-482-4473

12) **Exporting to Japan: Japan Export Information Center (JEIC)**
The Japan Export Information Center (JEIC) provides business
counseling services and accurate information on exporting to
Japan. The JEIC is the point of contact for information on
business in Japan, market entry alternatives, market
information and research, product standards and testing,
tariffs, and non-tariff barriers. The center maintains a
commercial library and participates in seminars on various
aspects of Japanese business. Contact: Japan Export
Information Center, U.S. Department of Commerce, Room 2320,
Washington, DC 20230; 202-482-2425; Fax: 202-482-0469;
(www.ita. doc.gov/regional/geo_region/japan/jeic.html}.

13) **Office of Export Trading Company Affairs**
The Office of Export Trading Company offers various information as
well as promoting the use of export trading companies and export
management companies; offers information and counseling to
businesses and trading associations regarding the export industry; and
administers the Export Trade Certificate of Review program

which provides exporters with an antitrust "insurance policy" intended to foster joint export activities where economies of scale and risk diversification are achieved. Contact: Office of Export Trading Company Affairs, U.S. Department of Commerce, 14th and Constitution Ave., NW, Room 1104, Washington, DC 20230; 202-482-5131; Fax: 202-482-1790.

14) **U.S.-Asia Environmental Partnership**

US-AEP is a comprehensive service to help U.S. environmental exporters enter markets in the Asia/Pacific region. It is a coalition of public, private and non-governmental organizations which promotes environmental protection and sustainable development in 34 nations in the Asia/Pacific area. Contact: U.S.-Asia Environmental Partnership, 1720 I St., NW, Suite 700, Washington, DC; 202-835-0333; Fax: 202-835-0366; E-mail: {usasia@usaep.org}; {www.usaep.org}.

15) **Business Information Service for the Newly Independent States (BISNIS)**

BISNIS provides "one stop shopping" for U.S. firms interested in doing business in the Newly Independent States (NIS) of the former Soviet Union. Information is available on commercial opportunities in the NIS, sources of financing, up to date lists of trade contacts as well as on U.S. Government programs supporting trade and investment in the region. BISNIS publishes a monthly bulletin with information on upcoming trade promotion events, practical advice on doing business with NIS and other topics. Contact: BISNIS, U.S. Department of Commerce, 1401 Constitution Ave. NW, Room 7413, R-Business, Washington, DC 20230; 202-482-4655; Fax: 202-482-2293.

16) **Technical Assistance with Transportation Concerns**

The Department of Transportation provides technical assistance to developing countries on a wide range of problems in the areas of transportation policy, highways, aviation, rail and ports. It also supports AID in the foreign aid development program. Contact: International Transportation and Trade: Bernard Gillian, 202-366-4368; Fax: 202-366-7417; Federal Aviation Administration:

202-267-3173; Fax: 202-267-5306; {www.faa.gov}; Federal Highway Administration: Kennith Wylde, 202-366-0605; Fax: 202-366-9626; {www.fhwa.dot.gov}; Federal Railroad Administration: Ilona Williams, 202-493-6130; Fax: 202-493-6171; {www.fra.gov}; Maritime Administration: 202-366-5773; Fax: 202-366-3746; {marad.dot.gov}; Office of International Aviation: Paul Gretch, 202-366-2423.

17) **"First Business"**
The "First Business" television program is a half-hour long monthly televised business program sent by satellite to more than 100 countries highlighting innovation and excellence in U.S. business. The program consists of segments on new products, services, and processes of interest to overseas buyers and promising research. "First Business" is produced by Worldnet Television, a division of the International Broadcasting Bureau. Contact: Worldnet Television, 202-619-1783; Fax: 202-205-2967; E-mail: {worldnet@ibb.gov}.

18) **Environmental Technology Network for Asia (ETNA):**
ETNA matches environmental trade leads sent from U.S.-Asia Environmental Partnership (USAEP) Technology Representatives located in 11 Asian countries with appropriate U.S. environmental firms and trade associations that are registered with ETNA's environmental trade opportunities database. U.S. environmental firms receive the trade leads by Broadcast Fax system within 48 hours of leads being identified and entered electronically from Asia. Companies may register online to join ETNA's 2400 firms and associations. Contact: Environmental Technology Network for Asia, US-AEP, 1720 I St., NW, Suite 700, Washington, DC 20006; 800-818-9911; Fax: 202-835-8358; {www.usaep.org/ouractiv/etna.htm}.

19) **Automated Trade Locator Assistance System:**
The SBAtlas is a market research tool that provides free of charge
two types of reports: product- specific and country-specific. The
product report ranks the top 35 import and export market for a
particular good or service. The country report identifies the top 20
products most frequently traded in a target market. This service is
free of charge. SBAtlas is available through SBA district offices,
Service Corps of Retired Executives (SCORE) office, and Small
Business Development Centers, to get the address and phone number
to the nearest office call 1-800-U-ASK-SBA.

20) **Export Contact List Service (ECLS):**
This database retrieval service provides U.S. exporters with names,
addresses, products, sizes and other relevant information on foreign
firms interested in importing U.S. goods and services. Similar
information is also available on U.S. exporters to foreign firms
seeking suppliers from the U.S. Names are collected and maintained
by Commerce district offices and commercial officers at foreign
posts. Contact your nearest district Commerce office located in this
book or call 1-800-USA-TRADE.

Trade Fairs and Missions

Trade fairs, exhibitions, trade missions, overseas trade
seminars, and other promotional events and services are
sponsored by the Export Promotion Services Group, U.S.
and Foreign Commercial Services, U.S. Department of
Commerce, 14th and E Streets, NW, Room 2810,
Washington, DC 20230; 202-482-6220. This office or one of
its field offices, which are listed later in this chapter, can
provide additional details on these activities.

1) **Industry-Organized, Government-Approved Trade Missions:**
Such missions are organized by trade associations, local Chambers of
Commerce, state trade development agencies, and similar trade-
oriented groups that enjoy U.S. Department of Commerce support.

2) **Catalog Exhibitions:**
Such exhibitions feature displays of U.S. product catalogs, sales brochures, and other graphic sales materials at American embassies and consulates or in conjunction with trade shows. A Department of Commerce specialist assists in the exhibition. Call 202-482-3973; Fax: 202-482-2716.

3) **Video Catalog:**
This catalog is designed to showcase American products via videotape presentation. This permits actual product  demonstrations giving the foreign buyer an opportunity to view applications of American products. Federal specialists participate in these sessions. Call 202-482-3973; Fax: 202-482-0115.

4) **U.S. Specialized Trade Missions:**
These missions are distinct from those mentioned above since the U.S. Department of Commerce plans the visits and accompanies the delegation. They are designed to sell American goods and services as well as establish agents or representation abroad. The Department of Commerce provides marketing information, advanced planning, publicity, and trip organization. Call 1-800-USA-TRADE.

5) **U.S. Seminar Missions:**
The objective here is to promote exports and help foreign representation for American exporters. However, unlike trade missions, these are designed to facilitate the sales of state-of-the-art products and technology. This type of mission is a one to two day "seminar" during which team members discuss technology subjects followed by private, sales-oriented appointments. Call 1-800-USA-TRADE.

6) **Matchmaker Trade Delegations:**
These Department of Commerce-recruited and planned missions are designed to introduce new-to-export or new-to-market businesses to prospective agents and distributors overseas. Trade Specialists from Commerce evaluate the potential firm's products, find and screen

contacts, and handle logistics. This is followed by an intensive trip filled with meetings and prospective clients and in-depth briefings on the economic and business climate of the countries visited. Contact: 202-482-3119; Fax: 202-482-0178; {www.ita.doc.gov/uscs/uscsmatc.html}.

7) **Investment Missions:**
These events are held in developing countries offering excellent investment opportunities for U.S. firms. Missions introduce U.S. business executives to key business leaders, potential joint venture partners, and senior foreign government officials in the host country. Call Investment Missions, 202-336-8799; Fax: 202-408-5155.

8) **Foreign Buyer Program:**
This program supports major domestic trade shows featuring products and services of U.S. industries with high export potential. Government officials recruit on a worldwide basis qualified buyers to attend the shows. Call Export Promotion Services, 202-482-0481; Fax: 202-482-0115.

9) **Trade Fairs, Solo Exhibitions, and Trade Center Shows:**
The Department of Commerce organizes a wide variety of special  exhibitions. These events range from solo exhibitions representing U.S. firms exclusively at trade centers overseas to U.S. pavilions in the largest international exhibitions. Call 1-800-USA-TRADE.

10) **Agent/Distributor Service (ADS):**
Looking for overseas representatives to expand your business and boost your export sales? Commerce will locate, screen, and assess agents, distributors, representatives, and other foreign partners for your business. Contact: 1-800-USA-TRADE; {www.ita.doc.gov/uscs/uscsads.html}.

11) **Trade Opportunities Program (TOP):**
The Trade Opportunities Program (TOP) provides companies with current sales leads from international firms seeking to buy or

represent their products or services. TOP leads are printed daily in leading commercial newspapers and are also distributed electronically via the U.S. Department of Commerce Economic Bulletin Board. Call 1-800-STAT-USA, 202-482-1986; Fax: 202-482-2164; {www.ita.doc.gov/uscs/ uscstop.htm}.

12) **Gold Key Service:**
This customized service is aimed at U.S. firms, which are planning to visit a country. Offered by many overseas posts, it combines several services such as market orientation briefings, market research, introductions to potential partners, and interpreters for meetings, assistance in developing a sound market strategy, and an effective follow-up plan. Gold Key Service is available in 70 of the world's best export markets for fees ranging from $150-$600. Call 1-800-USA-TRADE; {www.ita.doc.gov/uscs/uscsgold.html}.

Special Programs for Agricultural Products

The following programs are specifically aimed at those who wish to sell agricultural products overseas. Agricultural exporters should also be sure not to limit themselves only to programs under this heading. Programs listed under other headings can also be used for agricultural products.

1) **Office Space for Agricultural Exporters:**
The Foreign Agriculture Service (FAS) maintains overseas agricultural trade offices to help exporters of U.S. farm and forest products in key overseas markets. The facilities vary depending on local conditions, but may include a trade library, conference rooms, office space, and kitchens for preparing product samples. Contact: Foreign Agriculture Service, U.S. Department of Agriculture, 14th

and Independence Ave. SW, Washington, DC 20250, 202-720-7420; Fax: 202-205-9728; {www.fas.usda.gov}.

2) **Foreign Market Information:**
    A special office serves as a single contact point within the Foreign Agriculture Service for agricultural exporters seeking foreign market information. The office also counsels firms that believe they have been injured by unfair trade practices. Contact: Trade Assistance and Promotion Office, U.S. Department of Agriculture, 14th and Independence Avenue, SW, Washington, DC 20250, 202-720-7420; Fax: 202-720-3229.

3) **Export Connections:**
    The AgExport Action Kit provides information which can help put U.S. exporters in touch quickly and directly with foreign importers of food and agricultural products. The services include trade leads, a *Buyer Alert* newsletter, foreign buyer lists, and U.S. supplier lists. This bi-weekly newsletter, distributed by USDA's overseas offices, can introduce your food and agricultural products to foreign buyers around the world. *Buyer Alert* reaches more than 15,000 importers in 75 countries. Last year, *Buyer Alert* helped generate confirmed export sales of $100 million. Contact: AgExport Connection, Ag Box 1052, U.S. Department of Agriculture, FAS/AGX, Washington, DC 20250, 202-690-3421; Fax: 202-690-4374. Export Kit: {www.fas.usda.gov/egexport.html}. Buyer Alert: {www.fas.usda.gov/agexport/banews.html}

Export Regulations, Licensing, and Product Standards

Talk to ELVIS — Bureau of Export Administration (BXA)

BXA is responsible for controlling exports for reasons of national security, foreign policy, and short supply. Licenses on controlled exports are issued, and seminars on U.S. export regulations are held domestically and overseas. Contact:

Bureau of Export, U.S. Department of
Commerce, 14th St. and
Pennsylvania Ave., Room 2705 (for
mail), Room 1099 (for visitors),
Washington, DC 20230; 202-482-
4811; Fax: 202-482-3617; {www.bxa.doc.gov}; or BXA
Western Regional Office, 3300 Irvine Ave., Suite 345,
Newport Beach, CA 92660; 949-660-0144; 949-660-9347.

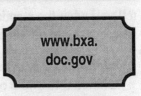

www.bxa.
doc.gov

Export license applications may be submitted and issued
through computer via the *Export License Application and
Information Network (ELAIN)*. The *System for Tracking
Export License Application (STELA)* provides instant status
updates on license applications by the use of a touch-tone
phone.

The *Export Licensing Voice Information (ELVIS)* is an
automated attendant that offers a range of licensing
information and emergency handling procedures. Callers
may order forms and publications or subscribe to the *Office
of Export Licensing (OEL) Insider Newsletter*, which
provides regulatory updates. While using ELVIS, a caller has
the option of speaking to a consultant.

Office of Export Licensing	202-482-8536
	Fax: 202-482-3322
ELAIN	202-482-4811
STELA	202-482-2752
ELVIS	202-482-4811
Export Seminars	202-482-6031

The National Institute of Standards and Technology provides
a free service that will identify standards for selling any
product to any country in the world. This federal agency will

tell you what the standard is for a given product or suggest where you can obtain an official copy of the standard.

> ***National Center for Standards and Certification***
> National Institute of Standards and Technology
> Building 820, Room 164
> Gaithersburg, MD 20899
> 301-975-4040
> Fax: 301-926-1559

Cheap Office and
Conference Space Overseas

If you are traveling overseas on a business trip, you may want to look into renting office space and other services through the American Embassy. Depending on the country and the space available, the embassy can provide temporary office space for as low as $25 per day, along with translation services, printing, and other services. Meeting rooms, seminar or convention space along with promotion services, mailings, freight handling, and even catering may be available in many countries. Contact the Department of Commerce/US & FCS field office, which is listed later in this chapter, or the appropriate country desk officer at the U.S. Department of Commerce in Washington, DC.

Other Services, Resources, and
Databases

The following is a description of some of the additional services and information sources that can be useful to anyone investigating overseas markets:

1) **Help in Selling to Developing Nations:**
   The U.S. Agency For International Development (AID) provides information to U.S. suppliers, particularly small, independent enterprises, regarding purchases to be financed with AID funds. U.S. small businesses can obtain special counseling and related services in order to furnish equipment, materials, and services to AID-financed projects. AID sponsors *Development Technologies Exhibitions*, where technical firms in the U.S. are matched up with those in lesser-developed countries for the purpose of forming joint ventures or exploring licensing possibilities. AID provides loans and grants to finance consulting services that support project activities related to areas such as agriculture, rural development, health, and housing. Contact: Information Center, U.S. Agency for International Development, Ronald Reagan Bldg., Washington, DC 20523; 202-712-4810; Fax: 202-216-3524; {www.info.usaid.gov}.

2) **Foreign Demographic Profiles:**
   The Government Printing Office has a publication called the CIA *World Factbook*. Produced annually, this publication provides country-by-country data on demographics, economy, communications, and defense. The cost is $29 (GPO: 041-015-00173-6). Order by contacting Superintendent of Documents, Government Printing Office, Washington, DC 20402; 202-512-1800; {www.gpo.gov}.

3) **Counseling and Licenses:**
   The Office of Exporter Services is responsible for counseling exporters, conducting export control seminars, processing license applications and commodity classifications, and for publishing changes to the Export Administration Regulations. Contact: Office of Exporter Service, U.S. Department of Commerce, 14th and Pennsylvania Ave., NW, Room 2725, Washington, DC 20230; Eileen Albanese, 202-482-0436; Fax: 202-482-3322. Export Counseling Division: Laverne Smith, 202-482-4811; Fax: 202-482-3617.

4) **Help With Selling Commodities Abroad:**
   The Foreign Agricultural Service is charged with maintaining and expanding export sales of U.S. agricultural commodities and products. Staff can provide information on foreign agricultural production, trade and consumption, marketing research including areas of demand for specific commodities in foreign countries, and analyses of foreign competition in agricultural areas. Other services include financing opportunities, contributing to export promotion costs, and testing market assistance. This office also handles U.S. representation to foreign governments and participates in formal trade negotiations. Contact: Foreign Agricultural Service, U.S. Department of Agriculture, 14th and Independence Ave., S.W., Room 4647, South Building, Washington, DC 20250, 202-720-7420; {www.fas.usda.gov}.

5) **International Prices:**
   Export price indexes for both detailed and aggregate product groups are available on a monthly basis. Price trends comparisons of U.S. exports with those of Japan and Germany are also available. Contact: International Prices Division, Bureau of Labor Statistics, U.S. Department of Labor, 2nd Massachusetts Ave., NE, Room 3955, Washington, DC 20212, 202-606-7100.

6) **Identifying Overseas Opportunities:**
   The International Trade Administration (ITA) of the Commerce Department assists American exporters in locating and gaining access to foreign markets. It furnishes information on overseas markets available for U.S. products and services, requirements that must be fulfilled, economic conditions in foreign countries, foreign market and investment opportunities, etc. Operations are divided into four major areas:

❑ **International Economic Policy:** promotes U.S. exports geographically by helping American businesses market products in various locations abroad and by solving the trade and investment problems they encounter. This office is staffed by Country Desk

Officers knowledgeable in marketing and business practices for almost every country in the world. Contact: Office of International Economic Policy, ITA, U.S. Department of Commerce, Washington, DC 20230, 202-482-3022; {infoserv.ita.doc.gov}.

❏ **Export Administration:** supervises the enforcement provisions of the Export Administration Act, and administers the Foreign Trade Zone Program. Personnel in its export enforcement and its administration, policy, and regulations offices can offer technical advice and legal interpretations of the various export legislation which  affect American businesses. Assistance in complying with export controls can be obtained directly from the Exporter Counseling Division within the Bureau of Export Administration (BXA) Office of Export Licensing in Washington, DC, 202-482-4811; Fax: 202-482-3617; {www.bxa.doc.gov}.

BXA also has field offices that specialize in counseling on export controls and regulations:

Western Regional Office	949-660-0144
Northern California Branch Office	408-998-7402

❏ **Trade Development:** advises businesses on trade and investment issues, and promotes U.S. exports by industry or product classifications. Offices offer assistance and information on export counseling, statistics and trade data, licensing, trading companies, and other services. Contact: Office of Trade Development, ITA, U.S. Department of Commerce, Washington, DC 20230, 202-482-1461; Fax: 202-482-5697.

❏ **U.S. and Foreign Commercial Service:** provides information on government programs to American businesses, and uncovers trade opportunities for U.S. exporters. They also locate representatives and agents for American firms, assist U.S. executives in all phases of their exporting, and help enforce export controls and regulations. They operate through 47 district offices located in major U.S. cities and in 124 posts in 69 foreign countries. In addition, a valued asset of the U.S. and Foreign Commercial Services is a group of about 525 foreign nationals, usually natives of the foreign country, who are employed in the U.S. embassy or consulate and bring with them a wealth of personal understanding of local market conditions and business practices. U.S. exporters usually tap into these services by contacting the Department of Commerce/US & FCS field office in their state (listed later in this chapter), or Office of U.S. and Foreign Commercial Service, U.S. Department of Commerce, Washington, DC 20230; 1-800-USA-TRADE.

Or contact regional directors at:

Africa, Near East	202-482-4925
Asia and Pacific	202-482-5251
Europe	202-482-5638
Japan	202-482-4527

7) **Latest News on Foreign Opportunities:**
In addition to technical reports on foreign research and development, National Technical Information Service sells foreign market airgrams and foreign press and radio translations. A free video is available explaining NTIS services. Contact: National Technical Information Service, U.S. Department of Commerce, 5285 Port Royal Rd., Springfield, VA 22161, 703-605-6000; Fax: 703-605-6900; {www.ntis.gov}.

> **A free video is available explaining NTIS services.**

8) **Planning Services for U.S. Exporters:**
In its effort to promote economic development in Third World countries, the Trade and Development Program finances planning services for development projects leading to the export of U.S. goods and services. A free pamphlet is available that describes the planning services offered by the Trade and Development Program. To obtain a copy, contact: U.S. Trade and Development Program, Department of State, Room 309 SA-16, Washington, DC 20523-1602, 703-875-4357.

9) **Terrorism Abroad:**
Assistance is available to companies doing business abroad to assess current security conditions and risk in certain cities and countries that may pose a threat. Over 1600 U.S. companies are already affiliated with the OSAC. The OSAC has numerous publications on security guidelines available from its website at {ds.state.gov/osacmenu.cfm}. Contact: Overseas Security Advisory Council (OSAC), U.S. Department of State, Washington, DC 20522-1003, 202-663-0533; Fax: 202-663-0868; E-mail: {osca@dsmail.state.gov}.

10) **Trade Remedy Assistance Office (TRAO):**
The Center provides information on remedies available under the Trade Remedy Law. It also offers technical assistance to eligible small businesses to enable them to bring cases to the International Trade Commission. Contact: ITC Trade Remedy Assistance Center, U.S. International Trade Commission, 500 E St. SW, Washington, DC 20436, 202-205-2200; Fax: 202-205-2139.

11) **International Expertise:**
Staff in the following offices will prove helpful as information sources regarding the international scope of their respective subject areas:

Economics:
International Investment, Bureau of Economic Analysis, U.S. Department of Commerce, 1441 L St., NW, Washington, DC 20230, 202-606-9800; {www.bea.doc.gov}.

Productivity and Technology Statistics:
Bureau of Labor Statistics, U.S. Department of Labor, 2 Massachusetts Ave., NE, #2150, Washington, DC 20212, 202-606-5654; Fax: 202-606-5679; {www.bls.gov}.

Investments and Other Monetary Matters:
Office of Assistant Secretary for International Affairs, U.S. Department of the Treasury, 1500 Pennsylvania Ave., Washington, DC 20220, 202-622-2000; Fax: 202-622-6415.

Population:

International Program Center, Bureau of Census, U.S. Department of Commerce, Room 205, Washington Plaza, Washington, DC 20233, 301-457-1403.

Population Reference Bureau, Inc., 1875 Connecticut Ave., NW, Suite 520, Washington, DC 20009, 202-483-1100; Fax: 202-328-3937; E-mail: {popref@prb.org}; {www.igx.org/pub}.

Country Development:

Inter-American Development Bank, 1300 NY Ave., NW, Washington, DC 20577, 202-623-1000; E-mail: {pic@iadb.org}; {www.iadb.org}.

International Monetary Fund, 700 19th St. NW, Washington, DC 20431, 202-623-7000; Fax: 202-623-6278; E-mail: {publicaffairs@ifm.org}; {www.imf.org}.

World Bank, 1818 H St. NW, Washington, DC 20433, 202-477-1234; Fax: 202-522-1159; {worldbank.org}.

12) **National Trade Data Bank (NTDB):**
This is a "one-stop" source for export promotion and international trade data collected by 17 U.S. government agencies. Updated each month and released on CD-ROM, the Data Bank enables a user with an IBM-compatible personal computer equipped with a CD-ROM reader to access over 100,00 trade documents. It contains the latest Census data on U.S. imports and exports by commodity and country; the complete Central Intelligence Agency (CIA) *World Factbook*; current market research reports compiled by the U.S. and Foreign and Commercial Service; the complete Foreign Traders Index which has over 60,000 names and addresses of individuals and firms abroad interested in importing U.S. products; and many other data services. It is available for free at over 900 Federal Depository Libraries and can be purchased for $35 per disc or $360 for a 12-month subscription. Contact: Economics and Statistics

Administration, U.S. Department of Commerce, Washington, DC
20230; 202-482-1986; Fax: 202-482-2164;
{www.state.usa.gov/tradtest.nsf}.

13) **Global Demographics:**

The International Program Center at the
Census Bureau compiles and maintains up-to-
date global demographic and social
information for all countries in its
International Data Base, which is accessible to U.S. companies
seeking to identify potential markets overseas. Contact Systems
Analysis and Programming Staff, Bureau of the Census, Room 109,
Washington Plaza 2, Washington, DC 20233; 301-457-1403.

14) **International Energy Database:**
The Office of Fossil Energy forwards prospective energy-related
leads to the Agency for International Development (AID) for
inclusion in its growing trade opportunities database in an effort to
reach an extended audience seeking energy-related trade
opportunities. For more information on the Fossil Energy-AID
Database contact: The Office of Fossil Energy, U.S. Department of
Energy, 1000 Independence Ave. SW, Washington, DC 20585, 202-
586-6503; Fax: 202-586-5146; {www.fe.doe.gov}.

15) **Online Economic Bulletin Board (EBB):**
This computer-based electronic bulletin board, is an online source for
trade leads as well as the latest statistical releases from the Bureau of
Census, the Bureau of Economic Analysis, the Bureau of Labor
Statistics, the Federal Reserve Board, and other federal agencies.
Subscribers pay an annual fee, plus cost per minute. Contact: EBB,
Office of Business Analysis, U.S. Department of Commerce,
Washington, DC 20230, 202-482-1986;
{www.ita.doc.gov/uscs/uscsebb.html}.

16) **Free Legal Assistance:**
The Export Legal Assistance Network (ELAN) is a nationwide
group of attorneys with experience in international trade who provide
free initial consultations to small businesses on export related

matters. Contact: Export Legal Assistance Network, Small Business Administration, 1667 K St., NW, Suite 1100, Washington, DC 20006; 202-778-3080; Fax: 202-778-3063; {www.fita.org/elan}.

17) **Global Learning:**
U.S. Department of Education, Business and International Education Programs. The business and international education program is designed to engage U.S. schools of business language and area programs, international study programs, public and private sector organizations, and U.S. businesses in a mutually productive relationship which will benefit the Nation's future economic interest. Approximately $3.6 million annually is available to assist U.S. institutions of higher education to promote the Nation's capacity for international understanding. Typical grantee activities include executive seminars, case studies, and export skill workshops. For more information contact: Office of Higher Education Programs, U.S. Department of Education, 600 Independence Avenue, SW, Washington, DC 20202; 202-401-9778.

18) **Export Counseling — SCORE:**
The Small Business Administration can provide export counseling to small business exporters by retired and active business executives. The Service Corps of Retired Executives (SCORE) is an overly
 active organization with over 12,400 volunteers and 389 SCORE chapters. Members of SCORE, with years of practical experience in international trade, assist small firms in evaluating their export potential and developing and implementing basic export marketing plans. Two of SCORE's most helpful programs are its weekly low cost workshops and its e-mail counseling. For more information, contact your local Small Business Administration (SBA) office listed in the government pages of your telephone book, or National SCORE Office, 401 Third St. SW, 6th Floor, Washington, DC 20024; 800-634-0245; Fax: 202-205-7636; E-mail: {score@sba.gov}; {www.score.org}.

19) **Department of Energy — Office of International Affairs and Energy Emergencies:**
The Department of Energy (DOE) promotes U.S. exports of energy goods, services, and technology primarily through participation in The Committee on Renewable Energy Commerce and Trade, and The Coal and Clean Technology Export Program. The following is a list of the Department of Energy's programs and the corresponding telephone numbers to call for more information.

❂ **Committee on Renewable Energy Commerce and Trade (CORECT):**
Through the concept of "one-stop shopping" potential exporters can receive comprehensive advice on potential markets, financing and information on export guidelines. Call the Office of Conservation and Renewable Energy, 202-586-8302; Fax: 202-586-1605.

❂ **Coal and Technology Export Program (CTEP):** The Coal and Technology Export Program (CTEP) serves as a reservoir for international information on U.S. coal and coal technologies, as the Department of Energy's intra-departmental coordinator, and as the USG inter-agency liaison for coal companies and technology firms. Call 202-586-7297.

❂ **The Export Assistance Initiative:** This entity in the Bureau of International Affairs has been designed to help identify overseas opportunities for U.S. companies, identify and attempt to alleviate discriminatory trade barriers, and identify possible financing alternatives for U.S. companies. Call 202-586-1189.

20) **Fax Retrieval Systems**
A number of offices offer documents on demand, delivered directly to a fax machine 24 hours a day. These automated systems each have a menu of available documents that can be sent to a fax machine by dialing from  a touch-tone phone and following directions. Below is a list of offices that offer this program:

Uruguay Round Hotline: This Fax retrieval system is located at the International Trade Administration and has information on the GATT agreement. Document #1000 is the menu of available information packets. A series of prompts will allow you to enter: 1, 1, 2, 2. This system allows retrieval for information on the Uruguary Round, service sector reports, state opportunities reports, industry sector highlight reports, and tariff and harmonization decisions. 1-800-USA-TRADE.

Center for Eastern European Business Information Center (CEEBIC): This Fax system has 5 main menus. Menu document #1000 has export and financing information. Document #2000 has a menu of documents relating to export and investment opportunities and upcoming trade events. A listing of Eastern European country information is available on menu document #3000. Document menus #4000 and #5000 have information on the *Eastern Europe Business Bulletin*, and the *Eastern Europe Looks For Partners* publications; 202-482-5745.

Business Information Service for the Newly Independent States: There are 3 menus available through BISNIS. Menu number 1, document #0001 has trade and investment opportunities and trade promotion information. Menu number 2, document #0002 has industry and country specific information, and financing alternatives. Menu number 3, document #0003, has information on BISNIS publications; 202-482-3145.

Office of Mexico: The main menu for Mexico is document #0101. There is also a menu of labeling and standards requirements (document #8404). Information on documents relating to the certificate of origin and rules of origin under NAFTA is document #5000. A complete NAFTA tariff schedule is on document #6000. Begin by selecting "1" when prompted. 202-482-4464 or 202-482-1495.

Office of Canada: The main menu for Canada is document #0101. The fax retrieval system offers menus on NAFTA rules of origin, customs information, and tariff schedules. 202-482-1495 or 202-482-4464.

Office of Africa, Near East, and South Asia: A list of documents covering the nations of North Africa and the Middle East is document #0100. Africa is #3000 and South Asian countries is #4000; 202-482-1064.

Overseas Private Investment Corporation: This system has information on OPIC project finance and political risk insurance programs; 202-336-8700.

Office of Latin America and Caribbean Basin: This fax retrieval system is maintained by the ITA. Select "2", Index Code: 1 to receive country fact sheets, key contacts, tariff and duty information, and trade programs. This system covers Southern Cone, Andean, Central American and Caribbean Basin countries. 202-482-2521.

21) **International Visitors Program**
Foreign individuals or groups are brought to the U.S. for about one month. The programs feature visits by business leaders and foreign government officials who have the opportunity to meet with their U.S. counterparts. Contact: Office of International Visitors, U.S. Information Agency, 301 4th St., SW, Room 255, Washington, DC 20547; 1-800-650-9822; Fax: 202-205-0792.

22) **International Company Profiles (ICP)**
The ICP, run by the U.S. Department of Commerce, provides

Background
Checks

thorough background checks on all potential clients to reduce the risk of entering new business relationships. U.S. embassies and consulates abroad will conduct this investigation for you at a reasonable rate and return the results in approximately one month. Commercial specialists will then give a trained opinion of a possible relationship between yourself and the subject firm. All requests are held within the strictest of confidences. For more information, contact your local Export Assistance Center.

23) **National Telecommunication and Information Administration (NTIA)**
The NTIA, through its Office of International Affairs, provides technical guidance, aids in stabilizing international telecommunications issues, deploys new technology into international markets, and works to improve global communications and expand trade opportunities for the U.S. Contact the Office of International Affairs at the NTIA: Office of International Affairs, National Telecommunications & Information Administration, Room 4701, U.S. Department of Commerce, 1401

Constitution Ave., NW, Washington, DC 20230; 202-482-1866;
Fax: 202-482-1865, {www.ntia.doc.gov/oiahome/oiahome.html}.

Read All About It: Helpful Publications

The Government Printing Office (GPO) has many titles to
choose from. For a listing, contact the GPO (listed below) by
mail or phone and ask for the Foreign Trade and Tariff
Subject Bibliography (SB-123; 021-123-00405-1).

Government Printing Office
Superintendent of Documents
Washington, DC 20402
202-512-1800
www.access.gpo.gov/su_docs

Basic Guide to Exporting:

This publication outlines the sequence of steps necessary to
determine whether to, and how to, use foreign markets as a source of
profits. It describes the various problems that confront smaller firms
engaged in, or seeking to enter,
international trade, as well as the
types of assistance available. It
also provides a guide to
appraising the sales potential of
foreign markets and to
understanding the requirements
of local business practices and
procedures in overseas markets.
The booklet is available for $13
(GPO: 003-009-00604-0) from: Superintendent of Documents, U.S.
Government Printing Office, Washington, DC 20402, 202-512-1800;
Fax: 202-512-2250.

Commercial News USA:

This publication describes a free export promotion service that will

publicize the availability of your new product to foreign markets of more than 150 countries, and test foreign market interest in your new product. There is a small fee. Contact Commercial News USA: Associated Publications International, 317 Madison Ave., New York, NY 10017; 212-490-3999; Fax: 212-986-7864; {www.cnews.com}.

Export Programs: A Business Directory of U.S. Government Resources:

This guide provides an overview of U.S. government export assistance programs and contact points for further information and expertise in utilizing these programs. Contact: Trade Information Center, U.S. Department of Commerce, Washington, DC 20230, 1-800-872-8723.

Business America:

The principal Commerce department publication for presenting domestic and international business news. Each monthly issue includes a "how to" article for new exporters, discussion of U.S. trade policy, news of government actions that may affect trade, a calendar of upcoming trade shows, exhibits, fairs, and seminars. The annual subscription is $47 in the U.S., $4 for any single copy. (GPO: 703-011-0000-4-W). Contact: Superintendent of Documents, Government Printing Office, Washington, DC 20402, 202-512-1800.

Key Officers of Foreign Service Posts: A Guide for Business Representatives:

Lists the names of key State and Commerce officers at U.S. embassies and consulates. Cost is $3.75 per copy (GPO: 044-000-0299-3). Contact: Superintendent of Documents, Government Printing Office, Washington, DC 20402, 202-512-1800.

Export Trading Company (ETC) Guidebook:

This Guidebook is intended to assist those who are considering
starting or expanding exporting through the various forms of an ETC.
The Guidebook will also facilitate your review of the ETC Act and
export trading options and serve as a planning tool for your business
by showing you what it takes to export profitably and how to start
doing it. Cost is $15 (GPO: 003-009-00523-0). Contact:
Superintendent of Documents, Government Printing Office,
Washington, DC 20402, 202-512-1800.

Foreign Labor Trends:

Published by the Department of
Labor, these are a series of reports,
issued annually, that describe and analyze labor trends in more than
70 countries. The reports, which are prepared by the American
Embassy in each country, cover labor-management relations, trade
unions, employment and unemployment, wages and working
conditions, labor and government, international labor activities, and
other significant developments. Contact: Office of Foreign Relations,
Room S 5006, 200 Constitution Ave., NW, Washington, DC 20210,
202-523-6257, 202-219-6257. This publication is also available from
the GPO for $1.50-$2.00.

ABC's of Exporting:

This is a special issue of Business America that takes you step by
step through the exporting process. It explains the federal agencies
and how they can help, as well as providing a directory of export
sources. This publication is free and is available by contacting Trade
Information Center, U.S. Department of Commerce, Washington, DC
20230, 1-800-872-8723.

Ag Exporter:

Monthly magazine published by the U.S. Department of Agriculture's
Foreign Agricultural Service (FAS). The annual subscription cost is
$27 (GPO: 701-027-00000-1). Contact: Superintendent of
Documents, Government Printing Office, Washington, DC 20402;
202-512-1800.

AID Procurement Information Bulletin:

This publication advertises notices of intended procurement of AID-financed commodities. The subscription cost is free. Contact: USAID's Office of Small and Disadvantaged Business Utilization/ Minority Resource Center, Washington, DC 20523-1414; 703-875-1551.

Breaking into the Trade Game: A Small Business Guide to Exporting:

The Small Business Administration has created this comprehensive guide to exporting. A must have for all exporters, new and experienced. This guide is available from the SBA website: {www.sba.gov/oit/txt/finance/pubs.html}.

U.S. Department of Commerce/ US & FCS Field Offices

Trade experts from the US & FCS are available to help you from 47 district offices and 21 branch locations throughout the U.S. The ITA trade specialists are also available at any of the 51 District Export Councils nationwide to assist U.S. firms export.

Alabama
Birmingham: 950 22nd St., North, Room 707, Birmingham, AL 35203; 205-731-1331; Fax: 205-731-0076.

Alaska
Anchorage: 3550 W. 7th Ave., Suite 1770, Anchorage, AK 99501; 907-271-6237; Fax: 907-271-6242.

Arizona
Phoenix: 2901 N. Central Ave., Suite 970, Phoenix, AZ 99501; 602-640-2513; Fax: 602-640-2518.

Arkansas
Little Rock: 425 West Capitol Ave., TCBY Tower Building, Suite 700, Little Rock, AR 72201; 501-324-5794; Fax: 501-324-7380.

California
Los Angeles: 11500 Olympic Blvd., Suite 975, Los Angeles, CA 90064; 310-235-7104; Fax: 310-235-7220.
Newport Beach: 3300 Irvine Ave., Suite 305, Newport Beach, CA 92660; 949-660-1688; Fax: 949-660-8039.
San Diego: 6363 Greenwich Drive, San Diego, CA 92122; 619-

557-5395; Fax: 619-557-6176.

San Francisco: 250 Montgomery St., 14th Floor, San Francisco, CA 94104; 415-705-2310; Fax: 415-705-2297.

Colorado
Denver: 1625 Broadway, Suite 680, Denver, CO 80202; 303-844-3246; Fax: 303-844-5651.

Connecticut
Middletown: 213 Court St., Suite 903, Middletown, CT 06457; 860-638-6950; Fax: 860-638-6970.

District of Columbia
Served by Baltimore, MD, ITA office.

Delaware
Served by Philadelphia, PA, District Office.

Florida
Miami: 5600 NW 36th St., Suite 617, Miami, FL 33166; 305-526-7425; Fax: 305-526-7434.

Clearwater: 1130 Cleveland St., Clearwater, FL 33755; 727-441-1742; Fax: 727-449-2889

Tallahassee: 107 W. Gaines St., Collins Bldg., Room 366G, Tallahassee, FL 32399; 850-486-6469; Fax: 850-487-1407.

Orlando: 200 E. Robinson St., Suite 695, Orlando, FL 32801;

407-648-6235; Fax: 407-648-6756.

Georgia
Atlanta: 285 Peachtree Center Ave., NE, Suite 200, Atlanta, GA 30303; 404-657-1900; Fax: 404-657-1970.

Savannah: 6001 Chatham Center Dr., Suite 100, Savannah, GA 31405; 912-652-4204; Fax: 912-652-4241.

Hawaii
Honolulu: 1001 Bishop St., Suite 1140, Honolulu, HI 96813; 808-522-8040; Fax: 808-522-8045.

Idaho
Boise: 700 W. State St., 2nd Floor, Boise, ID 83720; 208-334-3857; Fax: 208-334-2787.

Illinois
Chicago: 55 W. Monroe, Room 2440, Chicago, IL 60603; 312-353-8045; Fax: 312-353-8120.

Rockford: 515 N. Court St., P.O. Box 1747, Rockford, IL 61110-6247; 815-987-8123; Fax: 815-987-8122.

Indiana
Indianapolis: 11405 N. Pennsylvania St., Penwood One, Suite 106, Carmel, IN 46032; 317-582-2300; Fax: 317-582-2301.

Iowa

Des Moines: 501 Locust St., Suite 100, Des Moines, IA 50309; 515-288-8614; Fax: 515-288-1437.

Kansas

Wichita: 209 E. William, Suite 100, Wichita, KS 67202; 316-269-6160; Fax: 316-269-6111.

TradE SpEcialists

Kentucky

Louisville: 601 W. Broadway, Room 636B, Louisville, KY 40202; 502-582-5066; Fax: 502-582-6573.

Louisiana

New Orleans: 365 Canal St., New Orleans, LA 70130; 504-589-6546; Fax: 504-589-2337.

Maine

Portland: Maine International Trade Center, 511 Congress St., Portland, ME 04101; 207-541-7300; Fax: 207-541-7420.

Maryland

Baltimore: 401 E. Pratt St., Baltimore, MD 21202; 410-962-4539; Fax: 410-9624529.

Massachusetts

Boston: World Trade Center, Suite 307, Boston, MA 02210; 617-424-5990; Fax: 617-424-5992.

Michigan

Detroit: 211 W. Fort St., Suite 2220, Detroit, MI 48226; 313-226-3650; Fax: 313-226-3657.

Grand Rapids: 301 W. Fulton St., Suite 718-S, Grand Rapids, MI 49504; 616-458-3564; Fax: 616-458-3872.

Minnesota

Minneapolis: 45 South 7th St., Suite 2240, Minneapolis, MN 55402; 612-348-1638; Fax: 612-348-1650.

Mississippi

Raymond: 704 E. Main St., Raymond, MS 39154; 601-857-0128; Fax: 601-857-0026.

Missouri

St. Louis: 8182 Maryland Ave., Suite 303, St. Louis, MO 63105; 314-425-3302; Fax: 314-425-3381.

Kansas City: 2345 Grand St., Suite 650, Kansas City, MO 64108; 816-410-9201; Fax: 816-410-9208.

Montana

Missoula: Montana World Trade Center, Gallagher Business

Bldg., Suite 257, Missoula, MT 59812; 406-243-2098; Fax: 406-243-5259.

Nebraska
Omaha: 11135 O St., Omaha, NE 68137; 402-221-3664; Fax: 402-221-3668.

Nevada
Reno: 1755 E. Plumb Lane, #152, Reno, NV 89502; 702-784-5203; Fax: 702-784-5343.

New Hampshire
Portsmouth: 17 New Hampshire Ave., Portsmouth, NH 02801; 603-334-6074; Fax: 603-334-6110.

New Jersey
Trenton: 3131 Princeton Pike Building 4, Suite 105, Trenton, NJ 08648; 609-989-2100; Fax: 609-989-2395.

New Mexico
Santa Fe: New Mexico Department of Economic Development, P.O. Box 20003, Santa Fe, NM 87504; 505-827-0350; Fax: 505-827-0263.

New York
Buffalo: 111 W. Huron St., Room 1312, Federal Building, Buffalo, NY 14202; 716-551-4191; Fax: 716-551-5296.
New York: 6 World Trade Center, Room 635, New York, NY 10048; 212-466-5222; Fax: 212-264-1356.

North Carolina
Greensboro: 400 W. Market St., Suite 400, Greensboro, NC 27401; 336-333-5345; Fax: 336-333-5158.

Ohio
Cincinnati: 36 E. 7th St., Suite 2650, Cincinnati, OH 45202; 513-684-2944; Fax: 513-684-3227.
Cleveland: 600 Superior Ave., East., Suite 700, Cleveland, OH 44114; 216-522-4750; Fax: 216-522-2235.

Oklahoma
Oklahoma City: 301 Northwest 63rd St., Suite 330, Oklahoma City, OK 73116; 405-608-5302; Fax: 405-608-4211.
Tulsa: 700 N Greenwood Ave., Suite 1409, Tulsa, OK 73106; 918-581-7650; Fax: 918-594-8413.

Oregon
Portland: Suite 242, One World Trade Center, 121 SW Salmon St., Portland, OR 97204; 503-326-3001; Fax: 503-326-6351.

Pennsylvania
Pittsburgh: 1000 Liberty Ave., Room 2002, Pittsburgh, PA 15222; 412-395-5050; Fax: 412-395-4875.

Philadelphia: 615 Chestnut St.,
Suite 1501, Philadelphia, PA
19106; 215-597-6101; Fax:
215-597-6123.

Puerto Rico
San Juan: Room G-55 Federal
Building, Chardon Ave. San
Juan, PR 00918; 787-766-
5555; Fax: 787-766-5692.

Rhode Island
Providence: One West Exchange
St., Providence, RI 02903;
401-528-5104; Fax: 401-528-
5067.

South Carolina
Columbia: 1835 Assembly St.,
Suite 172, Columbia, SC
29201; 803-765-5345; Fax:
803-253-3614.
Charleston: 81 Mary St.,
Charleston, SC 29403; 843-
727-4051; Fax: 843-727-
4052.

South Dakota
Siouxland: Augustana College,
2001 S. Summit Ave., Room
SS-44, Sioux Falls, SD 57197;
605-330-4264; Fax: 605-330-
4266.

Tennessee
Nashville: 404 James Robertson
Pkwy., Suite 114, Nashville,
TN 37219; 615-736-5161;
Fax: 615-736-2454.
Memphis: 650 E. Parkway S, Suite
348, Memphis, TN 38104;
901-323-1543; Fax: 901-320-
9128.
Knoxville: 601 W. Summit Hill,
Knoxville, TN 37902; 423-
545-4637; Fax: 423-545-
4435.

Texas
Dallas: 2050 N. Stemmons Pkwy.,
Dallas, TX 75207; 214-767-
0542; Fax: 214-767-8240.
Austin: 1700 Congress, Austin, TX
78711; 512-916-5939; Fax:
512-916-5940.
Houston: 500 Dallas, Suite 1160,
Houston, TX 77002; 713-718-
3062; Fax: 713-718-3060.

Utah
Salt Lake City: Suite 105, 324 S.
State St., Salt Lake City, UT
84111; 801-524-5116; Fax:
801-524-5886.

Vermont
Montpelier: National Life Bldg.,
Drawer 20, Montpelier, VT
05620; 802-828-4508; Fax:
802-828-3258.

Virginia
Richmond: 400 N. Eighth St., Suite
8010, Richmond, VA 23240;
804-771-2246; Fax: 804-771-
2390.

Washington
Seattle: 2001 6th Ave., Suite 650,
　　Seattle, WA 98121; 206-553-
　　5615; Fax: 206-553-7253.

West Virginia
Charleston: 405 Capitol St., Suite
　　807, Charleston, WV 25301,
　　304-347-5123; Fax: 304-347-
　　5408.

Wisconsin
Milwaukee: 517 E. Wisconsin
　　Ave., Room 596, Milwaukee,
　　WI 53202, 414-297-3473; Fax:
　　414-297-3470.

Wyoming
Served by Denver, Colorado,
　　District Office.

State Government Assistance to Exporters

Last year state governments spent approximately
$40,000,000 to help companies
in their state sell goods and
services overseas. This figure
increased almost 50% over the
previous two years. During the
same period of time, federal
monies devoted to maximizing
companies' export capabilities

remained virtually constant. This is another indicator of how
the states are fertile sources of information and expertise for
large and small businesses.

The underlying mission of these offices is to create jobs
within their state. Usually their approach is to help
companies develop overseas marketing strategies or to offer
incentives to foreign companies to invest in their state. The
major state trade development programs and services are
outlined below.

Information USA, Inc.

1) **Marketing Research and Company Intelligence:**
All of the states can provide some degree of overseas marketing information. The level of detail will depend upon the resources of the state. Thirty-five states (except for California, Hawaii, Idaho, Kansas, Maryland, Minnesota, Nebraska, Nevada, New Jersey, New York, South Dakota, Texas, Washington, West Virginia, and Wyoming) say they will do customized market studies for companies. Such studies are free or available for a small fee. For example, the Commonwealth of Virginia will do an in-depth market study for a company and charge $1,000. They estimate similar surveys done by the private sector cost up to $20,000. Virginia relies on MBA students and professors within the state university system who get credit for working on such projects.

Even if a state does not perform customized studies, the trade office within a Department of Economic Development will prove to be an ideal starting place for marketing information. Some states, which do not undertake comprehensive studies for prospective exporters, will do a limited amount of research for free. These offices can also point to outside sources as well as the notable resources at the federal level that may be able to assist. And those states with offices overseas also can contact these foreign posts to identify sources in other countries. Moreover, many of the offices have people who travel abroad frequently for companies and also work with other exporters. Such bureaucrats can be invaluable for identifying the exact source for obtaining particular market or company intelligence.

2) **Company and Industry Directories:**
Many states publish directories, which are helpful to both exporters and researchers. Some states publish export/import directories which show which companies in the state are exporters and what they sell as well as which are importers and what they buy. Because many of the trade offices are also interested in foreign investment within their state, many publish directories or other reference sources disclosing

which companies in their state are foreign owned, and by whom. Other state publications may include export service directories which list organizations providing services to exporters such as banks, freight forwarders, translators, and world trade organizations. Some also publish agribusiness exporter directories, which identify agricultural-related companies involved in exporting.

3) **Free Newsletters:**

All but four states (i.e., Florida, Kentucky, Ohio, and North Carolina) generate international newsletters or publish a special section within a general newsletter on items of interest to those selling overseas. These newsletters are normally free and cover topics like new trade leads, new rules and regulations for exports, and details about upcoming overseas trade shows. Such newsletters can also be a source for mailing lists for those whose clients include exporters. We haven't specifically investigated the availability of such lists, but remember that all states have a law comparable to the federal Freedom of Information Act, which allows public access to government data.

4) **Overseas Contacts:**

Finding a foreign buyer or an agent/distributor for a company is one of the primary functions of these state offices. How they do this varies from state to state. Many sponsor trade fairs and seminars overseas to attract potential buyers to products produced in their state. The more aggressive trade promotion offices may organize trade missions and escort a number of companies overseas and personally help them look for buyers or agents. Many will distribute a company's sales brochures and other literature to potential buyers around the world through their overseas offices. Some states work with the federal government and explore general trade leads and then try to match buyers with sellers. Others will cultivate potential clients in a given country and contact each directly.

5) **Export Marketing Seminars:**
Many of the states conduct free or modestly priced seminars to introduce companies to selling overseas. Some of the courses are held in conjunction with the regional International Trade Administration office of the U.S. Commerce Department. The course may be general in nature, for example, *The Basics of Exporting*, or focused on specific topics such as *International Market Research Techniques*, *Letters of Credit*, *Export Financing*, or *How to do Business with Israel*.

6) **State Grants and Loans for Exporters:**
Many states offer financial assistance for those wishing to export. Some states even provide grants (money you do not have to pay back) to those firms which cannot afford to participate in a trade mission or trade fair. This means that they provide money to those companies that are just trying to develop a customer base overseas. More typically the state will help with the financing of a sale through state-sponsored loans and loan guarantees, or assistance in identifying and applying for federal or commercial export financing.

7) **Trade Leads Databases:**
Because these offices provide mostly services, there are not many opportunities for them to develop databases. However, their trade leads program is one area where a number of offices have computerized their information. These databases consist of the names and addresses along with some background information on those overseas companies that are actively searching or might be interested in doing business with companies within the state. The number of leads in such a system could range from several hundred to five or ten thousand. None of these states seem to have made such information available on machine readable formats to those outside the office. But, in light of state Freedom of Information statutes, it may be worth making a formal inquiry if you have an interest. The states that have computerized their trade leads include: Alabama, Arkansas, Arizona, California, Colorado, Connecticut, Delaware, Florida, Georgia, Hawaii, Illinois, Indiana, Iowa, Maine, Michigan, Maryland, Minnesota, Mississippi, Missouri, Nebraska, New Jersey,

New York, North Carolina, North Dakota, Ohio, Oklahoma, Oregon, New Hampshire, Pennsylvania, Puerto Rico, Rhode Island, South Dakota, Tennessee, Texas, Utah, Virginia, Washington, West Virginia, and Wisconsin.

State International Trade Offices

The foreign cities in parentheses after the telephone number are those locations where the state maintains a trade office.

Alabama
International Development and Trade Division, Alabama Development Office, 401 Adams Ave., Montgomery, AL 36130, 334-242-0400, 800-248-0033; Fax: 334-353-1330; E-mail: {idinfo@ado.state.al.us}; {www.ado.state.al.us/trade.htm}. (Stuttgart, **Germany**; Seoul, **Korea**; Tokyo, **Japan**; Jerusalem, **Israel**).

Alaska
Office of International Trade, Department of Commerce and Economic Development, 550 W. 7th Ave., Suite 1770, Anchorage, AK 99501, 907-269-8110; Fax: 907-269-8125; {www.commerce.state.ak.us/trade}. (Tokyo, **Japan**; Seoul, **Korea**; Taipei, **Taiwan**; Sakhalinsk, **Russia**).

Arizona
International Trade and Investment Division, Department of Commerce, 3800 N. Central, Suite 1500, Phoenix, AZ 85012, 602-280-1371; Fax: 602-280-1305; {www.commerce.state.az.us/itrade/itrade.shtml}. (Hermosillo, **Mexico**; Mexico City, **Mexico**; Tokyo, **Japan**; Taipei, **Taiwan**; London, **UK**; Munich, **Germany**).

Arkansas
International Marketing, Arkansas Industrial Commission, One State Capitol Mall, Little Rock, AR 72201, 501-682-2460; Fax: 501-324-9856; {www.1800arkansas.com}. (Brussels, **Belgium**; Tokyo, **Japan**; Mexico City, **Mexico**; Kuala Lumpur, **Malaysia**).

California
California State World Trade Commission, 801 K St., Suite 1926, Sacramento, CA 95814, 916-324-5511; Fax: 916-324-5791 (Tokyo, **Japan**; London, **UK**; **Hong Kong**; Frankfurt, **Germany**; Mexico City, **Mexico**; Taipei, **Taiwan**; Jerusalem, **Israel**; Seoul, **Korea**; Johannesburg, **South Africa**).

Export Development Office, One World Trade Center, Suite 990, Long Beach, CA 90831, 562-590-

5965; Fax: 562-590-5958; E-mail: {expdev@commerce.ca.gov}, {commerce.ca.gov/international}.

Colorado
International Trade Office, Department of Commerce and Development, 1625 Broadway, Suite 900, Denver, CO 80202, 303-892-3850; Fax: 303-892-3820; E-mail: {ito@governor.state.co.us}; {www.state.co.us/gov_dir/govnr_dir/ITO/intl_trade_gov.htm}. (Tokyo, **Japan**; London, **UK**; Guadalajara, **Mexico**).

Connecticut
International Division, Department of Economic and Community Development, 505 Hudson St., Hartford, CT 06106, 203-258-4285; Fax: 203-529-0535; {www.state.ct.us/ecd/international/}. (Tokyo, **Japan**; Taipei, **Taiwan**; **Hong Kong**; Mexico City, **Mexico**).

Delaware
Delaware Development Office, International Trade Section, 820 French St., Carvel State Building, 3rd Floor, Wilmington, DE 19801, 302-577-8464; Fax: 302-577-8499; {www.state.de.us/dedo/departments/trade/intnt.htm}.

District of Columbia
D.C. Office of International Business, 717 14th St. NW, Suite 1100, Box 4, Washington, DC 20005, 202-727-1576; Fax: 202-727-1588.

Florida
Office of International Affairs, Florida Department of State, The Capitol, Tallahassee, FL 32399-0250; 850-414-1727; Fax: 850-414-1734; E-mail: {intrel@mail.dos.state.fl.us}; {oir.dos.state.fl.us}. (Toronto, **Canada**; Taipei, **Taiwan**; Seoul, **Korea**; Frankfurt, **Germany**; Tokyo, **Japan**; London, **UK**; Sao Paulo, **Brazil**; Mexico City, **Mexico**).

Georgia
International Trade Division, Suite 1100, 285 Peachtree Center Ave., Atlanta, GA 30303, 404-656-3571; Fax: 404-651-6505; {www.georgia.org}. (Brussels, **Belgium**; Tokyo, **Japan**; Toronto, **Canada**; Seoul, **Korea**; Mexico City, **Mexico**; **Malaysia**; Sao Paulo, **Brazil**; Shang Hai, **China**; Jerusalem, **Israel**; Johannesburg, **South Africa**; Taipei, **Taiwan**).

WORLD TRADE

Hawaii
Business Development and Marketing Division, Department of Business and Economic Development, P.O. Box 2359, Honolulu, HI 96804, 808-587-2584; Fax: 808-587-3388; {www.

hawaii.gov/dbedt/trade/greg.html}.
(Tokyo, **Japan**; Taipei, **Taiwan**).

Idaho
Division of International Business,
Department of Commerce, 700 W.
State St., 2nd Floor, Boise, ID
83720, 208-334-2470; Fax: 208-
334-2783; {www.idoc.state.id.us/
information/exportinfo/index2.
htm}. (Guadalajara, **Mexico**;
Taipei, **Taiwan**; Tokyo, **Japan**;
Seoul, **Korea**).

Illinois
International Business Division,
Illinois Department of Commerce
and Community Affairs, 100 W.
Randolph St., Suite 3-400,
Chicago, IL 60601, 312-814-7179;
Fax: 312-814-2370; {www.
commerce.state.il.us/Services/
International/International.htm}.
(Brussels, **Belgium**; Causeway
Bay, **Hong Kong**; Tokyo, **Japan**;
Warsaw, **Poland**; Mexico City,
Mexico; Budapest, **Hungary**).

Illinois Export Council and Illinois
Export Development Authority,
321 N. Clark St., Suite 550,
Chicago, IL 60610; (Export
Council) 312-793-4982;
(Development Authority) 312-793-
4995.

Indiana
International Marketing, Department of Commerce, One North
Capitol, Suite 700, Indianapolis, IN
46204, 317-232-8845; Fax 317-

232-4146; {www.state.in.us/doc/
indiresidents/ intmarket}. (Tokyo,
Japan; Mexico City, **Mexico**;
Toronto, **Canada**; Taipei, **Taiwan**;
Beijing, **China**; Seoul, **Korea**;
Amsterdam, **Netherlands**).

Iowa
Department of International Trade,
Iowa Department of Economic
Development, 200 East Grand
Ave., Des Moines, IA 50309, 515-
242-4743; Fax: 515-242-4918;
E-mail: {international@ided.
state.ia.us}; {www.state.ia.us/
government/ided/intl}. (Frankfurt,
Germany; Tokyo, **Japan**).

Kansas
Kansas Department of Commerce,
700 SW Harrison St., Suite 1300,
Topeka, KS 66603, 785-296-4027;
Fax: 785-296-5763; {kansas
commerce.com/0306international.
html}. (Tokyo, **Japan**; Brussels,
Belgium; Sydney, **Australia**; **UK**).

Kentucky
International Trade, Cabinet for
Economic Development, 2400
Capitol Plaza Tower, 500 Mero St.,
Frankfort, KY 40601, 502-564-
2170; Fax 502-564-7697; {www.
edc.state.ky.us/kyedc}. (Tokyo,
Japan; Brussels, **Belgium**).

Louisiana
Office of International Marketing,
P.O. Box 94185, Baton Rouge, LA
70804-9185, 225-342-4319; Fax:
225-342-5389; {www.lded.state.

la.us}. (Mexico City, **Mexico**; Taipei, **Taiwan**; **Netherlands**; Frankfurt, **Germany**).

Maine
International Trade Center, 511 Congress St., Portland, ME 04101, 207-541-7400, Fax: 207-541-7420, {www.mitc.com}.

Maryland
U.S. Export Assistance Center, World Trade Center, 401 East Pratt St., 7th Floor, Suite 2432, Baltimore, MD 21202, 410-962-4539; Fax: 410-962-4529. (Brussels, **Belgium**; Yokohama, **Japan**; **Hong Kong**)

Massachusetts
The Massachusetts Export Center, Fishpier West, Building 2, Boxton, MA 02210, 617-478-4133; Fax: 617-478-4135; {www.state.ma.us/export}. (Berlin, **Germany**; Jerusalem, **Israel**; Mexico City, **Mexico**; London, **UK**; Guangzhou, **PRC**; Rio de Janeiro, **Brazil**; **Singapore**).

Massachusetts Trade Office State Transportation Building, 10 Park Plaza, Suite 3720, Boston, MA 02116, 617-367-1830; Fax: 617-227-3488; E-mail: {moiti@state. ma.us}; {www.magnet.state.ma.us/moiti/}.

Michigan
International Trade Division, International Trade Authority,

Michigan Department of Commerce, P.O. Box 30105, Lansing, MI 48909, 517-373-6369; Fax: 517-335-2521; {michigansbdc.org/intlrsrc.html}. (Toronto, **Canada**; **Hong Kong**; Brussels, **Belgium**; Tokyo, **Japan**; Mexico City, **Mexico**; Harvae, **Zimbabwe**).

Minnesota
Minnesota Trade Office, 1000 Minnesota World Trade Center, 30 E. 7th St., St. Paul, 55101, 800-657-3858, 651-297-4222; Fax: 651-296-1290; E-mail: mto@state. mn.us}; {www.dted.state.mn.us}. (Oslo, **Norway**; Stockholm, **Sweden**; London, **UK**; Paris, **France**; Frankfurt, **Germany**; **Hong Kong**; Osaka, **Japan**; Budapest, **Hungary**; Tokyo, **Japan**; Taipei, **Taiwan**; Brussels, **Belgium**).

Mississippi
Department of Economic and Community Development, P.O. Box 849, Jackson, MI 39205, 601-359-6672; Fax: 601-359-3605 (Seoul, **Korea**; Frankfurt, **Germany**; Taipei, **Taiwan**).

Missouri
International Trade, Department of Economic Development, 301 W. High St., Room 720C, P.O. Box 118, Jefferson City, MO 65102, 573-751-4855, Fax: 573-526-1567; E-mail: {missouri@mail.state. mo.us}, {www.ecodev.state.mo.us/

intermark}. (Tokyo, **Japan**; Dusseldorf, **Germany**; Seoul, **Korea**; Taipei, **Taiwan**; Guadalajara, **Mexico**; London, **UK**).

Montana

International Trade Office, Montana Department of Commerce, 1424 9th Ave., Helena, MT 59620, 406-444-4112; Fax: 406-444-2903; {www.state.mt.us}, {commerce.state.mt.us}. (Taipei, **Taiwan**; Kumamoto, **Japan**).

Nebraska

Department of Economic Development, 301 Centennial Mall South, P.O. Box 94666, Lincoln, NE 68509, 402-471-3111; Fax: 402-471-3778; {international.ded. state.ne.us}.

Trade Offices

Nevada

Commission of Economic Development, 108 E. Proctor St., Capital Complex, Carson, NV 89710, 775-687-4325; Fax: 775-687-4450; {www.state.nv.us/ businessop}.

New Hampshire

International Trade Resource Center, Department of Resources and Economic Development, 601 Spaulding Turnpike, Suite 29, Portsmouth, NH 03801, 603-334-6074; Fax: 603-334-6110; {www.ded.state.nh.us/oic/trade}.

New Jersey

Division of International Trade, Department of Commerce and Economic Development, 20 West State St., 12th Floor, Trenton, NJ 08625, 609-633-3606; Fax: 609-633-3672; {www.nj.njbrc.org}. (Tokyo, **Japan**; London, **UK**; Mexico City, **Mexico**).

New Mexico

Trade Division, Economic Development, 1100 St. Francis Dr., Joseph Montoya Building, Santa Fe, NM 87501, 505-827-0307; Fax: 505-827-0263; {www.edd. state.nm.us/TRADE}. (Mexico City, **Mexico**).

New York

International Division, Department of Trade and Economic Development, 1515 Broadway, 51st Floor, New York Department of Economic Development, New York, NY 10036, 212-827-6200; Fax: 212-827-6279 (Tokyo, **Japan**; London, **UK**; Milan, **Italy**; Toronto and Montreal, **Canada**; **Hong Kong**; Frankfurt, **Germany**).

North Carolina

International Division, Dept. of Commerce, 430 N. Salisbury St., Raleigh, NC 27611, 919-733-7193; Fax: 919-733-0110; {www. commerce.state.nc.us/commerce/ itd}. (Dusseldorf, **Germany**; **Hong Kong**; Tokyo, **Japan**; London, **UK**; Dubai, **United Arab Emirates**; Toronto, **Canada**).

North Dakota
International Trade Specialist, Department of Economic Development and Finance, 1833 E. Bismarck Expressway, Bismarck, ND 58504, 701-328-5300; Fax: 701-328-5320; {www.growingnd.com/itp_prog.html}.

Ohio
International Trade Division, Department of Development, 77 S. High St., P.O. Box 1001, Columbus, OH 43216, 614-466-5017; 614-463-1540; E-mail: {itd@odod.ohio.gov}, {ohiotrade.tpusa.com}. (Brussels, **Belgium**; Tokyo, **Japan**; **Hong Kong**, Toronto, **Canada**; Mexico City, **Mexico**; **Israel**).

Oklahoma
International Trade Division, Oklahoma Department of Commerce, 700 N. Greenwood Ave., Suite 1400, Tulsa, OK 74106, 405-594-8116, Fax: 405-594-8413; {www.odoc.state.ok.us/HOMEPAGE/internat.nsf}. (Seoul, **Korea**; Mexico City, **Mexico**; **Singapore**; Antwerp, **Belgium**; Ho Chi Mnh City, **Vietnam**; Beijing, **China**; Taipei, **Taiwan**).

Oregon
International Trade Division, Oregon Economic Development Department, One World Trade Center, Suite 300, 121 Salmon St., Portland, OR 97204, 503-229-5625; Fax: 503-222-5050;

{www.econ.state.or.us/intl/it.html}. (Tokyo, **Japan**; Seoul, **Korea**; Taipei, **Taiwan**).

Pennsylvania
Department of Commerce, Office of International Trade, 464 Forum Building, Harrisburg, PA 17120, 717-787-7190, 888-PA-EXPORT, Fax: 717-234-4560; {www.dced.state.pa.us/PA_Exec/DCED/international/officeof.htm}. (Frankfurt, **Germany**; Tokyo, **Japan**; Brussels, **Belgium**; Toronto, **Canada**).

Puerto Rico
Fomexport, P.O. Box 362350, San Juan, PR 00936-2350, 809-758-4747, ext. 2785, Fax: 809-764-1415; {www.ddec.govpr.net}.

Rhode Island
International Trade Office, Department of Economic Development, 7 Jackson Walkway, Providence, RI 02903, 401-277-2601; Fax: 401-277-2102; {www.sec.state.ri.us/bus/REIX.htm}. (Mexico City, **Mexico**).

South Carolina
International Business Development, South Carolina State Department of Commerce, P.O. Box 927, Columbia, SC 29202, 803-737-0400; Fax: 803-737-0818; {www.callsouthcarolina.com/InternationalTrade.htm}. (Tokyo, **Japan**; Frankfort, **Germany**; Seoul **Korea**; London, **UK**).

South Dakota

South Dakota International Business Institute, 1200 S. Jay St., Aberdeen, SD 57401, 605-626-3098, Fax: 605-626-3004; {www.state.sd.us/goed}.

Tennessee

Tennessee Export Office, Department of Economic and Community Development, Rachel Jackson Building, 320 Sixth Ave. North, 7th Floor, Nashville, TN 37219, 615-741-5870, 800-342-8470, 800-251-8594; Fax: 615-741-5829.

MARKETING

Texas

Office of International Marketing, Texas Department of Commerce, 410 E. 5th St., 3rd Floor, Austin, TX 78701, 512-472-5059, Fax: 512-320-9674. (Mexico City, **Mexico**; Frankfurt, **Germany**; Tokyo, **Japan**; Taipei, **Taiwan**; Brussels, **Belgium**; Seoul, **Korea**).

Utah

International Business Development Office, 324 S. State St., Suite 500, Salt Lake City, UT 84111, 801-538-8737, Fax: 801-538-8889; {international.state.ut.us}. (Tokyo, **Japan**).

Vermont

Vermont World Trade Office, 60 Main St., Suite 102, Burlington, VT 05401, 802-865-0493, 800-305-8321, Fax: 802-860-0091; {www.vermontworldtrade.org}.

Virginia

Virginia Economic Development Partnership, P.O. Box 798, 901 E. Byrd St., Richmond, VA 23218, 804-371-8123, Fax: 804-371-8860, E-mail: {exportva@vedp.state.va.us}, {www.exportvirginia.org}. (Tokyo, **Japan**; Frankfurt, **Germany**; **Hong Kong**; Mexico City, **Mexico**)

Washington

Domestic and International Trade Division, Department of Trade and Economic Development, 2001 Sixth Ave, 26th Floor, Seattle, WA 98121, 206-956-3131; Fax: 206-956-3151; {www.trade.wa.gov}. (Tokyo, **Japan**; **Canada**; Shanghai, **China**; Paris, **France**; Primorski Krai, **Russian Federation**; Taipei, **Taiwan**).

West Virginia

West Virginia Department of Development, Capitol Complex Bldg. 6, Room 517, 1900 Kanawha Blvd., Charleston, WV 25305, 304-558-2234; Fax: 304-558-1957, {www.wvdo.org/international}. (Tokyo, **Japan**; Nagaya, **Japan**; Munchen, **Germany**; Taipei, **Taiwan**).

Wisconsin

Bureau of International Business Development, Department of Development, P.O. Box 7970, 201

W. Washington Ave., Madison, WI 53707, 608-267-0587; Fax: 608-266-5551; {www.commerce.state. wi.us/Com-International.html}. (Frankfurt, **Germany**; **Hong Kong**; Mexico City, **Mexico**; Toronto, **Canada**; Tokyo, **Japan**; Seoul, **Korea**; **South Korea**).

Wyoming
International Trade Office, Department of Commerce, 4th Floor N., Barrett Building, Cheyenne, WY 82002, 307-777-7576; Fax: 307-777-5840.

Overseas Travel: Business or Pleasure

The following sources and services will be helpful to anyone who is on business or vacation in any foreign country:

1) **Travel Overseas on Government Expense:**
   The U.S. Speakers Program will pay experts, who can contribute to foreign societies' understanding of the United States, to travel abroad and participate in seminars, colloquia, or symposia. Subjects relevant to the program include economics, international political relations, U.S. social and political processes, arts and humanities, and science and technology. To see if you qualify contact: U.S. Speakers, Office of Program Coordination and Development, U.S. Information Agency, 301 4th St. SW, Room 550, Washington, DC 20547, 202-619-4764.

2) **Citizens Arrested Overseas:**
   The Arrest Unit at the State Department monitors arrests and trials to see that American citizens are not abused; acts as a liaison with family and friends in the United States; sends money or messages with written consent of arrestee; offers lists of lawyers; will forward money from the United States to detainee; tries to assure that your rights under local laws are observed. The Emergency Medical and Dietary Assistance Program includes such services as providing vitamin supplements when necessary; granting emergency transfer for emergency medical care; and short-term feeding of two or three meals a day when arrestee is detained without funds to buy his or her

own meals. Contact: Arrests Unit, Citizens Emergency Center, Overseas Citizens Service, Bureau of Consular Affairs, U.S. Department of State, 2201 C St. NW, Room 4817, Washington, DC 20520, 202-647-5225; Fax: 202-647-5226; {travel.state.gov/arrest.html}.

3) **Citizens Emergency Center:**
Emergency telephone assistance is available to United States citizens abroad under the following circumstances:

Arrests: 202-647-5225; (see details above)

Deaths: 202-647-5225; {travel.state.gov/deathrep.html}; notification of interested parties in the United States of the death abroad of American citizens; assistance in the arrangements for disposition of remains.

Financial Assistance: 202-647-5225; {travel.state.gov/money.html}; repatriation of destitute nationals, coordination of medical evacuation of non-official nationals from abroad; transmission of private funds in emergencies to destitute United States nationals abroad when commercial banking facilities are unavailable (all costs must be reimbursed).

Shipping and Seamen: 202-647-5225; {travel.state.gov/where.html}; protection of American vessels and seamen.

Welfare and Whereabouts: 202-647-5225; {travel.state.gov/where.html}; search for nonofficial United States nationals who have not been heard from for an undue length of time and/or about whom there is special concern; transmission of emergency messages to United States nationals abroad. The Welfare and Whereabouts website lists all of the questions that will need to be answered upon calling the service. For other help contact: Overseas Citizen Services, Bureau of Consular Affairs, U.S. Department of State, 2201 C St. NW, Washington, DC 20520, 202-647-5225.

4) **Country Information Studies:**
For someone who wants more than what the typical travel books tell about a specific country, this series of books deals with more in-depth knowledge of the country being visited. Each book describes the origins and traditions of the people and their social and national

attitudes, as well as the economics, military, political and social systems. For a more complete listing of this series and price information, contact Superintendent of Documents, Government Printing Office, Washington, DC 20402, 202-512-1800.

5) **Foreign Country Background Notes:**

Background Notes on the Countries of the World is a series of short, factual pamphlets with information on the country's land, people, history, government, political conditions, economy, foreign relations, and U.S. foreign policy. Each pamphlet also includes a factual profile, brief travel notes, a country map, and a reading list. *Background Notes* is also available online at {www.state.gov/www/background_notes/index.html}. Contact: Public Affairs Bureau, U.S. Department of State, Room 4827A, 2201 C St. NW, Washington, DC 20520, 202-647-2518 for a free copy of *Background Notes* for the countries you plan to visit. This material is also available from Superintendent of Documents, U.S. Government Printing Office, Washington, DC 20402, 202-512-1800. Single copies cost from $1.25 to $2.50. Order online at {accessgpo.gov/su_docs/sale/prf/ prf.html}.

6) **Foreign Language Materials:**

The Defense Language Institute Foreign Language Center (DLIFC) has an academic library with holdings of over 100, 000 books and periodicals in 50 different foreign languages. These materials are available through the national interlibrary loan program, which can be arranged through your local librarian. Contact: {pom_www.army.mil}.

7) **Foreign Language Training:**

The Foreign Service Institute is an in-house educational institution for foreign service officers, members of their families and employees of other government agencies. It provides special training in 50 foreign languages. Its instructional materials, including books and tapes, are designed to teach modern foreign languages. Instruction books must be purchased from Superintendent of Documents, U.S. Government Printing Office, Washington, DC 20402, 202-512-1800; {www.gpo.gov}. Tapes must be purchased from the National Audiovisual Center, National Archive, NTIS, Springfield, VA 22161, 1-800-788-6282 or 703-487-8400; {www.ntis.gov/nac}.

8) **Free Booklets for Travelers:**
The following booklets and guides are available free of charge:

Travel Information: Your Trip Abroad:
Contains basic information such as how to apply for a passport, customs tips, lodging information, and how American consular officers can help you in an emergency. Contact: Publications Distribution, Bureau of Public Affairs, U.S. Department of State, 2201 C St. NW, Room 5815A, Washington, DC 20520, 202-647-9859.

Customs Information:
Provides information about custom regulations both when returning to the U.S. as well as what to expect when traveling to different parts of the world. Contact: Customs Office, P.O. Box 7118, Washington, DC 20044; {www.customs.ustreas.gov}.

Visa Requirements of Foreign Governments:
Lists entry requirements of U.S. citizens traveling as tourists, and where and how to apply for visas and tourist cards. For Americans attempting to gain visas in other countries, Consular Affairs maintains a listing of the requirements for acquiring a visa in each country and which countries are not currently not accepting visas. Contact online at {travel.state.gov/foreignentryreqs.html}. Contact: Passport Services, Bureau of Consular Affairs, U.S. Department of State, 1425 K St. NW, Room G-62, Washington, DC 20524, 202-647-0518; E-mail: {usvisa@state.gov}; {travel.state.gov/visa_services.html}

9) **Passport Information:**
U.S. citizens and nationals can apply for passports at all passport agencies as well as those post offices and federal and state courts authorized to accept passport applications. Due to the cost of maintaining passport services, the National Passport Information Center created a fee-financed call center with two options. 900-225-

5674 charges 35 cents per minute for all calls. 888-362-8668 charges a flat rate of $4.95 per call. To avoid these charges, the NPIC has created a detailed website containing passport applications, statistics, information on how to add pages, replace a lost or stolen passport, renew an old passport, and get a listing of fees for services as well as all post offices handling passport affairs. {http://travel.state.gov/passport_services.html}.

10) **Travel Warnings:**
Before traveling, it is always a good idea to be aware of any travel warnings for your destination. All travel warnings, general warnings, and public announcements are listed by country and are available on the Bureau of Consular Affairs website at {travel.state.gov/travel_warnings.html}. These warnings may also be heard by telephone at any time by dialing 202-647-5225, or by utilizing an automated fax retrieval system at 202-647-3000.

Franchising: How To Select The Best Opportunity

Franchising could be for you, according to a study conducted by Arthur Andersen & Company of 366 franchise companies in 60 industries. They reported that nearly 86% of all franchise operations opened in the previous five years were still under the same ownership; only 3% of these businesses were no longer in business.

The U.S. Commerce Department reports that from 1971 to 1987, less than 5% of franchises were terminated on an annual basis. In contrast, a study conducted by the U.S. Small Business Administration from 1978 to 1988 found 62.2% of all new businesses were dissolved within the first six years of their operation, due to failure, bankruptcy, retirement, or other reasons.

While we are sure you are beginning to entertain the idea of owning a new business, franchising is not risk free and needs to be entered into with a degree of caution. Therefore, you need to take measures to protect yourself. The following organizations and publications will help you find the right franchise for you.

Organizations

Federal Trade Commission (FTC)
Bureau of Consumer Protection
Division of Marketing Practices
Pennsylvania Avenue at 6th Street, NW
Washington, DC 20580
202-326-3128
www.ftc.gov

Buying a franchise or a business opportunity may be appealing if you want to be your own boss, but have limited capital and business experience. However, without carefully investigating a business before you purchase, you may make a serious mistake. It is important to find out if a particular business is right for you and if it has the potential to yield the financial return you expect.

A Federal Trade Commission (FTC) rule requires that franchise and business opportunity sellers provide certain information to help you in your decision. Under the FTC rule, a franchise or business opportunity seller must give you a detailed disclosure document at least ten business days before you pay any money or legally commit yourself to a purchase. This document gives 20 important items of information about the business, including: the names, addresses, and telephone numbers of other purchasers; the fully-audited financial statement of the seller; the background and experience of the business's key executives; the cost required to start and maintain the business; and the responsibilities you and the seller will have to each other once you buy. The disclosure document is a valuable tool that not only helps you obtain information about a proposed business, but assists you in comparing it with other businesses.

If you are not given a disclosure document, ask why you did not receive one. Some franchise or business opportunity sellers may not be required to give you a disclosure document. If any franchise or business opportunity says it is not covered by the rule, you may want to verify it with the FTC, an attorney, or a business advisor. Even if the business is not required to give the document, you still may want to ask for the data to help you make an informed investment decision.

Some Important Advice From The FTC

1. **Talk to owners**. They can be valuable sources of information. The disclosure document must list the names and addresses of current owners and operators. Ask them how the information in the disclosure document matches their experiences with the company. A list of references selected by the company is not a substitute for a list of franchises or business opportunity owners.

2. **Investigate claims about your potential earnings**. Some companies may claim you'll earn a certain income or that existing franchisees or business opportunity purchasers earn a certain amount. Companies making earnings representations must provide you with the written basis for their claims. Be suspicious of any company that cannot substantiate its earnings representations in writing. Sellers also must tell you in writing the number and percentage of owners who have done as well as they claim you will. Keep in mind that broad sales claims about successful areas of business — "Be a part of our four billion dollar industry," for example — may have no bearing on your likelihood of success. You also have to realize that once you buy the business, you may be competing with franchise owners or independent business people with more experience.

3. **Shop around**: compare franchises with other business opportunities. Some companies may offer benefits not available from the first company you considered. The *Franchise Opportunities Handbook*, published annually by the U.S. Department of Commerce, describes more than 1,400 companies that offer franchises. Contact those that interest you. Request their disclosure documents and compare their offerings.

4. **Listen carefully to the sales presentation**. Some sales tactics should signal caution. For example, if you are pressured to sign immediately "because prices will go up tomorrow," or "another

buyer wants this deal," slow down. A seller with a good offer doesn't use high-pressure tactics. Under the Rule, the seller must wait at least 10 business days after giving you the required documents before accepting your money or signature on an agreement.

5. **Be wary if the salesperson makes the job sound too easy**. The thought of "easy money" may be appealing, but success generally requires hard work.

6. **Get the seller's promises in writing**. Any oral promises you get from a salesperson should be written into the contract you sign. If the salesperson says one thing but the contract says nothing about it or says something different, the contract is what counts. If a seller balks at putting oral promises in writing, be alert to potential problems and consider doing business with another firm.

7. **Consider getting professional advice**. Ask a lawyer, accountant, or business advisor to read the disclosure document and proposed contract. The money and time you spend on professional assistance and research — such as phone calls to current owners — could save you from a bad investment decision.

Filing a Complaint

Although the FTC cannot resolve individual disputes, information about your experiences and concerns is vital to the enforcement of the *Franchise and Business Opportunities Rule*. The time to protect yourself is before you buy rather than after. Only fifteen states give you private rights to sue, and there is often a limited ability to recover. A franchiser knows your financial situation, and can often outwait you. Many franchise owners have no money left to hire a lawyer to try to recoup their losses.

Online

The Federal Trade Commission Online at {www.ftc.gov} offers a wide range of information and assistance for the franchisor.

To file a complaint with the FTC, or request a complete list of publications, contact the following addresses:

> The Consumer Response Center
> Federal Trade Commission
> Washington, DC 20580
> 202-FTC-HELP (382-4357)
> Online Complaint Form can be found at
> {www.ftc.gov/ftc/complaint.htm}

or

> Franchise and Business Opportunity Complaint
> Federal Trade Commission, Room 238
> Washington, DC 20580

Rules and Regulations of Franchising

By using this web address, {www.ftc.gov/bcp/franchise/ netfran.htm}, you will be able to access vital information listed under these main topics:

Regulatory Reform: Franchise Rule Review
Before You Buy: Franchise and Business Opportunity Pamphlets
*Consumer Alert: Enforcement "Sweeps" Target Business Opportunity
    Fraud*
Your Legal Rights: Guide to the FTC Franchise Rule
Franchise Rule Text: 16 CFR Part 436
State Disclosure Requirements: Franchises and Business Opportunities
Know The Risks: Summary of Recent Enforcement Cases
How To Comply: Recent Staff Advisory Opinions
Franchise and Business Opportunity FAQS

All FTC pamphlets are available online at {www.ftc.gov/bcp/ menu-fran.htm}.

State Agencies Administering Franchise Disclosure Laws

California (filing required)
Franchise Division, Department of Corporations, 1115 11th St., Sacramento, CA 95814; 916-445-7205.

Hawaii (filing required)
Franchise and Securities Division, State Department of Commerce, P.O. Box 40, Honolulu, HI 96813; 808-586-2722.

Illinois (filing required)
Franchise Division, Office of Attorney General, 500 South Second Street, Springfield, IL 62706; 217-782-4465.

Indiana (filing required)
Franchise Division, Office of Secretary of State, One N. Capitol St., Suite 560, Indianapolis, IN 46204; 317-232-6576.

Maryland (filing required)
Franchise Office, Division of Securities, 200 St. Paul Place, 20th Floor, Baltimore, MD 21202; 301-576-6360.

Michigan (notice required)
Antitrust and Franchise Unit, Office of Attorney General, 670 Law Building, Lansing, MI 48913; 517-373-7117.

Minnesota (filing required)
Franchise Division, Department of Commerce, 133 East Seventh St., St. Paul, MN 55101; 651-296-6328.

New York (filing required)
Franchise and Securities Division, State Department of Law, 120 Broadway, 23rd Floor, New York, NY 10271; 212-416-8211.

North Dakota (filing required)
Franchise Division, Office of Securities Commission, 600 East Boulevard, 5th Floor, Bismarck, ND 58505; 701-224-4712.

Oregon (no filing)
Corporate Securities Section, Department of Insurance & Finance, Labor and Industries Bldg., Salem, OR 97310; 503-378-4387.

Rhode Island (filing required)
Franchise Office, Division of Securities, 233 Richmond St., Suite 232, Providence, RI 02903; 401-277-3048.

South Dakota (filing required)
Franchise Office, Division of Securities, 910 E. Sioux Ave., Pierre, SD 57501; 605-773-4013.

Franchising

Virginia (filing required)
Franchise Office, State Corporation Commission, 1300 E. Main St., Richmond, VA 23219; 804-371-9276.

Washington (filing required)
The Department of Financial Institutions, Securities Division, P.O. Box 9033, Olympia, WA 98507-9033; 360-902-8760; Fax: 360-586-5068; {www.wa.gov/dfi/securities}.

Wisconsin (filing required)
Franchise Office, Wisconsin Securities Commission, P.O. Box 1768, Madison, WI 53701; 608-266-3364; {www.wdfi.org}.

State Offices Administering Business Opportunity Disclosure Laws

California (filing required)
Consumer Law Section, Attorney General's Office, 1515 K St., Sacramento, CA 92101; 916-445-9555.

Connecticut (filing required)
Department of Banking, Securities Division, 44 Capitol Avenue, Hartford, CT 06106; 203-566-4560 ext. 8322.

Florida (filing required)
Department of Agriculture and Consumer Services, Room 110, Mayo Building, Tallahassee, FL 32301; 904-488-2221, 800-342-2176 (in-state only).

Georgia (no filing required)
Office of Consumer Affairs, No. 2 Martin Luther King Dr., Plaza Level, East Tower, Atlanta, GA 30334; 404-656-3790.

Illinois (filing required)
Illinois Security Department, Lincoln Tower, 520 S. Second St., Suite 200, Springfield, IL 62701; 217-782-2256.

Indiana (filing required)
Consumer Protection Division, Attorney General's Office, 219 State House, Indianapolis, IN 46204; 317-232-6331.

Iowa (filing required)
Securities Bureau, Second Floor, Lucas State Office Building, Des Moines, IA 50319; 515-281-4441.

Kentucky (filing required)
Attorney General's Office, Consumer Protection Division, 209 St. Clair, Frankfort, KY 40601; 502-573-2200.

Louisiana (bond filing required)
Office of the Attorney General, Consumer Protection Division, 2610-A Woodale Blvd., Baton Rouge, LA 70804; 504-342-7900.

Maine (filing required)
Banking Bureau, Securities Division, State House, Station 121, Augusta, ME 04333; 207-624-8551.

Maryland (filing required)
Attorney General's Office, Securities Division, 200 St. Paul Pl., 20th Floor, Baltimore, MD 21202; 301-576-6360.

Michigan (notice required)
Consumer Protection Division, Department of the Attorney General, 670 Law Building, Lansing, MI 48913; 517-373-7117.

Minnesota (filing required)
Department of Commerce, Registration Division, 133 East 7th Street, St. Paul, MN 5501; 651-296-6328.

Nebraska (filing required)
Department of Banking and Finance, P.O. Box 95006, Lincoln, NE 68509; 402-471-2171, 402-471-3445.

New Hampshire (filing required)
Attorney General's Office, Consumer Protection Division, State House Annex, Concord, NH 03301; 603-271-3641.

North Carolina (filing required)
Department of Justice, Consumer Protection Division, P.O. Box 629, Raleigh, NC 27602; 919-733-3924.

Ohio (no filing required)
Attorney General's Office, Consumer Fraud and Crime Section, 25th Floor, State Office Tower, 30 East Broad Street, Columbus, OH 43266-0410; 614-466-8831, 800-282-0515 (in-state only).

Oklahoma (filing required)
Oklahoma Department of Securities, Suite 860 First National Center, 120 N. Robinson St., Oklahoma City, OK 73102; 405-280-7700; Fax: 405-280-7742; {www.securities.state.ok.us}.

South Carolina (filing required)
Secretary of State's Office, P.O. Box 11350, Columbia, SC 29211; 803-734-2169.

South Dakota (filing required)
Division of Securities, 910 E. Sioux Ave., Pierre, SD 57501; 605-773-4013.

Texas (filing required)
Secretary of State's Office, Statutory Documents Section, P.O. Box 13563, Austin, TX 78711; 512-475-1769.

Utah (filing required)
Consumer Protection Division, 160 East 300 South, Salt Lake City, UT 84111; 801-530-6601.

Virginia (no filing required)
Consumer Affairs Office, 101 North 8th Street, Richmond, VA 23219; 804-786-0594, 800-451-1525 (in-state only).

Top 30 Fastest Growing Franchise Companies	
1. McDonald's	16. Miracle Ear Hearing Systems
2. Burger King Corporation	17. Future Kids Inc.
3. Yogen Fruz Worldwide	18. Papa John's Pizza
4. 7-Eleven Convenience Stores	19. Holiday Inn Worldwide
5. Jani-King	20. Choice Hotels International
6. Subway	21. Proforce USA
7. Baskin-Robbins USA Co.	22. Domino's Pizza Inc.
8. Coverall North America Inc.	23. KFC
9. Arby's	24. Church's Chicken
10. Taco Bell	25. Orion Food Systems Inc.
11. Dunkin Donuts	26. Great Clips Inc.
12. Carlson Wasgonlit Travel	27. ReMax International
13. Jazzercise Inc.	28. Super 8 Motels Inc.
14. Blimpie Corporation	29. Coldwell Bankers Res. Affil., Inc.
15. Mail Boxes Etc.	30. Jiffy Lube

Washington (filing required)
Department of Financial Institutions, Securities Division, P.O. Box 9033, Olympia,
WA 98507-9033; 206-753-6928.

Publications

International Franchise Association (IFA)
1350 New York Avenue, NW
Washington, DC 20005-4709
202-628-8000
Fax: 202-628-0812
E-mail: ifa@franchise.org
www.franchise.org

Founded in 1960, the International
Franchise Association (IFA) has
more than 600 franchiser members,
including thirty-five overseas in
more than 60 different industries.
IFA members are accepted into the organization only after meeting
stringent requirements regarding number of franchises, length of time in
business, and financial stability. The IFA offers about twenty-five
educational conferences and seminars yearly, including an annual
convention and a legal symposium. There is a program on financing and
venture capital designed to bring together franchisers and franchisees.
Each year the association also sponsors several trade shows, open to the
public, so that franchisers may attract potential franchisees.

The IFA has created the Institute of Certified Franchise Executives (CFE)
and the IFA Educational Foundation. Both organizations are set to educate
the franchiser and collect vast amounts of franchising knowledge.
Between 1998 and 1999, the classes offered by the CFE more than
doubled. The ICFE Brochure is available online at {www.franchise.
org/edufound/cfe.paf}.

The International Franchise Association publishes the following
publications, which you can order by phone: 1-800-543-1038 from 9:00
am - 4:00 pm (EST), on the IFA website {www.franchise.org/books/
bookstore/bookstore.asp}, or order by fax: 412-741-1142. You may pre-

pay with a credit card through fax, phone, or web, but make sure to include all credit card information and know that all sales are final.

To Help You Franchise Your Business
How To Be A Franchisor - $8
Financial Strategies For The Growing Franchisor - $24
The Franchise Bible - $19.95
Franchise Organizations - $29.95
The Franchise Advantage: Make It Work For You - $30
The Guide To Franchising - $28.50
Target Success - $5.95

To Help You Choose A Franchise
Choosing Your Own Franchise Information - $29.95
Franchise Opportunities Guide - $15
　　(The *Franchise Opportunities Guide* is also available online at
　　{www.franchis.org/fog.asp})
The Top Franchises Available - $16.95
Investigate Before Investing - $6
The 20 Most Frequently Asked Questions About Franchising - $5
Guide to Negotiating a Business Lease - $15.95
The Franchise Bible - $19.95
Guide to Selecting the Best Entity to Own and Operate Your Business -
　　$15.95
How To Buy and Manage A Franchise - $11
Financing Your Franchise - $18.95
The Franchise Survival Guide - $24.95

Franchisee Information
Franchising: The Bottom Line - $44.95
Public Relations For the Franchisee: How to Create Your Own Publicity -
　　$21

For Franchisers
The Franchise Cooperatives Handbook - $45
*Advisory Councils: Effective Two-Way Communications For Franchise
　　Systems* - $10
Starting Your Own Business - $12.95
The Tortoise Wins Again - $12

Multiple-Unit Franchising - $27.50
You Can't Teach a Kid to Ride a Bike at a Seminar - $23.95
The Franchise Relations Handbook - $35
Wealth Within Reach - $25
Franchising: The Business Strategy That Changed the World - $19.95

Audio/Visual Information
The UFOC Guidelines (VHS) - $145
The National Franchise Mediation Program (VHS) - $60
In Pursuit of Excellence (VHS) - $35
Franchising: How To Be In Business For Yourself, Not By Yourself
    (VHS) - $ 49.95
The Franchise Success System - Choose the Right Franchise! (audio set
    and workbooks)- $49.95
Target Success (audio set and workbook) - $39.95
Opportunities in Franchising (audio) - $35.00

Reference Materials
The Future of Franchising: Looking 25 Years Ahead to the Year 2010 -
    $10
Glossary of Franchising Terms - $4
Franchising World magazine - $18 (call for quantity and international
    prices)
New! *Study of Franchised Unit Turnover* - $75
New! *International Expansion by U.S. Franchisors* - $75

Legal Information
Franchise Sales Compliance Guide - $225
Fundamentals of Franchising - $120
Building Franchise Relationships: A Guide to Anticipating Problems,
    Resolving Conflicts, and Representing Clients - $79.95
Mergers and Acquisitions of Franchise Companies - $69.95
The Franchise Trademark Handbook - $69.95
New! *Accounting and Tax Aspects of Franchising* - $120
International Franchising - Newly Revised 1996 Edition! - $195
International Franchising Law - $280
The Franchise Industry (CCH Tax Transactions Library) - $40
Covenants Against Competition in Franchise Agreements - $125
Franchising: An Accounting, Auditing, and Income Tax Guide - $140

Minority Business Development Agency
U.S. Department of Commerce
14th and Constitution Ave, NW, Room 5053
Washington, DC 20230
202-482-5061
Fax: 202-482-2678
www.mbda.gov

The Minority Business Development Agency (MBDA) was started in 1969 in order to provide management, technical assistance, information and advice on business matters to enterprising members of socially or economically disadvantaged individuals (though not limited to these groups of individuals). The MBDA

www.mbda.gov/
rroom.html

can help to identify sources of financing and assist in the preparation of financial and bonding proposals for those looking to purchase, begin, or expand a business.

The MBDA has held an annual celebration, Minority Enterprise Development Week (MED Week), since 1983. Here, over 1,000 minority owned business owners convene for networking sessions, seminars, award ceremonies, a congressional reception, trade fair, and more. MED Week is co-sponsored by the MBDA and the Small Business Administration.

The Minority Business Development Agency's website: {www.mbda.gov/rroom.html} (available in both Spanish and English) houses an electronic reading room accumulated by the MBDA Research Division as well as private providers. The library is consistently being updated.

Minority Business Development Agency Development Centers

Minority Business Development
Agency of Atlanta
401 W. Peachtree St., NW
Suite 1715
Atlanta, GA 30308
404-730-3300

Fax: 404-730-3313
States Served: Alabama, Florida, Georgia, Kentucky, Mississippi, North Carolina, Puerto Rico, South Carolina, Tennessee, and the Virgin Islands

Minority Business Development
Agency of Chicago
55 E. Monroe St., Suite 1406
Chicago, IL 60603
312-353-0812
Fax: 312-353-0191
States Served: Illinois, Indiana,
Iowa, Kansas, Michigan,
Minnesota, Missouri, Nebraska,
Ohio, and Wisconsin.

Minority Business Development
Agency of Dallas
1100 Commerce St.
Room 7B-23
Dallas, TX 75242
214-767-8001
Fax: 214-767-0613
States Served: Arkansas, Colorado,
Louisiana, Montana, New Mexico,
North Dakota, Oklahoma, South
Dakota, Texas, Utah, and
Wyoming.

Minority Business Development
Agency of New York
26 Federal Plaza, Room 3720
New York, NY
212-264-3262
Fax: 212-264-0725
States Served: Connecticut,
Delaware, Maine, New Hampshire,
New Jersey, New York,
Pennsylvania, Rhode Island,
Vermont, Virginia, Washington,
D.C., and West Virginia.

Minority Business Development
Agency of San Francisco
221 Main St., Room 1280
San Francisco, CA 94105
415-744-3001
Fax: 415-744-3061
States Served: Alaska, American
Samoa, Arizona, California,
Hawaii, Idaho, Nevada, Oregon,
and Washington.

Did You Know?...

According to the International Franchise Association:

- ➡ A new franchise opens every 8 minutes of each business day.
- ➡ 1 of every 12 businesses is a franchise.
- ➡ By the year 2000 total franchise sales could reach $1 trillion dollars.
- ➡ Franchise sales account for 40.9% of all retail sales.
- ➡ In 1992, franchise chains created approximately 21,000 new business format franchises. In contrast, more than 220,000 new businesses failed last year, resulting in over 400,000 job losses.
- ➡ According to a 1991 Gallup Poll an overwhelming 94% of franchise owners say that they are successful. Seventy-five percent of franchise owners would do it again while, only 39% of Americans would repeat their job or business.

➡ Based on the Gallup Poll survey, the average total investment
   cost, including fees and any additional expenses, was $147,570.
   Fifty-six percent reported total investment cost under $100,000
   while 26% reported total investment cost over $100,000.
➡ Based on the Gallup Poll survey, the average gross income
   before taxes of franchisees is $124,290. Forty-nine percent
   reported gross income of less than $100,000 and 37% reported
   gross income of more than $100,000.
➡ By the year 2000, an astounding 35-50 percent of all retail sales
   will pass through a franchise chain.

Women's Franchise Network
(WFN)

The Women's Franchise Network (WFN) was created by the IFA in order to provide an international networking forum for the exchange of ideas, resources and experiences among women in franchising. Information from the WFN is available online at {www.franchise.org}.

The WFN recently opened its National Women's Business Center in Washington, DC. This is a nonprofit training center, catering to women interested in franchising. Together with the U.S. Small Business Administration's Office of Women's Business Ownership, a scholarship fund has been created to allow women to train in their chosen business related field, regardless of economic standing. The Women's Business Center has a national network of educational programs and opportunities. To schedule an interview and gather more information, contact:

National Women's Business Center
1001 Connecticut Avenue, NW, Suite 312
Washington, DC 20036
202-785-4922

According to a recent report by the National Foundation for Women's Business Ownership:

Greatest Challenges:	
Being taken seriously	38%
Maintaining growth	21%
Proving capability	18%
Male dominated atmosphere	13%
Balancing life	12%
Biggest Rewards:	
Mistress of own fate	45%
Control over destiny	26%
Building a business	20%
Helping people	15%
Being with a movement	15%
Independence, freedom	13%
Achievements recognized	12%

Important Business Resource Numbers for Women according to the White House Office for Women's Initiatives and Outreach

President's Interagency Committee on Women's Business Enterprise:
202-219-6611
(Call for information and assistance on women entrepreneurial issues).

Department of Labor Women's Bureau: **202-205-6673**
(Call for information concerning economic and international issues)

U.S. Small Business Administration Office of Women's Business Ownership: **800-532-1169**
(specifically created to help women entrepreneurs)

Department of Transportation Short-Term Lending Program: **202-512-1800**
(Call for an application for a short-term loan, favorable to women in small business)

The White House Office for Women's Initiatives and
Outreach: 202-456-7300; Fax: 202-456-7311

Other Resources

The Smart Business Supersite
www.smartbiz.com
The Smart Business Supersite makes an effort to be all information and
very little show. Here, you will find news briefs, monthly columns,
tips for business owners, listings of trade shows, relevant articles,
reports, books, products, and listings of suppliers, all for the savvy
entrepreneur.

Be the Boss
www.betheboss.com
Be The Boss wants to know if you're ready to be your own boss! If
you are, this site can help with International and National Franchise
Expo information, information on how to get started in the franchise
business, lists of conferences, trade shows, and seminars, information
on existing franchises and the ability to post yours.

Small Business Administration
www.sba.gov
The U.S. Small Business Administration offers vast information on
franchises. Through their website, you will be able to access
information on topics such as SBA sponsored training courses, special
events in your local area (through a regional map located at
{www.sba.gov/regions/states.html}, Minority Enterprise Development
Staff, Public Information officers, and the location of Business
Information Centers.

Office of Advocacy
www.sba.gov/advo/research
The U.S. Small Business Administration's Office of Advocacy is
constantly conducting studies on franchising and U.S. businesses in
general. All research published since 1995 is available. A helpful
search engine allows you to find the information you seek quickly and
easily. You may also contact the Office of Advocacy at 202-205-6530.

The Franchise Registry:
www.franchiseregistry.com

After years of the U.S. Small Business Administration's involvement with franchisors, franchisees, and lenders, the SBA created the Franchise Registry. Through this registry, the SBA will be able to enable lenders as well as its SBA offices to verify a franchise system's eligibility through the Internet! This will severely quicken the entire process of eligibility for financial assistance. Utilizing the registry reduces the red tape of the whole process as well as the time and cost for all involved. All applications may now be completed online through this site.

Native American Program:
The Native American Program (NAP) was created by the Minority Business Development Agency (MBDA) to meet the special needs of Native American firms and individuals; entering, expanding, or maintaining their place in the competitive market. The NAP program is handled on a national level by Juanits Berry of the MBDA at 202-482-0404. Native American Business Development Centers have been created across the nation to answer questions and offer assistance to those Native Americans involved in the Business Industry.

Local Centers and Contacts

Arizona NABDC
953 East Juanita Ave.
Mesa, AZ 85204
602-545-1298
Fax: 602-545-4208
www.ncaied.org/nabdc.htm

Asheville NABDC Satellite Office
Eastern Band of Cherokee Indians
70 Woodfin Place
Suite 305
Park Place Offices
Asheville, NC 28801
828-252-2516
Fax: 828-497-9009

California NABDC
National Center for American
Indian Enterprise Development
11138 Valley Mall, Suite 200
El Monte, CA 91731
626-442-3701
Fax: 626-442-7116
www.ncaied.org/nabdc.htm

Minnesota NABDC
The Minnesota Chippewa Tribe
P.O. Box 217
Facility Center, Tract 33
Cass Lake, MN 56633-0217
218-335-8928
Fax: 218-335-7712

New Mexico Statewide NABDC
All Indian Pueblo Council, Incorp.
3939 San Pedro NE, Suite D
Albuquerque, NM 87190-3256
505-889-9092
Fax: 505-889-8238

North Carolina Cherokee NABDC
Eastern Band of Cherokee Indians
Alquoni Building
Box 1200
Cherokee, NC 28719
828-497-2952

North/South Dak)ota NABDC
3315 University Drive
Bismarck, ND 58504-7596

701-255-6849
Fax: 701-255-2207

Northwest NABDC
934 North 143rd St.
Seattle, WA 98133
206-365-7735
Fax: 206-365-7764
www.ncaied.org/nabdc.htm

Oklahoma NABDC
T3RC Associates
616 South Boston, Suite 304
Tulsa, OK 74119
918-592-1113
Fax: 918-592-1217

Franchise Business Network:
www.franchise.org/welcome_about/fbn.asp
The Franchise Business Network was created in 1996 by the IFA in order to bring franchise communities together locally, while assisting the Association in building its network nationally.

Local Centers and Contacts

Boston
Chairman and CEO
Super Coops
180 Bodwell St.
Avon, MA 02322
508-580-4340

Chicago
Chairman Joan Zwit
PB Amoco Corporation
700 E. Randolph Road
Suite 1907B
Chicago, IL 60601
312-856-6820

Houston
Chairman, Gail Schubot
Strasburger & Price
2800 One Houston Center
1221 McKinney Street
Houston, TX 77010
713-951-5660

San Diego
Chairman Tom Herskowitz
Executive Vice President, Mail
Boxes, Etc. USA, Inc.
6060 Cornerstone West
San Diego, CA 92121
therskowitz@mbe.com

619-455-8954
Fax: 619-597-6076
www.fbnsd.com

South Florida
Chairman Karen Shelledy
Vice President, Franchise
Services, Arby's Inc.
1000 Corp. Drive
Fort Lauderdale, Fl 33334
954-351-5132

Washington, DC
Contact Paul Rocchio
Grassroots Manager
International Franchise
Association
1350 New York Ave., NW
Suite 900
Washington, DC 20005
paul@franchise.org
202-662-0776

Women's Entrepreneur And Business Start Up Resources

Want to start a business or need help with your current one? There are hundreds of both government and private organizations willing to lend a hand. You can take courses, find mentors, network, or get assistance in finding loans and contracts. Here are some great starting places to help you on your way to becoming your own boss!

Research A Federal Database

The Women's Bureau is exclusively concerned with serving and promoting the interests of working women. Central to its mission is the responsibility to advocate and inform women directly and the public as well, of women's work rights and employment issues.

One of their services is the Women's Bureau Clearinghouse, a computerized database and resource center responsive to women's workplace issues. The Clearinghouse provides no cost, in-house database searches on employer sponsored dependent care options, bibliographies, Federal and State government resources, and non-profit organizations. They also offer the Fair Pay Clearinghouse to assist employees and employers who want to improve wage-setting practices by valuing the work done by a majority of women workers in the United States.

For general information, contact U.S. Department of Labor, Women's Bureau, 200 Constitution Avenue, W, Room No. S-3002, Washington, DC 20210; 800-827-5335 (general information); Fax: 202-219-5529; 202-219-4486 (Women's Bureau Clearinghouse); 800-347-3741 (Fair Pay Clearinghouse); {www.dol.gov/dol/wb/}.

Instant Networking

You can receive information, training, and opportunities for online networking to women business owners wherever you are at any time of the day. The Online Women's Business Center (OWBC) provides these services through an Internet site.

ONLINE WOMEN'S BUSINESS CENTER

This "virtual" women's business center works in unison with, and as an extension of, more than 54 Women's Business Centers (WBC) throughout the United States that have contributed actively to its creation. The combined efforts of the WBCs and OWBO create unlimited possibilities for reaching women who want instant access to information, personal guidance and insight into business management skills, particularly if they do not have a WBC nearby or if their current employment prevents them from visiting a WBC during operating hours. OWBC was developed on behalf of the U. S. Small Business Administration's (SBA) Office of Women's Business Ownership (OWBO) and several corporate sponsors who joined forces in a unique public/private partnership.

For more information, contact Online Women's Business Center, Paula Aryanpur, Project Director, Bill J. Priest Institute for Economic Development, 1402 Corinth Street, Suite 209, Dallas, TX 75215-2111; 214-565-0447; Fax: 214-565-7883; {E-mail: virtual@onramp.net}; {www.onlinewbc.org}.

Assistance With Entrepreneurial Issues

The President created the White House Office for Women's Initiatives and Outreach in June of 1995 to better serve and listen to his constituents. The office serves as a liaison between the White House and women's organizations, listening to women's concerns and proposals and bringing these ideas to the President and others in the Administration.

Inside and outside the White House, the office advocates issues that are important to women. The office schedules events and speeches for White House officials and presidential appointees and holds events and roundtables to amplify the President's pro-woman, pro-family agenda. The President's Interagency Committee on Women's Business Enterprise can provide you with information and assistance on women entrepreneurial issues.

For more information, contact Office for Women's Initiatives and Outreach, Room 15, O.E.O.B., Washington, DC 20502; 202-456-7300; Fax: 202-456-7311; 202-205-6673 (women entrepreneurial issues); {www.whitehouse. gov/WH/EOP/Women/OWIO}.

Camps For Entrepreneurs

The mission of the National Education Center for Women in Business is to promote women and business ownership on the national level by conducting collaborative research, providing education programs and curriculum development and serving as an information clearinghouse for women entrepreneurs.

You could benefit by participating in two different Camp Entrepreneur(r) programs, a one-day executive education conference for women, a program for college students, breakfast forums, a series of six 3-hour workshops, and more. For more information, contact Seton Hill College/The National Education Center for Women in Business, Seton Hill Drive, Greensburg, PA 15601; 412-830-4625; 800-NECWB-4-U (632-9248); Fax: 412-834-7131; {E-mail: info@necwb.setonhill.edu}; {www.necwb.setonhill.edu/}.

JOIN FELLOW WOMEN ENTREPRENEURS NATIONALLY

1. The *National Association of Women Business Owners* is a member operated, dues-based organization in which women entrepreneurs gain valuable experiences, information, business and leadership training and recognition. NAWBO propels women entrepreneurs into economic, social, and political spheres of power by strengthening and promoting economic development, creating changes in business culture, building alliances, and influencing policymakers.

    The organization currently has over 75 chapters. Many chapters offer educational programs to help women start and grow a successful business. As an example, the St. Louis, Missouri chapter offers Successavvy which includes course topics on: Do I Really Want To Be In Business, Writing a Business Plan, Basic Accounting for Your Business, Writing a Marketing Plan, and When and How to Use Professionals.

    Membership is open to sole proprietors, partners and corporate owners with day-to-day management responsibility. Those who do not live in a chapter area join as at-large members. For more information, contact NAWBO Headquarters, 1100 Wayne Avenue, Suite 830, Silver Spring, MD 20910; 301-608-2590; Fax: 301-608-2596; NAWBO Information Service Line: 800-55-NAWBO (556-2926); {E-mail: national@ nawbo.org}; {www.nawbo.org}.

2. The *National Foundation for Women Business Owners* (NFWBO) is a central source of information and statistics on women business owners and their businesses providing non-profit research, leadership development and entrepreneurial training. Their web site has a large collection of related links.

   Contact National Foundation for Women Business Owners, 1100 Wayne Avenue, Suite 830, Silver Spring, MD 20910-5603; 301-495-4975; Fax: 301-495-4979; {E-mail: NFWBO@worldnet.att.net}; {www.nfwbo.org/index.htm}.

3. The *National Women Business Owners Corporation*, a not-for-profit corporation, was established to increase competition for corporate and government contracts through implementation of a pioneering economic development strategy for women business owners. NWBOC is a sister organization to the National Association of Women Business Owners (NAWBO) and the National Foundation for Women Business Owners (NFWBO).

The NWBOC Network was established to provide critical information about corporate and government contracts and

NWBOC

systems to women suppliers. NWBOC has streamlined the often cumbersome task of locating information and technical assistance about corporate, and federal, state and local government contracting through one-stop electronic access.

In an increasingly complex and competitive business world, the NWBOC Network offers women business owners a significant competitive advantage. For more information, contact NWBOC, 1100 Wayne Ave., #830, Silver Spring, MD 20910; 561-848-5066; Fax: 561-881-7364; {E-mail: info@wboc.org}; {www.wboc.org/}.

NETWORK WITH OTHER BUSINESSWOMEN

1. The mission of the *American Business Women's Association* is to bring together businesswomen of diverse occupations and to provide opportunities for them to help themselves and others grow personally and professionally through leadership, education, networking support and national recognition.

   ABWA believes education and training are key to helping women grow personally and professionally. The Association supports education by providing continuing education programs and products, which enhance members business skills. Members receive discounts on a variety of products and services, including career-focused books and audiotapes, seminars by national seminar providers and computer application classes. The ABWA also provides education and skill building services to assist members just beginning their career.

For more information, contact American Business Women's Association, 9100 Ward Parkway, P.O. Box 8728, Kansas City, MO 64114-0728; 816-361-6621; Fax: 816-361-4991; {E-mail:abwa@abwahq.org}; {www.abwahq.org/}.

2. The *National Association for Female Executives* is the largest businesswomen's association in the United States. NAFE's mission: to empower its 150,000 members through education, networking, and public advocacy.

Whether you work for yourself or another company, NAFE is always here to help you get ahead in your career. The association, with its 200 networks in cities across the country, their magazine, *Executive Female*, and this web site all have one goal: to provide resources and services that will help you achieve career success and financial security.

For further information, contact NAFE, P.O. Box 469031, Escondido, CA 92046-9925; 800-634-NAFE (634-6233); {E-mail: nafe@nafe.com}; {www.nafe.com/}.

Training On An International Level

The Centre for Development and Population Activities (CEDPA) is a women-focused nonprofit international organization founded in 1975. CEDPA's mission is to empower women at all levels of society to be full partners in development.

All CEDPA activities are designed to advance gender equity. Working with partner nongovernmental organizations and networks in more than 37 countries, CEDPA designs, implements, monitors, and evaluates projects in family planning and reproductive health, family life education, women's participation in empowerment, youth services, and international advocacy for women and girls.

The Women in Management (WIM) leadership training workshop is CEDPA's flagship capacity-building initiative. During this five-week tuition-based workshop, WIM participants from around the world hone leadership and management skills with peers for a dynamic dialogue. This training program is designed for women working in government, non-governmental, and community-based  organizations who design, manage, and evaluate gender-equitable development programs and women working in a wide range of professions who have demonstrated leadership potential in areas related to gender-equitable development. The goal of the Women in Management program is to enhance women's leadership capacity for managing strategic responses to health, economic, education, and other development challenges.

For more information, contact Workshops Coordinator, CEDPA, 1717 Massachusetts Avenue, NW, Suite 200, Washington, DC 20036; 202-667-1142; Fax: 202-332-4496; {E-mail: ketty@cedpa.org}; {www.cedpa.org/}.

Network and Train with Professional Women of Color

1. *Professional Women of Color* (PWC) is a non-profit organization that provides workshops, seminars, group discussions as well as networking sessions to help women of color more effectively manage their personal and professional lives. There is $50 annual membership fee to join PWC. Contact Professional Women of Color, P.O. Box 5196, New York, NY 10185; {E-mail: www.pwconline.org/}.

If you would like to become
more self-sufficient, check out
the economic entrepreneurial
centers run by the *National
Council of Negro
Women* (NCNW). For
more information, contact
National Council of Negro
Women, Christine Toney,
Executive Director, Lucenia
Dunn, Director of Programs, 633 Pennsylvania Avenue,
NW, Washington, DC 20004; 202-737-0120; Fax: 202-
737-0476; {E-mail: ncnwbpdc@ erols.com};
{www.ncnw.com}.

HELP FOR
WORK AT HOME MOMS

Mothers' Home Business Network (MHBN) provides
information, ideas, and inspiration to moms who choose to
work at home. They publish two newsletters: *Home
Working Mothers* (annual) and *Kids and Career* (twice a
year).

MHBN provides literature on how to juggle your time
between raising children and running a successful business,
as well as a "fraud detector" for evaluating home business
opportunities. Contact: Mothers' Home Business Network
(MHBN), P.O. Box 423, East Meadow, NY 11554; 516-
997-7394.

For Entrepreneurial Girls

Independent Means is the leading provider of products and services for girls' financial independence. Their target group is girls under twenty who are true individuals, following their own path and pursuing their own dreams. They run An Income of Her Own Entrepreneurship Conferences, Camp $tart-Up, and after-school programs all over the United States and sponsor a National Teen Business Plan Competition.

Contact: Independent Means, 126 Powers Ave., Santa Barbara, CA 93103; 800-350-1816; {E-mail: contactus@ independentmeans.com}; {www.independentmeans. com/}.

Financial Concerns

Women Incorporated is a national non-profit organization designed to improve the business environment for women through access to capital, credit, business discounts and products, and financial services. They also provide assistance in preparing loan application and other basic business start-up training.

For more information, contact Women Incorporated, 333 South Grand Ave., Suite 2450, Los Angeles, CA 90071; 800-930-3993; 213-680-3375; Fax: 213-680-3475; {www.womeninc.com/}.

Other Organizations that provide information on self-employment and microenterprise development:

1. *National Association for Female Executives*, 30 Irving Place, New York, NY l0003; 212-477-2200.

2. *Association for Enterprise Opportunity*, 320 North Michigan Avenue, Suite 804, Chicago, IL 60611; 312-357-0177.

3. *The Corporation for Enterprise Development*, 777 North Capital Street, NW, Suite 801, Washington, DC 20002; 202-08-9788.

4. *The Self-Employment Learning Project*, 1333 New Hampshire Avenue, NW, Suite 1070, Washington, DC 20036; 202-736-5807.

5. *Women's Economic Development Program*, The Ms. Foundation, 120 Wall Street, 33rd Floor, New York, NY 10005; 212-742-2300.

Websites
for Women Entrepreneurs

1. *Advancing Women's* mission is create a network for women to share career strategies, to provide employment opportunities and cutting edge resources that power women's success. For more information, visit **{www.advancingwomen.com/}**.

2. *Field of Dreams* operates a participative website that assists women business owners to evaluate, develop, and implement secondary or alternative business options, and to be trained and active participants in computer technological advances. FOD provides a secure place to learn, begin networking, and build business relationships for further business development and electronic commerce for tomorrow's success. The organizing team presents training programs and assists the organization of rural women in business owners to develop skills for business planning and implementing new business opportunities.

   Participants are better able to prepare a business plan; develop incubator groups to address operations, finance, marketing, and human resource components affecting the success of a business operation; determine a process for implementing and monitoring the progress of a business plan. For more information, visit **{www.fodreams.com/home.html}**.

3. *The Biz Resource Site* exists to provide support and information to small business owners and aspiring entrepreneurs. Weekly biz tip updates keep information in an easy-to-use format, and the links to other business sites can provide a good starting point for new businesses seeking assistance. Visit **{www.bizresource.com/}**.

4. *Women Entrepreneurs Online Network's* mission is to create a network of women entrepreneurs who will tutor and support each other, share their insights and skills, and help newcomers gain the opportunity and exposure needed to succeed in modern commerce. For more information, contact  Women Entrepreneurs Online Network, 11259 Fisher Avenue, Warren, MI 48089-3004; 810-754-6731; Fax: 810-757-1105; {E-mail: rozey@weon.com}; **{http://weon.com/}.**

5. *Women's Wire* is a popular Internet service concerned with all aspects of womanhood. They offer a section for small business owners that contains information on starting up, money matters, networking central and trade-show information, tips on growing and managing the company you founded, office essentials, space, stuff and more nitty-gritty. For more information, visit **{www.womenswire.com/smallbiz/}.**

6. *BWNi.com* serves as a starting place for business opportunities. What BWNi.com offers ranges from procurement opportunities in both the government and the private sector, to resources for businesses in both the United States and globally, and to access to the tools to use the internet and e-commerce to expand a business. For more information, contact Business

Women's Network interactive, 1146 19th Street, NW, Washington, DC 20036; 202-466-8209; 800-48-WOMEN (489-6636); Fax: 202-833-1808; {E-mail: bwn@tpag.com}; **{www.bwni.com/}.**

7. *An Income of Her Own* on-line is a place where teen

women can learn about pursuing their dreams through entrepreneurship. They offer imaginative and unique programs and products related to economic empowerment for young women. For more information, visit **{www.anincomeofherown.com/}.**

8. *Black Women On the Web* is a virtual community of minority women entrepreneurs and business owners. Their website offers information and advice, networking and support. Do not miss their resource center. For more information, visit **{www.dtshop.com/bwow/}.**

9. *Digital-Women* was created for women in business, business women and all women around the globe looking for a place to gather resources, free business tips, free sales tips, free marketing tips, home business ideas, and a place to network with other business women and women owned businesses. For more information, visit **{www.digital-women.com/}.**

State-by-State Programs Providing Entrepreneurial Assistance for Women

Alabama

Assistance For Your New or Existing Business
The *Women's Business Assistance Center* - a private, nonprofit corporation - is located in the Center for Entrepreneurial Excellence. This is a former school campus, which was purchased and renovated by the City of Mobile and Mobile County. It is now a business incubator and training center. The executive director of the WBAC is also owner of the Women's Yellow Pages of the Gulf Coast. The WBAC provides training seminars and one-on-one counseling for the South Alabama and Northwest Florida area (see also Florida). Contact: Women's Business Assistance Center Inc. (WBAC), Kathryn Cariglino, Executive Director, 1301 Azalea Road, Suite 201A, Mobile, AL 36693; 334-660-2725; 800-378-7461; Fax: 334-660-8854; {E-mail: wbac@ceebic.org}; {http://ceebic.org/~wbac}.

Alaska

Help for Women-Owned Microenterprises
WOMEN$ Fund is a micro-enterprise training and microlending program for women entrepreneurs in Anchorage. Consistent with the National YWCA's mission to empower women and girls and to eliminate racism, the programs of the YWCA of Anchorage promote independence, knowledge and self-esteem, especially for low-income and minority women. WOMEN$ Fund's mission is to secure financial independence for women through the provision of capital and technical assistance. By providing individual mentoring, training classes in entrepreneurship and technical  assistance, and seed money for women-owned small businesses, WOMEN$ Fund empowers low/moderate-income, single-parent and minority women in Anchorage and surrounding Alaska communities through economic self-sufficiency. Contact: The YWCA of Anchorage, WOMEN$ Fund, Kathryn J. Maieli, Program Director, Sharon Richards, YWCA Executive Director, 245 West Fifth Avenue, P.O. Box 102059, Anchorage, AK 99510-2059; 907-274-1524; Fax: 907-272-3146; {E-mail: ywcaak@Alaska.NET}.

Network With Alaskan Women Online
The *Alaska Women's Network's* purpose is to further the empowerment of Alaska women through sharing of information, education and support and

through encouraging the development of skills that will enable women to
assume leadership roles in building a better world. To achieve this purpose,
they maintain a statewide communications network between Alaskan women
and women's organizations, through electronic means that can be a valuable
resource in helping you identify job training opportunities. Point your browser
to {www.juneau.com/akwomen/network.html}.

Arizona

Self-Employment Training For Women and Minorities

Are you a low-income individual who would like to start or expand a small
business? The *Self-Employment Loan Fund, Inc. (SELF)* is a private non-profit
organization that can provide you with training, technical assistance, and loan
access. The training sessions are ten to fourteen weeks in length with the
outcome a completed business plan. Upon the completion of the business plan,
participants are eligible for SELF's peer lending process, called Borrower's
Circles. These circles of three to eight individuals provide an avenue for
support, debt repayment, and continuing business education. SELF serves all
of Maricopa County and will soon be providing services in Graham and Gila
counties. For more information, contact Self-Employment Loan Fund, Inc.
(SELF), Jean Rosenberg, Director, Andrea Madonna, Project Manager, 201
North Central Avenue, Suite CC10, Phoenix, AZ 85073-1000; 602-340-8834;
Fax: 602-340-8953; {E-mail: self@uswest.net}.

Arkansas

Training and Credit For Self-Employed People

The mission of the Good Faith Fund's *Arkansas Women's Business Center* is to
widen the profile of future entrepreneurs to include women, minorities and
dislocated workers through the delivery of credit and credit services and to
raise the income levels of low-income and self-employed people. Services
include business skills training (with special modules for childcare providers), a
"Women's Biz" mentoring program, loan packaging assistance, and Internet
training. The AR WBC also organizes regional peer support groups who meet
monthly. Contact Arkansas Enterprise Group, Good Faith Fund's Arkansas
Women's Business Center, Penny Penrose, Executive Director, Maria Jones,
Project Director, 2304 W. 29th, Pine Bluff, AR 71603; 870-535-6233; Fax:
870-535-0741; {E-mail: ppenrose@ehbt.com}; {E-mail: mjones@ehbt.com}.

California

Rebirth for Entrepreneurs

The *Renaissance Entrepreneurship Center* comprises a unique, multicultural
marketplace of entrepreneurs. Diversity-ethnic, social and economic-is a
critical factor for the center's success. This diversity generates a synergy that
translates to business income: 60 percent of Renaissance graduates report doing

business with one another. A 10-year impact study by the Federal Reserve Board of San Francisco in 1997 revealed that 87 percent of businesses started through this program are still in operation (compared to the national average of 38 percent). Services include an incubator facility, loan packaging and links to credit resources, core business planning, introduction to business, and advanced action-planning classes. Graduates of Renaissance programs receive a one-year free membership in the San Francisco Chamber of Commerce, peer support, mentoring, events and a business expo. Contact Renaissance Entrepreneurship Center, Claudia Viek, Executive Director, 275 Fifth Street, San Francisco, CA 94103-4120; 415-541-8580; Fax: 415-541-8589; {E-mail: claudia@rencenter.org}.

Get The Help You Need To Start Your Own Business

1. *Women's Enterprise Development Corporation (WEDC),* previously known as California AWED, began in 1989 with SBA funding to assist the growing number of women business owners in Los Angeles. It has been awarded a new grant to meet the unique needs of the San Gabriel Valley area of Southern California. The center focuses on serving the fast-growing Latina and Asian populations, with training offered in Spanish, Chinese (both Mandarin and Cantonese), Khmer, Vietnamese, Armenian and English. Programs and activities include entrepreneurial training at the start-up, mid-size and rapid-growth levels; meetings and consultations; procurement and contracting assistance; direct micro-lending assistance and assistance in procuring SBA loans; and entrepreneurship services for youths. In addition to a full-time facility, WEDC uses a "circuit rider" project manager for outreach, to provide counseling within communities. WEDC also employs a "biz-tic" for business counseling that lays out a program for each student, then enables her to understand the end goal of the engagement, the steps necessary to get to that goal, and the benefits of each step. Contact Women's Enterprise Development Corporation (WEDC), Dr. Philip Borden, Executive Director, 235 East Broadway, Suite 506, Long Beach, CA 90802; 562-983-3747; Fax: 562-983-3750; {E-mail: wedc@aol.com}.

2. Orange County has the third largest concentration of women-owned businesses in the nation (ranking just behind New York and Los Angeles). AWED Orange County follows the same AWED curriculum described above which includes the core program, plus a two-hour pre-business seminar and a monthly group counseling program. For more information

Women's Enterprise Development Corporation, Linda Harasin, Acting Executive Director, 2301 Campus Drive, Suite 20, Irvine, CA 92715; 310-983-3747; Fax: 310-9830-3750.

Enhance Your Business Skills Close To Home

If you live in lower-income communities around San Francisco, particularly Fruitvale, San Antonio and Central East Oakland, the *Women's Initiative for Self Employment* can provide you with training and technical assistance in establishing your own business. The English language program consists of a two-week business assessment workshop, a fourteen-week business skills workshop and a four-week workshop on writing a business plan. The Spanish language program parallels the English but is in modular format. WI also offers business support services including one-on-one consultations, peer networking and support groups, and special  seminars. They provide training in locations close to their client base, in shopping centers, etc. Contact Women's Initiative for Self Employment (WI), Barbara Johnson, Executive Director, 450 Mission Street, Suite 402, San Francisco, CA 94105; 415-247-9473; Fax: 415-247-9471; {E-mail: womensinitsf@igc.apc.org}; {E-mail: wioakland@igc.apc.org} (Oakland Site); {E-mail: wialas@igc.apc.org} (Spanish Site).

Career and Microenterprise Development for Low-Income Women

North Coast Opportunities, Inc., a community action agency serving Mendocino County, formed a partnership with Mendocino College and the Ukiah Community Center's WEST Company to provide low-income women with job training, job placement, self-employment training, and the other supportive services necessary to achieve self-sufficiency. The *Bright Center Low-Income Women's Project* integrates personal development, life skills training, and case management into a comprehensive program of employment training and microenterprise development services. For more information, contact Ernie Dickens, Executive Director, North Coast Opportunities, Inc., 413 North State Street, Ukiah, CA 95482; 707-462-1954; Fax: 707-462-8945.

Micro-Business Assistance

Coalition for Women's Economic Development provides credit and technical assistance services to low- income women in the Los Angeles area through a micro-business workshop, a solidarity circle program and a revolving loan fund. The solidarity circle program is modeled after Accion International's model, which forms groups of borrowers in order to provide peer support and exchange and encourage loan repayment. For more information, contact Coalition for Women's Economic Development (CWED), 315 West 9th Street, Suite 705, Los Angeles, CA 90015; 213-489-4995.

Help With Procurement for Advanced Business Owners
The *Women Business Owners Corporation* (WBOC) forecasts and develops business opportunities in the government and major corporate markets for women business owners. WBOC also assists women suppliers in marketing their goods and services and acquiring the skills necessary to succeed in these markets. The SBA's Office of Women's Business Ownership has provided the initial funding for development of the WBOC Procurement Institute and procurement training to women suppliers through WBOC's world wide web site. Contact Women Business Owners Corporation, Kathleen Schwallie, President, 18 Encanto Drive, Palos Verdes, CA 90274-4215; 310-530-7500; Fax: 310-530-1483.

Help For Northern CA Small Business Owners
WEST Company serves micro enterprise owners in rural Northern California. Through their Build a Better Business training and consulting program, they assist clients in developing a business plan for both start-up and expansion purposes. They make individual and peer loans; assist with the formation of business networks; and have started a cross generational technology mentoring program. For more information, contact:
1. West Company, Sheilah Rogers, Executive Director, 367 North State Street, Suite 201, Ukiah, CA 95482; 707-468-3553; Fax: 707-462-8945.

2. West Company, Carol Steele, Loan Fund Manager, 340 North Main Street, Fort Bragg, CA 95437; 707-964-7571; Fax: 707-961-1340.

Network And Learn From Other Women In Management
Women In Management (WIM) is a nonprofit educational corporation for the advancement of women into management positions. Open to everyone, regardless of your place on the career path, WIM's annual membership costs only $65 per person. They host monthly meetings in the Southern California area for managers, entrepreneurs, administrative assistants, the self-employed and anyone who would like to make contacts, develop leadership skills, establish rewarding relationships and advance their career. They also offer scholarships for education to their members. WIM does not have a permanent address, since all of their board positions are on a volunteer basis and the people who fill the positions change annually. You can reach them at 800-531-1359 or through their web site at {www.wimworks.com} or by {Email: mail@WIMworks. com}.

Training and Technical Assistance
Women's Initiative for Self Employment (WISE) provides business training and technical assistance in English and Spanish to low-income women in the San Francisco Bay Area. The English language program consists of a 2-week

business assessment workshop, a 14-week business-skills workshop and a 4-week workshop on writing a business plan. The Spanish-language program parallels the English, but is in modular format. WI also offers business support services, including one-on-one consultations, peer networking and support groups, and special seminars. Contact Women's Initiative for Self Employment (WISE), Barbara Johnson, Executive Director, 450 Mission Street, Suite 402, San Francisco, CA 94105; 415-247-9473; Fax: 415-247-9471; {E-mail: womensinitsf@igc.apc.org}

Spanish Site: 1398 Valencia St., San Francisco, CA 94110; 415-826 5090; Fax: 415-826-1885; {E-mail: wialas@igc.apc.org}

Oakland: 11611 Telegraph Ave., Suite 702, Oakland, CA 94612; 510-451-3415; Fax: 510-451-3428; {E-mail: wioakland@igc.apc.org}.

North Coast Entrepreneurial Women

The *Women Entrepreneurs Institute (WEI)* is a non-profit organization without walls - a volunteer board of business women collaborating in partnership with local businesses, economic development organizations, training institutions and local government to provide education, support and resources for women and youth who are interested in starting and/or growing business on the North Coast. They offer large evening networking events, a series of workshops designed for women in business, a Women in Leadership Conference, a peer lending program, a quarterly newsletter, and Business Connections - the networking arm of WEI that meets regularly. For more information, contact Women Entrepreneurs Institute, 818 F. Street, Eureka, CA 95501; 707-443-4625; {www.redwood-country.com/ WEI/}.

Find A Mentor
The *Center to Develop Women Entrepreneurs* is a non-profit organization located within San Jose State University's College of Business. They seek to provide women entrepreneurs with the courage and direction to open or grow their own business by matching carefully screened aspiring and existing women entrepreneurs with individually selected mentors from a broad volunteer pool of seasoned women business owners, as well as professionals and corporate women. They also conduct scholarly research on the impact of gender and mentoring on entrepreneurship through systematic data collection and interviewing of the women in our program. For further information, contact Jacqueline C. Simon, Chief Executive Officer, Center to Develop Entrepreneurs, San Jose State University, College of Business BT 053, One

Washington Square, San Jose, CA 95192-0220; 408-924-5863; Fax: 408-924-3419; {E-mail: cdwe@cob.sjsu.edu}; {www.cob.sjsu.edu/dept/cdwe/CDWE.html}.

Colorado

Referrals

The *Women's Economic Development Council* is a Governor-appointed advisory council to the governor and the Women's Business Office regarding women's business issues. They may be able to offer you valuable referrals on women's business issues. For more information, contact Women's Economic Development Council, 1625 Broadway, Suite 1701, Denver, CO 80202; 303-572-5496.

Network

The *Colorado Women's Business Office (WBO)* has developed a network to connect women from all parts of the state with resources and information about starting and growing their own businesses. For more information, contact Colorado Women's Business Office, Elaine Demery, Director, 1625 Broadway, Suite 1710, Denver, CO 80202; 303-892-3840; Fax: 303-892-3848; {E-mail: elaine. demery@ state.co.us}; {www.state.co.us/gov_dir/ wbo/bnew_ad.html}.

Economic Community of Women

The mission of the *Colorado Women's Chamber of Commerce* is to create an economic community for women in commerce through education and training, information exchange, and partnerships and alliances. They accomplish this through a variety of programs including business roundtables, a newsletter, a membership directory, a resource library, government procurement assistance, and a number of activities and functions that change monthly. For more information, contact Colorado Women's Chamber of Commerce, 13949 W. Colfax Avenue, Denver West Office Park, Building 1, Suite 107, Golden, CO 80401; 303-235-2766; Fax: 303-235-2767; {E-mail: Info@CWCC. org}; {www.cwcc.org/}.

Women Leaders

The Colorado Women's Leadership Coalition recognizes and supports the leadership of women. This is accomplished by providing a network of support and strength for individual women to realize their leadership potential, and by building a coalition among women's organizations in order to exercise the collective strength of women as individuals and facilitate their ability to take appropriate action in economic, social and political arenas. They offer many opportunities for leadership training and education through the annual conference, a quarterly newsletter, monthly programs, and other events. For more information, contact Sondra Aksamit, CWLC Administrator, 7084 S. Cherry Drive, Littleton, CO 80122; 303-221-7434; {E-mail: SondraSA@aol.com}; {www.gossamer-moon.com/cwlc/}.

Training for Low-Income Entrepreneurs
1. The *Mi Casa Resource Center* for Women provides quality employment and education services that promote economic independence for low-income, predominantly Latina women and youth. Services include educational counseling, job-readiness and job-search training, life-skills development, job placement, and nontraditional and computer skills training. Entrepreneurial training is provided through either the "Evening Entrepreneurial Training Program" or "Project Success." Individuals learn how to start a business and develop a business plan, with microloans available to program graduates. Youth development, dropout prevention, leadership training and responsible decision-making are provided through three youth programs: Mi Carrera (My Career), Mi Camina (My Road) and Fenix (teen-pregnancy, AIDS and STD prevention program). Contact Mi Casa Resource Center for Women, Inc., Mi Casa Career Development and Business Center for Women, Agnes Talamantez Carroll, Director of Business Development, Gayle Warner, Director of Program Development, 700 Knox Court, Denver, CO 80204; 303-573-1333; Fax: 303-607-0872; {E-mail: acarroll@micasadenver.org}; {www.micasadenver.org}.

2. Mi Casa has received a new grant to expand their services to Colorado Springs with a satellite program in Pueblo, a predominantly Hispanic community. There are few employment opportunities in Pueblo, outside of low-wage hourly service and retail positions, and many have a difficult time achieving and sustaining self-sufficiency. Mi Casa collaborates with the Women's Resource Agency to provide services. Mi Casa offers training geared specifically toward women on public assistance and also offers their evening program in Spanish. Monthly seminars are open to clients and graduates of their training programs and mentoring is available through "Tuesday Tune-Up" seminars and weekend roundtables. Transportation and child-care assistance, as well as clothing and other emergency services, are also provided. Contact Mi Casa Colorado Springs/Pueblo, Agnes Talamantez Carroll, Director of Business Development, 571 Galapago Street, Denver, CO 80204; 303-573-1302; Fax: 303-607-0872: {E-mail: acarroll@micasadenver.org}.

Connecticut

Business Training
Entrepreneurial Center of Hartford's College for Women serves potential start-up and established women business owners throughout Connecticut, with

special emphasis on women who are socially and economically disadvantaged. This is a collaboration with People's Bank and the Connecticut Development Authority. The University of Hartford provides the self-assessment workshops and conducts a 16 week intensive business training program. People's Bank and the Connecticut Development Authority provide assistance in seeking access to capital. The center offers the "Trickle-Up Program," an international fund that provides seed capital of up to $750 to qualified clients for start-up, a grant that does not have to be paid back. The center provides technical assistance for all graduates for the life cycles of their businesses, collaborating statewide with economic development organizations. This program is the first of its kind nationally, linking a state agency, private corporation and a non-profit to a formal partnership. Contact: The Entrepreneurial Center of Hartford's College for Women at the University of Hartford, Jean Blake-Jackson, 50 Elizabeth St., Hartford, CT 06105; 860-768-5618 or 5681; Fax: 860-768-5622; {E-mail: blakejack@mail.hartford.edu}.

Southwestern Assistance
Women's Business Development Center (WBDC) serves women from all social and economic backgrounds throughout southwest Connecticut, and collaborates with other community agencies to target socially and economically disadvantaged clients. In addition to one-on-one counseling, the training courses include: Finance a Business, Launch a Business, and The Business Toolbox, as well as the Experienced Entrepreneur: Leveraging Growth, Government Procurement and Camp Entrepreneur: A Mother/Daughter Experience. Collaborating with the Urban League of Southwestern Connecticut, Inc., and the YWCA OF Greenwich, WBDC is developing an innovative summer camp program for girls between the ages of 11 and 14. Contact Women's Business Development Center (WBDC), Fran Pastore, 400 Main Street, Suite 410, Stamford, CT 06901; 203-353-1750; Fax: 203-353-1084; {E-mail: wbdc@ferg.lib.ct.us}.

Delaware

The Old Reliable
The *YWCA of New Castle County, MicroBusiness Chamber of Commerce* builds on a favorable working relationship with the Working Capital Program, the state's largest micro-enterprise program, which has been led by the YWCA and has made 400 microloans since 1995. The combined effort uses lessons and materials from the Working Capital Program, offers peer and individual lending, and focuses on creating access to the marketplace. It also established the MicroBusiness Chamber of Commerce to provide networking and institutional support and to work closely with the existing chamber. In additional, the YWCA, which has strong local support, offers career counseling, a group savings program for low-income families, and childcare

services. Contact YWCA of New Castle County, MicroBusiness Chamber of
Commerce, Mary Dupont, Olakunie Oludina, Director, MicroBusiness CoC,
233 King Street, Wilmington, DE 19801; 302-658-7161; Fax: 302-658-7547;
{E-mail: oso@ diamond.net.udel.edu}; {E-mail: Mary_dupont@diamond.net.
udel.edu}.

District of Columbia

All Kinds Of Opportunities For Women in DC
You are fortunate to live near the *National Women's Business Center*. They
have many programs for women at all stages of business development
including: Introduction to Business Ownership; Making it Happen; Up and
Running; Marketing: Getting Results; Managing a Business with
Accountability; Federal Procurement Series; The Advanced Training Institute;
The Business Council; The Roundtable; The Business Laboratory; and The
Bottom Line. The National Women's Business Center, located in downtown
Washington, DC also has an office at the SBA District Office, co-located with
a Small Business Development Center sub-center to maximize the exposure to
and utilization of business training and counseling with several SBA resource
partners. Contact National Women's Business Center, Beth Cole, Executive
Director, Arlinda Halliburton, Director, Patti Berens, Director, 1250 24th
Street, N. W., Suite 350, Washington, DC 20037; 202-466-0544; 202-466-
0581; SBA office 202-606-4000, Extension 278; {E-mail: wbc@patriot.net};
{www.womenconnect.com/ womensbusinesscenter}.

Business Development

*Get The Help You Need To Start
Your Own Business*

Founded in 1976, the *American Woman's
Economic Development Corporation* is the premier national not-for-profit
organization committed to helping entrepreneurial women start and grow their
own businesses. Based in New York City, AWED also has offices in Southern
California, Connecticut and Washington, DC. Join over 100,000 women who
have benefited from formal course instructions, one-to-one business
counseling, seminars, special events and peer group support. AWED's goal is
to increase the start-up, survival and expansion rates of small businesses.
Contact American Woman's Economic Development Corporation (AWED),
Suzanne Tufts, President and CEO, 71 Vanderbilt Avenue, Suite 320, New
York, NY 10169; 212-692-9100; Fax: 212-692-9296.

Florida

Grow Your Own Business
The *Women's Business Development Center* can provide you with quality
business education, technical assistance and access to capital. Their focus is for
women, minorities, low- and moderate-income individuals who are starting or

growing their own businesses. Business education programs incorporate both traditional and non-traditional methods of learning. In classroom settings, business owners and professionals teach participants about entrepreneurship, market research, financial analysis and business planning. Non-traditional programs include one-on-one business counseling, a Mentor/Protégé program, business specialty workshops and networking forums. The Center also assists clients with preparation of loan packages and will present loans to financial institutions. The Center has been designated an intermediary for the SBA Women's

Prequalification Loan Program and has a satellite office in downtown Miami at the SBA's Business Resource Center. Social skills training for women on welfare have been initiated and will be offered with dual goals of enhancing employability as well as providing the first step to self-employment. For more information: Women's Business Development Center (WBDC), Christine Kurtz-White, Director, 10555 West Flagler Street, Room 2612, Miami, FL 33174; 305-348-3951, 305-348-3903; Fax: 305-348-2931; {E-mail: obermann@fiu.edu} (Program Coordinator); {E-mail: rojasm@fiu.edu} (Financial Consultant).

Find A Mentor For Your Women Owned Business Endeavor
The mission of the Women Business Owners Of North Florida is to create and recognize opportunities to lift up the successes of women in the business world, both individually and collectively. What this means for you is that WBO will support your vision with practical educational opportunities and with mentors who offer encouragement, advice and networking assistance. Contact Women Business Owners Of North Florida, P.O. Box 551434, Jacksonville, FL 32255-1434; 904-278-9270; {www.jaxwbo.org/}.

Assistance For Your New or Existing Business
This expansion of the *Women's Business Assistance Center* in nearby Mobile services an area that includes Escambia and Santa Rosa counties, two of the most populous counties in the far northwestern reaches of the state, as well as Okaloosa County, which includes Eglin Air Force Base. Twenty-five percent of clients are socially and economically disadvantaged, with scholarships available to cover any fee-for-service programs. The center also targets the area's military spouses and military retirees, especially focusing on women retiring from the military who are considering business ownership as a second career. In addition to training, counseling, mentoring and video-conferencing, the center will expand its service in the third year to provide "circuit-rider training" to the Fort Walton Beach area. They also expect to outfit a van with

computers, reading materials and videos for outreach to distant communities, and to produce videotaped class segments to sell as a source of revenue. Contact Women's Business Assistance Center, Inc. (WBAC), Kathryn Cariglino, Executive Director, 301 Azalea Rd., Suite 201A, Mobile, AL 36693; 334-660-2725; Fax: 334-660-8854; {E-mail: wbac@ceebic.org}.

Georgia

Start Your Own Business

If you are planning, expanding or strengthening a business, the *Women's Economic Development Agency* program is for you. It is a 21-seminar series for women business owners, lasting two-and-one-half hours each week. WEDA also provides mentoring and one-on-one counseling. The majority of clients are African-American women; however, it is open to all individuals. Topics covered in the training program include marketing, business planning, accounting and finance, contract negotiation, and domestic and international procurement. Women's Economic Development Agency (WEDA), Joyce Edwards, Chairperson for Board, 675 Ponce de Leon Avenue, Atlanta, GA 30308; 404-853-7680; Fax: 404-853-7677; {E-mail: dorothy.fletcher@ internetmci.com}.

Atlanta Training

Greater Atlanta Small Business Project (GRASP) gives a hand up to women in the city of Atlanta and in Fulton County, about half of whom are African Americans. GRASP offers three program tracks, depending on the needs and preferences of each woman: "The New Horizon Track" is a hands-on business-development program for women transitioning from welfare to work. "The Education/Training/ Information Track" offers Internet and other computer training and access, a small business resource center, access to training programs of numerous other small business service providers, and twice-monthly workshops on topics of interest to most women and not currently available from other local service providers. "The Advanced Business Performance Track" invests an intensive level of management and technical assistance in well-established women-owned businesses selected for their overall growth potential, and also includes start-ups with unusually strong management capacity and/or market niche. The team assigned to each client comprises an experienced, successful businessperson, an accountant and an attorney. GRASP partners with TEKnowledge, Inc., a minority-owned technology firm that responds to user questions and problems regarding technology or other issues as needed. In addition, GRASP oversees a cooperative for the purpose that markets products and services of women-owned businesses to corporations, government procurement offices and specific consumer markets. Contact Greater Atlanta Small Business Project

(GRASP), Maurice Coakley, CEO, 55 Marietta Street, Suite 2000, Atlanta, GA 30303; 404-659-5955; Fax: 404-880-9561; {E-mail: m_coakley@ graspnet.org}.

Hawaii

Helping You Re-tool Your Career
With experience in working with Samoan, Fijian, Hawaiian, Korean, Japanese, Filipino and Chinese populations, the Women's Financial Resource Center (WFRC) is well positioned to serve the ethnically and culturally diverse Hawaiian population. Under WFRC's program, each client receives an individual assessment, which includes training in writing business plans, a marketing study group, and a monthly networking and information meeting. WFRC provides special topic workshops, such as Designing Brochures and Flyers, Taxes for the Small Business Owner, Taking the 'Starving' Out of Artist, and Starting a Home-Based Business. The center has also entered into a partnership with the Chamber of Commerce of Hawaii to provide distance/ correspondence training. WFRC plans to have subcenters on at least two other islands. Contact The Women's Financial Resource Center (WFRC), Laura Crites, Director, 1111 Bishop Street, #204, Honolulu, HI 96813; 808-522-8136; Fax: 808-522-8135.

Idaho

Find Your Mentor
Women's Entrepreneurial Mentoring Systems, Inc. serves all women throughout the state, with special outreach to socially and economically disadvantaged clients. Specific outreach plans are proposed for finding, assisting and encouraging women who own or wish to start home-based businesses. Special problems for women with disabilities who want to start businesses are also addressed. Some training is provided by WEMS, while other assistance is provided through the BIC, OSCS, SCORE, SBDC and the Boise Chamber of Commerce, all of which share the facility. WEMS was created as a result of the WNET Program and provides a monthly Mini-WNET mentoring group online. Contact Women's Entrepreneurial Mentoring Systems, Inc. (WEMS, Inc.), Beverly Kendrick, President, LaDonna Baker, Project Director, P.O. Box 190893, Boise, ID 83719-0893; 208-377-4627 (Kendrick); 208-378-7002 (Baker); Fax: 208-888-0398; {E-mail: kathyroma@aol.com}.

Illinois

Management Training
Founded in 1976, *Women in Management* was developed by a group of women in business to meet the need for training and support seminars for woman managers and women seeking management positions. The Near West Cook

County Chapter was founded in 1991. Theirs is a membership organization. For more information, contact Patricia Davis, President, PRO Office Services, Oak Park, IL 60302; 708-386-3717; Fax: 708-848-4099; {E-mail: riz@megsinet.net}; {www.oprf.com/WIM/index.html}.

Other chapters in Illinois include:
1. Women In Management Incorporated, 30 N Michigan Ave. # 508, Chicago, IL 60602-3404; 312-263-3636.

2. Women-In-Management Incorporated, 2203 Lakeside Dr. # B, Deerfield, IL 60015-1265; 847-295-0370.

Assistance in Chicago

Women's Self Employment Project (WSEP) provides credit, technical assistance and training through an individual lending program, a group lending program (the Full Circle Fund) and an Entrepreneurial Training Program. WSEP's services are targeted to low and moderate income women in the Chicago area.

Its goal is to assist these women to achieve self- sufficiency through self-employment. For more information, contact Women's Self Employment Project (WSEP), 166 West Washington, Suite 730, Chicago, IL 60613; 312-606-6255.

Women Entrepreneurs in Chicago

The *Women's Business Development Corporation* can provide you with a variety of entrepreneurial training courses and seminars: one-on-one counseling; financial assistance and loan packaging for micro-loans, the SBA Prequalification Loan Program and other SBA and government loan programs including the mentor/protégé program. They also offer WBE certification and private and public sector procurement; annual conference and Women's Buyers Mart; and extensive advocacy and policy development for women's economic and business development issues. Founded in 1986, the WBDC serves women business owners in the greater Chicago area, and advocates for women business owners nationwide. WBDC provides services through a local bank's "Wheels of Business" van, which travels to low-income neighborhoods to offer training and counseling. Contact Women's Business Development Center (WBDC), Hedy Ratner and Carol Dougal, Co-Directors, Linda Darragh, Project Director Extension 22, 8 South Michigan Avenue, Suite 400, Chicago, IL 60603; 312-853-3477; Fax: 312-853-0145; {E-mail: wbdc@aol. com}.

Women in Franchising

Women in Franchising, Inc. (WIF) is the nation's leader in assisting prospective women and minority entrepreneurs in all aspects of franchise business

---

ownership. Founded in 1987 and located in Chicago, Illinois, WIF has developed specialized skill and knowledge in the evaluation, financing and purchase of franchised businesses. WIF offers expertise in the development, coordination and implementation of franchise business training seminars and workshops on a national basis. Women in Franchising educates women, minorities and the physically challenged about franchising, and trains franchisers in marketing and development in these special markets. Contact Women In Franchising Incorporated, 53 W Jackson Blvd. # 205, Chicago, IL 60604-3607; 312-431-1467; 800-222-4WIF (222-4943); Fax 312-431-1469.

Resource
The State of Illinois maintains a hotline where you can ask questions pertaining to your small business. Contact Illinois Small Business Hotline; 800-252-2923.

Indiana
Help For Women and Minorities
Are you an Indiana woman or minority who owns a business? The *Women and Minorities in Business Group (WMBG)* offers counseling for emerging and mature businesses. Client needs are determined, evaluated and advised at no cost. Services include: workshops and seminars, direct counseling, information clearinghouse and referral source, and general information including statistics regarding women- and minority-owned businesses. They also administer the Minority Outreach Resource Executive (MORE) Program in six regions. Apply Through: Indiana Small Business Development Corporation (ISBD Corp.), 1 N Capitol Ave. # 1275, Indianapolis, IN 46204-2025; 317-264-2820.

Self-Employment Training for Daycare Workers
The goal of *Eastside Community Investments (ECI)* is to create jobs and improve the quality of housing in a disadvantaged section of Indianapolis. It has pioneered an innovative self-employment program for day care providers and also is a participant in the demonstration program to provide self-employment services to women on AFDC. For more information, contact Eastside Community Investments (ECI), 3228 East 10th Street, Indianapolis, IN 46201; 317-633-7303.

Self-Employment Services

Fort Wayne
Fort Wayne's Women's Bureau Inc.
(FWWBI) serves Fort Wayne plus nine counties in the northeast corner of Indiana, six of which are part of the Fort Wayne metropolitan area and three that are primarily rural. They reach out to low-income and Hispanic women, and women with disabilities. FWWBI training includes comprehensive financial, management and marketing assistance, as well as government

procurement and "Owning Your Business," parts I and II. They provide workshops and training, including all the services of the SBA, through the SBA home page and the Online WBC. They offer full-time bilingual services for all program areas. FWWBI works with AARP to identify ways the program can meet the unique needs of senior women who need or want to continue working and want to explore entrepreneurship. In cooperation with local services, they provide signing interpreters for the hearing impaired and transportation for people with physical disabilities. Contact Fort Wayne's Women's Bureau Inc. (FWWBI), Betty Tonsing, Ph.D., Executive Director, 303 E. Washington Blvd., Fort Wayne, IN 46805; 219-424-7977; Fax: 219-426-7576; {E-mail: fwwb@fwi.com}.

Iowa

Would You Like To Be Self-Employed?
The Institute of Social and Economic Development focuses on minorities, women, people with disabilities and low-income individuals. This is a consortium of all the major business-development organizations in the state; it serves every level of women business owners in a unified and intensive way. They encourage self-sufficiency through the growth of a small business and other self-employment opportunities. They can provide services for any person who wants to start or expand a business employing up to five employees, including the owner. For more information, contact Institute of Social and Economic Development, 1901 Broadway, Suite 313, Iowa City, IA 52240; 319-338-2331; Fax: 319-338-5824;
{E-mail: cpigsley@ised.org}; {www.ised.org}.

Kansas

Study Profiles of Successful Entrepreneurs
The mission of the *Huck Boyd National Institute for Rural Development* is to enhance rural development by helping rural people help themselves. In addition to conducting rural policy studies, the Institute offers presentations encouraging grass-roots community self-help throughout the state. To encourage entrepreneurship, the Institute has compiled and broadcast over 200 profiles of entrepreneurs, community leaders, and others who have created hundreds of jobs in more than 89 of the 105 counties. For more information, contact Huck Boyd National Institute for Rural Development, 216 Call Hall, Manhattan, KS 66506-1604; 785-532-7690; Fax: 785-532-7036; {E-mail: huckbyd@ksu.edu}; {www.ksu.edu/huckboyd/92ksprof.htm}.

Kentucky

Lots of Programs
Midway College's Center for Women, Diversity, & Leadership serves the Lexington metropolitan area and the rural Danville-Boyle County area with

expansion to other areas of the state by "distance learning" and other techniques. The University works in close coordination with local agencies to reach out to welfare-to-work, low income and minority populations. They coordinate with other women's colleges that have SBA-funded women's business centers-Columbia College in South Carolina and the University of the Sacred Heart in Puerto Rico to employ innovative, coordinated approaches to the Hispanic business community and to welfare-to-work programs. Programs include Taking Off: Launching Your Small Business, Advancing Your Business, technical workshops on selling to the government, sources of capital, and mentoring and team building. In addition to offering a directory of online computer training programs, they provide discussion groups for small office/home office businesses. Minutes of quarterly mentoring meetings and transcripts of events are posted online where participants or those unable to attend can join to continue discussions. They also provide specific interactive course materials and an online business library page with recommended readings and resources, and links to discounted materials. The University will present an annual award for outstanding achievement by a woman

Women Entrepreneurs for Economic Development

entrepreneur in Kentucky that will include an invitation to an honorary fellowship to speak at college events during the next year. Contact Midway College, Center for Women, Diversity, & Leadership, Dr. David Arnold, 512 East Stephens Street, Midway, KY 40347-1120; 606-846-5811; Fax: 606-846-5787; {E-mail: darnold@midway.edu}.

Louisiana

Help For Women Entrepreneurs
Women Entrepreneurs for Economic Development, Inc. (W.E.E.D.) was founded in 1989 by three businesswomen. Since their inception, W.E.E.D. has assisted over 200 women to become economically self-sufficient. They assist women in the Orleans Parish area of New Orleans. Its "NxLevel for Business Start-Ups" offers a hands-on, commonsense approach to developing a small business. Contact Women Entrepreneurs for Economic Development Inc. (W.E.E.D.), Paula Pete, Executive Director, Cynthia Beaulieu, Director of Training, 1683 North Claiborne Avenue, New Orleans, LA 70116; 504-949-8885; Fax: 504-949-8885; {E-mail: webc@bellsouth.net}.

Women Small Business Owners Assistance
The *Women's Business Center* is a program that was developed by the Southeast Louisiana Black Chamber of Commerce (SLBCC) to assist women in Jefferson Parish, but serves nine other parishes including: Orleans, St. Bernard, St. Tammany, St. James, St. John the Baptist, St. Charles,

Tangipahoa, Plaquemines and Washington. The Center can provide you with training, counseling and mentoring to aid and encourage the growth and development of small businesses, owned and controlled by women. Many of the clients served through the Center have started their own businesses. The Center is located in JEDCO West, an incubator program in Harvey, LA. For more information, contact Southeast Louisiana Black Chamber of Commerce (SLBCC), Women's Business Center, Laverne Kilgore, Director, 2245 Peters Road, Suite 200, Harvey, LA 70058; 504-365-3866; Fax: 504-365-3890; {E-mail: wbc200@bellsouth.net}; {www.gnofn.org/~slbcc/ wbc}.

Women Business Owners
Women Business Owners Association works to establish women business owners as an integral and influential element of the business community and promotes the success of women-owned businesses. Greater New Orleans area

business owners wanting to exchange information and share experiences formed WBOA as an organization consisting of women who own businesses and associates who support women in business. WBOA was created to: foster training, technical assistance and other learning opportunities oriented toward your needs, encourage, support, and represent women-owned businesses, cultivate economic stability of women-owned businesses, and initiate and support legislation benefiting small businesses. For more information, contact WBOA, P.O. Box 8326, Metairie, LA 70011; 504-456-0505; {www.wboa.org/Default.htm}.

Maine

Help For Fledgling Women Owned Businesses
Coastal Enterprises, Inc. (CEI) is a private non-profit community development corporation that provides financing and technical assistance to Maine businesses that provide income, ownership or employment opportunities to low income people. One of their programs is The Women's Business Development Project (WBDP) that emerged from CEI's experience in assessing women's business owners' needs, and providing women's business owners with training, technical assistance, financing and advocacy. If you have already started your own business anywhere in Maine, they can help you. You can benefit from CEI's counseling, as well as their capacity to provide access to capital through its SBA Microloan Program, the SBA Women's Pre-Qualification Loan Program and other resources. For more information, contact Coastal Enterprises Inc. (CEI), Women's Business Development Program (WBDP), Ronald Phillips, President, Ellen Golden, Senior Project Manager, P.O. Box

268, Wiscasset, ME 04578; 207-882-7552; Fax: 207-882-7308; {E-mail: efg@ceimaine.org}; {www.ceimaine.org}.

Janet Roderick, Women's Business Counselor, Betsy Tipper, Telecommunications Business Counselor, 7 North Chestnut Street, Augusta, ME 04330; 207-621-0245; Fax: 207-622-9739; {E-mail: jmr@ceimaine.org}; {E-mail: eat@ceimaine.org}; {www.ceimaine.org}.

Self-Employment Training for Displaced Homemakers
The *Maine Displaced Homemakers Program's* primary goal is to help prepare disadvantaged women to participate fully in the state's changing economy through innovative pre-employment and self-employment training and support services. For more information, contact Maine Displaced Homemakers Program, Stoddard House, University of Maine, August, ME 04330; 207-621-3432.

Maryland
Run Your Own Transportation Business
AdVANtage II is a van service and entrepreneurial training program sponsored by Sojourner-Douglass College and funded by a grant from the Baltimore City Department of Social Services. You can receive the training and follow-up support services needed to establish and maintain your own transportation business. They will also help you become certified as a Minority Business Enterprise. In turn, you will provide van services to up to 500 welfare-to-work customers, enabling them to commute to job assignments not served by existing transportation providers. For more information, contact AdVANtage II, Sojourner-Douglass College, 500 N. Caroline St., Baltimore, MD 21205; 410-276-9741.

Training For Low-Income Entrepreneurs
Women Entrepreneurs of Baltimore, Inc. (WEB), can polish your skills through an entrepreneurial training program designed to help economically disadvantaged women become self-sufficient through business development. The main components of the WEB program are: an intensive three-month business skill training course; mentoring; financing strategy development; community networking; resource sharing; and professional business consultation. For more information, contact Women Entrepreneurs of Baltimore, Inc. (WEB), Amanda Crook Zinn, Chief Executive Officer, 28 East Ostend Street, Baltimore, MD 21230; 410-727-4921; Fax: 410-727-4989.

Rural Assistance
Women's Business Institute Inc. serves start-up and established businesses, including socially and economically disadvantaged women in rural

communities in Maryland, West Virginia and Pennsylvania. Services include one-on-one counseling, Internet training, "First Step" for welfare-to-work clients, "Premier FastTrac," parts I and II, "Contracting Dollar$ and Sense," and "Entrepreneurship 101," as well as loan packaging and mentoring. Each participant receives a training manual and booklet that contains printouts from the Online Women's Business Center and lists of Internet addresses with brief content descriptions pertinent to the program. The center will investigate how to modernize its distance learning programs by partnering with universities, colleges and learning centers. Contact Women's Business Institute Inc., Beatrice Checket, CEO, 10 S. Howard Street, 6th Floor, Baltimore, MD 21201; 410-266-8746; {E-mail: checket@juno.com}.

Massachusetts

Minority and Women Business Assistance
In addition to their work certifying companies as minority or women-owned or controlled, and publishing a directory listing of verified firms, the *State Office of Minority and Women Business Assistance (SOMWBA)* also offers technical assistance. This means you could benefit from management seminars and workshops for minority and women entrepreneurs on a wide variety of

Personal Development Workshops

business topics. For more information, contact Business Development Office, 1 Ashburton Pl. # 2101, Boston, MA 02108-1519; 617-727-3206; 800-5-CAPITAL; {www.state.ma.us/mobd}.

Get Help With Starting Your Own Business
The *Center for Women & Enterprise, Inc. (CWE)* is a non-profit educational organization whose mission is to empower women to become economically self-sufficient and prosperous through entrepreneurship. The first center of its kind in Massachusetts, CWE provides courses, workshops, round tables, one-on-one consulting, and loan packaging assistance to women who seek to start and/or grow their own businesses. While services are open to everyone, scholarships target low-income women. For more information, contact Massachusetts Center for Women & Enterprise Inc., Andrea Silbert, Director, 45 Bromfield Street, 6th Floor, Boston, MA 02108; 617-423-3001ext. 222; Fax: 617-423-2444; {E-mail: info@cweboston.org}; {http://asilbert@cweboston.org}.

Michigan

All Kinds of Services for Women Seeking Self-Employment
The *Women's Initiative for Self-Employment (WISE)* Program provides low-income women with the tools and resources to begin and expand businesses.

The WISE Program can provide you with a comprehensive package of business training, personal development workshops, credit counseling, start-up and expansion financing, business counseling, peer group support, and mentoring. The creation and expansion of businesses is only one goal of this program. The WISE Program was also designed to fight poverty, increase incomes, raise self-esteem, stabilize families, develop skills and spark a process of community renewal. For more information, contact Ann Arbor Community Development Corporation Women's Initiative for Self Employment (WISE), Michelle Richards, Executive Director, 2008 Hogback Road, Suite 2A, Ann Arbor, MI 48105; 313-677-1400; Fax: 313-677-1465; {E-mail: mrichards@miceed.org}.

Break Through Barriers
Grand Rapids Opportunities for Women (GROW) is a non-profit economic development organization that provides women from diverse backgrounds -- many of whom are facing social or economic barriers -- with opportunities to develop the skills and acquire the knowledge needed to achieve financial independence. Focusing on small businesses, GROW can provide you with entrepreneurial training needed to start a small business as well as the follow-up services needed to sustain and expand a business. Since starting a business often affects all aspects of a woman's life, GROW is committed to providing group and individual support for both business and personal development. Contact Grand Rapids Opportunities for Women (GROW), 25 Sheldon SE, Suite 210, Grand Rapids, MI 49503; 616-458-3404; Fax: 616-458-6557; {E-mail: grow@voyager.net}.

Help In Detroit
Detroit Entrepreneurship Institute, Inc. (DEI) serves businesses owned by welfare recipients, dislocated workers and other women with low to moderate incomes who are seeking self-sufficiency through entrepreneurship. Among the nation's 25 largest cities, Detroit was ranked as having the highest rate of poverty; one in three urban residents lives below the poverty line. Two of DEI's long-term (11-week) classes are "Self-Employment Initiative," open to welfare recipients, and "Enterprise Development Initiative," open to low- to moderate-income general public, dislocated workers, and women with disabilities. The state of Michigan partnered with the Corporation for Enterprise Development and secured a two-year waiver to protect the welfare benefits of DEI participants. The waiver allows participants to earn business income and accumulate assets while continuing to receive their grants and medical benefits during the start-up phase of their businesses. Contact Detroit Entrepreneurship Institute, Inc. (DEI), Cathy McClelland, CEO, 455 W. Fort Street, 4th Floor, Detroit, MI 48226; 313-961-8426; Fax: 313-961-8831; {E-mail: deibus@aol.com}.

Educational Meetings

In the ten years of its existence, *Alliance for Women Entrepreneurs* has become an important resource and advocate for West Michigan women business owners, providing outstanding educational meetings for women at all levels of entrepreneurship, from start-up to mature businesses. AWE membership gives members a solid support base for networking with other business owners, and the organization works to provide current information on legislation, political issues and trends at the state and national levels that will impact on small business. And from the beginning, the organization has the support of the state and community officials and leaders. Contact AWE, PO Box 1201, Grand Rapids, MI 49501; Reservation Line: 616-224-9366.

Minnesota

Employment and Business Services For Women

If you are looking for direction or assistance in developing your career, searching for employment, starting or expanding a business, *WomenVenture* is the resource for you. They can help you identify your career direction, make a career change, enter/re-enter the workforce or try for that perfect job. They can also help you get started with a new business idea or grow an existing business. Their career development services are on a sliding fee scale and include individual consulting, Myers-Briggs Type Indicator, and Strong Interest Inventory. Classes include Career & Life Planning for Women and How to Ace an Interview. There is also a Career & Employment Transition Group for Women. Specific training programs include a program geared towards challenging the boundaries of men's work through pre-apprenticeship training and placement programs in construction or printing. Another program prepares women for jobs that require minimal training or experience, but offer good pay and benefits, in such fields as banking, administrative support, food service and many other areas. They offer training in resume development; personal empowerment; sexual harassment prevention; interviewing techniques; job search strategies; job placement; job retention support; library and computer access. For more information, contact WomenVenture, 2324 University Avenue, St. Paul, MN 55114; 651-646-3808; Fax: 651-641-7223.

Women's Business Training

If your new or existing business could benefit from expert technical assistance, *Women in New Development* may be right for you. They can assist you in your business goals through one-on-one counseling, classroom training (using a variety of workshop formats), an annual regional Women's Business Conference, and through several networking organizations. Since 1969, WIND has served the small business communities of Beltrami and Cass Counties in rural northwestern Minnesota. WIND provides technical assistance to new and existing businesses. In addition, WIND also provides training services to eight additional counties in northwestern Minnesota in collaboration with the Northwest Minnesota Foundation. For more information, contact Women in New Development (WIND), Susan Hoosier, WIND Coordinator, 2715 15th Street NW, P.O. Box 579, Bemidji, MN 56601; 218-751-4631; Fax: 218-751-8452; {E-mail: bicap@northernnet.com}.

Help For Women Business Owners
This site is located in rural Minnesota on the White Earth Reservation. They provide one-on-one counseling and the following training seminars: Starting a Business; Customer Service; The Business Plan; Organized Record Keeping; Entrepreneurial Peak Performance; Effective Management; The Marketing Plan; Entrepreneurial Confidence; Preparing for Financing. This site networks with the demonstration sites in Fargo, ND and Bemidji, MN to plan conferences and special programs. For more information, contact Women's Business Center, White Earth Reservation Tribal Council, Mary Turner, Director, 202 South Main Street, P.O. Box 478, Mahnomen, MN 56557; 218-935-2827; Fax: 218-935-9178.

Technical Assistance
The *Minnesota Women's Business Center* provides technical assistance to new and existing businesses. Services are provided through one-on-one counseling, classroom training (using a variety of workshop formats), an annual regional women's business conference, and through several networking organizations. The center also provides training services to twelve additional rural counties in northwestern Minnesota, in collaboration with the Northwest Minnesota Foundation. Contact Minnesota Women's Business Center, A division of The People Connection, Bonnie Stewart, Director, 226 East 1st Street, Fosston, MN 56542; 218-435-2134; Fax: 218-435-1347; {E-mail: wind@means.net}.

WOMEN'S BUSINESS CENTER

Mississippi

Entrepreneur Training For Women of Color
If you live in Mound Bayou or Ruleville in Bolivar County and would like to become more self-sufficient, check out the economic entrepreneurial centers run by the *National Council of Negro Women (NCNW)* in those areas. For more information, contact Mississippi Women's Economic Entrepreneurial Project (MWEEP), Jo Thompson, Director, 106 West Green Street, Mound Bayou, MS 38762; 601-741-3342; Fax: 601-741-2195 or 601-335-3060; {E-mail: jthompson@tecinfo.com}; {www.ncnw.com}.

Training For Low-Income Women in the Delta

Mississippi Action for Community Education (MACE) oversees the Mid-Delta Women's Entrepreneurial Training and Technical Assistance Program (WE-TAP). Given the limited opportunities for traditional employment in this area, WE-TAP creates alternative and non-traditional means of economic support for low-income women. You can benefit from programs such as Project New, a business incubator project, or their women's entrepreneurial program, Project Jump Start. Their ultimate goal is to create self-sufficiency and build wealth particularly for low-income women residing in the Mississippi Delta. Contact Mississippi Action for Community Education (MACE), Mid-Delta Women's Entrepreneurial Training and Technical Assistance Program (WE-TAP), Ruby Buck, President, 119 South Theobald Street, Greenville, MS 38701; 601-335-3523; Fax: 601-334-2939.

Missouri

Women Entrepreneur Training Program

Through the Continuing Education Division, *St. Louis Community College* offers educational opportunities filling a variety of community needs in numerous locations throughout the metropolitan area. The Florissant Valley Campus handles all of the inquiries regarding the Woman Entrepreneur Training Program, however, all of the classes are held at the Meramec Campus located at 11333 Big Bend Blvd. in Kirkwood. For more information on courses, workshops and mentoring for women who want to start or expand a small business, contact Continuing Education, Saint Louis Community College, 3400 Pershall Road, St. Louis, MO 63135-1499; 314-95-4586.

Help In Impoverished Neighborhoods

Grace Hill Neighborhood Services serves areas consisting entirely of impoverished neighborhoods with residents at or below poverty level, high crime and high school dropout rates, evident drug and gang presence, and deteriorating properties. This project's comprehensive regional scope includes St. Louis and three counties. The center's first concern is outreach and marketing to make women aware of their services. Long-term training for start-up and existing businesses is subcontracted through a Small Business Development Center. They also run a business incubator and provide a listing of approved local suppliers who offer discounts to women business owners. The center also maintains a listing of women's businesses, so they can patronize one another's companies. Because of their special focus on welfare-to-work participants and low-income working women, they hold a monthly online chat group of disadvantaged clients from around the country. Contact Grace Hill Neighborhood Services, Betty Marver, Managing Director of Social Services, 2600 Hadley, St. Louis, MO 63106; 314-539-9506; Fax: 314-214-8938.

Montana

Training For Business Women Business Owners

Montana Women's Economic Development Group (WEDGo) hosts business workshops that cover basic or advanced business concepts. Business owners learn from experienced trainers in a relaxed, interactive setting. The training uses real-world information, featuring local business owners as speakers.

Trainers emphasize practical problem solving that most business owners can carry out independently. They also help you network through marketing alliances that link similar businesses to work together on efforts that include market research, promotion, distribution and advertising. Alliances they have developed include tourism business, childcare business, arts and commercial sewing sectors.

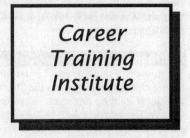

Career Training Institute

For more information, contact Women's Opportunity & Resource Development Inc., Rosalie S. Cates, Director, 127 N. Higgins, Missoula, MT 59802; 406-543-3550 ext. 19; Fax: 406-721-4584; {E-mail: mcdc@montana.com}.

Assistance for Low-Income Entrepreneurs

The *Human Resource Development Council of Bozeman (HRDC)* offers microbusiness training, technical assistance, and loan funds for low-income entrepreneurs. A community action agency serving Gallatin County in southwestern Montana has developed a partnership to improve an existing microbusiness incubator program by providing crucial, but previously lacking, loan funds to low-income people seeking to pursue microbusiness enterprises. For more information, contact Jeffrey K. Rupp, Executive Director, Charles Hill, Project Director, Human Resource Development Council, 321 East Main Street, Suite 300, Bozeman, MT 59715; 406-587-4486; Fax: 406-585-3538.

Rural Training

The *Career Training Institute* targets 12 counties, extending from the Helena area north to the Canadian border and encompassing 30,403 square miles. Because the targeted area is very rural, the Career Training Institute offers training classes in four strategically located areas: Lewistown, Great Falls, Browning and Helena. Contact Career Training Institute, Sheila Hogan, Executive Director, Maureen Garrity, Project Director, 347 North Last Chance Gulch, Helena, MT 59601; 406-443-0800; Fax: 406-442-2745; {E-mail: mgarrity@ixi.net}.

Counseling and Loans
Montana Community Development Corporation provides counseling, loans and loan packaging to clients in western Montana. Professional staff have worked with hundreds of large and small businesses. MCDC has provided over $1 million in direct business financing, and has packaged and facilitated commercial loans in that amount each year. Contact Montana Community Development Corporation, Rosalie S. Cates, Executive Director, 127 North Higgins, Missoula, MT 59802; 406-543-3550; Fax: 406-721-4584; {E-mail: mcdc@montana.com}.

Nebraska

The mission of the *Nebraska Center for Entrepreneurship* is to enable and inspire entrepreneurs by exceeding their needs through untraditional and traditional learning strategies. The Center hosts a Global Conference on Creative Entrepreneurship (GCCE) which brings together talented entrepreneurial students from around the world to study entrepreneurship, to create an international business network of entrepreneurs, and to promote international understanding and cultural awareness. Their International Business Plan Competition encourages new venture creations by college students who present their business plans to prominent business leaders and venture capitalists serving as judges. An internship program provides opportunities for college students to be matched with successful entrepreneurs who have similar interests. Internships allow the student to earn college credit while working for a successful company in a practical entrepreneurial environment. For more information, contact Nebraska Center for Entrepreneurship, 209 CBA, University of Nebraska-Lincoln, Lincoln, NE 68588-0487; 402-472-3353; {E-mail: ddoughty@unl.edu}; {www.cba.unl.edu/additional/ent/index.html}.

Nevada

Self-Employment Training For Low-Income Individuals
1. You can participate in training programs designed to open the door to self-sufficiency through self-employment. The *Nevada Self-Employment Trust* serves Clark County that includes Las Vegas, North Las Vegas, Henderson, Boulder City and Mesquite. They were founded in 1991 by the Nevada Women's Fund to enhance the economic opportunities of low-income individuals. Since their classes began in January 1992, over 300 low and moderate-income individuals in Nevada have successfully participated in NSET's training programs. They can also help you capitalize your new business as NSET is a microlender under SBA's microloan program. For more information, contact Nevada Self-Employment Trust, 1600 E. Desert Inn Road, #209, E. Las Vegas, NV 89109; 702-734-3555; Fax: 702-734-3530.

2. *Nevada MicroEnterprise Initiative* is a similar program whose
    mission is to enhance the economic self-sufficiency and quality
    of life of low- to moderate-income individuals through
    entrepreneurial training, business technical assistance
    and loans for new and expanding businesses
    throughout the State of Nevada. These programs
    are designed to give you economic power by
    providing the most comprehensive entrepreneurial
    services. NMI's programs provide women and men
    with business skills as well as life skills. Contact
    Nevada MicroEnterprise Initiative (NMI), Virginia
    Hardman, Project Director, 1600 East Desert Inn Road, Suite 209E, Las
    Vegas, NV 89109; 702-734-3555; Fax: 702-734-3530; {E-mail:
    nmilavegas@aol.com}; or Nevada MicroEnterprise Initiative (NMI),
    Elizabeth Scott, Program Coordinator, 116 East 7th Street, Suite 3, Carson
    City, NV 89701; 702-841-1420; Fax: 702-841-2221; {E-mail:
    lizs@cbrcnmi.reno.nv.us}.

Just For Women
The *Nevada Women's Business Resource and Assistance Center* provides
services specifically geared to low- to moderate-income women throughout
Nevada and uses the services of other providers throughout the state to leverage
its resources. The center integrates personal development and leadership into
its programs, as necessary components of business success. In a six-week pre-
startup course, participants assess their own skill levels and the feasibility of
their ideas; determine startup costs, pricing and break-even points; and address
licensing and other startup concerns. If, at any point in the training, a client
determines that entrepreneurship is not for her, she can refocus on finding
employment with the center's assistance; such a decision is also seen as a
success by the center. If she does decide to open a business, she takes an eight-
week course that helps her develop a solid business plan. An additional course
helps existing businesses address the challenges of growth, and an alumni
program develops leaders and mentors from graduates and provides ongoing
educational opportunities. Contact Southern Nevada Certified Development
Company, The Nevada Women's Business Resource and Assistance Center,
Allison Loftus, Executive Director, 2770 S. Maryland Parkway, Suite 212, Las
Vegas, NV 89109; 702-732-3998; Fax: 702-732-2705; {E-mail:
loftus@aol.com}.

New Hampshire
Women Entrepreneurs Take Note
The *Women's Business Center, Inc.* is a collaborative organization designed to
encourage and support women in all phases of enterprise development. They

provide you with access to educational programs, financing alternatives, technical assistance, advocacy and a network of mentors, peer advisors and business and professional consultants. They can address your women-owned business needs through several targeted programs: Seminars for Women Entrepreneurs; WBC Newsletter; Monthly Peer Advisory Meetings; Internet for Small Business Workshops; and The Entrepreneur's Network. For more information, contact Women's Business Center, Inc., Connie Dove, Executive Director, 150 Greenleaf Avenue, Unit 8, Portsmouth, NH 03801; 603-430-2892; Fax: 603-430-3706; {E-mail: info@womenbiz.org}.

New Jersey

Many Job Services
The *Kean Office of Continuing Education* offers career counseling, vocational interest testing (Strong, Myers-Briggs), resume consultation, workshops on starting your own business, and job enhancement. Fees range from $25-75. For more information contact Kean Office of Continuing Education, 1000 Morris Ave., Union, NJ 07083; 908-527-2211.

New Mexico

Learn To Be Self-Sufficient
The *Women's Economic Self-Sufficiency Team (WESST Corp.)* assists low-income and minority women throughout New Mexico. They can offer counseling and mentoring through professional volunteers including attorneys, accountants, insurance agents and benefits counselors. If you decide to start a new business, they can assist you in obtaining capital funds, as WESST Corp. is a micro-lender under SBA's micro-loan program. Their focus encompasses the area of Las Cruces and Farmington, New Mexico, with program services provided to women in Dona, Ana, Luna, Otero and Sierra counties, with limited outreach to El Paso, Texas. Contact their main office or locate the office nearest you below: New Mexico Women's Economic Self-Sufficiency Team (WESST Corp.), Agnes Noonan, Executive Director, 414 Silver Southwest, Albuquerque, NM 87102; 505-241-4760; Fax: 505-241-4766; {E-mail: wesst@swcp.com}; {Agnes Noonan's E-mail: agnes@swcp.com}.

Other locations:
1. WESST Corp. - Sante Fe, NM, Marisa Del Rio, Regional Manager, 418 Cerrillos Road, Suite 26, Sante Fe, NM 87501; 505-988-5284; Fax: 505-988-5221; {E-mail: sfwesst@swcp.com}.

2. WESST Corp. - Taos, NM, Dawn Redpath, Regional Manager, Box 5007 NDCBU, Taos, NM 87571; 505-758-3099; Fax: 505-751-1575; {E-mail: redpath@laplaza.org}.

3. WESST Corp. - Roswell, NM, Roberta Ahlness, Regional Manager, 200 West First, Suite 324, Roswell, NM 88201; 505-624-9850; Fax: 505-622-4196; {E-mail: wesst@rt66.com}.

4. WESST Corp. - Las Cruces, NM, Jennifer Craig, Regional Manager, 691 South Telshor, Las Cruces, NM 88001; 505-522-3707; Fax: 505-522-4414; {E-mail: jencraig@zianet.com}.

5. WESST Corp. - Farmington, NM, Joretta Clement, Regional Manager, 500 West Main, Farmington, NM 87401; 505-325-0678; Fax: 505-325-0695; {E-mail: 4business@acrnet.com}.

New York

Get The Help You Need To Start Your Own Business

Founded in 1976, the *American Woman's Economic Development Corporation* is the premier national not-for-profit organization committed to helping entrepreneurial women start and grow their own businesses. Based in New York City, AWED also has offices in Southern California, Connecticut and Washington, D. C. Join over  100,000 women who have benefited from formal course instructions, one-to-one business counseling, seminars, special events and peer group support. AWED's goal is to increase the start-up, survival and expansion rates of small businesses. Contact American Woman's Economic Development Corporation (AWED), Suzanne Tufts, President and CEO, 71 Vanderbilt Avenue, Suite 320, New York, NY 10169; 212-692-9100; Fax: 212-692-9296.

Rochester

The *Rochester Women's Network* was founded in 1978 and is the largest network of its kind in the country. Its mission is to foster the growth and advancement of women in the workplace. Membership offers to more than 850 members, as well as the community-at-large, challenging, stimulating programs, a wealth of valuable benefits, and continuing support, both personally and professionally. For more information, contact Rochester Women's Network, 39 Saginaw Dr., Rochester, NY 14623; 716-271-4182; Fax: 716-271-7159; {www.rwn.org}.

Train To Start Your Own Business

The *Entrepreneurial Assistance Program* can provide you with classroom instruction and individual counseling, business plan development for minorities, women, dislocated workers, public assistance recipients, public housing recipients. They serve those seeking to start a new business or who have owned a business for five years or less. For more information, contact

Empire State Development Office, Entrepreneurial Assistance Program, 633 3rd Avenue, New York, NY 10017; 212-803-2410; {www.empire.state.ny.us}.

Training and Loans For New Women Business Owners
The *Women's Venture Fund, Inc.* is based on a radically simple idea: empowering women, particularly low-income women to create new businesses by making micro-loans available to them, and then ensuring their success through their mentoring and training component. The Fund makes micro-loans to entrepreneurial women who cannot get funding through conventional sources. If you have great ideas, but desperately need small loans, business planning, and the moral support it takes to develop a business into reality, contact Women's Venture Fund, Inc., Maria Semidei-Otero, President, 155 East 42nd Street, Suite 316, New York, NY 10017; 212-972-1146; Fax: 212-972-1167.

North Carolina
Loans and Technical Assistance
Affiliated with the Self-Help Credit Union, this program is a partner with local organizations in the *North Carolina Urban Microenterprise Program*. The Center also provides small to medium-sized loans and technical assistance to businesses and projects that address the economic needs of rural, minority, female, and low-income people in the state. For more information, contact Center for Community Self-Help, 413 East Chapel Hill Street, Durham, NC 27701; 910-683-3615.

Referrals and Resources
The *North Carolina Center for Women Business Owner's* mission is a first-step resource and referral agency for women. The center has a variety of empowerment programs for women; high local credibility, with an eight-year history serving women and families; and strong local partnerships. It runs a successful entrepreneurial enterprise that provides ongoing training on product-development, pricing and marketing, and support through its retail outlet for home-based women's businesses. Nearly one third of their clients are socially and economically disadvantaged and are from both inner city and rural areas; other clients are military spouses from two nearby bases. Contact The North Carolina Center for Women Business Owners, Barbara Baker-Davidson, Director, 230 Hay Street, Fayetteville, NC 28301; 910-323-3377; Fax: 910-323-8828; {E-mail: WCOF2@ aol.com}; {www.wcof.org}.

North Dakota
Assistance For Women Business Owners
The *Women's Business Program* offers a wide variety of services. They can assist you by providing counseling and technical assistance for women

entrepreneurs; by maintaining a database of women-owned businesses; by administering the women's incentive grant program; by certifying women-owned businesses for federal and state contracting; by supporting the Women's Business Leadership Council; by providing information and support through trade shows and conferences; and by serving as an information clearinghouse on economic development service providers. For more information about WBDP, contact Tara Holt, ND Women's Business Program, 418 East Broadway, Suite 25, Bismarck ND 58501; 701-258-2251; Fax: 701-222-8071; {E-mail: holt@btigate.com}.

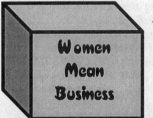

Business Assistance in Rural Areas and Indian Reservations
Through partnership with SBA resources, colleges and universities, and other service providers, the *Women and Technology Program* provides a support structure within North Dakota to provide business-development and technical assistance, financial advice, business education, and market planning, primarily via distance learning. Their targeted population is Native Americans and welfare-to-work participants. They address areas such as home-based businesses, international trade, franchising and legal issues. Distance learning, video conferencing, workshops and seminars are also available via BICs and Tribal BICs. The center uses all local resources to provide training in a three-year tier; 13 organizations have been identified in the first tier. Using modern technology, this project reaches women in rural areas and on Indian reservations, as well as women with disabilities. Contact Technology Transfer, Inc., Women and Technology Program, Tara S. Holt, Project Director, 1833 East Bismarck Expressway, Bismarck, ND 58504; 701-258-2251; Fax: 701-258-7514; {E-mail: holt@gcentral. com}.

Programs for Women To Advance Career Skills
The mission of the *Women's Business Institute* is to improve the opportunities for economic and business growth for women in North Dakota, Minnesota and the surrounding region. Numerous programs and services are available to women interested in advancing their business and career skills. Programs offered by the Women's Business Institute include monthly training classes, activities such as "Women Mean Business" networking events, coaching and counseling (including "Business Success" mentoring teams) and marketing/purchasing opportunities. In addition, the WBI hosts annual events such as the Business Technology Expo, a full day training conference, and a home-based business conference and trade show. Regular activities include computer classes, and courses in management, marketing, financing and entrepreneurial

confidence. Contact Women's Business Institute (WBI), Penny Retzer, Director, 320 North Fifth Street, Suite 203, P.O. Box 2043, Fargo, ND 58107-2043; 701-235-6488; Fax: 701-235-8284; {E-mail: wbinstitute@corpcomm.net}; {www.rrtrade.org/women/wbi}.

Ohio

Statewide Assistance For Women

The Ohio Women's Business Resource Network is a statewide effort to assist women business owners and promote successful women's business ownership. This umbrella organization promotes the sharing of information, technical assistance and education among its member organizations. OWBRN seeks to provide consistent baseline services to women across the state. Contact Ohio Women's Business Resource Network (OWBRN), Mary Ann McClure, Director, 77 South High Street, 28th Floor, Columbus, OH 43215-6108; 614-466-2682; 800-848-1300 Ext. 62682; Fax: 614-466-0829; {E-mail: owbrn@eurekanet.com}.

The following centers are all graduated members of OWBRN:

1. *Women's Organization for Mentoring, Entrepreneurship & Networking, (WOMEN) & Women's Network Inc.,* Julie Sparks, Executive Director, Women's Network, South Main Street, Suite 235, Akron, OH 44311-1058; 330-379-9280; 330-379-2772; Fax: 330-379-9283; {www.womennet.org}.

2. *Women's Business Resource Program of Southeastern Ohio*, Debra McBride, Project Director, Ohio University, 20 East Circle Drive, Suite 155, Technology and Enterprise Building, Athens, OH 45701; 740-593-1797; Fax: 740-593-1795; {E-mail: aa428@seorf.ohiou.edu}.

3. *Pyramid Career Services*, Mary Ellen Hess, Executive Director, Elaine Sherer, MBA, Program Manager, 2400 Cleveland Avenue North, Canton, OH 44709; 330-453-3767; Fax: 330-453-6079; {E-mail: pyramid@ezo.net}.

4. *Glenville Development Corporation Micro-Enterprise Program*, Rosalind Brewster, Micro-Enterprise Development Officer, 10640 St. Clair Ave., Cleveland, OH 44108; 216-851-8724; Fax: 216-851-8941.

5. *Central Ohio Women's Business Development Center*, Leslie Weilbacher, Director, 317 N. High Street, Columbus, OH 43215-3065; 614-225-6910; Fax: 614-469-8250; {E-mail: lweilbacher@columbus.org}; {www.columbus.org/busi/sbdc/index.htm}.

6. *Ohio Women's Business Development Council, Inc.,* Linda Steward, Director, 462 W. Broad St., Columbus, OH 43215; 614-621-0881; 877-238-6081; Fax: 614-621-2633; {E-mail: lsteward@network.com}/

7. *Women's Development Center,* Evelyn France, Executive Director, 42101 Griswold Road, Elyria, OH 44035; 440-324-3688; Fax: 440-324-3689.

8. *Women's Entrepreneurial Network,* Linda Fayerweather, Liaison, 1605 Holland Rd., Suite A3, Maumee, OH 43537-1630; 419-897-9799; Fax: 419-897-9776; {E-mail: lindafay@glasscity.net}.

9. *Women Entrepreneurs Inc.,* Angelita Moreno Jones, President, Gartlett Bldg., 36 East 4th Street, Suite. 925, Cincinnati, OH 45202; 513-684-0700.

Western Reserve Business Assistance

If you are a woman business owner, the Western Reserve Business Center for Women can assist you by providing information and support to help you flourish including: home-based business assistance; referrals, networking and mentoring; sources of financing; Western Business Enterprise (WBE) Certification Assistance; and government contract assistance and alternatives to assisted living. Also offered are dynamic training programs such as: Building Sales and New Business; Basic Business Skills; Personal Selling Skills; Promoting Self-Confidence; Time Management; Goal Setting; Developing Focus and Strategy; Evaluating Your Business Idea; Researching Your Market; Building Sales and New Businesses; Products/Services; Financial Statements; Taxes and Record-keeping; Employee/Contractor Issues; and Improving Internal Operations. The Western Reserve Business Center for Women serves Medina, Portage, Stark, Summit and Wayne Counties. Contact Western Reserve Business Center for Women, Karen Franks, Director, University of Akron, Community and Technical College, M/185V Polski Building, Room 185, Akron, OH 44325-6002; 330-972-5592; Fax: 330-972-5573; {E-mail: kdf@uakron.edu}.

Business Center

The Women's Business Center is part of an Enterprise Center sponsored by Ohio State University Extension. The Women's Business Center focuses on rural transition issues and alternative income sources. In the statewide network, this Center is one of the international trade assistance centers. For more information, contact Enterprise Center /Women's Business Center, Dr. Don McFeeters, Executive Director, Kendra Conley, Coordinator, Women's Business Center, Ohio State University, 1864 Shyville Road, Piketon, OH

45661; 614-289-3727; 800-860-7232; Fax: 614-292-1953; {E-mail:
enterprise@agvax2.ag.osu.edu}; {www.ag.ohio-state.edu/~prec/}.

Northwest Women Business Support
The *Northwest Ohio Women's Entrepreneurial Network* sponsors training for
start-up businesses and seminars for existing women business owners. They
are developing an "Expert Team Review" program that allows women-owned
businesses to meet with a panel of successful women business owners to
discuss problems with their business plans. For more information, contact
Northwest Ohio Women's Entrepreneurial Network, Linda Fayerweather,
Director, 5555 Airport Highway, Suite 210, Toledo, OH 43615; 419-381-7555;
Fax: 419-381-7573; {E-mail: lindafay@primenet.com}.

Oklahoma
Entrepreneur Camp
The *Women's Business Center* is an "entrepreneurial training camp" where a
team of small business supporters are committed to help those who want to
help themselves and their businesses. They offer you a complete one-stop
resource toolbox. Entrepreneur-led educational experiences will empower you
with knowledge and develop every aspect of your small business skills. They
create opportunities to build business-support networks and
connect their community's entrepreneurs with one
another. Through their alliance with the Small
Business Administration and the First National
Bank of Bethany, they can provide you with
access to capital once you are in their program.
Other monthly programs include: Connections -
Building Business Networks; Quest for Capital;

Intro. to the Internet and Entrepreneur 101. Bi-monthly programs offered are:
Camp Cash Flow and Jungle Marketing. Each Fall and Spring semester, they
offer Premier FastTrac I and Premier FastTrac II. For more information,
contact Women's Business Center, Working Women's Money University
(WWMU), Lori Smith, Director, 234 Quadrum Drive, Oklahoma City, OK
73108; 405-232-8257; Fax: 405-947-5388; 405-842-5067; {E-mail: lori@wbc-
okc.org}; {E-mail: charlotte@wbc-okc.org}.

Oregon
Break Through Barriers
Southern Oregon Women's Access to Credit (SOWAC) provides business
training, mentoring and financing services for women and men with barriers
including low-income Hispanic entrepreneurs and very rural entrepreneurs.
Join more than 288 students who have participated in their training program or
65 businesses which they have helped startup or expand in Jackson and

Josephine counties. As a training graduate, you may apply to SOWAC's Mentor Program to receive assistance from an experienced person who volunteers expertise over a six-month period, and/or for a SOWAC business loan of up to $25,000. SOWAC is funded by the SBA Office of Women Business Ownership, private foundations, client fees, interest income and local contributions. For more information, contact Southern Oregon Women's Access to Credit (SOWAC), Mary O'Kief, Director, 33 North Central, Suite 209, Medford, OR 97501; 541-779-3992; Fax: 541-779-5195; {E-mail: jasmith@sowac.org}; {E-mail: geninf@sowac.org}; {www.sowac.org}.

Business Assistance for Native Americans By Native Americans
Organization of Native American Business & Entrepreneurial Network (ONABEN) is a non-profit public benefit corporation created by Northwest Indian Tribes to increase the number and profitability of private enterprises owned by Native Americans. ONABEN offers training, individual counseling, assisted access to markets and facilitated access to capital for its clients. Each of the ten tribes hosting an ONABEN Service Center pays annual dues of $2,500 plus 40% of the cost of operating their site. The sites, located on reservations in Oregon, Washington and California, deliver services to all citizens regardless of tribal affiliation. Some have up to 40% of users coming from the surrounding non-Native community. For more information, contact ONABEN - A Native American Business Network, Patrick Borunda, Director, 520 Southwest 6th Avenue, Suite 930, Portland, OR 97204; 503-243-5015; Fax: 503-243-5028; {E-mail: borunda@onaben. org}; {www.onaben.org}.

Find A Supportive Environment
Women Entrepreneurs of Oregon has been providing education, professional support and networking opportunities for women business owners throughout the state of Oregon since 1981. Their purpose is to empower members so they may run more successful and profitable businesses. They offer a supportive environment that encourages learning through the sharing of experiences with other women in business. For more information, contact Women Entrepreneurs of Oregon, P.O. Box 1784, Clackamas, OR 97015; 541-786-9817; 800-947-9817; {E-mail: jwalton@cratus.com}; {www.cratus.com/weo/}.

Pennsylvania

Empowering Women Entrepreneurs
The *Women's Business Development Center (WBDC)* is dedicated to the economic empowerment of women. The Center enables women to launch new businesses and to more successfully run their existing businesses. If you are a start-up, emerging or established woman entrepreneur, they offer you a unique continuum of supportive services including: Premier FastTrac I & II, comprehensive course work culminating in the development of a viable

business plan for each entrepreneur; individualized business consulting in management, marketing, and financial matters; loan packaging; procurement and certification assistance. By offering a full range of services and utilizing the expertise of successful women business owners to deliver its programs, the Women's Business Development Center will be the Greater Philadelphia Region's focal point for women's economic empowerment opportunities. For more information, contact Women's Business Development Center (WBDC), Geri Swift, President, 1315 Walnut Street, Suite 1116, Philadelphia, PA 19107-4711; 215-790-9232; Fax: 215-790-9231; {E-mail: wbdc@erols.com}.

Women's Rural Business Incubator

The *Women's Enterprise Center (WEC)* serves the Pittsburgh area and plans to establish a second location in rural Washington County. WEC is a rural incubator offering home-based memberships. The services they provide include a "Passport for Services," a personalized written tool that sets goals and objectives, registers customers for specific services and resources, and articulates measurable and quantifiable outcomes. Group consults provide a peer-to-peer forum. SBDCs will sub-contract for some of the technical assistance. Links to other resources, including SBA loan programs, will also be provided. The center will also explore cooperative marketing among women-owned businesses engaged in related industries on the Internet. Contact Allegheny West Civic Council, Inc. Women's Enterprise Center (WEC), Chloe Velazquez, Business Services Director, 901 Western Avenue, Pittsburgh, PA 15233; 412-321-5660; Fax: 412-321-5673; {E-mail: hunterfa@sgi.net}.

Network

Since 1989, the *Women's Business Network, Inc. (WBN)* has been a networking organization of enthusiastic women business owners and professionals committed to integrity of performance and service and the creative exchange of business. Over 300 members of the Women's Business Network belong to local chapters that meet twice a month in various locations throughout Southwestern Pennsylvania. These chapter meetings provide each member time to network, to market her business, and to learn and discuss various aspects of running a successful business. In addition to the regular chapter meetings, the Women's Business Network sponsors a number of social and educational activities throughout the year that give members an opportunity to network within the entire organization. These include the annual holiday breakfast in December, the annual dinner in May, the annual meeting in June, an annual retreat, educational seminars and other organization-wide networking events. WBN also co-sponsors special events with other professional organizations. For more information, contact Women's Business Network, Inc., 2400 Oxford Drive, Village Square, Bethel Park, PA 15102; 412-835-4566; {E-mail: what@sgi.net}; {www.wbninc.com/}.

Alliance for Women Entrepreneurs
Female entrepreneurs have overcome many of the obstacles that block the path to success. *Small Business Association of Delaware Valley's Alliance for Women Entrepreneurs (AWE)* exists to give Delaware Valley businesswomen a network they can turn to at times of trouble, as well as triumph. They offer educational programs, a resource center, and a forum for group members. For more information, contact SBADV-AWE, 867 Sussex Blvd., P.O. Box 800, Broomall, PA 19008; 800-533-3732; {www.bestofpa.com/sbadv/nfawe.htm}.

Puerto Rico
Help For Women Entrepreneurs
The *Women's Business Institute (WBI)* at University of the Sacred Heart, Center for Women's Entrepreneurial Development (CWED) offers technical assistance to women interested in establishing a business. If you are a woman business owner, they provide a place to expose and share ideas, objectives and experiences. The WBI will contribute to the social and economic development of women through training on empowerment and business ownership as an alternative to attain economic independence. For more information, contact Women's Business Institute (WBI), Universidad Del Sagrado Corazon, (The University of the Sacred Heart), Joy Vilardi de Camacho, Director, Center for Women's Entrepreneurial Development, P.O. Box 12383, San Juan, PR 00914-0383; 787-728-1515 Extension 2560; 787-726-7045; Fax: 787-726-7077; {E-mail: womenbiz@caribe.net or carms@caribe.net}.

Rhode Island
Business Training For Low-Income Women
Center for Women & Enterprise, Inc., Rhode Island is a new venture of CWE Boston, 70 percent of whose clients are women of low and very low incomes and 35 percent of whom are women of color. CWE RI helps women access financing through banks and SBA loan-guaranty programs. Entrepreneurial courses include Fast/Trac, GROW (Getting Right On With It Groups), TEAM (The Executive Advisory Meeting), workshops, seminars, networking groups, plus one-on-one counseling. CWE RI is a national clearinghouse for women and financing, providing technical assistance on SBA loan programs and directing women business owners to local SBA resource partners. CWE RI offers "Turbo Day" once a year, a day-long program of high-impact workshops, each geared to a specific level of business experience. Workshops include Shoestring Marketing, Power Negotiating, Super Sales Strategies, Show Me the

Money, Personnel: Everything You Wanted to Know But Were Afraid to Ask. Until the center is located in downtown Providence, RI, you can contact them at Center for Women & Enterprise, Inc., Rhode Island (CWE RI), Andrea Silbert, CEO, 1135 Tremont Street, Suite 480, Boston, MA 02108; 617-536-0700 (temp); Fax: 617-536-7373 (temp); {E-mail: info@cweboston.org}; {E-mail: asilbert@cweboston.org}.

South Carolina

Help For Women Entrepreneurs
The mission of the *Center for Women Entrepreneurs at Columbia College of*

 *South Carolina* is to expand economic opportunities for women by advancing entrepreneurship and providing resources to assist in successful business start-ups, maintenance of growth, and exploration of new business opportunities. You could benefit from services that include individual consultations, management and technical assistance, annual women's conference, round table luncheon series, resource guides, seminars and workshops, and internships. The focus on communications through the Online Women's Business Center enables the project to serve not only mature women ready to start businesses or women already in business, but young female entrepreneurs in high schools. As local support for this project can attest, the Center for Women Entrepreneurs is an active advocate of collaborative ventures among resources that support women entrepreneurs. For more information, contact Center for Women Entrepreneurs, Columbia College of South Carolina, Susan Davis, Project Director, Ms. Sam McKee, Director of Grants, 1301 Columbia College Drive, Columbia, SC 29203; 803-786-3582; Fax: 803-786-3804; {E-mail: susdavis@colacoll.edu or smckee@colacoll.edu}; {www.colacoll.edu}.

South Dakota

Entrepreneur Training For Women
If you are or would like to be an entrepreneur in South Dakota, the *Entrepreneur's Network for Women* may be for you. The program offers you toll-free phone counseling, training seminars in management, marketing, financing, government contracting and entrepreneurial confidence. Networking sessions, a group mentoring program and Business Success Teams are offered at many locations in the state. The Network publishes a quarterly newsletter and holds an annual spring conference. The Network works in cooperation with the Women's Business Institute in North Dakota and is a division of the Watertown Area Career Learning Center, which is further described below. For more information, contact Watertown Area Career Learning Center, The Entrepreneur Network for Women (ENW), Kay Solberg, Executive Director, Becky Doerr, Business Specialist for ENW, Kay Tschakert, Career

Specialist/Financial Officer, 100 South Maple, P.O. Box 81, Watertown, SD 57201-0081, 605-882-5080; Fax: 605-882-5069; {E-mail: network4women@basec.net}; {www.network4women.com}.

Native American Assistance

Located on the Pine Ridge Indian Reservation, the Latoka Fund's mission is to support the development of private Latoka-owned and operated businesses on the reservation by providing financial and technical assistance and by fostering personal development. Its circle banking project uses a group lending methodology inspired in part by the Grameen Bank. For more information, contact The Latoka Fund, P.O. Box 340, Kyle, SD 57752; 605-455-2500.

Tennessee

All For the Women Business Owner

Located in Nashville, the *Women's Resource Center* offers on-site business-counseling services, training programs and technical assistance to women business owners in Middle Tennessee, which includes 21 counties. Through the consortium of sister National Association of Women Business Owners (NAWBO) chapters, and a corporate partnership with BellSouth and the Tennessee Economic Development Center, the Women's Resource Center provides training programs statewide through satellite, two-way interactive videoconferences and the Internet. For more information, contact The National Association for Women Business Owners (NAWBO)-Nashville Chapter, Janice S. Thomas, Executive Director, 1112 8th Avenue South, Nashville, TN 37203; 615-248-3474; 615-256-2706; {E-mail: tnwrc@bellsouth.net}.

Texas

Assistance For Women Business Owners

The *Texas Center for Women's Business Enterprise* is a public/private initiative dedicated to the entrepreneurial success of Texas women. If you are thinking about starting a business or already own one and would like to expand it, TxCWBE can help you. As a member of this new generation of entrepreneurial women, they will prepare you for business success by dealing with topics including: certification information, internet training for small businesses, business plans, loan assistance referral program, women's construction network, and consortium and contributing partners. Conveniently located in the capital city, TxCWBE has served Texas women for over six years. In 1996, Texas ranked 2nd out of the 50 states with 552,000 women-owned businesses, employing over 1 million people and generating $129.6 billion in sales. In addition to providing current training for today's businesses, the TxCWBE has also assisted in capitalizing women-owned businesses with $13 million in bank loans. For more information, contact:

1. Texas Center for Women's Business Enterprise (TxCWBE Austin),
   Michele Pettes, Executive Director, Two Commodore Plaza, 13th Floor,
   206 East 9th Street, Suite 13.140, Austin, TX 78701; Mailing Address:
   P.O. Box 2044, Austin, TX 78768; 512-472-8522; 888-352-2525; Fax:
   512-472-8513; {E-mail: txcwbe@txcwbe.org}; {E-mail: michele@
   txcwbe.org}; {www.txcwbe.org}.

2. Texas Center for Women's Business Enterprise (TxCWBE Temple)
   Temple/Killeen, Michele Pettes, Executive Director, P.O. Box 1992,
   Temple, TX 76503; 254-773-4815; 888-352-2525; Fax: 254-773-4967;
   {E-mail: txcwbe@txcwbe.org}; {E-mail: michele@txcwbe.org};
   {www.txcwbe.org}.

Fort Worth
The *Fort Worth Women's Business Center* is located in the Business Assistance
Center, which is a consortium of 13 service providers established in February
1995 to serve start-up and established small businesses in the Dallas/Fort
Worth area. The FW WBC addresses the needs of women business owners and
potential women entrepreneurs, through roundtables, discussion groups,
mentoring programs, networking opportunities and training support. By
leveraging local community resources, the center has assisted in the creation of
over 3,350 jobs and has facilitated over $133 million in business loans from
local banks, SBA loan programs and other community-based loan programs.
Contact Fort Worth Women's Business Center, Catherine Simpson, Director,
100 E. 15th Street, Suite 400, Fort Worth, TX 76102; 817-871-6009; Fax: 817-
871-6031; {E-mail: dcw@ci.fort-worth.tx.us}; {E-mail: Csimpson@
fwbac.com}.

Hispanic and Immigrant Populations Take Note
The *Women's Empowerment Business Center (WEBC)* serves a largely poor
and Hispanic immigrant population in four counties that have an
unemployment rate of 20 percent and where a third of the adult population does
not have a high school education. Services are available in both English and
Spanish. The WEBC is located at the SBA's one-stop capital shop in Edinburg,
Texas, and works closely with other agencies and service organizations.
Clients located in the Enterprise Zone have access to revolving loan funds.
WEBC services are integrated with various banks, municipalities, enterprise
centers, micro lenders and chambers of commerce. Contact Rio Grande Valley
Empowerment Zone Corporation, Women's Empowerment Business Center
(WEBC), Candi Roxas, Director, University of Texas-Pan American Annex,
2412 S. Closner, Edinburg, TX 78539; 956-316-2610; Fax: 956-316-2612; {E-
mail: webc@panam.edu}.

Chamber for Women
The San Antonio Women's Chamber of Commerce is dedicated to promoting
the growth and economic development of women, and achieving the integration
of women in leadership roles. Contact Women's Chamber of Commerce, P.O.
Box 460706, San Antonio, TX 78246; 210-299-2636.

Utah

Training for Women's Business Owners
1.   You can receive training to help you establish or expand your business in
     a program established by the Utah Technology Finance Corporation
     (UTFC) dubbed the *Utah Office of Women's Business Ownership*.
     Training is available both in Salt Lake City and in outlying areas of the
     state. In addition, they maintain a database of women business owners in
     the state of Utah. UTFC administers the SBA microloan program for
     Utah. For more information or to locate a service provider near you,
     contact Utah Technology Finance Corporation, Kathy Thompson, 177
     East 100 South, Salt Lake City, UT 84111; 801-364-1521 ext. 3; Fax:
     801-364-4361.

2.   The *Women's Business Center* at the Chamber supports the success of
     women business owners throughout Utah with counseling, training and
     loan packaging assistance. With more
     than 30 committees and task forces,
     the Chamber provides you with
     unique networking opportunities as
     well as a full service export assistance program. Their onsite high-
     tech center offers access to the internet and all types of business software.
     Women business owners can access help with marketing, management,
     finance and procurement. There is a modest fee for some services, but
     scholarships and specialized training are available for socially or
     economically disadvantaged women. Contact the Women's Business
     Center at the Chamber, Salt Lake Area Chamber of Commerce, Nancy
     Mitchell, Assistant Director, 175 East 400 South, Suite 600, Salt Lake
     City, UT 84111; 801-328-5075; Fax: 801-328-5098; {E-mail:
     nmitchell@slacc.org}; {www.saltlakechamber.org}.

Vermont

Training For New And Existing Women Business Owners
The *Women's Small Business Program* offers a continuum of services to
women seeking to identify, start, stabilize and expand a small business. You
could benefit from services that include: Getting Serious, a workshop to
determine a business idea and whether business meets personal goals; Star-Up,
a 15 week intensive course to develop a business plan and business

management skills; Working Solution, topic specific workshops for micro-business owner; and a graduate association to foster ongoing networking and access to information. They also offer comprehensive skills training and the opportunity to connect with other women entrepreneurs. Grants and scholarships for training are available to income eligible women. For more information, contact Economic Development Department, National Life Dr., Montpelier, VT 05602; 802-828-3211, 800-341-2211; Fax: 802-828-3258; {www.state.vt.us/dca/economic/developm.htm}.

Entrepreneurial Training

Northeast Employment and Training Program was incorporated in 1978 as a non-profit agency for the purpose of delivering educational and charitable programs to low-income Vermonters. One of their offerings is the Vermont Entrepreneurial Training Program, a classroom training program providing an in depth look at starting and operating a business. It is taught over Vermont Interactive Television and in individual classrooms. The program is regularly scheduled in September, January and April, but can and will be taught on demand. The program is divided into modules of which students may take all or any one. The costs of individual modules range from $25 to $200. The course information is project based along the creation of a business plan. Students are not graded on work performance, but do a self-analysis of learning. For more information, contact Northeast Employment and Training Program, P.O. Box 186 Johnsbury, VT 05819-0186; 802-748-8935; Fax: 802-748-8936; {www.vt-neto.org/index.html}.

Basic to Advanced Training

The *Vermont WBC* focuses on economically disadvantaged women, including welfare recipients, and ensures access for people with special needs or disabilities, those in rural areas, and women interested in agriculture. Training ranges from basic to  advanced, and services include financial and loan assistance, loan packaging, management and marketing assistance, and working with individual woman business owners. WNET mentoring roundtables meet once a month. A six-hour seminar on wholesale tradeshows is also available in two locations, and the center holds an annual business showcase and conference. A subcontract with CyberSkills Vermont provides Internet training and assistance. Programs are also offered on Vermont's Interactive Television Network. Contact Trinity College of Vermont, Women's Small Business Program/Vermont Women's Business Center, Pam Greene, Director, 208 Colchester Avenue, Burlington, VT 05401; 802-846-7164; Fax: 802-846-6587; {E-mail: pgreene@charity.trinityztvt.edu}.

Virginia

Entrepreneurial Center

The *Old Dominion University Entrepreneurial Center* provides research and educational services to innovative, high growth and/or technology driven Virginia businesses. They offer a tutorial based program that provides business assistance to individual companies that are starting, expanding, or attempting to turn business in different or more profitable directions. They also support entrepreneurial and innovative companies through the location and creation of risk capital funds, small business assistance programs, management training programs, information clearinghouses, community education concerning economic development, and linking regional higher education to the private sector. For more information, contact Old Dominion University Entrepreneurial Center, ODU-NSU Higher Education Center, Norfolk, VA 23529, 804-683-3524; Fax: 804-431-4739; {E-mail: ectr@infi.net}; {www1.infi.net/ectr/index.htm}.

Technology Entrepreneurs

Virginia's Center for Innovative Technology increases the Commonwealth's economic competitiveness and quality of life by advancing the development of Virginia as a technology state and by creating and retaining technology-based jobs and businesses. CIT has a vast network of technical assistance programs in place to help you build and grow your technology-based business. Their assistance covers most aspects of the technology lifecycle from concept to prototype to market. They can also help you access and improve existing technologies to use in your business. To locate the regional center nearest you or for more information, contact Center for Innovative Technology, Suite 600, 2214 Rock Hill Road, Herndon, VA 20170; 800-3-TECHVA (383-2482); 703-689-3000; Fax: 703-689-3041; {E-mail: wolfgang@cit.org}; {www.cit.org/}.

Student Entrepreneurs

Have you ever wondered if you have what it takes to be an entrepreneur? Have you ever dreamed of owning your own business? Do you just want to learn more about business in the real world? The *Association of Collegiate Entrepreneurs (ACE)* at Virginia Tech is a group of motivated college students from all majors with these goals in mind. If you have ever wondered what it takes to make your own business, then ACE is the place for you. Benefits and activities include meetings, leadership, guest speakers, networking, conferences, and more. For more information, contact Virginia Tech, Association of Collegiate Entrepreneurs, Blacksburg, VA 24061; 540-231-6000 (General Information); {www.vt.edu:10021/org/ace/}.

Virgin Islands

Change Your Life Through Entrepreneurship
Nearly one in four Virgin Islanders does not speak English as a primary language. About one in three Virgin Islanders lives in poverty and single women account for 50 percent of the heads of households. The *St. Croix Foundation for Community Development* helps these women change their lives through entrepreneurship. In its first year of funding, the SCFCD is running two repeated training programs for six months each. They cover how to write a business plan, loan strategies-accessing capital for start-ups and expansions-as well as basic accounting, record-keeping, small business management and marketing, and computer and Internet training. Group counseling sessions are held twice a month, with sessions relating to the ongoing course of study. Mentoring and networking groups are also available. Two-hour seminars cover topics such as The 3D's: Dedication, Discipline, Due Diligence, It's All Attitude, Arts and Crafts for Profit, The Government Procurement Process, and Over the Money Hurdle, Moving from Local to Global. Four full-day conferences are also held each year. For more information, contact St. Croix Foundation for Community Development, Inc. (SCFCD), Yvette DeLaubanque, Program Director, Suite 202, Chandler's Wharf, Gallows Bay, St. Croix, U.S. Virgin Islands 00820; 340-773-9898; Fax: 340-773-8727; {E-mail: stxfound@worldnet.att.net}.

Washington

Training Assistance For Women and Minority Business Owners
You can access resources and technical assistance to start or expand your business through the *Minority & Women Business Development* program. MWBD can provide you with entrepreneurial training, contract opportunities, bonding assistance, export assistance, and access to capital for start-ups or expanding businesses in the minority and women's business community. For more information, contact Minority & Women's Business, 406 Water St. SW, Olympia, WA 98501-1047; 360-753-9693 or Community Trade & Economic Development, 906 Columbia St. SW, Olympia, WA 98501-1216; 360-753-4900; {http://access.wa.gov}.

Business Assistance For Native Americans and Others
ONABEN *ONABEN - A Native American Business Network*, is a non-profit public benefit corporation created by Northwest Indian Tribes to increase the number and profitability of private enterprises owned by Native Americans. ONABEN offers training, individual counseling, assisted access to markets and facilitated access to capital for its clients. Each of the ten tribes hosting an ONABEN Service Center pays annual dues of $2,500 plus 40% of the cost of operating their site. The sites, located on reservations in Oregon, Washington and

California, deliver services to all citizens regardless of tribal affiliation. Some have up to 40% of users coming from the surrounding non-Native community. For more information, contact ONABEN - A Native American Business Network, Sonya Tetnowski, OWBO Coordinator, 3201 Broadway, Suite C, Everett, WA 98201; 425-339-6226; Fax: 425-339-9171; {E-mail: sonya@onaben.org{; {www.onaben.org}.

Assistance For Rookies Through Experts
The *Community Capital Development Program* is distinguished by its approach to three general categories of assistance: the seasoned entrepreneur (in business 3-5 years), the business owner (in business 3 years or less), and the start-up (including refugee and immigrant women on welfare, and welfare-to-work participants). The center has strong local partnerships, its own in-house loan fund, and substantial funding from the city of Seattle. For more information, contact Community Capital Development, James L. Thomas, CEO, Ruth-Ann Halford, VP, P.O. Box 22283, 1437 South Jackson Street, Suite 302, Seattle, WA 98122-0283; 206-324-4330; {E-mail: ruthannh@ seattleccd.com}; {E-mail: suzannet@seattleccd.com}; {E-mail: jimt@seattleccd.com}.

West Virginia
You Can Work At Home
If you live in rural West Virginia and would like to learn about alternative approaches to economic development such as networks of home-based business entrepreneurs, the *Center for Economic Options* can help. This is a non-profit, statewide, community-based organization that promotes opportunities to develop the economic capacity of West Virginia's rural citizens, particularly women, and communities. The Center creates unusual approaches to economic development including home-based business support and works with communities to help build support for small and micro-businesses. For more information, contact Center for Economic Options, Inc., Pam Curry, Executive Director, 601 Delaware Avenue, Charleston, WV 25302; 304-345-1298; Fax: 304-342-0641; {E-mail: wvmcoptns@citynet.net}; {www.centerforeconoptions.org/}.

Wisconsin
Access Business Education or Lending Programs
The *Wisconsin Women's Business Initiative Corporation* is an economic development corporation providing quality business education, technical assistance and access to capital. They consult, educate and mentor small and micro-businesses throughout Wisconsin. You could benefit from approximately 200 business courses and workshops offered in Milwaukee, Madison, Racine/Kenosha, Green Bay/Fox Valley, Beloit/Janesville annually. Topics include business planning, entrepreneurship, management, marketing,

finances, and the Internet. In addition, if you are a woman, person of color, or low-income individual who owns or can demonstrate the ability to operate a small business, they can provide access to loans of $100-$25,000 to help you along.

1. In Milwaukee, contact Wisconsin Women's Business Initiative Corporation, 2821 N. Fourth Street, Milwaukee, WI 53212; 414-263-5450; Fax: 414-263-5456.

2. In Madison, contact WWBIC - Madison Office, 217 S. Hamilton Street, Suite 201, Madison, WI 53703; 608-257-7409; Fax: 608-257-7429; {E-mail: info@wwbic.com}; {www.wwbic.com} and {www.onlinewbc.org}.

Statewide Chapters
The *Wisconsin Women Entrepreneurs* is the largest statewide organization for established businesses with the following chapters: Fox Valley, Racine/Kenosha, Rock Valley, South Central, Central (Stevens Point area), Coulee Region (La Crosse area) and Metro Milwaukee. They provide monthly programs, training seminars, mentor committees, membership directory, and an annual conference. For more information, contact Wisconsin Women Entrepreneurs, 6949 N. 100th Street, Milwaukee, WI 53224; 414-358-9290; 800-993-8663.

Child Care and Home Based Business Assistance
Western Dairyland's Women's Business Center (WDWBC) serves four counties in western Wisconsin. The city of Eau Claire, the largest population center in the service area, has the lowest per capita personal income of any metropolitan area in the state, while the predominantly rural nature of the service area hampers business and economic development. WDWBC projects that at least 75 percent of its clients have incomes at or below 150 percent of the poverty level. WDWBC provides start-up assistance, access to a loan guarantee fund, intensive follow-along services to regularly monitor progress, and continued access to a lending library of computers and related equipment. Owners of existing businesses receive customized technical assistance, including business-plan development, accessing financing from local lenders, SBA Loan Prequalification and MicroLoan programs, marketing assistance, Internet training, etc. Two types of business are especially targeted: child-care and home-based businesses. The center also shares information on Western Dairyland's sewing and textile manufacturing network, a model for flexible manufacturing that allows several

micro-businesses to obtain contracts and produce products that no one of the businesses could handle on its own. For more information, contact Western Dairyland's Women's Business Center (WDWBC), Renee J. Walz, Business Development Director, 23122 Whitehall Road, P.O. Box 45, Independence, WI 54747; 715-985-2391x211; Fax: 715-985-3239; {E-mail: rwalz@win. bright.net}.

Wyoming

A Good Resource
The *Wyoming Commission for Women* can assist you with a number of employment issues as well as offer you referrals. Their mission is to work to improve the quality and equality of life for Wyoming's women. The Commission For Women focuses its actions on the needs and concerns of Wyoming women in the following areas: Educational opportunities, Employment, Family and community, Public policy, Legal rights and responsibilities. For more information, contact Wyoming Women's Center, 1000 West Griffith, P.O. Box 20, Lusk, WY 82225; 307-334-3693; Fax: 307-334-2254; {http://wydoe.state.wy.us/wcwi/}.

New Program
The *Wyoming Women's Project* serves all women throughout the state, especially those who are economically and socially disadvantaged, seeking referrals from churches and the Wyoming Department of Family Services. This project started with the first statewide women's conference held in Wyoming in 25 years, from a resolution to set up a micro-credit program for women with low and moderate incomes to help them start their own businesses. In its first year, the program will be publicized through mini-conferences, a web site and a toll-free number. Micro-credit loan peer groups and women mentors provide ongoing support, and some training is subcontracted to the state SBDC. By the fifth year, the center hopes to open a subcenter in either Casper or Riverton, near the Wind River Indian Reservation. For more information, contact Wyoming Women's Project of the Wyoming Coalition Against Domestic Violence & Sexual Assault, Ann McCullough, Project Director, P.O. Box 236, Laramie, WY 82073; 307-745-3059; Fax: 307-755-5482; {E-mail: anniemac@vcn.com}.

Index

A

Advanced Technology Program, 132
Africa
    fax retrieval system, 862
Agency for International Development
    (AID), 838, 853
Agent Distributor Service (ADS), 841, 848
AgExport Action Kit, 850
Agriculture Department, 131
Airline Deregulation Act, 130
Alabama
    business assistance, 189
    business financing, 190
    disadvantaged business enterprise
        contacts, 87
    exports, 192
    federal procurement assistance, 733
    Intermediary Relending Program, 510
    inventor's resources, 796
    microloan programs, 558
    procurement office, 753
    rural development office, 532
    Small Business Development Centers,
        498
    tax incentives, 190
    unconventional loan programs, 583
    venture capital, 689
    venture capital clubs, 678
    women and minorities, 192, 925
    women's business centers, 53
    women's business ownership
        representative, 44
    women's commission, 116
Alaska
    business assistance, 193
    business financing, 194
    disadvantaged business enterprise
        contacts, 87
    exports, 196
    federal procurement assistance, 734
    grants, 177
    Intermediary Relending Program, 510
    inventor's resources, 797
    microloan programs, 577
    procurement office, 753
    rural development office, 532
    Small Business Development Centers,
        499
    tax incentives, 196

    women and minorities, 925-926
    women's business centers, 54
    women's business ownership
        representative, 44
    women's commission, 117
American Business Women's Association
    (AWBA), 915-916
Arizona
    business assistance, 198
    business assistance programs, 646
    business financing, 199
    disadvantaged business enterprise
        contacts, 87
    exports, 200
    federal procurement assistance, 734
    Intermediary Relending Program, 510
    inventor's resources, 797
    microloan programs, 558
    procurement office, 753
    rural development office, 532
    Small Business Development Centers,
        499
    tax incentives, 200
    unconventional loan programs, 583
    venture capital, 689
    women and minorities, 200, 926
    women's business centers, 54
    women's business ownership
        representative, 44
    women's commission, 117
Arkansas
    business assistance, 201
    business assistance programs, 646
    business financing, 202
    disadvantaged business enterprise
        contacts, 87
    exports, 204
    federal procurement assistance, 734
    Intermediary Relending Program, 510
    inventor's resources, 798
    microloan programs, 558
    rural development office, 532
    grants, 163
    procurement office, 753
    Small Business Development Centers,
        499
    tax incentives, 203
    unconventional loan programs, 584
    venture capital, 689
    venture capital clubs, 678
    women and minorities, 926

Index

Index

Index

P

microloan programs, 573
procurement office, 756
rural development office, 535
Small Business Development Centers,
504
tax incentives, 422
unconventional loan programs, 633
venture capital, 716
venture capital clubs, 682
women and minorities, 962-963
women's business centers, 74
women's business ownership
representative, 50
women's commission, 122
State business listings. *See* individual states
State Department
country experts, 834
Subcontracting. *See* freelancing
Surety bonds, 726

T

Technical assistance grants, 130
Temporary Assistance for Needy Families
(TANF), 544
Tennessee
business assistance, 423
business financing, 425
disadvantaged business enterprise
contacts, 91
exports, 429
federal procurement assistance, 742
grants, 148, 149
Intermediary Relending Program, 527
inventor's resources, 819
microloan programs, 574
procurement office, 756
rural development office, 535
Small Business Development Centers,
505
tax incentives, 429
unconventional loan programs, 634
venture capital, 716
women and minorities, 430, 963
women's business centers, 74
women's business ownership
representative, 50
women's commission, 122
Texas
business assistance, 432
business financing, 433
disadvantaged business enterprise
contacts, 92
exports, 435
federal procurement assistance, 742

grants, 164
Intermediary Relending Program, 528
inventor's resources, 820
microloan programs, 574, 580
procurement office, 756
rural development office, 535
Small Business Development Centers,
505
tax incentives, 434
unconventional loan programs, 634
venture capital, 717
venture capital clubs, 682
women and minorities, 963-964
women's business centers, 75
women's business ownership
representative, 50
women's commission, 122
Trade Adjustment Assistance Program, 130
Trade Development, Office of, 855
Trade Opportunities Program (TOP), 848
Trade Remedy Assistance Office (TRAO),
857
Trademarks, 784
registering, 786
researching, 784-785
Transportation Department, 82-92, 131
exporting assistance, 844

U

U.S. and FCS Field Offices listing, 867-872
U.S. and Foreign Commercial Service, 855-
856
U.S. Speakers Program, 883
U.S.-Asia Environmental Partnership, 844
Uruguay
fax retrieval system, 861
Utah
business assistance, 436
business financing, 437
disadvantaged business enterprise
contacts, 92
exports, 439
federal procurement assistance, 743
grants, 178, 179
Intermediary Relending Program, 528
inventor's resources, 821
microloan programs, 575
procurement office, 757
rural development office, 536
Small Business Development Centers,
505
tax incentives, 438
unconventional loan programs, 635
venture capital, 719